Cormac McCarthy

Cormac McCarthy

AN AMERICAN APOCALYPSE

Markus Wierschem

Michigan State University Press · *East Lansing*

Michigan State University Press
East Lansing, Michigan 48823-5245

Library of Congress Cataloging-in-Publication Data
Names: Wierschem, Markus, author.
Title: Cormac McCarthy : an American apocalypse / Markus Wierschem.
Description: East Lansing : Michigan State University Press, [2024] |
Series: Studies in violence, mimesis, and culture | Includes bibliographical references and index.
Identifiers: LCCN 2023021733 | ISBN 9781611864823 (paperback) |
ISBN 9781609177508 | ISBN 9781628955156
Subjects: LCSH: McCarthy, Cormac, 1933-2023—Criticism and interpretation. | Apocalypse in
literature. | American fiction—20th century—History and criticism. | American fiction—
21st century—History and criticism.
Classification: LCC PS3563.C337 Z95 2023 | DDC 813/.54—dc23/eng/20230620
LC record available at https://lccn.loc.gov/2023021733

Cover design by David Drummond, Salamander Design, www.salamanderhill.com.
Cover art is original oil painting by billi_kasabova. iStock.

Visit Michigan State University Press at *www.msupress.org*

With love to my mothers and fathers—in body and mind, heart and soul.

Contents

Acknowledgments

Humans have a thing for recasting the passage of time in space. That's what any watch does, as its arms chase the hours and minutes around the clock. Marking our time on this earth, we speak of the journey of life. For each of us, that journey consists in becoming who we are. "We ourselves are our own journey," says Cormac McCarthy. So, in a way, is any book written, any book read. The book you are reading now has been a part of my life's journey for a decade. It was almost left unfinished. Not all journeys reach their destination, and some take us longer than we thought they would when we took those first fateful steps. Along the journey, the road changes beneath us, as does the landscape around us. That is what life is. We are going places we never expected to see. We make choices. We are met with challenges and obstacles, but also friendly guides who help us overcome them. We encounter fellow journeymen and sometime companions. Roads cross and diverge. Some are lost along the way. All of them are owed thanks.

I am grateful to the Studienstiftung des deutschen Volkes, whose grants allowed me to pursue my research both in Germany and the United States. Thanks to their conferences, I was able to meet many outstanding young scholars whose work and personalities proved equally humbling and inspiring. I also wish to thank my fellow Cormackians of the Cormac McCarthy Society, especially Rick Wallach, who hosted me on my way to the McCarthy Archives in San Marcos, talking great music, Japanese cinema, and rote Grütze. Credit likewise goes to the participants of "Cormac McCarthy between Worlds," the 2016 Berlin conference hosted by James Dorson, Julius Greve, and myself, where we discussed many of the ideas explored here with such wonderful scholars as Dianne Luce, Stacey Peebles, Bryan Giemza, and Patrick O'Connor. Furthermore, I thank my fellow Girardians and COV&R members, who welcomed both me and my work with open hearts and minds. Particularly, I wish to thank Ann Astell as well as Andrew and Stephen McKenna, who have been outstanding in their encouragement and in discussing some of the ideas put forth in this book. Thanks go likewise to my editors at MSU Press, Bill Johnsen, Anastasia Wraight, Caitlin Tyler-Richards, and Catherine Cocks. Their understanding, patience, and support helped me to bring this journey to an end after a particularly long and dark stretch of the road.

Then, there are those traveling companions whose words and presence will linger, even after, in some cases, ways have long since parted. Here, I have to mention Geoff Hamilton, who first set me on the trail of Cormac McCarthy, and David Fitzgerald, who shared long days at the archive, as well as some terribly unhealthy yet seriously delicious pancakes at the Alamo. I owe a debt of gratitude to my colleagues at the University of Paderborn, especially Jarmila Mildorf, Miriam Strube, and the members of her doctoral seminar, particularly Lena Schneider, Alexandra Hartmann, and Marcin Chichocki. Their critical feedback made this a better book. Most affectionately, for their love and friendship, interest, patience, and support, I wish to thank my love, Elena Resch, as well as Jeniffer Zorn, Marc-Anton André, Benjamin Koch, Nikolas Isensee, Nadine and Christian Hellweg, Sarah Meier-Böke, Martina Fischer, Serap Cig, Björn Martin, Kassandra König, Isabel Borkstett, Maria Goeth, Maria Robaszkievicz, and Maria Wierschem. Special thanks go to Anna-Sophie Jürgens, whose contagious enthusiasm and imagination have made her my favorite conspirator in all things entropically artistic, and Daniel-Pascal Zorn, whose insight and friendship shaped the path of this book in more ways than I can mention here.

As time passes and the road leaves its marks on us, there are finally those that led our way when we could not yet see it. Gratitude and appreciation only begin to express the debt I owe to Peter Freese, whose guidance, wisdom, and scholarly model have been a constant inspiration in my life and to this book from its inception to its conclusion. Having passed in 2020, he never lived to see its publication. Neither did my stepfather, Konrad, who took me in as a child of two and raised me with all the love he would give to his own son, my brother Thomas. I can likewise never repay the love and patience of my mother, Gabriele, nor my father, Hans-Joachim, who found a way to raise me with all the love a child could hope for, even as his and my mother's own paths diverged. To all of them, in this journey and the ones to come: I carry you with me, as you carried me.

Some portions of this book have appeared as articles in the following publications:

- "The Other End of The Road: Re-Reading McCarthy in Light of Thermodynamics and Information Theory," *Cormac McCarthy Journal* 11.1 (2013): 1–22.
- "'It's More True, but It Ain't as Good': Searching for Truth in the Death-Deferring Dialogue of McCarthy's The Sunset Limited," in *Imaginary Dialogues in America*, edited by Till Kinzel and Jarmila Mildorf (Heidelberg: Winter, 2014), 327–47.
- "'Some Witless Paraclete Beleaguered with All Limbo's Clamor': On Violent Contagion and Apocalyptic Logic in Cormac McCarthy's Outer Dark," *Contagion: Journal of Violence, Mimesis and Culture* 22 (2015): 185–202.
- "At a Crossroads of Life and Death: The Apocalyptic Journey(s) of Cormac McCarthy's Fiction," in *The Journey of Life in American Life and Literature*, edited by Peter Freese (Heidelberg: Winter, 2015), 159–85.

Abbreviations

The following abbreviations are used for works consistently referred to in this book. All references to these sources appear in parentheses following citations.

Cormac McCarthy

APH   *All the Pretty Horses*

BM   *Blood Meridian*

CG   *Child of God*

COU   *The Counselor*

CP   *Cities of the Plain*

CRO   *The Crossing*

NC   *No Country for Old Men*

OD   *Outer Dark*

OK   *The Orchard Keeper*

R   *The Road*

SL   *The Sunset Limited*

SM   *The Stonemason*

SUT   *Suttree*

WM   *Whales and Men*, archival manuscript

René Girard

BE   *Battling to the End*

DBB   *To Double Business Bound*

DDN   *Deceit, Desire and the Novel*

GR   *The Girard Reader*

ISS   *I See Satan Fall Like Lightning*

SG	*The Scapegoat*	**Richard Slotkin**		
TE	*A Theater of Envy*	*FE*	*The Fatal Environment*
TH	*Things Hidden Since the Foundation of the World*	*GN*	*Gunfighter Nation*
		REG	*Regeneration through Violence*
VS	*Violence and the Sacred*		

A Note on Citations, Translations, Spelling, and Punctuation

Archival materials from the Cormac McCarthy Papers of the Wittliff Collection's Southwestern Writers Collection are indicated by parenthetical reference to the collection, box, folder, and page where pagination exists (otherwise noted as n.p.). Translations of non-English works are mine or have been adopted from the respective source documented in the bibliography. In the case of direct quotations from McCarthy's works, I have retained McCarthy's syntax, punctuation, and spelling, as well as its nonstandard idiosyncrasies, for example, his rare use of commas, lack of quotation marks, and omission of apostrophes in contractions like "cant," "dont," etc. Characters (e.g., quotation marks, em vs. en dashes) in citations from other works have been standardized.

Introduction

An American Apocalypse?

Once there were brook trout in the streams in the mountains. You could see them standing in the amber current where the white edges of their fins wimpled softly in the flow. They smelled of moss in your hand. Polished and muscular and torsional. On their backs were vermiculate patterns that were maps of the world in its becoming. Maps and mazes. Of a thing which could not be put back. Not be made right again. In the deep glens where they lived all things were older than man and they hummed of mystery.

—Cormac McCarthy, *The Road*

Thus read the final words of *The Road*, Cormac McCarthy's tenth and, until most recently, last novel. In it, the Earth's biosphere has been turned into a wasteland of ashes. Civilization lies in ruins, mankind itself has all but vanished, and its last survivors prey on each other for want of any other food resource. What remains is but the fading memory of a world that has been lost: a living, breathing world embodied by trout in mountain streams, which once were there and now are no more. The brown and green marble patterns of the trouts' scaled backs suggest "maps of the world in its becoming," and so the remote origins of life itself. Still, as they no longer hum, as we witness the world in its undoing, we are left with another mystery: Where have the trout gone, and where mankind? Where, for that matter, has *life* gone? The silence of *The Road* yields no answers. We only feel the mystery. And in the ubiquity of death, we too partake in the loss of that which cannot "be made right again," asking ourselves how it could come to this. Or whether it had to. Whether the road leading to the end had always already been laid out before us.

Existential questions like these come with the eschatological territory: Presenting an exquisitely bleak vision of the end of the world as we know it, *The Road* falls firmly into the literary tradition associated with that ominous epithet, *apocalyptic*. Of course, tales of the end times are a dime a dozen. Visions of the last days have been shaping religious thought through millennia and across cultures. They foretell of preordained cataclysmic change, earthshattering catastrophes, and all-consuming battles between the forces of good and evil. For some religions, these catastrophes are part of a spiritual process that is the judgment of humanity itself, its damnation or salvation. Apocalyptic texts hence constitute a prophetic genre. As such, they are an integral part of Judeo-Christian scripture. The apocalyptic texts of the Bible include the book of Daniel, parts of the prophetic writings of Isaiah, Ezekiel, and Jeremiah, and sections of the synoptic Gospels. Yet it is the last book of the Bible, St. John's book of Revelation, which begins with that eponymous word *apocalypsis* (Gk. unveiling, revelation), that dominates our perception of the genre to such an extent that some, like Harold Bloom, judge its resonance "[o]ut of all proportion to its literary strength or spiritual value" (1992, 162). Still, by its dense, terrifying imagery and symbolism articulating a vision of destruction, the Second Coming of Christ, the final battle at Armageddon, and the Last Judgment, Revelation became synonymous with the genre. In Meyer Howard Abrams's concise formula: "In its late and developed form an apocalypse [. . .] is a prophetic vision, set forth in arcane and elaborate symbols, of the imminent events which will bring an abrupt end to the present world order and replace it by a new and perfected condition of man and his milieu" (38).[1]

Like the trout-back maps in McCarthy's elegy, genuinely apocalyptic writing articulates a certain view of the world, of life, and of history as endowed with teleological purpose. While other cultures often envision the unfolding of time as an eternal cycle of birth, death, and rebirth following the rhythms of night and day or the cycle of seasons, the Abrahamic religions hold to a view of history as finite, as moving along a carefully laid out, providential path that began in the Garden of Eden and that moving along a few, incisive key events, will lead to the unmaking of the old world and the creation of a new and better one. In this design from Genesis to Revelation, the utopian destination in perfection is inextricably built into the "fortunate fall" of the beginning.

Nowadays, the popularity of end-of-the-world stories and postapocalyptic scenarios is at an all-time high. However, the religious monopoly on doomsday visions has long since been broken. Instead, the peddlers of these tales are the creators of Hollywood blockbusters like *Terminator 2: Judgment Day*, *Armageddon*, *The Matrix*, *The Day After Tomorrow*, or *2012*; celebrated television series like *The Walking Dead*; and acclaimed video games like *The Last of Us* or the *Fallout* franchise. They are the public intellectuals who alert us to the risks of rapid technological advancement. They are the scientists and activists warning us about the effects of overpopulation, ecological exploitation, and climate change. Last but not least, they are the artists, the poets, playwrights, and novelists, who compel us to confront the existential and ethical questions that envisioning the end of days should entail.

Among these artists turned eschatologists, few have gone to chart the abyss of human behavior and unflinchingly returned its gaze to shape our vision of apocalypse as has the Irish American Cormac McCarthy. Writing in obscurity for twenty-five years, he is today considered not only one of America's greatest living writers but also the heir apparent to the grand literary tradition of authors like Herman Melville and William Faulkner, whose best work, even as its catastrophes and revelations remain localized, has even been imbued with a profound sense of the apocalyptic. That being said, it is best to begin by confronting McCarthy's apocalypse on its own terms: To find an explanation for the annihilation we witness in *The Road*, we need look no further than the novels that precede it.

Here, the shape that the common death assumes is commonly one of violence. Naturally, more can, has been, and will yet be said about McCarthy's themes, his artistic vision, and the philosophical implications of a body of fiction that warranted his induction into the American Philosophical Society in 2012. And yet, for any first-time reader of *Blood Meridian* (1985)—a book that Bloom called "the authentic American apocalyptic novel" (2000, 254)—the overwhelming impression will be that of the boundless carnage rendered there. Similar things may be said about McCarthy's other novels, all of which are to a greater or lesser extent saturated with violence and an atmosphere of decay, ruin, and death. Essentially, the world of his fiction from his early short stories on has always been a world dominated by these forces. And McCarthy would not have it any other way: "Death is the major issue in the world. For you, for me, for all of us. It just is. To not be able to talk about it is very odd" (Woodward 2005, 98).

Even so, to many, the artistic centrality McCarthy awards to death and violence will appear exceedingly bleak. It is easy to forget that they are not the whole story. As the disappearance of the brook trout bearing the intricate patterns of life emergent reminds us, the "major issue" of death presupposes another mystery—that of life itself. Ultimately, it is not simply death, but rather the polarity between life and death that is at the core of McCarthy's vision. It is not surprising, then, that McCarthy resorts to an apocalyptic mode: no other form of writing forces existential issues across disciplines as uncompromisingly and on a scale that links the fate of the individual to that of the species. Quoth the author at the climate change conference in Santa Fe, anno 2007: "Of course it's relevant—we're all going to die" (Kushner). In interrogating McCarthy's life work, patterns and themes emerge that characterize his individual creations as elements of a larger and, I argue, consistent and systematic apocalyptology that is without peer in contemporary American literature. Understanding the logic and design of his apocalypse is the purpose of this book.

Before we proceed to the structure and methodology of this study, I want to address a few key questions to contextualize McCarthy's literary eschatology within the general evolution of the apocalyptic genre and American apocalyptic thought in particular. First and foremost, in looking at McCarthy's work, are we actually dealing with something that can meaningfully be characterized as an *apocalypse*? Arguably, much of contemporary apocalyptic art barely warrants the name. We have seen a massive expansion of the cataclysmic catalogue our stories draw from, ensuring the continuing adaptability of the mode to the zeitgeist. However, this expansion has diluted the subversive sociopolitical and spiritual explosiveness originally held by a genre that once constituted "gospel for bad times" (Freese 1997, 21).[2] Today, when natural disasters, zombies, or self-conscious machines tear down civilization every other week, the genre amounts to little more than a label for any other scenario involving large-scale destruction.

What is more, in such secular scenarios, we are frequently dealing with a "cropped apocalypse" (Vondung 12)—one limited to the destruction of the world while eschewing its restoration and perfection. The utopian hope that gave a meaning to the ordeal has been lost, as has the notion of history as a providential plot with a beginning, a middle, and an end—the "essential tension between old and new, destruction and renewal, threat and promise" (Freese 1997, 27). Paradoxically, we have thus raised the stakes, rendering threats more pervasive and tangible, at the same time that we have commodified and in so doing tamed the apocalypse, reducing it to a constant, mildly ominous background noise. Like any other product, it is consumed without urgency or inspiring either the reflection or collective action that the end of the species might otherwise be expected to inspire. In this respect, McCarthy's fiction presents an exception, for it retains a deeply unsettling quality: whatever demons rage there rage unexorcised. Is this quality a consequence of a dispassionate, scientific outlook, a nihilistic view of life even? Or is it, to the contrary, that McCarthy's apocalypse retains a religious core, however fragile? Finally, does it retain the twofold outlook and historical view that is a staple of genuine apocalypticism?

Interrogating the general apocalyptic character of his work, a second major concern is whether it makes sense to describe McCarthy's as a specifically *American* apocalypse. Differently put, to what extent do the writings of as quintessentially American an author as McCarthy reflect the history of apocalyptic thought in what may well be "the most apocalyptic of nations" (Bloom 1992, 160)? From the beginnings of European presence in the New World, Christian eschatology exerted a tremendous influence. Frequently, colonial American writers cast the blossoming nation as an active agent in a history of salvation. In "A Model of Christian Charity" (1630), John Winthrop famously envisioned the Massachusetts Bay Colony as a shining city upon a hill, and so invoked not only the Sermon on the Mount but also the heavenly city of St. John's prophecy. New England Puritans followed suit, casting America as the place where New Jerusalem would arise. About a century later, Jonathan Edwards speculated that the revivals of the Great Awakening were signs of the end times, before the American Revolution and the emergence of an independent republic opened the doors to a religiously unaffiliated, "civic millennialism" that would drive American expansionism and its sense of manifest destiny (Boyer 36).

In the decades following the Revolution, decidedly religious millennial movements—like the Millerites, Seventh-day Adventists, and Jehovah's Witnesses—would time and again predict the end of the world, only to be disappointed time and again (Bloom 1992, 71, 159–63). Disproven prophecy, it seems, matters but little to the ongoing vitality of the genre. As Frank Kermode points out in his seminal *The Sense of an Ending,*

> The great majority of interpretations of Apocalypse assume that the End is pretty near. Consequently the historical allegory is always having to be revised; time discredits it. And this is important. Apocalypse can be disconfirmed without being discredited. This is part of its extraordinary resilience. It can also absorb changing interests, rival apocalypses [...]. It is patient of change and of historiographical sophistications. (8)

Consequently, notions of the End have lost their "naïve *imminence*" and have instead become *immanent* (Kermode 6). The millennial tradition continues to this day, regaining urgency in light of issues like climate change. Thus, in 1992, Bloom mused that "[t]he American Religion, always millennial, will soon enough engage us all in fearful expectations of finality" (268). Indeed, at the close of the twentieth century, such expectations remained a vibrant strand in American popular religion, as upward of half of the American populace believed in the Bible offering "an explicit plan of history's end" while would-be eschatologians continue to twist scripture to fit contemporary events, social realities and political entities into their end-time dramas (Boyer 36).

A number of fault lines thus emerge between secular and religious eschatologies. Plainly, apart from "the strongest poets, from Dante and Spenser through Milton on to Blake and Shelley," the vision of Revelation continues to captivate "the quacks and cranks of all ages down to the present moment in America" (Bloom 1992, 162).³ Apocalyptic discourse in the United States and elsewhere seems largely a monopoly of fundamentalist groups. The indictment of René Girard is thus quite appropriate:

> The only Christians who still talk about the apocalypse are the fundamentalists, but they have a completely mythological conception of it. They think that the violence of the end of time will come from God himself. They cannot do without a cruel God. Strangely, they do not see that the violence we ourselves are in the process of amassing and that is looming over our own heads is entirely sufficient to trigger the worst. They have no sense of humor. (*BE* xvi)

Of all religious texts other than cosmogonic narratives, apocalyptic tales are perhaps the ones most explicitly aligned with *myth*. But insofar as they pertain to the future, they also contain a host of realistic potentialities, a sense in which the events they describe may yet come to pass. Taking these issues seriously, an all-too-literal and mythical interpretation of scripture must be left behind. Where, then, does Cormac McCarthy stand in this respect?

Syncretic Eschatology:
The Curious Case of Cormac McCarthy

Following the writers he admires—Dostoevsky, Faulkner, Melville—Cormac McCarthy delves deeply into the unconscious of his culture, its history and myths. Embedded in the greater narratives of his novels, one finds many a story of events passed, anecdote of local color, and allegory or parabolic tale nigh biblical in tone. Yet McCarthy is no fundamentalist. Though raised in a Catholic family that "went to church on Sunday," McCarthy does not remember the topic of religion "ever even being discussed" (Jurgensen). On the other hand, his affinity for the company of scientists and yearlong engagement at the Santa Fe Institute hardly failed to shape his world view. In fact, McCarthy resists the false choice between science and religion. Instead, he professes his admiration of William James's *The Varieties of Religious Experience* (Wallace 138) while acknowledging the ambiguity of his own position:

"I have a great sympathy for the spiritual view of life, and I think that it's meaningful. But am I a spiritual person? I would like to be. Not that I am thinking about some afterlife that I want to go to, but just in terms of being a better person" (Jurgensen).

McCarthy's fiction likewise reflects this uncertain ontology. Spearheaded by Vereen M. Bell, early scholarship still identified McCarthy's novels as either ambiguously or consummately nihilistic. In contrast, later scholars around Edwin Arnold find in his work "a profound belief in the need for moral order, a conviction that is essentially religious" (1999, 46).[4] While Arnold still shies away from turning McCarthy into an "overtly Christian writer," Bryan Giemza argues for reading him as "overtly Catholic" (160), though a Catholic examining his beliefs through heretic positions. Still others adopt an intermediary position. John Cant characterizes McCarthy as a "religious writer in a Godless world," who accommodates the scientifically as well as the spiritually minded by depicting man as cast into an "absurdist universe" that is "the product of a consciousness that has lost its religious belief but retained a religious cast of mind" (15). Running across these discourses is a strain of scholarship, led by Leo Daugherty and Dianne Luce, that views McCarthy as a postmodern peddler of gnostic myth, or else a representative of the "neo-gnosticism of twentieth century existentialism" (Luce 2009, viii).

Conclusively, in the first book-length discussion of the issue of *Religion in Cormac McCarthy's Fiction*, Manuel Broncaro isolates "the religious scope of his fiction" as perhaps "the most controversial issue in Cormac McCarthy studies" (3). The picture Broncaro paints is one of manifold, interwoven systems:

> McCarthy critics seem to be divided between those who find a theological dimension in his works and those who reject such an approach, on the grounds that the nihilist discourse characteristic of his narrative is incompatible with any religious message. Whatever the critical stand, however, the religious elements in McCarthy's fiction are pervasive: anchorites and hermits, priests and ex-priests, prophets and heretics, pilgrims and penitents, martyrs and virgins, dilapidated churches and missions, Christian and Native American symbols, biblical names and allusions, and saintly and devilish individuals, are too conspicuous to be ignored and too recurrent to respond to anything but an overarching design. (4)

In the following, I argue that this "overarching design" identifies McCarthy's work as an apocalypse. While saturated in American mythology and Judeo-Christian tradition, this apocalypse is simultaneously bolstered and complicated by a profound scientific awareness. In a word, McCarthy's eschatology is fundamentally syncretic.

At the same time, the apocalyptic and religious dimensions in McCarthy's fiction are undeniably bound up with the fact of violence. While *Blood Meridian* is often singled out as rivaling epics like the *Iliad* for its rendering of bloodshed, its notoriety tends to occlude the contextual complexity of violence in McCarthy's work. Locale and period may vary—from Appalachian mountain hamlets to the streets of Knoxville, from the plains of a Southwestern past to the ash-covered roads of an indefinite future—yet all of McCarthy's landscapes are marked by the mementos of death and mortal struggle. Such are the tests his protagonists face, and the stuff they themselves are made of. Not seldom are they killers of men, not yet fully grown into adulthood, cowboys and outlaws, orphaned sons and sometimes fathers, but all alike outcasts and restless wanderers marked by violence, *homo necans* and *homo viator* in a single gestalt.

And yet, it would be a mistake to confuse McCarthy with "Bret Easton Ellis and all the other talk show hosts of darkness" (Greiner 2007). For, while his list of good writers may preclude "anyone who doesn't 'deal with issues of life and death'" (Woodward 1992, 31), McCarthy's concerns are far from postmodern excess or shocking for the sake of shock. Instead, the quality that shines through consistently is a deep conviction that "violence is pretty ugly," which seems to spring from childhood experience as much as the study of history: "You grow up in the South, you're going to see violence" (Kushner). And yet, among McCarthy's more puzzling statements on any subject is the following proposition: "There's no such thing as life without bloodshed. [...] I think the notion that the species can be improved in some way, that everybody could live in harmony, is a really dangerous idea. Those who are afflicted with this notion are the first ones to give up their souls, their freedom" (Woodward 1992, 36).

What are we to make of these words? For one, the idea that life and bloodshed are inextricably tied can be seen as either a neutral accidence or an essential condition of contemporary life. We may avert our eyes, we may displace and dissimulate it through markets and institutions, yet the fact is that to sustain life and often mere comfort, blood is inevitably shed by, on behalf of, and finally with the quiet consent of _us_. What other meanings these words hold only become explicit once their scope is widened to include human civilization through time.

Implicitly, the second part of McCarthy's statement already expands our view by introducing the "dangerous idea" of improving the species and living in harmony. At first, this indictment seems radically at odds with either our at least nominal ideal of nonviolence or the humanist's belief in the potential of people for intellectual and moral growth. A self-identified pessimist, McCarthy is liable to make his readers skeptical of such faith. Perhaps though, his skepticism is directed less at ideas of learning and change as such, than the kind of utopian vision imposed from without. Whether the latter is wrapped in religious, sociopolitical, or technocratic garb, he seems to suggest, the desire behind those lofty visions all-too-easily turns totalitarian and destructive of human freedom. The danger as demonstrated by nationalist and communist projects of the twentieth century would be that in building utopia, its builders resort to the very violence they seek to expunge in the quest for human perfection.[5]

McCarthy's brand of pessimism is naturally at home within contemporary, secular apocalypticism. Human freedom of self-realization has come to imply a freedom of self-destruction. Today, the origins of annihilation are to be sought not in some divine wrath, but in human nature. And while McCarthy often dramatizes violence in terms of the sacred, the face of violence in his work bears distinctly human features. Simone Weil held that scripture articulates a theory of man before it articulates a theory of God. If this is so, changes to our view of humanity will be reflected in our visions of its end. In the curious case of Cormac McCarthy, we are thus initially stuck between a biblical rock and a secular hard place. This conflict only resolves itself once exegesis is yoked to an anthropological hypothesis. Coming out of the bloodiest century in human history, McCarthy's work suggests a future that he predicted "would be a lot more violent." It is hence not surprising that for him it is our own "violence and neglect" that may seal our fate: "We're going to do ourselves in" (Kushner). Our utopian prospects dashed, what hope remains cannot evade the challenge of McCarthy's eschatology. It conforms to neither our traditional biblical nor our manifold secular and scientifically informed visions of the end. Instead, what we get is an exceedingly syncretic apocalyptic middle-ground that reflects the human condition in the face of both first and last things.

This middle ground is a manifestation of a more universal outlook than can initially be surmised. Since 1992, when Cormac McCarthy first opened up to the public and Richard B. Woodward of the *New York Times*, readers have known that out of his manifold interests, "McCarthy would rather talk about rattlesnakes, molecular computers, country music, Wittgenstein—anything—than himself or his books" (1992, 30). In recent years the frequency of interviews McCarthy grants has increased considerably. Still, little has changed about his documented preference for the company of scientists or his reluctance about discussing his art. Out of McCarthy's scarce comments about the writer's craft, it is his begrudging admission of "the ugly fact" that "books are made out of books" and that "[t]he novel depends for its life upon the novels that have been written" that has garnered the most critical attention. Conversely, his ostensibly straightforward preoccupation with "issues of life and death" as the author's true calling has left less of an impression, as has his view of the novel as being able to "encompass all the various disciplines and interests of humanity" (Woodward 1992, 30–31).

Taken as a kind of "minimal poetics," the two latter propositions hint at a literary program that is the more remarkable for being formulated in an age that has alternately lamented or celebrated the death of the form McCarthy so unabashedly champions, that is, the novel. This is so because, in these statements, one finds the seeds of its apotheosis: as a human *artifact* in the literal sense as "a thing made with skill," the McCarthyan novel ideally contains within itself endless potentialities that include yet transcend both the sum of their parts and the purview of even the most inclusive scientific theory of everything. In the words of *The Crossing*, McCarthy's most overtly poetological work, the implicit ontology of this poetics may well be articulated as follows:

> The story [. . .] can never be lost from its place in the world for it is that place. And that is what was to be found here. The corrido. The tale. And like all corridos it ultimately told one story only, for there is only one to tell. [. . .] For this world also which seems to us a thing of stone and flower and blood is not a thing at all but is a tale. And all in it is a tale and each tale the sum of all lesser tales and yet these also are the selfsame tale and

contain as well all else within them. So everything is necessary. Every least
thing. This is the hard lesson. Nothing can be dispensed with. Nothing
despised. Because the seams are hid from us, you see. The joinery. The way
in which the world is made. [. . .] And those seams that are hid from us are
of course in the tale itself and the tale has no abode or place of being except
in the telling only and there it lives and makes its home and therefore we
can never be done with the telling. Of the telling there is no end. [. . .] And
[. . .] in whatever other place by whatever other name or by no name at all I
say again all tales are one. Rightly heard all tales are one. (*CRO* 143)

While the depth of this vision can only be unraveled as we progress through
McCarthy's work, it is hard not to be struck with its aspiration to totality: in
the McCarthyan tale at its most accomplished, microcosm and macrocosm
reflect and resonate within one another as literary fractals. Here, all is one
and one is all, the whole contained within and informing each of its parts,
and every part integral to the whole. In this literary matrix, the act of storytelling itself is fundamentally bound up in shaping and, in a sense, founding
whatever world its characters inhabit. It is a poetics characterized by, firstly,
its universal scope and, secondly, its firm belief in unguessed elemental connections pertaining to each work's structure, theme, and plot, down to the
style and grammar of McCarthy's prose.

Once we consider in conjunction these disparate elements, which pertain to both to plot and theme and the operative level of storytelling itself,
what comes to light is exactly "the joinery," the "seams" of the whole hidden in the tale itself. And in McCarthy's ontology, that tale is ultimately the
world itself, the living, breathing world perceived and lived in, so long as
the telling continues. This poetics is developed throughout his work, and
so unifies it. The teleology of this work, I claim, identifies it as essentially
apocalyptic. For the complexity of its unified vision notwithstanding, the
dynamics and vital force of the McCarthyan novel without fail derive from
and unfold within the coordinates of order and disorder, good and evil, and
life and death weighed upon a universal scale.

Now, it stands to reason that our engagement with literature *as such*—
rather than a singular motif or aspect—is guided best by that theoretical map
that most fully explicates and answers to the central concerns of the work in
question. Dealing with a poetics such as McCarthy's, our approach should

be similarly syncretic and integrative. Practically, this means that we need to be able to relate, as Andrew McKenna puts it, "the operations of signs to the machinations of the socius" (10). In McCarthy's case, it is pertinent to include his well-known yet critically underappreciated interest in the processes of the natural world as a third dimension. What we need for an appreciation of the scope and depth of McCarthy's literary vision is a holistic approach bridging the gaps between what C. P. Snow called "the two cultures," between the natural and the human and social sciences. It is necessary to explicate the relation between humans and the world they perceive and live in, the dynamic interactions of humans among themselves, and the way in which these relations relate to one another on the literary level of the joinery that unifies the *world-as-tale*.

Perhaps it is foolhardy to attempt such a thing. Certainly, it is beyond the scope of any one book. Theory by nature tends toward reduction, quite necessarily so. We are at an impasse, however, with a literature that makes a point of its aspirations to totality, the notion that "Every least thing" is necessary, that "Nothing can be dispensed with." No single reading or theory of art, no matter how universal, can match and exhaust the capacities of its object, nor is this finally desirable. Does this mean the project ought to be abandoned? Falling inevitably short of explaining everything, the goal must rather be to define a unified field of literary inquiry as well as the conditions of such inquiry, and to do so while integrating past scholarship and remaining open enough to accommodate future, more specialized perspectives.

Toward a Unified Poetic Field: Outline and Methodology

This book is organized into a theory chapter and five analytic chapters. Superficially, these chapters follow the Southern/Pastoral, Western, and post-Western phases in McCarthy's work. In actuality, they represent steps in the deepening anthropological examination that informs the development of his apocalypse. After laying the theoretical foundation, the subject of chapters two and three is the early novels *The Orchard Keeper* (1965) and *Child of God* (1973), which focus on the dynamics between individuals and the pastoral communities they are a part of. Stakes are raised in the fourth

and fifth chapters, which anachronistically begin with *Outer Dark* (1968),
McCarthy's second novel and first properly apocalyptic work. It is here that
we are confronted with the logic behind the forces that compel us to self-
destruction and the role of Christianity in this process. What is implicit in
Outer Dark is then spelled out and applied to history in *Blood Meridian*
(1985). Its position within the American canon and as McCarthy's most discussed work notwithstanding, I contend that its challenge has been understated, reflecting our potential future within the bloody mirror of America's
frontier past. Finally, the final chapter jumps ahead two decades, looking at
the postapocalypse of *The Road*, to offer, paradoxically, a saving grace at the
moment that life is fading away.[6]

In the theory chapter following this introduction, I outline the "unified
poetic field" that will allow for a systematic, integrative reading of McCarthy's
novels under the aspects of myth, violence, and entropy. I conceive of these
aspects not as isolated bits, but as parts of an intricate thematic-aesthetic
triad permeating, structuring, and unifying McCarthy's oeuvre. Between the
three, it is possible to interrelate the operations of language and storytelling,
myth and literature, to the threat of escalatory violence between individuals
and communities, and to align both with the theological, ecological, and
scientific concerns that inform McCarthy's cosmology. Exploring these
dimensions methodologically takes the form of close reading and multidisciplinary structural analysis. What makes this integrative approach possible
is a number of structural analogies and ways in which the dynamics outlined
within each field parallel one another and intersect in central points. The
intersection visited most frequently will be that of *order and disorder*, which
represents a sublimation of the more fundamental McCarthyan opposition
of *life and death*.

Relating the processes of literary signification to the world of human
culture and the world of nature, this "unified poetic field" approach will first
examine the dimension of myth as the one most directly involved in the
operations of literature and narrative. As a common theme, I advance a position that conceives of myth as a culturally constitutive, narrative conceptual-
ization of the passage from disorder to order and vice versa. In this passage,
violence emerges as instrumental. The second element of the triad, violence,
will be approached primarily through René Girard's mimetic theory. Adopting this perspective serves to situate McCarthy not simply in a line with the

usual American suspects of Melville and Faulkner, but also in a more broadly Western tradition spearheaded by such writers as Sophocles, Shakespeare, and Dostoevsky. Specifically, mimetic theory offers interpretive strategies highlighting conflictual relationships, the violent dynamics between crowds and individuals, as well as their textual representations, and finally the operation of forces of cultural disintegration and reconstitution.

In contrast, myth and entropy constitute discursive fields, mimetic theory represents the sole systematic approach in my reading. Since Girard's "teaching and research were always interdisciplinary" (*GR* 5), it is particularly suited to accommodate the integrative nature of McCarthy's poetics.[7] His unorthodox interpretation of Judeo-Christian tradition put Girard at odds with both believers and atheists, even as its basis in anthropology arguably accommodates either perspective. Given the importance of said tradition in the work of fellow Catholic McCarthy, mimetic theory can serve as a guide not just to McCarthy's violent anthropology but to his "heretical" thought as well. This is not to say that McCarthy's work is directly informed by Girard. In truth, the development of his apocalypticism prefigures the major steps of mimetic theory by several years. As McCarthy's literary anthropology will be found to reflect Girard's, the independence of their findings only strengthens the plausibility of what either of them has to say.

Finally, reflections on the second law of thermodynamics and the evolution of its central concept of entropy, which can provisionally be described as the tendency of the world to disorder, further complicate McCarthy's apocalypse. They do so by adding a scientific dimension to eschatology that is poetically less incongruous than it may seem at first, illuminating the pervasive impression of man's cosmic insignificance in his work. In addition, the second law supplies another way of thinking about order, disorder, and difference—all of which emerge as central terms in the conversation about myth and violence. It is the aspect that most directly pertains to the foundation of structure and meaning.

Regarding this selection of theories to fill in the unified field, the question of originality arises. It may be objected that discourse on entropy in literature had its high time in the 1990s, that the study of myth has not generated any major paradigm since the end of structuralism, and that mimetic theory, being first formulated in the 1960s and 1970s, is similarly outdated and never really caught on in the way that other paradigms did. Additionally, with regard to McCarthy, there have been various discussions of myth as well as of violence, and there have even been select Girardian readings. Nevertheless, I contend that despite their age, these theories have something important to offer not just for reading McCarthy, but for literary and cultural criticism as a whole.

So what exactly is new in this "unified poetic field" approach? Generally, two responses are possible, the first being one accepting the inherent premise of the primacy of originality. Though fashioned from known elements, the syncretic approach itself certainly has its original points to make. It is in analyzing the interrelationships between its elements that it can offer new insights. As I have indicated, scientifically informed analyses remain a rare sight in McCarthy criticism, and while myth has been explored, these explorations largely deal with it predominantly as a subject, rather than the operation or structure of the literary text. Finally, what Girardian readings of McCarthy there are remain almost exclusively in the realm of *Violence and the Sacred*, as though the turn to Judeo-Christian scripture, which fundamentally shaped the subsequent development of mimetic theory, never occurred. Much work remains to be done here.

The second response is to turn the question against itself by interrogating its premise. A strength of the integrative approach I propose is that while it remains open to future discussions of, for instance, social issues like race, class, or gender, it can inform such inquiries in fundamental ways that are not true the other way around. This is so to the extent that it deals with interdividual and transhistorical as well as pre- and transcultural dynamics. Put differently, it deals with first things, with principles and universals. In this respect, this book cannot help being painfully out of step with the zeitgeist of cultural studies and literary scholarship, which, for some time now, have been geared first and foremost toward what is purportedly new or original, and socially toward individualism and the unceasing (re)production of differences, large or small, essential or cosmetic, real, symbolic, or phantasmatic. Conversely, thought on reconciliation, unity, and identity as shared humanity is often relegated to a niche existence, even where its necessity is acknowledged.

The irony in this reproduces the dilemma of modern society as described by Girard in 1961. In distinguishing between romantic and novelistic writers, he draws the following analogy: "Novelists see little value in romantic individualism which, despite vain efforts to hide it, is always a product of opposition. Modern society is no longer anything but a *negative imitation* and the effort to leave the beaten path forces everyone inevitably into the same ditch" (*DDN* 100). The imperative that our methodologies, theories, and objects be ever fresh and original finds a formidable antidote in mimetic theory. For the latter exposes the inherent romanticism of this imperative, suggesting provocatively that, more often than not, our constant pursuit of being *en vogue* is motivated less by what constitutes a worthy cause, or simply good scholarship, than by the vain desire to outdo our academic rivals and distinguish ourselves as unique and original voices in the crowd.

Even dispensing with this critique, it can hardly be argued that novelty and originality should be the be-all and end-all of literary criticism. As a field, literary and cultural studies depend on tradition as much as innovation, which, more often than not, turns out to be the rediscovery of what, in T. S. Eliot's words, "has been lost / And found and lost again and again" (2004a, 182). I am not making claims to originality, absolute truth, or explaining everything. A better way to assess the merit of a theory is to demonstrate how well it works when its ideas and methods are adopted. What is more, as McKenna argues in *Violence and Difference*, theories need to be cross-read and tested against one another in order "to decide what theory accounts for the best in literature as well as, concomitantly, what literature accounts best for what makes us human and for what goes on among us, including what makes us behave in ways we regard as inhuman" (22). The yardstick of any literary theory then must finally be "how much literary substance it really embraces, comprehends and makes articulate" (*DDN* 3). That is the true test to which this study must submit.

As stated, my interest here is first and foremost in understanding McCarthy's apocalypse. This vision represents the most pressing formulation of "issues of life and death," the bare-bones, naturalistic facts of which precede, transcend, and in some regards unify more particular and context-sensitive categories of race, class, gender, or religious denomination. In radical fashion, it ties the survival of the individual to that of the species and further challenges us to justify that survival in the face of the damage we have caused to ourselves and the world we live in. It is the logic behind the McCarthyan apocalypse that needs to be understood: its causes, its dynamics, and the way it stretches back unto a time when the ancestors of *homo sapiens* first killed one of their own and along which it extends forth into the ashen wastes of an uncertain future. A notion not to be shaken, too, this goes beyond a literary fiction, encompassing instead the real possibility that it is for McCarthy. As fellow novelist Madison Smartt Bell once put it, at his most urgent and insightful, McCarthy delivers "pronouncements on the order of what Job heard from the whirlwind" (2000, 5). In other words, in McCarthy's hands, the apocalyptic mode returns to a mode of prophecy. Through it, literature itself becomes a matter of life and death.

CHAPTER 1

Sanguinary Signifiers

The Dis|Orderly Language of Myth, Violence, and Entropy

> For this world also which seems to us a thing of stone and
> flower and blood is not a thing at all but is a tale. [. . .]
> So everything is necessary. Every least thing. [. . .] Because
> the seams are hid from us, you see. The joinery. The way in
> which the world is made. [. . .] And those seams that are
> hid from us are of course in the tale itself and the tale has
> no abode or place of being except in the telling only.
> —Cormac McCarthy, *The Crossing*

In this chapter, I delineate the theoretical map that unfolds a unified poetic field allowing for an integrative reading of Cormac McCarthy's oeuvre in light of his overarching concern with life and death. On a thematic level, this concern manifests itself as a relation between "humans to the world" on the one hand, and a relation of "humans to their fellow humans" on the other. The first is realized chiefly in *The Crossing*'s vision of the "world as a tale," that is, as *myth*. The second puts into focus the prevalence of *violence* in his fiction. Yet, McCarthy reminds us, we also need to look at "the joinery" and trace the "seams that are hid from us"—hidden in the story itself. So our approach needs to enable us to look at how McCarthy's fiction relates these relations to one another. On this operative level and prime domain of literary criticism, the discussion of life-and-death issues will be reconceptualized from the perspective of order and disorder, which here denotes the concept of *entropy*.

Drawing on narratology, mimetic anthropology, psychoanalysis, historiography, and thermodynamics and information theory, the kind of interdisciplinary, kaleidoscopic approach pursued here by necessity involves a change of frameworks, or languages. Consequently, it exemplifies Heinz von Foerster's insight that "the amount of order, or of complexity" that we discover "is unavoidably tied to the language in which we talk about these phenomena. That is, in changing languages, different orders and complexities are created" (179). Labyrinthine though they initially appear, such complexities are an integral part of the architecture of McCarthy's fiction. After considering the relations of myth, violence, and entropy, we will investigate the interplay of these elements. In particular, this requires a look at thematic intersections and structural analogies in which the dichotomy of *order* and *disorder* (dis|order) takes center stage as an abstraction of the McCarthyan opposition par excellence—that between *life* and *death*.

To understand McCarthy's apocalyptic vision, we need to understand not simply its thematic poles, but also the dynamics of psychological, social, natural, and semiological processes unfolding between them in the poetic joinery of human interests and disciplines that is the ideal of the McCarthyan novel. Like the thread of Ariadne, McCarthy's words and fiction will constantly guide us along the hidden seams of his work on our way through this uncharted maze. In particular, this applies to those works that do not receive full analyses in the following chapters but that nonetheless prove illuminating in context.

The World as Tale:
Myth and Literature

All is telling. Do not doubt it.
—Cormac McCarthy, *The Crossing*

Discussing a body of literature as deliberately about the nature of narrative as McCarthy's, it seems altogether fitting to begin this discussion by telling a story from the continent McCarthy's ancestors made their home. The following is a tale told by the Tlicho or Dogrib nation of northwestern Canada: A woman has sexual intercourse with a dog. Eventually giving birth to six puppies, she is expelled by her tribe. Forced to look for food for herself and her offspring, she discovers one day that the puppies are actually human children who shed their dog skins whenever she leaves. She tricks them into thinking she left again, only to sneak back and hide away their dog skins. Forced to remain fully human, her children become the ancestors of the Dogrib and of all mankind.[1]

The Dogrib's tale is easily recognized as the kind of story commonly referred to as a myth. As is often noted and reflected in titles like *Myth, Legend, Dust: Critical Responses to Cormac McCarthy* and *Cormac McCarthy and the Myth of American Exceptionalism*, this makes them a type of tale that McCarthy's oeuvre is deeply invested with. One of his avowed motives for moving to the Southwest was his fascination with the mystique of the West: "There isn't a place in the world you can go where they don't know about cowboys and Indians and the myth of the West" (Woodward 1992, 36). Yet, whether one considers the Southern Appalachian or the Southwestern period of his career, McCarthy's works consistently draw on the themes and motifs of classical and modern, European and regional American mythologies, with some scholars maintaining that his novels are essentially *mythoclastic*—investigating the mythologies of their culture in order to interrogate, invert, and deconstruct them.

McCarthy's mythic eclecticism ranges from the smaller scale of legends, folktales, and corridos to the grander traditions of "the pastoral" and "the frontier."[2] By itself, such interest is hardly remarkable. Similar fascination has been a mainstay of Western literature, inspiring poets from Ovid and Dante Alighieri to Shakespeare and Johann Wolfgang von Goethe to James Joyce and T. S. Eliot, and informing works of art from the *Iliad* and *The Metamorphoses* to *Apocalypse Now* and *Star Wars*. As with any of these, it is what McCarthy does with the myths that he employs that is important. "Mythology, the body of inherited myths in any culture, is an important element of literature, and [. . .] literature is a means of extending mythology. That is, literary works may be regarded as 'mythopoeic,' tending to create or recreate certain narratives which human beings take to be crucial to their understanding of their world" (Coupe 4). In fact, myth is often considered the fountainhead of literature.³ Conversely, literature is never fully rid of myth. Instead, it displaces it to a lesser or greater extent by means of its various modes and genres, according to ruling ideals of verisimilitude and "canons of morality or plausibility" (Frye 1971, 365)—from the most to the least mimetic (here, *representational*) modes (Coupe 159–64). Characterizations of McCarthy as a mythoclast who deconstructs Western mythologies thus need to be reexamined according to the degree to which his narratives remain themselves mythical, especially where violence is concerned.

Yet before this dimension of McCarthy's novels can be explored, we need to ask: What exactly is a myth? Mythography, the study of myths and of the process of mythopoesis, provides a variety of answers. In fact, it offers about "as many definitions of myth as there are myths themselves" (Morales 2).⁴ Rather than adding yet another definition, it thus seems more productive to explore some of the more pertinent ideas. In this way, we can begin to open up a shared horizon for the underlying dimension of myth in McCarthy.

A good place to start is taking a look at the meanings attached to the word itself. In everyday speech, *myth* may refer to a commonly held belief that is factually untrue and usually known to be so. It is a myth that lightning never strikes twice, that women are worse drivers than men, that Washington never told a lie, or that Cormac McCarthy ended up at the Santa Fe Institute because "he rode up on a mule one day [. . .] and the mule died" (Kushner). What these examples reflect but barely is the *narrative* mold of myth. Many mythographers, notably Lévi-Strauss and Barthes, locate it on a linguistic or semiological level. They tell us that "myth *is* language" that "to be known [. . .] has to be told" (Lévi-Strauss 1963, 209), and that it is a "type of speech" (Barthes 109). Etymologically, *mythos* means exactly that: word, speech, fable, narrative. Myth shares this meaning with another Greek word, *logos*, but whereas "the former came to signify fantasy," the latter was increasingly denoted as "rational argument" (Coupe 9). In a way, the everyday view of myth is thus confirmed: a myth is a story that is fantastic, but certainly not true.

Still, to say that myth is "an untrue tale" does not yet say much. Paradoxically, next to "illusory stories," David Leeming identifies another, simultaneously valid view of myth as "containers of eternal truth" (xii)—a truth, that is, beyond the facts of history. Similarly, we might take the meaning of myth to be symbolic rather than historical or literal. In this quality, myth functions much like the Mexican corrido, which, as one of McCarthy's characters proclaims, "does not owe its allegiance to the truths of history but to the truths of men" (*CRO* 386). Now, the notion of truth necessarily implies an idea of representation, the referent of which is generally (a view of) the world and the people who inhabit it: "Mythic narratives are the sacred stories that are central to cultural identity because, for the cultures to which they belong, these religious myths convey some significant truth about the relationship between human beings and the source of being" (Leeming xi).

In sum, myth is thus a quasi-religious tale that is charged with both the epistemological task of making sense of the world that surrounds us, and the task of establishing our personal and cultural identity and place within that world. Across cultures, this endeavor produces a vast array of different characteristics. The various templates for myth narrative can be distinguished by the paradigmatic nature of their plots—for example, *cosmogony, fertility myth, heroic myth,* or *deliverance myth.*[5] While different mythographers privilege different paradigms, for Mircea Eliade, myth at its purest takes the shape of cosmogony:

> The myth, then, is the history of what took place *in illo tempore*, the recital of what the gods or the semidivine beings did at the beginning of time. To tell a myth is to proclaim what happened *ab origine*. Once told, that is, revealed, the myth becomes apodictic truth; it establishes a truth that is absolute. [. . .] The myth proclaims the appearance of a new cosmic situation or of a primordial event. [. . .] It is for this reason that myth is bound up with ontology. (95)

For Eliade, myth commemorates "dramatic irruptions of the sacred into the world." These irruptions constitute the founding events of (a) reality. What comes into being may well be the world as a whole, but it may also be "only a fragment—an island, a species of plant, a human institution" (Eliade 95, 97), or, as in the Dogrib myth, the founding of a community and the establishment of a law (e.g., the prohibition of bestiality).

In myth, the founding of a reality is thus retraced and symbolically reenacted as narrative. Some of the best-known creation myths thus also tie the spoken word to the act of creation itself: Just consider the book of Genesis, where God's verbal commands directly create and shape the world, or the Gospel of John, where "the Word" is at once the divinity incarnate and the source and the way from and through which everything is made (see Jn. 1:1–5).[6] Naturally, this idea of a *creatio ex nihilo* through words has long exerted an irresistible fascination on poets and writers, who find their art reflected there. So too, in a mystical dream of McCarthy's *The Crossing*, we are presented with the vision of a God "weaving the world. In his hands it flowed out of nothing and in his hands it vanished into nothing once again. Endlessly" (*CRO* 149). Appropriately, the Latin word for a woven fabric is none other than *textum*, and as such, the world in McCarthy appropriately materializes as a delicate fabric of words, a tale. To recall, the world itself, "which seems to us a thing of stone and flower and blood is not a thing at all but is a tale" (*CRO* 143). In the literal sense, nothing could be more mythic than this conception. Yet it also rings true to our shared experience, which is itself accessible through the stories we tell ourselves *about* ourselves. However, these stories run deeper than the innocent fantasies we often take them to be.

Modern Myth and the Question of Function

Myths are stories we tell ourselves about the world, and more importantly about *where*, *how*, and *who* we are in the world. As such, these stories exemplify in prototypical fashion one of the central insights of narratology: how we see ourselves and the world around us is shaped by narrative, as "man naturally seeks to understand his world in order to control it, and his first act in compassing this end is an act of the mind or imagination" (*REG* 7). If our thinking itself is circumscribed and structured by language, language being the primary medium we "think in," we are just as dependent on the regulating operations of storytelling when it comes to ordering our daily experience. At their most mythic when telling of the foundation of reality, myths are "the most basic expressions of a defining aspect of the human species—the need and ability to understand and to tell stories to reflect our understanding" (Leeming xi–xii) of the world.

Remarkably, in an age that has made us thoroughly insecure about our ability to grasp reality and articulate meaning, Cormac McCarthy has repeatedly expressed a profound respect for the epistemological (and in the mythical sense, ontological) primacy of language. In a key passage of

The Crossing, he writes that "the narrative is itself in fact no category but is rather the category of all categories for there is nothing which falls outside its purview. All is telling. Do not doubt it" (463). Admittedly, this apotheosis of storytelling belongs to one of McCarthy's recurring "wise hermits." Ever pending between madness and revelatory insight, these figures provide the closest thing to an authorial presence, but are of course not identical with the author. Even so, Douglas Wager, who worked with McCarthy on the failed stage production of *The Stonemason*, confirms that the view expressed here is, in fact, McCarthy's: "He talked about how narrative is basic to all human beings, how even people who are buried alive go over their life stories to stay sane. Verification of one's story to someone else is essential to living, he said; our reality comes out of the narrative we create, not out of the experiences themselves" (Arnold 2000, 145).[7] Our equation, then, is that as stories do for an individual, so myths do for a culture.

A problem with the religious conception that reverberates in McCarthy's vision of a god weaving a *world-as-text* and that has dominated our discussion of myth thus far is that it approaches its limits in dealing with modern myths. Most mythographers focus exclusively on ancient mythology. Some, like E. B. Tylor, even hold that mythmaking is restricted to a premodern, or at least presecularized, stage. Contrary to this, works like Barthes's *Mythologies* and Slotkin's frontier trilogy suggest that we remain myth-making animals. But can the narratives of wrestling, the face of Greta Garbo, the brain of Albert Einstein, or the Citroën DS 19 accurately be described in terms of myth? For that matter, can the seemingly indestructible American dream, or the "myth" of the frontier? If so, what in these new myths relates them to the old ones, especially when the religious or sacred subjects of these tales are discounted or dispensed with?

Addressing such categorical problems, Robert Segal has suggested that the complex question of what a myth is can be parsed into questions about the *origin, subject matter,* and *function* of myth (2–3). The last of these is perhaps the most difficult to answer. It is also the most interesting one. To answer it implies answers to the question of *why* mythmaking does or does not endure today. One factor that distinguishes authentic myths from stories of discernible authorship, as well as folktales, legends, or corridos of anonymous origins, is that the events and characters they speak of require a high level of "*collective* recognition to become *mythic*" (Morales 3). From this, it can be inferred that the events and people thus mythified are not only significant, myth itself performs an important task. The function it serves is vital to its community. In this sense, myths can be described as "active agents" predicated on people using them in a "continual process of telling and retelling, of provoking and responding, of critiquing and revising" (Morales 115).

All in all, there is nothing that keeps myth from serving any number of functions.[8] Most of them are easily compatible and complementary. Thus, one could be content with Don Cupitt's succinct summary that "the work of myth is to explain, to reconcile, to guide action or to legitimate" (cit. in Coupe 6). Still, it is worth considering whether there is not something that unifies the various functions myth serves—from the purely epistemological to the psychological or developmental, to the levels of social cohesion, pragmatic action, or legal sanction. If such a basic function can be distilled, it will be a factor that generically defines myths across cultures, continents, and time periods. While I argue that there is such a common denominator, there is no straightforward way to address it without taking a look at the way myth relates to history and ideology. Incidentally, this look also surveys the status of modern myths in the American context, the context of McCarthy's stories.

History, Ideology, and the American Frontier

When he left the streets of Knoxville and the Appalachian mountain ranges for the plains and deserts of the Southwest, Cormac McCarthy joined his voice to a chorus of writers and artists devoted to telling the grand narrative of America in its conception. While that narrative has been a staple of movies and dime novels rather than great literature, its centrality in American identity is beyond doubt. Thus, Richard White argues, the "Wild West" can effectively be considered a piece of modern cosmogony:

> When we try to think of a common story, of a story which we invent about America, we lay that invention in the West. There is no section of America which is less American than any other section, but there are stories that become more American than other stories because we tell them as stories which can include all of us. [...] It probably is an illusion. There's no single experience in the West or any place else. But we fight so much about those

stories because those stories deeply matter. Not because of what happened in the West but of what happens right now, what matters right now. (Ives, 1:45:57–1:47:04)

Talking about the West as America's oldest, most distinctive myth, we cannot avoid talking about the frontier. From the founding of Jamestown in 1607 at the latest, the frontier has been practically synonymous with the West, up to the census's declaration of its closure in 1890. In his seminal study of the frontier in American history, Richard Slotkin traces the evolution of this myth from its beginnings with the arrival of the first English colonists in the New World, through its reformulations in the age of expansion, to what he calls a crisis of American mythography in the wake of the Vietnam War. Like McCarthy, he proceeds from the premise that like our compulsion to tell stories, on which it builds, mythmaking is a "primary attribute of the human mind" (*REG* 4). Being both a psychological and social operation, myths distinguish themselves from other stories through their collective nature and the spiritual investment we, as a culture, have in them. A mythology can thus be described as "a complex of narratives that dramatizes the world vision and historical sense of a people or culture, reducing centuries of experience into a constellation of compelling metaphors" (*REG* 6).

In the American context, few metaphors have proven as compelling and enduring as that of the frontier. Ever since 1893, when Frederick Jackson Turner called the Western frontier "the line of most rapid and effective Americanization" (4), this metaphor has been seen as encapsulating the decisive factor in the formation of American identity. For the individual, it expressed the idea of the West as a region where "the man on the make" could go to make or mend his fortunes. For the young American nation, it embodied the notion of progress by conquest of the wilderness and its "savage" inhabitants, a divinely sanctioned process that would bring about the reinvigoration of the Anglo-Saxon race.

American development has exhibited not merely advance along a single line, but a return to primitive conditions on a continually advancing frontier line, and a new development for that area. American social development has been continually beginning over again on the frontier. This perennial rebirth, this fluidity of American life, this expansion westward

with its new opportunities, its continuous touch which the simplicity
of primitive society, furnish the forces dominating American character.
(Turner 2)

While the Puritan settlers envisioned America as a New Canaan or a shining city upon a hill that would redeem the sins of old Europe, the idea of
"perennial rebirth" puts into focus the themes of resurrection and continual
renewal. It is as mythological a theme as any, evoking Frazer's and the Cambridge anthropologists' idea of fertility rites and the cycle of seasons as a
basic template for mythical narratives, and Eliade's idea of a generative event
that "happened once, but which also happens all the time" (Armstrong 111).
America, too, was an arcadian garden—according to Henry Nash Smith,
"for the imagination, the Garden of the World"—and so an idea that, since
it expressed "the assumptions and aspirations of a whole society" (124), was
decidedly mythic in character.

If the Western frontier was, in Turner's phrase, "the meeting point
between savagery and civilization" (3), the pastoral garden constituted one
of these poles. Geographically, it lay east of the frontier in the established
colonies. Yet its true teleological destination lay eternally west, representing
a "refuge from tyranny and corruption, a safety valve for metropolitan discontents, a land of golden opportunity for enterprising individualists, and an
inexhaustible reservoir of natural wealth on which a future of limitless prosperity could be based" (GN 30). The frontier merged ancient pastoralism,
with its circular structure and notions of fertility, with the progress-oriented
and by extension apocalyptic teleology of expansive development and per-
fectionism. The "master symbol of the garden" with its notions of fertility,
growth, and bucolic bliss dominated during the age of Jeffersonian agrarianism, which centered around "the heroic figure of the idealized frontier
farmer armed with that supreme agrarian weapon, the sacred plow" (Smith
123). The Jacksonian age of expansion that followed focused on the wilderness that lay on the other side of the frontier. The new paradigm brought
into focus the themes of progress through conquest and "savage war," which
was in equal parts "a mythic trope and category of military doctrine" (GN
12). In this revised American myth, the heroes are not the founding fathers,
but "the rogues, adventurers, and land boomers; the Indian fighters, traders,
missionaries, explorers and hunters who killed and were killed until they had

mastered the wilderness," and only then "the settlers who came after" and "the Indians themselves" (*REG* 4).

While individual authors contribute to mythopoesis, it is an essentially communal process that draws on a people's collective historical experience. In this sense, it can be said that "the culture as a whole acts as author," and the myths it produces over generations acquire "a symbolizing function that is central to [its] cultural functioning" (*FE* 373, 16). The process through which history is shaped into myth is one of continuous retelling and narrative adjustment, as a culture's historical experience evolves over time. In the case of the frontier myth, the original ideological task was accounting for and justifying the foundation of the colonies, as well as to serve as a beacon by which the Puritan colonists defined themselves as Americans against the Englishness they left behind and the foreignness of the natives they encountered in the New World. With the expansion of the colonies, the myth was gradually adapted "to account for [America's] rapid economic growth, [its] emergence as a powerful nation-state, and [its] distinctively American approach to the socially and culturally disruptive processes of modernization" (*GN* 10). Nevertheless, as the everyday association of myth with falsehood suggests, myth is anything but a faithful representation of history. As the same stories are told and retold time and again, they are conventionalized, and abstracted, "until they are reduced to a set of powerfully evocative and resonant 'icons' [. . .] in which history becomes a cliché" (*FE* 16). In Barthes's terms, mythification turns history into nature:

> Myth does not deny things, on the contrary, its function is to talk about them; simply, it purifies them, it makes them innocent, it gives them a natural and eternal justification [. . .]. In passing from history to nature, myth acts economically: it abolishes the complexity of human acts, it gives them the simplicity of essences, it does away with all dialectics, with any going back beyond what is immediately visible, it organizes a world which is without contradictions because it is without depth [. . .], it establishes a blissful clarity: things appear to mean something by themselves. (143)

The timeless quality and appeal of myth has its roots in this "simplicity of essences." Myth's naturalization of history goes hand in hand with a widening of the frame of reference to which it applies. Establishing a metaphoric bridge between past and present, every new context in which the tale is invoked actualizes and adds to its significance through "creative acts of transmutation and associative linkage" (*FE* 435), highlighting conflict, irony, and moral lessons over less dramatically conducive elements. In essence, myth is thus "history successfully disguised as archetype" (*FE* 13). Simplification notwithstanding, if myths merely remained popular stories, they would be largely unproblematic. However, in their mythic shape, these stories may "reach out of the past to cripple, incapacitate, or strike down the living" (*REG* 5).

In the dramatic, conflict-driven tale of myth, the figure of the hero-protagonist—in our case the American in passage—naturally conjures up that of the villain-antagonist. In the mythical perception, this antagonist often assumes a face less human than monstrous: "Myths define enemies and aliens and in conjuring them up they say who we are and what we want, they tell stories to impose structure and order" (Warner 1994, 19). In the frontier myth's opposition of civilization and a hostile wilderness, the Indian was associated with the latter, and thus with barbarism and savagery. Following the emerging "calculus of capitalism," this meant that the Indian came to be treated as "an aspect of the world of resources—a tree to be cleared off so the field can be farmed" (*FE* 80). As with any act of communication, there is inevitably something lost in the process. For Girard, it is the identity behind the monsters of mythological violence; for Slotkin, it is the complexity of historical reality, which is always more painful and bewildering than either history or myth articulate.

Myth's distortions go further yet. Though rooted in past experience, its language falsifies historical memory in a fundamental way. While certain myths may represent historical details accurately, "what is lost when history is translated into myth is the essential premise of history—the distinction of past and present itself" (*FE* 24). Because of this, myth can provide "a scenario for response to events whenever it is successfully invoked" (*REG* 562). In other words, myths do not simply rest at distorting the past; they articulate an implicit or explicit "recipe for action" in the present.[9] These recipes are provided by the respective myth's hero-models: "Mythic space is a metaphor of history, and the heroes in a functioning mythological system represent models of possible historical action" (*GN* 88). It is in this way that a culture's myths are accomplice to its ideology. Unlike openly argumentative vehicles such as manifestos, speeches, or sermons, myth expresses ideology indirectly. The language it employs is metaphorical and suggestive. Its narrative movement "implies a theory of history (or even of cosmology), but these ideas are offered in a form that disarms critical analysis" (*GN* 6), because they are packaged in the form of stories and historical memory. "Myth does not argue its ideology, it exemplifies it" (*FE* 19).[10]

Overall, the effect of mythic concealments, distortions, and imperatives adds up to the creation of a compelling grand illusion Slotkin calls *the fatal environment*. Adopted from Walt Whitman's "From Far Dakota's Cañons,"[11] an early text that fostered what evolved into the myth of "Custer's Last Stand," the fatal environment encompasses the notion

> that Custer's death completes a meaningful myth-historical design, a grand fable of national redemption and Christian self-sacrifice, acted out in the most traditional of American settings. [. . .] And it is essential to the illusion of this myth that Custer's fate seem somehow implicit in the environment, a moral and ideological lesson which seems to emerge from the very nature of things—as if Nature or God composed the story and assigned its meaning, rather than men. (*FE* 11)

Here, we thus find expressed the mythic operation of channeling a phantasmatic perception of events toward real effects in a people's psyche. Through narrative, environments and events are imbued with meaning beyond fact or history. Given their apparent source in the laws of nature or divine providence, a landscape or historical context assumes symbolic significance, and a sequence of events and actions come to appear as inevitable—as *fatal*. "By turning history into myth, we transform random events into a chain of events directed by a will greater than our own, one that is determined and preordained" (Hedges 23–24).

Consequently, what is finally concealed and denied by myth is that "the substance of mythic materials and genres is provided by human authors" (*FE* 15). As the truth of human authorship is removed, so too are all implications of human fallacy, culpability, and responsibility. This provides myth with its problematic aura of inevitability. "Myth is constituted by the loss of the historical quality of things: in it, things lose the memory that they once were made" (Barthes 142). It is in this sense that all mythical objects and even modern, secular myths retain religious qualities. The only way out of this fatal environment of expectations and imperatives is to demystify both our myths and the process of mythmaking itself. As we shall see, though, the way of demystification is strewn with its own pitfalls.

From Chaos to Cosmos

Looking at the American frontier relates the workings of myth to history and ideology. As a narrative the political allegiances of which are statistically on the right, myth argues ad verecundiam. It tells its adherents not only to whom a given object—a sacred relic, a piece of land, a position of power, etc.—belongs, but to whom it belongs *rightfully* by divine mandate, venerable tradition, purported merit, or the presumed will of the people.[12] In this sense, myth can be said to be concerned with establishing and/or legitimizing a "hierarchy of possessions" (Barthes 155) the conflictual dimension of which becomes central in mimetic theory. Yet the more elementary notion turns out to be that of order and disorder. This dichotomy is an attribution of the mind that perceives the world, more so than a property of the world itself. In shaping our understanding, the simplifications involved in mythopoesis amount to establishments of a lower-grade order in the overwhelming complexity of the present.

   At this point, it is helpful to return to the subject matter of myth. While much can be said about similarities that exist across mythologies, the mythical leitmotif par excellence has to be the emergence of a cosmos, of a world ordered and arranged according to reason, out of an a priori state of chaos. Early texts such as Hesiod's *Theogony* (ca. 700 BC) still envision *chaos* as an unfathomable empty void, an indefinite abyss that existed before everything else (ll. 116–38). The work of Anaxagoras, Plato's *Timaios*, and Ovid's *Metamorphoses* redefine chaos as an amorphous primordial matter that serves as the stuff of creation:

> It was a rude and undeveloped mass,
> that nothing made except a ponderous weight;
> and all discordant elements confused,
> were there congested in a shapeless heap. (Ovid, ll. 5–8)

Both ideas merge in the West's premier creation myth, the book of Genesis. There, the earth is initially *tohu wa bohu*, "without form and void" (Gn. 1:2), until God, in successive creative acts, separates and thus orders day and night, seas and heavens, and creates dry land, plants, animals, and finally the first humans. Chaos and nothingness thus seem closely related. Both can be conceptualized solely from a position of existence and order respectively.

Not all creation myths unfold so peaceably. Order, quite often, comes at the cost of conflict. In the Babylonian *Enuma Elish*, the god-hero Marduk slays the older sea and chaos goddess Tiamat and consecutively divides her corpse into heaven and earth. It is the murder of Ymir, the primeval, hermaphrodite giant of Norse mythology, that provides the raw material from which the gods fashion the world. Similarly, the primordial first man Purusha of the Indian Rig Veda offers himself up as sacrifice to make the world and social castes of ancient Indian society. And the Chinese giant Pangu works himself to death over the course of thirty-six thousand years during which he separates yin and yang, heaven and earth. After death, his body gives rise to mountains, rivers, winds, forests, and all the elements of the *cosmos*. The theme of sacrificial or violent death as an origin also finds itself on a smaller scale: In the Abrahamic religions, Cain, the first murderer, is also the first city builder. Likewise, the founding of Rome coincides with the vengeful murder of Remus by Romulus.

In sum, the subject matter of these cosmogonic myths ranges from cataclysmic battles between gods and giants to mundane fratricide and more or less voluntary (self-)sacrifice. In myth, violence and chaos serve as the fertile soil for life and the ordered world. It is striking, too, that the tales that exhibit this pattern originate in vastly different cultures, time periods, and geographical regions. Their remarkable parallels cannot be explained away by any sort of interdependence or exchange, even adjusting for the extraordinarily long half-life of myth: The existence of the pattern is nothing if not astounding, especially as it would appear to clash with the boundlessness of narrative creativity in the rich variety of cultural contexts:

> On the one hand it would seem that in the course of a myth anything is likely to happen. There is no logic, no continuity. Any characteristic can be attributed to any subject; every conceivable relation can be found. With

myth, everything becomes possible. But on the other hand, this apparent
arbitrariness is belied by the astounding similarity between myths collected in widely different regions. Therefore the problem: if the content
of a myth is contingent, how are we going to explain the fact that myths
throughout the world are so similar? (Lévi-Strauss 1963, 208)

Indeed, the improbable similarities of supposedly fantastic constructions of
the cultural imagination present a riddle to mythography. One answer may
lie with Eliade's proposition that myth originates in a momentously creative
event. Yet, at this stage, the nature of this event is difficult to pin down, as
is an answer to the question of how such events could have been so similar
across cultures as to produce the patterns discerned.

One answer is Carl Gustav Jung's hypothesis that mythical stories arise as
a function of the human psyche and a supposed *collective unconscious*, which
harbors all the images or *archetypes* from which myth is allegedly fashioned
(Jung 7–10).[13] Another answer in the "quest for the invariant" is provided by
Claude Lévi-Strauss's structuralist approach (1995, 8). Like Jung, he posits
that "myths get thought in man unbeknownst to him" (1995, 3), yet Lévi-
Strauss goes beyond most psychoanalysts in making good on Jacques Lacan's
claim that "the unconscious is structured like a language" (2006c, 737). So
Lévi-Strauss takes us back to the etymological root of myth in asserting that
the nature of myth partakes in the Saussurean dimensions of both *langue*
and *parole*. The "operational value" of myth, he posits, is rooted in its structure, which persists through its actualizations in past, present, and future.
The structure is built on invariant, synchronic and diachronic "constituent
units" or "bundles of relations," called *mythemes*. Reminiscent of Slotkin's
"constellations of compelling metaphors" (*REG* 6), mythemes function akin
to phonemes, morphemes, and sememes, but "belong to a higher and more
complex order," persisting "at the sentence level" (Lévi-Strauss 1963, 211–12).

To Lévi-Strauss, the thought expressed in mythic narratives organized
around mythemes progresses from the perception of oppositions toward the
reconciliation of these oppositions. "Myth is a form of language, and language itself predisposes us to attempt to understand ourselves and our world
by superimposing dialectics, dichotomies, or dualistic grids upon data that
may in fact be entirely integrated. And underneath language lies the binary

nature of the brain itself" (Doniger viii). In this way, the ubiquity of the mythematic opposition of *chaos* and *cosmos* becomes explicable. Myth is not simply a creative undertaking but also an intellectual one, and so characterized, in Wallace Stevens's memorable phrase, by a "blessed rage for order" (130). As we shall see, this rage regularly threatens to devour order itself. Still, the establishment of order is common to "all the intellectual undertakings of mankind," suggesting that there is "a basic need for order in the human mind" (Lévi-Strauss 1995, 12). Here we arrive at the elementary function of myth.

In his 1923 essay on "*Ulysses*, Order and Myth," T. S. Eliot tellingly referred to the poet's attempt "of controlling, of ordering, of giving a shape and a significance to the immense panorama of futility and anarchy which is contemporary history" as "the mythical method" (1975, 177–78). Whatever the paradigm, and whether or not we assume that the function of myth is to explain the world, to establish cultural identity, to prescribe modes of appropriate behavior by offering recipes for action, to provide insight into the sacred truths of the cosmos, to reconcile humans with the dramatic facts of suffering and death, or to legitimate a given status quo—all such paradigms and all such relations presuppose a superordinate "passage from disorder to order" (Girard 1984, 80). Myth is instrumental in narratively processing and facilitating this passage, as it is in consolidating the order at its terminus. Reflexively, myth orders its adherents to leave the order it establishes alone.

"The shape of the road is the road" (*CRO* 230), McCarthy writes. In the end, what distinguishes myth from other forms of narrative is not its themes or scope, but that the mythical *subject matter* par excellence cannot be separated from its collective and basic cultural *function* of ordering the world. This ordering function of the tales we tell—inherent in and indispensable to all narrative, the reflexive epistemology of which helps us discern the order that it establishes in the first place—finds its original expression in myth. Returning to the beginning of this chapter with another McCarthyan phrase, we can say that the "order in creation" that we see is that which we have put there, "like a string in a maze, so that [we] shall not lose [our] way" (*BM* 245). Myth *is* that string. And yet it is also, in a way, the maze, for it can trap us in its architecture, exposing us to the violent monsters within. Their frightening masks, we shall find, hide nothing but our own distorted visage.

A Fundamental Anthropology:
The Mimetic Theory of Violence and Culture

The ends of all ceremony are but to avert bloodshed.
—Cormac McCarthy, *The Crossing*

As the cosmogonic tales of our forefathers suggest, violence is as old and older
still than myth itself. Frequently, it becomes its subject. In turn, the effects
of myth—particularly its leveling of historical complexities, including the
sensory immediacy of bloodshed—shape the ways violence manifests itself
within the world. On the communal level, violence often assumes mythical
qualities. So much is apparent in war, the media distortions of which, especially in its early stages, provide case studies in Slotkin's fatal environment. As
war unfolds, it tends to be mythologized as it becomes part of the historical
narrative. Conversely, the history of civilization is often framed in terms of
conflict. Just so, Heraclitus suggested "war" or "strife" as a universal mover
and first principle of change in the world of men: "War is the father of all and
the king of all; and some he has made gods and some men, some bound and
some free" (Kirk, Raven, and Schofield 194). The endurance of this principle
was attested, too, by Edward Gibbon, whom McCarthy invokes in *The Sunset Limited*, and who spoke of history as "little more than the register of the
crimes, follies, and misfortunes of mankind" (102). About two hundred years
after Gibbon, William and Ariel Durant soberingly calculated that of "the
last 3,421 years of recorded history only 268 have seen no war" (81).

Paradisiac mythologies notwithstanding, there is no reason to assume
that prehistory was more peaceful: *homo sapiens* has ever also been *homo
necans*. As Sigmund Freud saw, the inherent challenge of violence only
becomes the more pressing when, post Enlightenment, we are forced to reconcile its dominance with the ideal of human rationality:

> [M]en are not gentle creatures who want to be loved, and who at the most
> can defend themselves if they are attacked; they are, on the contrary, crea-
> tures among whose instinctual endowments is to be reckoned a powerful
> share of aggressiveness. As a result, their neighbor is [. . .] someone who
> tempts them to satisfy their aggressiveness on him, to exploit his capacity

for work without compensation, to use him sexually without his consent, to seize his possessions, to humiliate him, to cause him pain, to torture and to kill him. *Homo homini lupus.* Who, in the face of all his experience of life and of history, will have the courage to dispute this assertion? (1961, 68–69)

Blood Meridian's Judge Holden would no doubt second, yes, even celebrate this image of man. Yet, if in the light of the record, we accept our wolf-nature as fact and fate, a new set of problems unfolds: What is the origin of violence? Is it a product of nature, or is it culturally determined in some fundamental way? Is violence wholly irrational, or does it have its reason(s) and purposes? What levels of human interaction does it pertain to, and to what effects? Finally and vitally: How is violence kept in check?

Conceptually, a good starting point in answering these questions, is Slavoj Žižek's categorical distinction between one purely subjective and two objective forms of violence. *Subjective violence* is the directly visible violence of "clearly identifiable agent[s]," demanding our attention as "a perturbation of the 'normal,' peaceful state of things." As such, it is experienced against an objective, apparently peaceful normalized zero-level of violence. There, we find first *symbolic violence*, which extends from "cases of incitement and of the relations of social domination reproduced in our habitual speech forms" to the more fundamental dimension of "language as such, to its imposition of a certain universe of meaning." Myth narrative falls into this category. The second distinction here is the *systemic violence* that is conditional to "the smooth functioning of our economic and political systems." More directly than its symbolic form, systemic violence breeds "what otherwise seem to be 'irrational' explosions of subjective violence" (Žižek 2009, 1–3).

Exemplarily addressing the subjective and systemic dimensions of violence, Thomas Hobbes famously proceeded from the premise that the natural condition of man was in fact one of war, "and such a war, as is of every man, against every man" (84). This condition was to be overcome through human rationality: by means of a *social contract* in which people surrender some of their natural freedoms to a "common power to keep them all in awe" (Hobbes)—that is, the state, the eponymous *Leviathan* (1651) of his work, which would protect its citizens and regulate their relations. In contrast, Freud envisioned the process of civilization in mythological terms, as the constant struggle between two opposing drives within man: *Eros*, "whose purpose is to combine single human individuals, and after that families, then races, peoples and nations, into one great unity, the unity of mankind," and an aggressive or death drive, which is expressed in "the hostility of each against all and of all against each" (1961, 81–82), and which Freud's students called *Thanatos*.[14]

These theories are but two among a vast number of attempts at coming to grips with the challenge of violence. Influential as they all have been within their fields, most of these attempts bear the character of localized analysis rather than systematic theorization. Among them, genuine theories like Freud's or Hobbes's fall somewhat short for relying on largely axiomatic constructs (e.g., the death drive, the social contract). Others pertain to isolated aspects of the problem only. None of them provides a framework that integrates the evolutionary as well as the psychological, symbolic, and systemic dimensions of violence, and so would allow for holistic analysis. Finally, none of them provides a compelling answer to that great mystery of how, when confronted with a violent inclination infinitely disruptive of social relations, it was possible for civilization to emerge and endure in the first place.

Mimetic theory, the life's work of René Girard, has been dedicated to addressing just these problems. In sum, Girard proposes "a morphogenetic hypothesis concerning the generation of social and cultural order" (Fleming 41)—a theory of the role of violence and religion in human evolution that addresses the subjective, as well as the systemic and symbolic, dynamics of violence. Since his theory originates in literary analysis, it is also singularly suited to apply to the fiction of McCarthy. In the following, I will trace the first two of three major steps in the development of mimetic theory: firstly, the discovery of *mimetic desire*, which identifies subjective violence as a consequence of rivals clashing around a mutually desired object, potentially affecting the entire social system, and secondly, the resolution of such crisis through what he calls the *scapegoat mechanism*.

The Imitative Animal

To follow Girard's argument about the role of violence in human culture, it is essential to first get a grasp of what is arguably the central concept of his theory: the notion of mimetic desire. A self-identified Darwinist, Girard posits that the evolutionary transition from primates to humans and the development of human culture—what he calls the process of hominization—is instrumentally driven by an intensifying neurological specialization toward imitation (Gk. *mimesis*). Today, asserting the "centrality of imitative behavior in human social and cognitive development" (Fleming 10), while perhaps not a matter of course, may not seem too outrageous a claim either. Developmental psychologists like Andrew Meltzoff have demonstrated that "infants are able to imitate immediately at birth," and so have made compelling arguments that being both "preverbal and pre-representational," this "intersubjective capacity for imitation" must be "the starting state of human cognition and sociality" (Garrels 2011b, 239). In the 1990s, the discovery of mirror neurons and their confirmation in humans only reinforced this argument, revitalizing interest in mimesis.[15] Yet, in the 1960s, the centrality Girard awarded to imitation was neither evident nor fashionable, proving largely "antithetical to [...] the predominant and overarching view of Western philosophical and scientific thinking [...] that humans are fundamentally self-enlightened or autonomous beings" (Garrels 2011a, 2).

Historically, there certainly existed a tentative concept of man as *homo mimeticos*.[16] Yet our understanding is skewed by the influence of Plato's theory of ideas and Aristotle's subsequent emphasis on art as imitative of nature, limiting it to an aspect of representation. Generally considered a form of gregariousness and social cohesion rather than division, even prescient forerunners on mimetic thought like William James thus conceived of imitation as independent from feelings like jealousy and envy. Girard's great innovation is unifying them as particular manifestations of imitation itself with his concept of *mimetic desire*. To the idea of imitation as *representation*, he adds the dimension of *appropriation*: "It is obvious that appropriation figures formidably in the behavior of human beings [...] and that such behavior can be copied" (*TII* 8). In addition to our ability to learn languages, behavioral patterns, and various skills by imitating others, Girard contends that we should also think of desire as rooted in imitation: "We must understand that desire itself is essentially mimetic, directed toward an object desired by [a] model" (*VS* 146)—that is, a person who is imitated in his apparent desires. In this, mimetic desire is distinct from the "the sexual origin of desire" posited in psychoanalysis, as well as from basic "animal needs for hydration, shelter, rest, and nutrition," which for Girard do not suffice to constitute desire, though they "may serve as pretexts" for its formation (Fleming 10–11).

While Girard later expanded his focus to anthropology and theology, it is from literature that he derived his initial hypotheses. Based on his readings of novelists like Miguel de Cervantes, Marcel Proust, and Fyodor Dostoevsky, and later, playwrights like Sophocles, Euripides, and Shakespeare, he suggests that whereas we tend to think of desire as *according to Oneself,* that is, as directed toward an object of our choosing, the truth of the matter is that we unwittingly desire *according to Another*. Reflecting the view of humans as self-enlightened beings, the psychology of literary heroes frequently espouses a conception of desire as original and autonomous. Like McCarthy's Suttree, most of us pride ourselves on our individuality, affected as we are by a more or less "subtle obsession with uniqueness" (*SUT* 113). In contrast, Girard argues that to believe in the autonomy of desire is to fall prey to a form of (self-)deception, a "romantic lie." Great works like *A Midsummer Night's Dream, Don Quixote, À la recherche du temps perdu,* or *Notes from the Underground*—and, we shall see, practically all of McCarthy's novels—reveal the "novelistic truth" about the decidedly prosaic, unoriginal nature of desire: "We learn what to desire [. . .] by copying the desires of others" (Fleming 5).

Perhaps this concept of desire is best illustrated when contrasted with Freud's, the most famous expression of which is the Oedipus complex. Frequently diagnosed in the parental relations of McCarthy's fiction, any reinterpretation of the complex is of analytical import as well. At its core, Freud's theorem proposes that boys between the age of three and five come to sexually desire their mother—the "incest wish"—and seek to assume the place of their father: the "patricide wish." Only at a later stage is the resolution of the complex achieved through identification with (and symbolic internalization of) the father, the representative of the law, authority, and the budding superego that prohibits such cravings.

Like our everyday idea of it, this concept of desire is essentially *bipolar,* oriented toward an inherently desirable object, the prime example of which is the mother. In contrast, mimetic desire is *triangular*. It involves a process of mediation between a subject (or disciple), a model (or mediator), and an object selected largely arbitrarily. This process "detaches desire from any predetermined object, whereas the Oedipus complex fixes desire on the maternal object" (*VS* 180). Structurally, it is thus no different from any other process of mimetic desire and resulting rivalry. In contrast to Freud though, the sequence of identification and desire is reversed in mimetic mediation, desire being linked to and viewed as the consequence of mimesis. The son copies the desire of his model, which happens to be the father. "The identification is a desire *to be* the model that seeks fulfillment [. . .] by means of appropriation; that is, by taking over the things that belong to his father" (*VS* 170).

For Girard, most objects we crave are not desirable as such. They do not telegraph their inherent desirability. As in the thought of Lacan, triangular desire is consequently centered more on the Other than on the object: "Human desire [. . .] is always 'desire of the Other' in all the senses of that term: desire for the Other, desire to be desired by the Other, and especially, desire for what the Other desires" (Žižek 2009, 74). Hence, it is an admired model's desire, "real or presumed, which makes [an] object infinitely desirable in the eyes of the subject" (*DDN* 7). This is what Girard calls *mediation*. Beyond our animal needs, all desire can be said to have always already been mediated, be it by the models that surround us in our daily lives or the enchanting worlds we are constantly exposed to by the media.

Desire may be mediated *externally*, if the subject or "disciple" is separated from "the model" or "mediator" by a certain irreducible distance in time, space, or social rank. In myth, this distance is reflected by the models and recipes of action provided by gods and heroes. Where no such distance exists, desire is mediated *internally*. This is the sphere of conflict. At the point where the internally mediated desire of model and disciple collide, it turns them into rivals. Their relationship may become conflictual for two reasons. Firstly, their roles are reciprocal since "the disciple can also serve as a model, even to his own model." Invariably, the model is a disciple of other models. Secondly, the mediator of desire emanates a contradictory double imperative—"Imitate me!" and "Do not imitate me!"—the latter of which can be read as "Do not appropriate my object" (*VS* 147).[17] The model for any given desire thus simultaneously becomes the obstacle (Gk. *skandalon*) to its fulfillment.

The irony of desire is that the object recedes from view as the relationship between model and disciple intensifies. In this, the object functions similarly to the logic of *objet petit a* in Lacanian psychoanalysis—designating an essential void or lack in the psyche, satisfaction of which remains forever out of reach.[18] For the true goal of desire, Girard posits, is not the object, but rather a certain quality of the model, which is on some level perceived as a superior being:

> Once his basic needs are satisfied (indeed, sometimes even before), man is subject to intense desires, though he may not know precisely for what. The reason is that he desires *being*, something he himself lacks and which some other person seems to possess. The subject thus looks to that other person to inform him of what he should desire in order to acquire that being. If the model, who is apparently already endowed with superior being, desires some object, that object must surely be capable of conferring an even greater plenitude of being. It is not through words, therefore, but by the example of his own desire that the model conveys to the subject the supreme desirability of the object. (*VS* 146)

As the object itself holds little value, and the desire of the subject is rather directed toward something immaterial, the model's apparent "fullness of being" (*TH* 97), Girard also speaks of *metaphysical desire*. "The object is only a means of reaching the mediator. The desire is aimed at the mediator's *being*" (*DDN* 53).

Driving home this point, McCarthy, too, repeatedly shows that even where there are no material objects, one may still compete for something as elusive as "truth." So do Black and White in *The Sunset Limited*, who—as mimetic doubles to the core—increasingly resemble one another in adopting each other's phrases and gestures and switching roles as their debate unfolds.[19] So too do the theodicy-haunted anchorite of *The Crossing* and his rival, the Mormon turned priest turned witness and narrator, who only through their rivalry and after the anchorite's death becomes finally "himself" (*CRO* 140). While the argument between the two is ostensibly about the nature of God, the eventual realization is that ultimately,

> what we seek is the worthy adversary. For we strike out to fall flailing through demons of wire and crepe and we long for something of substance to oppose us. Something to contain us or to stay our hand. Otherwise there were no boundaries to our own being and we too must extend our claims

until we lose all definition. Until we must be swallowed up at last by the very void to which we wished to stand opposed. (*CRO* 153)

One's being is thus defined in relation to that of another, which one strives to incorporate. This explains why, when the object of rivalry *is* acquired, its fascination evaporates. Naturally so. For the model bested loses its status for the disciple, who turns his or her searching gaze toward new objects and models. Of either, there is no scarcity: secularized and democratized, modern society is rife with internally mediated desire as the barriers of social class, sex, and gender become increasingly permeable and the distance between disciples and potential models decreases. This is not an idiosyncrasy of the information age, but rather, as Alexis de Tocqueville knew, a consequence of the rising egalitarianism of modern democracies.[20]

Increasing equality signals the proliferation of models. It results in a foreshortening of the distance between subject and mediator, a multiplication and intensification of desire. If anything, Girard argues, desire is less substantial and more ephemeral today as the great ideologies of modernity continue to promise metaphysical autonomy: "God is dead, man must take his place. Pride has always been a temptation but in modern times it has become irresistible because it is organized and amplified in an unheard of way" (*DDN* 56). The striving for earthly objects demarcated by our models invariably ends in disappointment, because those objects inevitably fail to bestow the metaphysical plenitude we attribute to them. We are thus perpetually confronted with the void of existential particularity, inadequacy, and lack of definition. Still, the "promise remains true for Others. Each one believes that he alone is excluded from the divine inheritance and takes pains to hide this misfortune" (*DDN* 57). So we keep on desiring and looking for models. It is in this first sense that "men become gods in the eyes of each other" (*DDN* 53).

For Girard, the proper image of the human condition is therefore not Albert Camus's Sisyphus. Instead, "each of us is his own cask of the Danaïdes, which he tries in vain to fill" (*DDN* 261). Like the quest for the Holy Grail, the quest of desire is unceasing, both because we misunderstand the true goal of our desire and because that goal may be unachievable. McCarthy thus writes in *Whales and Men*: "We are arks of the covenant and our true nature is not rage or deceit or terror or logic or craft or even sorrow. It is longing" (130). As the image of the covenant suggests, the conception of "longing" here marks a metaphysical, ultimately religious intent that at once underlies and distinguishes it from its worldly actualizations, aiming for what will finally sate our insatiable hunger for *being*.

One strategy of dealing with this problem may be to renounce desire itself and with it the world and company of others. This is the ascetic withdrawal of McCarthy's many hermits and anchorites. Yet, as the theological dispute of hermit and priest in *The Crossing* exemplifies, withdrawal from the world is no guarantee of remaining free from scandal. Later, we will see that there is yet another way, one that invariably hinges on a profound moment of revelation and emerges at exceedingly rare, yet all the more significant points in McCarthy's stories. On a literary level the emergence of such possibilities can be related to the evolution of the Oedipal theme as identified by John Cant, that is, the changing relationships between fathers and sons in McCarthy's novels. On a metaliterary level, it reflects the issue of authorial anxiety of influence, that is, McCarthy's relationship with *his* literary fathers and *models* in finding his own voice as a writer. Read this way, his work becomes an ongoing reconciliation with "the ugly fact" that "books are made out of books" (Woodward 1992, 31), in his quest to carve out his place within the literary pantheon. Yet what is true of human history is also true to the immediate experience of reading McCarthy's fiction: the most probable outcome in the clash of human desires is violence.

When Degree Is Shaked

So far, mimetic desire appears as the disciple's "cannibalistic" drive to assume the model's status, its being. There is a sense, too, that when desires converge on the same object, they are bound to clash in ways ever in danger of escalating, as Hobbes claimed: "If any two men desire the same thing, which nevertheless they cannot both enjoy, they become enemies; and in the way to their end [. . .] endeavor to destroy, or subdue one another" (83). Originally aroused by mimesis, desire between rival-obstacles in turn only intensifies imitation. It manifests as a feedback loop, rendering opponents increasingly alike in their game of one-upmanship. Left unchecked, this game tends to escalate—from competitive behavior to the symbolic or verbal exchange of hostilities to the actual physical exchange of blows. This intersubjective dynamic has profound repercussions on a broader, social scale.

Again, we do not usually think of mimesis as conflictual. This is so, partially because we tend to restrict it to a representational function, partially because we tend to view it as promoting sociability and gregariousness, as indeed it often does.[21] Violence and aggression instead tend to be essentialized as part of "human nature." In contrast, the concept of mimetic desire locates a primary origin of conflict less within than in-between subjects: violence is not an essence—it emerges *interdividually*. What is inborn is simply a compulsion toward imitation that pervades all areas of social life, placing us under the double bind of acquisitive mimesis. As such, it serves as a breeding ground for conflict, and its imitative quality explains why, once unleashed, violence is so contagious.

What is more, there is a tendency to idolize the models of our desire, whose violence actually becomes a marker of their status. Desire thus "clings to violence and stalks it like a shadow because violence is the signifier of the cherished being, the signifier of divinity" (*VS* 151). Its transcendent quality relates violence to Girard's idea of *the sacred*. We have encountered a similar idea before. To recall, Eliade's analysis of mythic thought is that "creation springs from an abundance," "an excess of power," or "a surplus of ontological substance," the subject of myth ultimately being "this sacred ontophany, this victorious manifestation of a plenitude of being" (97). Yet the gods of myth do not merely create. Frequently, they visit catastrophe upon the human world. Eliade's view of the sacred as a creative event must be broadened to include cataclysmic potentialities. To Girard, it encompasses

> all those forces whose dominance over man increases or seems to increase in proportion to man's effort to master them. Tempests, forest fires, and plagues [. . .] may be classified as sacred. Far outranking these, however, though in a far less obvious manner, stands human violence—violence seen as something exterior to man and henceforth as a part of all the other outside forces that threaten mankind. Violence is the heart and secret soul of the sacred. (*VS* 31)

In its move toward externalization, Girard's sacred resembles less Eliade's than Slotkin's idea of the "fatal environment," the central effect of which is the obfuscation of human authorship and agency. The sacred functions like a smokescreen behind which humans hide their own violence. It is

characterized by what Walter Benjamin calls "mythical violence," a manifestation of the gods' existence, that is, their being (55). So we begin to understand why mimetic desire—at heart ever a metaphysical desire for being—is
attracted to and strives to incarnate "violence triumphant" (*VS* 151). Whatever the contest, the violence of the victor settles matters effectively, ending
all argument about right and wrong, and proclaiming instead the essential
superiority of its wielder.

Still, even in the nuclear age, the threat of violence to society would be
limited if it expended itself in a single act. Yet history and the blood feuds
of so many Montagues and Capulets tell another tale. Mimetic desire and
violence not only feed into each other, they dramatically shape one another
as they do the rivals caught in their web. The prime expression of this is vengeance. So long as there remains one who can exact retribution, there is no
natural end to violence. If it is frequently compared to wildfires or epidemics,
that is because it "is easily 'caught' by others" (Fleming 46), often drawing
in even those trying to halt its proliferation.[22] Each violent act calls forth
its own response: "Vengeance professes to be an act of reprisal, and every
reprisal calls for another [. . .]; in almost every case it has been committed in
revenge for some prior crime. Vengeance, then, is an interminable, infinitely
repetitive process. Every time it turns up in some part of the community, it
threatens to involve the whole social body" (*VS* 14–15).

Vengeance is thus what society must avert above all. According to Girard,
societies throughout history have confronted this threat with various preven-
tive strategies and curative measures. While modern society frequently relies
on the operation of a legal system, in archaic communities it falls especially
to prohibition and ritual to prevent or at least direct violence into "appropriate" channels, prohibiting the mimesis of rivalrous acquisition and, where
this fails, containing the ensuing mimesis of violence.[23] Significantly, these
measures "fall within the domain of religion, where they can on occasion
assume a violent character," as is the case with sacrifice: "Violence and the
sacred are inseparable" (*VS* 19).

Frequently, the smooth operation of prohibitions, laws, and the authority of regulating institutions is dramatically reduced times of upheaval
and profound systemic change. Vice versa, violence itself can weaken the
systems set up to combat it. While natural catastrophes, epidemics, and
economic or humanitarian crises test any society, a central problem is the

sense of confusion that inevitably results and often turns people against their neighbors. Structurally, this is due to what is perhaps the consequence of conflictual mimesis most difficult to grasp, that is, "the progressive erosion of differences between mimetic antagonists" (Fleming 42). Put simply, the more rivals struggle to differentiate themselves, the more they come to resemble one another through their actions guided by the reciprocal logic of their engagement, up to the point where they can be described as *doubles*.

Such undifferentiation is especially pronounced in times of interstate or civil war, yet it is also observable in the rise of social movements. The more radical the movement, the more it works according to totalitarian principles, as Arendt observed: "Whoever is not included is excluded, whoever is not with me is against me, so the world loses all the nuances and pluralistic aspects that have become too confusing for the masses" (1997, 380–81). In war, all who oppose us are lumped into one undifferentiated mass. Seen so, war is also a force of social cohesion, as it "reduces the headache and trivia of daily life. The communal march against an enemy generates a warm, unfamiliar bond with our neighbors, our community, our nation, wiping out unsettling undercurrents of alienation and dislocation" (Hedges 9). This reduction of complexity mirrors the reduction of historical realities at work in mythical narratives. Myth and war are natural bedfellows.

So compelling is their intoxication that they may initially sway even dissidents and pacifists. It promotes a sense of union among a people that is a natural extension of the mimetically driven loss of self in crowds noted by William James. "It is perfectly true that in military as well as revolutionary action 'individualism is the first (value) to disappear'; in its stead, we find a kind of group coherence which is more intensely felt and proves to be a much stronger, though less lasting, bond than all the varieties of friendship, civil or private" (Arendt 1970, 67). The euphoria of any mass movement exerts a powerful mimetic imperative. In the case of war, this imperative necessarily affects more than one nation; it spreads like a disease because war "is a form of contact that [. . .] once adopted by some, must of necessity be adopted by all," and so "tends to stamp a certain sameness on human cultures" (Ehrenreich 134). What observations are made on the subjective level, between individuals, thus also hold true on the systemic level, within and between communities: here as there, the mixture of mimesis and violence radically reduces the social distance between rival individuals, groups, or nations, aligning them in opposing dyads while foreshortening the reciprocity of hostile exchange, and so rendering opposing parties increasingly alike.

In myth, the alignment of mimetic antagonists is narratively reflected through Oedipal relations, as well as doubles, doppelgängers, enemy twins, and rival siblings such as Cain and Abel, Polyneices and Eteocles, or Romulus and Remus. All such constellations feature heavily in McCarthy. Interestingly, they do so frequently in direct juxtaposition with reflections and mirror images, emphasizing symmetry. A prime example is *Suttree*. In a dream, the eponymous protagonist finds himself assailed by a dark figure, whom he initially mistakes to be his father but later finds to be his son (28). More than his troubled relationship with his family, it is Suttree's preoccupation with his stillborn twin brother that gives the lie to his naïve claim to uniqueness. The dead twin haunts him as his "mirror image," and perhaps, too, in his frequent visions of "Antisuttree" reflected off glass, and later, in the woods, of "some doublegoer, some othersuttree" (*SUT* 14, 28, 287). His is but one among a multitude of such configurations. Even as unlikely a dyad as youthful hero John Grady Cole and the ancient dueña Alfonsa in *All the Pretty Horses* can be productively read as mimetic rivals. Their competition to shape the life of Alejandra, John Grady's beloved and Alfonsa's niece, manifests itself chiefly in verbal exchanges accompanied by games of chess. The dueña's claim to social and parental authority—"In this matter, I get to say" (137)—makes her an obstacle for the young pair's race- and class-defying love. Yet it is McCarthy's subtle choice of making both left-handed and paralleling John Grady's cheek scar to Alfonsa's missing fingers that identifies both as rival-doubles: in more ways than would initially appear, they are *alike*.

Even so, the idea of conflict as emerging from a lack rather than an intolerable surplus of difference may seem counterintuitive. Such is to be expected. Where they come into conflict, mimetic antagonists will perceive nothing but differences. Thus White, the professor of *The Sunset Limited*, insists upon the singularity of his own death-wish even among the suicidally depressed. Initially, this is true also of Suttree, who emphatically lashes out at the suggestion that he is similar to either his father, his uncle, or his living brother: "We're not alike. [...] I'm not like you. I'm not like him. I'm not like Carl. I'm like me. Dont tell me who I'm like" (*SUT* 18). History also is full of examples of individuals, and even whole nations, who—with the benefit of hindsight—can be identified as having unwittingly partaken in conflictual mimesis and undifferentiation. So, at the height of the Cold War, most Americans would have failed to see their nation as a mirror image of the USSR, even as the symmetry of the arms race propelled the world toward mutually assured destruction. The red scare and communist witch-hunts effectively undermined the values and civil liberties they purported to protect. Historically, fear of the communist Other thus drove the United States blindly into a pursuit of ideological purity that reflected that of the Soviet Union. "From within the system, only differences are perceived; from without, the antagonists all seem alike" (*VS* 159).

It is not just rivals' tendency to essentialize and exaggerate difference that obstructs their view of identity. Prominent examples notwithstanding, the principle of violence resulting from similarity runs counter to the assumptions of most cultural theory, which tends to explain "conflict in terms of unmanageable differences [...] rather than the absence of those differences" (Fleming 43). Through the lens of mimetic theory, the perspective can be productively reversed. Once we do so, what comes into focus is the dimension of social order as the house built on the foundation of the system regulating difference: "Order, peace, and fecundity depend on cultural distinctions; it is not these distinctions but the loss of them that gives birth to fierce rivalries and sets members of the same family or social group at one another's throats" (*VS* 49).[24]

The abstract effect of mimetic rivalry is an erosion of difference, which sets the conditions for and perpetuates the vicious circle of reciprocal violence. When this dynamic becomes systemic, Girard speaks of a sacrificial crisis in the context of archaic societies and, more generally, of a mimetic crisis. The crisis centers around the structural element of difference itself, which is simultaneously the product, the operative logic, and the result of the system of cultural mediation. In this way, crisis affects interpersonal relationships, institutions, social norms, and hierarchies, disturbing the symbolic operations of ideology, religion, and law. Thus, it puts the entire social structure at risk: "The sacrificial crisis can be defined, therefore, as *a crisis of distinctions*—that is, a crisis affecting the cultural order. This cultural order is nothing more than a regulated system of distinctions in which the differences among individuals are used to establish their 'identity' and their mutual relationships" (*VS* 49). Its causes may range from *external* (epidemics, drought, flood, famine, war) to *internal* ones (political, religious, or social conflicts). Yet fictional and historical accounts of crisis often bespeak a similar experience. It is firstly a social one—one of the "absence of difference, the lack of cultural differentiation, and the confusion that results" (*SG* 13).

In the violent worlds of McCarthy's novels, we frequently encounter just such phenomena of systemic disintegration. General poverty, the encroachment of modernity that sweeps away traditional ways of life, the corruption of law, and sudden eruptions of violence permeate all of the Appalachian works. It is not solely ecocritical sensitivity either that has McCarthy submerge the towns of Red Branch and Sevierville in disastrous floods or that makes the polluted Knoxville River a central motif of *Suttree*. Similarly, the blood-drenched deserts and ruined churches of *Blood Meridian*, the spatiotemporal lack of definition that characterizes the world of *Outer Dark*, and the postapocalyptic wasteland of *The Road* can productively be read as literary examples of a crisis of distinctions. Such catastrophic backgrounds provide a glimpse into the experience of crisis and one more way in which McCarthy's fiction and literature in general partakes in myth.

To recall, this sense of violent confusion—the tension of dis|order—is the mythological theme par excellence. Myths communicate confusion and violence through various symbols and narrative constituent units, what Lévi-Strauss calls *mythemes*. On the one hand, one is struck by the frequency of epidemics and natural disasters. The latter emphasize the collective scale of the catastrophe, yet occlude the social dimension of reciprocity. On the other side of the spectrum, one finds highly individualized crimes—like regicide, patricide, fratricide, incest, bestiality, or blasphemy—motifs, that is, that emphasize both violence and the disintegration of social norms involved in the process. Consequently, Girard classifies such crimes and catastrophes as mythic *symbols of desymbolization.*

How, exactly, do these symbols articulate the crisis? In the Dogrib myth from the beginning of this chapter, the mytheme used is the intermingling of human and animal that evokes the paradox of an unwritten prohibition against bestiality the transgression of which establishes the law in the first place. The myth of Oedipus exemplifies both types of motifs in the plague that afflicts the city of Thebes and the accusations of patricide, regicide, and incest that Oedipus alone is supposedly guilty of: "The act of regicide is the exact equivalent, vis-à-vis the polis, of the act of patricide vis-à-vis the family. In both cases the criminal strikes at the most fundamental, essential, and inviolable distinction within the group. He becomes, literally, the slayer of distinctions" (*VS* 74). Another classical rendition of *sacrificial crisis* is the rivalry between King Pentheus and Dionysus and the madness of the Maenads in Euripides's *The Bacchae*. The Maenads have left Thebes for the wilderness during the time of the Dionysian ceremonies, where they live among beasts, engage in orgiastic rituals, and eventually ravage neighboring cities. Misled by his rival, Pentheus's contestation of Dionysus's divinity results in his being torn to pieces by the women, including his own mother, while he is dressed up as a woman. Dionysus thus embodies the levelling of distinctions between sexes, animals, humans, and gods and triumphantly emerges as the herald of undifferentiation and "god of decisive mob action" (*VS* 134).

The common theme of these tales is the joining of subjective violence with systemic catastrophe as forms of symbolic undifferentiation. In their depiction, myths transform outbursts of subjective violence into symbolic violence. One last, yet particularly insightful early modern dramatization of such crises is Ulysses's famous speech in the first act of Shakespeare's *Troilus and Cressida*. Laying siege to Troy, the Greek army has been internally ruptured, its loyalties split by the open rivalry and contempt between Agamemnon and Achilles. Ulysses addresses his king regarding the "fever" (1.3.595) of demoralization and insubordination that has "infected" the Greeks. His speech (1.3.534–97) ventures from the state of the army to the physical order of the planets to the social order of human societies. Its core amounts to nothing less than a poststructuralist diagnosis *avant la lettre* of the elementary systemic function of difference, which here goes by the name "degree":

> O, when degree is shaked,
> Which is the ladder to all high designs,
> Then enterprise is sick! How could communities,
> [...]
> But by degree, stand in authentic place?
> Take but degree away, untune that string,
> And, hark, what discord follows. Each thing meets
> In mere oppugnancy. (1.3.560–70)

The image of the untuned string suggests a piece of music, which relies on the sequence and distinctness of its notes, on clear rhythms, melodies, and

harmonies not to become a discordant cacophony.[25] So too without "degree,"
everything is plunged into chaos. The stars, which normally circle Sol, just
as the soldiers in the Greek army obey their king, do now wander "in evil
mixture to disorder" (l. 554), causing plagues, storms, earthquakes, general
upheaval, and even mutiny and patricide. Even moral concepts such as "right
and wrong" "lose their names" (ll. 575–77), and so become meaningless.

The meltdown Ulysses describes is hence more than a poetic illustration
of the Elizabethan chain of being (Watt 36). Instead, Shakespeare presents a
treatise on the basic principle of any kind of order that goes beyond the minimal complexity (or maximum simplicity) of an amorphous mass. It is the
criterion of degree—of *differentiating difference*—that, once shaken, affects
and may even unravel all system and order.

> [A]ll particular degrees or differences [...] are specifications of a single dif-
> ferential principle, Degree with a capital D, upon the integrity of which the
> stability of cultural systems and even their existence depend. [...] Degree,
> that is, the cultural order, is transcendental, but in a peculiarly finite and
> fragile way that makes it highly vulnerable not to the stars but to human
> conflict. It has no other reality than the respect it inspires. If this respect
> turns to disrespect at the top, contagion is sure to follow and Degree will
> quickly dissolve in the undifferentiation of mimetic rivalry. (*TE* 162, 164)

Once the crisis of distinctions passes a certain point, the institutions that
uphold order and stability are increasingly perceived as "little more than
additional parties in the same struggle, rather than as its impartial arbitra-
tors" (Fleming 46). Degree or difference, after all, are nothing that exists in
any material sense, but only as an ordering function in people's minds.

Once more, Girard's thought resonates with that of Arendt. She posits
that political power, "the human ability [...] to act in concert," lies with the
rational agency of the unified group, to which the authority of institutions,
which rely on "recognition by those who are asked to obey," is subordinate
(1970, 44–45). This explains why violence spreads "in the void" of genuine
power: where power persists, violence is unnecessary. In turn, the erosion
of political power and institutional authority only propagates violence,
further destabilizing an already shaky system. So, when degree or difference

disappears, everything moves toward relations of violent reciprocity, as described by Ulysses: "Each thing meets in mere oppugnancy." Still, the symbolic but effective role of degree gives rise to an apparent paradox: "*Degree* is more than the source of all stable meaning, more than the mechanism of differentiation in the sense of modern theory; it is a paradoxical principle of unity among men. I call it paradoxical because it is disunity, separation, distance, hierarchy. Why should a principle of separation be a principle of union?" (*TE* 164).

The Origins of Culture

In the third part of *The Crossing*, Billy and Boyd Parham visit a Mexican town that currently hosts a traveling opera troupe. Watching their show, they see a motley-clad man kill both the prima donna and "another man perhaps his rival with a dagger" (*CRO* 219). As the brothers meet the troupe a little later, Billy asks them about the meaning of the play. Regarding the clichéd love-triangle, the actress picks up on Billy's suggestion that the murderous clown "was just jealous," admitting jealousy to be the obvious and tiresome motivator in the perpetual restaging of the same drama: "To be killed night after night. It drains one's strength. [. . .] [E]ven to be jealous is a test of one's strength. Jealous in Durango and again in Monclova and in Monterrey. Jealous in heat and in rain and in cold. Such a jealousy must empty out the malice of a thousand hearts, no?" (*CRO* 229). The mundane love-triangle is instantly recognized as driven by the jealousy of rivals, yet the reiterative quality of the play itself points back to the ritual origins of drama and the ways in which these processes recycle and finally exhaust themselves.[26] Concurrently, it is the ritual origins of the drama of civilization that concern us now.

Socially the problem of violence is twofold, as society needs to contain both revenge and the undifferentiation involved in the breakdown of social order. Specifically, the feedback loop between mimesis and violence raises the issue of how society reemerges from violent disorder, and how, going back, it could emerge in the first place. Going further, if mimetic theory presents a "fundamental anthropology" as Girard claims, it also has to confront a charge familiar from our discussion of myth: The differences between cultures seem too overwhelming to allow for holistic theorization. The burden of argument is in outlining the pattern of violence, crisis and its resolution, tracing it across cultures. Girard's answer to this problem is the hypothesis of a sudden realignment of reciprocal violence against a common victim that he dubs *the scapegoat mechanism*. This concept, which was developed together with that of the sacrificial crisis in *Violence and the Sacred*, forms the second major step in the development of mimetic theory.

To recall, one half of societal strategies in dealing with runaway violence is constituted by *prohibitions*. In character, prohibitions are antimimetic, especially in archaic societies: "Prohibited objects are first of all those that might give rise to mimetic rivalry, then the behaviours characteristic of its progressively violent phases, finally individuals who appear to have 'symptoms' thought to be inevitably contagious, such as twins, adolescents at the stage of initiation, women during their menstrual period, or the sick and the dead, those excluded temporarily from the community" (*TH* 19). Yet cultural order is not immutable. Even under normal circumstances, laws, customs, and prohibitions are subject to change, some changes being more controversial or disruptive than others. In times of crisis, prohibitions often fail outright. Usual codes of behavior and even the law itself may be suspended as social order deteriorates.

So the threat of runaway violence remains. In contrast to other animals, who are ruled by dominance patterns and natural breaking mechanisms that prevent serious injury or death in their procreational competition, there is no innate limit to human violence. Girard's solution to the problem revolves around the "physics of violence" itself. He suggests that social order, once abandoned, must be reintroduced in the wake of "a non-conscious intensification and polarization of violence itself [. . .] directed at a randomly selected victim" (Fleming 47). At first sight, this claim seems to run against what was argued all along: If violence first casts society into a vicious cycle of violent retribution and social destructuralization, how then can it suddenly expend itself in one final act? How can violence, which sets people at one another's throats, suddenly reunite them?

What sheds light on this conundrum is the investigation of a class of practices often discredited as based on illusory premises: rituals. Rituals constitute the second half of the strategies archaic society employs to deal with internal violence. They are instrumental in the task "of transforming the conflictual disintegration of the community into social collaboration" (*TH* 20). Of particular interest is ritual sacrifice. Across cultures, the common denominator in the latter is an act of *substitution* regarding the receptacle of violence (*VS* 3–4). Indeed, the latter is often interchangeable. Even in everyday life, people will vent their bottled-up frustration on something or someone other than the original source of that frustration when the latter is untouchable, out of reach, or unknown. What is a common in human interaction is institutionalized as the modus operandi of sacrifice: "When left unappeased, violence seeks and always finds a surrogate victim. The creature that excited its fury is abruptly replaced by another, chosen only because it is vulnerable and close at hand" (*VS* 2).[27]

Such substitution goes some way in relieving the strain of violence. Just so, in early anthropological accounts of various African tribal cultures, sacrifice comes to the fore as "a deliberate act of collective violence performed at the expense of the victim and absorbing all the internal tensions, feuds, and rivalries pent up within the community" (*VS* 7). Girard extrapolates that the original purpose of sacrifice—ultimately of ritual, prohibitions, and religion in general—is to contain or cleanse the violence that would otherwise devour the community *through* an act of violence.[28] Speaking with McCarthy, the inherent paradox of this is beautifully expressed in two aphorisms: "A ritual includes the letting of blood" (*BM* 329), and yet, "The ends of all ceremony are but to avert bloodshed" (*CRO* 359).

Two pillars bearing the roof of cultural order, prohibition and ritual are thus joined in a unity of purpose: "Prohibitions attempt to avert the crisis by prohibiting those behaviours that provoke it, and if the crisis recurs nonetheless, or threatens to do so, ritual then attempts to channel it in a direction that would lead to resolution" (*TH* 25). How does ritual achieve this catharsis? If Girard is correct, sacrificial practices are modeled upon the resolution of the original (respectively, the preceding) crisis. However, the mechanism at its core lies in behavioral patterns stretching back to humanity's evolutionary beginnings. Its salutary effect can be attributed to the operation of aggravated mimesis itself. At some point, the mimetic violence that once infected and divided the members of a community, making them doubles of each other, is transformed through the emergence of a mutual animosity directed at a foe shared by all: "If violence is a great leveler of men and everybody becomes the

double [...] of his antagonist, [...] anyone can at any given moment become
the double of all the others; that is, the sole object of universal obsession and
hatred" (*VS* 79).

Once the crisis progresses beyond a certain threshold, the only thing that
can stop the oscillation of violence between antagonists is an act of collective violence directed against an opportunistically selected victim. "A single
victim can be substituted for all the potential victims [...] for each and every
member of the community" (*VS* 79). While anyone can serve as a potential
victim, the part is most often played by marginal individuals or groups, for
the simple reason that they are the least prone to incite vengeance, excluded
as they are from the social bonds that link most members of the community.
Appearing sufficiently "other" even at the height of undifferentiation, these
outsiders or pariahs—often foreigners or minorities—are singled out by
virtue of their perceived or artificially imposed difference.[29]

In *The Scapegoat*, Girard elaborates on the nature of victims and the
various signs used to single them out. Among others, they include physical criteria such as sickness, madness, deformities, accidental injuries, and
disabilities in general (17–18). Abounding with characters existing on the
margins of society, McCarthy's novels feature a number of such scapegoats,
including Marion Sylder and Arthur Ownby in *The Orchard Keeper*, Culla
and Rinthy Holme in *Outer Dark*, *Child of God*'s Lester Ballard, *Suttree*'s
Harrogate, *Blood Meridian*'s the Kid, and even John Grady Cole in *All the
Pretty Horses*, Billy Parham's brother Boyd in *The Crossing*, or Magdalena in
Cities of the Plain. Historical examples invoked by Girard include the Greek
pharmakoi—a class of prisoners kept for the explicit purpose of being sacrificed for the polis—women, and children, as well as the disabled and royalty
such as Marie Antoinette. After all, the selection is not restricted to the lower
ranks of society. Once again, the paradigmatic example is Oedipus: not only
the king, but also a foreigner who is suffering from "swollen feet" that physically singles him out, he is a walking catalogue of victimage markers.

Typically, the accusations leveled against the chosen fall into the categories of violent crimes, sexual crimes (e.g., rape, incest, bestiality), and religious
crimes, both of which transgress the strictest of social taboos (*SG* 15). What
these charges have in common is that the crimes they invoke are constitutive:
they designate offenses that negate elementary distinctions of cultural order.
Furthermore, unlike an epidemic, a drought, or even an economic depression,

the victims and alleged crimes are accessible to corrective action by the mob, by the crowd mobilized against a common foe. By definition, the mob "seeks action but cannot affect natural causes. [. . .] Those who make up the crowd are always potential persecutors, for they dream of purging the community of the impure elements that corrupt it" (*SG* 16). Once the dynamic behind the accusations is understood, it is hard not to see it at work wherever racism and xenophobia rear their heads. Any accusation may serve:

> The slightest hint, the most groundless accusation, can circulate with vertiginous speed and is transformed into irrefutable proof. The corporate sense of conviction snowballs, each member taking confidence from his neighbor by a rapid process of mimesis. The firm conviction of the group is based on no other evidence than the unshakable unanimity of its own illogic. The universal spread of "doubles," the complete effacement of differences, heightening antagonisms but also making them interchangeable, is the prerequisite for the establishment of violent unanimity. For order to be reborn, disorder must first triumph. (*VS* 79)

Retrospectively, the "selection process" is determined by whatever accusation acquires a critical mass—and sticks. Entered into nonvolitionally and unconsciously by the social actors (Fleming 53), it is this dynamic of mimetic polarization and surrogate victimage that constitutes the scapegoat mechanism. Originating in the Yom Kippur rite of sending goats loaded with the community's sins into the desert, today the term significantly implies that the accused are truly innocent, or at least no more culpable than anyone else. By definition, having a scapegoat means not being aware that you have one. Therein lies its effectiveness.

This effectiveness is twofold: what differentiates the victim from former victims of violent crisis is its status as the one that heralds the end of violent reciprocity. It does so firstly by virtue of its perceived difference from the rest of the community. This "virtue" reintroduces the notion of difference itself, that same crucial element of cultural order lost in the wake of the crisis. Yet more directly involved than this epistemological process is a second, pragmatic operation: The surrogate victim serves as catalyst in the transformation of reciprocal violence into unanimous violence. Through lynching and collective murder, the Hobbesian "all-against-all" is transformed into an

"all-against-one," as the victim is blamed for the collective maladies that have
befallen the community. Since its victimization by the mob, now reunified
by shared enmity to the scapegoat, brings about a sudden end of violent reciprocity, the surrogate victim is then reinterpreted in a different light:

> It is not enough to say that the surrogate victim "symbolizes" the change
> from reciprocal violence and destruction to unanimous accord and con-
> struction; after all, the victim is directly responsible for this change [. . .].
> From the purely religious point of view, the surrogate victim—or, more
> simply, the final victim—inevitably appears as a being who submits to
> violence without provoking a reprisal; a super-natural being who sows vio-
> lence to reap peace; a mysterious savior who visits affliction on mankind in
> order subsequently to restore it to good health. (*VS* 86)

It is this resolution of the crisis that is ritually reenacted in the institution of
sacrifice, and that is narratively transformed in myth. The function of sacrifice is "to perpetuate or renew the effects of this mechanism; that is, to keep
violence outside the community" (*VS* 92). In retrospect, the salutary effects
of collective murder provide compelling if false proof of the victim's guilt,
at once confirming and justifying the community. At different stages, the
victim is hence attributed either pernicious or beneficial traits. This explains,
for instance, the mysterious double nature of the gods. Likewise, the double
transformation is what constitutes the difference between Oedipus the
criminal of *Oedipus Rex* and Oedipus the guarantor of prosperity of *Oedipus
at Colonus*. The surrogate victim is initially seen as the cause of social collapse, plague, and violence, guilty of the worst of crimes, and later perceived
as a savior whose death or exile carried the seeds of cultural reinvigoration.

The mythic dimension of this operation will be explored later on. For
now, the preliminary conclusion is that only violence can put a stop to violence. As one Mexican vaquero explains to John Grady Cole in *All the Pretty
Horses*, though "war had destroyed the country [. . .] men believe the cure for
war is war as the curandero prescribes the serpent's flesh for its bite" (111).
Actually, the operations of violence are more fundamental still: the victim is
written into the very matrix of the system. "If the surrogate victim can inter-
rupt the destructuring process," Girard reasons, "it must be at the origin of
the structure" (*VS* 93). Thus he advances a version of Freud's *founding murder*

thesis, the anthropological concept of "the crime that founds the rule of the Law itself, the violent gesture that brings about a regime which retroactively makes this gesture itself illegal/criminal" (Žižek 2008a, 58).

In *Totem and Taboo* (1913), Freud envisions the young males of the Darwinian primal horde banding together and murdering the tyrannical primal father, who keeps the desired females to himself (see 1950, 174–81). Out of remorse, the rebellious sons then renounce the women and establish sexual prohibitions, particularly the rule of exogamy. With these rules they lay the religious foundation of culture: the ritual totem of the dead father ever presiding over his rueful sons. Their "memorable and criminal deed," Freud claims, was thus "the beginning of so many things—of social organization, of moral restrictions and of religion" (1950, 176). In claiming that society was "based on complicity in the common crime" (1950, 181), Freud was thus perhaps "the first to maintain that all ritual practices, all mythical implications, have their origins in an actual murder" (*VS* 201).

In contrast to Freud, however, Girard argues that the father does not truly explain anything. If humans erect a culture of prohibitions and rituals on the corpse of the totemized victim, this is *not* because the victim is the father. The transformative impression the collective murder made on the community "is not due to the victim's identity per se, but to his role as unifying agent" (*VS* 214). Literally a matter of life and death—the survival of individual and community—the pacifying effects of collective murder provide a more compelling rationale for the subsequent totemization of the victim and the ritual establishment of surrogate victimage than any sort of emotional ambivalence and deferred obedience. Nor is incestuous desire within the tribe itself the problem. Rather, it is the violence of heightened reciprocity and rivalry resulting from incest that must be prohibited.

Another difference from Freud that allows Girard to integrate his theory of the "process of hominization" into the theory of evolution and contemporary ethology is that the drama of collective murder is not to be thought of as a unique occurrence. Not unlike the opera company's recurring play of murderous jealousy that Billy and Boyd Parham witness in *The Crossing*, scapegoating and sacrifice must be interpreted as a *generative process* occurring in conjunction with sacrificial crises, and repeating itself over hundreds of thousands of years. Hominization can be conceived as progressing in consecutive cycles and stages that allow for the domestication of progressively increasing and intense mimetic effects, separated from one another by crises that would be catastrophic but also generative in that they would trigger the founding mechanism and at each step provide for more rigorous prohibitions within the group, and for a more effective ritual canalization toward the outside. In this sense it becomes conceivable that human infancy could become more and more vulnerable and prolong itself for a period corresponding to the growth of the brain [. . .]. One can also see that at each step more and more elaborate institutions would favor a new mimetic level, which would bring about a new crisis and thus continue on in a spiral movement that would progressively humanize the anthropoid. (*TH* 95–96)

The unifying effect of collective violence against a single victim becomes the blueprint for ritualistic sacrifice, meant to trigger and repeat the salutary effects of this murder in times of crisis. Like the restaging of a drama, what must originally have been a spontaneous occurrence is institutionalized, repeated, and refined over generations. Going even further, Eric Gans has hypothesized that the consecutive, unanimous gestures of attraction to and deferral from the victim demarcate the latter as at once desirable and taboo, and that this constitutes the starting point of what can be considered genuinely "human" signification, or, as the title of his book suggests, *The Origin of Language* (1981).

In sum, the surrogate victim—or rather, the *first* collective victim(s)— is thus conceptualized as the fountainhead of human culture. Certainly, Girard's and Gans's claims regarding human evolution are only hypotheses. Yet, much like the theory of evolution, they offer consistent explanations regarding the behavior of humans to this day and make sense of much of the puzzling records and artifacts of our prehistory. What is clear is that the neurophysiology of the human brain allows for a level of mimesis well beyond the capabilities of any animal. In the absence of animalistic dominance hierarchies or breaking mechanisms, the contagious violence that results from mimetic competition must have presented a formidable problem to the early humanoid. Rather than through the spectral presence of Freud's primal father, or the metaphysics of Eros and Thanatos, both cultural genesis and disintegration can be explained through a single, highly observable "drive"—*mimesis*.

As Aristotle claimed, imitation characterizes man above all animals and leads to predictable patterns of behavior. It is thus that Girard can call himself a Darwinian, his hypotheses scientific. In human sociality, mimesis approaches the formal qualities of a principle or law of nature in the natural sciences. In this still metaphorical sense, Girard can speak of mimetic dynamics as "a kind of social physics" (*BE* 184)—providing both the organizing and disorganizing principles of social order, the latter of which manifests itself, in cybernetic terms, as an exacerbation and runaway of positive feedback. Recalling the mythical subject and function par excellence, we can say that the scapegoat mechanism produces the social analog of a "thermodynamic wonder," of an ordered system emerging from chaos.

Before exploring this world of metaphor, it is to actual physics that we must now turn. Thematically, this turn provides yet other ways through which we look at the world and ourselves.[30] Critically, it prepares a shift toward the operative level of texts. Also, it introduces a new language or discourse suited to address questions of order and disorder. This step, to recall von Foerster's argument, necessarily introduces another layer of complexity, creating new orders, and perhaps setting us on the trail of the hidden seams of McCarthy's work. Fortunately, such a discourse already exists. It centers around a word frequently (mis)taken for a synonym of disorder itself. That word is *entropy.*

Order and Disorder: A Short History of Entropy

I think that truth has no temperature.
—Cormac McCarthy, *The Counselor*

Since Cormac McCarthy's first interview with Richard B. Woodward in 1992, scholars have been aware of his fascination with the natural sciences. He studied physics and engineering in college, and his preference for the company of scientists over that of artists is well documented. Perhaps the foundations of McCarthy's scientific leanings may be traced back to his grandfather John Francis, an entrepreneur and machinist "interested in how things worked" (Kushner) after whom he later named his own son. In any case, since becoming writer in residence at the Santa Fe Institute, known for its inter- and multidisciplinary study of complex-adaptive systems, McCarthy has been able to indulge his scientific interests, notably engaging in dialogue with some leading voices in science today. Among others, particle and string physicist Lisa Randall and Nobel Prize winner and personal friend Murray Gell-Mann acknowledge McCarthy's input in their books *Warped Passages* (x–xi) and *The Quark and the Jaguar* (xv).[31] Clearly, science plays an important role in McCarthy's intellectual life.

Remarkably little of it has made an impact on our assessment of McCarthy's work, though. The study of what I call "the scientific McCarthy" (2013, 1) still constitutes one of the largely uncharted territories on the map of McCarthy scholarship. Part of this may be due to lack of scientific expertise, part of it due to an unquestioned notion that McCarthy's books "show no sign of being shaped by high-flown scientific thought" (Woodward 2005, 100).[32] Whatever the case, McCarthy has primarily been viewed as the heir of Herman Melville, Ernest Hemingway, and William Faulkner: an author of myth and bloodshed, a writer of apocalypses. Yet hidden before our very eyes is also a writer in a complementary, scientific tradition of thought initiated by the formulation of the second law of thermodynamics, the central implication of which is the continuous dissipation of energy, or the increase of *entropy*. The universal implications of the second law, in particular the running down and eventual *heat death* of the universe, resonate strongly with the notion of human insignificance and cosmic indifference in McCarthy's novels. Moreover, the entropic main theme of the world's tendency toward disorder and man's struggle to come to terms with it have been a hallmark of his writing at least since *The Orchard Keeper*, as we shall yet see.

This is more than simple thematic resonance. While McCarthy's scientific interest and the inclusion of a chapter on entropy in *The Quark and the Jaguar* already suggest McCarthy's familiarity with the second law, this inference can be confirmed as fact. In the archival first draft of *The Road*, he mentions "the cold of space" in direct conjunction with the second law's projection of the universal "Heatdeath" (91/87/6, 219).[33] Even two decades earlier, in the first draft of *Whales and Men*, the philosophizing aristocrat Peter invokes "the cold hand of entropy." Obviously, McCarthy decided against including such dead giveaways in his final drafts. This suggests entropy is less of an explicit theme in the way of violence or Western history, and instead a part of the tale's "hidden joinery"—part of those thematic, aesthetic, and structural concerns that unify his work more so than regional or historical localizations. As a theme, entropy only assumes centrality in *The Road*. Yet, even early on, entropy is a constant within his work. Integrating it into the larger discussion serves to characterize McCarthy's eschatology as an elaborate fusion of various traditions of thinking about the end. The groundwork for this integration is laid in the following.

Thermodynamics and the Heat Death of the Universe

In his 1959 lecture on *The Two Cultures*, the physicist and novelist C. P. Snow famously compared knowledge of the second law to having read a work of Shakespeare's. In his talk, Snow bemoaned what he saw as a general scientific illiteracy in the humanities. Still today, the use of *entropy* in the humanities and social sciences often amounts to little more than a vague, scientifically sketchy label for gradual dissolution, or the final result of said processes, disorder itself (Freese 1997, 197–202). Thermodynamics can hardly be counted as part of the education of the literary scholar, let alone McCarthy's general readership. Even physicists sometimes find the concept of entropy "puzzlingly opaque" (Freese 1997, 12), and Peter Atkins admits to "serious doubts about whether Snow understood the law himself" (37), only to reassert its status as "one of the all-time great laws of science" (xii). The history of the second law of thermodynamics is thus tinged with the irony that "few physical concepts have caused as much confusion and misunderstanding" (Lovelock 2000b, 2) as one that came to be understood as disorder itself. Yet its significance is likewise beyond doubt.

It is impossible to treat the history and metamorphoses of the Second Law in detail here. Nor can I hope to offer more than a layman's perspective. Nonetheless, assuming a condition of overall ignorance of a concept as consequential as the second law, an introduction of three central aspects is in order: (1) the formulation of the second law and the concepts of entropy and heat death, together with their initial reception; (2) the shift from classical to statistical thermodynamics and the ensuing connection of entropy

and dis|order; and (3) the shift from energy to information, which set off
additional metamorphoses. This short history will allow us to connect it to
mythography and mimetic theory.

In the first half of the nineteenth century, the Industrial Revolution
with its soaring interest in the development of steam engines led to the
establishment of thermodynamics, the branch of physics that deals with the
properties of energy and its conversions into different forms, most notably
work and heat.[34] The German physician Julius Robert Mayer was among the
first to establish that energy can be neither created nor destroyed, but only
exchanged and transformed. Specifying conservation as a principle, the first
law of thermodynamics states that the internal energy within any *isolated
system* remains constant. Systems in nature, however, are rarely isolated,
interacting with their surroundings to a greater or lesser extent. Hence, they
fall into a spectrum of *open systems*, able to exchange energy and matter with
their environment, and *closed systems*, which exchange only energy.[35] It is
primarily with regard to the latter that the first law is mathematically stated
as $dU = \delta Q - \delta W$. The differential in a system's internal energy (dU) is equal
to the amount of energy added as heat to the system (δQ) minus the amount
of work (δW) it performs on its environment.

Initially, the second law was formulated in seeming contradiction to
the conservation principle. Nicolas Sadi Carnot (1796–1832) and William
Thomson (1822–1907), the later Baron of Kelvin, established that there
was effectively no such thing as a lossless transformation of energy—be it
thermal, electric, mechanical, or else. "No cyclic process is possible in which
heat is taken from a hot source and converted completely into work" (Atkins
41). In other words, in any transformation, a certain amount of energy is
inevitably and irreversibly "lost" to the surroundings in the bound form of
henceforth unusable heat. Searching for a suitable term for this loss, the German physicist Rudolf Julius Emanuel Clausius (1822–88) in 1850 coined the
pseudo-Greek neologism *entropy* to refer to the "transformation content"
or "measure of the mechanical unavailability of energy in a closed thermodynamic system" (Freese 1997, 97).[36] Simply put, the greater the entropy of
a system, the less energy free to do work it will contain as that energy is dissipating as heat. In mathematical terms, Clausius's equation today is written
as $dS = \delta Q/T$, meaning that the change in a system's entropy is "the result

of dividing the energy transferred as heat by the (absolute, thermodynamic) temperature at which the transfer took place" (Atkins 47). Thus,

> when a colder body absorbs an amount of heat Q from a hotter body at temperature T, an amount of entropy $S = Q/T$ is gained by the former and lost by the latter. Because $S = Q/T$ becomes larger when T becomes smaller, the colder body necessarily gains more entropy than the hotter body loses, and this means that entropy necessarily increases in all closed physical systems which are not in equilibrium. (Freese 1997, 97)

Applying his findings to the universe at large, Clausius restated the first and second laws of thermodynamics as "the energy of the world is constant," and "the entropy of the world approaches a maximum" at thermal equilibrium. From a human perspective, the consequence derived from these two laws is rather bleak: the quantity of energy in the universe is constant; however, in every process or exchange, free energy is degraded into bound energy, into heat dissipating in space. Consequently, at some point all free energy in the universe will have been converted into bound energy. At this stage of maximum entropy, the temperature of the universe will be at equilibrium. Concurrent with the lack of any heat differential, no free energy will be left that could be converted into work.

Everything thus tends toward a state of maximum entropy at a temperature close to absolute zero. Hermann von Helmholtz called this state the *Wärmetod* or "heat death" of the universe. In a lot of American fiction, this projection is frequently misinterpreted as an apocalyptic vision of universal conflagration (Freese 2004, 336). Conversely, McCarthy clearly understands its implications. For one, the cooling world he creates in *The Road* approximates Helmholtz's scenario. Yet he incorporates his scientific knowledge into other concerns as well. Early drafts of *Whales*, apart from referencing the "cold-hand of entropy" also contain the scientific metaphor of humans "labor[ing] in a heatdeath of the soul and of the heart" (91/97/1, n.p.). What would such death imply? Clearly, it carries Helmholtz's prediction beyond the boundaries of physics and its understanding of energy.[37] Spiritual, psychic, and social concerns are metaphorically unified: more than the body's inevitable progress toward death and decomposition, there is such a thing as an entropy of the soul, an entropy, too, of compassion, of love itself.[38] Since the heat death spoken of is singular, do we have to assume that one entails that of the other? What domains other than the ethics of religious and social interaction might we imagine as the shared site of such death? Finally, since "labor" is a form of energy and is still ongoing, would not this suggest that while heat death looms large, resistance may not be futile? Within McCarthy's unified field, these questions are interrelated. Yet conceptual implications remain vague for now.

Whatever concrete shapes it assumes in McCarthy's fiction, Helmholtz's final state projection elevated the scientific fact of entropy, "a cosmic memento mori, pointing to the underlying cause of the gradual decay of all things physical and mental" (Arnheim 9). Slowly but inexorably, Isaac Newton's clockwork universe is running ever down and down till all processes of nature cease. And life ends. Rather than the Christian Apocalypse, it was now entropy that in Arthur Eddington's memorable phrase, provided the *arrow of time*. And while both paradigms envision a linear progression of history toward a final state, the second law does not promise renewal, or a continuation of life in the kingdom of heaven. Its version of perfection is eternal stasis.

In retrospect, Helmholtz's depressing vision likely sparked the mythologization of the second law.[39] Upon its initial formulation in the mid-nineteenth century, however, its dire implications put the second law radically at odds with the zeitgeist. After all, Charles Darwin's theory of evolution and the rapid progress of the Industrial Revolution promised just the opposite of continuous decline—namely "a transition towards higher order, heterogeneity, and organization" (Bertalanffy 41). The objection is worth pondering. If everything tends toward disorder, how do we explain that all around us, we see complexity and organization emerge? Patterns of order range from the spiral arms of our galaxy to the mineral organization of crystals, through the biological diversification of plant and animal life, up to the dazzling neural network of our own brains. Truly, order seems to be all around us.

As we have seen in discussing myth, such patterns are attributions of the mind. Yet even granting that we are compelled to find order in just about anything, few would altogether do away with the notion of order as such. Even the word "dis-order" implies that, in thinking about these matters, order comes first: Attributions of either state can only be articulated from a position of relative order, just as much as we can communicate notions of life and death solely from the position of life. Incidentally, *life* in particular must be seen as the most glaring violation of the second law: "What is physically amazing is that living organization and living order exist" (Morin 105).

The contradiction dissolves once we recall that the law applies firstly to isolated and closed systems. Living organisms are open systems. The maintenance of *homeostasis*, that is, the ability of a system to retain internal equilibrium while adapting to a changing environment, requires energy. The cost of our bodies performing their work and keeping their internal entropy low is the ingestion of energy (or low grade entropy), taken from our environment. "Thus, living systems, maintaining themselves in a steady state, can avoid the increase of entropy, and may even develop towards states of increased order and organization" (Bertalanffy 41). The net result, however, is the raising of entropy in the environment, that is, an increase in the sum total of entropy. Inescapably, the heat death of the universe still looms.

Apart from Darwin's theory, the cast of nineteenth- and early twentieth-century challenges to the second law featured a number of objections, opposing concepts, logical and formal refutations, voiced by some of the major thinkers of the age.[40] None of them stuck. Yet this did not dissuade people from looking for a loophole within the lawbook of nature. The most famous attempt at a solution, while originating in the same hallowed realm as Clausius's initial discovery and Helmholtz's foreboding vision of doom, eventually morphed into something rather unscientific. An exercise in demonology not unlike the goats of Yom Kippur. A myth.

Maxwell's Demon, or from Energy to Information

It was a thought experiment by physicist James Clerk Maxwell (1831–79) that should bring forth the most influential attempt at refuting the second law by far. Challenging the inevitable, Maxwell conceived of a container filled with gas and divided into two compartments. Considering the varying internal energies and speeds of molecules within the gas, he conceived of a kind of trapdoor between the compartments. Then he appointed a "doorkeeper." Admitting only the fast-moving, high-energy molecules, this entity would separate them from the slow, low-energy molecules. The resulting effect approximates a perpetual motion machine: whereas the temperature in the first chamber drops, the temperature in the second chamber continuously rises. Hence, by using naught but the internal speed of molecules, it should be possible to create the thermal disequilibrium necessary to, say, fuel an engine. Finally, the absolute reign of entropy was challenged. Little did it matter either that while Maxwell preferred to think of his doorkeeper as more of a valve, much to his chagrin, his anthropomorphized, antientropic brainchild only achieved notoriety, after a remark by Kelvin, as "Maxwell's Demon."

This baptism heralded the birth of something akin to a thermodynamic philosopher's stone. Maxwell's Demon occupied the world of physics and information theory well into the late twentieth century, to be exorcized time and again, more or less decisively. Not only did it provoke a century of discussion, revision, and conjecture, it marked the "inscription into scientific discourse of a new attitude toward chaos and disorder" (Hayles 1990, 32). Part of this was Maxwell's realization that the second law "only referred to matter *en masse* and, consequently, was not universally but only statistically true" (Freese 1997, 107). This realization contained the germ cells for the paradigm shift from traditional to statistical mechanics, and even prefigured central elements of information theory.

The shift took place toward the turn of the century, when the existence of atoms was still contested. Switching from the macroscopic perspective of classical thermodynamics (i.e., bulk mechanics) to the microscopic level of atoms and molecules, the Austrian physicist Ludwig Boltzmann (1844–1906) reconceptualized entropy in terms of statistical mechanics, focusing now on the *probable* behavior of myriads of atoms and molecules. In the words of Max Planck, Boltzman's work made "the hypothesis of elementary disorder [...] the real kernel of the principle of increase of entropy" (50). Doing so, he augmented Helmholtz's vision of the heat death of the universe by a dimension of molecular chaos. The equation that became Boltzmann's epitaph— $S = k \log W$—redefined the entropy of an isolated system as proportional to the logarithmic probability of certain microstates within the macrostate of that system, "specifying the amount of randomness or disorder in a system" (Freese 1997, 111). Put simply, Boltzmann related the tendency of energy to dissipate to the observation that in nature, *disorder* is much more probable than *order*.[41]

It is here that the culturally momentous but confusing and scientifically problematic identification of entropy with disorder comes fully into focus. A first complication is the aforementioned agency of the observer making attributions of dis|order from a position of limited knowledge. Early on, Maxwell himself had already insinuated that "confusion, like the correlative term order, is not a property of material things in themselves, but only in relation to the mind which perceives them" (220). Secondly, there is a linguistic, or rather conceptual, problem: in their everyday usage, the meaning of terms such as "order," "disorder," "chaos," "organization," or "complexity" not only differs from how they are used in physics and other sciences, they also carry decidedly positive and negative connotations. Essentially, they imply a certain aesthetic judgment, rooted in the evolutionary process.

> Order is a prerequisite of survival; therefore the impulse to produce orderly arrangements is inbred by evolution. The social organizations of animals, the spatial formations of travelling birds or fishes, the webs of spiders and bee hives are examples. A pervasive striving for order seems to be inherent also in the human mind—an inclination that applies mostly for good practical reasons. (Arnheim 3)

In statistical thermodynamics, the term "order" applies to the probability of the microstates of a system.[42] By extension, speaking of social or cultural entropy, we are using metaphors complicated by a slew of factors. Not the least of these is the fact that while improbable orderly arrangements are subject to entropic dissolution, a certain heterogeneity—a difference of temperatures and energy levels—both within and between the system and its environment, is indispensable to evolution. Disorder and the cycle of organization and disintegration are necessary parts in the genesis of life's complex orders, as Edgar Morin explains:

> The omnipresent disorder not only opposes order to create disorganization, but, strangely also cooperates with it. As a matter of fact, aleatory meetings that suppose agitation, and thus, disorder, help to generate physical organization (nuclei, atoms, heavenly bodies), and actually generated the first living creatures. Disorder cooperates with the generation of organizational

order. [. . .] [D]isorder, present at the origin of organizations, continually
threatens them with disintegration. This threat originates either from the
outside (destructive accident), or from the inside (increase of entropy). [. . .]
[A]uto-organization, which characterizes living phenomena, contains in
itself a permanent process of disorganization which it transforms into a
permanent process of reorganization until [. . .] final death. (102)

An increase in entropy and disorder is a natural by-product of the processes
that make life possible. Conversely, a state of random molecular distribution
across lower energy levels corresponds to minimal entropy. It may reasonably
be called orderly. Yet it is the lowest kind of order, an order of homogeneity
and without complexity. So too, if a human body is at thermal equilibrium
with its surroundings, it is usually dead. Clearly, these metaphors, illuminating and productive as they may be regarding the workings of systems and the
art of scientifically savvy writers such as McCarthy, need to be applied with
a certain care.

A second transformation of the second law took place around five
decades after Boltzmann. A side effect of developments in an area that at first
sight had little to do with either branch of thermodynamics, it may be characterized as a shift *from energy to information*. In 1948, the mathematician
and cryptographer Claude E. Shannon of Bell Telephone Laboratories published "A Mathematical Theory of Communication." In this seminal treatise,
he provided the framework and vocabulary to describe processes of encoding
and transmitting data and thus laid the foundation for the burgeoning field
of information theory.[43] Primarily concerned with the technical problems
of communication, the significance of Shannon's paper was enhanced by
linking the concept of information to Boltzmann's probabilistic conception
of entropy. In establishing a way to measure "how much information is 'produced' [. . .] or better, at what rate information is produced" in a communication process, he suggested "quantities of the form $H = -\Sigma\, p_i \log p_i$ as measures
of information, choice and uncertainty" (Shannon and Weaver 50). Legend
has it that Shannon followed mischievous advice by John von Neumann and
elected to call this quantity entropy.[44] Pointing out that "the form H will be
recognized as that of entropy as defined in certain formulations of statistical
mechanics," he acknowledged the isomorphism of his equation to that of
Boltzmann (Shannon and Weaver 48, 50, 51).

To be sure, the realization that there was a connection between entropy and information had had its precursors in the work of Maxwell, and had been made explicit in 1929 by Leó Szilárd. Szilárd later became one of the leading minds behind and an eventual opponent of the Manhattan Project developed in part in McCarthy's home state of Tennessee. Years prior, he had reinterpreted Maxwell's Demon as an information processor. Szilárd found that the demon would have to obtain information about which molecules to let through, and that in conducting his measurements, he would actually use more energy—or increase his own entropy—than could ever be gained (Freese 1997, 176–80). Szilárd's work was picked up again in the 1950s by the physicist Léon Brillouin, and again in the 1980s by computer scientists Charles H. Bennett and Rolf Landauer. Their work linked *the process of observation* to the necessity of *storing information*, which eventually will have to be erased again: "The conclusion is that information is a physical phenomenon, subject to the laws of thermodynamics" (Floridi 66). Shannon gave this relation its mathematical foundation.

Although information and entropy are clearly linked to one another, the relation established is far from uncontested. One source of confusion is that "information" in the Mathematical Theory of Communication (MTC) is tied to randomness and uncertainty, and as divorced from meaning or what a message expresses as "order" in Boltzmann's statistical thermodynamics is from common notions of organization. In MTC information "has nothing to do with meaning," but deals with the statistical probabilities of "a whole ensemble of messages" rather than a single message (Shannon and Weaver 27), the objective being efficiency in encoding and transmitting data.[45]

Fascinating as the conundrums involved are, none of them need particularly concern us here.[46] What is important are the broader implications of Shannon's equations for the kind of communication process that interests the student of culture and literature. They are succinctly summarized by Norbert Wiener, the father of cybernetics:

> Messages are themselves a form of pattern and organization. [. . .] Just as entropy is a measure of disorder, the information carried by a set of messages is a measure of organization. In fact, it is possible to interpret the information carried by a message as essentially the negative of its entropy, and the negative logarithm of its probability. That is, the more probable

the message, the less information it gives. Clichés, for example, are less
illuminating than great poems. (21)

To make matters worse, as in any act of transmission, a message is subject to
the possibility of errors, distortions, gaps, and what information theorists call
noise. The term describes additional, unwanted, senseless data that intrude
and disturb the official message. These data may cause the message to lose
organization and thus information that cannot be regained. This other,
inevitable *loss in translation*, Wiener points out, is "the cybernetic form of
the second law of thermodynamics" (78).

Perhaps the literary applicability of these ideas may seem questionable.
Yet McCarthy demonstrably and frequently draws attention to phenomena
of *noise*, processes of symbolic erasure, and uncertainties. Sometimes one
of his barely literate characters is faced with words, symbols, or artifacts
unintelligible to them. At other times, characters like Lester Ballard or the
Judge purposely erase or destroy such artifacts and traces, either for the sake
of destruction or to create palimpsests upon which to inscribe their own
designs. On the metaliterary level, McCarthy's frequent use of arcane diction
and obscure xenologisms sends scholars to consult the *Oxford English Dictionary*. His use of languages other than English demands additional translation work, and so does figuring out the complex, initially confusing plot
structures of novels like *The Orchard Keeper*. Even his characteristic narrato-
rial voice, which at first seems to tend toward omniscience, approaches severe
limitations. These range from the oft-noted inaccessibility of his characters'
inner lives to unsolvable questions on the magnitude of what bird sung at a
certain point (*OD* 62, 183). The frequency of "uncertainty markers"—like
the adverbial *perhaps*—in many such cases draws explicit attention to these
practically inconsequential details. The effect, however, is one of unease at a
level perhaps barely conscious, yet nagging: If the narrator is not even sure
about such trivia, how can we trust him in more elementary matters?

Finally, there is also a larger issue at stake that pertains to the nature of
literature and art as such. Wiener's opposition between great poetry and clichés, meaningful messages and accidental noise, points toward the centrality
of entropy and information in the process of *artistic* communication: For
what is a poem, painting, film, novel, piece of music, performance, or video
game, if not the communication of some message or meaning, even if that

meaning is subjective? Great art is inscribed with the enduring potential of possibility, of *making* a difference. Even where the meaning of the message is apparent chaos, the very notion of a message by necessity implies that of intent, and so of meaning, which cannot be conceived of without order. Art is therefore inherently antientropic. Thus, we may begin to appreciate such seemingly hyperbolic statements as Atkins's claim that the second law "illuminates why anything—anything from the cooling of hot matter to the formulation of a thought—happens at all" (xii). And it is here, too, that we can redirect the discussion of entropy into that of the unified poetic field.

A Fourth Vision:
The Interplay of Myth, Violence, and Entropy

> Perhaps in the world's destruction it would be
> possible at last to see how it was made.
> —Cormac McCarthy, *The Road*

In our quest to trace the hidden seams of McCarthy's fiction, a common thread so far is that order and disorder, chaos and cosmos, are less rigidly opposed than we commonly assume. Patterns and structures, their emergence, organization, or dissolution are as fluid as are the meanings contained within and contingent upon these patterns. Being constructions of the perceiving mind, they are circumscribed by what we, as imperfect observers, do or do not know about what seems like chaos, or the role of disorder in producing order. We need to refocus our perspective to include these factors. As Edgar Morin proposes:

> The necessity of conceiving together the notions of order and disorder in their complementarity, their concurrence, and their antagonism, poses to us exactly the problem of thinking the complexity of physical, biological and human reality. Yet to do that, it is necessary [. . .] to imagine a fourth vision [. . .] that will have our own vision for its object [. . .]. We have to look at the way we understand order, the way we understand disorder, and envisage ourselves looking at the world, that is, include ourselves in our

vision of the world. [. . .] [T]he real field of knowledge is not the pure
object, but the object viewed, perceived and co-produced by us. The object
of knowledge is not the world, but the community Us/World, since this
world is part of our vision of the world, which is itself part of the world.
(99–100, 106)

Emboldened by such trailblazing models as *Reflection in the Waves* (2019),
Pablo Bandera's exploration of mimetic theory and quantum mechanics,
perhaps we are now able to open up something approaching such "a fourth
vision." How we relate perspectives and patterns emerging between myth,
violence, and entropy and bring them to bear on our view of the world is
itself reflexively constitutive of *meaning*. We must now make explicit some
of these meanings and, in doing so, provide a roadmap of intersections and
bifurcations, crossroads and transgressions between these disparate horizons.
Whereas before, the starting point was mythology, the sequence is now
reversed, proceeding from entropy, through violence, to myth. Doing so will
make it possible to trace the contours of McCarthy's apocalypticism.

Intersections and Bifurcations

Historically, through the doors opened by Boltzmann and Shannon, the concept of entropy entered various disciplines such as genetics, economics, geo-
science, and systems and chaos theory. Culturally, Norbert Wiener's *Human
Use of Human Beings* (1950) presented a popular milestone by establishing
entropy as pertaining to both the material and the symbolic. Effectively, he
became the first to convincingly argue for "the intriguing possibility of relating a given state of language to the concomitant state of the world" (Freese
1997, 194), and thus to call attention to the social and artistic implications of
the second law.[47] Principles that apply to physical and informational systems
may thus also cast light on similar dynamics that affect biological, social,
ecological, and economic systems.

Entropy started out as a concept in thermodynamics. From there, it
made its way into information theory, and from there to practically everywhere else. Given these tectonic shifts in the application of entropy, grand
statements such as Atkins's view that the second law is "not only [. . .] a basis
for understanding why engines run and chemical reactions occur," but also "a

foundation for understanding those most exquisite consequences of chemical reactions, the acts of literary, artistic, and musical creativity" (37), assume a certain plausibility. In the arts and social sciences, "entropy" is often used to describe phenomena of disorder and dissolution on the sociological or environmental level.

John Cant, Georg Guillemin, and Jay Ellis have each hinted at entropic dynamics at work in McCarthy's fiction.[48] In particular, it is Cant's notion of "cultural entropy"—which echoes quasi-historiographers like Oswald Spengler and Henry Adams, and a jesting Lévi-Strauss's idea of reconceptualizing anthropology as *entropology*, the study of cultural decay (cf. Freese 1997, 218–19)—that suggests the systemic meltdown Girard calls a mimetic or sacrificial crisis. It would seem that cultural entropy could be substantiated by giving it a theoretical foundation in mimetic theory. To recall, mimesis is a process that erodes and negates differences between people who imitate one another both in their desires and in acting upon them. In a mimetic crisis, which is ever a crisis of distinctions, this process accelerates and intensifies to flatten social orders. Just as in thermodynamics, where a heat differential is needed for the transformation of energy, without difference there can be no biological evolution toward more complex, living structures. As it is in the realm of nature, so it is in that of culture: differentiation is a conditio sine qua non of structural order and complexity.

A "difference which makes a difference" is exactly the criterion that Gregory Bateson suggested to define "the elementary unit of information" (459). This elementary unit of distinction, Floridi points out, is the *datum*, which is "ultimately reducible to a *lack of uniformity*" (23). Functionally, information is part of any act of communication the content of which produces change within a system. In the case of feedback in communication theory, this kind of operation may be "self-corrective either toward homeostatic optima [i.e., *negative feedback*] or toward the maximization of certain variables [i.e., *positive feedback*]" (Bateson 315). In the first case, the system is stabilized; in the second it is put on the path of profound change—of evolution, revolution, or disintegration.

This view of information ties the ordering difference produced by the victimage mechanism to the informational processes of what I call *violentropy*. In a sacrificial crisis, the engine of disintegration is violence itself. On the individual level, the final violence of death subjects the body to the entropy of organic decomposition. On the social level, mimesis erodes the distinct identities between individuals and causes institutions and values to deteriorate. This in turn leads to more violence. In cybernetic or system-theoretical terms, this anthropological observation, which describes the phenomenon of vengeance on a communal level, constitutes a positive feedback loop leading to a runaway toppling the entire system (*TH* 292).

> If imitation tends to contaminate the urge to possess, to acquire, to be master of something or even of someone, it will be an essential, perhaps *the* essential cause of conflict and misunderstanding between people. Thus, mimetic desire appears to be not only the principle of learning, but mostly the principle of feedback between individuals, leading two, or more, of them to be caught in what Gregory Bateson would probably have called a "symmetrical escalation." [. . .] [I]n sociological disorder, when it exceeds the cultural boundaries, either the system will be able to contain the disorder through repressive means of some kind, or there will be a runaway effect, which might cause the breakdown of the entire sub-system or even system. [. . .] [T]hese breakdowns themselves, even though they can be described as "sociological disorder," do have a structure, an order, which is very simple and which consists of more and more symmetry, more and more reciprocity. The breakdown is the result of the exacerbation of another type of mimetic exchange, of blows, insults, neurotic or psychotic symptoms, etc. (Oughourlian 72, 74)

It bears repeating that when physicists talk about order, they do *not* talk about purposive structures, but rather about "an improbable arrangement of elements, regardless of whether the macro-shape of this arrangement is beautifully structured or most arbitrarily deformed," whereas disorder "signifies the dissolution of such an improbable arrangement" (Arnheim 15). Conversely, when Girard speaks of mimetic snowballing leading to a social meltdown, he is envisioning something that might more aptly be described as a breakdown of cultural distinction, metaphorically as *social* or *cultural entropy*. The social "function" of difference is to regulate and dissimulate conflictual mimesis in sociocultural exchange, to set people at a proper distance from one another. When this distance folds in on itself, mimetic reciprocity skyrockets, and cultural exchange is reorganized in more immediate and symmetrical patterns. It is this progress toward immediacy and symmetry in social relationships that Girard calls "'disorder,' even though formally they are a kind of order" (1984, 86).

Of course, in finding analogies between social and physical disorder, one should not only consider the breakdown but also the genesis of order. While the initial theorization of entropy focused on its dire implications, systems and chaos theory point to the phenomenon of systems emerging from apparent disorder. In fact, the existence of life and its evolution testify to the existence of what Wiener called "local and temporary islands of decreasing entropy in a world in which the entropy as a whole tends to increase" (36). Being exceedingly improbable, these insular orders represent a sort of thermodynamic wonder. In *Order Out of Chaos*, Ilya Prigogine and Isabelle Stengers shed light on the origin of these islands:

> We now know that far from equilibrium, new types of structures may originate spontaneously. In far-from-equilibrium conditions we may have transformation from disorder, from thermal chaos, into order. New dynamic states of matter may originate, states that reflect the interaction of a given system with its surroundings. We have called these new structures *dissipative structures* to emphasize the constructive role of dissipative processes in their formation. (Prigogine and Stengers 12)

Prigogine, who in 1977 received the Nobel Prize in Chemistry for the discovery of these *dissipative structures*, actually touched upon the connections between his discoveries and mimetic theory, arguing that "a similar type of interaction appears at all levels of evolution" and most significantly at the "social level," where the evolutionary time scales "are obviously much shorter" than those in biology or astronomy (Prigogine 42, 57, 60).[49]

The phenomenon of order reemerging from chaos finds its social equivalent in the operation of the *scapegoat mechanism*. The latter is the key to the "spontaneous" self-organization and (re)constitution of the social system. Yet the most astonishing parallels emerge when considering the scapegoat in conjunction with Maxwell's Demon. Recalling his working principles, N. Katherine Hayles casts the demon in appropriate robes as a *mythical imp* who presided over a box of ideal gas divided by a partition. The Demon's task was to sort the molecules by opening and closing a shutter in the partition allowing only the fast molecules to pass through. The resulting separation created a temperature differential, which in turn could be converted into work. [...] Like guardians of portals to other realms in ancient myths, the Demon is a liminal figure who stands at a threshold that separates not just slow molecules from fast but an ordered world of will from the disordered world of chaos. On one side is a universe fashioned by divine intention, created for man and responsive to his will; on the other is the inhuman force of increasing entropy, indifferent to man and uncontrollable by human will. (1990, 7, 43)

Interestingly, Hayles even briefly considers the demon in the terms of scandal and sacrifice. What is truly astounding though is how the design of Maxwell's thought experiment reflects the sacrificial structure of surrogate victimage. The demon operates in a homogeneous gas, the victim in the social realm of an undifferentiated mass of mimetic doubles who are—in mythic and biblical parlance—*possessed* by one another. Out of their respective molecular and social disorders, the sorting agency of demon or scapegoat transforms these masses, in the one case dividing fast- from slow-moving molecules, in the other realigning violent reciprocity into violent unanimity. And whereas the demon thus creates the heat differential necessary to perform work, the sacrificial victim establishes the social harmony conditional to the rebirth of cultural order and in the same breath reintroduces a similarly elementary difference-making-a-difference, that is, information: *us vs. them, inside vs. outside* the group, *before vs. after* the crisis. Following the generative logic of the primal murder, it is these central binary digits of information that are the elementary units of social order.

The demon and the victim thus occupy structurally analogous positions. They perform analogous work, leading to analogous effects: one organizes *molecules* (Lat. small mass), the other individuals and masses of people. Both effect a difference that maintains or reestablishes the operation of the system. So the scapegoat and sacrificial victim in Girard's theory works precisely and practically as the demon in Maxwell's thought experiment turns out, in reality, *not* to work. For the demon will always pay with an increase in entropy greater than the amount of energy made available through his agency. The payment in Girard's theory is the lifeblood of the victim, which nourishes the life of the community. There is an additional caveat, though: as we shall see, even the sacrificial reduction of social entropy eventually exhausts itself; in an ironic way, the analogy is even closer than it appears at first.

Yet another parallel may be drawn by considering the twentieth-century reinterpretation of the demon as an information processor. As I have only hinted, Girard's theory, like that of Lévi-Strauss, potentially extends to the very origins of culture, and so of signification and language itself. Unlike Lévi-Strauss and the information theorists, Girard would not start with the binary digit as the basic constituent of information though:

> One cannot imagine starting with a structuralist system containing two differential elements that have the same degree of value. There is a simpler model that is uniquely dynamic and genetic—but also completely ignored. This is the model of the exception that is still in the process of emerging, the single trait that stands out against a confused mass or still unsorted multiplicity. (*TH* 100)

This exception becomes flesh in the scapegoat, the victim blamed for the crisis and later glorified for resolving it, for countering the process toward entropy, of violence running wild. But how can we imagine the original emergence of *signs*? The relation is rudimentary in Girard's own writings. It centers around the "original victim"—the father in Freud—who becomes the catalyst for "a new degree of attention, the first non-instinctual attention" (*TH* 99) of the primate community gathering around the corpse. This attention results from the "maximal contrast between the releases of violence and its cessation, between agitation and tranquility"—with "the cadaver of the collective victim" (*TH* 99) becoming a new kind of object—a *transcendental signifier* that kicks off the process of hominization. This original scene of culture has been theorized more thoroughly by Eric Gans. Exploring Girardian *difference* in conjunction with Derridean *différance* (i.e., deference and differentiation), Andrew McKenna summarizes the argument as follows:

> The natural act of appropriation is a reflex on the part of all; it thereby becomes a gesture, indeed, a sign, for it designates the victim as desirable— and as forbidden. All imitate this movement toward the victim because all

desire the victim, if only out of reflex imitation of movement toward the
victim prior to anything like desire. It is the confluence of these movements
that ensures the victim's inaccessibility, indeed, that makes the victim an
object of desire in the first place—or rather in the second place, every
desire being a second to another. The object that all desire is perforce the
one that none dares appropriate. To designate the victim is to designate it
as both desirable and taboo in one and the same movement or moment.
[. . .] The victim is holy, sacralized by its deferred possession, which alone
accords peace to the group. [. . .] Gans's formal theory enables us to conceive the movement from the natural to the cultural, which is to say first
and foremost the sacred, in this originary deferral. (70–71)

To the pacification produced by communal murder, which Girard claims is
the origin of culture, one can thus add the processes of attraction and deference as the beginning of *signification*, of human language itself. Concurrently,
in his essay "The Kekulé Problem," McCarthy ponders the possibility "that
language is a totally evolutionary process. That it has somehow appeared in
the brain in a primitive form and grown to usefulness. Somewhat like vision,
perhaps. [. . .] I dont know. But all indications are that language has appeared
only once and in one species only. Among whom it then spread with considerable speed. [. . .] The ur-language of linguistic origin out of which all
languages have evolved" (26–27). Even the elementary principle of both the
emergence of signification and institutionalized sacrifice is one and the same:
substitution. "The simple understanding that one thing can be another thing
is as the root of all things of our doing" (29).

And so it becomes possible to combine the Lacanian notion of the
unconscious being structured like a language and the Girardian idea that
it is structured "like a lynching" (McKenna 5). Socially and symbolically,
the victim becomes the original difference producing further differences, a
genuine bit of *evolutionary information* in the process of hominization. We
need to acknowledge the possibility that, from the very start, our signifiers
have been drenched in blood. Symbolic violence, in this respect, may go far
beyond what we usually assume.[50] These analogies allow us to relate natural
processes to social and semiological processes, and hence to the operations of
myth, ideology, and literature. It will come as no surprise that the role of violence in these processes—be it subjective, systemic, or symbolic—is central.

Reading the work of Cormac McCarthy, what is radically foregrounded is the disordering effect of violent reciprocity. Where its destructuration is contextualized or symbolically framed not just in subjective and social, but in explicitly thermodynamic and/or informational terms, as it frequently is by McCarthy, we can rightfully speak of *violentropy*.

Nonetheless, this should not be taken to mean that thermodynamic entropy, informational entropy, and violentropy—which relates these concepts to the mimetic dynamic of violence—are related in a way that is scientifically measurable or quantifiable. Even the question of whether informational and thermodynamic entropy are merely relatable, analogous, isomorphic, or one and the same is still subject to debate. Once we take the step into the realm of culture, such uncertainties increase tenfold. Like Michel Serres, Girard warns us not to confuse metaphors with explanations—only to briefly endorse such a metaphor himself:

> Describing the problem in terms of entropy, and negentropy is very attractive to modern minds, which have a penchant for thinking that metaphors taken from scientific disciplines can function as explanations, when they are simply another way of articulating the problem. The secret underlying cultural "negentropy" is the victimage mechanism and the series of religious imperatives it engenders. (*TH* 294)

That being said, the parallels are too numerous and striking to be ignored.[51] Finally, violentropy pertains not to actual and measurable dynamics, but to the literary ones established in McCarthy's universal poetics. What I *do* suggest, though, is that in the overall aesthetic of McCarthy's fiction, entropy features formidably and in multiple shapes—thermodynamic, informational, environmental, cultural—and that it cannot be separated from the violence that pervades his works. The element yet missing in this triad, of course, is that of myth.

Crises Resolved and Reimagined

Eliade held that the authentic event of myth is cosmogony, the act that founds reality itself. Now, the vision of a crisis resolved, of culture reemerging out of a violent chaos, certainly serves to color in the contours of this ominous notion. If sacrificial rituals can be called more or less abstract reenactments of a crisis that have been modeled on its solution, myths are "the retrospective transfiguration of sacrificial crises, the reinterpretation of these crises in the light of the cultural order that has arisen from them" (*VS* 64).[52] Most cosmogonic myths envision the battle between an ancestral hero and a primeval monster or godhead whose slain body becomes the world or gives birth to the community. Alternatively, they may tell of the deliberate labor and death, the outright self-sacrifice, or the expulsion of the godhead. All these myths can be seen as reflecting the reemergence of a social order from a crisis of distinctions through the unifying effects of sacrificial violence.

Seen so, the violence of myth is a reflection of actual violence. Somewhere behind the heroes and monsters of myth and legend lie the stories of victims made scapegoats, ritually expelled or sacrificed by their communities to stabilize the social order. Likewise, the double nature of the gods and heroes corresponds to different stages of viewing the victim: Apollo is the god of pestilence and the god of medicine. Oedipus the tyrant "causes" the plague of Thebes; Oedipus the outcast sage will bless the community where he lies buried. The zoophiliac transgression of the Dogrib woman gives birth to half-canine shapechangers, but she not only retroactively founds the law she transgressed but gives birth to mankind itself. In ancient Greece, an entire class of people, the *pharmakoi*, was designated by a word that means both poison and remedy. Myth frequently dramatizes such double-transformations.

In *The Crossing*, McCarthy provides a wonderful example of the compulsive nature of this mythical reinterpretation *in progress*. In the third part of the novel, Billy and Boyd Parham recover some of the horses that have been stolen from their family farm and taken to Mexico. Despite the documents designating the horses as their property, they are pursued and confronted by a one-armed man and his henchmen working for the landowner who now claims possession of their horses. As they refuse to surrender the animals, the *manco*, reaching for his gun, accidentally falls off his horse and breaks his neck. This leads to a wild chase between the brothers and his henchmen. Boyd is shot and takes refuge with a Mexican family where he recovers. Upon visiting him later, Billy finds Boyd is fast becoming idolized as some kind of local hero, as the villagers shower him with gifts and he lies on his sickbed "among his offerings like some feastday icon" (*CRO* 303). The stories that begin to circulate about the brothers' exploits take this adoration to yet another level:

> The workers believed that his brother had killed the manco in a gunfight in the streets of Boquilla y Anexas. That the manco had fired upon him without provocation and what folly for the manco who had not reckoned upon the great heart of the güerito. They pressed [Billy] for details. How the güerito had risen from his blood in the dust to draw his pistol and shoot the manco dead from his horse. They addressed Billy with great reverence and they asked him how it was that he and his brother had set out upon their path of justice. (*CRO* 317–18)

What McCarthy shows here is a rudimentary myth in the making. As readers, we know the truth of the matter. The irony is that what *really* happened is inconsequential in comparison to the tales spun around a wholly accidental escalation of events, a dispute about the rightful ownership of a few horses. What matters is the villagers' deep sense of conviction. Their stories make Boyd and Billy heroes to be revered, while the handicapped *manco* in his lethal misfortune assumes the more negative aspect of the scapegoat. The religious locals' conviction is that "Hay justicia en el mundo" (*CRO* 318). From this, even Billy's own account will not dissuade them. The charm of the myth pattern is stronger, as the locals' tale grafts itself onto an older corrido of a young, fair-haired American, coming from the north to seek justice:

> I heard the tale of the güerito years ago. Before your brother was even born.
>   You dont think it tells about him?
>   Yes, it tells about him. It tells what it wishes to tell. It tells what makes the story run. The corrido is the poor man's history. It does not owe its allegiance to the truths of history but to the truths of men. It tells the tale of that solitary man who is all men. It believes that where two men meet one of two things can occur and nothing else. In the one case a lie is born and in the other death. (*CRO* 386)

Of course, the binary dilemma between death and a lie does not have to be accepted, as we shall yet see. In the archaic and folklike context of the corrido, however, it may indeed be so. Consequently, as Billy rightly replies, "It sounds like death is the truth" (*CRO* 386). In a way, it is. The clash of rivals compels either the death of the system of mimetic antagonists, or the hidden truth of the collective murder of the scapegoat. The "truth of men" is built on self-deception regarding their own violent agency, their culpability. This deception is the same as the mythical cover-up, which entails a second act of symbolic violence—a "lie" born to cover up the violence underlying the system itself.

As it turns out, the monsters and the founders and cultural heroes are one and the same. According to Girard, myths should thus be interrogated and evaluated critically as *texts of persecution*. History, then, may be reinterpreted as humanity's awakening to the prevalence of scapegoating, and the concurrently declining effectiveness of the practice. The resulting accounts of persecution, whether mythically opaque or historically transparent, are grounded in real acts of violence. As such, they often exhibit common mythemes or stereotypes:

- a *state of crisis* marked by chaos, violence, and undifferentiation, and codified in such *motifs* as epidemics, floods, droughts, etc.
- *accusations* of crimes that transgress fundamental regulations and symbolically abolish "difference," for example, of parricide, incest, bestiality, etc., leveled against
- a *monster* or individual who is marked by signs of physical and/or moral deformity and held responsible for the crisis, which finally leads to
- the (*re*)*birth of order* into the culture after the supposed culprit is killed, expelled, or sacrificed.

Naturally, not all myths display all of these elements. Over time, the process of (re)telling inevitably mutates the tale. Elements are deemphasized or lost altogether. Regardless, as myths originate and persist on a *cultural* level and are bound up with defining that culture's cosmos and identity, they remain invested with its perspective. In other words, myths are told from the perspective of the persecutors, of the victimizers, the "winners of history." The narratives produced are naturally skewed in their favor—created to both vilify the victims and exonerate the community of their murder.

We need not rely solely on ancient or indigenous myth to argue the universality and persistence of mimetic violence, scapegoating, and their mythic transformation. The case would be much improved if we could trace the pattern in the mythology of a modern culture closer to our own. Luckily, we have already become acquainted with such a mythology.

The Frontier Revisited

Earlier, I introduced the work of Richard Slotkin to establish the basic function of myth and how it interacts with history and ideology. Focusing on *narrative*, Slotkin stresses that myth provides a culture with a common language, that is, a shared perception of the world and its place in it. In comparison, Girard argues that a culture's myths tell the tale of the reemergence of social order from crisis. At first sight, these statements seem unrelated. Yet we may ask: Is there any point when a culture is more in need of a common language, an identity, and a conception of the world than at its (re)birth from chaos?

Myth flattens historical complexity, distorts a people's view of the world, and silences the voices of the victims of history. Seen so, it is a prime manifestation of informational entropy. And yet, myth is nothing if not *a tool for establishing order* on a cultural level. All cultural institutions, including myth and religion, can be seen as aiming to keep violence outside the community. They do so by exporting it, by projecting it outward against an enemy who either is or is made to appear markedly different. Just so, the early colonists redefined themselves as Americans by differentiating themselves from both their English kinsmen and the "savages" they encountered in the New World. In later years, the existence of the frontier with its seemingly inexhaustible resources and free land would be seen as a safety valve against the civil disorder and strife that plagued the European metropolis.[53] The common denominator in these cases is the spirit of unity achieved through the organization of the inhabitants of a community along the same lines. This effect is far from being solely economic. Turner saw this quite clearly, pointing out a particular consolidating agent: "Particularism was strongest in colonies with no Indian frontier. This frontier stretched along the western border like a cord of union. The Indian was a common danger, demanding united action" (14).

These are more than just analogies. The principle expressed by Turner is the same extrapolated by Girard and Slotkin, and is the same asserted by

McCarthy's Judge Holden when he claims: "What joins men together [...] is not the sharing of bread but the sharing of enemies" (*BM* 307). Further similarities emerge in the recipes for action provided by our mythic heroes, which constitute explicit models of external mediation, or else the structural similarity between Slotkin's *fatal environment* and Girard's *sacred*, both of which cast man as at the mercy of forces beyond his control. Both thus obfuscate the knowledge of human agency, an obliviousness crucial to the functioning of both myth and the channelization of violence through scapegoating. Yet the most striking convergence is revealed in Slotkin's typology of the frontier myth, which early on functioned as a myth of *initiation*. Asserting the colonists' need to reconcile the heritage of Europe with the daily experience of American reality, Slotkin argues that this need inspired attempts to "cut through the conventionalized mythology to get back to the primary source of blood-knowledge of the wilderness, the 'Indian' mind" (*REG* 17). Initiation is essentially a personal experience. In colonial American society, through the shared "experience of acculturation and of nation building" (*REG* 473), it was made a social one as well. Initially, this was expressed in four distinct narrative formats: conversion, sacred marriage, exorcism, and, finally, regeneration through violence.

Of these four, the last is by far the most influential in shaping the relationship between the American Indians and the white settlers and their offspring. Originally, the myth envisions the figure of the hunter who leaves the security of his community on a quest into the realm of the wilderness. There, the hunter tracks and kills his game, which is then consumed in a "eucharist of the wilderness," renewing both hunter and community in the process: "The final expression of such a relationship is the domination, destruction, and absorption of one by the other [...]. The myth of the hunter [...] is one of self-renewal through acts of violence" (*REG* 554, 556). This paradigm complies with both of Girard's central concepts: mimesis and scapegoating. In dealing with both the wilderness and natives, contemporary writers like William Smith suggested that indeed "the proper way to live in America [was] to imitate the Indian" (cit. in *REG* 231). The American Indian came to serve as the primary though ambivalent model for the Puritan in search for a new identity and a way to master the wilderness. In mimetic terms, what was desired was the very *being* of the American Indian, "whose patriotism, independence, and love of liberty [made] him the model of the ideal American" (*REG* 231). Further proof of this is found in the motif of cannibalism:

> In one sense [the Puritans] did wish to cannibalize the Indian—to take into themselves [. . .] his ability to live within the environmental laws of the wilderness. [. . .] [B]eginning with the acquiring of special powers by consuming parts of the slain (heart, hand), [cannibalism] culminates in the total absorption of the eater and the eaten in each other, a total sharing of identities. [. . .] The preference for images of Indian cannibalism and rape reflects a growing Puritan belief that the only acceptable communion between Christian and Indian, civilization and wilderness, was the communion of murder, hunger, and bloodlust. (*REG* 90, 125)

The relation of Puritans to Indians thus provides a textbook example of *metaphysical* desire. A focal point in McCarthy's work starting with *Outer Dark*, the cannibalistic expression of mimetic desires converging on a common object—here mastery of the wilderness as the way to American identity—results in the gradual exacerbation of violent reciprocity. Caught in a vicious circle of myth and mimesis, Puritans were "likely on the battlefield to respond to Indian savagery with savagery in kind, to meet massacre with massacre, burning with burning, atrocity with atrocity" (*REG* 137). This violent dynamic was expressed in the concept of "savage war," driven by what Mark Twain called the "spirit of massacre" (*FE* 522).[54]

When looking for a scapegoat, the American Indian, too, provided the obvious choice for the Puritans and generations to follow: "The Puritans viewed the Indians as projections of the evil within themselves, as well as agents of an external malice" (*REG* 178). The sacrificial act, then, is to be found in "savage war," which was "the most acceptable metaphor for the American experience" (*REG* 68) as it offered dramatic contrast and the simplicity of direct conflict. By substituting the traditional English differential markers of class and religion for those of culture and race, this metaphor symbolically and practically achieves the unifying effects at work in scapegoating: "In American mythology, the Indian war also provides a symbolic surrogate for a range of domestic social and political conflicts. By projecting the "fury" of class resentment outward against the Indian, the American expands his nation's resources and thereby renders class struggle unnecessary" (*GN* 13).

In later wars, much the same held true for Mexico, the Philippines, and Vietnam.[55] In the totalitarian logic of war, the necessity is always that the attacker has already been attacked, that the violence he unleashes has been "forced" upon him by the Other. Yet mysteriously, whereas this illogic has prevailed throughout most of history, we are in a position today to perceive it as the act of scapegoating that it is. So what exactly has changed?

Judeo-Christian Revelations

Demonization of the Other is decisively easier to spot in texts of historical persecutions than in mythological accounts: "The face of the victim shows through the mask in the texts of historical persecutions. There are chinks and cracks. In mythology, the mask is still intact; it covers the whole face so well that we have no idea it is a mask" (*SG* 37).[56] But how is it possible that after centuries we are suddenly able to discern the patterns of communal violence and identify the workings of the scapegoat? How is it that more than any other before it, our age is dominated by a practically universal concern for victims? To ask these questions is to acknowledge the comparative infertility of mythogenesis today. Indeed, the myriad stories organized into the mythology of the American frontier may constitute a last residue of genuine culturally generative mythmaking. Clearly though, the human compulsion to tell stories remains as strong as ever. Again, what has changed?

The solution to this conundrum demarcates a third major step in the development of mimetic theory. Specifically, Girard posits that what allows for our identification of scapegoats is an epistemological leap rooted in a tectonic shift of perspectives from the many to the few, from the view of the community to the experience of the victim. While modern thought jumps almost by default to the achievements of the Enlightenment, he claims that the actual reason for this profound shift in perspective, in the West, is a heritage of Judaism and Christianity.[57] Endorsing Simone Weil's view that the Bible presents an anthropology first and a theology second, he finds both Testaments characterized by a deep awareness of man's mimetic being and an exceeding sympathy for the persecuted. Thus, the Yahweh of the Pentateuch takes vengeance out of human hands when he marks the original murderer Cain with his protective ward. He outright abolishes human sacrifice in the story of Abraham and Isaac. Joseph, after being sold into slavery by his brothers, who envy him for their father's favor, forgoes vengeance once the tables are turned and embraces them. And the last of the Ten Commandments, after prohibiting the coveting of one's neighbor's house, wife, servants, livestock, and so on, comes out against coveting anything that is one's neighbor's (Ex. 20:17)—and thus against envious coveting, read, *mimetic desire* as such (*ISS* 11).

While traces of an ancient wrathful God in the Old Testament are undeniable, there is an equally undeniable tendency to cast off this concept. Thus, the book of Psalms constantly performs a narrative "shift from the persecutors to the victims, from those who are making history to those who are subjected to it" (*SG* 104). Significantly, calamity-stricken Job resists the mimetic temptation of accepting the accusations of his community and even his wife, who believe his ill-luck to be a divine punishment. Yet in his trial before them, Job stalwartly insists that God is his "witness" or "defender," testifying for him (Job 16:19). God is opposed to Satan, whose role in "Job" is often compared to that of a legal persecutor, and whose name fittingly connotes any adversary or accuser, as does the Greek *diábolos*. In accordance with Job's tale, the Talmud establishes a principle reportedly often invoked by Emmanuel Levinas: "If everyone is in agreement to condemn someone accused, release him for he must be innocent" (*ISS* 118).

In Bateson's terms, we could say that these texts introduce a new type of information or "message" into mythical thought, and that this information makes a profound difference, reprogramming the system relying on collective violence from the ground up. If the Old Testament prefigures this message, it is fully articulated in the texts literally designated as "good news"—that is, the Gospels. In telling about the life of Jesus, these texts establish a new model to be imitated. Two prominent examples are Jesus's cure of the demoniac of Gerasa, which looms large in McCarthy's *Outer Dark*, and the mimetic contagion of *antiviolence* that is the effective result of Jesus's famous appeal to a group of men out to stone an adulteress: "Let him who is without sin among you be the first to throw a stone at her" (Jn. 8:7). In particular, though, it is the Crucifixion narratives that attract Girard's attention. From Caiaphas's sacrificial rationale that "it is better [. . .] that one man should die for the people, not that the whole nation should perish" (Jn. 11:50), to Pilate's *ecce homo* and admission of finding Jesus guiltless (Jn. 19:6), the Gospels leave no doubt about the innocence of the accused. Against the scapegoat, they pit the lamb of God. Yet the central moment that reveals the charm of myth to demystify it is Jesus's prayer on the Cross:

> The mythic process is based on a certain *ignorance* or even a *persecutory unconscious* that the myths never identify since it possesses them. The Gospels disclose this [. . .] in several explicit definitions of the persecutory unconscious. The most important of these we find in the Gospel of Luke, the famous prayer of Jesus during the Crucifixion: "Father, forgive them because they don't know what they are doing" (23:34). (*ISS* 126)

At least since Frazer, critics of Christianity have emphasized similarities of scripture with older, pagan myths, discrediting the Bible as a form of cultural plagiarism. Conversely, fundamentalists ignore such evidence to insist on the literal truth and the originality of the Gospels. In contrast to either group, Girard stresses both the continuity and the enormous breaks of the Bible with the tales and tropes of archaic religion. What is finally unique about the Judeo-Christian tradition is the *representation* and evaluation of collective violence, persecution, and victimization. In the Gospel of Luke, Jesus quotes a Psalm: "The stone that the builders rejected has become the cornerstone" (Lk. 20:17; see Ps. 118:22).

> The entire edifice of culture rests on the cornerstone that is the stone the builders rejected. Christ is that stone in visible form. [. . .] The Cross is the supreme scandal not because on it divine majesty succumbs to the most inglorious punishment—quite similar things are found in most religions— but because the Gospels are making a much more radical revelation. They are unveiling the founding mechanism of all worldly prestige, all forms of sacredness and all forms of cultural meaning. (*TH* 429)

This is why to Girard the Judeo-Christian heritage is genuinely and funda- mentally mythoclastic: it unveils the innocence of the victim. Doing so, it dismantles the generative principle on which the house of culture is built. With the Crucifixion, Jesus's innocence, and so, by extension, that of all victims of collective violence, is revealed. If Christ's death can be called a sacrifice, it is the sacrifice to end all sacrifice. With the unconscious made conscious, from there on out, people will be less and less capable of denying what they are doing.

Crossroads to the End

There is one final element that is central to our reading of Cormac McCarthy's work as an apocalypse peerless in all of English literature. Firstly, it has to do with the destructuralization of the social system of differences, the *sacrificial crisis*. Secondly, it involves what Slotkin calls a "crisis of mythography." Informed by the reinterpretation of myth through the lens of Judeo-Christian scripture, we now begin to understand that the latter is a subset to the former, and that the world McCarthy portrays in his novels is finally characterized by both.

The crisis of mythography—which is perhaps more aptly a *crisis of mythopoesis*—constitutes a state in which the myths that used to express a culture's world vision come into an irresolvable conflict with the experience of recent events. Events like My Lai can shock a culture into facing the hidden evils and fateful errors its myths have caused.[58] Socially, the effects of such a shock to a culture's myths can be hazardous, as William H. MacNeill asserts: "Discrediting old myths without finding new ones to replace them erodes the basis for common action that once bound those who believed into a public body, capable of acting together" (cit. in *GN* 626). Considering the social unrest that disturbed American metropolises in the "Long Hot Summer of '67" in convergence with the escalation of the war, what may otherwise sound overdramatic appears like a fairly accurate assessment:

> [O]ur penetration and demystification of the system necessarily coincides with the disintegration of that system. The act of demystification retains a sacrificial quality and remains essentially religious in character for at least as long as its fails to come to a conclusion—as long, that is, as the process purports to be nonviolent, or less violent than the system itself. In fact, demystification leads to constantly increasing violence, a violence perhaps less "hypocritical" than the violence it seeks to expose, but more energetic,

more virulent, and the harbinger of something far worse—a violence that knows no bounds. (*VS* 24–25)

Now, the demystification of Western myth seems to be a goal McCarthy explicitly pursues in his work. At the very least, it is one of its effects. Scholars have thus often described him as a *mythoclast*. Guinn claims that McCarthy "subverts the myths upon which culture rests, calling all certainty into question" (109). Cant says that McCarthy "implicitly and consistently attacks the myth of the pastoral in all its forms," recasting myth "to attack what he sees as the false and destructive cultural constructs of American exceptionalism in particular" (6). But what if McCarthy's project went further yet? If his novels indeed constitute a consistent apocalyptology, concerned with first and last things rooted in human nature, McCarthy's vision is firstly one of totality. As it does in *The Road*, it implicates the entire world. Secondly, it also articulates a model of history.

We have encountered three such models, one clearly cyclical, one clearly final. The first is the model of myth, which is identified with the archaic, the pastoral, with the cycles of nature, and with Nietzsche's idea of *eternal return*. Socially, this is the model underlying sacrifice. From an evolutionary perspective, the first victim and its sacrificial descendants, cast out again and again, represent a first fundamental bit of information, one truly making a difference. It is the victim as the fountainhead of culture and evolutionary impulse kick-starting the process of hominization. The second, chronologically newest, and scientific (yet culturally mythicized) model is that of the second law of thermodynamics. In physics, it casts the increase of entropy and the heat death of the universe as the arrow of time. In the realm of information, it projects confusion and a totality of *noise*.

Seen so, the teleology of entropic decline seems at odds with the circularity of myth. Yet the finality of the second law includes circularity as well: ecologically, the law underlies the cycle of composition and disintegration of open, living systems, their "maintenance" at the cost of their environment, their development into more complex orders, and the final fate of all such order. While this entropy is the measure of a nonhuman principle, a law of science, McCarthy's notion of a "heatdeath of the soul and of the heart" (91/97/1, n p.) at least implies a precarious spirituality with all-too-human consequences. Seen so, rather than a straight line, finality is the outcome of an ongoing downward spiral.

The third model is that of eschatology. The apocalypse envisions at once a revelation and exacerbation of violence before the perfection of the kingdom of heaven. The latter arrives as the consequence of a new type of message, a new bit of genuine, phylogenetic *information* articulated by the Gospels. From a secular, a-theistic perspective, this model appears as but another myth, though it implies finality rather than circularity. From the view of mimetic anthropology, though, the apocalypse is not a myth, but instead the consequence of the demystification of sacrifice and the scapegoat mechanism. In this light, the apocalyptic texts of the Gospels are a prognosis rooted in a view of humanity, rather than Providence:

> A scapegoat remains effective as long as we believe in its guilt. Having a scapegoat means not knowing that we have one. Learning that we have a scapegoat is to lose it forever and to expose ourselves to mimetic conflicts with no possible resolution. This is the implacable law of the escalation to extremes. The protective system of scapegoats is finally destroyed by the Crucifixion narratives as they reveal Jesus' innocence, and, little by little, that of all analogous victims. (*BE* xiv)

Revelation entails a radical *freedom of choice* that becomes the more precarious the more this "message" spreads and the less humanity can rely on sacrificial delusion to dissimulate and channel its internal violence. The knowledge of the scapegoat's innocence lays open the founding violence at the origin of the system, including the historical, violent failures of Christianity heeding its own message.

In a single image that gives shape at once to Morin's idea of a "fourth vision" as well as my interpretation of a "unified poetic field" and the McCarthyan *world-as-tale*, we might imagine ourselves as on a long road (see figure). Like McCarthy's protagonists, we are *homines viatores*. As a species, our journey in the historical narrative can be interpreted as a process of growing awareness of the forces that compel us to violence, the ways it figures into the ways we impose order upon the chaos of our existence, and in which this order dissolves back into chaos and violence. We are at a crossroads, with

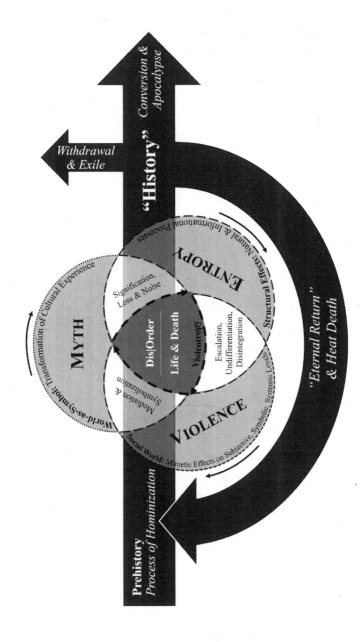

FIGURE. Outline of a "Unified Poetic Field" and the Apocalyptic Logic of Cormac McCarthy's Novels

choices to be made: with the stories we tell ourselves about ourselves and the world as our guides, how we interact with our fellow human beings as well as our environment will decide which way we will go as a species. We have to flesh out these choices as McCarthy presents them.

The first choice, as ever, remains that of how we manage subjective, systemic, and symbolic violence. We are thus at once radically free today not to choose violence at the same time that violence is a greater threat than it has ever been. Violence itself is as contagious as ever. The clamor of mimetic violence reverberates the stronger as we enter the cacophony of globalized communication. "Where else, but from the industrialized world, did the suicide hijackers [of September 11, 2001] learn that huge explosions and death above a city skyline are a peculiar and effective form of communication? They have mastered the language. They understand that the use of disproportionate violence against innocents is a way to make a statement" (Hedges 8). War may be a force that gives us meaning, and so, to be sure, is myth. But the meaning they produce is without substance, the sense of place they provide to us in our opposition to a common foe is short-lived and shallow. It is impossible today to believe—collectively, consistently—in the essential evil of our enemies.

> The knowledge we have acquired about our violence, thanks to our religious tradition, does not put an end to scapegoating but weakens it enough to reduce its effectiveness more and more. This is the true reason why *apocalyptic* destruction threatens us, and this threat is not irrational at all. The rationality enters more profoundly every day into the concrete facts of contemporary history, questions of armament, ecology, population, etc. (*ISS* 184)

What the writers cited here agree on is that the models of myth are mediators of violence. Subjective, systemic, and symbolic at once, this violence, in the globalized world, can be associated with a number of escalating phenomena of decline, erosion, and undifferentiation. It produces dis|order on reciprocally interconnected levels:

> · *culturally*, of all systems and institutions of social order, identity, and meaning; the proliferation of rumor and noise in old and new media

(so-called fake news, troll culture, postfactual reality, etc.); the loss of
the ability to communicate and mediate positions of disagreement;
the formation of extreme positions and ideological echo-chambers;
the frantic search for, defense, blaming, and impersonation of victims
as the new discursive strategy;

· *politically*, of the division between government and globalized corporate interests, and the representative power of old parties; the rise of
extremist and populist movements and governments; the rise of civil
and interstate war; streams of political refugees;

· *socioeconomically*, of the institutions and regulations curtailing corporate and individual desire; to the rise of economic crises in which
profits are privatized and catastrophic losses are socialized, resulting
in the ongoing undifferentiation of the middle class into the poor,
and so the rising divide between haves and have-nots;

· *environmentally*, of the ecosystem and biodiversity as a result of
pollution, the exploitation of limited resources, and the exacerbation
of climate change; a rise in environmental catastrophes, as well as
streams of environmental refugees; etc.

In sum, it is what I call *violentropy*. I stress again that this is a concept that
pertains to literary and cultural representation. How productive such a recal-
ibration of looking at these phenomena could be for analyses in other fields is
another matter. Culturally, the finality of the second law in the human world
has more to do with the eternal return of mythology than with the linearity
of Judeo-Christian eschatology. In the wake of revelation, the sacrificial effectiveness of scapegoating increasingly approaches that of Maxwell's Demon,
which is to say: *nil*. For the longest time, sacrifice constituted a social *perpetuum mobile*. Today, this is no longer the case. Violentropy must increase and
eventually overrun a system built on a cyclical transformation and expulsion
of violence at the expense of its victims. Lest the Judeo-Christian message
be wiped away together with its secular humanist offshoots, there can be no
return to the blissful, Dionysian ignorance of mythical scapegoating.

All things considered, reading Cormac McCarthy as a mythoclast—an
author whose work forces us to look beyond the illusions of myth, strips it
of its divine garb, and unveils the violence at its core—one has to take into
account that such a reading may be precarious to author and reader alike.

After all, if what we found is true, such writing and reading alike means entering a devil's triangle of violence, myth, and entropy. If there is in fact "no life without bloodshed" (Woodward 1992, 36) and "all is telling" (*CRO* 463), as McCarthy claims, to take violence and myth seriously means one cannot rest at undermining the mythic foundations of a culture. Neither can it be sufficient to halt at a revisionist reproduction of myth that simply inverts its role assignments but retains its basic premises. How McCarthy's work addresses these problems is what we shall explore now on our journey into the heart of darkness, the heart of light.

CHAPTER 2

Dissolved in a Pale
and Broken Image

Pastoralism, Mimesis, and Dis|Order in *The Orchard Keeper*

And the Lord God planted a garden in Eden, in the east,
and there he put the man whom he had formed. And out
of the ground the Lord God made to spring up every tree
that is pleasant to the sight and good for food. The tree
of life was in the midst of the garden, and the tree of the
knowledge of good and evil.
        —Genesis 2:8–9 (ESV)

It was in 1959, in the fall issue of a students' literary magazine of the University of Tennessee called *The Phoenix*, that a four-page story called "Wake for Susan" announced the first literary foray of a certain C. J. McCarthy Jr. Only two years prior, at age twenty-four, McCarthy had returned to Knoxville and university life. An initial enrollment in 1951–52 had been cut short and consecutively seen him join the air force for four years, two of which he spent stationed in Alaska hosting a radio show and pursuing an extensive, self-guided reading program. While his second enrollment also ended prematurely and without McCarthy attaining his liberal arts degree, the years from 1957 to 1960 bore witness to his first published efforts as a writer. In "Wake for Susan," he asked readers to follow the story of a young man dreaming of

romance with a girl long dead and buried. A second story was published in
the March edition of *The Phoenix* in 1960. "A Drowning Incident" tells of a
young boy getting back at his father for drowning the family dog's puppies
by hiding the turgid carcass of one of the puppies in his baby sister's crib. His
short stories won McCarthy the Ingram Merrill Award for creative writing in
both years, cementing his resolve to become a writer: "I never had any doubts
about my abilities. I knew I could write. I just had to figure out how to eat
while doing this" (Woodward 1992, 31).

While still a student at the University of Tennessee, McCarthy began
work on what would become *The Orchard Keeper*, taking it along as he left
Tennessee, moved to New Orleans, to Ashville, North Carolina, and finally
to Chicago, where he finished the novel earning his daily bread at an auto
parts store. In 1962, he sent the manuscript to Random House—"the only
publisher I [McCarthy] had heard of" (Woodward 1992, 31)—where it eventually fell into the care of Albert Erskine, who had previously edited Ralph
Ellison, Eudora Welty, Robert Penn Warren, and William Faulkner.[1] The
novel, which in the meantime bore such alternative titles as *Toilers at the Kiln*,
The Apple Orchard, Hourglass and Fiddle, and *Such Hawks, Such Hounds*, was
finally published as *The Orchard Keeper* in May of 1965 and went on to win
the Faulkner Foundation Award for the best first novel (91/1/1, n.p.).

Reviews in the national press were mixed, generally lauding McCarthy's
prose and noting his thematic debt to Faulkner while articulating confusion
as to the novel's structure and its characters' motivations. Katherine Gauss
Jackson found the novel demanding and "often difficult to follow," yet also
"an evocative exposition of the transiency of life" and ultimately "well-worth
the concentration it deserves" (112). Similarly, Granville Hicks, while judging
the plot's development "erratic" and some of McCarthy's techniques "tiresome," noted his narrative power and "gift for vivid description" (35–36).
Most positively, Walter Sullivan praised McCarthy's prose as "magnificent,
full of energy and sharp detail and the sounds and smells of God's creation,"
and perceptively realized that associations with other Southern writers were
"fleeting and prove to be false," singling out McCarthy as "like nobody so
much as he is like all the writers who have gone before him" (1965, 721). On
the negative end of the spectrum, the *New York Times*'s Orville Prescott
judged that McCarthy "submerges his own talents beneath a flood of

imitation" of Faulkner, and while he acknowledged the "torrential power" of the writing, he ultimately disparaged the novel as "an exasperating book [...] a jumpy, disconnected narrative" (45).

Indeed, *The Orchard Keeper* is a complicated book, if less so with regard to its themes than to its narrative structure and presentation. Frequently, it is associated with the literary traditions of naturalism and (late) modernism, and genres such as the Southern gothic, the historical romance, or the bildungsroman. Scholars have suggested a whole number of issues associated with various and often overlapping artistic programs. Depending on whether the focus lies more on theme or form, these programs range from "a meditation upon the irrelevance of the human in the impersonal scheme of things" (Bell 1988, 10), to the establishment of Appalachian Tennessee as an area both worthy of literary consideration and distinct from the South of William Faulkner and the agrarian school of writers, to an exploration of the "twin motifs of connection and disconnection" (Jarrett 11) pertaining to individual and community as well as to past and present. Finally, the novel is frequently read as a dramatization of the clash between civilization and wild nature in connection with the parallel conflict between and "interpenetration of different lives and cultures" (Cant 63), specifically between urbanized modernity and more rural, archaic ways of life often associated with the tradition of the pastoral.

In particular, it is the latter interpretations that my reading takes as its point of departure. Providing a twofold perspective on both ecological and social issues, the pastoral tradition can provide an entry into those mythic patterns that govern the interaction of humans with one another and the world, and which underlie McCarthy's work. At the same time, the aesthetic effects to which he employs the symbolic and thematic vocabulary of these traditions bespeak a deep epistemology of order and disorder, life and death, that already shapes up to be a pure, if yet unrefined, expression of McCarthy's universal poetics. Following an analysis of the texts' dis|orderly form, themes, and aesthetics through the pastoral lens, and rooting them in the historical context of Tennessee, I will put into focus the undiscovered mimetic dynamics of the novel, which will unearth some more of its mythic substance and recast it in a different light. In retrospect, these various patterns must appear not only as the starting point of McCarthy's career proper, but also as the germ cells from which grows Cormac McCarthy's apocalypse. All of it begins with *The Orchard Keeper*.

The Ruined Orchard:
Pastoralism and Programmatic Dis|Order

The main action of *The Orchard Keeper* takes place during the Depression years from around 1934 to 1941 and centers around the fictional mountain community of Red Branch. Primarily, the narrative follows the lives of three men.[2] Early in the novel, in 1934, Marion Sylder, a young whiskey-runner and local philanderer, kills Kenneth Rattner in self-defense and dumps his body into an insecticide pit close by the abandoned, eponymous orchard. Rattner's body is discovered by the aging hermit Arthur Ownby, who, rather than alerting the authorities, keeps watch over the unknown corpse for the next seven years. In 1940, both men's paths cross with that of young John Wesley Rattner, the son of the man Sylder killed, neither of the three being aware of their connection.

While at base level the novel is the story of these three men and the decline of the community they are a part of, it makes for a challenging, sometimes frustrating reading experience: its storylines branch out, diverge, and intersect, jump back and forth in time and space, and spread throughout the novel's four sections, twenty-one chapters, and prologue. These storylines frequently shift in focalization between the musings of an already fairly defined extradiegetic third-person narrator typical of McCarthy's later novels, a number of characters both central and marginal, and, in a few instances, a feral cat. Due to these shifting focalizers—often in combination with pronouns that refer to no identifiable antecedent—its at times exuberant stylistic lyricism, and what appears like a complete disregard for the unities of time, place, and action, the novel poses considerable difficulties. Add to this the initial opacity of the novel's central images, the often inscrutable motivations of its characters, and a number of apparent plot holes, and one is easily inclined to agree with Prescott's criticism or Bell's assertion that "by Jamesian standards *The Orchard Keeper* is a shambles" (1988, 11). Consequently, the question is raised whether these apparent flaws are due to an overambitious young novelist's failure to reign in his considerable powers of expression, or whether they are integral to the novel's design. I propose that the latter is the case.

Southern Pastoralism and Narrative Form

As if to force the issue, *The Orchard Keeper* opens with a prologue that at first sight bears no relation to the narrative that follows. The prologue presents the image of an elm tree "down and cut to lengths," its sections "spread and jumbled" on the ground (*OK* 3). A stocky white man and a black man are working on cutting it down further, while a young bystander is watching attentively. As they saw into one log, the workers are confronted with a mangled and twisted wrought-iron fragment of a fence that the white man says has "growed all through the tree" (*OK* 3). Aside from the man's dialect, which hints that the scene takes place somewhere in the South, the time and locale are unidentifiable. It is the first of a number of prominent images that few readings of *The Orchard Keeper* can dispense with discussing. For first-time readers, it is an image that defies them to make sense of it, "an interpretive problem that hovers over the main action of the book" (Ellis 2006, 43). Are we to take tree-and-fence-intertwined as a sort of leitmotif? If so, what does it express? That the tree has been felled and cut by the work of man may be seen as an early nod in the direction of pastoral or ecocritical traditions, especially as the elm is a classical tree of pastoral poetry. In the same vein, its penetration by the fence is a first example of Leo Marx's famous *machine in the garden*, or, viewed neutrally, of "the theme of man and nature interfused" (Bell 1988, 6).

A related aspect is introduced by the workers' assumption that it is the fence that has grown through the tree. This can be taken as a dramatically ironic example of anthropocentric hubris and ignorance, as readers realize that it must have been the tree that has grown around the fence.[3] Adding to the lack of context, the worker's statement raises the suspicion that something may have confounded conventional epistemology, as if the order of things had been upset. In "Narrative as Spatialized Perception of History," Matthew Horton argues that the image of the dissected tree is in fact programmatic for the novel, anticipating "the fractured surface and disordered sequence of the narrative to follow" and even reflecting the tension and "juxtaposition of rhythmic order and dissolution" (285–86), down to the level of syntax and meter. As I will show, this is one of the central points of *The Orchard Keeper*'s aesthetic: as readers, we are constantly forced to create an order, both structural and thematic, out of a narrative that is profoundly concerned with challenging that very order. In performing this kind of labor, it thus constantly draws attention to how, in Bell's words, "we become ironic metaphysicians making order out of random data" (1988, 25). That is to say, the dis|order of the novel is programmatic.

If we agree to read the prologue as an artistic program, it follows that *The Orchard Keeper* is a novel deeply concerned with the dramatic and aesthetic tension between order and disorder or, as Horton writes, "between coherence and dissolution" (289). Nevertheless, its design itself is by no means random. The novel's final chapter reveals the place and time of the prologue to be that of Red Branch's cemetery, seven years after the events of the main storyline. The unidentified young man of the prologue is likely none other than John Wesley, who has paid a visit to his mother's grave and witnessed the workers' removal of the tree and section of the fence. This framing device allows for the possibility that the novel's tale is in fact his own. Save for the prologue and final chapter, John Wesley's extradiegetic position is the same as the narrator's vis-à-vis the story that happens in between.[4] Like the fence growing through the tree, his "hallucinated recollections" and memories of "things done [. . .] and dreamt" (*OK* 245) may have informed and merged with the narrator's voice in what has gone before. Such order materializes only at the end of the narrative though. Its impact on the interpretation can be appreciated only on repeated readings.

Later, I will say more about tree and fence as well as McCarthy's framing of the novel. For now, let it suffice to say that in reading McCarthy's apprentice novel, it becomes clear that the central themes and many of the techniques that would become hallmarks of his writing are already present in ovular form. But whereas later works are more openly philosophical, more explicitly mythical, and more drastically violent, *The Orchard Keeper*'s aesthetic is sensual rather than didactic, emphasizing the complexity of the whole rather than highlighting any singular one of its intricately connected elements. Here as in later works, one finds at the core the essential opposition of life and death, which the novel envisions as a powerful tendency toward decay, dissolution, and disorder. Here already, this tendency becomes all but graspable, firstly, in the novel's use of pastoral imagery, which is deeply tied up with its dramatization of violence. Secondly, it extends to the act of reading itself. The complications of the latter, vis-à-vis this novel, are best understood as a constant negotiation and mixture of realistic and historical elements on the one hand, and a more allegorical and mythic layer that permeates the "real world," as the fence does the tree.

As in the two novels that would follow, one of the central artistic choices in McCarthy's contemplation of time and decay is *The Orchard Keeper's* employment and variation of the rich, and in America predominantly Southern, tradition of the pastoral genre. As Lewis Simpson argues in *The Dispossessed Garden*, the popular mythology of America is essentially one of progress as represented by advancing science and technology, the rise of commerce and capitalism, and the gradual emergence of a middle class, "together with a tendency to level the orders of the social structure," but there exists in the pastoral a powerful and no less mythical tradition of "responses to the dispossession of the integral and authoritative community [. . .] by modern history." The objective of these responses, in art as in real life, was to establish "places of permanence" (Simpson 1975, 1–2), which, drawing on the classical tradition of Theocritus's bucolic poetry and Virgil's *Eclogues* as well as Puritan Christianity, were envisioned as some sort of idyllic garden set against both the wilderness and the urban environment of the city. Thus, the pastoral presented a rich source of themes and symbols particularly appealing to the antebellum South. After all, as John Grammer summarily observes, the latter had always envisioned itself "as a refuge from all the ills to which European culture was heir—from politics, commerce, corruption, war and, ultimately, from time itself," offering instead "the promise of changeless order" (31).

At a first glance, McCarthy's Red Branch—situated in the Tennessee valley east of Knoxville, where the "small ridges and spines of the folded Appalachians [. . .] contort the outgoing roads to their liking" and where "on a clear day you can see the cool blue line of the watershed like a distant promise" (*OK* 10)—suggests such a secluded idyll. A closer look dispels any such notions. Red Branch assumes a decisively less promising character, emphasizing not timeless order, but instead the processes of growth and

decay, projected at once into the prehistoric past and an ominous future. On
the one hand, corn fields stand "parched and sere, stalks askew in defeat,"
the clay "cracks and splits in endless microcataclysm" under an "infernal sky,"
and the forest floor "has about it a primordial quality, some steamy carbon-
iferous swamp where ancient saurians lurk in feigned sleep" (*OK* 11). On
the other hand, there is the "cynical fecundity" of nature that threatens to
overgrow Increase Tipton's "jerrybuilt shacks" (*OK* 11) that constitute the
first glimpse of the actual township itself: "Even the speed with which they
were constructed could not outdistance the decay for which they held such
affinity. Gangrenous molds took to the foundations before the roofs were
fairly nailed down. Mud crept up their sides and paint fell away in long white
slashes. Some terrible plague seemed to overtake them one by one" (*OK* 11).

Consequently, *The Orchard Keeper* presents no simple pastoral ideal, but
reflects the development of Southern literature from the early nineteenth-
century agrarian writers' regretful yet defiant depiction of the disappearance
of "a distinctive agrarian Southern culture," through Faulkner's reinterpretation of Southern patriarchy as tragedy, to Flannery O'Connor's and Eudora
Welty's realistic yet satirical look at rural Southern cultural life in which the
disappearance of the Old South has already become a matter of course (Jarrett 10).

The decay the poorly built houses are subjected to is mirrored by the
undifferentiated nature of the families who inhabit them. Neither part of the
ethnically mixed group of Mellungeons specific to northeastern Tennessee
nor "exactly anything else," the inhabitants reproduce with "frightening pro-
lificness," and move in and out of the area, "each succeeding family a replica
of the one before" (*OK* 12). More than anything else, they are defined by their
very anonymity and lack of defining characteristics. This group represents
but one portion of the inhabitants of Red Branch. The novel does not speak
of them again, unless perhaps in reference to "the strange race" that remains
in Red Branch after the original inhabitants are "fled, banished in death or
exile, lost, undone" (*OK* 246).

Overall, these families' vague foreignness, lack of cultural definition, and
abject living conditions can be taken as suggestive of the dissolution of the
pastoral realm, without being necessarily couched in or confined by pastoral
symbolism. Even this early in the novel, McCarthy introduces what Girard

would call *symbols of desymbolization*: there are the subtle hints at natural disaster and a sense of contagious disease, as well as repetition and replication as regards the apathetic and definitively undefined community of shack dwellers. In sum, we find a general tendency toward undifferentiation and decline of order. While the extent and import of this setting is still elusive, it is worth pointing out that even on the first pages of his first novel, McCarthy already sketches a thematic line and draws upon an array of symbols that he will remain true to for the rest of his writing career.

The Invasion of the Machine

The flipside of the internal decay invoked by the first glimpse of Red Branch is the concomitant invasion of the pastoral garden by "the machine," that is, by the embodiment of the forces of progress and history that in Leo Marx's analysis transformed "a rustic and in large part wild landscape [. . .] into the site of the world's most productive industrial machine" (343). Evidently, *The Orchard Keeper*'s pastoralism is further complicated by the fact that Red Branch cannot comfortably be described as a garden, nor is it likely to ever have been one: its principal pastoral locus, the orchard of the novel's title, whose "Edenic connotations link it to humanity's old dream of the return to the garden, sanctuary from labor, history, change, and death" (Luce 2009, 29) has in fact gone to ruin about twenty years before the events of the main storyline—due to a lack of keepers to harvest its peaches.[5] Now its insecticide pit, whose mere presence negates the ideal of a life in harmony with nature right from the start, harbors the corpse of a murdered man. Hence, it serves as the novel's recurrent pastoral *et in arcadia ego*—the reminder of the presence of death in the paradisiac garden. The orchard itself is overshadowed by an ominous metal tank, simultaneously the clearest and yet the most mysterious representation of technocratic modernity in the novel.

Elements of Christian theology may be invoked as "an effective framework of meaning and the illusion of a less chaotic world" (Prather 45), but are consistently subverted and negated, both arcadian and biblical idylls denied. Neither does Red Branch conform to the ideal of Jeffersonian agrarianism. In fact, the only farm that is prominently featured is the one the younger Arthur Ownby inhabited together with his wife Ellen. A subject of the older

Ownby's reveries, it becomes the subject of what Georg Guillemin calls "an allegory on the death of Ownby's pastoral dream" (2004, 32). In my view, at least for Ownby, there is not much allegory to this scene, though: it is the real thing. Details are sketchy as this past is glimpsed but briefly through Ownby's fragmentary memory. Apparently, Ellen runs off with a Bible sales-man. Ownby is so devastated by this loss that he lets his farm go to waste, his lifestock starve and die until the air is filled with "an outrageous stench [. . .] a vile decay" (*OK* 155). His self-destructive mourning period concludes with his symbolic burial of Ellen's clothes and his abandoning the farm and with-drawal to the life of the mountain hermit that readers initially get to know.

Clearly, McCarthy's Red Branch is no Jeffersonian agrarian paradise, but closer in spirit to "a micro-frontier where mechanized civilization and 'official' progressive culture meet and combat both what is left of the natural environmental matrix and the mountain pastoral world" (Luce 2009, 29). It constitutes the kind of barely cultivated, half-wild location that Leo Marx has described as a middle ground "somewhere 'between,' yet in transcendent relation to, the opposing forces of civilization and nature" (23). This tenuous in-between position finds its expression in the social hub of the community, the Green Fly Inn (Cant 66; Grammer 33). Erected "on a scaffolding of poles over a sheer drop" and partly "nailed to a pine tree that rose towering out of the hollow," the inn is always threatened by collapse, sometimes "career[ing] madly to one side" only to "slowly right itself and assume once more its nor-mal reeling equipoise" (*OK* 12–13). It is as though the inn were itself some living system, barely maintaining homeostasis by negative feedback. The text could even be said to support such a cybernetic reading (Gk. *kybernetiké techne*—the art of steersmanship), as to the patrons "the inn was animate as any old ship to her crew" (*OK* 13). Without overinterpreting the locale, the inn's central feature is certainly its rugged yet cordial atmosphere, "a solidar-ity due largely to its very precariousness" (*OK* 13).[6]

Insofar as McCarthy's apprentice novel is still invested in the vocabulary of traditional pastoralism, the presence of encroaching technology is evident throughout. So too is the presence of a burgeoning modern consumer cul-ture and cash economy that has largely replaced the more barter-oriented trading still practiced by some, like Ownby. In part, the inhabitants of Red Branch are unwitting accomplices to the machine's invasion, a particularly poignant example being Marion Sylder. As Guillemin points out, "it is he who encroaches upon the city with his untaxed liquor and his outlaw morality, he who introduces urban commodities and customs to the village of Red Branch, his machine that invades the garden" (2004, 22). Particularly, Sylder's changing cars are precarious vehicles, not only disturbing the quiet of the forest and scattering gravel into the woods "like grapeshot" (*OK* 19), but also being the means to his smuggling operations, evasion of the authorities, and amorous adventures at the beginning of the novel.[7] Ordering his boots through a mail-order catalogue, buying a new pair of socks every week and ceremoniously burning the old, Sylder is an early example of conspicuous consumption and throw-away consumerism, an "affluent son [...] bearing no olive branch but hard coin and greenbacks," whose return ushers in "an era of prosperity, a Utopia of paid drinks" (*OK* 29) for the patrons of the Green Fly Inn.

At the same time, it would be a mistake to regard Sylder as the sole culprit, nor does his relation to nature seem particularly exploitative.[8] He is but one representative of a larger process that has its firm basis in the social and geographical realities ruling "one of, if not *the* most economically, culturally and imaginatively dispossessed areas within a larger region," that is, the South, which in terms of literary engagement "has historically reveled in these factors" (Walsh 2003, 32). Luce's detailed investigation of the backgrounds of McCarthy's first novel provides a conclusive overview of a number of events and processes in the late nineteenth- and early twentieth-century history of east Tennessee, leaving no doubt about their effects. Among such national factors as the onset of the Great Depression in 1929 and the beginning and end of Prohibition in 1919 and 1933 respectively, the three regional developments that stand out most are the ecological impacts of logging, the creation of the Great Smoky Mountains National Park, and the foundation of the Tennessee Valley Authority (TVA). A part of promoting the interests of railroad companies in the late nineteenth and early twentieth centuries, massive industrial logging drastically altered and destroyed regional wildlife habitats, leading to a spread of wildfires and an erosion of the topsoil that in turn exacerbated flooding (Luce 2009, 6). As local farmers were "semi-agrarian and strongly dependent on the ecosystem of the forest," its decline in turn led to a reduction in the size of families and a diminishment of their self-sufficiency, simultaneously creating "a new dependence on manufactured goods and consumption of processed foods" (Luce 2009, 6, 7).

In 1934, the creation of the Great Smoky Mountains National Park, while actually meant to counter the damages of logging as well as to create some tourism revenue, led to the displacement of over 250 mountain communities, dispersing them into the hardship of an economy right in the middle of the worst depression in U.S. history. Another fateful change was the creation of the TVA in 1933. A part of Franklin Roosevelt's New Deal, it proved ultimately more detrimental and damaging to the region and its inhabitants than the Depression itself. In pursuit of its goals, which were primarily the promotion of industrial growth, the production of electricity, as well as flood control, the TVA launched various engineering projects, chief of which was the erection of a system of dams and locks that regulated the river system. As a result, thousands of acres of some of the best farmlands, cemeteries, and other cultural and historical landmarks were submerged together with smaller streams and rivers. This led to the extinction of several species and the displacement of 13,499 families and between 72,000 to 80,000 individuals, permanently altering the sociocultural makeup of the region and fostering a new, deep mistrust of and resentment toward the federal government.[9]

With his family's move to Knoxville in 1937, McCarthy's childhood and youth provided ample opportunity for him to witness firsthand many of the monumental changes coming to the region. Since Charles McCarthy Sr.'s work as a lawyer for the TVA was what likely inspired the move in the first place, young Cormac's life in the region itself was involved in the forces that forever transformed east Tennessee.[10] It comes as no surprise, then, that the effects of many of these developments echo throughout the novel. Sylder's consumerism as well as the presence of a disused loom in the Rattner house point toward the increased dependency of the region on outside goods. In addition, the presence of the "strange race" (*OK* 246) that has taken over the region by the end of the novel as well as that of several members of the prominent Tennessean Tipton family can be read as inconspicuous allusions to the regional displacement of locals that took place in the wake of the creation of the TVA and the national park. Though *The Orchard Keeper*'s landscapes vibrate with the flora and fauna of the region—all the more so when compared to later novels—experienced "watcher[s] of the seasons and their work" (*OK* 90) like Ownby notice the disappearance of mink, muskrat, bobcat, and panther. In fact, the younger Ownby's past work for the railroad involved blasting a trail through the valley and was thus actively involved in the destruction.

Birds are not exempt from the onslaught of modern technology, either. Hanging from a light wire, "dangling head downward and hollowed to the weight of ashened feathers and fluted bones," an electrocuted owl stares at Ownby and the reader alike "from dark and empty sockets, penduluming softly in the bitter wind" (*OK* 143). For the boys around Warn Pulliam, dynamiting birds is the cause of wonder and stuff of boyish adventure. Having surrendered a hawk at the Knoxville courthouse and subsequently buying traps with the dollar he has been paid, John Wesley realizes only toward the end of the story that the animal has "no value or use" to modern society "other than the fact of [its] demise" (*OK* 233). Thus the bounty theme, which Wallis Sanborn argues functions as an expression of "man's ceaseless desire and attempt to control the natural world" (2006, 13), can be seen as another instance of the intrusion of the machine into the garden.

The most extensive marker of environmental decline, however, is the devastating flood that befalls Red Branch, swallowing fence posts, half-submerging the flats of Little River, and launching a veritable invasion of aquatic and aerial wildlife (*OK* 173–74). If one can assume that all of these more and less visible signs of natural decline are in fact the combined result of the processes outlined above, it follows that it is a mistake to assume, as Guillemin does, that "the pastoral realm of the novel is hardly overrun by progress but very much intact" (2004, 21). In this quality, the world of *The Orchard Keeper* is quite realistic, as major events can rarely be traced back to a single cause. Nevertheless, Guillemin is right insofar as the dissolution of Red Branch is not solely due to the forces of progress: the wilderness itself continuously assaults and reclaims human constructs, a process that includes not only Tipton's shacks and the flooded houses, but more sturdy constructs such as the Rattners' log cabin and Mildred Rattner's headstone, which only three years after her death, is already "glazed with lichens and nets" (*OK* 245). Finally, there is yet another, intracommunal dimension of the breakdown that needs to be addressed.

Mimesis and Violence:
The Disintegration of Red Branch

The interpretive problems of *The Orchard Keeper* can largely be understood as effects of two different narrative modes—one adhering to the primacy of realism and history, the other beholden to mythic symbolism—that interpenetrate one another. Guillemin is thus also correct in another sense: to read the flood as a result of logging, ruthless environmental exploitation, and the well-intended but disastrous activities of the TVA is to view it from an exclusively realistic mindset. Rather than by pastoralism, this view is informed by the sociogeographic history of the region. Admittedly, to do so is quite appropriate: starting with his debut, McCarthy frequently employs the ugly facts of history as a chief weapon in his arsenal for achieving his mythoclastic ends. John Cant argues that his apprentice novel stands out in McCarthy's oeuvre, as he deems both its characters and action "entirely believable in a way that is not true, or meant to be true, of later texts. Although *The Orchard Keeper* attacks America's myth of the pastoral it is not in itself an anti-myth" (66). Nevertheless, although this assessment is thematically accurate, it underaccentuates the way in which McCarthy's prose frames important parts of the world his novel depicts.

The Mythical Flood and Boyhood Shenanigans

The dramatization of the flood that opens the fourth section and catastrophic conclusion of the novel provides a vivid case in point. Structurally, it represents a climax in the events of the novel, as it occurs shortly before the arrests of Ownby and Sylder, the latter of which it directly precipitates. Lasting a biblical seven days, it is preceded by a raging storm that rains down "a plague of ice" and turns the dust road into "geysers of erupting mud," bends and defoliates trees as if "on some violent acceleration of the earth's turning," and renders the wooden paths a "maelstrom of riotous greenery" (*OK* 171–72). On his way to the orchard, Ownby is knocked unconscious by a lightning's impact into a nearby chestnut: "A clash of shields rings and Valkyrie descend with cat's cries to bear him away" (*OK* 172). The Norse mythology invoked here is interwoven with biblical imagery evoking several of the ten plagues in the book of Exodus: the earth itself seems to be bleeding, as blocked gullies overflow with "water of a violent red" and "r[u]n red and livid as open wounds," frogs, fish, and other wildlife invade the nether regions of Red Branch, and, as in Exodus, fence posts disappear into the flood "like the soldiers of Pharaoh" into the red sea (*OK* 173–74). These are not the sole biblical allusions in this chapter either, as the newest "attraction" in Mr. Eller's store is a litter of kittens whose "eyes were closed and festered with mucus as if they might have been struck simultaneously with some biblical blight" (*OK* 180). These passages may be called magical, mythical, charged with sacred violence; a thing they are *not* is realistic.

Insofar as the three pages depicting this deluge involve the destruction of fences and the splitting of trees, one is inevitably reminded of the novel's opening image of the fence that has "grown" into the tree. Seen as a (anti) pastoral symbol, the image belongs in a tradition that has its roots in Greco-Roman culture. One of the crucial differences with regard to the pastoral world as seen by the Abrahamic religions is a fundamentally different concept of time and history itself. As I have shown in the theory section of this study, the cosmogonic hypothesis par excellence is that of an original *chaos* becoming *cosmos*. With regard to the human world, M. H. Abrams points out, there also existed a second, "primitivist view" of an original golden age from which history represented an ongoing decline, yet the view prevalent in "the sophisticated thinking of philosophers, historians, and political theorists, as well as poets," was a third one, namely "the theory of cycles."

> The overall course of events is from bad to better to best to worse to worst to better, and so on, time without end. Some proponents of this theory held a view of eternal recurrence, maintaining that the kinds of things that have happened before will happen again, as time brings the world back to the corresponding phase in the cycle of human values, or even that each individual being will recur and each particular event will in due course be reenacted. (Abrams 34)

Pertaining to different stages of prehistory and the historical process itself, these three ideas were by no means mutually exclusive. Mythographers have proposed that the cyclical concept of time itself is openly reflected in the structure of pagan ritual. As Mircea Eliade argues in *The Sacred and the Profane*, rituals, festivals, and other rites are shaped according to a mode of "sacred time." In contrast to the "profane time"—the "ordinary, temporal duration" of daily life—sacred time is *reversible* in the sense that [. . .] it is a primordial mythical time made present," with rites and festivals representing "the reactualization of a sacred event" (68–69), which is the founding event of reality. Sacred time is thus aligned, if not necessarily identical, with cyclical history. It is this ontology that underlies the world of Red Branch, which in some respects is closer to the pagan *sacred* mindset than the *profane* modernity of the United States that envelops and eventually overwhelms Red Branch.

It may be but a coincidence that in certain tribal communities, like the Polynesian Tikopia, the "passage from profane to sacred time" (Eliade 86) is ritually effected by the splitting of a piece of wood. Even so, this coincidence highlights rather beautifully how sacred time overlaps with the pastoral ideal that we have in the mysterious fusion of tree and fence that opens and closes the novel: "The elm and iron have fused inextricably, and, as a result, symbolize a transitional age in history defined by overlapping, interrelated, and clashing times. To separate those times, to slice through them in the same way as the rest of the tree, proves to be impossible" (Horton 288). Eliade's conception of the religious consciousness will easily be seen as identical, or at least congruous, with the dominant perspective of Ownby and, partially, the older John Wesley of the frame, insofar as their perception shapes the narrative voice and even the structure of the novel itself.

The point is not so much that McCarthy had a particular ritualistic tradition in mind in dramatizing his flood or opening the novel with the image of a split tree, but rather that the *novel* is at least partly informed by incongruent epistemologies. *The Orchard Keeper*, then, alternates between realistic or naturalistic and more mythical and symbolic modes of presentation. What unites both modes is that they investigate mimetic processes and their results. While the naturalistic mode pays exquisite attention to the details of imitative behavior and the search for proper models, the mythical mode, much as in later novels, is primarily dedicated to the violent and disruptive side of these processes. Viewed this way, Red Branch appears not only as a disappearing pastoral middle-ground or regressive microfrontier, but as the first in a series of fictional societies imploding in the wake of a crisis, even as it is slowly absorbed in the progress of forces representing mainstream America.

The flood provides a memorable case in point. According to Girard's theory, floods and epidemics, such as the one afflicting Eller's kittens, serve to symbolize and may be seen as an actual external occasion or starting point of the social upheaval of the sacrificial crisis. In Greek tragedy, myth, and what he calls *texts of persecution*, they symbolize the collective confusion and lack of differentiation involved in the crisis. Like the plague, the flood "is less than theme, structure or symbol, since it symbolizes desymbolization itself" (*DBB* 152). As a mythical motif, the flood provides a concrete image for "the deterioration of human relations at the heart of the community and with a shift toward reciprocal violence" (*TH* 13) the propagation of which it expresses in the guise of a natural catastrophe.

Of all this, the flood in *The Orchard Keeper* is exemplary. Yet the argument that links it to a hypothetical sacrificial crisis enveloping Red Branch requires more evidence, such as can be gathered only by looking at the significant social relations in the novel. These relations are fashioned in the more realistic, "profane" mode. The exploits of young John Wesley and his friends are enlightening. These characters have their rough analogues in McCarthy's childhood friends. Some of their fictional trials, such as the "exploding birds" episode, were actually "lifted almost wholesale from [their] associations and sundry misadventures" (Gibson 26).[11] Hence, the authentic feel of these parts is not remarkable in itself. Nevertheless, it raises the question of whether the attention to mimesis displayed in these episodes is a conscious choice on McCarthy's side, or whether he simply retold things as he experienced them. In either case, the adventures of the boys prove particularly rich and revealing as they illustrate both the gregarious and potentially destructive aspects of mimesis through the unadulterated behavior of children. The boys proudly display or talk of their possessions, such as Warn's leashed and half-domesticated turkey buzzard, the ancient musket of Boog's grandfather, or John Wesley's declaring that his coon dog "makes as good a tree dog as they is goin," which significantly is a verbatim adoption of Sylder's words (*OK* 112, 134). Similarly, their boastful accounts of their adventures in nature bespeak a playful rivalry as they "try to outdo each other in their mastery of bragging and scatology" (Hall 69).

But the boys' humorous and innocent competition has a darker side to it. Warn's snub at Boog for confusing bugles and beagles is a first hint, and Boog follows the model provided by Warn, tellingly adopting the correction

later (*OK* 135, 142). While not internally disruptive, the childlike imitation of external models, too, involves certain hazards. On two occasions of
building a fire, the boys first utilize "a old Indian trick" (*OK* 137) and later,
in the cave, strive to emulate what they imagine is "the way the cave-men
used to do" (*OK* 140), almost smoking themselves out in the process. What is
most illuminating is the boys' conversation about whites, blacks, and Native
Americans. Their discussion is quite explicitly framed as a search for models:

> Which'd you rather be, Boog asked John Wesley, white or Indian?
> I don't know, the boy said. White I reckon. They always whipped the
> Indians.
> Boog tipped the ash from his cigarette with his little finger. That's so,
> he said. That's a point I hadn't studied.
> I got Indian in me, Johnny Romines said.
> Boog's half nigger, said Warn.
> I ain't done it, Boog said.
> You said niggers was good as whites.
> I never. What I said was *some* niggers is good as *some* whites is what I
> said. [...]
> I had a uncle was a White-Cap, Johnny Romines said. You ought to
> hear him on niggers. He claims they're kin to monkeys. (*OK* 140)

This remarkable exchange is one of the comparatively few passages in McCarthy's oeuvre where race is overtly an issue. Taking place in a cave littered with
"inscriptions" and "hieroglyphs" and evoking the Darwinian theme of man's
shared ancestry with apes—though the latter is attributed solely to blacks—
not only does the conversation expose the systemic racism of the society the
boys are a part of and that McCarthy grew up in, it also argues the ironically universal tendency of humans to differentiate between the peoples of
the earth and to attach value judgments to their discrimination. Their racial
essentialism assumes a relation between such accidental factors as skin color
and cultural heritage on the one hand and the metaphysical value of a human
being on the other. In their quest for superiority, for uniqueness, they naïvely
ignore the universal bonds shared by all. Boog's remark that "*some* niggers
is as good as *some* whites," complicated though it may be by being framed
as a rebuttal to the challenge of *his* ancestry, is at once the most egalitarian

and markedly "discriminating" position, simultaneously abolishing sweeping claims to collective superiority, while distinguishing between individuals and their qualities.

The boys' natural search for models to emulate becomes more problematic when viewed against the background of the society they are a part of. In their early teens at best, they are already immersed in the hunting and gun culture of Red Branch. The sight of the boys carrying shotguns and rifles and "buying shells not by the box but by fours and sixes and lending to the bustle [of Eller's store] a purposeful and even militant air" (OK 142), does not raise so much as an eyebrow among adults. That their shenanigans do not register as "subjective violence" among their elders is not simply a sign of pedagogic laxness, but bespeaks the fact of what Žižek calls the objective, systemic "zero level" of violence—the "violence inherent to this 'normal' state of things" (2009, 2). The culmination of growing up in this environment is represented by such acts as Warn shooting a gun in a tunnel to kill a skunk, which some critics have seen as a symbolic rape of the earth (Luce 2009, 36), and the act of dynamiting birds out of mere curiosity and playful mischief.

The effects on the reader are initially humorous and, on second thought, terrifying, as one recognizes the sinister play of imitation. Using the transformer of an electric train to set off a stolen dynamite cap, the boys' bird blasting chronologically repeats and narratively foreshadows Ownby's accidental killing of panther cubs in his work of dynamiting for the railroad company, decades ago. Thus, "Warn, Johnny, and Boog model their acts on and unconsciously parody the adult culture they are preparing to join," and this culture is one that neglects "stewardship or enlightened coexistence" with nature "in favor of utilitarian ownership and even paramilitary assault" (Luce 2009, 35–36). The exception is John Wesley. Initially attracted to the lures of technocratic modernity, in the end, he consciously rejects its morality in favor of the models provided by Sylder and the older, wiser Ownby.

Monstrous Doubles

It hardly requires the mimetic approach to see that the comparatively harmless destruction caused by the children is symptomatic of a culture that has normalized a certain degree of violence. To an extent, this is true of any society. Though tame and subdued when compared to later novels' carnage, the ways in which *The Orchard Keeper* dramatizes violence leaves no doubt as to its pervasiveness. It is waged by the agents of progress and representatives of the industrial order as well as the people of Red Branch; yet, it would also seem that McCarthy, at this stage, still believes in a clear difference between agents. What is more, violence is also shown as an integral part of the realm of the sacred, of undomesticated nature itself. In most of these instances, it is predominantly represented in mythical terms.

Discounting acts that can be called violent only with some abstraction, such as the dissection of the tree in the prologue, the first prominent act of violence occurs after the overburdened porch of the Green Fly Inn collapses. Insofar as the inn stands pars pro toto for Red Branch as a whole, partial collapse and violent eruption function as both symptom and prefiguration of the more encompassing disintegration of the community. The immediate result of this accident for the affected patrons is the loss not of their lives but of their dignity and, it will turn out, of their money, which the opportunistic Kenneth Rattner steals from their lost trousers and jackets. As the survivors return "torn, unclothed and crushed [. . .] looking like the vanquished in some desperate encounter waged with sabers and without quarter," the atmosphere of the inn suddenly "seethe[s] with an inchoate violence." Consequently, "two factions" form and fall "upon each other murderously" to fight "far into the night" (*OK* 25–26).

The episode is interesting in several respects. First so in that there is no apparent reason for the murderous brawl; while one might suspect misdirected outrage over Rattner's theft as a possible cause, Mrs. Eller's account does not identify the theft as the origin of the fight, which chronologically seems to antedate its discovery. Second, rather than mentioning just a violent brawl, McCarthy suggests a distinct symmetry between the two factions. Third, like the ill-defined "not Mellungeons" inhabiting Tipton's shacks, the factions are remarkable for their very lack of characteristics, of distinctions. Before the accident we were given at least three distinct individuals with the tale-spinning Ef Hobie, the barman Cabe, and Kenneth Rattner. With the accident, people become a "knot of men," a "mass" that "Cabe and a few others" are trying to untangle (*OK* 25), before they, too, are lost to the distinguishing eye of McCarthy's narrator.

The only one who consistently remains apart from the group is Kenneth Rattner, the man who profits from the accident. Having moved from

Maryville to Red Branch only four days prior, his family represents a group of outsiders who illegally squat in an abandoned log house. At the Green Fly, Rattner remains to himself, sinister in his isolation as he evades the looks of the others, "seeking [. . .] that being in the outer dark with whom only he held communion, smiling a little to himself, the onlooker, the stranger" (*OK* 24). As is the case with Culla Holme in *Outer Dark*, the novel that is anticipated here, other figures like the storekeeper at the beginning of the novel or the barman in Jim's Hot Spot always regard Rattner with a mixture of suspicion and disgust. Retrospectively, their caution seems justified: Even at his first appearance, Rattner lies constantly and steals from the gas station grocery store. He has abandoned his wife and kid for over a year, and he may well go on to rob and perhaps kill the man who gives him a ride on his way to Atlanta. At least, he tries as much with Sylder in the confrontation that brings about the novel's central act of violence.

A closer look reveals the relationship between Rattner and Sylder to be that of *mimetic doubles*. Sylder is actually the character who, as victim, perpetrator, and spectator, is involved in most of the acts of violence in the book. At the outset, he can arguably be said to be a scoundrel. Not only is he on the wrong side of the law with his illegal whiskey smuggling, he is also a philanderer, even something of a sexual predator.[12] His fatal encounter with Rattner is effectively the consequence of another fight. He loses his job at the local fertilizer plant for getting into a fight with a certain Aaron Conatser, whom he engages rather casually—"not out of any particular dislike [. . .] or even in any great anger, but only to get the thing over with, settled," and because Conatser is similar to him in that he is "the only man in the plant his size" (*OK* 30). As with the anonymous free-for-all at the Green Fly Inn, the lack of any particular motive or occasion is a subtle hint to the essential vacuousness of mimetic rivalry: the only object at stake in this confrontation, at best, is personal prestige.

Losing his job sends Sylder on a temporary escape from Red Branch, during which he meets Rattner at a roadhouse outside of Atlanta. Narratively, the encounter and in fact their relationship as a whole is framed in terms of symmetry. Symmetry begins with the syllabic equivalence and cadence of their names, affects their shared position both as roamers with a questionable relation toward the law, and extends to such minute details as Rattner's pretense to owning a 1934 V8 Ford involved in his deception of the clerk in the grocery store. As it turns out, this is the *same* brand and likely even the actual car Sylder owns at this point.[13] Most likely, it is also Sylder's "nice autymobile" (*OK* 34) that Rattner desires and that serves as the object-cause of their confrontation. Both men have hurt their legs, Rattner cutting himself on a barbed-wire fence and Sylder limping slightly as a result of his fight with Conatser, and on their respective escapes from and returns to Red Branch both get drunk at Jim's Hot Spot. It is almost as if both men were mirror images of each other. So too, upon entering the road house both men *do* look into an actual mirror: Rattner is "surprised to see himself, silhouetted in the doorframe"; Sylder gazes upon his "hollow-eyed and sinister" reflection (*OK* 22, 32), which effectively provides him "a glimpse of the violent outlaw Rattner in himself" (Luce 2009, 52).[14] Finally, their encounter is prefigured by the spectacle of "two men circling warily with clenched bottles" (*OK* 32), and upon commencing their nightly journey, they will gaze at each other in the reflecting glass of the car's windshield "like enemy chieftains across a council fire" (*OK* 36).

Evidently, McCarthy takes great care to draw attention to the doppel-gänger theme. Even minor figures, such as "a man and his son" who briefly threaten to discover Sylder's murder when they stop by to offer help, appear as such, one being "heavy and red, with creased skin, the younger a tall and thinner duplication" (*OK* 42). The near perfect symmetry of the entire confrontation between Sylder and Rattner, as told from Sylder's view, exhibits all the mechanisms of mimetic doubling. In this, Rattner, who remains an anonymous stranger, assumes the increasingly mythological role of the monstrous double:

> The subject watches the monstrosity that takes shape within him and outside him simultaneously. In his efforts to explain what is happening to him, he attributes the origin of the apparition to some exterior cause. Surely, he thinks, this vision is too bizarre to emanate from the familiar country within, too foreign in fact to derive from the world of men. The whole interpretation of the experience is dominated by the sense that the monster is alien to himself. The subject feels that the most intimate regions of his being have been invaded by a supernatural creature who also besieges him without. (*VS* 165)

Identifying Rattner as a monstrous double, my analysis builds on that of Luce who also regards Rattner as a character who straddles the fence between realism and allegory, representing an early example in McCarthy of "the double who ambiguously represents a main character's darkest self, yet who also menaces him physically" (2009, 53). Effectively, Rattner becomes a supernatural creature once Sylder opens the door of his car to find him inexplicably sitting there "as if conjured [...] simultaneously with the flick of light," inducing in him not just the disgust and suspicion Rattner typically meets with, but "a profound and unshakable knowledge of the presence of evil, of being for a certainty called upon to defend at least his property from the man already installed beneath his steering wheel" (*OK* 33).[15]

How does Sylder arrive at this conviction? Since he serves as the main focalizer in this passage, objective answers are hard to come by, but the mimetic perspective suggests his utter inability to recognize himself in his anonymous opposite. Even as a careful reading strongly suggests their similarity and kinship of character, Rattner to Sylder appears solely as the monstrous other. Again, "from within the system, only differences are perceived; from without, the antagonists all seem alike" (*VS* 158). And yet, it requires a conscious effort on the part of the reader to escape the narrative system created by the totalizing focalization of Sylder's perception, as well as a looking beyond the immediate encounter itself to see what is really going on.

Rattner is gradually dehumanized in Sylder's eyes, and so in the reader's: his lips purse "carplike" as he smokes a cigarette, his "puffy fingers" remind Sylder of "baby possums [...] blind and pink" as they crawl over his arm during their fight, and upon his death, Rattner's hands clench up "like a killed spider," his eyes staring "owlishly" (*OK* 36, 39, 40). Narratively, he becomes a figure destabilizing the boundary between human and animal. Like the mythical wampus cat that haunts Ownby's dreams, he is a monster. His face in the windshield has the look of "some copper ikon, a mask, not ambiguous or inscrutable but merely discountenanced of meaning, expression" (*OK* 36). As Girard tells us, the essence of masks is that they are "beyond differences; they do not merely defy differences or efface them, but incorporate and rearrange them in original fashion. In short, they are another aspect of the monstrous double" (*VS* 168). In this way, McCarthy already sets up the sacrificial role the deceased Rattner will play after his death.

At the same time, contextual analysis alerts us to the fact that this kind of view involves the unconscious distortions of mythology. Though quite effective in evoking both Sylder's and the reader's disgust, the strategy McCarthy uses is by no means particular to this episode: metaphors and similes animalizing humans, personifying animals, or transforming inanimate objects like Sylder's car, the sun, or the moon in either way, abound in the novel. In general these tropes suggest both our animal nature and essential oneness with the natural world as part of the early McCarthy's effort to overcome an anthropocentric point of view. Yet their ordinariness, that is, the commonplace frequency with which they occur, also suggests Rattner may simply not be quite as monstrous and abnormal as he appears. In sharp contrast to the expressionless mask seen before, Sylder notes a look of terror on Rattner's face, which he feels is "not his doing either but the everyday look of the man" (*OK* 39). It is exactly in these moments that the mask of the double slips to allow for a glimpse at the human face behind it. And what we glimpse is fear.

Equally, these instances call for a reading against the grain of both the text and McCarthy criticism in general. To the extent that the account of their lethal confrontation is focalized through Marion Sylder, it is unreliable. And yet, there is a point when Sylder relaxes his grip around his double's throat, and both men speak. Rattner begs Sylder for his life: "For Christ's sake, he gasped. Jesus Christ, just turn me loose" (*OK* 39). Sylder responds with a threat, yet for the fraction of a moment, there seems to be the chance that their struggle could be resolved. Then, Sylder sees Rattner looking at his hurt shoulder—and kills him. The text is ambiguous on this point, but Rattner's fatal look suggests two possible interpretations: One is that the look is a reminder of the damage Rattner has already done with his initial assault, making the killing an act of reprisal. Another is that Sylder interprets the look at his hurt shoulder as a search for weakness in preparation for a final attack, which leaves him with no doubt that he *has* to kill Rattner. The reader is likely to side with Sylder in his assessment of the other as dangerous, not just because Sylder serves as focalizer, but because the text has already shown Rattner as a thief, and suggested that he has robbed and possibly assaulted the man who gives him a ride to Atlanta (*OK* 15). The fact of the matter, though, is that the narrative never *shows* Rattner committing a murder. After his initial attack on Sylder has failed, his first impulse is that of flight.

Furthermore, in that fatal exchange of looks that directly precedes Sylder's murder, the phrasing with its unclear referentiality of pronouns suggests that it is actually Sylder who first looks at his own shoulder, and that Rattner instinctively follows this look: "Then he saw his shoulder, saw the man looking at it" (*OK* 40). Consequently, what Sylder interprets as preparation for an attack may in fact be none. Even if it were, what directly precedes Rattner's look is Sylder's threatening answer to his plea for mercy. All in all, the suspense in the buildup to the actual encounter is largely the consequence of the strain Sylder feels. From first laying eyes on him, he expects Rattner to attack, and combined with his disgust, this alertness prompts him to interpret each of Rattner's actions in this light. Rattner himself is likely to pick up on these signals, and in turn interpret them as hostility.

The symmetry of doubles caught in the logic of reprisals gives rise to an interesting possibility: every act of reprisal professes to be the response to some previous attack. Hence, could it be that caught in the perpetual fear evidenced by his "everyday look," Rattner might have interpreted Sylder's own caution, suspicion, and aversion to him as preparation for an attack, causing him to launch a preemptive strike? One cannot help but wonder what the confrontation would have read like had it been told from Rattner's point of view. Might we not be more inclined to excuse or at least explain his behavior as a reaction—born out of fear—to Sylder's hostility? Inevitably, the vile creature Sylder and others see in him would be *humanized*, while the compelling sense of necessity in Sylder's reaction would be relativized to an extent. What can be anticipated here is a shift of perspective that will be offered in *Child of God* and *Outer Dark*. Whatever position is assumed though, the end of Rattner's life is but the beginning of his significance for the novel.

Mythic Transformations and the Threat of Vengeance

As we have seen, in creating the figure of Kenneth Rattner, McCarthy chose to endow him with both realistic and mythological traits, with the latter overlaying the former in the perception of those whom Rattner encounters. A newcomer and essentially a foreigner to the community of Red Branch, Rattner consistently remains apart from his fellow men, whom he preys upon for their money and other property. Therefore he embodies some of the qualities that according to Girard predispose him for the role of sacrificial victim. This is essentially what Guillemin suggests when he briefly associates him with "the *pharmakon*, that is, the scapegoat creature in Greek mythology, who contaminates the community, and whose sacrificial death induces a collective catharsis" (2004, 26).

How appropriate is this association? Left to rot in the orchard's insecticide pit, Rattner not only serves as the pastoral *et in arcadia ego* of the novel, he is metonymically designated as "the moral equivalent of a pest" (Luce 2009, 43) or, as Guillemin says, a contaminant. And yet, for all his lying and stealing, Rattner's threat is first and foremost one to Sylder, his double, not a collective one. Concomitantly, to the twenty-year-old Sylder the killing of Rattner represents a rite of passage. As Leslie Fiedler has observed, "in the United States, it is through murder rather than sex, death rather than love, that the child enters the fallen world" (22).[16] Traditionally, this kind of initiation involves a kind of symbolic catharsis. After he has disposed of Rattner's body, it is not only the putrid stench of decay that induces the "spume of vomit" to roil up in him, and forces Sylder to his knees, "retching" (*OK* 44–45). Emesis is part of the standard symbolic vocabulary of tales of initiation, evoking the cleansing of the initiate, and projecting the (at least partial) shedding of his old existence and symbolic rebirth into a new identity.[17] Rattner's murder "initiates a process of self-examination" in Sylder, signaling "an awakening into greater technical consciousness" (Luce 2009, 54). This means nothing else than that it functions as his initiation into another order.

Girard contends that, at bottom, the goal of initiatory rites is the same as that of sacrifice and of all rituals: all rites—including those purportedly subversive Dionysian festivals of obligatory excess and debauchery, of which today's carnivals are but a tame and impotent shadow—are finally geared toward the preservation of the status quo. Rather than its sacrificial resolution, though, rites of passage are modeled on the crisis itself:

> Instead of avoiding the crisis, the neophyte must advance to meet it. [...]
> Instead of fleeing the most painful and terrifying aspects of reciprocal violence, he must submit to each and every one of them in the proper sequence.
> The postulant must endure hardship, hunger, even torture, because these ordeals were part of the original experience. In some instances it is not

enough to submit to violence; one must also inflict violence. [. . .] Indeed, in many societies the ultimate act of initiation is the killing of an animal or a human being. [. . .] The purpose of rites of passage, then, is to graft onto the model of the original crisis any burgeoning crisis brought into being by a sudden outbreak of undifferentiation [. . .]. In subjecting [the younger men] to rites of passage the culture is trying to induce a state of mind favorable to the perpetuation of a differentiated system. (VS 283–85)

Seen in this light, Sylder's disgust with Rattner is reflective of his "profound revulsion against his own violence" (Luce 2009, 53), which he will henceforth direct into more acceptable, less antisocial channels, as is shown by his dedication to the collaborative practice of the coon-hunt in the second half of the novel.

With the death of his monstrous double, Sylder becomes a comparatively well-adjusted member of the community. He quits his philandering, gets married, and most importantly takes John Wesley under his wing. Though he continues his whiskey runs, Sylder's criminal energies are henceforth directed against those agents of modern society that threaten Red Branch.[18] That Rattner would effect this profound change in Sylder, then, is not in conflict with his cultural role as *pharmakon*, but its exact analogue on the individual level. As Sylder's brief clash with Conatser suggests, their particular pairing can also be read as the sign of the spread of doubles characteristic of the mimetic crisis, as are the factions battling in the Green Fly Inn. After Rattner's death, the archaic order of Red Branch will hold for another seven years. Only then will Rattner fully cross the threshold into the realm of myth.

John Wesley hardly remembers his father, knowing him primarily through his mother's talks. The devoutly religious Mildred Rattner keeps his portrait in a "scrolled and gilded frame" to look down upon them, and "Captain Kenneth Rattner" watches as "soldier, father, ghost" (OK 61). Quite in contrast to the parasitic thief and liar the reader gets to know, she idealizes him as "a Godfearin man," a war hero, and "a provider" whose pride would not let him accept government aid. In sum, she creates an idol so glorious that—she leaves no doubt—John Wesley could be proud were he to "make half the man he was" (OK 66, 73).[19] Such idolization is typical of the mythical postmortem transformation of the victim whose death has resolved the mimetic crisis. When the body is eventually discovered, Legwater's frantic and hapless sifting of the ashes for the platinum plate Rattner allegedly carried in his head suggests that the legend Mrs. Rattner weaves around her lost husband has caught on in the community. "The father figure is viewed as an oppressive monster during his life but is transformed at death into a persecuted hero" (*VS* 204). As it turns out, Kenneth Rattner "wadn't no war hero" (*OK* 240) but a criminal wanted in several states, and for Legwater the effect of the message is one giving him "the incredulous and empty expression common to victims of tragedy, disaster and loss" (*OK* 241).[20]

Though the tenor of the latter episode is grotesquely humorous, there is a pernicious aspect to the legend, too: Mildred Rattner makes John Wesley swear an oath of vengeance "You goin to hunt him out. When you're old enough. Goin to find the man that took away your daddy. [. . .] You swear it, boy. [. . .] You won't never forget. [. . .] Never long as you live" (*OK* 66–67). Set shortly after the murder, the scene would lead the first-time reader on to expect a revenge plot, but as Bell has rightly asserted, this expectation is never fulfilled, only cited and played with: at least initially, we are as readers, like John Wesley's mother, "trapped in a plot" (Bell 1988, 13)—a mythic revenge plot, to be exact. If I am correct, part of McCarthy's agenda is to shatter this narrative pattern, to disenchant the lure of *vengeance*.

Ironically, the morality behind the vow John Wesley's mother pressures from him is the polar opposite of the one the actual murderer of his father asks for. As he visits his surrogate father in prison, John Wesley finds Sylder has been subjected to a brutal beating by Constable Gifford and his men. Outraged, John Wesley says he is "goin to get the son of a bitch," and Sylder asks him "to stay away from Gifford [. . .]. Swear it?" (*OK* 211, 213). The argument between the two involves the logistics of exchange, balance, and reciprocity. Feeling guilty because he believes that Sylder got beat up for protecting him against the bullying Gifford after he confiscated his traps, John Wesley is fully intent on exacting revenge. Sylder first tries to address the boy on his terms, claiming that him and Gifford "are square" (*OK* 213), that balance is restored. When he realizes that he cannot convince the boy this way, Sylder formulates a message aimed at shattering what is a fundamental element of any mythical narrative and most literature, namely, the idea of the hero-protagonist: "You want to be some kind of goddamned hero. Well, I'll tell ye, they ain't no more heroes. [. . .] *You understand that?*" (*OK* 214).[21]

Perfectly in tune with McCarthy's mythoclastic project and the markers of what Girard would call a novelistic (*romanesque*) rather than a romantic (*romantique*) piece of literature, this is nonetheless a painful message to absorb—for John Wesley, for the sympathetic reader, and for Sylder himself. It is further complicated by the fact that Sylder's thoughts belie his words:

> He sat up, half rose from the cot, would call him back to say That's not true what I said. It was a damned lie ever word. He's a rogue and a outlaw hisself and you're welcome to shoot him, burn him down in his bed, any damn thing, because he's a traitor to boot and maybe a man steals from greed or murders in anger, but he sells his own neighbors out for money and it's few that deep in the pit, that far beyond the pale. (*OK* 214–15)

Of course, the considerable agony involved in not calling John Wesley back is testament first and foremost to Sylder's wish to save the boy from any harm an ill-advised attack on Gifford would cause him. On a deeper level, it articulates a fundamental insight that separates men like Sylder from men like Gifford, the old order from the new: for those who understand violence, the urge to vengeance has to be resisted—at whatever personal a cost.

Of Metal Tanks and Wampus Cats

The Orchard Keeper is a book steeped in mythological subtexts. So, in naming his fictional mountain community Red Branch, McCarthy consciously invokes the half-mythological Red Branch Circle of his ancestral Ireland's ancient tribes as Barbara Brickmann has shown. Thereby already, the Irish American author subtly suggests that his Appalachian mountain town is an archaic society where life follows values and traditions different from the rest of modern American society. Between the two Red Branches, Brickmann identifies the shared, central traits of an emphasis on lineage and a basic equality between members of the ruling families; among the tribes, these factors "created incredible rivalries" and long-standing, intergenerational feuds between families (58). Vengeance was thus a threat to the stability of the Irish clans—and so it is to the fictional Red Branch McCarthy modeled upon them. To recall, in quasi-archaic communities such as McCarthy's Red

Branch, the threat of violent reciprocity is potentially an existential one. It is this social susceptibility to violence that, I argue, informs the single most important action of the novel.

One reason for archaic societies' vulnerability to vengeance is that they could not comfortably rely on a complex legal system to dissimulate reciprocal violence. Situated "beyond the dominion of laws either civil or spiritual" (*OK* 16), neither can Red Branch. Scholars have widely established the novel's antinomian sympathies, which, given the less-than-glorious history of the Tennessee Valley Authority and the general Southern distrust of government, are not surprising. A look at the agents of modern legal order within the novel is sufficient to provide justification on a subjective level as well: For who wants to put his faith in the law if the law were represented by such alternatingly incompetent, corrupt, or downright cruel agents as Constable Gifford or the "humane officer" Legwater? Apart from Sylder's most severe accusation that Gifford "sells out his neighbors" (*OK* 215), he abuses his police authority on several occasions, pressuring John Wesley to tell on the elusive whiskey runner, and vengefully beating up a restrained and defenseless Sylder. Legwater is another bully who shoots dogs in front of children and kills Ownby's old hound Scout merely out of frustration at his own foolishness.[22] The agent who arrests Ownby awaits him "with the composed disinterest of a professional assassin" (*OK* 202), breaks his "druidic" walking staff, and is deaf to his pleas to take Scout along. Finally, the social worker who visits Ownby in the asylum chooses the framework of his equally standardized forms and patronizing institutional rhetoric over a real conversation. Despite unmistakable demonstrations to the contrary, he is apparently also incapable of realizing that Ownby is of sound mind.

Obviously, between the people of Red Branch and the representatives of the larger world of Knoxville and by extension the 1930s and 1940s United States, there exists a fault line not only of ways of life, but of moralities. In sum, there is little to add to the analyses of Luce and Ragan, who posit that the agents representing the incursion of institutional bureaucracy and technocratic modernity upon Red Branch's traditional way of life "have lost their humanity in their thoughtless allegiance to civilization's norms" (Luce 2009, 36) and embody values that "are faceless, exploitative and aligned with powers accountable to neither individual responsibility nor community standards" (Ragan 21). There is yet another disparity—glimpsed in the wanton cruelty of Legwater and the vengeful brutality of Gifford—that separates the new order from the old. This difference hinges upon the *quality* of the violence employed and fully emerges when comparing the behavior of the agents of the law to that of such characters as John Wesley, Sylder, and especially Arthur Ownby.

An antinomian, tall tale-spinning hermit and guardian of Red Branch's cultural memory, "Uncle Ather's" precursors include such literary and actual personalities as Joel Chandler Harris's Uncle Remus, James Fenimore Cooper's Leatherstocking, Henry David Thoreau, and, most closely, the celebrated local Tennessean figure of Lemuel Ownby.[23] Once he discovers Rattner's body in the insecticide pit of the orchard, he does not report it to the authorities. Instead, he keeps watch over it for seven years, ritualistically covering the corpse with cedar branches cut upon each consecutive winter solstice.[24] Often identified as a shaman- or druidlike character, he is the character most attuned to the closely related forces of nature and the sacred. The heavily fragmented flashbacks to his past suggest a similar but more extreme transformation than Sylder's: Ownby's dynamiting work for the railroad leads to the death of two panther cubs, and to his adoption of the remaining third. As a consequence, his farmstead is visited upon by the panther mother who kills several of his livestock and terrifies his wife Ellen.[25] The terror ends with Ownby's surrender of the cub.

It is this experience that sets off Ownby's transformation into the "old hierophant" (*OK* 148) that dazzles John Wesley and Warn Pulliam with his regional tales of "painters."[26] Hierophany according to Mircea Eliade describes "the manifestation of something of a wholly different order" (11), which is the order of the sacred. Much like the wampus cat—another monstrous chimaera between woman and animal that haunts Ownby's sleep—the panther mother is less a real than a mythic creature, a frightening avatar of the forces of nature, and manifestation of the wholly other and sacred, or, as Ownby simply states, "no common kind of painter" (*OK* 157). In the aftermath of its visitation, Ellen leaves Ownby for a Bible drummer, and though the state of affairs remains nebulous, it appears that Ownby, trying to win her back from his rival, is actually shot in the process.[27] Following Ellen's loss, he lets his whole farmstead go to waste, but, as Guillemin surmises, "the violence of letting his livestock perish [. . .] is directed more against Ownby's own ego than against the beasts, for it copies the destruction of his pastoral and romantic

self" (2004, 33).[28] Confronted with the destructiveness of desires, the price
he pays—or rather, the insight he arrives at—manifests as a withdrawal from
human interaction. He is the first and most fleshed out of the wise or mad
hermits that will appear time and again in McCarthy's fiction.

And so Ownby becomes the guardian of Red Branch, the eponymous
orchard keeper, and the one character of the novel who truly understands
violence. His privileged insight reveals itself in two confrontations: the first
is Ownby's assault on the ominous government tank that has been installed
atop the orchard mountain; the second is his shootout with the police who
have come to arrest him for "Destruction of Government Property" (OK
218). Although it is contingent upon the first, I will begin with this second
act of violence. Following Ownby's initial resistance to arrest, it is the agents
of the law who fire the first shot. They unload a veritable bullet storm on
his home, destroying the cabin but failing to subdue him. In contrast, his
actions are slow and thoughtful. His three shots, deliberately aimed low so
as not to kill anyone (OK 187), hit their marks and temporarily chase off
his assailants. On their third attempt to apprehend him, they make up for
their mindlessness in excessive force, using teargas, storming the house from
multiple sides—and wounding one of their own in the process. The scene is
almost farcical in its impact, not just because Ownby is long gone, but for the
sheer disproportion of force and effect between the two sides. Whereas the
representative of the old order uses violence in a controlled, almost surgical
manner, the agents of modernity wage it excessively, but in the way of the
local boys setting a wild fire in their cave. They are like the sorcerer's apprentice, unleashing "invisible and malevolent spirits" (OK 186) beyond their
control and ultimately harmful to themselves.

The end of the story is, of course, that once Ownby is apprehended, he
is additionally charged with "Assault with Intent to Kill" (OK 218) in four
cases. He is thus misjudged in his intentions and made a scapegoat for the law
agents' own incompetence. Worse yet, according to Mr. Eller, they are even
"liable to thow [Rattner's murder] off on him to save huntin somebody else"
(OK 235). Of course, Ownby is not ritually killed by the collective, but rather
declared mad and incarcerated in an asylum. In certain respects, this amounts
to the same thing, the purported troublemaker is excluded and locked away.

As clear as the dynamic of this violent exchange is, as initially opaque
are the motives behind the elder Ownby's other central act of violence, his

assault on the "government tank" (*OK* 168). Few other items in *The Orchard Keeper* have evoked as much critical speculation. Hypotheses as to the actual usage of the tank range from such relatively inconsequential roles as the storage of water or whiskey, to the infinitely more sensitive function of storing nuclear waste for the nearby Oak Ridge facility, and, following the more recent identification of the real-life model for the "tank" as a local Federal Aviation Administration nondirectional radio beacon situated in the area where McCarthy grew up, the regulation of civilian and military air traffic. However, all of these suggestions are somewhat unsatisfactory in one way or another, either because they take too little account of the text itself, because they make for a rather weak motive for Ownby's actions, or because they involve more or less glaring anachronisms that McCarthy would likely have avoided.[29]

Consequently, if one agrees that the actual use of the tank is indeterminable, its literary significance must then be sought in its symbolic dimension. Scholars have overwhelmingly read the tank as a traditional "machine in the garden" motif and cogently reasoned that the shooting articulates an act of antinomian defiance against the exploitative encroachment of modern society into the quasi arcadian paradise. In this reading, Ownby is cast as a latter-day Luddite or literary precursor to the Unabomber, Ted Kaczynski. While his act is undoubtedly one of resistance, I believe it is not simply "modernity" or "technology" that Ownby lashes out against. The symbolic value of the tank assumes real depth only when swapping the pastoral for a related, yet more explicitly ritualistic frame of reference.

The government tank is another literary hybrid presence. It exists between the realistic and the mythic. The neutral, factual description of a "squat metal tank that topped the mountain [. . .] on high legs," which is surrounded by a fence "with red signs" and has a "polished skin" (*OK* 51, 97), is starkly contrasted with the charged perceptions of Ownby and Sylder. Situated in the epicenter of a miniature wasteland, a "barren spot" where "not even a weed grew,"[30] the tank to Ownby appears as "fat and bald and sinister," as a "great dome" standing "complacent, huge" (*OK* 93). In the inherent intertextuality of McCarthy's oeuvre, these attributes relate the phallic tank to *Blood Meridian*'s equally phallic Judge Holden, whose skull is described as a "lunar dome" (*BM* 335) and whose stature, corpulence, and complete hairlessness recall the tank's massive size and polished metal "skin."

Like the Judge, the tank has its prototype in actual historical models. And yet, it is larger than life, its origins mythically superelevated to be placed on a prearchaic, Hadean time scale, the tank "seeming older than the very dirt, the rocks, as if it had spawned them of itself and stood surveying the work, clean and coldly gleaming and capable of infinite contempt" (*OK* 93). The latter description prefigures Holden's characterization of war as something both older than man and as indifferent to his opinions and rational enterprises as stone (*BM* 248). Like the Judge, the tank seems to evoke the presence of the precultural principle of the sacred, differently put, of mythic violence itself.

It is worth pursuing this line of thought. Ownby is not the only one who feels the menace of the tank. To Sylder there is "something ghastly and horrific about it" as it trembles under Ownby's shots "like a thing alive" (*OK* 97). There is but one entity in *The Orchard Keeper* that emanates a similar, ominously threatening aura of repulsion and dread. This entity is Kenneth Rattner. The government tank and the dead father, who is interred in the "concrete tank" (*OK* 52) of the insecticide pit, are related not only by their geographical proximity to the orchard, but also by paradigmatic kinship. The nature of this kinship is a religious one: the ritualistic manner in which Ownby goes about in his care of Rattner's body "evokes sacrifices and burial rites performed by druids on consecrated occasions" (Brickmann 62–63) and equally informs his preparatory circumcision of his shotgun shells, and the "evenly spaced" shots he fires marking the tank with a "huge crude X" (*OK* 96–97). Significantly, the "copper ikon" (*OK* 36) of Rattner's face in Sylder's windshield is recalled in the tank's description as a "great silver ikon" (*OK* 93). To this religious framing, one may add Rattner's identification with the *pharmakon* and the Oedipal theme Cant has traced throughout McCarthy's oeuvre, including *The Orchard Keeper*.

From these deliberations, it is then but a small step to identify the tank's role as that of the totem as described in Sigmund Freud's *Totem and Taboo*. Consequently, the tank can be read as a symbolic substitute for Rattner, who himself recalls Freud's murdered primal father. To recall: in his mythically distorted murder by his sons, the latter becomes the cultic germ cell of social evolution, and his literary heritage, according to Freud, is none other than the hero of Greek tragedy, cast out by the chorus (1950, 193). There is thus a literary game of substitution going on here: in the otherwise cryptic reference of a member of *The Orchard Keeper*'s explicitly designated "chorus of

elders"—a group of old men meeting around Eller's store, who significantly
appear solely in the chapter in which Ownby shoots it—the tank "ain't so
much that as it is one thing'n another" (*OK* 115).[31] This other, surplus thing,
I suggest, is nothing other than the principle of *sacrificial substitution* itself—
the surrogate victim or scapegoat that Rattner embodies and that the tank
consequently symbolizes.

If this seems still implausible, one needs to take into account that such
mythical substitutions are par for the course in the novel. Interestingly, these
transformations often concern cats. Ownby's panther is one such example, yet
the more significant example is the mythical wampus cat of Tennessean folklore. The story of the wampus cat is one other myth that would have delighted
René Girard. According to Native American legend, the monstrous cat was
born from cultural transgression of a curious Indian woman who, cloaked in
the pelt of a mountain cat, secretly spied on the sacred hunting rituals of the
male members of the tribe. As she was discovered, the tribe's medicine man
subsequently punished her crime by transforming her into the half-female,
half-feline wampus cat. The scapegoating pattern of a *marginal figure* (the
woman) charged with a *transgression* (her illegitimate observation of the
rites) that abolishes fundamental *distinctions of the cultural order* (e.g., gender
roles), and who is subsequently collectively punished and transformed into
a supernatural being embodying human and animal qualities—an excluded
monstrosity—is fulfilled beautifully (Schlosser 94; Sanborn 2006, 30).[32] In
this legend, we discover again the kind of mythological transformation we
already saw at work in the depiction of the flood.

What, then, do these patterns of sacrificial exclusion and substitution
imply regarding the connection of the tank and the murdered father, Kenneth Rattner? Simply put, the same kind of transformation is at work: that
the totem assumes the shape of the machine in the garden rather than an
animal surely befits the technocratic character of the society it embodies and
that is in the process of supplanting Red Branch. Individual transgressions
against it, like Ownby's assault, are duly punished: they represent rebellion
against the founding principle of the cultural order. What McCarthy's text
offers here is the intriguing possibility of reinterpreting the pastoral motif of
the machine in the garden as but another transformation of the dead, Freudian, primal father, who in his transformation into the totem constitutes but a
special case of the sacrificial *pharmakon*—of the victim expelled or murdered

to achieve the cathartic communal cleansing and ritualized in the practice of sacrifice.

It shall not be concealed, however, that there is an apparent contradiction in character psychology that this reading the tank as a substitute for Rattner provokes: after all, Ownby's assault on the *symbolized* victim seems at odds with his cyclical care for the *actual* victim. In the latter case, a violent crime is kept a secret; in the former case an offense is committed for all to see, a fact that Ownby seems to be counting on (*OK* 229). What then is the rationale of Ownby's actions? The answer to this question and to any doubt as to Rattner's function as *pharmakon* is to be found in an element of the sacrificial crisis that I have not yet touched upon. Wampus cat and panthers aside, the flood that heralds the final decline of Red Branch coincides with the first narrative appearance not only of Eller's "blighted" kittens, but of a fourth prominent feline: a little stray cat that roams the partially submerged landscape and is carried off by an owl, eliciting a wail from above that unsettles Mr. Eller.

Eller's bewilderment is an expression of the sense that the flood has upset the natural order of things in some fundamental way: cats should not fly. What is more, the cat is explicitly set up as another manifestation of Rattner. In his final conversation with John Wesley, Arthur Ownby reveals his belief that the souls of dead people may possess the body of a cat, especially if the person drowns or does not receive a proper burial. His thoughts make the connection between the cat and Rattner, whose corpse was recently discovered and got set on fire, explicit: "I don't have to fool with him no more except he ought not to of got burnt [...] but it's done now and he's gone, that had to of been him Eller was supposed to of heard" (*OK* 228). The association is not just Ownby's: even upon Rattner's second appearance in the book, he is already described as "catlike" (*OK* 15).

What, then, does it mean that the death of the cat coincides with the flood that almost directly ensues the discovery and burning of Rattner's corpse? Skeptical readers may doubt that correlation signifies causation in this case, yet McCarthy held both in mind, as an undated letter to Albert Erskine clearly shows: a handwritten side note specifies that the "cat's death should trigger [the] general decline of everybody" (91/1/1, n.p.). It goes without saying, though, that it is exactly *not* the death of a mere feral cat, but of a creature McCarthy has consciously linked, by mythic association, with the dead father and the totemized machine in the garden, the government tank. Chief among these implications is the resurfacing of the victim that Ownby kept hidden for so long. It goes hand in hand with the intensification of the crisis, the *desymbolization* that is symbolized by the flood.

As with the three principal players in Sophocles's *Oedipus Rex*—Oedipus, Creon, and the seer Tiresias—the paradoxical objective of both of Ownby's violent acts is thus ultimately to contain the figurative plague that has infected Red Branch. His intent is to stem the rising tide of violence: "Ever man loves peace and a old man best of all" (*OK* 229). Rattner's killing *has* to be kept a secret, for the revelation of the murder would unleash the ultimate threat of vengeance as invoked by John Wesley's mother upon the archaic community. What likewise has to be resisted, however, is the cult of violence rooted in the sacralization and mythological transformation of the victim as symbolized by the tank. The latter is the totem of a *new* societal framework that—even as it indulges in illusions of progress and enlightenment—has little of the old order's cautious vigilance vis-à-vis the dangers it engages. So, whereas Ownby is in control of his violence, the agents of the new order wage it excessively, without control or restraint. Finally, although it is anachronistic and untenable in any practical sense, critics' frequent association of the tank with the ultimate violence inherent in the atomic bomb and the Oak Ridge facility, though factually impossible, is surprisingly accurate in a symbolic sense. Their "essence," it can be said, is one and the same.

Ownby's words to the social agent prove more revealing than they initially appear: "Why not jest up and ast me? [. . .] Why I done it. Rung shells and shot your hootnanny all to hell? I could tell you why—and you stit wouldn't know. [. . .] But not knowin a thing ain't never made it not so" (*OK* 221).[33] On one level, this comment can simply be read as an attribution of the social agent's ignorance to the traditional ways of Red Branch that must perceive Ownby's attack simply as the futile and irrational deed of a senile rabble-rouser. But "not knowin" that the cultural order and peace is bought with a collective murder, in Girard's theory, is elementary to the generative effect of the victim, which depends on this ignorance. It is precisely the lack of knowledge of Rattner's murder that keeps the peace within the community of Red Branch and that makes the positive relationship of John Wesley to Ownby and Sylder possible in the first place. It needs to stay a secret.

This explains Ownby's "presentiment of ruin" (*OK* 158) at discovering the (unexplained) immolation of Rattner's body, and likewise the parallel "bile-sharp foretaste of disaster" (*OK* 168) that strikes Sylder with the sudden question of the motive behind Ownby's assault. Ownby knows that he can no longer keep the murder a secret, with all that this entails. Sylder's sense of foreboding approaches yet never quite reaches the same awareness of the principles upon which the society symbolized in the tank operates and that provides the rationale of Ownby's actions. The old man's prediction of "real calamity afore this year [i.e., 1941] is out" (*OK* 225) must not be thought to refer solely to the attack on Pearl Harbor and the United States' entrance into World War II, as is usually assumed (Prather 39; Cant 60), but rather as the assertion of the overall pattern of violence. As John Wesley tells Ownby, even in 1941, the original community of Red Branch has already largely vanished (*OK* 227). In 1948, all that will be left of them is "myth, legend, dust" (*OK* 246).

Dis|Orderly Aesthetics:
Narrative Epistemology and the Place of the Observer

Summing up the insights of this analysis so far, the transformations of mythic and pastoral symbolism of *The Orchard Keeper* ought to be regarded, effectively, as a reflection of more fundamental, heretofore unguessed anthropological constants. These behavioral patterns are governed by the logic of mimetism and the violence that results from it. Characters like Sylder and particularly Ownby are sensitive to or aware of mimetic dynamics to an extent. Yet their response is still largely a *mythic* one. Insofar as violence is a factor, in the literal sense, of both social disorder and order, it is thus worth considering to what extent the text reflects this theme on a structural and aesthetic level.

This analysis began with the motif of tree and fence intertwined and the image of the tree cut to lengths, its sections spread across the lawn. The doubly complicated motif has been interpreted, on the one hand, as a sign of the novel's antipastoralism and, on the other hand, as a model for the narrative design of the text itself. The effect of this design is an attempt at expanding the limits, set out famously in Gotthold Ephraim Lessing's "Laokoon" (1776), of literature as decidedly temporal. In Horton's words, McCarthy attempts "to spatialize an inherently temporal art; to fragment and reorder the chronological path of history; to narrate a story as one would saw and stack wood" (288). This reordering of history can be related to the divergent conceptions of time, specifically Ownby's mythic cycles and the linear logic of progress-oriented modernity. Yet the ordering of time and nonsequential storytelling form merely a part of a larger aesthetic of order and disorder and the complicated epistemology that are the earliest, full articulation of McCarthy's universal poetics. It is to this dimension of the text that the remainder of this chapter is dedicated.

Late in the novel, having temporarily eluded the authorities and briefly resettled in the wilderness of the "harrykin," Arthur Ownby enjoys a moment of respite that directly precedes his final arrest. He contemplates the sublime beauty of the Tennessee valley:

> Through a gap in the trees he could see the valley far below him where the river ran, a cauldron in the mountain's shadow where smoke and spume seethed like the old disturbance of the earth erupting once again, black mist languid in the cuts and trenches as flowing lava and the palisades of rock rising in the high-shored rim beyond the valley—and beyond the valley, circling the distant hoary cupolas now standing into morning, the sun, reaching to the slope where the old man rested, speared mist motes emblematic as snowflakes and broke them down in spangled and regimental disorder, reached the trees and banded them in light, struck weftwork in the slow uncurling ferns—the sun in its long lightfall recoiled again in leafwater. (*OK* 200–201)

This sensual moment provides not only a fine example of McCarthy's celebrated landscapes but, more importantly, an interpretive key to the structure and aesthetic of *The Orchard Keeper* as a whole. Initially, one is easily submerged in McCarthy's stream of words, mistaking them perhaps for the actual stream of consciousness of the narrator as focalized through Ownby's eyes. Upon closer inspection, one realizes that there are only two principal objects being described here, namely the valley and the sun above. Whereas

Ownby serves as the perceiving subject in the first part of the sentence, he gradually assumes the quality of yet another object, almost incidental to his place on the slope, as the sun takes over the role of subject only to surrender it again in the paratactical appendage at the end of the sentence. Apart from being the source of *life* on earth, the sun has a special place in cultural history not only as a cult object but also as a central symbol of epistemology, from before Plato's cave to the proverbial age of enlightenment. Here, its progress seems to both discover and produce *order* in nature as it unveils the valley and breaks down the mountain mists, strikes rather than reveals the complex textures of the ferns that unfold under its warming rays.

On the other hand, the sun uncovers something paradoxical: beyond the macroscopic level of the mists, there exists an oxymoronic "regimental disorder." Military associations aside, if something were regimental, it would appear to be highly structured and involve both a certain redundancy of arrangements and, possibly, a higher level of complexity through the incorporation of smaller structures into a larger one. This, however, is the *opposite* of disorder. What complicates the matter further is that the striking sun itself seems to be the originator rather than revelator of said disorder. Finally, the position of the observer is put into question as McCarthy's prose involves a profound decentering of the narrative point of view, overturning the anthropocentrism inherent in Jamesian standards to evoke "a world without a point of view and without the temporary illusion of one" (Bell 1988, 14).

Consequently, the passage raises the issue of whether order and disorder are discovered or invented, in other words, whether it is "due to the insufficiency of the resources or capacities of the human mind [. . .] which prevents it from finding the hidden order behind the apparent disorder," or whether it is "the objective character of reality itself" (Morin 103), and thus to what extent we, as observers, have to include ourselves in the observation. The remarkable passage thus turns out to be not only an indicator of questions that will punctuate McCarthy's work through the years, but also an apt metaphor for the reading experience of *The Orchard Keeper* in particular. In short, it creates the kind of "fourth vision" that Morin and Heinz von Foerster request as a prerequisite for a modern epistemology that includes the human within a community of us-and-the-world.

The solar revelation of paradoxical dis|order illustrates how traditional pastoral readings fail to fully grasp the complexity of McCarthy's vision.

Addressing this problem, Guillemin cogently describes it as an "incipient ecopastoralism" that overcomes traditional anthropocentric nostalgia for the pastoral paradise through the "principal commitment of the narrative consciousness [. . .] to a certain wilderness perspective" (2004, 22–23). On the level of narrative point of view—the novel's shifting perspectives, the cat episodes, as well as the numerous incantatory passages where the narrative consciousness attains a quality one may associate with nature itself serving as focalizer—*The Orchard Keeper* thus achieves an effect not unlike that which McCarthy's celebrated formal strategy of *optical democracy* achieves on the syntax level. David Holloway describes optical democracy as a poetic mode or style that

> has been latent in McCarthy's style since *The Orchard Keeper*, but which has only emerged as a dominant form in the later western novels. [. . .] As defined and practiced in *Blood Meridian*, the style of "optical democracy" connotes a writing that renders all preference among objects "whimsical" (moral preference, epistemological preference, aesthetic or political preference), until anything beyond the uniform facticity of the moment is crowded from view. Optical democracy is a kind of writing that verges on deep ecology in its reduction of all that is animate and inanimate to a dead level of equivalence: ostensibly, that is, it is a writing in which a man and a rock become equally "thinglike." (2002, 35)

While Holloway's view of McCarthy's aesthetic as one of "late modernism" primarily utilizes a Marxist perspective that emphasizes the material basis of all processes in his novels, Arnold's attestation of "a larger and more pantheistic view" (2002a, 7) or Guillemin's use of *animism*, "understood as the conviction that all things animate and inanimate share in existential equality" (2004, 16), provide a better starting point for characterizing the vibrant world of *The Orchard Keeper*. Another interpretive approach pointing in the same direction is Ellis's invocation, via Carolyn Merchant, of sixteenth-century organismic theory to understand the apparent confusion of the metal of the fence of the prologue "growing into the tree." This view, deeply rooted in a day-to-day experience probably not unlike that of characters such as Arthur Ownby or John Wesley Rattner, understood the earth itself as alive and "emphasized interdependence among the parts of the human body, subordination of individual to communal purposes in family, community, and state, and vital life permeating the cosmos to the lowliest stone" (cit. in Ellis 2006, 63).

The direction of all of these interpretations is clear: if his apprentice novel teaches us anything, it is that in McCarthy's literary worlds, virtually all things are somehow interrelated, equally though not always simultaneously subject to processes of growth and decay in a highly complex system approaching, literarily, the mystery of *life*. The latter, he seems to say, can never be fully understood, the reason being that there are always multiple interconnected perspectives, without a privileged, encompassing view that totalizes, in a final, hierarchical order, all possible knowledge and interpretation of the facts of life. Nowhere is this more apparent than in McCarthy's manipulation of time. As Horton demonstrates, the stories of Rattner and Sylder—told, as they are, in the first two chapters—start off at different points in time only to catch up with one another in their confrontation, which violently slows down the passage of time to highlight the traumatic nature of the experience.

When violence finally erupts with Rattner's attack, its impact is at once realistic, traumatizing, and grotesque. The struggle is suspended in a kind of "somnambulant slow motion as if time itself were running down," hypercharging and sensitizing Sylder's perception to such horrific details as Rattner's jaw "coming down not on any detectable hinges but like a mass of offal, some obscene waste matter uncongealing," and as he gains the upper hand, strangling Rattner "like squeezing a boil," he notices the widening of his opponent's eyes, the "loll of tongue," and feels Rattner's windpipe "collapse like a dried tule" (*OK* 39–40). Taken seriously, the effects of the scene on both Sylder and the reader amount to what William Prather, drawing on Albert Camus and Wolfgang Kayser, identifies as the sensation of the absurd, that is, of the clash between "a human desire for order and meaning" and the sudden revelation of the existential world "through the loss of anthropocentric illusions" (Prather 38). The realization congruent with this revelation is that our world is fundamentally not just and orderly, but grotesque. Perhaps such a disturbing experience is what confrontation of the sacred amounts to in a secularized world?[34]

At another point, we see Sylder drive off after witnessing Ownby's shooting of the tank in what according to the growth of vegetation and Ownby's seasonal memories (*OK* 88–89, 96–97) must be summer, to him crashing his car into an icy creek and being saved by John Wesley, who, after "pushing time" (*OK* 65) till November, is out there collecting his traps. Narratively, Sylder drives off in summer and crashes his car in late autumn. McCarthy thus seamlessly juxtaposes "discontinuity in time" and "continuity in space" (Horton 294), a technique that, once noticed, cannot fail to thoroughly disorient the reader. This kind of manipulation goes way beyond the vagueness of the novel's timescale and jumbled chronology, and is further complicated yet when considered against the background of the mythical perception of sacred time that characterizes Ownby's superficially biblical, but certainly mythic conception of seven-year cycles.[35]

Apart from a general pastoral framework that provides the mythic backdrop for the tragic decline of Red Branch and much of the symbolic vocabulary of *The Orchard Keeper*, the discussion so far has shown that even as early as 1965, social relations and their more violent expressions in McCarthy's work are already characterized by an underlying mimetic structure. A Girardian reading raises our awareness of another level of human interaction, such as the playful rivalry and search for models John Wesley and his friends engage in, as well as the deeper mechanisms and bias of perspective behind the confrontation between Sylder and his monstrous double Rattner, whose status as *pharmakon* becomes a prototype for later, more fully realized scapegoats. Equally, it can serve to interrelate many elements that otherwise remain disconnected and in the process make intelligible the acts, words, and thoughts of characters like Ownby and Sylder.[36]

Even so, there remains a whole bundle of riddles and open questions that the mimetic perspective cannot fully account for, making for an indeterminate core and overall air of mystery that is hard to penetrate.[37] Chief among the novel's riddles are the often inscrutable causes of momentously important events and the closely related, frustrating epistemological problem of how characters *know*: How do the police know that it was Ownby who shot the tank? How is Rattner's corpse discovered? Is it because of the fire? Is that fire somehow caused by the out-of-control cave fire of the boys, or do Warn and John Wesley set the pit aflame on their drunk journey home from Ownby's hut as the tracks he finds may indicate? If so, did they see Rattner's corpse and report it, only to never bring this crucial fact up in later conversations? Or, is the discovery of the body due to a larger investigation of the area in the course of either the flood or Ownby's arrest? Did Ownby, in the end, give up the secret he so stalwartly kept for so long, as the conversation in Eller's store seems to infer? What leads people to think that the decomposed and burned remains in the pit are actually Rattner's, even as they allow for some "room for speculatin" (*OK* 235)? How does Legwater "know" of the supposed platinum plate in Rattner's head, and how does Gifford know it is not actually there? How does Gifford know it was Sylder who beat him up as his "revenge" implies? Finally, how does Ownby, who has long left the area and is then shut away in an asylum, know about Mr. Eller hearing the "flying cat"?

How indeed. Minute details in the novel *may* help us to infer answers to some of these questions, but even those involve a degree of uncertainty and conjecture: Ownby may have admitted that he shot the tank on the police's first attempt at questioning him, and also told them about the corpse given that his mystical seven-year period of care has passed. People do not actually know it is Rattner's corpse, Legwater likely suffers from an idée fixe planted by Mildred Rattner's tales of her husband, and Gifford knows better from police reports. He may infer it was Sylder who beat him from learning his identity as the local whiskey runner. Yet such answers are anything but certain, and other questions remain flat-out unanswerable, reminding us of Bell's assessment that the experience and position of the reader becomes that of "ironic metaphysicians making order out of random data" (1988, 25). To be sure, this position is privileged in some respects: unlike John Wesley, Arthur Ownby, and Marion Sylder, we can go back and forth in narrated time and are able to perceive the flow of narrative from a bird's-eye view, as it were. Thus we can see (or rather establish) the intricate web of connections that composes the novel's narrative design.

Twice in this analysis, I have touched upon the role of the prologue's image of the cut tree and fence: once at the outset to give an idea of the narrative situation of the novel and to introduce the image's thematic and structural implications for reading it in the light of the pastoral tradition and as a narrative more generally concerned with the breakdown of order; and a second time to illustrate the novel's simultaneous investment in contrasting epistemologies that can be identified with a profane and a pagan, sacred perception of the world and that correspond to a spectrum of more realistic and more mythical modes of storytelling. A third and final look at the image will deepen our understanding of both these aspects and reveal a different layer of meaning yet.

The narrative frame of the novel has been identified with the reflection of John Wesley looking back upon the formative experience of his youth in Red Branch: "The act of narration affords him an opportunity to reorder his past, a chance to recontextualize fragments of memory, an occasion to fill gaps in personal knowledge with passages of imagination and hallucination" (Prather 40).[38] But the narrative thus created is asymmetrical, because the novel's closing chapter formally is not an epilogue. It is a part of the novel's fourth section and not presented in italics as are both the novel's flashbacks and the prologue itself. Therefore it exists on another narrative plane. According to Jay Ellis, writing about *Spatial Constraints and Character Flight*, this break of expectation is by design as "to have given us an epilogue [. . .] would have been an act of closing off the narrative, fencing it in, as it were" (2006, 62). Part of the frame is missing, yet as John Wesley's final departure "through the gap in the fence, past the torn iron palings and out to the western road" (*OK* 246) illustrates, the structural openness of the narrative reflects its thematic movement. John Wesley's move not only situates him in a long line of Americans, real and imagined, setting out westward for a new beginning, but anticipates the flights of Suttree, the Kid, and other McCarthy characters, as well as his own move to the Southwest.

Ellis likens McCarthy's best landscapes to "narrative particle accelerators: now and then a crack in the tunnel allows a character to fly out into darkness" (2006, 56). Another analogy may aptly serve us to make a point concerning the epistemological dimension of *The Orchard Keeper*. In leaving a gap in both the fence and frame of his novel rather than completely closing off and isolating his story, McCarthy chooses to give us an *open narrative system*. Metaphorically, he thus allows for exchanges of matter and thought and thus provides a fitting image for the ordering act of reading that in his best works is a constant and fluctuating process of creating ever more complex and intricate structures out of the "random data" they present us. However, these structures seem to constantly disintegrate again before our very eyes, forcing us to acknowledge that they come at both his and our own expenditure of creative energy, and like any system, are subject to entropy. Simply put, making sense of this novel is a demanding task for a human mind compelled to create order in the thick of what may appear to be a chaos.

As Horton points out, there exists, within the narrative proper, another frame of sorts, represented by two passing vehicles. The first is glimpsed by Kenneth Rattner, who sees "a small shapeless mass" emerging in the distance "like something seen through bad glass," which eventually gains "the form and solidity of a pickup truck" only to revert "into the same liquid shape by which it came" (*OK* 7). By contrast, the second vehicle is an old wagon carrying an "aged Negro" and drawn by a "ruined and ragged mule" that slowly passes the older John Wesley "as if under the weight of some singular and unreasonable gravity," whose gaze follows them as they "dissolve[e] in a pale and broken image" (*OK* 244). This second frame presents us with two images of dissolution that, once again, illustrate the novel's thematic and aesthetic program: First of all, the pastoral mindset recognizes the contrast between an image of technocratic modernity overtaking the past on the one hand, and the representation of the older order slowly fading away on the other. Secondly, in Horton's reading, the images are part of McCarthy's project of spatializing the temporal act of storytelling, the awareness of "how the passage of time, even the narrative itself, tends to defy coherence or containment in shape" (292). Thirdly, drawing on both analyses, it can be asserted that the visual succession of chaotic masses taking shape and then dissolving again encapsulates not only the rise and fall of the pastoral community but, more generally, the formation and dissolution of any sort of structure against the progress of time in the direction of increasing *disorder*.

Finally, on a metalevel, they relate to the epistemological challenges of the time acts of reading and interpretation. So, if the vision of the first vehicle can be read as a reference to Paul's First Epistle to the Corinthians—"For now we see through a glass [i.e., a mirror], darkly; but then face to face: now I know in part; but then shall I know even as also I am known" (KJB, 1 Cor. 13:12)—it implies not only a sinister appropriation of the epistle chapter's praise of love in its application to Rattner's mirror image, Sylder, but an apt characterization of the reading experience itself. At first one sees only "a shambles," or, in Prescott's critique, a "jumpy, disconnected narrative" (45). Gradually, principles of organization emerge, connections are made by theme or motif, events are placed in time, hypotheses formed, tested, and then corroborated or abandoned. Ultimately though, the reader finds that there is a point beyond which interpretation must remain incomplete: too dazzling is the complexity of the whole. What emerges is a structurally complicated narrative matrix that both thematically and aesthetically is fundamentally concerned with questions of dis|order on virtually every level, stretching from the integrity of the human mind to the individual's place in society, nature, and the cosmos, extending to the status of values and morality in the wake of historical progress, and beyond to the acts of storytelling and reading themselves. Each of these levels is consistently shown as being subject to the threat of disintegration. At the very bottom of the structure, however, lies the common core of the interplay of life and death, the nucleus around which all of McCarthy's writing revolves.

CHAPTER 3

Order in the Woods and in Men's Souls

Gothic Psychomythology and Scapegoating in *Child of God*

Then children were brought to him that he might lay his
hands on them and pray. The disciples rebuked the people,
but Jesus said, "Let the little children come to me and
do not hinder them, for to such belongs the kingdom of
heaven."
   —Matthew 19:13–14 (ESV)

With 1965's *The Orchard Keeper* and its tale of pastoral trauma and a murderous secret at the heart of a small mountain community, Cormac McCarthy
had introduced himself as a writer in the tradition of Flannery O'Connor
and William Faulkner. Three years later, his second novel, *Outer Dark*,
which will be discussed in the next chapter, probed yet darker territories as
it traced the doom-haunted nightmare journeys of a destitute and ostracized
pair of incestuous siblings. Confronted with the novel's oppressive gloom,
transgressive subjects, and grisly violence, readers found that McCarthy had
firmly embraced the Southern gothic tradition. Published in 1973 as the

third of his Appalachian novels, *Child of God* only cemented this notion, albeit in a setting less surreal than *Outer Dark*'s, and closer to the naturalism of McCarthy's apprentice novel.

Critical reactions, once again, were decidedly mixed. While some reviewers like Anatole Broyard were astonished "to see how a good writer can make us care about a bad character," and how talent could "find the humanity behind the inhuman" (45), others were utterly shocked by and even disgusted with it. Thus, Richard Brickner found the book "lacking in human momentum or point," and its protagonist "so flattened by fate" and disconnected from the readership that he was "beneath the reach of tragedy" (334). The book again became the subject of controversy in 2007, when a fourteen-year-old student at a Texan high school chose *Child of God* for a book report, and parental complaints sparked the provisional suspension of his English teacher (see Brown). In 2013, James Franco's independent film adaptation of the novel evoked a range of responses from both critics and audiences.[1] So *Child of God* remains divisive to this day.

Given the novel's subject matter, extreme reactions are par for the course. *Child of God* depicts not only the dire poverty, social isolation, and murderous sexual deviance of its barely literate and psycho-narratively inscrutable protagonist, Lester Ballard, but does so before a naturalistic background of general deprivation, in which interpersonal relations are characterized almost exclusively by verbal and physical abuse. In a way, it exemplifies all the bad clichés that exist about "hillbillies" and Southern "white trash." Nevertheless, *Child of God* exceeds the grasp of a mere study in human perversion. Broyard's declaration of feeling empathy with the novel's cross-dressing necrophiliac murderer Ballard is characteristic of a reading experience shared by many, which summarily may best be described as one of profound ambivalence typical of "the uncanny" (Madsen 17).

Uncanny ambivalence can only partially be explained by the operations of (Southern) gothic fiction, however. In my view, it is the effect of a more general twofold agenda of destabilization, whose other half is constituted by the novel's mythoclasticism. The latter undercuts the pastoral illusions of Jeffersonian agrarianism by showing how McCarthy's protagonist becomes the degenerate hunter that is the dark, nightmarish reflection of the frontier myth's rugged American hero. Simultaneously,

Child of God also humanizes its protagonist by depicting him as a product of his violent environment and revealing a much more relatable side to Ballard, identifying him as a prime example of the mythical scapegoat. What is thus established is a distinctive sense of kinship between Ballard, his troubled community, and ultimately, the reader herself. In this, McCarthy ultimately performs a revelatory task on a smaller scale, preparing the stage for later, grander unveilings.

Much Like Yourself, Perhaps: Psychology, Myth, and the Gothic

The action of *Child of God* takes place over an only vaguely determinable time period between 1945 and 1965 and is set in the mountainous area of Sevier County in eastern Tennessee. Arranged in three consecutive parts composed of fifty-two predominantly short chapters, the novel tells the story of Lester Ballard, a social outcast who, evicted from his home and falsely accused of rape, slowly descends into necrophilia and serial murder. The first section comprises close to half of the entire narrative and carefully introduces setting and characters, depicting Ballard's family background as well as his history with the community of Sevier County. The second and third parts chronicle his crimes and eventual downfall or, alternatively, his precarious redemption.

More akin to the naturalistic *The Orchard Keeper* than the surreal and allegorical *Outer Dark*, the events of *Child of God* are steeped in both regional and national history. Its historical investment begins with its protagonist. The character of Lester Ballard was inspired by a murder case that took place in northern Georgia in 1963, for which one James Blevins was put on trial. A second source of inspiration was the serial murderer and "Plainfield necrophile" Ed Gein, who had already inspired the character of Norman Bates in Robert Bloch's *Psycho* (1957) and Alfred Hitchcock's 1960 movie adaptation of that novel (Luce 2009, 144; Schafer 116). Together, these sources seem to have supplied McCarthy with many of the elements of *Child of God*. Apart from the murders, necrophilia, fetishism, the community's propensity to lynch violence, and the enormous role voyeurism plays on multiple levels of the novel, not the least of these elements is the title itself, which was likely drawn from an utterance of a compassionate priest, who described Gein as "a child of God."[2]

So when we initially meet Gein's literary progeny in McCarthy's twenty-seven-year-old Lester Ballard, he is introduced to us as the offspring of "Saxon and Celtic bloods. A child of God much like yourself perhaps" (*CG* 4). At first sight, this phrase implies little more than "a seeming appeal to the democratic egalitarianism at the center of American political rhetoric and to the [...] Christian doctrine of the fundamental equality of all souls" (Jarrett 36). In certain areas of the South, however, the phrase "child of God" can imply that someone is "not right in the head" (Bell 1988, 68). Certainly, this meaning befits Ballard better than the implications the phrase carries in the Bible, where it is connected to the "little children" to whom the kingdom of heaven belongs, as well as to the the peacemakers of the beatitudes, who "shall be called the children of God" (Mt. 5:9; 19:13–14). Over the course of the next two hundred pages, we witness Ballard turn from an isolated backwoods voyeur spying on others' lovemaking to an accidental necrophiliac, and finally to a man killing to satisfy his needs.[3] To add insult to injury, the narratively intrusive proposition that this "practitioner of ghastliness," this "part-time ghoul" (*CG* 174) should be "much like yourself"—to many readers—must seem well-nigh outrageous. And yet, it is perhaps the single most important phrase of the entire book. In it converge the novel's gothic aesthetic, its religious perspective, and its anthropological outlook, which this reading explicates.

What McCarthy introduces here is also the first and essential element in a poetics of destabilization and transgression. Philip Simpson identifies this trait as central in the textual agenda of both the gothic novel and the serial killer subgenre: "The Gothic is rife with ambiguity, sexual perversion, decenteredness, self-referentiality, repetition, and breakdown of boundary" (2000, 28; see also Bruhm 263). In the case of *Child of God*, these motifs and devices oscillate between the poles of psychology and myth. The first is necessary to make McCarthy's protagonist believable and, to some extent, relatable. The second is elementary in assessing Ballard's place in American mythology as well as his role as the mythic, Girardian scapegoat, of which he is one of the clearest examples in all of McCarthy's fiction.

Eye Spy with My Deviant I:
Voyeurism, Mimesis, Identity

By and large, critics have found psychological approaches, if not the language of psychology per se, inadequate in illuminating McCarthy's characters. While his novels "convey to us vividly the speech, manners, and values of the area's people, the climate, the nature of the land, its animals living their own separate life," his characters often appear to be "almost eerily unselfconscious" and largely devoid of thought (Bell 1988, 4). Most of the time, McCarthy's characteristic third-person narrator merely observes the action. It is only on the rarest of occasions that the reader is allowed a fleeting glimpse into a character's psyche.[4] With its rendering of Lester Ballard, *Child of God* serves as a prime example of this strict narrative adherence to the observable. Paradoxically, the novel is at the same time perhaps McCarthy's most psychoanalytically suggestive work in its portrayal of Ballard's progressing alienation from his community and the slow disintegration of his personality.

Interspersed in the first part of the novel are seven chapters in which anonymous inhabitants of Sevier County relate their personal experiences with Lester. These chorus-like witness accounts provide much of what readers learn about Ballard and his family's history. For instance, the folk narrator of the second account remembers how Ballard once gave a bloody nose to one of his schoolmates for refusing to recover a lost soft ball (*CG* 18), thus depicting young Lester as a child inclined to violence early on. What is more, John Lang points out, they go some way in humanizing Lester, by providing or at least suggesting "psychological insights into his later behavior" (105). After all, while the community is well informed about Lester's crimes, given that these accounts are clearly told a posteriori, looking backward, for the first-time reader, Ballard has yet to commit any crime. Hence, he appears principally as a wretched victim of his circumstances, as well as that of the self-same community that keeps retelling the tales of his villainy. What is revealed in these accounts is a personal history of abandonment and traumatic experiences, even before Lester's forced dispossession of his family home.

In the third vignette, the community narrator tells of the suicide of Ballard's father, after his wife had eloped with another man: "[Lester] com in the store and told it like you'd tell it was rainin out. We went up there and walked in the barn and I seen his feet hangin. We just cut him down, let him fall in the floor. Just like cutting down meat. He stood there and watched, never said nothin. He was about nine or ten year old at the time" (*CG* 21). Deprived of both mother and father, Lester is left to fend for himself. Significantly, it is never specified whether or not a member of the community takes custody of the young orphan. This has led Jay Ellis to suggest that Lester "seems to have been left there until he is deemed old enough to be kicked off without any bother to the community" (2006, 80).[5] In any case, the passage represents the first instance in an ongoing experience of loss and abandonment that characterizes much of Lester's life. Moreover, it introduces the sense of trauma that seems to resonate still in Ballard's later crimes. Years later, a "rope hanging from the loft" (*CG* 4) in the barn, possibly the same his father hanged himself with, serves as the reminder of an event Lester has presumably never come to terms with: "They say he never was right after his daddy killed hisself" (*CG* 21).

In the communal narrator's relation of the event, Lester appears as speechless and emotionally numb as he is through much of the novel. For the most part, he is unable to articulate his feelings, and when he does, it is usually in the form of obscenities. Instead, perhaps triggered by the grotesque and traumatizing sight of his father dead in the barn, whose eyes "run out on stems like a crawfish and his tongue blacker'n a chow dog's" (*CG* 21), Lester becomes a voyeur. Once attention is directed to it, the prevalence of voyeurism in *Child of God* is overwhelming.[6] In fact, the novel's opening lines, which depict a caravan of musicians and showmen arriving for the auction of Ballard's farm, are nothing less than a vivid description of Ballard's visual perception. Sharing this perception with the readers, the text then directs their narrative gaze at the watcher of this spectacle himself: "His eyes are almost shut against the sun and through the thin and blueveined lids you can see the eyeballs moving, watching" (*CG* 4). Later, Ballard is found masturbating at the sight of a couple having intercourse in a car: "On buckling knees the watcher watched" (*CG* 20).

In the present age, the term "voyeurism" has become an apt and oft-cited diagnosis of Western society's total immersion in the visual stimuli and celebrity stories that its mass media broadcast twenty-four hours a day. In its original, medical definition, voyeurism, or scopophilia, describes the derivation of sexual pleasure through the act of spying on the sexual activities of others. As a paraphilia, it is significantly symptomatic of subliminal conflicts and psychological disorders originating in childhood or youth (O'Shea 10). Seen so, Ballard appears as the prototypical voyeur, who "has not reached full sexual maturity, but has stopped in his development on the behavioral level of an adolescent" (O'Shea 12). In this, he is still childlike. Functionally, the early formation of Ballard's voyeurism constitutes a decisive first step in his journey of progressing deviation from socially acceptable spheres of behavior. Thus, he moves from watching couples' copulations to performing necrophilic sex acts and finally to killing people to satisfy his desires.

Indications that something may in fact be dangerously wrong with Lester's vision can be found from the start. After his attempt to stop the auction of his farm is thwarted by the blow of an axe to his head that may have caused him lasting neurological damage (Ellis 2006, 74), Ballard "never could hold his head right" (CG 9) again. Yet the problem goes deeper than that. Even the semantics of the gaze as such already hold a quality of menace. On Ballard's part, this menace is to objectify and render lifeless the beheld subject. Most clearly, it is articulated by the connection of the gaze to Ballard's omnipresent rifle, which serves as a fairly unoriginal Freudian phallic symbol. A great shot, Ballard hits "anything he [can] see" (CG 57), and as his deviance progresses, several women become the victims of both his gaze and his rifle, which factually turns them into dead objects to satisfy his blooming necrophilia. Following Laura Mulvey's influential characterization of the male gaze as either voyeuristic or fetishistic (13–14), we can say that Ballard's sexual objectification arguably combines both. This becomes most explicit in his treatment of his first "victim," a dead woman he finds and brings home. "He took off all her clothes and looked at her, inspecting her body carefully, as if he would see how she were made. He went outside and looked in through the window at her lying naked before the fire" (CG 91–92). Naturally, such scenes lend themselves to charges of misogyny, which are occasionally leveled against the novel and its author and will become part of this reading further on.

Others clearly feel the menace of Ballard's gaze. At the county fair, a young girl "saw the man with the bears watching her and she edged closer to the girl by her side" (CG 65). In turn, the gaze of others presents a threat to Ballard. Falsely accused of rape, he encounters his supposed victim, who upon seeing him "starts to laugh. Ballard is craning his neck to see her. She comes through the door and stands looking at him" (CG 51). At this, Ballard "looks down at his knee" (*CG* 51) and begins to scratch it nervously. The discomfort thus expressed results from an utter defenselessness toward the intrusive power of another's inspecting gaze, a power manifest in the threat of castration, as the woman rages: "I'll kick his goddamned cods off" (*CG* 52). This threat is symbolically realized when John Greer, the man who has purchased the auctioned off family estate, shoots off Lester's arm and, in doing so, takes away his ability to use his phallic rifle. In a twofold mythical sense, Greer hence bears the traits of Sigmund Freud's tyrannical father, first dispossessing and then castrating his son.

That being said, one must not mistake the predominance of voyeurism in *Child of God*, to which one might add Luce's analysis of Lester's necrophilia as combining traits of both *true necrophilia* and mutilating *necro-sadism*, as a simple casebook study in paraphilia.[7] If McCarthy's novel can be read as what Bruhm defines as a "contemporary Gothic" novel—purposefully employing, modifying, and subverting the insights of psychoanalysis to make its own disquieting points—the unconscious desires Lester's voyeurism expresses, too, "center on the problem of a lost object. [. . .] That loss is usually material [. . .], but the materiality of that loss always has a psychological and symbolic dimension to it" (263). Be it by his own agency or that of others, Ballard loses his parents, his home and surrogate home, his first dead beloved, and even the stuffed animals he wins at a shooting gallery. Upon retrieving his rifle, which he had feared he had lost on one of his mountain trips, Ballard exclaims, "You'd try it, wouldn't ye?" (*CG* 132), revealing his expectation—conditioned by past bereavements—to be left and abandoned by all he holds dear.

So it is the trauma of loss, abandonment, and rejection that constitutes Lester's experience. What is truly missing for him, however, goes beyond the loss of his home or even his parents. According to Bruhm, the desire to look, in the gothic genre tradition, "is ultimately the desire to find that which has been lost, that which will unify an otherwise fragmented subjectivity" (264). More than anything else, Ballard seems to be looking for companionship, or, in other words, a place within his community. Consequently, Lester's increasingly grotesque attempts to establish social bonds go hand in hand with the escalating dissolution of his identity. While voyeurism may be the necessary starting point for his descent into necrophilia and serial murder, it is *not* sufficient to explain its logic. After all, scopophilia is per se an ersatz gratification (O'Shea 12).

It is here that mimetic theory provides a more grounded explanation of the psychology behind Lester's unraveling. As Gary Ciuba, whose exemplary Girardian reading informs my own, explains: "Voyeurism and fetishism act out the paradox of mimetic desire. They objectify the beloved so that [. . .] she entices even as she impedes; indeed, she entices because she impedes, for the object of desire becomes more desirable the more that it is denied" (2007, 174).[8] Girard labels this psychological dynamic one of "existential masochism" that exemplifies the ultimately *metaphysical* bend of mimetic desire. Existential masochism seeks not pain or humiliation as such, but rather the awe that is the supreme signifier of the rival-model's perceived superiority and divine fullness (*DDN* 182).

To be sure, young Ballard can hardly be said to have been fully socialized: "Lester has never achieved even elementary maturity and is therefore without discipline or taboo, has never passed over from the child's fictional world into the adult's world, where fact expresses itself in the otherness of other people" (Bell 1988, 61). For the greater part of the novel, he seems so ignorant of his wrongdoing that one is tempted to attribute to him a child's innocence. If this is true though, his state is, as Bell attests, "a parody of innocence, as his ramshackle squatter's house and his caves will become parodies of home, odd versions in turn of stability and arrested time" (1988, 61). While few models were present in young Lester's socialization, the primary model Ballard's father provided his son with culminated in masochistic self-slaughter. His suicide, Ciuba suggests, was likely driven by the loss of his wife to another rival: "Violence is Ballard's true patrimony. The son may even be haunted by a kind of hereditary death wish, a desire to sacrifice his life in order to rejoin the missing father" (2007, 171). Indeed, the night before he assaults his rival and symbolic tyrant father Greer, Ballard "thought he heard a whistling as he used to when he was a boy in his bed in the dark and he'd hear his father on the road coming home" (*CG* 170). As he falls asleep, he is haunted by a starkly beautiful dream vision of his own impending end. Consequently, Ballard's attack on Greer, which heralds the closing of the novel, has sometimes been interpreted as a kind of suicide attempt (Jarrett 42; Bell 1988, 60).

In the first part of the novel, however, Ballard is still looking for other models. As he is excluded from the sexual plenitude that surrounds him, his search materializes as spying upon the lovers' trysts at Frog Mountain. It is here that Ballard finds a first model for his Southern masculinity in the "dark incubus" (*CG* 20) Bobby. The latter embodies "an ecstatic fullness" (Ciuba 2007, 174) that is affirmed by his lover's cries of passion, which move from her lover to the divine and then collapse into excremental profanity: "O Bobby, O god, [. . .] O shit, said the girl" (*CG* 20). In Girard's terms, Ballard and Bobby become mimetic rivals, and the voyeuristic disciple "tries to reassert his superiority through racial degradation" (Ciuba 2007, 175): "It's a nigger, whispered Ballard. [. . .] A nigger" (*CG* 20). Yet in the end it is Ballard who is chased away by Bobby, the model signifying to him the fullness of being, the divine identity that he craves.

Ballard then moves on to Reubel the junkyard keeper's promiscuous daughters, who continuously tease and embarrass him. Afterward, another significant object of his romantic endeavors is represented by the Lane family's nameless daughter, whose mentally impaired child Billy is incidentally one of Ballard's own doubles.[9] And in an earlier episode, he finds a half-naked woman sleeping by the roadside. Interestingly enough, it is the only time in the novel we see him reaching out with compassion: "Ain't you cold?" (*CG* 42). His extended kindness notwithstanding, the encounter escalates and eventually lands him in jail. There, he tries to bond with another prisoner who "cut a motherfucker's head off with a pocketknife" (*CG* 53). When Ballard professes, "All the trouble I ever was in [. . .] was caused by whiskey or women or both," he is explicitly framed as imitating others, the reasoning behind his statement being that "he'd often heard men say as much" (*CG* 53). His attempt at male bonding is, however, as unsuccessful as his efforts at courtship.

All in all, Ballard is continuously thwarted in his attempts to find a romantic partner and establish kinship with others. This frustration culminates in a grotesque conjunction of voyeurism, mimesis, and necrophilia. Hunting for squirrels on Frog Mountain, he discovers a half-naked pair in a running car. They turn out to be dead from carbon monoxide poisoning. Again, one is struck by the powerful conjunction of voyeuristic imagery and mimetism, though it is hardly surprising as the latter "requires the look or gaze to be exercised" (*TH* 117). The woman's eyes stare "with lidless fixity," while the man's eyes gaze "sightlessly" out of "the disarray of clothes and the contorted limbs" (*CG* 86).[10] Taking a closer look at her, Ballard engages in mimetic rivalry with the dead man, whose "penis, sheathed in a wet yellow condom, [is] pointing at him rigidly" (*CG* 88). Ballard pushes him aside "with a dull loathing," and—with the dead man "watching him from the floor of the car" (*CG* 88)—has intercourse with the corpse of the woman. The rivals switch roles: Lester assumes the model's divine author-ity, and the former model is reassigned the place of the passive onlooker (Ciuba 2007, 176).

In the end, what should provide Ballard with a sense of identity turns out to be its complete dissolution, as the differences between living and dead are lost in the deadly constellation of mimesis, necrophilia, and serial mur-der. Like another Norman Bates, Ballard begins to wear the underclothes and later the dresses of his female victims, becoming "a gothic doll in illfit clothes" (*CG* 140). Shortly thereafter, the progressing erosion of his self is described in terms of schizophrenia, dissociative identity disorder, and—notably—demonic possession: "Whatever voice spoke to him was no demon but some old shed self that came yet from time to time in the name of sanity, a hand to gentle him back from the rim of his disastrous wrath" (*CG* 158). As Ballard attempts to kill Greer, he sets upon him like "an apparition created whole out of nothing" (*CG* 173). Here, he is referred to only as an "it," some-thing indefinite much like "monstrous" baby Billy. Finally, when Ballard gets shot and the wig he loses turns out to be a human scalp, the disintegration of Lester's identity between the poles of man/woman, dead/living, and victim/victimizer is complete. At this point, he is truly the embodiment of "imita-tion run amok" (Ciuba 2007, 177)—a "slayer of distinctions" (*VS* 74), or else the incarnation of distinctions slain.

Caught in the Myth:
Lester Ballard's Mythic Models

In terms of mimetic anthropology, Lester Ballard provides a more clear-cut and condensed example of the operations of imitative desire and its con-flictual potentialities than the characters of *The Orchard Keeper*. In addi-tion to illuminating the psychological forces and desires at work within the protagonist of *Child of God*, the mimetic perspective is useful, too, in uniting our view of the novel's psychology with the materialist subtext several scholars identify as running through the text. In turn, materialisti-cally focused interpretations can help to expand our understanding of the

subversive, critical nature of McCarthy's creation by placing its protagonist
before both a sociohistorical background and a national mythology that
provide another set of models.

Mimesis, Materialism, Necrophilia

As David Holloway observes, there exists a strong link between Lester's
progressing psychological aberration and alienation from his community
and the "structuring role of commodity and private property relations," as
communal bonds are shattered "by the logic of bourgeois commodification"
(2002, 127, 128). It follows that the protagonist's exploits, specifically his
necrophilia, reflect this ideology. Even in one of the earliest serious treatments of the novel, William Schafer remarks that Lester's increasingly psychotic actions "are rough parodies of 'normal' life: he courts women, takes
them as brides, is obsessed with them. He tries to regain his lost property; he
wishes to be a landowner, a man of property like others" (117). While its core
story could reasonably be taking place in another rural setting and at another
time, it is therefore not by accident that *Child of God* is set in the 1950s and
1960s, when "the American way of living emerged and with it came an added
emphasis on materialism and the growing importance of household appli-
ances, technological wonders, and 'stuff' in general as ways to define yourself
and true happiness" (Madsen 25).

In this milieu converge the individual operations of mimetic desire on
the one hand, and its culturally transferred sublimations on the other, which
consist in the social glorification of materialistic aspects within that grand
myth that is the American dream. The first looks for a sense of identity and
metaphysical fullness in attaining the objects of wealth and prestige that
apparently confer this fullness to the divinized model. The second is an
expression of the actions of the equally deified "bitch-goddess of success"
(Freese 1994, 273), who merges secularized notions of Calvinist predestination with social Darwinist ideas of the survival of the fittest, and thus elevates
the property, wealth, and success one enjoys into the prime determinants of
one's social status, identity, and sense of place. Taking into account their
roots in notions of salvation and providence, the aura of which they still
cling to, one can interpret these materialistic and success-oriented aspects
of the dream as a collective, externally mediated manifestation of desire, just

as the American sense of mission and manifest destiny that *Blood Meridian* dramatizes can be interpreted as another such mediation. In all three cases, metaphysical desires attach themselves to certain objects—self-fulfillment, wealth and success, the advancement and perfection of the nation, and so on—that are seen as advancing the self, whether that self is an individual, a corporation, or a nation state, and provide a fertile ground for conflicts both physical and symbolic.

For the novel, the initial expropriation and "unhousing" (Ellis 2006, 70) of Ballard that sets off his psychotic descent is the operative case in point. At the auction of his family estate, the auctioneer CB loudly and at some length praises the value of the property as a sound future investment: "Friends, they is no limit to the possibilities on a piece of property like this. [. . .] A piece of land like this here I sincere believe will give ye ten percent on your investment. And maybe more" (*CG* 5–6). After his brief interference is violently cut short by Buster's blunt axe blow, the auction continues "like nothing never had happen" (*CG* 9), ending with John Greer's purchase of the land. In a sense, Lester's later attempt at regaining his family farm from Greer is therefore part mimetic retaliation for his violent expropriation, part expression of his equally material and social longing for a place within the mythical and social order. In erecting his little necropolis in the caves, he pursues the same goals. Here as there, he is always following only what models his society provides:

> Lester is emblematic of the society from which he arises. [. . .] While far from middle class America, the novel's Sevier (significantly pronounced "Severe") County is a mountain valley of ashes [. . .] whose inhabitants hoard material remains or dead and deadening material; Lester's sifting the ashes of his burned cabin for the remains of his first beloved [. . .] reflects the materialistic orientation of his culture. The ruthless opportunism of Lester's near-neighbors, who legally cheat him of material goods in the auction of his farm or in the barter of watches, is implicated in the formation of Lester's necrophilia. From this society in which the weak are dispossessed, Lester learns to take possession of others forcibly. [. . .] Lester's shooting and hoarding his human victims is an extension of the same impulse: he expends his talents and efforts in amassing material goods— much like ourselves, perhaps. (Luce 2009, 161–62)

Sociologically, there is a clear sense in which Lester's lethally literal objectification of women holds up a grotesque mirror to a society in which "women's bodies are normatively defined [...] as commodity matter" (Holloway 2002, 129). Some readers have understandably called either Lester or the novel as a whole misogynist, and taken this either positively as an implicit critique of patriarchal values or else negatively as its expression and unreflected endorsement of such values by the author himself.

Psychologically though, Ellis asserts, such materialistically underpinned criticism lacks empathy toward Lester and ultimately fails to elucidate his character beyond adding the charge of misogyny to his already impressive catalogue of character flaws.[11] After all, Ballard's necrophilia is motivated by more than the satisfaction of sexual needs, directed not at arousal through death but rather toward human warmth, as Luce points out (2009, 178–79). Psychologically, the illusion of live interaction is a vital component of necrophilia, which Ellis consequently deems an inherently skewed and inaccurate term: Ballard "loves the dead by pretending they are alive, and that they have not rejected him," and he does so by imaginatively reinserting them into hallucinated "living social arrangements" (2006, 83), which is precisely what renders his interactions with the dead at once pathetic and unsettling.

Certainly, he is no flesh-hacking, corpse-mutilating necro-sadist like Ed Gein, at least not until late in the book where he goes from wearing his victim's clothes to wearing their scalps. Instead, he may more appropriately be reinterpreted in terms of Hillary Gamblin's more empathetic and psychologically nuanced feminist reading as a necromantic. Ballard is still unsurprisingly stuck in the patriarchal gender roles of his time, yet it is not as though his victims were solely sex objects. His first found "girlfriend" he outright romances, telling her "everything he'd ever thought of saying to a woman. Who could say she did not hear him?" (CG 88–89). He buys her dresses, lingerie, lipstick, and as he arranges her for another night, he carefully dresses her, brushes her hair, and paints her lips. "He would arrange her in different positions and go out and peer in the window at her. After a while he just sat holding her, [...] talking to her" (CG 103). What we find in this conjunction of voyeurism and necrophilia is a grotesque imitation of idealized domesticity:

> In an uncanny way, Lester is finally able to be the middle-class husband
> with the perfect stay-at-home wife that loves him unconditionally and cer-
> tainly will never leave him. He is certainly attracted by the sexual encoun-
> ters with this woman. But perhaps he is even more drawn to *the image* of
> her as she is framed in the window. In this instance, the window functions
> eerily like a suburban picture window. From the outside looking in, Lester
> sees the ultimate image of domesticity which is quite disturbing to us.
> There is something entirely unhomely (*unheimlich*) about this instance of
> the homely (*heimlich*). (Madsen 23–24)

Upon Lester's abduction from the hospital, the image of domesticity returns
in another picture-window scene, showing a man with his wife and children.
Ballard is extended some small kindness reflecting and verbally echoing his
own initial kindness toward the sleeping lady in an earlier episode: "Aint' you
cold," a man asks, and Ballard is handed a pair of overalls that "were soft and
smelled of soap" (*CG* 180). In the novel's otherwise harsh naturalism and set
against the threat of Lester's being lynched, this minimalistic scene is one of
the few moments of respite and comparative beauty for both Ballard and the
assaulted reader, no less so for its melancholy aura as it has Ballard once again
peering in from the outside, breathing in the elusive scent of his innermost
wishes.

Finally, such scenes also accentuate the sense of the Freudian uncanny
(*das Unheimliche*) that prevails earlier on and that is another essential aspect
in the novel's gothic mode of transgression and destabilization. In essence,
Lester's voyeurism and his necrophilia are as disturbing as they are because
they reflect our own voyeuristic and materialistic tendencies back at us, making his social abnormality a dark mirror of our own normality. In this way,
McCarthy makes us uncertain about how to regard either him or ourselves as
we realize the unfulfilled and all-too-human needs and longings at the root
of his aberration.

From Yeoman to Degenerate Hunter

My discussion of *Child of God* so far has focused primarily on its psychological elements, which assign the novel a place in the contemporary gothic

landscape and bring into play the first half of the Girardian logic that seems to underlie Ballard's rampage. The second half of this logic centers around another set of models that features prominently in Ballard's search for identity, namely the mythical pairing of farmer and hunter. It is through a discussion of these oppositional figures that the novel's positioning within American mythology, specifically the frontier and pastoral tradition, can be asserted.

The foundations for the stature of the farmer in American mythology were laid in the first two decades of the nineteenth century, the era of Jeffersonian democracy. In this era, America conceived of herself as a primarily agrarian nation, and saw the European metropolis as a cesspool of vice, decadence, and corruption. An antithesis of the mercantile city dweller, the ideal American citizen had to be "a free individual, living on his own land, independent of others for the necessaries of life yet depending on his fellow citizens (and society in general) for protection, law, and civilized amenities" (*FE* 70). For Thomas Jefferson, this embodiment of civic virtue and the "best social base of a democratic republic" (Hofstadter 27) was none other than the yeoman farmer. In his *Notes on the State of Virginia* (1782–83), Jefferson famously proclaimed:

> Those who labour in the earth are the chosen people of God, if ever he had a chosen people, whose breasts he has made his peculiar deposit for substantial and genuine virtue. It is the focus in which he keeps alive that sacred fire, which otherwise might escape from the face of the earth. (290)

With the onset of the Jacksonian era and the progress of industrialization, the ideal of an agrarian nation faded away together with its hero, who was replaced by the figure of the hunter as exemplified by such real and unreal (but equally mythical) figures as Daniel Boone and James Fenimore Cooper's Natty Bumppo. The only places where the role of the farmer retained some of its stature were parts of the South, which "guided by pastoral and republican imperatives, [. . .] persistently attempted to portray itself as a region somehow outside of time and change, a permanent refuge of order in a chaotic world" (Grammer 31).

This is the tradition to which McCarthy's child of God is heir. The problem is that, in the midst of the twentieth century, its heroic ideal is thoroughly outdated. As K. Wesley Berry shows in his essay "The Lay of the Land," the naturalistically rendered mountainscapes of Appalachian Tennessee that McCarthy depicts in both *The Orchard Keeper* and *Child of God* show obvious "evidence of ecological disease" (55). *Child of God* in particular is set in a time period in which small-farm subsistence agriculture in the southern regions of Appalachia—an area that in 1930 still "had the heaviest concentration of self-sufficient farms in the country" (cit. in Berry 62)—has disappeared almost completely.[12] In the 1940s and 1950s, years of economic depression and ruthless exploitation by the coal and timber industry had depleted most of the soil in this area, and the timber on Ballard's family land is tellingly low as it has been cut in the previous decades. One likely result of this exploitation, the quasi-biblical flood of the novel, not only recalls the flood of *The Orchard Keeper* but suggests 1957 as a likely date for the novel's main action (Luce 2002, 171–72).[13]

Ballard's closest associates include the whiskey maker Fred Kirby and the junkyard keeper Reubel. Apart from John Greer, farmers are conspicuously absent in the novel, as are farm-grown foods (Berry 65). Clearly, it is not a good time for "those who labor in the earth." The folk narrators' anecdotal tales certify that people do not know anymore how to handle their animals. Ballard is no exception.

> He had this old cow to balk on him, couldn't get her to do nothin. He pushed and pulled and beat on her till she'd wore him out. He went and borry'd Squire Helton's tractor and went back over there and thowed a rope over the old cow's head and took off on the tractor hard as he could go. When it took up the slack it like to of jerked her head plumb off. Broke her neck and killed her where she stood. (*CG* 35)

Ballard "has not inherited agricultural wisdom," nor has he "cultivated vegetables for years" (Berry 64). Most of his meals are improvised, ranging from potatoes roasted over a lamp with a coat hanger to stew made of squirrels and turnips. Nonetheless, readers will surely still sympathize with him as he is evicted from his family's farm home.

As in *The Orchard Keeper*, realistic concerns overlap with mythic and ritualistic realities. Accompanied by a caravan of musicians and entertainers, the auction begins as a festive rite of exclusion as the auctioneer praises the future of the property and the value of real estate. In the auctioneer's words, the land "needs some improvin" (*CG* 6). Still, the auction is framed in strictly capitalist terms as "the soundest investment you can make" (*CG* 6), which indicates that it is not virtuous, long-term Jeffersonian cultivation for the common good he has in mind, but rather the exploitation of the land for personal gain. As Ballard interferes to prevent the impending loss of what he sees as his property, the auction quickly deteriorates into a "holiday-gone-wrong" that will "inaugurate a new cycle of revenge" (*VS* 125; Ciuba 2007, 182–83). From the mythical, pastoral perspective, "the scene in which the yeoman farmer loses his property is the one which pastoral republics dread—the moment when death enters their world. [. . .] The sheriff and the auctioneer [. . .] are figures of modernity, of time; Lester casts himself as a reactionary, still hoping to resist the tides of history" (Grammer 39).[14] When Lester protects his property against the county officials, he is acting in perfect accordance with the mythic role assigned to the yeoman farmer: "An armed man, prepared to defend the country and his own liberty and property, was for our ancestors the ideal republican citizen" (Grammer 39).[15] With this initial dispossession, however, this mythic role model is denied to Ballard, and he is deprived "of the identity, means of sustenance and place of status that the founding myth of his culture regards as his birthright" (Cant 94).

What is left to him is the other American model, the role of the frontiersman, which harkens back to the mythic hunter: "McCarthy is rewriting the American pastoral type of the frontiersman, of the American Adam, whose formative experience is regeneration through the confrontation with, and survival in, the American wilderness" (Guillemin 2004, 39; see also Jarrett 41). In spite of his neighbors' hostility and the indifference of nature, Ballard is independent, resourceful, and persevering—qualities that allow him to endure in the wilderness. Consequently, a harsh reality has endowed him with a harsh view of it. Watching two hawks couple, the only thing that occurs to him is that "all things fought" (*CG* 168). In another scene, he witnesses the death struggle of a hunted boar, watching their

> ballet tilt and swirl and churn mud up through the snow and [. . .] the lovely blood welter there in its holograph of battle, spray bursts from a ruptured lung, the dark heart's blood, pinwheel and pirouette, until shots rang and all was done. A young hound worried the boar's ears and one

lay dead with his bright ropy innards folded upon the snow and another whined and dragged himself about. (*CG* 69)

Whether it is that the language of this scene, which clearly cannot be Ballard's, reflects the narrator's point of view, or that Ballard's perception bleeds into the narrator's to aestheticize this spectacle of violence, there is a strong sense that the wilderness surrounding Ballard is just as violent as he himself. Scenes like these or the scene where Ballard's second home is invaded by a pack of wild dogs suggest a reversion to a Hobbesian state of nature and a Darwinian logic of survival of the fittest. Ballard *needs* to be the hunter, and his ever-present rifle is a powerful reminder of his role. So it is his prowess with this lethal tool that gains him a modicum of respect from his neighbors: at the shooting gallery, it wins him the stuffed animals that will be his "companions" for a while, as well as the admiration of a small crowd.

However, stuffed animals and squirrels are all that this latter-day Daniel Boone can hunt for. Eventually his pent-up violence turns against his fellow humans. He becomes the degenerate hunter of frontier nightmare J. Hector St. John de Crèvecoeur wrote about in his *Letters from an American Farmer*: "The chase renders them ferocious, gloomy, and unsociable; a hunter wants no neighbour, he rather hates them because he dreads the competition" (76).[16] Whereas the original hunter of myth tried to engage in a "sacred Eucharist" with an often female-coded representative of the wilderness to revivify his community, the communal ties of this degenerate hunter have been severed and the female element has moved out of reach. If, wading through a flooded creek, "the rifle aloft in one arm," Lester is compared to "some demented hero or bedraggled parody of a patriotic poster come aswamp" (*CG* 156), it is because in a real sense he is exactly that (Schafer 115–16). In Ballard's case, the independence and ascetic solipsism associated with the frontier hero metastasize into the pathological narcissism and hubris of what Simpson regards as his modern, gothic heir: the serial killer.

Narcissus vs. Adam

Another instance of the novel's merging of visual metaphor and the semantics of the gaze with mythological contents is its frequent evocation of the fabled figure of Narcissus. Several times in the novel, Ballard catches sight of himself in reflecting surfaces as well as other people, and is repeatedly found talking to himself. Closest to the mythical tale is an episode in which Ballard drinks from a pool of water and then, studying his visage, "halfway put his hand to the water as if he would touch the face that watched there but then he rose" (*CG* 127). In the Greek myth, Narcissus famously drowns in his own watery reflection, making his a cautionary tale of multiple failures that works on the allegorical levels of both psychology and epistemology. Firstly, it is a warning against undue and exaggerated valuation of the self to the exclusion of the other, for it exemplifies the self-destructive consequences of such solipsism. Secondly, it expresses an epistemological failure: Narcissus fails to discern the illusory nature of the reflection, paradoxically revealing a simultaneous absence of self-awareness at the height of self-glorification.

With regard to mimetic theory, the Narcissus myth is interesting as it reproduces the failure of mimetic rivals to recognize themselves in their respective double. In turn, Narcissus's failures resonate meaningfully in the life of Lester Ballard. In fact, he shares in them. To Luce, the narcissistic moments in *Child of God* suggest "the Platonic idea of the role of vision in achieving wisdom," and she consequently interprets Lester's moments of actual, physical reflection allegorically as "near misses, lost opportunities to see his own face truly," with the scene cited above showing "both his near-recognition of his 'proper substance and worth' and his pursuit of shadows or illusions" (2002, 181–84). These flaws of perception are not solely Lester's: On the narrative level, the Narcissus substrate serves as an ironic comment on the community's members' failure to recognize themselves in Lester, most explicitly so as he is abducted from the hospital by the lynch mob, and a man who carries a shotgun instead of Lester's rifle watches him through the glass of the truck he is held in (*CG* 181). On a metanarrative level, these scenes serve in turn as opportunities in the novel's invitation *to the reader* to recognize her or his own face in the visage of Lester.

Psychologically, Lester's exemplary Narcissus-moment occurs shortly after his first murder. It heralds the unraveling of his self at the same time as it parallels the outward escalation of his violence. Hence, it ties into what Simpson views as the perverted heirloom of the frontiersman's self-sufficiency, the antisocial element of which becomes the murderous hubris of the serial killer. Freud's concept of narcissism envisions it as an early stage of development in which the libido is not directed at other objects, but rather uses these objects to feed, exclusively, itself. Seen this way, Ballard's "wretched arrogance" (*CG* 41) and solipsism are a kind of regression to an earlier stage compared to his attempts to interact with others; eventually this culminates in a symbolic regression to a prenatal state in the caves of mother earth.

In Girard's reinterpretation of Freud, both object-directed desire and narcissistic desire are two sides of the same coin that is *mimetic desire*: "Narcissistic libido also does the same thing as all the others, after cleverly putting itself forward as a model. The narcissistic libido feeds on the desire that it directs toward itself" (*TH* 373). In contrast to the disciple who triumphs over his model and attains the object of his desire, only to find the model stripped of its former divinity and the object utterly devalued, the narcissist feeds on the desires of others, who are equally devalued in his eyes—much like Ballard's narcissistic turn entails his murderous objectification of others. The narcissist, then, seems himself the supreme model whose desires circle around a nucleus of total self-sufficiency: "This self-sufficiency is not an earthly thing; it is the last glimmering of the sacred. [. . .] Object-directed desire dreams of an intact narcissism because it dreams of the absolute and indestructible being who does violence to everything around it but suffers none itself. That is why, in Freud's terms, narcissism is libido itself—which is the same thing as energy and power, *energeia* and *dunamis* in the Greek" (*TH* 375–76).

So there exists an inherent connection, in narcissism, between the egotistical exultation of the self that depends on its own lack of self-awareness and sustains itself at the cost of others, and the violence that signifies the presence of divinity. Immersed in the wilderness, which according to Girard is the realm of violence and hence also of the sacred, the unhoused child Ballard now seeks to incorporate divinity itself. Being the slayer of distinctions, he now "blurs the distinction that is the source of all other distinctions. Ballard eliminates the difference between the pious regard for sacred violence and the desire to arrogate such heavenly fury for his own power [. . .] he makes transgression the very sign of his transcendence" (Ciuba 2002, 94).

In a word, this transgression is the original one, that is, *hybris* or *superbia*—of striving to be like God. Yet in tune with the Narcissus-theme, it does not involve the moment of self-recognition. Consequently, Lester becomes a serial killer. As he claims supreme violence in his first murder, he commands the lethally wounded Lane daughter to "Die, goddamn you," and in the next sentence we are told that "she did" (*CG* 119). In the following, Ballard symbolically assumes the power over nature as well, and the wording of the scene indeed suggests a certain parallelism to the murder as he tells "the snow to fall faster" and, again, we are told that "it did" (*CG* 139). Marching through the snow, Ballard's boots trample out "the prints of lesser life" (*CG* 140). In this manner, he not only expresses his superiority but symbolically reasserts the authority over life and death that he claims literally in his murders. Interestingly though, the purest expression of Lester's divine aspirations is a rather abstract one. Sowing chaos and destruction, and finally coming to embody undifferentiation itself, his strongest desire ironically seems to be for order:

> Coming up the mountain through the blue winter twilight among great boulders and the ruins of giant trees prone in the forest he wondered at such upheaval. Disorder in the woods, trees down, new paths needed. Given charge Ballard would have made things more orderly in the woods and in men's souls. (*CG* 136)

To some extent, Ballard's wish is likely the outcome of his reduction to aimless wandering and cave-dwelling, a result of his forced homelessness and frustration at his constant rejection by society. To him, these experiences challenge the notion of a divinely ordered cosmos as he considers himself "so grievous a case against the gods" (*CG* 189). Hence, he presumes that he would do a better job.

Though often rather in passing by the wayside of their own interpretive paths, several critics have noticed this central facet of McCarthy's creation. For instance, Michael Madsen states that "Lester attempts to create order out of chaos" (24), Steven Frye acknowledges "the innate human desire to stand against the apparent chaos of seeming forms" (2009, 45), and the Platonic-Gnostic perspective of Dianne Luce suggests to her that Lester's "longing for order derives from the immortal part of his soul" (2002, 187). As so often, the complexity of Lester's wish is defined within a syncretic spectrum of psychological and mythological reference points. It relates at once to the state of nature (the woods) and his own psyche, insofar as he has internalized nature's upheaval and reverted to the precultural wilderness state of the frontiersman. Yet it also includes an element of the social and religious in his contemplation of the disorder in "men's souls."

Only a few pages later, the extension of Ballard's wish is fleshed out as voicing the existential dilemma of discerning some kind of order in a cosmos that seems utterly devoid of it. Watching "the hordes of cold stars sprawled across the smokehole" of his cave, he wonders "what stuff they were made of, or himself" (*CG* 141).[17] In pursuing his quest, Ballard employs a double strategy that entails firstly *looking* for order, such as when he is stargazing or inspecting his first dead beloved "as if he would see how she were made" (*CG* 91–92), and secondly attempting to actively *create* it. In a rudimentary way, the former strategy relates Ballard to the realm of philosophical observation, as Luce's discussion of Greek myth within the novel demonstrates. The second role is more genuinely rooted within American mythologies of the frontier and the pastoral. Endowed with childlike innocence and blissful unawareness of the right and wrong of his deeds, this child of God, who can be traced "back to Adam" (*CG* 81), is not only a failed farmer and misplaced frontiersman, but also a perverted mirror-image of the purely literary type that informs the depictions of either of these semimythological figures.

In his late eighteenth-century *Letters from an American Farmer*, Crèvecoeur had already conceived of the American as a fundamentally new man who had left behind all ties and allegiance to past European existence (86–70). But it was probably with R. W. B. Lewis's classic study that the literary heroes who rose from the tales of the New World experience became subsumed within the prototypal figure of the eponymous *American Adam*. In describing this figure of national myth as an "individual standing alone, self-reliant and self-propelling, ready to confront whatever awaited him with the aid of his own unique and inherent resources," Lewis also delivers a fitting exposition of the qualities that characterize Lester Ballard. Furthermore, like the morality of both the American and the biblical Adam, Ballard's "moral position [is] prior to experience"—and thus "fundamentally innocent" (Lewis 5). As with the asocial tendencies of the frontiersman, McCarthy's mythoclastic take on this heroic type presents an extreme picture of what was always a part of its distinctly American character:

> The American Adam operates as a variation of the pathetic fallacy, transferring the inferred innocence of the wilderness to the representative American identity. Within its setting of primitive wilderness, *Child of God* reverses Lewis's thesis. Unlike Thoreau at Walden Pond, Ballard's isolation

in nature neither regenerates nor restores a lost innocence; it corrupts this
contemporary inversion of the American Adam. (Jarrett 41)[18]

Jarrett is right in identifying the inversion. Yet McCarthy's point is less the
failure of nature to restore innocence.[19] Rather, the point is to reveal the violent potentialities inherent in said innocence by having the cultural hero not
bring order and regeneration, but sow the seeds of chaos and destruction.
Being barely literate, Ballard lacks the semiotic ordering power of language
manifest in the original Adamic act of naming, preferring instead to let his
rifle do the talking. Thus, Jarrett rightly asserts that his attempts to order his
life work primarily "through a violence projected on others" (41), and Ciuba
observes that "each of [Ballard's] murders disorders the world in order to
reorder it as a dominion according to his own desires" (2007, 176).

In sum, the conditions that nurtured the pastoral and frontier myth with
their respective heroes have long since disappeared. And yet, the charm of
these myths remains unwavering. In clashing with the realities of Ballard's
time, it leads him onto a path of destruction. Differently put: against the
entropy of a violent environment, which reflects upon the entropy of his
violent psyche, Ballard sets his blasphemous wish to become himself godlike.
His vision of dominion appears to find its grotesque (literally *grotto-esque*—
of a cave) realization in the timeless order and immutable permanence of his
cave necropolis, which relates it to the mythic ideal of the pastoral, Edenic
garden outside history that the South tried to incorporate. The antipastoral
disappearance of the farmer, the narcissistic hubris of the displaced frontiersman, and the perversion of the American Adam are thus all aspects in the
larger argument that constitutes McCarthy's confrontation of American
myth with its dark potentialities and historical realities.

The Physics of Mortality:
Necrobiosis and Maxwell's Demon

While the necrophilic delusion is one of the deads' vitality, the pastoral
garden has always been haunted by the specter of death. A taint in Adamic
and pastoral visions that reflects on Ballard's own flawed vision is the

fact that the dead body is manifestly perishable to the point of sensory assault—hence a need for new corpses. The final unearthing of his victims records the putrefaction and molecular disintegration of the dead body in effectively revolting detail, noting the "sour [. . .] faint reek of ammonia," the falling "gray soapy clots of matter," and the dripping "gray rheum" of the bodies (*CG* 196). In Ballard's caves, there is in fact no timeless order of stone and death. To the contrary, *Child of God* shows death as "the ultimate assault to the flesh. It causes carefully delineated physiological structures to lose their systematic wholeness until they achieve the final indistinction of dust" (Ciuba 2002, 96).

Going beyond the immediate scope of his mimetic reading, Ciuba calls the level of detail McCarthy devotes to necrobiotic dissolution, in conjunction with his imagery of weighty corpses dangling stiffly from ropes in rigor mortis, the novel's "physics of mortality" (2007, 179). Plain yet poetic, the phrase proves to be more accurate than Ciuba implies. My reference above to the entropy of the environment and the psyche is only partially metaphorical: in McCarthy's work-long meditation on the vital dynamics of order and disorder that unfold between the conceptual intersections of personal identity, society, nature, and narrative, *Child of God* is the first novel that explores the actual *physical* underpinnings of dis|order. Whereas the spatiotemporal construction, shifting narrative perspectives, and incipient style of "optical democracy" in *The Orchard Keeper* articulate the question of the status of order between ontological fact and epistemological construction, and *Outer Dark* metaphorically conjoins the dynamics of heat with the violent social tendency to disorder in the imagery of satanic fires, *Child of God* pays attention to the thermodynamic process itself. In this, the conjunction of heat exchange, work, and necrophilia is central, as is McCarthy's subtle invocation of yet another quasi-mythical, yet scientific figure.

A secondary theme of *Child of God* paralleling Ballard's reaching for community is constituted by the recurring imagery of his seeking warmth. Likely to be lost in scientifically undiscerning appreciations of the novel's naturalism, such imagery nonetheless punctuates the text with unfailing regularity, as we see Lester building fires or looking for natural sources of heat. In fact, there are several of these images that explicitly concern themselves with issues of energy storage or the thermodynamic transfer between

hot and cold bodies. Shortly before he will extend his single kindness in asking the woman he finds by the road "Ain't you cold," Ballard is found sitting
with his back to the sun "as if he'd store the warmth of it against the coming
winter" (*CG* 40). In the scene where he watches the mating hawks to realize his fundamental principle that "all things fought," he is similarly shown
leaning against a rock "and soak[ing] the warmth from it" (*CG* 169). With
much of the novel set in winter, Ballard is constantly battling the elements.
Losing his second home to the accidental fire he sets, he climbs onto the
hearth "for the warmth of it" against a night of "six below zero" (*CG* 102),
that is, minus twenty-one degrees Celsius. After he crosses a flooded river,
the effect of his exposure to water and coldness leaves him alternately "half
frozen" next to his fire, suffering from "hot pains" with the nearby creek feeling hot, yet also "shivering with his arms crossed" (*CG* 159), his convulsing
muscles fighting hypothermia as his body tries to raise its temperature. While
they are exemplified rather than explicated, heat exchange and storage are
clearly a recurrent theme in *Child of God*.

From a thermodynamic perspective, Ballard's second home in Waldrop's remote forest cabin is an important location, for it is the setting of
several scenes that firstly establish the connection between warmth, work,
and order, and that secondly associate the dynamics of heat and cold with
Ballard's necrophilia. After all, though violence dominates the second half
of the novel, it would be wrong to assume that it is Ballard's only means
in trying to order his life. One may hardly consider Ballard a champion of
cleanliness, yet his first act upon moving into the cabin is an act of house-
keeping: he sweeps the floor of "old newspapers" and mud as well as dried
animal excrement and insect husks, removes a hornets' nest, closes the open
window, and sweeps the chimney (*CG* 13). Having used his workforce and
makeshift instruments to clean up his new home, he consequently burns
the newspapers, evoking a direct correlation between work, order, and fire.
The day's work behind him, he replenishes himself with a meal of sliced
potatoes heated over a lamp.

Together with the scenes quoted above, these instances paint as complete a picture of basic, macroscopic thermodynamics as one could wish
for. Energy is absorbed as heat from the environment, ingested as food
and excreted again in degraded form (*CG* 13) by the open system of the

body, or else converted to work expended in countering nature's tendency to disorder.[20] In addition, the subtle links these naturalistically rendered scenes establish by connecting physical and emotional states—such as the metaphoric association of physical and emotional warmth—contrast the inherent life-preserving and destructive potentials of fire. Thus, they serve to unify the novel's investigation of physical processes with its dramatization of the mimetic dissolution of the psyche within the larger disorder of the social structure. Since all of these processes are interlinked within an intricate matrix that unfolds paradigmatically as well as by structural analogy and effective causation, this complex artistic vision may be described as that of *violentropy*. In condensed form, this concept is made tangible by the image of Ballard's rifle put next to the fireplace (*CG* 101); later, Ballard even puts the rifle in the fire to thaw its frozen action (*CG* 158–59).

Admittedly, there is a possibility that these episodes are purely incidental to the novel's naturalistic outlook, the "brutal scarcity" Holloway regards as articulating "the merely biologic (or factical) status of the human condition" (2002, 125). In my view, however, they constitute evidence of the scientific sensitivities of a still aspiring author who studied physics and engineering and "was good at it"—even if he was not good enough to satisfy "his own personal extravagant ego" (Kushner). Even if one doubts that these aspects are part of the novel's consideration of the general themes of disorder in the natural and human world, they are at the least testament to McCarthy's awareness of the thermodynamic processes going on, the implications of which a work like *The Road* makes explicit.

What is more, in the discussion of the equally physical, social, and psychological dimensions thermodynamic imagery entails in *Child of God*, the pivotal episode has yet to be mentioned. After Ballard has found his first "dead girlfriend," he hides her in the other room and later the attic of his new home, storing her "away from the heat for keeping" (*CG* 94). In the night that sees the enactment of his ne*cromantic* domestic fantasy, he sets up a fire in the hearth against the freezing winter night. Jay Ellis's spatially focused analysis of the ensuing processes is highly revealing:

> Outside, it is exceedingly cold. Inside, Ballard divides the house into two
> parts: he furiously heats the half in which he must dwell to stay alive, and

into which, at the right time, he brings the girl. The other half of the house is left cold, static, a storage space for time, and his hedge against the fact that the girl is dead. (2006, 86)

A house, two chambers in different thermal states, a change and exchange of energy induced by the agency of some intermediary party: what Ellis provides here is not just an accurate summary of Ballard's actions, but also the description of a thermodynamic scenario that bears striking resemblance to the thought experiment that became famous as Maxwell's Demon. While I have briefly discussed this idea before, it warrants more detailed analysis at this point. Positing that the second law of thermodynamics held statistical rather than universal validity, James Clerk Maxwell conceived of his "demon" as a finite, anthropomorphic entity (or else a valve) operating a door in a wall partitioning a container filled with gas, that is, an otherwise isolated system. The demon would open the door—or two doors, one on either side—only letting through the fast, high-velocity molecules on the one side, and only the slow, low-velocity molecules on the other. In this way, the demon could raise or decrease the temperatures in either compartment, creating the heat differential necessary for any kind of energy conversion or natural process to happen. Theoretically, the demon thus violated the tendency of an isolated system to approach thermal equilibrium, that is, the probable state of molecular disorder that the second law predicts.

But Maxwell's hypothesis carried in its wake larger implications still. It is worth recalling N. Katherine Hayles's characterization of the demon as a mythic guardian and "liminal figure who stands at a threshold that separates not just slow molecules from fast but an ordered world of will from the disordered world of chaos" and entropy (1990, 43). In McCarthy's imagination, Ballard assumes the position of the demon. Gathering wood, feeding the fire against the freezing cold outside, he moves his "dead girlfriend" from the cold storage space to the domestic room of his fantasy, laying her on the hearth. Gradually, he effects the transformation of the "frozen bitch" and her "wooden" rigidity (*CG* 102) into the proper image of romance and domesticity. Only once his beloved is limber enough can the necrophiliac lose himself in the fantasy of a life relationship with a partner that promises stability and the order of conventional social roles. Only where conditions are far from equilibrium can life develop—the illusion of life, in this case.

The analogy goes further yet: "Ballard will heat his passions with a fuel derived from the remainders of natural life, sacrificing them in the long run for a scene meant to stop time—for what the French call a 'little death'" (Ellis 2006, 86). Implicitly, Ballard's agency metaphorically connects the illusory orgasmic synchronicity of life and death with the pastoral idea of timeless order. Putting the last idea differently, he appears to momentarily halt the arrow of time that entropy represents by virtue of the second law's prediction of the irreversible progress to thermal equilibrium, molecular disorder, and death.

Speaking in Hayles's terms, Ballard, the child of God who will consecutively clothe himself in the transvestite garb of homicidal hubris, uses his exceedingly strong will to create, but for a moment, the fantasy of an ordered, meaningful universe that offers him the place that he is otherwise denied. But of course, like the demon, it is finally just that: a fantasy. At least as far as Maxwell's original concept is concerned, Ballard's agency diverges from that of the demon in important ways. Not only does he exert his energy as work, he draws energy from his surroundings in the form of firewood, and by his inclusion of "whole lengths of fencepost with sections of rotted wire" (*CG* 102), he overrides the cultural demarcation and discriminatory function of the fence, increasing disorder on another level.[21] Also, the life his deluded necrophilic imagination projects into the body of his beloved is manifestly an illusion: whether frozen or limber, she remains a corpse at equilibrium with her surroundings. Finally, in his pursuit of mastery—which peaks in his arrogant challenge to the exceedingly cold night: "Now freeze, you son of a bitch" (*CG* 103)—Lester overcompensates as he heats the cabin beyond its structural capacity to contain the thermal energy. Put differently, the feedback loop that exists between his heating the house and the cooling of the outside causes a runaway and the breakdown of the entire system: the cabin burns down, melting the snow that covers the ground around it that after a while, "beg[ins] to steam," and the fire leaves behind "only a blackened chimney with a pile of smoldering boards" (*CG* 105). Of his beloved, he finds "not so much as a bone. It was as if she'd never been," and whereas before Ballard might have appeared as the ultimate voyeur, his eyes are now "dark and huge and vacant" (*CG* 107).

The last image points us toward another, final analogy. Ballard's antientropic project clearly does not succeed. However, neither does the demon's.

Now, if Ballard somehow resembles the demon, the demon logically resembles Ballard also: like McCarthy's mountain voyeur, the demon relies for his work on his powers of observation. It is a supreme spectator, a voyeur par excellence. This fact became a central aspect in its later reconceptualization as "an information device" (Floridi 64) and its consecutive exorcism on these grounds by the work of Leó Szilárd, Léon Brillouin, and later Rolf W. Landauer and Charles H. Bennett. Floridi sums up the combined results of their work as follows:

> Any information collection, such as monitoring the location and speed of the particles, requires energy. [...] Once information has been collected, the demon must perform some information processing, such as calculating exactly when to operate the trapdoor, in order to work effectively and hence decrease the entropy of the system. But computation uses memory [...]. Therefore, as our demon keeps operating, the entropy will decrease, yet its memory storage will increase. [...] [T]here is one computational operation which is necessarily irreversible, namely memory erasure. So the demon will need energy to erase its memory and this energy is what pays the entropy bill of the system under the counter, so to speak. (Floridi 65; see also Hayles 1990, 44–48)

Significantly, Bennett's "Demons, Engines and the Second Law" (1987) compared the demon's record of past measurements to yesterday's newspaper taking up valuable space the cleaning up of which would neutralize any benefit their information might have carried. *Child of God* appeared a full fourteen years before Bennett's paper. In this respect, it is an almost uncanny coincidence that in envisioning a scenario that so thoroughly reflects the mechanics and failings of the demon, McCarthy would even include "old newspapers" (*CG* 14) and draw attention to their "old news of folks long dead, events forgotten" (*CG* 15), which are burned in the process of Ballard's cleaning up the place. Ultimately, the second law reigns supreme, whether it is considered in terms of energy or information. Such seems to be the final implication of Ballard's trampling out "the prints of lesser life" (*CG* 140), which is an operation of memory erasure even before it is a symbolic act of violence.

In the dazzling weblike complexity of the dynamics of disorder the narrative of *Child of God* weaves between physics and violence, there is one last aspect to consider. While it is perhaps no more than a curious aside that mimetic desire, in mythical texts, frequently manifests itself as a phenomenon of (demonic) possession, I have suggested that in a structural sense, the transformation of reciprocal to unanimous violence, and the consecutive reconstruction of communal order effected by the scapegoat mechanism, works a lot like Maxwell's Demon works—or rather, does *not* work—with regard to the elementary disorder of molecules. Perhaps now it is time to explore this suggestion. For this, Ballard's role within the community has to be addressed.

Lester Is Legend:
Scapegoating the *Child of God*

Up to this point, I have discussed the psychology of *Child of God*'s protagonist and located him within the landscape of American mythology. Whether or not Lester Ballard can also be considered a scapegoat is subject to debate. Vereen Bell seems to say as much when he points out that "no one in this community is even remotely like Lester," and then qualifies this statement in that "the difference along the human spectrum is one of degree, not kind, and that difference is sustained by an almost apprehensive overcorrection, as if by some effect of collective auto-hypnosis" (1988, 57). In contrast, Guillemin rejects such views as "less than plausible," finding that the text does not "allow for a classification of Lester as a scapegoat of the violent collective" (2004, 44, 43). To argue his point, he cites the reader's empathy with the trauma of dispossession, the incorporation of Lester into a background of other misfits and outsiders, and the absence of ritual purification.

Inasmuch as the scapegoat in question is that of mimetic theory, I must disagree with this assessment. First, the reader's empathy with Lester—granted its premise—in no way precludes his functioning as a scapegoat with regard to his community. Neither does his symbolic reintegration into the community, even if it is only the marginal space assigned to its misfits. In fact, the reincorporation of the scapegoat is a central part of its role; its functional effectiveness continues to depend on its symbolic liminality. What is more, the novel presents no more than a glimpse of what happens after Ballard's death. One can by no means be certain that his exclusion does *not* at least temporarily restore social order, yet in the light of the ubiquity of social disintegration, it certainly seems unlikely. Nevertheless, the failure of social regeneration would only bespeak the increasing ineffectiveness of scapegoating that becomes a central point in the apocalyptic turn of Girard's thought. Alternatively, this failure could simply indicate that the crisis in Sevier County has passed the point of no return.[22] Of course, that the mimetic crisis is actually a fitting term to describe the state of things in *Child of God* has yet to be demonstrated.

According to Girard, the scapegoat, or surrogate victim, needs to be (or, be made) sufficiently *similar to* but *separate from* those for whom he is substituted. Therefore, whether or not Lester Ballard can be considered a scapegoat in this sense rests on how the text positions him in relation to his community, and how that community is presented. To be sure, once he turns into a necrophiliac and serial killer, Lester seems like a deadly aberration. As the previous discussion has shown, however, he turns out that way for two reasons. First, his role in the grand American myth as a failed farmer and displaced frontiersman propels him toward this end: in the narrator's words, he is the product of "a race that gives suck to the maimed and the crazed, that wants their wrong blood in its history and will have it" (*CG* 156). Second, on a psychological level, Lester's primary experience has been characterized as one of loss, dispossession, and rejection.

This last aspect deserves greater emphasis, as it is here that his fellow beings are directly involved. Ballard possesses the markers that make him sufficiently different from the rest of his community, including markers of mental and physical deformity. For want of any living kin or friend who is not himself an outcast, he is missing essential social bonds with his community. It is the precondition for his death not to spawn a circle of revenge as he becomes subject to vigilante justice. Time and again, Lester is shown reaching out for companionship; time and again, he is rejected. Apart from his inept attempts at courtship, the most significant scene is the one in which he tries to partake in a mass at Sixmile Church. Once again, visual cues are key to interpretation. Ballard's entering "with his hat in his hand" (*CG* 31) indicates his genuine desire to fit in. Lester is willing to submit to the rules of customary piety, yet the astonished congregation and even the priest ignore him: "Ballard had a cold and snuffled loudly through the service but nobody expected he would stop if God himself looked back askance so no one looked" (*CG* 32). The implication is that the pariah is not accepted, even in the House of God. Hillary Gamblin notes: "That this incident takes place in a church illustrates the severity of the ostracism, as religion serves as a main structure for human interaction in Ballard's community; despite the Christian ideal of charity, the community continues to ignore Ballard's existence" (29). To me, the point is less that "God himself fail[s] to influence Ballard" (Gamblin 29), than that, as the conditional implies, the *all-seeing* one would and does *not* look at him—at least in the eyes of the community. To the would-be Christians of Sixmile Church, this child of God is an unwanted one.

In terms of the community's "apprehensive overcorrection" that Bell mentions, the stories told about Ballard and his ancestors seem to indicate that he is but the latest, most malignant growth in a rotten family tree. His grandfather Leland is said to have evaded the Union Army draft and to have been a member of the vigilante White Caps. His granduncle was hanged in Mississippi: "Goes to show it ain't just the place. He'd of been hanged no matter where he lived. [. . .] I'll say one thing about Lester though. You can trace em back to Adam if you want and goddamn if he didn't outstrip em all" (*CG* 81). The community's attempt to distance itself as much as possible from the Ballards and Lester in particular is fairly obvious. It is written into the program of scapegoating to present the victim "as a monstrous exception to the general run of mankind; he resembles nobody, and nobody resembles him" (*VS* 72). So, too, is the consecutive transformation of the scapegoat into a quasi-divine figure after its expulsion. Though Ballard is never divinized, an impoverished echo of the transformation resonates within the community's tales, as Giles notes: "As shocked and disgusted as they are by his actions, the community feels a degree of genuine pride in having produced the sinner of sinners" (123).[23] Lester is legend.

Nevertheless, the facts of his deeds seem to impede upon the argument for Ballard as a scapegoat. He is undoubtedly guilty of many crimes, the worst of which are his murders; however, there is no actual need that the scapegoat, or surrogate victim, be innocent. In fact, the victim may be as guilty as those

who make him or her a scapegoat (*VS* 202). In this regard, it is interesting to
see that communal violence in the form of accusation settles upon Ballard
before he has committed any major crime. Falsely accused of rape, assault,
and battery, he is summoned to the office of the county sheriff, who is ironically named Fate Turner. Before his encounter with the alleged victim turns
violent, she does not at all seem sure about her testimony. Asked if Ballard is
not "the one," she hesitates and then exclaims: "Well. Yes. He's the one, the
one . . . It's them other two sons of bitches I want jailed. This son of a bitch
here . . ." (*CG* 51). The only conclusion to be drawn from this exchange is
that it was actually somebody else, two other men in fact, who assaulted and
potentially raped the woman. Ballard is, in fact, a surrogate. Though charges
are dropped with the unexplained disappearance of the plaintiff and after he
has spent nine days in prison, Fate Turner predicts his later crimes: "I guess
murder is next on the list ain't it? Or what things is it you've done that we
ain't found out yet?" (*CG* 56). Even before Lester becomes a murderer, he
appears as a pariah, surrogate victim, and scapegoat. In this case, the act of
scapegoating actually assumes the shape of a self-fulfilling prophecy, anticipating—and perhaps inspiring—the crimes that judicial violence professes
to be a response to.

In the Midst of Crisis:
The Community of Sevier in Sevier County

As much as *Child of God* is the story of its protagonist, it is also that of the
community that has rejected him. If Lester Ballard can be characterized as a
scapegoat and surrogate victim, then the state of the community should be
describable in terms of the sacrificial crisis. This crisis, once again, is essentially a crisis of distinctions, a failure of social order. On a literary or mythical
level, this crisis manifests itself through *symbols of desymbolization*, such as
rampant epidemics and natural catastrophes on the one hand, and incest or
patricide on the other. The first pairing stresses the crisis's collective character; the second expresses the disappearance of difference and hierarchy. To
be sure, on both the environmental and social level, these signs abound in
McCarthy's novel.[24] Consequently, Ballard's mayhem has to be understood
not as "an isolated aberration in a culture that otherwise works effectively"

to keep the contagion of violence at bay, but rather as "part of a more wide-spread crisis in Sevier County" (Ciuba 2007, 180–81).

The discussion above has already established that the soil and vegetation of Sevier County bear the marks of severe exploitation. In addition the novel's landscapes show widespread signs of environmental pollution. Frog Mountain is littered with "flattened beercans and papers and rotting condoms" (*CG* 20), and the muddy path leading to Reubel's junkyard is "packed with tins trod flat, with broken glass. The bushes strewn with refuse" (*CG* 26). At the same time, human constructs fare no better in this wilderness. Cars lie "upturned at either side of the road like wrecked sentinels" (*CG* 26); an old truck is rusting in the honeysuckle. As Guillemin has argued, these instances constitute variations on the machine in the garden motif, which here as elsewhere in McCarthy suggest "a shared tendency to entropy" (2004, 15). Likewise, the outhouse of Ballard's transitional home lies "collapsed in a shallow hole where weeds sprouted in outsized mutations," and the house itself is partly overgrown with "weeds high as the house eaves" (*CG* 13) and littered with the excrement of wild animals. The polluted, deteriorating environment is a mirror of society. On both levels, one finds signs of the disorder against which Ballard pits his will and projects his wrath.

Ecological and cultural entropy appear in union as the city of Sevierville is swept under by a disastrous flood. In this, the novel recalls the mythically inflated flood of *The Orchard Keeper*, though here mythical meanings are attached by the inhabitants of Sevierville rather than the narrator. While it is only the latest in a number of historically documented floods and major fires, the citizens attribute additional meaning to this particular flood. The sheriff jokingly asks his deputy if "You ain't seen a old man with a long beard buildin a great big boat anywheres have ye?" (*CG* 161), thus linking it to the biblical story of Noah's ark. Another citizen, Mr. Wade, tells of an old woman who claims the flood is "a judgment. Wages of sin and all that. I told her everybody in Sevier County would have to be rotten to the core to warrant this. She may think they are, I don't know" (*CG* 164). Indeed, though one man remarks that "trouble ought to make people closer" (*CG* 161), one learns earlier in the chapter that several goods, mostly guns, were stolen from the hardware store, and a woman, upon hearing about people gone missing, exclaims: "I never knew such a place for meanness" (*CG* 164). The sheriff's laconic answers—"Some people you cain't do nothin with" and "It used to be worse" (*CG* 162, 164)—downplay the matter. At this point, the reader has seen enough violence and depredation to know better.

After all, the signs of chaos and disintegration are pervasive on the social level, and violence seems to lurk just below the surface of the quotidian. Perhaps the most prominent mythic indicator of social breakdown, the motif of incestuous sexuality features prominently in *Child of God*, too, though it is not elementary to the plot as it is in *Outer Dark*. It is in the family of Reubel, the junkyard keeper, that the connection of incest, mimesis, and undifferentiation is most pronounced. To be sure, the family evokes many of the "poor white trash" stereotypes connected to the South. Reubel himself cannot say which of his nine daughters is "the oldest or what age" (*CG* 26). They bear names like Urethra, Cerebella, and Hernia Sue that he has adopted from a medical dictionary. While this might have "at least brought the differentiation of language to Reubel's nondescript progeny," the novel assigns none of the names to any particular daughter, and thus "they all dissolve into each other, becoming as indistinguishable for the reader as they are for their father" (Ciuba 2007, 184). Consequently, at the junkyard, cultural entropy runs rampant.

The same point is stressed in the daughters' promiscuous behavior. Like Marcel Proust's coquettes and young girls, the "sorority of junk" (Ciuba 2007, 184) attracts the desires of many entirely anonymous suitors, who arrive and leave at "all hours in all manner of degenerate cars." One by one, the girls fall pregnant, and even the "twelve year old beg[ins] to swell" (*CG* 27). As a reaction to this, the father beats his daughters and randomly fires a shotgun into the nightly shrubbery to chase away potential suitors. The junkyard air is heavy with sexuality and violence. All culminates in the violence of incest. Catching one of his daughters in flagrante delicto, Reubel chases her lover away. Consequently, he is "so inflamed by desire like his daughter's that he sexually assaults his own flesh" (Ciuba 2007, 185)—essentially copying her lover, becoming his double.[25] He stops only after she pleadingly assures him that the boy did not "dump a load" (*CG* 28) in her. Reubel's assault violates the rule of exogamy; in his conjunction of violence and incest, he does as Lester Ballard does with his corpses, assaulting not only his daughter but difference itself. In the poignant words of Gary Ciuba, "the violence of the incestuous rape is the violence of the dump itself—the disintegration of all distinctions, the intermixture of identities, the commingling of what should be kept apart" (2007, 186).[26]

The other part of the sacrificial crisis, violence, also surfaces frequently in Sevier County. Anecdotes of escalating boxing matches with gorillas or competitive shooting for pigeons loaded with firecrackers are part of the novel's black humor, yet the accounts of historical Sheriff Tom Davis's struggle against the White Caps serve as reminders of a more serious, well-documented kind of lynch violence and frontier justice—another theme *Child of God* shares with *Outer Dark*. The White Caps were a local vigilante group in the 1890s that much like the Ku Klux Klan, "began as a moralistic movement by the community to enforce conventional standards of sexual propriety," but then "degenerated rapidly into a form of collective criminal violence" (Cant 92). In the novel, one of the younger deputies thinks "it sounded like a good idea [...]. Keep people in line," yet this kind of thinking is quickly debunked by an elderly man, who describes the White Caps as "a bunch of lowlife thieves and cowards and murderers" (*CG* 165). If *Child of God* alludes to an earlier sacrificial crisis in its presentation of the haphazard violence of lynch justice, the public hanging of Pleas Wynn and Catlett Tipton represents the ritualistic resurgence of order:

> I remember there was still holly boughs up and Christmas candles. Had a big scaffold set up had one door for the both of em to drop through. People had started in to town the evenin before. [...] You couldn't get a meal in town, folks lined up three deep. Women sellin sandwiches in the street. Tom Davis was sheriff by then. He brung em from the jail, had two preachers with em and had their wives on their arms and all. Just like they was goin to church. All of em got up there on the scaffold and they sung and everybody fell in singin with em. Men all holdin their hats. [...] Whole town and half of Sevier County singin I Need Thee Every Hour. Then the preacher said a prayer and the wives kissed their husbands goodbye and stepped down [...] and down they dropped and hung there a jerkin and a kickin for I don't know, ten, fifteen minutes. (*CG* 167)

In tune with Girard's conception of sacrifice, the references to churchgoing and Christmas, the presence of the priests, and the devout character that accompanies the hanging emphasize its ceremonial character. The sheer size of the crowd attending this event stresses the unanimity of this publicly administered and highly ritualized act of violence. At the same time, the conjunction of collective murder with Christian rite repeats the major theme readers encounter in *Outer Dark*, namely the theme of Christianity collapsing into patterns of mythical thought and sacrificial action. Finally, as the witness telling the story explains, the act brought about "the end of White Cappin in Sevier County," which "people don't like to talk about [. . .] to this day" (*CG* 167–68). A former crisis was thus in fact resolved; however, its memory, or, at least, the memory of a dark chapter in American local history, is suppressed.[27]

Clichéd though it sounds, history has a habit of repeating itself. Sixty to seventy years after the hanging of Wynn and Tipton, the community of Sevier County shows all-too-obvious symptoms of rampant social disintegration. In a sense, the enraged citizens who abduct Ballard from his hospital room represent a resurgence of the same vigilante spirit that inspired the White Caps. If this is the case, it is because in the world of McCarthy, as in that of Hobbes or Freud, the fact of violence is an immutable constant in life:

> You think people was meaner then than they are now? the deputy said.
> The old man was looking out at the flooded town. No, he said. I don't.
> I think people are the same from the day God first made one. (*CG* 168)

I'm Supposed to Be Here:
Reintegrating Lester Ballard

At this point, the lines of the mimetic logic that informs *Child of God* are clearly defined: Flood, pollution, incest, necrophilia, violence—all alike are part of the same disease that infects Sevier County. I have argued that this disease is best described, socially and mythologically, in terms of the mimetic crisis, and metaphorically in terms of cultural entropy, which has a strong physical grounding in the actual thermodynamic process. In all of these areas, there can be no doubt that in the eyes of the fictional community as in the eyes of the reader, the pivotal role falls to Lester Ballard. Scapegoat or not, for the novel to make its point, it is essential that Ballard be somehow reintegrated into the community.

The stories people tell each other about Lester and his crimes already point in this direction. Vaguely reminiscent of the chorus in classical drama, their local narrators provide an additional point of view as well as "a necessary comic relief to the dark events by invoking the existence of an alternate moral universe beyond that of Ballard and the McCarthy narrator's studious avoidance of moral commentary or judgment" (Jarrett 131). However, their function goes beyond that. Evidently told at some point after the events of the novel, the very telling of these stories implies "that Lester has become a part of the mythology of his region and has thereby achieved, ironically, a place in the community" (Bell 1988, 52). In spite of such arguments, a case can be made that in his role as his community's shared nightmare, Ballard is still confined safely to the margins of society as his burial "with others of his kind [at] a cemetery outside the city" (*CG* 194) suggests.[28]

For the reader, this is hardly enough, nor is it in accordance with the gothic agenda of destabilization the novel openly subscribes to when it programmatically proclaims Ballard to be "much like yourself, perhaps" (*CG* 4). Though Ballard may remain deviant on the level of the story, he needs to be normalized on the level of discourse. This is achieved through McCarthy's use of a narrative focus, which in keeping with the novel's presentation of its protagonist, is often rightly called *voyeuristic*. Through the novel's minute observation of detail, narrator and reader alike become themselves watchers of the watcher, objectifiers of the narrative subject: "Just like Lester in the role of voyeur [. . .] observing his potential victims, we as readers are voyeurs. But instead of merely gaining access into a strange and dark world, we are also gazing at ourselves and what we could potentially be" (Madsen 25). In my view, the dark mirror works both ways: just as we may realize our potential to become like McCarthy's child of God, we also recognize the undeniable signs of Lester's shared humanity with us. How then does McCarthy humanize him?

Finding the first dead woman, he whispers into her ear "everything he'd ever thought of saying to a woman" (*CG* 88). One does not know whether these are words of vulgarity or of tenderness and romance. Ballard repeatedly blushes in openly dealing with women's sexuality (*CG* 29). Buying underwear and makeup for his dead lover, "his face afire [...] his hands still crammed in his rear pockets" (*CG* 98), his body language betrays a boyish insecurity. Black humor does its fair share to alleviate otherwise horrifying realities. Forgetting for a minute the necrophilic background of the shopping spree, the scene is likely to inspire not just amusement, but recognition, as Madsen argues: "Certainly the experience of looking at rows of lingerie with eyes 'slightly wild as if in terror of the flimsy pastel garments' is one that many husbands and boyfriends will recognize" (23). Moments like these are geared to make us relate, empathize, and identify. Likewise, having sex with the first corpse, perhaps out of shame, perhaps to shield himself from the narrator's and thus the reader's gaze, Ballard "pull[s] the blanket over them" (*CG* 92).

In turn, as we watch Ballard in his crimes, we might even be said to enter into a sort of uneasy complicity with him, as some critics have suggested; at the very least, normalcy is approximated in these snapshots that either shield Ballard from the viewer's gaze or offer close-ups of his unmistakably human reactions. In another at once pastoral and entropic scene, Ballard is found crying at "the diminutive progress of all things in the valley, the gray fields coming up black and corded under the plow, the slow green occlusion that the trees were spreading" (*CG* 170). Is his an outcry of loneliness, or perhaps of lost innocence—inspired by the sheer beauty of creation or his symbolic exile from the Garden of Eden and the community of man? Ballard himself may not know. Yet the scene shows that he is neither a cold-blooded psychopath nor an emotionless monster. I agree with Lydia Cooper:

> If Ballard is permitted any semblance of interiority, it is only to make the point that he only *seems* inexplicable. All humans, the narrator seems to argue, are inexplicably vicious creatures. All humans are likewise haunted by the same desires for respect, for connection, for love. Critics who ignore the interior revelations in this novel are therefore implicated by the novel's thematic argument. (2011b, 44)

Just like Ballard is at a loss at what to make of the verbose demonstrations of the blacksmith teaching him to "dress" his axe (*CG* 70–74), there is little hint that Ballard understands himself, or realizes the gravity of his deeds.[29] Sanity rapidly fades as violence and necrophilia hold sway, and by the time he assaults Greer, Ballard has utterly lost himself. Oddly enough, the loss of his arm and his impending victimization at the hands of the outraged vigilantes who abduct him from his hospital bed seem to bring about his return to sanity and, finally, a certain sense of identity. On his flight through mountainous caves, Ballard loses his pursuers as well as himself, only emerging after five days. As a church bus drives by, Ballard recognizes a small boy

> looking out the window, his nose puttied against the glass. There was nothing out there to see but he was looking anyway. As he went by he looked at Ballard and Ballard looked back. [...] He was trying to fix his mind where he'd seen the boy when it came to him that the boy looked like himself. This gave him the fidgets and though he tried to shake the image of the face in the glass it would not go. (*CG* 191)

Critics have offered widely varying interpretations of this scene, viewing it alternatively as an analog of the Christian resurrection, a kind of conversion of Lester heralding his acceptance of "society's disparaging vision of him" (Evenson 55), or else along the lines of Gnosticism and the Narcissus theme as another refused epiphany and sign of Lester's final submission (Luce 2009, 283).[30] Personally, I find that the scene and its context are so rich in mythical, religious, and psychological allusion that an interpretation that combines these elements should be the most elucidating. In this respect, the scene is remarkably reminiscent of what Jacques Lacan conceptualized in his "mirror stage," a term by which he describes the formation of a child's *I* through the perception of its apparently complete reflection. Like the child in this model, Ballard sees himself in the reflection of the boy, the difference being that the *I* is not "precipitated in a primordial form" (Lacan 2006b, 76), but rather postmaturely excavated in the developed form of the man, who is less physically than cognitively and emotionally incapacitated.

Mythological implications practically jump off the page: Lacan claims that the mirror stage establishes "a relation between an organism and its reality" (2006b, 78). The "fidgets" Ballard feels are "signs of malaise and motor uncoordination," and like Lacan's child, the now one-armed Ballard suffers from "anatomical incompleteness" and is "covered all over with red mud" (*CG* 191), that is, the "humoral residues of the maternal organism" (Lacan 2006b, 78). It is no coincidence either that Ballard's "scene of recognition" takes place after his return from the caves, where he had wished for "some brute midwife to spald him from his rocky keep" (*CG* 189). The latter was described both as "the innards of some great beast," like Jonah's whale, and as a mythic *vagina dentata*, which is suggested by the caves' "slavered," "wet," "bloodred," and "organic" look (*CG* 135). All of this indicates that the scene is Lester's symbolic rebirth following a *regressus ad uterum matris terrae*. Only here does Ballard recognize himself, reflexively, as a conscious being, the relation between his "*Innenwelt* and the *Umwelt*" (Lacan 2006b, 78), and thus, finally, the guilt he has laden upon himself. Consequently, he turns himself in at the hospital: "I'm supposed to be here" (*CG* 192).[31]

The aftermath of Ballard's surrender is sobering. Probably ruled non compos mentis, Ballard is "never indicted for any crime" but committed to the Knoxville state hospital, next to the cell of "a demented gentleman who used to open folks' skulls and eat the brains inside with a spoon." Ironically, Ballard has "nothing to say to a crazy man" (*CG* 193). In a sense, his confinement to a mental home is another, modern version of the *pharmakos*, promising "social reinforcement against aberration" (2006, 112) as Ellis suggests: "In modernity, outcasts are not longer 'cast out.' Perhaps because we have so thoroughly filled even the most distant spaces, we instead constrain our outcasts" (2006, 110). In 1965, Ballard dies of pneumonia. Subsequently, his body is subjected to what Ciuba rightly identifies as a modern, scientific version of the Dionysian sacrificial rite that is the *sparagmos* (2007, 198):

> He was laid out on a slab and flayed, eviscerated, dissected. His head was sawed open and the brains removed. His muscles were stripped from his bones. His heart was taken out. His entrails were hauled forth and delineated and the four young students who bent over him like those haruspices of old perhaps saw monsters worse to come in their configurations. (*CG* 194)

The text's insistence that it is not his remains, but simply *Ballard* who is "scraped from the table into a plastic bag" (*CG* 194) stresses for a last time "Lester's humanness at the point at which it is irrevocably extinguished" (Bell 1988, 67).

Finally, for all the violence that is running wild in Sevier County, one can raise considerable doubts about the assertion that the novel ends safely within the confines of culture, as Ciuba suggests. Even in death, Ballard is interred with other outcasts and pariahs outside the city limits, and while "the discipline of medicine keeps the severing and slicing from becoming a gratuitous hacking of the flesh, [as] it transforms the violence inflicted on the cadaver into a way of educating a new generation of healers" (2007, 198), this education leads only to a vision of "monsters worse to come." Ballard's reintegration is restricted to the realm of local mythology. At least, that is, if—grounded in the knowledge of our shared humanity, even as that humanity assumes monstrous forms—McCarthy's novel does not itself represent another, redemptive form of integration.

CHAPTER 4

A Sense of Judgment

Myth, Christianity, and Cosmic Disorder in *Outer Dark*

But the children of the kingdom shall be cast out into
outer darkness: there shall be weeping and gnashing of
teeth.

—Matthew 8:12 (KJB)

Of McCarthy's early novels, *Outer Dark* (1968) to this day remains the most
opaque. In stark contrast to the other works of the Appalachian period, the
story's setting is unspecific. The first in a number of journey narratives to follow, the novel references locales that identify the broader region once more
as Tennessee and possibly parts of northern Georgia. One would be hard-
pressed, though, to identify concrete models for its disconnected locales, or
to chart its characters' itineraries as they make their ways through the wilderness and rural townships that seem to be barely connected to one another.
Hence, *Outer Dark*—which tells the tale of the incestuous siblings Culla and
Rinthy Holme, the birth and abandonment of their child, and the Holmes'
respective journeys in search of the boy and flight from parental responsibility—is "a significant departure from McCarthy's almost trademark tendency

of grounding his fictions in an actual time and place" (Luce 2009, 62). Told in alternating chapters, the siblings' separate journeys are punctuated by chapters involving the perspective of the itinerant tinker who finds their newborn son, as well as a handful of short vignettes or interchapters presented in italics. The latter detail the deeds of three nightmarish men who follow in Culla's wake, murdering several of his brief acquaintances. Like most of the novel's personnel, they are not fleshed-out characters but rather abstractly defined entities. For these reasons, the novel is often classified as parabolic, allegorical, or fairytale- or dreamlike in character.

Unconcerned with the weight of sociohistorical minutiae, *Outer Dark* assumes a more universal quality. To be sure, the setting is vaguely identifiable as Tennessee. Even so, the novel's mythical and allegorical or parabolic features, as well as its strangely claustrophobic aesthetics, suggest that its darkness extends far beyond a few counties in one or two states. So much is readily apparent. What is less clear are the implications of this ill-defined gestalt. The more encompassing of interpretations range from Bell's early estimation of *Outer Dark* as a nihilistic exploration of man's existential homelessness within an indifferent cosmos denying "the grids of understanding we habitually impose upon it" (Bell 1988, 38), and Jarrett's view of the novel as a meditation on the themes of alienation, isolation, and the disintegration of the family as grounded within the historical collapse of Southern patriarchy, to Grammer's and Guillemin's (anti)pastoral readings. More recently, Luce has advanced a gnostic interpretation of *Outer Dark* as a "tragedy of the fleshbound human spirit" (2009, 66) entangled in archontic *heimarmene*, and Cant asserts that the novel represents a literary scourging of "the inhuman violence and intolerance inherent in Protestant fundamentalism" (86) within McCarthy's mythoclastic treatment of American exceptionalism.

Where these varied readings intersect is in their preoccupation with the mythical and biblical symbolism of the novel—such as the Oedipal theme or the itinerant "grim triune" (*OD* 129) of mysterious and deadly men—often emphasizing one over the other.[1] Interestingly, little attention has yet been paid to the complications involved in the artistic interactions of ancient myth *and* Christian revelation. What the novel articulates in its focus on incestuous familial disintegration and vigilante justice, I think, is actually the failure and perversion of Christianity, which like other authorities becomes a party to the crisis it attempts to mediate. However, I argue, McCarthy's mythoclasticism goes way beyond an indictment of Protestant fundamentalism, or even Christianity at large: What is special in *Outer Dark* as opposed to the other works of McCarthy's Appalachian period is the apparent cosmic scope of its crisis, which follows a specific logic the novel formulates through its mediation of mythological and biblical symbolism. This logic is essentially an apocalyptic one, as will be explained in the following. For the discussion of both these sides of *Outer Dark*, Culla's opening dream is of crucial significance.

Darkened Sun, Different Stars:
Culla's Dream and Crowd Dynamics

As a starting point, much akin to *The Orchard Keeper* and *Child of God* with their troubled mountain communities, or *Suttree* with its decrepit McAnally Flats, the narrative of *Outer Dark* presents the reader with a society in turmoil. To the general impression of isolation, disconnection, and spatiotemporal displacement, one can add the presence of epidemics and flooding. Another aspect is the apparent spread of doubles that is a part of the erosion of personal individuality; as will be shown, this process involves Culla in particular. Above all, it is the story's opening that defines its persistent sense of endemic social chaos.

The frequent comparison of the logic of the tale with that of a dream readily suggests itself, since the narrative proper opens with Rinthy waking a screaming Culla from a nightmare.[2] The dream reads at once like an apocalyptic prophecy and a highly condensed account of a sacrificial crisis. In the dream, Culla finds himself in a square among "a beggared multitude" composed of lepers, the disabled, and the blind. All listen intently to the admonitions of "a prophet" who announces a coming solar eclipse and promises that "all these souls would be cured of their afflictions." To the apparent surprise of the prophet, Culla cries out, asking whether he, too, can be cured. The prophet answers in a tentative, twice-qualified affirmative: "Yes, I think perhaps you will be cured" (*OD* 5). The sun is eclipsed as foretold, yet as it does not return, the crowd grows restless and turns against the dreamer Culla, setting upon him "with howls of outrage" (*OD* 6).

As has been widely recognized, Culla's nightmare is instrumental in defining both the grotesque, darkly gothic aesthetics as well as the dreamlike feel and flow of the narrative to follow. Insofar as Culla's guilt-ridden psyche governs his dream, his waking "from dark to dark and into a night more dolorous" (*OD* 5) is usually taken as a sign that "like a curse that he has brought upon the world, he now has remade the world in his own blighted image" (Bell 1988, 39). That is, Culla turns his inner dark into an outer dark that not only envelops the afflicted of the dream, but extends beyond it by arranging the subsequent "experience of the novel as a kind of dream" (Luce 2009, 62) governed by a metanarrative consciousness that can in part be identified with Culla himself.[3]

Looking into the underlying cause of the eclipse, Ellis proposes that—whereas with the return of the sun a "magical healing of blindness and leprosy would have taken place"—not only does Culla's guilt cause the eclipse, but his crime of sibling incest "is so serious that it circumvents the pleading of the other supplicants" (2006, 115). This reading, while perfectly fitting with regard to Culla's psychology, is problematic in two respects, one of them being textual consistency, the other having to do with causation. Firstly, it contradicts the testimony of the unassuming and helpful blind man Culla meets in the closing chapter of the novel. Recounting an event that mirrors Culla's dream in all but the eclipse—afflicted crowd, healing preacher, one incurable, and all—he offers Culla the consolation that "may be he [the prophet] weren't no true preacher" (*OD* 241). In other words, it may not be Culla who causes the eclipse and prevents the catharsis of the crowd. To keep his reading consistent, Ellis has to exonerate the dubious would-be healer of Culla's dream at the cost of this blind man, who is one of the few hopeful presences of the novel. So, he discredits him as possibly "a false prophet," and a "devil trickster" akin to Judge Holden in *Blood Meridian*, who (fraudulently) topples the Reverend Green (Ellis 2006, 127–28). Secondly, the interpretation is based on the premise that the incest *truly* is at the root of the cosmic crisis enveloping the novel. Therefore, it falls in exactly the kind of mythological pattern of thought that, I argue, *Outer Dark* and McCarthy's work in general subverts and demystifies.

While the question of the cause behind the symbolic darkness that, a few specks of hopeful light notwithstanding, enshrouds most of the narrative is an interesting one, it is secondary to the exemplary mythical structure of the dream itself. The latter so far has not been explored, its equally parabolic and apocalyptic nature not yet fully grasped.[4] To the extent of this oversight, answers are bound to remain incomplete, vague, or in the realm of conjecture. For the dream does much more than simply set the desolate tone and initiate the longer, dreamlike journey of the novel. As a matter of fact, it serves as a structural model that integrates many of the central mythical elements that the subsequent narrative will explore in some of its crucial scenes.

To see this, one needs to pay closer attention to the details of the mise-en-scène and the dynamics of the dream itself, specifically its crowd dynamics. A "delegation of human ruin" (*OD* 5), the crowd is composed of people stricken with various afflictions, but overall remains amorphous and ill-defined. The sole exceptions are the prophet and Culla, who seems not to belong with these "pariahs" as the text labels them. A sense of epidemic pervades as the narration emphasizes "blind eyes [...] puckered stumps and leprous sores" (*OD* 5), and the crisis assumes a second, more cosmic dimension with the advent of the eclipse. Prefiguring the dark, entropic earth of *The Road*, Culla's dreamworld grows "chill" and then "cold and more black and silent," simultaneously purveying the sense of a deeper disorder that is both cosmic and temporal as the sky shows "the stars of another season." Subsequently, the situation escalates, with the crowd growing first restless, then desperate, and finally "seething and [. . .] mutinous." Suddenly, an accusation hangs in the air as "voices were being raised against him" (*OD* 6), and the crowd collectively turns on Culla, who only by being woken by Rinthy is saved from suffering—like Pentheus in *The Bacchae*—some dream version of the Dionysian *sparagmos*, of being torn limb from limb by the murderous crowd.[5]

Associations to Attic tragedy are reinforced when we consider that, in an early draft, McCarthy actually set the dream within "an ancient city" (91/8/1, 157), a sign that we find ourselves within the realm of archaic, sacrificial logic.[6] In truth, the dream thematically prefigures a number of lynchings and attempted lynchings that punctuate *Outer Dark* with a certain regularity, establishing the pattern and model for crowd dynamics in the novel. Once sufficiently enraged and given an object against which to vent its wrath and confusion, the formerly peaceful crowd *mob*ilizes, literally becoming a mob. If one excludes temporarily the psychological element of Culla's guilt, it seems in fact hard *not* to read this dream as an example of "mimetic snowballing"

(*ISS* 43) rapidly uniting the formerly confused crowd that always "seeks action but cannot affect natural causes" and "therefore looks for an accessible cause that will appease its appetite for violence" (*SG* 16).

A charge is raised. As if he could be held responsible for the eclipse, a single person is groundlessly blamed for the crisis. This person is Culla. His dream *sparagmos* not only thematically and structurally, but also linguistically reflects this terrible dynamic. In describing Culla as "caught up in the crowd" (*OD* 6), McCarthy uses the English equivalent of the Latin *in turba*. To recall, *turba* is the etymological root of many words across the Germanic and Romance languages—among them disturbance, trouble, and turbulence—that reveal "curious semantic analogies" between the sacrificial crisis Girard envisions and the contemporary scientific "language of order through disorder" (1984, 86), pointing toward certain shared qualities. More pertinently, the phrase is frequently used in ancient Roman texts, particularly in Livy's *History of Rome*, to refer to acts of crowd violence against outstanding individuals. For example, it features prominently in various versions of the respective deaths of the mythological enemy twins Romulus and Remus (*SG* 93).[7] Structurally, thematically, and semantically, then, Culla's dream introduces two major elements McCarthy explores throughout *Outer Dark*: the dynamics of the crowd transforming into a lynch mob, and a sense of acute crisis and pervasive disorder, which here assumes equally eschatological, cosmic, and social dimensions.

Oedipus Re-Imagined:
The Incest Motif and the Scapegoat

In examining the causes of the crisis, scholars have turned toward the myth that represents the flipside of the novel's Christian subtext, that is, to the incest motif and the Oedipal model of the story. As can already be inferred from the discussion of paternal figures in *The Orchard Keeper* and *Child of God*, the relation between father and son in McCarthy is a complicated and evolving one that has been the subject of various examinations. Beginning with the looming *absence présente* of the father in "A Drowning Incident," whose killing of the family dog's puppies incites the vengeful wrath of his young son, or the family-abandoning ways of Kenneth Rattner in *The Orchard Keeper*, and continuing to the drunk, broken, and barely present fathers of *Suttree*, *Blood Meridian*, and *All the Pretty Horses*, the early to mid McCarthy consistently portrays his paternal figures as weak, irresponsible, neglectful, threatening, tyrannical, or simply absent. "From the early Southern novels to those set in the Southwest, McCarthy's fiction enacts the death, absence or denial of the father" (Jarrett 21). With the possible exception of the child-murdering, pedophiliac yet paternalistic figure of Judge Holden, the character of Culla Holme constitutes the nadir of fatherhood in McCarthy. In him, we're thus haunted by the specters of both one of our archetypal myths and one of our fundamental taboos.

The Role of Incest

The predominantly negative portrayal of father figures and father–son relationships to some has suggested a reflection of tensions between Cormac and Charles McCarthy Sr.[8] Ellis biographically reads *Outer Dark* as "a confluence of the myth of Oedipus" and "the anxiety that a serious young writer hardly thirty years old may have felt at the birth of his first child" (2006, 114, 124), the name of Culla Holme possibly being a portmanteau of his first wife Lee Holleman and their son Cullen. Inspired by McCarthy's aforementioned acknowledgment of "fact that books are made out of books" (Woodward 1992, 31), another group has singled out the young writer's ambivalent stance of admiration and fear of influence with regard to his own literary fathers and their traditions, from which he seeks to emancipate himself.[9] In this view, the struggle to find his own literary voice for the early McCarthy involves the abandonment of "the structuring metaphors of the family romance and miscegenation by which Faulkner's fiction had defined the South and its past" (Jarrett 21). Essentially, this last view conceives of the writer's relationship to his literary ancestors as that between Amadis de Gaulle and Don Quixote, that is to say as one of *externally mediated* mimesis.

In sum, it is therefore hardly surprising that Oedipal themes have been a common thread running through practically all of McCarthy's novels from the beginning. Nowhere is this more apparent than in *Outer Dark*, which, for all intents and purposes, can be considered a retelling of the Greek myth.

Ellis and Cant have pointed out a number of intriguing parallels and variations. Chief among these is Culla's son's status as the "actual product of incest,
rather than its future perpetrator," and as living witness to an act of incest
that has already happened and thus presents a more "direct threat to Culla
than does the birth of Oedipus to King Laius," which substantiates his fear
that "the son's existence will eclipse his own" (Ellis 2006, 114–15).[10] Finding
parallels in the story of Oedipus and the plague that ravages the city of Thebes, critics have tended to regard the Holmes' violation of the fundamental
incest taboo as the metaphorical and/or actual cause of social upheaval in
Outer Dark. Jay Ellis posits that the novel's "gothic darkness and desolation
point directly to Culla Holme's breaking of an ancient taboo" (2006, 115).
Kenneth Lincoln regards the plot as "an apocryphal antiparable of inbred
sin" (41). Ann Fisher-Wirth sees the incest as "an archetypal, originary transgression" the significance of which "seems to extend far beyond the specific,
individual act" (139). Finally, John Ditsky muses that "it is almost as if these
two poor souls [. . .] had let loose all the demons in the world by the fact of
their fornication" (6).

Such causal attributions appear as a case of reasoning post hoc, ergo
propter hoc. They make sense, however, to the extent that they treat the incest
as a naturalistic phenomenon (rather than as a symbol) within a novel that
is otherwise read either as a warped dream or distorted record of the psycho-
pathology of its male protagonist, or else as a myth or fairy tale, where such
phenomena can disregard the laws of logic and natural causation to wholly
disproportionate effects. That is to say, they make sense insofar as incest is
interpreted *psychologically* or *mythically.* Outside such paradigms, though,
one has to ask the same question John Grammer asks: "How is it that incest
calls forth such dire retribution? And whence, in McCarthy's apparently
godless universe, does this retribution come?" (36). Consequently, another
school of critics has tended to regard the incest not as a cause, but as a symbol or symptom. In pastoral and Faulknerian interpretations, the incest thus
becomes a literary reflection of the breakdown of Southern patriarchy in the
wake of the Civil War and Reconstruction period, or, more generally, of "a
social order which, in its anxiety to avoid contact with the corrupting outer
world, ends by collapsing inward on itself" (Grammer 37–38).

As I have argued in my discussion of *The Orchard Keeper,* the collapse
of the pastoral order can both be accommodated by and further elucidated

within the anthropological concept of the sacrificial crisis. In his essay "Discovering Fourthspace in Appalachia," James R. Giles summarizes Girard's view of incest as "one of the oldest of human taboos [. . .] because, like murder, it assaults communal order in the most profound of ways. By destroying culturally accepted distinctions, it bequeaths chaos" (112). He interprets Culla's persistent refusal to name his son as a reflection of incest as "a sin too fundamentally unsettling to be acknowledged," and again ends with a causal attribution, namely that "Culla violated one of the most basic of cultural taboos and thus instigated a sacrificial crisis that profoundly threatens the social order" (120). While Giles's summary of the destructuring power of incest is apt, his conclusion, in blaming Culla, elides an essential insight of mimetic theory: firstly, the destructuring power is almost wholly symbolic; secondly, and more importantly, the accusation of incest itself is a part of the mythical distortions meant to exonerate the community from the collective violence it vents upon its scapegoats. Just like patricide, which *Outer Dark* replaces with infanticide, incest as a myth motif is at once a signifier of disintegration vis-à-vis the family, and the clichéd default accusation leveled against the alleged originator of the social crisis. It is not the actual *object* of the prohibition, nor is it the actual *cause* of the crisis. The latter must be sought in the fountain of reciprocal violence that springs from the well of mimetic rivalry and concomitant undifferentiation.

To take a step back, the elementary fact of the transgression may not be as clear-cut as is universally assumed. Time and again, we see Culla accused of crimes he did not commit, such as the murder of squire Salter and the ferry man, or the accidental death of Vernon in the hog stampede. Given these examples of his innocence, what exactly gives us the conviction he is guilty in this case? If we disengage ourselves but for a moment from the a priori assumption that there actually *was* an act of incest, we have to concede that we never actually witness the act. I would go so far as to claim that, in fact, there is nothing about the book's text but its dust jacket blurb to assure us that the incest took place: all of the evidence the text itself suggests is circumstantial or inferential.

One such piece of evidence is Rinthy's statement to the doctor that "I wasn't ashamed" (*OD* 156); a second is Culla's failure to deny the triune leader's assessment that "you got this thing here in her belly your own self" (*OD* 233). Yet the first statement could just as easily refer to the baby being born out of wedlock—the conversational subject that immediately precedes Rinthy's presumptive admission. And threatened as he is by the triune, Culla's silent lack of protest could be simply that, without necessarily implying admission. The most damning piece of evidence, no doubt, is Rinthy's single confessional "Yes" toward the tinker's probing questions—"It ain't hisn [Culla's], he said. [. . .] Is it?" (*OD* 193)—in their emotional dispute about the child's custody.[11] Before he implicitly concedes the truth by storming off to the haunting sounds of Rinthy's agonized sobs, the resentful, raging tinker sevenfold denies Rinthy's statement as a lie. By surmising "You'd try it woudn't ye? You lyin little bitch" (*OD* 194), he frames it as a ruse of hers to get him to surrender the child back to her. Add to this the novel's Oedipal resonance, the guilt that weighs so visibly on Culla as to inspire the suspicion of near everyone he meets, his paranoid refusal to let even a midwife come anywhere near Rinthy in her hours of labor, and finally his shameful act of abandoning the child in the woods, and all initial suspicion seems confirmed.

Still, if there is any lesson to be drawn from René Girard's and Sandor Goodhart's readings of *Oedipus Rex*,[12] it is to be suspicious about our suspicions: What if the tinker's initial reaction were the right one? When a helpful lawyer asks whether Rinthy is married, she seems uncertain: "No, she said. Then she looked up and said: I mean I ain't now. I was but I ain't now" (*OD* 150). In an earlier draft, she had yet replied with a plain "No" (91/8/1, 126). Yet the novel has Rinthy claiming to be "a widow," seemingly telling a lie that, however one views it, seems utterly unnecessary. But what if it were not a lie? Conversely, what if her forced confession toward the tinker were, in fact, a falsehood?[13] Prior to the child's birth, we know next to nothing about the siblings' past, the whereabouts of their own parents, or how they came to live in their remote cabin in the woods, in a county where nobody seems to know them. The Holmes' enigmatic past harbors a vast potential for explanations *other* than fraternal incest for how Rinthy could have conceived the child, including the death of an otherwise unknown husband, or perhaps another, paternal act of incest.[14] The provocative question implicit here is this: Could it be that for more than forty years, Cormac McCarthy has duped his entire readership?

We may be playing devil's advocate. Admittedly, the case against incest seems rather weak, but it is nonetheless a possibility to be admitted for reasonable doubt before the readerly jury.[15] It is a testament to the charm of the mythical pattern that so far no one seems to have entertained the idea that it never happened, and I will henceforth resume the consensus position that it did. My defensive stance, though, is in itself begging the true question, the one Grammer intuitively asks: Even if there was an act of incest, how could it possibly account for the crisis that has befallen the world? The answer is that *it cannot*—lest we are caught in myth, caught in the same structure that propels Culla to commit the graver sin of abandoning his newborn son in the woods. In the words of an earlier draft, Culla thus "broke the law of God" in order "to right the settin aside of man's law" (91/8/1, 146), yet it is the human law that is on the side of myth, the one that propels the sacrificial decision (Lat. *decidere*—to cut off) that initiates the action to follow.[16] The cause of the crisis must lie elsewhere.

Marks of the Victim in *Outer Dark*

Outer Dark abounds with examples of victims who are innocently drawn into the circle of accusation and punishment. Expectedly, it is upon strangers, marginal figures, and otherwise distinguished individuals that violence vents itself. Outside Culla's dream, two early examples follow in the wake of the murder of squire Salter and a number of recent grave robberies in Cheatham County. Initially, several men try to apprehend Culla; being unsuccessful, the vigilantes then substitute "two itinerant millhands" (*OD* 95), who are unceremoniously hanged in a field. Ironically, Culla is later hired to dig graves for them in "the place for buryin anybody that ain't spoke for" (*OD* 145)—likely a cemetery for the outcast and lawless not unlike Ballard's final resting place in *Child of God*. As strangers who are blamed for the death of squire Salter, they are clearly identified as scapegoats.

In another twist of fate, it is then none other than the man who previously insisted on leaving the corpses hanging for a few days as "kindly good advertisin for the public peace" (*OD* 141) who shortly thereafter joins these victims in their tree (*OD* 146). This man is the auctioneer Clark, who is identifiable by his "dirty white suit" (*OD* 139, 146). The fact that Clark is not only a businessman and storeowner but also an eminent town official exemplifies that it is not necessarily the lowest in the social ladder that become victimized. What is more, Clark is explicitly identified not just as representing but as *being* "the law" (*OD* 141). This articulates something fundamental about the power dynamics between institutional authority and the crowd: "The former usually get the better of the latter, but in times of crisis the reverse is true. Not only does the crowd get the upper hand but it also becomes a kind of melting pot in which even authorities that seem unshakable eventually collapse" (*SG* 115).

Lynchings and vigilante justice are an infamous fact of U.S. history, particularly in the South. So is the less overtly violent process of systemic corruption to which, as Dianne Luce's research has established, the idiosyncratic Tennessean Justice of Peace or Squire System was highly susceptible.[17] As to his portrayal of social authorities in crisis, McCarthy is both anthropologically and historically accurate. *Outer Dark* presents us with authorities thoroughly undermined by corruption, participating in the vigilante justice the legal system is supposed to contain, or else being wholly consumed in the process. The second squire, who abuses his legal authority to exploit Culla, is an example of the first case, squire Salter exemplifies the last scenario, and Clark fits either, first joining the lynch mob and then becoming its victim.

If we interpret the triune as the embodiment of the accusatory process of mobilized lynch violence, as I will do in the following, the line of their victims is extended further by Salter, by the reclusive snake-trapper Culla meets, and by the itinerant tinker himself, all of whom the triune murders in cold blood. Again, the snake trapper and the tinker share the decisive nonquality of lacking any social connections. The tinker openly addresses this lack and the fact of his ostracism. Having suffered at the hands of his fellow men, he resentfully claims Rinthy's "chap," essentially as a kind of compensation for his persecution:

> I give a lifetime wanderin in a country where I was despised. [...] I've not got soul one in this world save a old halfcrazy sister that nobody never would have like they never would me. I been rocked and shot at and whipped and kicked and dogbit from one end of this state to the other and you cain't pay that back. Them accounts is in blood and they ain't nothing in this world to pay em out with. (*OD* 192–93)

Hence, it is not far-fetched for Cant to associate the tinker with "the Wandering Jew, the mythic scapegoat for the death of Christ" (3), and Guillemin sees him as another double and older version of Culla (2004, 62–63) who, in the novel's final stage, appears as the one truly affected by Rinthy's prophecy, "You won't never have no rest" (*OD* 194).

From a Girardian perspective, what is remarkable up to this point is not just the sheer number of these actual victims. In keeping with the enduring eclipse of Culla's prophetic dream, none of these collective murders actually resolves the crisis. If anything, the darkness becomes thicker as the novel progresses. In fact, it may be the very inefficacy of sacrificial violence that calls for the murder of ever more victims.

This brings me to the two central victims of the text, namely Culla and his infant son. To recall, the selection of scapegoats is contingent upon the victim's simultaneous difference and basic similarity to the people of its community. The latter is basically a given, as violent undifferentiation of the crisis renders people one another's mimetic doubles, serving at once as a sign and condition of the crisis. In this spreading of doubles, Culla presents a true nexus. Both the tinker and the patriarchal leader of the triune are often regarded as his doubles, or rather psychological projections.[18] More importantly, Culla is repeatedly struck by his own reflection in watery surfaces and seems permanently tied up with his own shadow (*OD* 13, 28, 32, 47, 79, 131, 134, 242). After he has abandoned his son in the woods, it seems to the tinker who finds his erratic tracks "as if their maker had met in this forest some dark other self in chemistry with whom he had been fused" (*OD* 20). Upon their first meeting, the triune's leader insinuates doubts as to Culla's identity, "I think maybe you are somebody else" (*OD* 179), and in their second encounter, he even asserts Culla's fundamental sameness with everyone else (*OD* 235). At the same time, the Holmes' remote and isolated life in the woods places them at a sufficient distance from the rest of society that they do not share any social ties to speak of, a condition they share with most of the novel's victims.

Consequently, to view Culla, who is perpetually on the run and accused of crimes he did not commit, as a prime example of the mythical scapegoat practically suggests itself. In a novel that reverberates strongly with the Oedipal themes of maternal incest, patricide, and physical blindness, for which McCarthy substitutes sibling incest, infanticide, and spiritual blindness, Culla is a latter-day Oedipus, even limping toward the end of the narrative.[19] More to the point, like Oedipus, he is a scapegoat par excellence. In the episode of the Gadarene swine, which has yet to be analyzed, his would-be lynchers tellingly debate whether they should "hang him" or "thow him off the bluff" (*OD* 223), the latter being the preferential method of ritual execution reserved for the Greek *pharmakoi*.

As a victim Culla is surpassed solely by the son he abandons. The child becomes a surrogate for Culla himself as well as the final and true sacrificial victim of the novel. This role is laid out from the start, as Culla's view of his child is governed by mythical distortion of incestual dread. At his birth, the baby seems to him like something out of a nightmare, "a beetcolored creature," "a skinned squirrel" with an "old man's face" (*OD* 14–15) that he only refers to as an "it." Upon his disoriented return to the glade where he abandoned the child, he sees "a shapeless white plasm" that he "would have taken [. . .] for some boneless cognate of his heart's dread had the child not cried" (*OD* 17–18). Such distortion is possible in mythical perception, where "incestuous propagation leads to formless duplications, sinister repetitions, a dark mixture of unnamable things" (*VS* 75). Effectively, McCarthy's prose casts the child as a veritable amalgamation of the *crisis of distinctions*—as something amorphous defying all classification and not even differentiated by a name.

As the triune's leader tells Culla during their first meeting: "If you cain't name something you cain't claim it. You cain't talk about it even. You cain't say what it is" (*OD* 117). Their second confrontation counts among the most unsettling scenes in all of McCarthy. The child is found inexplicably burned, muted, and mutilated to the loss of one eye,[20] in place of which there is only an "angry red socket like a stokehole to a brain in flames" (*OD* 232). Culla cannot bear to look at his son. In his view, which governs the narrative perspective, the child has become something animalistic and monstrous, "a dressed rabbit, a gross eldritch doll with ricketsprung legs and one eye opening and closing softy like a naked owl's" (*OD* 235), seeming to constantly stare at him in silent accusation. The son is subsequently sacrificed, his throat ritualistically slit by the triune's leader—Culla's double—his blood cannibalized by the mute imbecile of the group: his own double. Yet, even after this ultimate, horrendous act of violence against the most innocent of victims, there is no indication that this sacrifice does anything to lift the darkness of McCarthy's second novel.

Some Witless Paraclete:
Apocalyptic Symbolism and Christian Failure

Little attention has been paid so far to the relation and interplay between mythical and Christian symbolism in *Outer Dark*. Scholarship tends to treat either to the exclusion of the other, or else makes no systematic distinction between the two. Perhaps such is to be expected within the context of secularized modernity, where following thinkers like Friedrich Nietzsche and James G. Frazer, Christianity is seen as just another mythology. In contrast, mimetic anthropology, which emphasizes both continuities *and* discontinuities between Christianity and ancient sacrificial religions, argues that Christianity, building on Judaism, *demystifies* mythology and pagan religion at a fundamental level. From that vantage, the failure of sacrifice in *Outer Dark* is not all that surprising.

In a slow revelation that starts in the Hebrew Bible and culminates in the narratives of the Passion, the secret workings of the sacrificial structure are exposed with the knowledge that the victim is a scapegoat, that she or he is innocent. This knowledge begins to assert itself in a general concern for victims that Nietzsche, in *Zur Genealogie der Moral*, identifies as the cultural legacy of Christianity and that he reviles as "slave morality" (2007, 266–77; *ISS* 173). However we evaluate it, granted the mimetic premise, this ethical and epistemological shift effectively undermines the sacrificial foundation on which society rests. With the Christian revelation, the historical narrative is fundamentally changed, as "no further sacralization is possible. No more myths can be produced to cover up the fact of persecution. The Gospels make all forms of "'mythologizing' impossible since, by revealing the founding mechanism, they stop it from functioning. That is why we have fewer and fewer myths all the time [. . .] and more and more texts bearing on persecution" (*TH* 174). In this view, the narrative consequence of the revelation, which transfers knowledge of the innocence of Jesus to that of other victims, is that as knowledge spreads, sacrificial society is increasingly incapable of fashioning real myths, instead producing only texts of persecution that are more readily identified as the fabrications of the murderers. This is so in part because the twofold metamorphosis of the scapegoat, first into a monstrosity and second into a quasi-divine savior, is cut short after the first transformation: We regularly fantasize monsters and abject others. We rarely transform them into gods anymore.

Another consequence is that in exposing the scapegoat, society is deprived of its ultimate response to crisis. At the one end of the revelatory process, Girard locates the Apocalypse, which thus ceases to be a divinely set capstone to history and instead is reenvisioned as a decidedly *human* spiral of mimetic conflict that inexorably veers toward total destruction. Such seems to be the logical conclusion of a now nuclear-powered and technologically enhanced humanity unable (or unwilling) to get rid of its violence other than in the form of a scapegoat. That is why, according to Girard, Jesus warns his disciples that he has come "not [. . .] to bring peace, but a sword" (Mt. 10:34; *ISS* 159). To this bleak outlook, the Gospels provide an alternative, utopian vision—elusive and untapped, yet persistent and ever-potential—in the kingdom of heaven. The latter, Girard holds, must be identified with an unconditional commitment to nonviolence and the commandment of charity and neighborly love.

Alas, to paraphrase Alfred Adler, it is easier to fight for one's ideals than to abide by them. In this regard, Christianity has historically failed. It is this failure that is at the heart of Christian apocalypticism. One does not have to delve too deeply into *Outer Dark*'s symbolism to see its signs everywhere. After walking for miles to get some food and sweets for Rinthy, Culla is turned away at a local store, the owner reasoning that "We still christians here" (*OD* 26). Giles points out McCarthy's "deliberate withholding of the uppercase C from 'christians,'" and argues along the same lines as Cant that the novel articulates a "condemnation of a southern Christian fundamentalism that denies support to those who exist outside it. Such 'faith,' McCarthy seems to imply, is divorced from any meaningful association with Christ" (114).[21] Certainly, the inhabitants of the novel's world are more preoccupied with appearances, for example whether a person has been "saved" or "baptized" (*OD* 109, 225), than with adherence to Christian ethics. Worse, the church itself becomes the gathering place for the lynch mob (*OD* 84), and a professed priest initially advocates hanging in favor of driving the wrongfully accused over a cliff because "Tain't christian" (*OD* 224). Like other authorities, Christianity is hollowed out to a mere shell of wholly peripheral social dictates, devoid of its original ethical core, and consequently absorbed in communal violence.

The inverse of this hollowing out is embodied by Rinthy Holme, who represents something closer to the ideals of the kingdom. Constantly associated with light and "described in terms of innocence and even a kind of virginal purity" (Arnold 1999, 48), she is often compared to Lena Grove in Faulkner's *Light in August* (Bell 1988, 34; Guillemin 2004, 86; Cant 86). Even though she seems ignorant of any formal religious education (or any education for that matter) and may not know whether she has "been saved" (*OD* 109), Rinthy, like no other character, embodies Christian virtues like humility, kindness, diligence, and most of all love. Culla is usually viewed with suspicion and even hostility; Rinthy—perhaps by way of positive mimesis—inspires the kindness of almost everyone she meets. In another sharp contrast to Culla, who even at being found out in his lie about the baby's death (*OD* 33) shifts the blame onto her, there is no sense in which she condemns, reviles, or misrepresents him to others. Where she has nothing good to say, she prefers to remain silent.

Furthermore, Rinthy abhors all violence, feeling "sinkened in [her] heart" (*OD* 116) about the two mill hands' deaths, even after she hears what they supposedly did. Arnold identifies her name as a diminutive of Corinth, relating it to Paul's First Epistle to the Corinthians (1999, 48). With its famous praise of faith, hope, and love (1 Cor. 13), Corinthians almost perfectly characterizes the humble, trusting, hopeful, and enduring Rinthy, whom Ann Fisher-Wirth further identifies with the *mater dolorosa*, the grieving Virgin Mary (134).[22] Though ending tragically, her path therefore offers a clear if not formally Christian alternative to that of Culla, which respectively entails a cyclical return of sacrificial violence and aimless wandering, and which, translated to a world where the sacrificial release has been suspended, threatens to drown in its own violence.

The inevitable choice between annihilation and love will find its climactic dramatization in *The Road*. Yet, it is with *Outer Dark* that McCarthy begins to spell out the apocalyptic implications of his view of human behavior, which are henceforth more fully realized in *Blood Meridian*. In this sense, Giles's observations and Cant's reading of the novel's mythoclastic project as an indictment of Southern Baptism and Protestantism hit the mark, but do not go far enough. The apocalypticism of *Outer Dark* is more complicated than it first appears. Its theme of judgment that many have noted extends beyond the suspicious and prejudiced reactions people display toward Culla, its instances of vigilante justice, and even the triune's theological nature as "agents of retribution and thus figures of judgment" (Arnold 1999, 49).

In the biblical sense the Apocalypse involves not simply the end of the world, and the literal revelation of God's plan, but the judgment of humanity as such, which is imagined as a final, divine act of jurisprudence. As I will argue in the following, what is really "on trial" in *Outer Dark* is the historical failure of Christianity as a whole, its failure to live up to its own principles, to sow peace and love, and to effectively rid the world of violence. What the novel consistently shows instead is Christianity reverting to mythical ways of thought and sacrificial modes of action; what it implies is the apocalyptic consequence of this failure that later works explore more fully, and on a larger scale.

Outer Darkness and Salt Gone Stale

The unending eclipse of Culla's dream is programmatic too, in that—barring a few hopeful specks provided by the presence of Rinthy in her "amnion of light" (Luce 2009, 80)—it is never truly lifted. Here, the titular metaphor of the "outer darkness" becomes important. As many critics have noted, the phrase comes from the Gospel of Matthew, where it is used by Jesus to denote a space opposite to the kingdom of heaven. Often seen as closely related to the last judgment, this darkness is usually associated, theologically, either with hell (Arnold 1999, 46) or, more generally, with a state of separation from God. The latter, Frye identifies as McCarthy's view of "the absolute condition of the human experience" (2009, 29). Repeatedly, Matthew refers to this "outer darkness" where "there will be weeping and gnashing of teeth": first in connection to the centurion of Capernaum (Mt. 8:12), and a second time in the parable of the royal wedding (Mt. 22:13). These instances are often read as valuations of true faith and adherence to the message of Jesus and the prophets—though their followers be gentiles—in contrast to those who are nominally "children of the kingdom" but do not act according to its ethics. In Dianne Luce's words, the phrase thus denotes "a spiritual state of pale belief or unconviction" (2009, 64).[23]

Considered within the context of the themes of blindness and spiritual ignorance, this interpretation correlates with Arnold's association of the phrase with the plight of the uncommitted of the third canto in Dante

Alighieri's *Inferno*, who are wanted by neither heaven nor hell, as well as with Revelation's condemnation of those who are "neither hot nor cold" and therefore spat out (Rv. 3:16)—both characterizations that Arnold finds "thoroughly applicable to Culla himself" (1999, 52–53). Arnold's suggestion is reinforced when, looking at the following verse, one finds that it also touches on the themes of blindness and delusion. The verse addresses those who think themselves rich and without need, but are truly "wretched, pitiable, poor, blind, and naked" (Rv. 3:17). Regardless of whether one reads the illusory wealth as a material or spiritual one, the phrase is further remarkable in that it provides a bridge to a third mention of "outer darkness" in the Gospel of Matthew.

This third, more ambivalent use of the phrase occurs in the well-known parable of the talents (Mt. 25:14–30). Therein, a certain master rewards two profitable servants and punishes an unprofitable one. Given its inherent resonance with the Calvinist belief in economic success as a sign of God's favor and personal predestination for salvation, which according to Max Weber's famous thesis played such an important role in the development of American capitalism, and finds its purest literary articulation in the Horatio Alger story, one is reminded of the figure of squire Salter in *Outer Dark*.[24] The squire self-righteously asserts that "shiftlessness is a sin" and espouses working "daybreak to backbreak for a Godgiven dollar" (*OD* 47), even as he himself exploits both Culla and his black servants. There is, then, a sense in which the triune, which seems to have emerged "out of a proletarian mural" (*OD* 35) and uses a hook brush in its killing of Salter, can be seen as partially enacting "a type of revenge against the ideology of the propertied classes, who associate wealth with morality and ignore their own exploitation of the lower classes" (Jarrett 28). The second, nameless squire of the text, who equally misuses his judicial authority to exploit Culla for trespassing, simultaneously endorses and questions the same ideology: "My daddy always claimed a man made his own luck. But that's disputable, I reckon" (*OD* 207). So, the association of the parable with the outer dark assumes a decidedly ironic quality, condemning exploitative greed as opposed to McCarthy's cardinal virtue of neighborliness.

Yet, insofar as one can relate this capitalist ideology to the parable of the talents in particular or to Christian ethics in general as squire Salter explicitly does, McCarthy's critique is less to be seen as part of a Marxist attack on

American capitalism, as Jarrett suggests, than as a part of the larger critique of Christianity gone astray.[25] As elsewhere in the novel, names are significant here: Divorced from the core virtue of charity, *Salt*er is a prime example of "the salt of the earth" mentioned in the beatitudes, which, gone stale and having lost "its saltiness," is hence "thrown out" and "trampled under people's feet" (Mt. 5:13), not unlike the unprofitable servant. Furthermore, Salter's name evokes the musical poems and prayers of the book of Psalms, the *Psalter*. What irony does it spell, then, that the *P*, which is in turn part of one of the oldest Greek Christograms in the ☧ (Gk. *Chi-Rho*), is silent, erased?[26]

As one can see, what the title metaphor of outer darkness suggests is a web consisting of the interrelated themes of blindness and ignorance, false beliefs, and lacking commitment on the side of believers. It is in this spirit, too, that McCarthy utilizes the biblical texts to articulate a subtle critique of capitalist ideology. The wider, apocalyptic implications of these connections are established by the contexts of the title's three uses in Matthew: The parable of the talents is followed by the announcement of the coming of the "son of man" and the last judgment, promising salvation to them that show charity and kindness to the least (Mt. 25:40). The story of the centurion is set immediately after Jesus heals a leper and just before the expulsion of the Gadarene swine. Finally, the parable of the royal wedding directly succeeds what is known as the parable of the vineyard and the wicked husbandmen, who brutalize and expel the servants of the vineyard's master and finally murder his son (Mt. 21:33–46). In this parable, exegetes suggest, Jesus refers to himself and the imminent Crucifixion.[27] The most significant phrase in this context is Jesus's enlistment of an image adopted from Psalm 118:22: "The stone the builders rejected has become the cornerstone" (Mt. 21:42). As I have noted, for Girard, as well as for Peter in his First Epistle to the Corinthians (1:2–8), the cornerstone is associated with the *skandalon* (Gk. snare, stumbling block) represented by the model-obstacle, and it refers to the founding victim. Christ's revelation of the latter is what throws a wrench into the machinery of collective violence (*TH* 429). Yet this does not abolish violence itself, as McCarthy shows.

A caveat is in order here. It is possible that McCarthy, then in his mid-thirties, may have been consciously or unconsciously responding to his own Catholic upbringing when composing *Outer Dark*. Given the novel's sheer wealth of apocalyptic implications, though, this may be crediting him with a kind of prescience bordering on the prophetic, predating even Girard's analyses of the subject. That being said, Girard credits *novelistic writers* with exactly this kind of awareness, particularly Fyodor Dostoevsky, who, to recall, counts among McCarthy's main influences.[28] Be that as it may, the novel's title metaphor emerges as multilayered and programmatic. As part of McCarthy's mythoclastic enterprise, its overall effect amounts to a sharp indictment of Christianity, the failure of which is, itself, apocalyptic.

The Eclipse and the Riderless Horsemen

Coming back to Culla's opening nightmare, one finds that the catastrophic solar eclipse overshadows not just the dream but figuratively the entire narrative. It forms but the first of many ominous symbols in a novel that is heavily invested with apocalyptic imagery. Cosmic phenomena such as solar eclipses or falling comets, across the ages and borders of otherwise disparate cultural mythologies, have often been interpreted as portentous signs and not infrequently associated with monumental changes, the end of an era, or of the world itself. A spectacle even today, the sheer enormity of the darkening of the warming and life-giving light in the sky to communities not disenchanted by astronomy presented a radical, hierophantic rupture in the otherwise unfailing circles of the sun, suggesting that the apparent order of the cosmos had been upset.[29] In the Judeo-Christian tradition, too, solar eclipses have long been an integral part of the symbolic inventory of apocalyptic texts, which in turn continue to exert their influence on Western literature.[30] Almost paradigmatically, the opening of the first seal in the book of Revelation (6:12), which heralds the true start of the events that lead to the end of the world and its perfection in the kingdom of heaven, is marked by both the advent of a solar eclipse and the appearance of the four horsemen of the Apocalypse.

Given McCarthy's investment in this kind of symbolism, it is a telling error that several critics refer to the novel's strictly pedestrian triune as "night riders" (Bell 1988, 43) and "menacing riders" (Grammer 35). More explicitly, Thomas Lask finds the triune "move about like the horsemen" (33), and William Schafer outright calls them "foot soldiers of the Apocalypse" (111). While the horsemen themselves may not appear in the novel, at least two of their steeds arguably do. Rinthy witnesses a first equestrian epiphany while camping under a bridge, where she is passed by a "burning horse" trailing "a wake of pale and drifting dust" to the sound of "iron caparisons" and "exploding" hooves (*OD* 97). She encounters the second horse after leaving the farmer she has briefly stayed with:

> It came out of the sun at a slow canter, in a silhouette agonized to shapeless-ness. She crouched in the bushes and watched it, a huge horse emerging seared and whole from the sun's eye and passing like a wrecked caravel gauntribbed and black and mad with tattered saddle and dangling stirrups and hoofs clopping softly in the dust and passing enormous and emaciate and inflamed and the sound of it dying down the road to a distant echo of applause in a hall forever empty. (*OD* 212)

While the color of the first horse is not mentioned, its description as "burning" evokes the second horseman (Rv. 6:4), whose steed's color is described as a (in some translations flaming or fiery) red.[31] He is usually identified as the incarnation of war or, more specifically, internal strife and civil war. This association, subtly bolstered by the horse's unusual "iron caparisons" and the explosions of its hooves on the bridge, is further substantiated when one considers that the horse's appearance is set directly after a vignette wherein the triune's leader incites a crowd to search for the murderers of squire Salter. In the same chapter, Rinthy, passing through a field, then encounters the grim result of this appeal to vigilantism in the shape of the two hanged mill hands.

The second, black horse—likely the same that terrifies Culla on the chaotic nightly ferry ride that carries him to the triune's campfire—by its "gauntribbed" and "emaciate" shape evokes the third horseman identified with starvation. Two of the four horsemen are thus at least implicitly present in *Outer Dark*.[32] At the same time, the second horse's black silhouette, seeming to appear "out of the sun," visually recalls the eclipse of Culla's dream and again calls attention to the dynamics of light, shade, and darkness within the novel. In this respect, it is perhaps significant that in both cases it is light-enveloped Rinthy who becomes a frightful, yet unharmed spectator to the apocalyptic horses' progress. After all, she is the character that most closely reflects Christian virtues.

What complicates this interpretation is the fact that while no horse-man is mentioned in the case of the "burning horse" and his presence is thus uncertain, the emaciated black horse evidently bears no rider. This could be taken as an indication that the forces the horsemen personify are undirected by any higher power. This hypothesis is corroborated by the image of the sounds dying away on a road that sequentially, though not grammatically, in the flow of the sentence, leads to a "hall forever empty" (*OD* 212). Read this way, the teleology and meaning of history implied in the Apocalypse are voided in favor of a nihilistic vision that replaces the biblical divine order with the indifference of a chaotic cosmos. This certainly is a possibility. Yet, as it is specifically this literal vision of apocalyptic violence as decreed *by* God that is discredited, to apply this reading is to fall back on an essentially mythical presupposition, even in its negation. The other possibility is a strictly anthropological interpretation of the cataclysm announced in the eschatological texts as an end brought on by *human* agency, its disorder being, in truth, a product of the escalation of reciprocal, violent undifferentiation in what could be understood as the ultimate sacrificial crisis.

Turbulent Waters and the Gadarene Swine

The narrative cosmos of *Outer Dark* contains potentialities for both fundamentalist and anthropological interpretations of the Apocalypse. In contrast, there is also a sense in which that same cosmos appears, in Bell's words, as "an incoherent and unrationalized gestalt of mass and process, without design or purpose, unless it is that some demented and unapproachable God invisibly presides" (1988, 38). I have already alluded to the novel's dreamlike displacement in time and space. Unable to determine either a point of departure, a destination, or anything beyond the vague regional vicinity of certain waypoints, the characters' journeys and the resulting reading experience are characterized by a profound sense of disorientation, of being lost in the dark.

Disorientation is prevalent in various scenes involving Culla. One is the final station of the novel, the swamp described as a Dantesque "landscape of the damned" and "garden of the dead," of which Culla can only wonder "why a road should come to such a place" (*OD* 242). In an earlier episode, he crosses a swollen "dark and oily" river that "tend[s] away into nothing" (*OD* 164). The stream seems to merge with the night skyline, so that the cable-drawn ferry's passengers—Culla, the ferryman, and a nameless horseman—"seemed to hang in some great depth of darkness" (*OD* 164), the ferry paradoxically appearing "to be racing sideways upriver against the current." The cable busts in "a loud explosion" (*OD* 165), setting the ferry loose on an uncontrollable ride that sends the other passengers and the frightened horse overboard. Effectively, the river becomes at once a kind of black hole and strangely animate force: it swallows the horse's fury "traceless as fire" beneath its waves and sucks away Culla's shouts for help that "fell from his mouth in a chopped bark" and amount "not even [to] an echo," leaving him "praying silent and godless in his heart" (*OD* 167).

As Luce observes, this "turbulent" and violent river is already prefigured in an earlier scene "when Culla carries his baby along the Chicken River with its 'swollen waters coming in a bloodcolored spume from about the wooden stanchions [. . .] with a constant and vicious hissing,' as if in commentary on his murderous endeavor" (2009, 86). She associates these scenes with the gnostic concept of *turbid water*, which expresses the gnostic perception of the "noise and turmoil of the cosmos" (Luce 2009, 83) that is the soul's prison. Interestingly, Gnosticism and mimetic theory intersect at this point: as I have indicated in my discussion of the eclipse, the words *turbid* and *turbulence* are etymologically related to the *turba*, the crowd whose violent crisis finds its collective mythical representation in floods, droughts, and epidemics, all of which abound in McCarthy's novels. It is not by turbulence and cosmic darkness alone that his perilous river crossing is linked to Culla's opening dream. His description of the river itself evokes the violent crowd as it alternates between silence and "the stammerings of the cloistered mad," going so far as to suggest the river is "looking for him [Culla]" (*OD* 167). Like the floods of *The Orchard Keeper* and *Child of God*, the turbid waters of *Outer Dark* serve as signifiers of violent chaos.

Yet the pivotal chapter establishing the connection between the violent *turba* and the turbid waters of cosmic disorder is McCarthy's reimagining of the biblical tale of the Gadarene swine, which is also known as Jesus's cure of the demoniac of Gerasa. Coming upon a large herd of hogs driven through a valley, Culla has an amicable conversation with Vernon, one of the herd's drovers. Inexplicably, the hogs suddenly panic and stampede, carrying Vernon over a nearby cliff and to their shared demise. In the aftermath Culla is accused of having caused the stampede and almost lynched, barely escaping with his life by jumping over the cliff and into a river.

While the miracle tale is universally identified as McCarthy's source, calling its import "obvious" (Luce 2009, 131) may be premature.[33] At first sight, the inversion of the biblical story of Jesus's exorcism of demons into a herd of swine seems evident: whereas in the Bible a herd of swine "is drowned in the sea by God for the sins of their owners," McCarthy has "the swine-herd [. . .] downed and drowned by the swine, so the swine-herd dies, while the swine survive" (Sanborn 2006, 61). However, this idea of simple inversion involves a few distortions: For one, it is but a single swineherd, supposedly the counterpart to the biblical demoniac, who is drowned, while a substantial number of hogs still perish with him. Furthermore, as the following discussion will show, neither does the Bible directly attribute the swine's demise to an act of God, nor is it the point of the episode that the swine are made scapegoats for the sins of their owners. In my view, McCarthy goes beyond merely inverting the biblical tale. To show this, we must consider the biblical model that is apparently inverted, the details of the scene itself, and finally the aftermath of the episode in *Outer Dark*.

The biblical episode occurs in all three synoptic Gospels, with some significant variations (Mt. 8:28–34, Mk. 5:1–20, Lk. 8:26–39). Traveling the gentile country of Gadara in east Jordan, Jesus and his disciples are approached by a naked, possessed man, or two men in Matthew's version. Stuck in a continual loop with the people of his community, whose repeated attempts to restrain the man fail, this demoniac has come to live among the tombs. The demon identifies himself: "My name is Legion: for we are many" (Mk. 5:9). Jesus then casts the demon(s) into a herd of swine, which run off a nearby cliff into the lake and drown. Seeing their demoniac clothed, calm, and restored to sanity scares the Gadarenes, and they ask Jesus to leave their country.

Several aspects are of note here. The Gadarenes' reaction differs markedly from that of other groups to Jesus's wondrous healings and exorcisms. According to Girard, this difference in reaction is a matter of cultural, or rather religious, context: the episode takes place outside the Jewish religious community and within a pagan one. Not only are the Gadarenes not happy about the cure of their demoniac, who so obviously disturbs the peace, they are outright upset. Interestingly though, "the drowning of their pigs disturbs them less than the drowning of their demons" (*SG* 174). Among some smaller details, the Gadarenes' strange reaction, together with clear indications in both Luke and Mark that the whole process of the demoniac's mad spells and his expulsion is cyclical in nature, leads to an interesting suggestion: The Gadarenes may not actually be trying all that hard to heal their demoniac. Rather, they prefer to keep on casting him out time and again.

Unsurprisingly, Girard's general appreciation of the Gospel texts as a revelation of "humanity's imprisonment in the system of mythological representation based on the false transcendence of a victim" (*SG* 166) interprets this case of demonic possession in the conceptual framework of the sacrificial crisis. Oscillating between states of lucidity and possession, between being bound and roaming freely, and between the life of the city on the one hand and life in the mountains, the wilderness, and the tombs on the other, the possessed negates the differences between freedom and captivity, city life and the wilderness, and life and death (*SG* 168). In stoning and expelling himself, he imitates collective forms of punishment. So finally do the possessed swine in hurling themselves off the cliff. Yet the central element is the simultaneous singularity and multiplicity of the demon:[34]

> The demons are in the image of the human group; they are the *imago* of this group because they are its *imitation*. [. . .] Legion symbolizes the multiple unity of society [. . .] but in the rightly famous sentence "My name is Legion; for there are many of us," it symbolizes that unity in the process of disintegration since it is the inverse of social development that prevails. The singular is irresistibly transformed into a plural, within the same single sentence; it marks the falling back of unity into mimetic multiplicity which is the first disintegrating effect of Jesus' presence. This is almost like modern art. *Je est un autre*, says Matthew. *Je* is all the others, says Mark. (*SG* 181–82)

The Gadarenes' displeasure about the successful cure of the man that they themselves pretended to wish for thus becomes intelligible. It is not the loss of their swine that upsets them—the latter are not even an issue that is brought up—but something more fundamental. Essentially, Jesus's healing of the possessed marks the termination of a time-tested social system, which retained its inner harmony by cyclically expelling the demoniac, who serves as the community's collective scandal and convenient, perpetual scapegoat.

As far as McCarthy's retelling of the episode in *Outer Dark* is concerned, even a cursory look beyond the mere structural properties of the action is sufficient to see that there is more going on than a mere reversal of the Bible tale. To begin with, the scene of the hapless drover's swine-borne plunge to his death again dramatizes the connection of flooding, social crisis, and mob violence. As Luce points out, the entire spectacle is heavily invested with the imagery of turbid water, with the hogs cast as "a weltering sea" (*OD* 213), a "howling polychrome tide" (*OD* 214), and repeatedly as a "flood" washing against the rock Culla climbs for refuge (*OD* 218). What has not sufficiently been considered is the crowd dynamic of the scene, which follows the pattern established by the opening dream and the triune leader's agitation of the crowd in the fourth interchapter. Vernon, now described as beyond "hope and [. . .] prayer," is caught up in a "pandemonium" that carries him off "like some old gospel recreant seized sevenfold in the flood of his own nether invocations or grotesque hero bobbing harried and unwilling on the shoulders of a mob stricken in their iniquity to the very shape of evil until he passed over the rim of the bluff and dropped in his great retinue of hogs from sight" (*OD* 218).

Like the flood of hogs, the poetic torrent of the whole passage is overwhelming at first, making palpable the chaos of the scene. Only gradually does one begin to unravel the mythical, social, and religious implications. First coined by John Milton in *Paradise Lost*, the word *pandemonium*, literally the seat of all demons, is originally the capital of hell, but today has come to signify "a place or state of utter confusion and uproar; a noisy disorderly place" (*OED*, 129). The description of Vernon as a gospel recreant or apostate "seized sevenfold" links him both to the theme of outer darkness as spiritual unconviction and to the biblical mark of Cain (Gn. 4:15–24) that is the Old Testament God's protective ward against escalatory vengeance, which the New Testament extends to the precept of forgiveness (Mt. 18:21–22). Both ward and precept are invalidated and cast aside in this scene, an impression that is fortified by the alternative image of Vernon as carried off not by panicky animals, but by a raging mob. Finally, the way the drover meets his demise, like the biblical tale it is based on, recalls the method of execution of the Greek *pharmakoi* as well as the most socially reviled Roman criminals, who were pushed off the Tarpeian Rock.

These details corroborate the interpretation of the scene as an inversion of the biblical text, but alter it in significant ways, too. Within a contagion of violent undifferentiation that is conceived as nothing less than (pan) demonic, *Outer Dark* overturns the biblical prohibition against vengeance and the law of forgiveness in favor of an ancient Greco-Roman mode of collective violence against a single victim. In this, McCarthy alerts us to the fact that the biblical tale is *already* an inversion of sacrificial violence: "It is not the scapegoat who goes over the cliff, neither is it a single victim nor a small number of victims, but a whole crowd of demons [...]. Normal relationships are reversed. The crowd should remain on top of the cliff and the victim fall over; instead, in this case, the crowd plunges and the victim is saved" (*SG* 179). In short, the inversion of *Outer Dark* is an inversion of an inversion, literally presenting a *re*version to an older mode of social action—though with a twist: after all, the scene constitutes only the first half of the novel's most significant and direct dramatization of Christianity's collapse into sacrificial violence.

A look at the aftermath of this scene only cements this interpretation, for it repeats exactly the same process. Initially, one is struck by the absolute peace that Vernon's death seems to have brought to the region within the space of two paragraphs: in stark contrast to the preceding chaos, it is now "a fine spring day" and the drovers are assembled in "indifferent conviviality" (*OD* 219). The harmony is short-lived. Following Culla's approach, an accusatory spiral unfolds with the same torrential power that drove the stampede. At first, he is reproached for not helping Vernon. But a few lines later, he is accused of being a "troublemaker" (*OD* 220)—literally as someone sowing disorder, confusion, and strife—and charged with starting the stampede in the first place. Ridiculously, Culla's situation takes another turn for the worse as the words "Peace be on all you fellers" mark the entrance of "a parson or what looked like one" (*OD* 221). The man asks Culla whether he caused the stampede, only to assert, without a shred of evidence: "I believe he run em off" (*OD* 222). By asking whether the drovers are intending to hang Culla, the alleged parson puts that idea in their heads in the first place, reinforcing it through constant admonition against it. And after initially asserting God's exclusive right to vengeance via Romans 19:12, he subsequently qualifies its prevalence as precluding "the strongest extremes" (*OD* 222).

Reservations and questions of guilt are then dropped altogether, all suddenly united in the conviction that "Everybody seen what e [Culla] done" (*OD* 222). Henceforth, it is only a question of whether it would be better to hang him or to send him over the cliff like the swine, which is discouraged (with absurd Girardian correctness) for religious reasons: "Tain't Christian" (*OD* 224). After that, Culla's religious affiliation, his baptism, and whether he is "too mean to be saved" (*OD* 225) are the sole remaining questions.

In sum, the scene presents an at once hilarious and horrifying textbook example of the accusatory spiral and the workings of the scapegoat mechanism. Against the absence of credible cause or substantial evidence, against Culla's reasonable protest, against the reader's knowledge of his innocence, the collective sense of conviction asserts itself by no other evidence than its unanimity. The thing that "possessed the hogs" (*OD* 221) is quite the same thing that now possesses the drovers, and the dubious preacher who should act in defense of the accused instead becomes the leader of the lynch mob. All Christian principles he may loudly display are unceremoniously swept under the rug, or worse yet perverted. "Tain't Christian," or, if it is, it is tainted Christianity. The irony is perfect when Culla escapes being hanged by himself enacting the *pharmakos* ritual by jumping off the cliff. And while one may chuckle with Giles at the "absurdist humor" of the scene, one cannot help to also recognize that the flipside of this "wonderful black comedy" (116–17) is the abject horror of lynch logic.

Cosmic Disorder and the Witless Paraclete

As the preceding analysis shows, *Outer Dark* consistently integrates phenomena of social disorder and mob violence within a framework of mythical, biblical, and gnostic imagery and allusion. The effect of this strategy points toward the diffusion of structure and category as such. In the logic of the novel, the return to sacrifice does not halt this disintegration, either: after jumping off the cliff to escape his would-be lynchers, Culla sees them moving "along the bluff with no order rank or valence to anything in the shapen world" (*OD* 227), though this could alternatively be seen as the result of a thwarted collective murder.

Next to the dream's eclipse, the original scene and possibly the metaphorical cause of all disorder is Culla's abandonment of his son in the woods. After leaving the infant in a glade of cottonwoods, Culla becomes "confused in a swampy forest" (*OD* 16). Prefiguring his later turbulent ferry ride, Culla's warped flight through the dark repeatedly leads him back to a creek that as if time's river were flowing backwards, carries his saliva "inexplicably upstream, back the way he had come," though the water itself seems "motionless" (*OD* 17). To Culla's horror, he ends up back in the glade where he has left the baby: "It howled execration upon the dim camarine world of its nativity wail on wail while he lay there gibbering with palsied jawhasps, his hands putting back the night like some witless paraclete beleaguered with all limbo's clamor" (*OD* 18). Culla has already lost his sense of both orientation and time in a dark wood that appears to bend and suspend the ordinary laws of physics. Now, he also loses his ability for coherent speech, as he is confronted again with the child that just like the incestuous act that has (purportedly) spawned it, serves as a supreme signifier of designification.

Even the scene's religious symbolism, "the language of McCarthy's own Catholic upbringing" (Frye 2009, 33), is employed to this end. The first term of interest is the compound noun "camarine world." Ann Fisher-Wirth identifies the camarine as a feature of church architecture denoting the little chapel or shrine behind the altar "where images are dressed and ornaments destined for that purpose are kept." She goes on to identify it with both the glade and the womb, judging that Culla "has arrived at the shrine or temple of existence" (131). Certainly, the scene taps into some fundamental dimension that includes but also transcends the confines of the purely symbolic: in leaving his newborn child to die, Culla visits his own incestuous sin upon an innocent. Like Pilate, he is repeatedly yet vainly trying to wash his hands of it as he does the blood of the child's birth (*OD* 15, 28). Expelling his own flesh and blood, he commits the crime that rather than the incestuous act, sets off the actual plot. He thus perpetuates the sacrificial patterns on which culture rests and that he himself will repeatedly nearly fall prey to. Finally, the entire world seems to be cursed by the child's howls of execration. If Culla's following disorientation and the testament of the novel as a whole reveal anything, it is that the sacrificial mechanisms meant to restore order and harmony are out of order.

In expressing this, the second religiously connoted image of the "witless paraclete" is of essential significance. Derived from the Greek *paraklētos*, the word is primarily used in the Christian Trinitarian tradition as a title for the Holy Spirit. Within the framework of Kristevan psychoanalysis, Fisher-Wirth reinterprets McCarthy's use of the word as referring to the patriarchal "champion of symbolic order" (132) that in Culla's horrific vision is subsumed in the Kristevan semiotic that constitutes another, pre-Oedipal, prelinguistic mode of communication identified with the mother. As was the case with Luce's gnostic view of turbid water, the feminist-psychoanalytic reading of the paraclete constitutes another important intersection with the interpretive lines of mimetic anthropology. After all, the operation of scapegoating may itself be reductively regarded as a collective social manifestation of Kristevan abjection, which is at once the psychological *process* of casting something out and the *state* of being outside the symbolic order in a "place where meaning collapses" because it is "what disturbs identity, system, order" (Kristeva 2, 4).[35]

Pitting order against disorder and aligning the scapegoat with the abject, my own reading overlaps with that of Fisher-Wirth in essential points. A fundamental difference, though, is the role assigned to the paraclete: for insofar as the symbolic order he represents is identified as that of the social order that expels, he is put in league with the murderers. This possibility exists, given that it is *Culla* who is grammatically compared to the paraclete. Nothing, however, could be farther from the meaning of the word, which is literally translated as comforter, helper, and, most importantly, the *advocate* for the defense (*OED*). In the New Testament, it is identified both with Jesus, who is man's "advocate with the Father" (1 Jn. 2:1), and the Holy Ghost supposed to accompany humanity as "another Comforter" and agent of revelation or "Spirit of truth" (Jn. 14:16–26) active in history. Mimetic anthropology further interprets this aspect of the paraclete as the knowledge attained through the Passion, that is, the historically active, myth-shattering knowledge of the victim's innocence.

> *Parakleitos*, in Greek, is the exact equivalent of advocate or the Latin *advocatus*. The Paraclete is called on behalf of the prisoner, the victim, to speak in his place and in his name, to act in his defense. The Paraclete is the universal advocate, the chief defender of all innocent victims, *the destroyer of every representation of persecution*. He is truly the spirit of truth that dissipates the fog of mythology. [...] Christ is the Paraclete, par excellence, in the struggle against the representation of persecution. [...] When Christ has gone, the Spirit of Truth, the second Paraclete, will make the light that is already in the world shine for all men, though man will do everything in his power not to see it. (*SG* 207–8)

What, then, does it mean that the paraclete in the forest clearing is "wit-less" and "beleaguered with all limbo's clamor" (*OD* 18)? If, as one lucid, early reviewer put it, *Outer Dark* shows society acting out "the old patterns of crime, punishment and sacrifice" (Lask 33), this bespeaks the paraclete's witlessness, reflected by Christianity's historical tendency to fall back into the mythological mindset of sacrificial violence. Yet it also testifies to his revelatory activity: we know that the victims are innocent, in the novel none more so than the Holmes' son. The child's expulsion, like the lynchings, fails to reinvigorate or cleanse the disintegrating social order. If anything, it only exacerbates its crisis—and McCarthy's "witless paraclete" is both the agent and witness to its baneful implications: "It is the Holy Spirit that teaches us that historical Christianity has failed and that the apocalyptic texts will now speak to us more than they ever have before" (*BE* 103).

Satan and the Unholy Triune

In discussing Christianity's disastrous reversion to the mechanisms of an older, sacrificial order, the three roving marauders of *Outer Dark* are central figures. Throughout the years, various roles and functions have been assigned to these frightening figures, interpreting them either *psychologically* as pater-nalistic and/or archontic doubles and Jungian shadows of Culla's infanticidal psyche (Jarrett 17; Luce 2009, 95; Hage 129), *allegorically* as pastoral figures of death and time or projections of evil within an allegorical compound char-acter (Grammer 35–37; Guillemin 2004, 61–62), *religiously* as manifestations of guilt and judgment or a parodic inversion of the holy trinity (Arnold 1999, 49; Spencer 83; Hillier 2006, 56), and lastly in combinations of these views. My own reading builds primarily on the religious interpretation, which mimetic theory corroborates and expands with an anthropological basis.

McCarthy criticism has chosen to refer to the three with an expression featured in their murder of the snake hunter. To the dying man, they appear "in consubstantial monstrosity" as "a grim triune" (*OD* 129). William Spen-cer has convincingly interpreted the three as an inversion and parody of the Holy Trinity, comprising a "triple allegory of evil" (91). Thus, the father is mirrored in the bearded man, who according to his own words (*OD* 233) "recognizes no bounds, no restrictions, no rules of any kind" and thus "allies himself with chaos"; Harmon, the only name-bearing member of the group,

is the Antichrist, bringing not harmony and reconciliation but instead harm
and violence; and the triune's nameless, mute member represents a "reversal
of the Holy Spirit [. . .] the transcendent, nonphysical fact of God" in "an
uncommunicating mute, ultimately a symbol of beast-like ignorance" (Spencer 89–90). Spencer's insightful reading fits perfectly into my view of the
novel as an encompassing critique of Christianity. As my reading has modi-
fied this critique through an anthropological lens, consistency demands that
the triune be viewed this way, too.

From this point of view, it can be said that the triune is not simply a
metaphysically enlarged representation of evil, but profoundly bound up in
the social turmoil the novel presents. Inexplicably violent figures from the
opening of the novel, the three kill seemingly without concern for race, class,
or age. They are also responsible for the desecration of three graves. This act
further marks them as figures of undifferentiation. Not content with stealing the burial clothes of the dead, they arrange the body of "what appeared
to have been an old man" (*OD* 87) to grotesquely share his coffin with a
recently murdered "negro sexton whose head had been cut half off and who
clasped him in an embrace of lazarous depravity" (*OD* 88). The triune's blasphemous act not only negates the lines between living and dead by exposing
the corpses to the eyes of both the crowd and an anthropomorphized sun
that seems "arrested with surprise" (*OD* 87), but also "violates the boundaries
that would have existed between these two men in life, suggesting nothing
less than homosexual miscegenation" (Ellis 2006, 119). Like the strange,
undefinable meat they offer Culla, the triune's deeds defy the very idea of
differentiation.[36]

In the interchapter succeeding this grotesque spectacle, another function of the triune is introduced. The bearded leader, wearing the disinterred
dead man's "shapeless" suit (*OD* 95), incites a largely faceless and anonymous
crowd over the murder of squire Salter and effectively shapes it into a lynch
mob. What is at first sight puzzling about this scene is that McCarthy does
not cast the leader as much of an agent provocateur. To the contrary, he
explicitly undermines his authority. The man appears more as a negative presence than anything, what with his lack of shirt, his bare feet, and "nothing
of his face visible but the eyes like black agates, nothing [. . .] gloss enough
to catch the light and nothing about his hulking dusty figure other than its
size to offer why these townsmen should follow him" (*OD* 95). Even so, the

night does not pass without the hanging of two traveling workers. How can this be explained? Indeed, there seems no particular urgency, authority, or force involved: neither inspiring instigator nor demagogue, the bearded man seems like the social equivalent of a black hole, a force swallowing light, mass, and people within its gravitational pull. But is it enough to assume, as Spencer does, that "the townspeople are so predisposed to rash violence that they are easily seduced and controlled" (89)?

Once the triune is seen as an inversion of the Holy Trinity, implying their opposition to God, Christ, and the Spirit, the association of the three with the devil is not far off, but it has to be balanced with McCarthy's insistence on the triune's apparent nonsubstantiality.[37] On the one hand, their scenes with Culla already cast them in an appropriately hellish imagery of fire and darkness. Supposedly like the devil's foot, the leader's boot is described as "cleft from tongue to toe like a hoof" (OD 176). On the other hand, the reader is consistently faced with the impression that the triune has no real presence, their shapes against the fire projected "outward into soaring darkness and with no dimension to them at all" (OD 168), least of all to its leader. Clothed in a "dark and shapeless suit" (OD 170), his eyes appear like "shadowed lunettes with nothing there" (OD 171), and at their second meeting, the narrative blatantly suggests that "[Culla] was looking at nothing at all" (OD 233). Acknowledging this apparent paradox, Guillemin, who associates the bearded man's refusal to surrender his name with Mephistopheles in Johann Wolfgang von Goethe's *Faust*, summarily describes him as "not simply *like* Satan, but one of his avatars," even while granting the triune "no existence outside Culla's mind and the narrative consciousness" (2004, 62). However, this position does not accommodate the perception of those the triune interacts with, at least to the extent that the whole narrative is not seen as a dream or severe case of dissociative identity disorder. In a nutshell, the question is how a purely illusory presence purportedly existing only in Culla's or the narrator's mind is not only perceived by others, but interacts with them to such murderous effects.

Guillemin's characterization is especially apt when seen in the context of the snake trapper's death. The latter—by his profession associated with the Edenic serpent—twice declares that he "wouldn't turn Satan away for a drink" (OD 117, 127), the second time directly preceding his murder by the leader, who poses as a minister. Reflecting upon his profession, the old man muses that snakes "must have some good in em" because of how "old geechee snake doctors use em all the time for medicines," and somewhat ambivalently asks: "But the devil don't do doctorin does he?" (*OD* 124). Does this not exactly encompass the role the triune plays in the sacrificial structure of the novel? In the mimetic reading of the Bible, the devil—which in the Hebrew *Satan* as well as the Greek *diábolos* literally means accuser—assumes a role that, like the mute member in Spencer's conception of the triune as an anti-Trinity, places him in opposition with the *paraclete*, the defender. As such, he is interpreted as the biblical personification of mimetic contagion and sacrificial violence, which the paraclete opposes by uncovering its machinations.

> [Satan] is a principle of order as much as disorder. [. . .] The Satan expelled is that one who foments and exasperates mimetic rivalries to the point of transforming the community into a furnace of scandals. The Satan who expels is this same furnace when it reaches a point of incandescence sufficient to set off the single victim mechanism. In order to prevent the destruction of his kingdom, Satan makes out of his disorder itself, at its highest heat, a means of expelling himself. (*ISS* 34–35)

The biblical Satan, then, embodies both the mimetic contagion of the crisis *and* its solution in turning the *all-against-all* of the crisis into the *all-against-one* of the single victim mechanism.[38] Seen as the symbol of mimetic violence and the chaos of the crisis, Satan becomes "his own antidote of sorts: he stirs up the mimetic snowballing and then the unanimous violence that makes everything peaceful once again" (*ISS* 43). This is the mimetic solution to Jesus's conundrum: "How can Satan cast out Satan?" (Mt. 12:26). The devil does indeed "do doctorin"—we see evidence of his medicine throughout the novel. Time and again, *Outer Dark* has impressively dramatized the accusatory spiral leading to unanimous violence: Culla's dream, the persecutions and lynchings, the reinversion of the Gadarene swine episode—which not by accident envisions the swine drovers as "disciples of darkness" bearing "satanic looks" (*OD* 218)—and finally, the sacrifice of Culla's son.

What needs to be understood is that like the paraclete, Satan and the triune are not a material, personal force. They are an externalized personification of the violent mechanisms at work in the crisis. Without penetrating its logic, Spencer nonetheless expresses much the same when he speaks of

McCarthy's "gradual surprise attack on the smug view that evil is an outside, inhuman force. Instead, readers are subtly encouraged to see evil as a tendency *within* human beings" (87). Thus the ease with which the leader manipulates the crowd, and thus, too, the triune's strange aura of nothingness, of having no true presence. Fitting Culla's question regarding their nature, the triune truly are a "what" (*OD* 234) rather than a who:

> The devil's "quintessential being," the source from which he draws his lies, is the violent contagion that has no substance to it. The devil does not have a stable foundation; he has no *being* at all. To clothe himself in the semblance of being, he must act as a parasite on God's creatures. He is totally mimetic, which amounts to saying *nonexistent as an individual self.* [...] Why do the Gospels in their most complete definition of the mimetic cycle, have recourse to a figure named Satan or the devil rather than to an impersonal principle? I think the principal reason is that the human subjects as individuals are not aware of the circular process in which they are trapped; the real manipulator of the process is *mimetic contagion itself.* There is no real subject within this mimetic contagion, and that is finally the meaning of the title "prince of this world," if it is recognized that Satan *is* the absence of being. (*ISS* 42, 69)

Something Beyond All Warming:
Outer Dark's Final Judgment

Ultimately, the apocalyptic decision of *Outer Dark* is realized as a trial between Satan, the accuser, and the paraclete, the defender. The novel's pivotal scene and climax is Culla's second meeting with the triune under the "baleful eyes of some outsized and mute and mindless jury" (*OD* 231) reflected in the recently murdered tinker's pans. In their first conversation, the triune head already insinuates Culla's involvement in a number of crimes, like the killing and robbing of the ferryman and rider as well as Salter, and implicitly indicts him for not "takin care of [his] own" (*OD* 181). In the second meeting, he assumes the role of both prosecutor and judge, putting Culla through a series of ever more penetrating questions and increasingly explicit accusations, culminating in the charge of incest. In effect, Culla is left only with the choice between accepting the charges, and thus possibly face execution at the hands of the rifle-carrying Harmon—whose name implies the command to "harm on"—or evading and denying everything in a series of negations and double negations: "Never figured nothing, never had nothing, never was nothing" (*OD* 233). At the same time, his satanic prosecutor asserts Culla's fundamental equivalence with everyone else, the quality that makes him a double and potential victim: "You ain't no different from the rest. From any man borned and raised and have his own and die" (*OD* 235).

Still, there seems to be a chance for redemption. "In McCarthy's highly moralistic world," writes Arnold, "sins must be named and owned before they can be forgiven" (1999, 54). Culla, too, is faced with this choice. As his trial draws to a close and matters turn toward the child, he becomes more evasive and hesitant, only reluctantly handing the mutilated child over to the leader and showing the same kind of half-hearted concern that he showed by covering the child in his blanket even as he abandoned it to die (*OD* 234–35, 16). Interestingly, his behavior suddenly seems to emulate his sister: for the first time, Culla refers to the son in Rinthy's endearing words as a "chap" (*OD* 236), and he verbatim repeats and thus effectively "imitates" her plea to the tinker, "You don't need him" (*OD* 191, 235). "What's his name?" asks the leader (*OD* 235). On an ethical level, for Culla to answer this question would be to claim his child and thus own up to both his sin and fatherly responsibility. By the same token, Lydia Cooper demonstrates that in all of McCarthy's Appalachian works the "linguistic affirmation of life is mirrored through the symbolic action of naming" (2011b, 45), which signifies the basic acknowledgment of the other's humanity. On the epistemological level, naming the child would imply a first, Adamic act of ordering, a creative act of differentiating a small piece of living world against the disorder, noise, and turbulence represented by the triune and their leader's position that "some things is best not named" (*OD* 175).[39]

In this context, it is remarkable to note how *Outer Dark* first sets up the different multilayered semantic dimensions of fire that will assume meaningful prominence in McCarthy's later works. In both encounters, the leader remarks how he likes to keep the fire up, seeing as "there might be somebody else" and one "never knows what all might chance along" (*OD* 175, 232), implicitly introducing the notion of (informational) uncertainty.

His urinating into the fire of the novel's opening scene results in "a foul white plume of smoke out of and through which they fought suddenly and unannounced" (*OD* 3), a brief internal clash that constitutes the inaugural act of violence in the novel. The dominant image, however, is one that—for lack of a better term—seems to articulate the entropy of hell's fires: "the man seemed to be seated in the fire itself, cradling the flames to his body as if there were something there beyond all warming" (*OD* 179). Within the triune's campfires, we thus find contained the germ-cell of the analogy later works draw more explicitly. That is, the metaphorical interface between thermodynamic entropy, the (informational) differentiating act of naming, and the *violentropy* of the exchange and transformation of violence produced by the satanic-mimetic processes of social systems that can only maintain or revitalize their order by "feeding" on the scapegoat, like open systems feed on the free energy (or *negentropy*) of their environments.

Much the same can be said of the cataclysmic eclipse of Culla's dream that is the simultaneous cause of both the cooling of the earth and the disturbance of the crowd that will consequently reorganize itself against Culla. The physical process is inextricably bound up with the social one, which in turn forces the ethical decisions that carry within them all sorts of apocalyptic implications. In the face of human evil, the tinker's question, "why God ain't put out the sun and gone away" (*OD* 192), thus articulates a possibility to be considered. Yet McCarthy makes him an example that knowledge of evil alone is not enough as the tinker himself contributes to that evil by withholding the foundling child from Rinthy's love. In contrast to the cold and dark of human meanness—in other words the "entropy of the heart and of the soul"—it is not by accident either that McCarthy in turn also associates the physical and spiritual phenomena with Rinthy, who, in her desperate plea with the tinker is seen standing in a "fading patch of light like one seeking warmth of it or grace" (*OD* 188).[40]

Faced with the choice between the positive mimesis of Rinthy's love, which inspires the kindness and helpfulness of everyone she meets, and the mimesis of sacrificial violence, Culla finally opts out—suggesting only to look for Rinthy who "would take [the child]" (*OD* 236) and name him as she wanted even when she thought it dead (*OD* 29). In not making a choice, he effectively chooses the latter. Consequently, the triune's leader doubles Culla's original, half-hearted attempt at infanticide in a cannibalistic "parody of Christian communion" (Giles 121). Using a knife from the very boots he had taken from Culla in their previous meeting, the leader slits the child's throat and hands it to the mute "as both meal and a sacrificial offering" (Jarrett 17). It is with good reason that Ellis calls this scene "more repulsive than anything in McCarthy's novels" (2006, 120). It is here that the true, abysmal horror of the sacrificial logic is exposed and put on full display.

What is represented in Culla's dreadful indecision and the cannibalistic communion that follows symbolizes a nadir of historical Christianity's failure. "Witless" (*OD* 236), just like the paraclete earlier, the mute consumes the child's blood and in this moment embodies more than anything the evil that springs from human ignorance and that resists the lesson of the Gospel revelation, though not fully. After all other victims have failed, the archaic sacrificial logic the novel exposes leaves only the blood of the most helpless and innocent life of all to cleanse it, to effect the catharsis and lift the crisis that has befallen its world. However, the two following chapters give no indication that this final, most horrific act of violence does any good. Whether the curse is lifted by this return to myth is more than doubtful.[41]

Akin to yet simultaneously unlike Oedipus, Culla seems doomed to "never [...] have no rest" (*OD* 241), never to find, as Cant says, his Colonus (76). This is only consistent with his nature as scapegoat in an age when the victim is no longer divinized but only ostracized. Cant's mythical reading of Oedipus as the "first philosopher" and champion of reason is of interest here. He argues that by solving the Sphinx/Great Goddess's riddle, Oedipus replaces matriarchal cyclic time with a patriarchal, linear conception of time that introduces both "the notion of death as an end" and by extension "the notion of history" that "informs both Old and New Testaments" (79). Gendered ascriptions aside, it is not inappropriate to associate the "cyclic" notion of time with that of the eternal return, of the death and rebirth of society that characterizes the sacrificial cycle of ancient culture, whereas the linear, historic conception finds its expression in the Apocalypse.[42] This means, however, that the role Cant assigns to Oedipus has to be reconsidered as well. After all, he is one of the prime examples of the vilified and subsequently glorified scapegoat and thus subject again to the "eternal return of [sacrificial] religions" (*BE* 63) that Judaism and Christianity break with. Perhaps the interpretation of the Oedipus myth as representing a new model of time goes too far.

In any case, there is no return to mythical ignorance, nor is Culla a perfect Oedipus analog. He does not find a Colonus, nor is he divinized. What can be expected from the apocalyptic logic of the story that has gone before is instead a restless cycle of accusation and persecution down a slope toward annihilation. It is circular in the way of a downward spiral, the teleology of which ends, nonetheless, in a drain. And yet there seems to be a shred of hope even for "gracelorn" Culla (*OD* 241), whose condition is finally that of humanity: as he limps, like Oedipus, toward the swampy "landscape of the damned" (*OD* 242), the final chapter pits his figurative spiritual and moral blindness against the actual blindness of both Oedipus and an enlightened, helpful wanderer. This blind stranger who purports to be "at the Lord's work" and believes in the plain self-evidence of "Word and flesh" (*OD* 240)—Jesus and the paraclete—offers a striking reevaluation of Culla's apocalyptic opening dream, whose prophet, he suggests, "weren't no true preacher" (*OD* 241). And while Culla's blindness lets him reject this second chance at escaping the outer darkness, the novel's phrasing that he "used to meet" (*OD* 239) this blind sage, whom Luce associates with a gnostic enlightener, suggests that this may in fact be but the first in a number of encounters (Luce 2009, 110; Arnold 1999, 54).

As he finds that the road the blind man travels leads into a swamp, Culla stands idly by. The novel's final sentence states that "someone should tell a blind man before setting him out that way" (*OD* 242). So the possibility of salvation remains. However, its attainment seems dependent on a decision, and *Outer Dark* is deeply pessimistic about Culla—and so, in our reading, humanity—making that decision. And with good reason: entering the perilous terrains of *Blood Meridian*, both outer and inner darkness become all but overpowering.

CHAPTER 5

Degeneration through Violence

The Apocalyptic Logic of *Blood Meridian*

If I wrote about violence in an exaggerated way, it was looking at a future that I imagined would be a lot more violent. And it is.

— Cormac McCarthy (Kushner)

At the end of *Suttree* (1979), the eponymous protagonist escapes the existential void of his former life in Knoxville's decrepit and soon-to-be-demolished McAnally Flats. Heading out on a highway westward, his flight likewise marks his evasion of the allegorical vision of the huntsman of death, who is stalking the city outskirts with his untiring hounds. Only three years prior to the publication of this novel, which it had taken him twenty years to complete and which is generally taken to be his most auto-biographical work, McCarthy himself had left Knoxville and moved to El Paso, Texas. For McCarthy, this move marked the pursuance of a long-held literary interest in the myth of the West: "I ended up in the Southwest because I knew that nobody had ever written about it. Besides Coca-Cola, the other thing that is universally known is cowboys and Indians. You can go to a mountain village in Mongolia and they'll know about cowboys. But

213

nobody had taken it seriously, not in 200 years. I thought, here's a good subject. And it was" (Jurgensen).

With the support of a McArthur Fellowship he received in 1981, McCarthy learned Spanish and began extensive research for his fifth novel, *Blood Meridian, or The Evening Redness in the West*. Published in 1985, the novel continued the trend of its precursors and received an initially mixed reception: some critics were alienated by McCarthy's parting with the Appalachian South; others praised him as a supreme stylist but frowned upon the novel's excessive violence (Arnold and Luce 7). In the *New York Times*, Caryn James captured both sides of the argument when she called the novel "a slap in the face, an affront that asks us to endure a vision of the Old West full of charred human skulls, [and] blood-soaked scalps," but stressed the "brilliance of the work's conception," concluding that "if *Blood Meridian* is [. . .] a failure, it is an ambitious, sophisticated one" (1985, 31). Today, the novel is frequently considered McCarthy's masterpiece, as well as an outstanding work of literature by an American in the last three decades.[1] The exceptional status of *Blood Meridian* in McCarthy's oeuvre is testified to by the lively debates it has spawned in over thirty years and the amount of critical attention it continues to generate.

Once confronted with its horrors, a basic question that every reader of *Blood Meridian* has to answer for her- or himself is that of how to read it. Hinging in part on the critical distinction between subject matter and theme, even as ostensibly basic a question as that of genre is still widely discussed. Set primarily in the immediate wake of the Mexican-American War (1846–48), the novel dramatizes the clash of three different cultures—Mexican, Indian, and U.S. American—and their historical struggle for hegemony over the Southwestern borderlands during the heyday of manifest destiny. Its twenty-three chapters chronicle the journey of its young protagonist, called "the Kid," who joins a gang of professional scalp hunters under the historical figure of John Joel Glanton and the enigmatic Judge Holden. Initially hired to fend off Chihuahua's marauding Apache tribes, the scalp hunters eventually turn rogue and go on a killing spree through the deserts of the Southwest until their own violent end. The novel's final chapters relate the later years of the surviving Kid, now called "the Man," and presumably end with his death at the hands of the Judge.

Given its subject matter, McCarthy's novel is quite obviously concerned with America's western past, but is it more of a revisionist or an anti-Western? Is the stuff that *Blood Meridian* is made of that of tragedy, or does it grow from the yet older literary soil of the heroic epic? Is it a form of historical romance, or a Gnostic tragedy, a Nietzschean treatment of man's will to power, a bildungsroman, a tale of violent initiation, or a picaresque novel of war?[2] Indirectly, questions about the novel's classification point us toward McCarthy's *universal poetics*, his firm belief in the novel as an eclectic, potentially omni-disciplinary exploration of human interests not bound to any one discipline. Keeping in mind the reductive nature of criticism in the face of art, the following reading is at least partially concerned with pointing out the interconnectedness of the "various [. . .] interests of humanity" (Woodward 1992, 30) that *Blood Meridian* unites. Yet whatever the ultimate angle, the central concern and prime challenge it poses to most readers surely remains the ubiquitous carnage that stains page after page in blood. In a sense, this challenge is more pressing and acute in 2022 than it was in 1985. It is more so still today than in 2000, when no less seasoned a scholar than Harold Bloom admitted to having flinched away from the novel's violence on his first attempts to read it. Significantly, Bloom would then go on to praise it not only as "the ultimate Western, not to be surpassed," and as "both an American and a *universal* tragedy of blood," but also as "the authentic American apocalyptic novel" (2000, 254–55).

In continuation of the investigation begun with *Outer Dark*, it is primarily to the third of Bloom's characterizations that I want to direct my attention in this chapter. Ample discussion exists situating the novel with respect to both the tragic tradition and the bloody history of American continental expansionism and its continuation in the twentieth century. Conversely, its apocalyptic dimension—which is also, I would argue, the universal dimension of whatever tragedy we may trace in its bloodshed—remains largely unexplored. Indeed, part of this chapter's argument is that in his first Western, McCarthy grapples with the same dynamics that he does in his second Appalachian novel, so much so in fact that these two can be said to stand in an intimate dialogue with one another. If the opening eclipse of *Outer*

Dark turned out to be the programmatic image of the novel, *Blood Meridian* provides examples that prove similarly illuminating.

Having left Chihuahua with their first contract and equipped with new weapons, Glanton's gang rides through some mountains where "the sun when it rose caught the moon in the west so that they lay opposed to each other across the earth, the sun whitehot and the moon a pale replica, as if they were the ends of a common bore beyond whose terminals burned worlds past all reckoning" (*BM* 86). On the following day, when entering the town of Corralitos, the riders happen upon a sight that to the reader of *Outer Dark* will be eerily familiar: "It had rained in the day and the windowlights of the low mud houses were reflected in the pools along the flooded road out of which great dripping swine rose moaning before the advancing horses like oafish demons routed from a fen" (*BM* 88). The first of these two scenes provides one of McCarthy's celebrated, intensely visual, and symbolically charged landscapes the crafting of which here reaches new heights of aesthetic achievement. In most cases in which the novel's apocalypticism is brought up, it is these catastrophic, often cosmically evocative desert landscapes that are put into focus, conjuring before the mind's eye the kind of sun-scorched "terra damnata" (*BM* 61) that the novel is set on, its "distant pandemonium of the sun" (*BM* 185).[3] Drawing parallels between the luminist paintings of Frederic Church and McCarthy's literary imagery, Jarrett points out:

> McCarthy's sunset is transformed into a similar apocalyptic scene by the attachment of a further detail, both realistic and allegorical: out of these clouds "rose little desert nighthawks like fugitives from some great fire at the earth's end." This reference to fire mimetically reinforces the color and heat of the desert sun in the landscape yet supplies a further allegorical context—that of the earth's holocaust, which will presage the end of the earthly time in the Christian apocalypse. [...] [T]he novel's predominant image clearly and unflinchingly establishes a poetics of Western violence associated with the apocalyptic decline of the sun over the Western landscape. In this context, the *blood meridian* of the title is used as an extremity, peak, or climax; the period covered by the events of the novel is chosen as the historical position when the bloodshed of the West is at its peak. (68)

While Jarrett's analysis of McCarthy's landscape imagery and the setting's historical violence is highly accurate, I contend the apocalypse the novel dramatizes extends well beyond the boundaries of symbolism. To return to the two passages I have cited above, the mimetic reading I have been applying casts both scenes as more than vaguely portentous exercises in apocalyptic literary landscaping.

In the first example, not only is the moon described as a replica—a copy or else a *double*—of the sun, the image also conjures up the relationship of violence that exists between the two. Together, sun and moon metaphorically constitute a "common bore beyond whose terminals burned worlds past all reckoning." In the image of this cosmic bore, the earth upon which the gang rides is accordingly cast as a bullet whose trajectory must end in so many holocausts. The second scene recalls the earlier "pandemonium" (*OD* 218) that is Culla Holme's confrontation with the Gadarene swine. If the scene in *Outer Dark* is to be read as an inversion of Jesus's cure of a demoniac-scapegoat, and thus as a kind of regression to an older, sacrificial mode of dealing with the communal violence that the demons represent, much the same could be implied here. Worse yet, the situation presents a kind of escalation as the porcine demon horde appears to rise again from its watery grave, figuratively letting loose the violence that had been cast out in the demon legion.

Admittedly, these little scenes or sceneries are, firstly, just two examples from a novel that presents us readers with a plethora of similarly evocative imagery. Secondly, neither of them has any bearing on the plot, nor do many, if any, of the examples that could be cited in their stead. Therefore, philosophical readings tend to emphasize the quasi-eschatological implications of Western decadence and the decline of Euro-American civilization, which find their expression in the novel's falling stars and solar "holocaust[s]" (*BM* 105), chief among which is the novel's alternate title of "The Evening Redness in the West" (Dacus 2009). Alternatively, recent ecocritical approaches tend to read the book's landscapes as expressions of McCarthy's aesthetics of *optical democracy*, and its supposed sublimation of anthropocentric concerns into more biocentric or posthumanist perspectives. From this point of view, readers are drastically confronted with man's cosmic insignificance, and the *apocalyptic* assumes primarily the shape of environmental catastrophe as a consequence of human negligence and exploitation. For the latter, the image of plains strewn with buffalo carcasses that governs the novel's final pages is of particularly haunting iconicity (Keller-Estes 107–32).

In my view, these readings complement and extend McCarthy's apocalyptic but miss the mark by factoring out the novel's central element. In the examples cited above, both the echo of *Outer Dark*'s Gadarene swine and the cosmic bore to burning worlds point toward the central role of violence in McCarthy's apocalyptic vision. Excluding this element makes our readings, in a way, curiously bloodless.[4] Conversely, distilling an ahistorical and irremediable violent essence either inside or outside of humans that drives them to the point of self-annihilation does little to unravel the complexity of McCarthy's eschatological vision, either. Doing so only remythologizes violence. Our critical shortcomings in properly ascertaining the role that violence plays in the novel's apocalypticism may stem from a certain reluctance—well justified in the light of McCarthy's "heretical" tendencies—to turn him "into an overtly Christian writer" (Arnold 1999, 46). Perhaps though, they stem even more so from a general reticence of critical thought today, secular *and* theological, to seriously engage matters of eschatology as diagnosed by René Girard. To recall, he asserts that "the apocalypse has to be taken out of fundamentalist hands" (*BE* 48) and reenvisioned as a radically real, inherently secular potentiality. McCarthy does just that.

Early on, in one of *Blood Meridian*'s explicitly "prophetic" episodes, the Kid and some of his comrades celebrate their signing up with Captain White's ill-fated Mexican filibuster, "foreseeing a night of drink, perhaps of love" (*BM* 38) that will end with the violent death of one of the group. At the local cantina, they are confronted by "an old disordered Mennonite" (*BM* 39) who warns them against carrying "war of a madman's making" into Mexico: "The wrath of God lies sleeping," he says. "It was hid a million years before men were and only men have power to wake it" (*BM* 40). While McCarthy's Mennonite recalls another prophet figure from another American apocalypse, Herman Melville's *Moby-Dick*,[5] the Mennonite's central image echoes the prophetic tradition invoked by Jesus in Matthew 13:35: "I will open my mouth in parables; I will utter what has been hidden since the foundation of the world." Likewise, the Mennonite's statements prefigure Judge Holden's proclamation of war both as godlike and as the human activity par excellence. Both the Judge and the Mennonite clearly regard the absolute violence of war as something divine—or, rather, *sacred*—that is unleashed and revealed, however, *not* by God, but by humans.

It will not surprise anyone who has read the novel that the demonic presence of the Judge, who in an early typescript still referred to himself as someone "who knows how to make sleepers wake" (91/35/9, 465), is at the innermost core of the revelatory process. Conversely, the role of Christianity and Christian revelation in the course of history has its own part to play in the implacable logic of violence. The latter *Blood Meridian* dramatizes rightly as escalation, with sights set unflinchingly on the end of our world. When compared to the novels discussed thus far, *Blood Meridian* considerably extends the scope of the subject matter present in McCarthy's Southern novels from the personal and regional to the cultural and national level. In short, it gives them "the epic dimension that has to be incorporated into any examination of American mythology" (Cant 158). It is with *Blood Meridian, or The Evening Redness in the West*, as well, that we gradually discover the apocalyptic center of McCarthy's mythoclastic project. The following discussion therefore represents a continuation of the readings I have proposed so far, and particularly of *Outer Dark*, which relates to *Blood Meridian* somewhat in the way that an architectural blueprint relates to the actual building, the text of a play to its dramatic performance. In *Blood Meridian*, the atemporal, prophetic *logos* of *Outer Dark* is actualized and enacted in history.

In the following, I will repeatedly focus on the text's mimetic elements: the by now familiar themes of rivalry between doubles (of which filial-paternal rivalry is particularly prominent), the relation between myth narrative and history, and the role of Christianity in that relation. In addition, *Blood Meridian* puts into focus a new element, that is, the contagion of violence that here follows a Clausewitzian logic of escalation to extremes. Exploring these elements will substantiate the larger critique of Enlightenment ideology, Western imperialism, and the frontier that Chris Dacus traces in the titular symbolism of *The Evening Redness* and that Bloom alludes to when he speaks of the "self-destruction of European consciousness, the decline of the West" (cit. in Josyph 2010b, 88). As the apocalyptic tradition provides a model of history, anyone attempting to reclaim this dimension of the text needs to firmly plant her feet in the context of America's frontier past. McCarthy's interrogation of this history and its mythology constitutes the first part of the following analysis. Once this quality has been established, the path is clear for evaluating the novel's properly eschatological dimension, which revolves both around the Judge's metaphysics of war and, once more, around the problematic status of Christianity. Ultimately, my approach seeks to explore *Blood Meridian*, perhaps for the first time, as what Bloom claims it is: a fundamentally, yet decidedly antifundamentalist, apocalyptic novel.

A History of Violence:
Blood Meridian and the American Frontier

While by McCarthy's own words, history may have been "little more than the frame" (cit. in Jillet 6) for his literary concerns, this analysis necessarily begins with a discussion of *Blood Meridian* as both a Western and a piece of historical fiction. As there exists already a wealth of scholarship discussing these aspects of the novel, the following analysis will remain cursory with regard to the complex matrix of ideological, economic, social, ethnic, scientific, and religious imperatives comprised by manifest destiny. Nor is my prime interest in the historical realities of the scalp-hunting business, or the relation of *Blood Meridian* to its various source materials such as Samuel Chamberlain's *My Confession*.[6] Instead, the focus is on the literary dynamic of the novel's confrontation of myth with historical "realities." As in the previous discussion, this dynamic is shown to be fundamentally mimetic.

Mythic and Initiatory Patterns

While "the revelation of the profound disorder at the heart of [America's] myths" (Spurgeon 83) is one of McCarthy's central concerns, this revelation is a gradual one. In exploring the mythic dimension of *Blood Meridian*, an analysis of its "hero" provides a natural starting point that allows the discussion to expand its scope gradually, following the themes McCarthy introduces through the Kid's eyes. In this, the latter serves as a kind of picaresque guide offering an unfamiliar perspective on the familiar world of the Western. In truth, the Kid is a figure suggestive of many, more or less allegorical, roles. For the moment, it is his status in the frontier myth that interests me.

The text starts out as classic a Western or American novel as has been written: Like Huck Finn "lighting out for the Territory," a young boy leaves his home to try his fortune in the West. To recapitulate, the frontier myth builds upon the ancient hunter-hero mythology that also informs the Campbellian monomyth and according to Slotkin can be summed up by the formula of *regeneration through violence*. The hunter-hero of the tale, Sarah Spurgeon points out, engages in a spiritual exchange with the wilderness, returning with a kind of boon or special knowledge that revitalizes his community. This basic template informs both the older literary form of the heroic epic and modern stories of individual initiation. In the context of the frontier, where it assumed the form of a culturally active myth, this narrative suggested that Americans had to regress to an earlier evolutionary stage in order to address the necessities presented by their environment. Historically, one does not have to look far to see the sacrificial logic at work: It was through the "heroic" conquest of the wilderness and its "savage inhabitants" that the growth, wealth, and progress of American civilization would be ensured.

In accordance with the demands of the tale, the protagonist of *Blood Meridian* is a young man simply called "the Kid." Born one hundred years before McCarthy, and sharing his Tennessee background, the Kid might initially be assumed to function as a stand-in for his creator, as does the connection to McCarthy's almost-namesake and fellow Irish American Henry McCarty, better known as Billy the Kid.[7] Conversely, the choice of withholding his actual name provides the Kid with more universal features, recalling such quasi-mythical figures as Clint Eastwood's "man with no name" in Sergio Leone's Dollar Trilogy. This characteristic places McCarthy's Kid in a tradition identified with the mythical hunter-hero and his American descendant, the frontiersman (*FE* 374–75). Even before such intertextual kinships and the implied ambiguity of the Kid's role come into play, the novel introduces the familiar McCarthyan theme of troubled ancestry and father–son relationships. The reader is called upon to "See the child" (*BM* 3), as the Kid is yet referred to.[8] He is born on the November night of the historic 1833 Leonids meteor shower, which many at the time thought a sign of the impending end of the world. Significantly, he descends from a folk "known for hewers of wood and drawers of water" (*BM* 3), and is thus marked as belonging to the lowest of social classes.[9] Though his drunkard father used to be a schoolmaster and "quotes from poets whose names are now lost," the child is illiterate. Instead, we are told that "in him broods already a taste for mindless violence. All history present in that visage, the child the father of the man" (*BM* 3).

As McCarthy's opening quotation of William Wordsworth's "My Heart Leaps Up When I Behold" suggests, the child's adult life path is mapped out early on: His first "act" at birth is to "carry off" his mother, symbolically abjecting her. Thus, he grows up a half-orphan in a land itself only half-civilized, as the surrounding Tennessean woods "harbor yet a few last wolves" (*BM* 3). As Barcley Owens points out, the uneducated child is hence introduced as a kind of "primal First Man" (29), perhaps another American Adam, though his illiteracy may imply that his power of naming and creating order through language is impaired. From the outset, McCarthy's child is deprived of the nurturing "maternal" element and at best improperly induced into the "paternal" sphere of the symbolic, of language. The Kid lacks all parental influence that could curb or direct his natural dispositions. Whereas Wordsworth's child is characterized by "natural piety" (246), the prime attribute of McCarthy's child is his "taste for mindless violence," which in an earlier draft was yet characterized in terms of acquisitive desire as "mindless rapacity" (91/35/3, 1).[10]

To a modern readership, these characteristics will make for an unflattering first impression. According to Slotkin though, the lack of culture and the "violent spirit of the warrior hero" are the very conditions of his access to a knowledge that transcends that of book culture and are finally quite "inseparable from the regenerative process" (*FE* 374–75), which the hero is supposed to effect in his community. Beyond his mythical role, the Kid's ignoble family background, his attempts to get by on menial work, theft, and begging (*BM* 15), and his inscrutable attitude toward the havoc caused by the Glanton gang also mark him with traits of the picaro figure in a novel Guillemin describes as a picaresque Western (2004, 85; Whitbourn ix–xix). This view perfectly corresponds with the novel's nature as both a journey narrative and an antimyth that forces its readers to reexperience the Old West from an unfamiliar, Martian perspective. In the second third of the novel, the Kid recedes into the background from being in the narrative focus, assuming the role of an observer or witness, which is what the Judge will hold against him.

In terms of mimetic theory, what is striking is that the Kid is missing all proper models that he could emulate. Thus, his ensuing journey can partially be characterized as his search for such models, for "the father" as it were. Consequently, the cultural and sociological levels of myth and picaresque are laced with the personal level of a coming-of-age or initiation story. In contrast to his aggressive tendencies, the child's face is described as "curiously untouched [. . .], the eyes oddly innocent" (*BM* 4). This is less the monstrously insane innocence of a Lester Ballard than the youth and lack of "sivilization," which again situates McCarthy's protagonist within a tradition of characters like Huck Finn and Faulkner's Ike McCaslin. So *Blood Meridian*'s child is at once the "innocent child," the "bad boy," and the "confused and searching adolescent in his precarious liminal state between the not yet lost innocence of the child and the not yet gained experience of the adult, who has yet to achieve the transition from the one world into the other, to suffer the [Adamic] fall into maturity effected by knowledge, to pass his *initiation*" (Freese 1998, 24). The individual experience of initiation in either tale or ritual reflects the larger dynamic of regeneration through violence at the level of myth. Girard points out that "in some societies the individual in passage is stripped of his name, his history, and his family connections; he is reduced to an amorphous state of anonymity" (*VS* 282). This perfectly describes the state of the Kid, who throughout the narrative will neither receive a name nor reach a definitive state of identity.

Socially speaking, the point of the trials and tribulations that are part of any initiation ritual or narrative is the integration of the young initiate into the existing social order, which is thus, quite literally, rejuvenated and continued by the infusion of "fresh blood" into an aging community. But the connection goes deeper. Firstly, Girard reasons that the crisis experienced by the individual in passage in fact replicates on a psychological level the larger social crisis: "The purpose of rites of passage [. . .] is to graft onto the model of the original crisis any burgeoning crisis brought into being by a sudden outbreak of undifferentiation" (*VS* 284). Secondly, much like the barely hidden sacrificial pattern of the sacred hunter myth that informs frontier mythology, the initiatory transformation in its unadulterated form is inextricably bound up with the infliction of violence:

> The postulant must endure hardship, hunger, even torture, because these ordeals were part of the original experience. In some instances it is not enough to submit to violence; one must also inflict violence. [. . .] Indeed, in many societies the ultimate act of initiation is the killing of an animal or a human being. [. . .] With regular repetition and a pattern of success, these rites are gradually transformed into simple tests or trials, becoming

increasingly "symbolic" and formalistic. The sacrificial nature of the rites
tends to become obscured with the passage of time until finally it is hard to
say what the symbols are intended to symbolize. (*VS* 283–84)

Setting out on what could be his personal journey from innocence to experience, McCarthy's child runs away from his home at the age of fourteen.
Like John Wesley Rattner or Cornelius Suttree before him, he leaves behind
the "pastoral landscape" (*BM* 4) of Tennessee. On his journey toward the
Western wilderness he passes through several spaces of transition where
he undergoes the metaphorical rites of passage. If in John Wesley's case, it
could already be suggested that initiation in American literature functions
"through murder rather than sex, death rather than love" (Fiedler 22), the
same applies doubly to the protagonist of *Blood Meridian*, who in contrast
to the boy-hero of *The Orchard Keeper* is actively spoiling for a fight. In New
Orleans, he engages in regular tavern brawls with traveling sailors: "They
fight with fists, with feet, with bottles or knives. All races, all breeds. Men
whose speech sounds like the grunting of apes. Men from lands so far and
queer that standing over them where they lie bleeding in the mud he feels
mankind itself vindicated" (*BM* 4).

   In another parallel to *The Orchard Keeper*, it is worth pointing out that
as in Marion Sylder's altercation with Aaron Conatser, no rationale is provided for the violence. Neither does the child seem to stand out in any way
among the crowd. He is described as "some fairybook beast," whose close-set
shoulders and big wrists and hands (*BM* 4) themselves suggest a somewhat
ape-like physiognomy. The child is eventually shot twice. He thus undergoes
the formulaic near-death experience—the first of several in fact—that signals
his initiation into the violent masculine culture of the Old West.[11] As Arnold
van Gennep outlines in *Les rites de passage* (1909), the child loses his previous
status and acquires a new one: "Only now is the child finally divested of all
that he has been. His origins are become remote as is his destiny" (*BM* 4).
Henceforth, the text refers to him as "the Kid."

   With his arrival in Nacogdoches, close to the geographical ninety-eighth
meridian, the Kid by and by enters one of the "arid lands" that Frederick
Jackson Turner defined as a natural border zone between civilization and
wilderness (8; Schimpf 2008, 15). Beyond this region, "the laws and regulations of civilized America didn't apply," giving way, in Rick Wallach's words,

to "the unbounded gratification of the libido" (cit. in Josyph 2010a, 93). In mythical terms, this land provides the perfect terrain where the frontier hero's tale of self-creation or recreation through violence can unfold: "Not again in all the world's turning will there be terrains so wild and barbarous to try whether the stuff of creation may be shaped to man's will or whether his own heart is not another kind of clay" (*BM* 4–5). The Kid's ensuing journey into this wilderness, that is, the frontier hero's double-quest for identity and the regeneration of his people, is thus framed as an investigation into questions of determinism, free will, and human nature itself. In sum, the basic parameters of the myth and the Kid's literary role are roughly delineated: part picaresque guide, part neophyte frontiersman, he is also searching for fathers, teachers, models. While much remains to be said about the Kid, the discussion will now shift to *Blood Meridian*'s dramatization of two major aspects of frontier history, which also shed more light on the mythical and actual models offered to the Kid. The first of these is the era of manifest destiny represented by the fictional character Captain White; the second is the "business" of scalp hunting.

Corrupted Heroism and Manifest Destiny

In 1883, Frederick Jackson Turner famously posited his thesis of the continuous cycle of expansive regression and advance on the western frontier as the guiding principle of American social evolution and the vital force in the shaping of the national character. Given its enormous cultural impact, it is more than a little surprising that in the developing field of mimetic theory with its discussion of violent mythologies, the American myth par excellence should be as curiously absent as it has been for the past fifty years. René Girard's preoccupation with myths whose origins lie hundreds and thousands of years ago, in the days of yore, as well as primarily in the Old World, has apparently precluded him and others, as far as I am aware, from writing at length about the relatively young mythology of the frontier, central as it has been to the forging of America's national identity.

Perhaps the parallels are rather too obvious to require mimetic explication. According to Turner, the evolution of the American character took shape against the background of the geographic and economic expansion of America's national borders, which guaranteed relative internal peace and social cohesion so long as there was a frontier behind which lay free land to occupy (32; *GN* 30). This peace was not purely defined in economic terms, though. Significantly, the formulation of Turner's thesis may be taken as a point in time onward from which we gradually came to realize that from the start, the fertilizer of America's growth—its "perennial rebirth" (2)—has been the lifeblood of its Native American, black, and Hispanic populations. When comparing the myth of the frontier to older mythologies in terms of mimetic theory, three factors deserve special emphasis:

1. the increasing number of victims necessary to produce the desired cultural revitalization or stabilization, in other words, the decreasing potency of sacrifice;
2. the dramatically shortened half-life of the power of (modern) myths to effectively repress or else sanctify the knowledge of victimization, a function that may in part be assumed by various more or less totalitarian ideologies;
3. the cultural upheaval, often conflictual and sometimes violent, that correlates with the disintegration of mythology and the revelation of the victim.

Turner clearly perceived the role played by "the Indian," whose perceived threat, real or illusory, called for "united action" and so served to unify colonies across the frontier as a "consolidating agent" (14). Turner and his contemporaries were still able to believe in a frontier myth powerful enough to repress or else ideologically rein in and justify the knowledge of the victims of expansionism. Today, we no longer have that luxury as our counternarratives and various historical revisionisms testify. To the contrary, the myth of the frontier, with its narrative core of regeneration through violence, only exposes the impotence both of sacrifice and of modern myths, at least in the Western world. It is thus that Bloom can rightly identify *Blood Meridian* as a "holocaust novel. The holocaust is of the Native Americans of the Southwest, but it is certainly a holocaust" (cit. in Josyph 2010b, 78). Not only did the victims of manifest destiny number in the tens and hundreds of thousands, the sacrificial pattern behind the slaughter is all-too-readily apparent.

With the erosion of myth, the role of ideology in justifying genocidal victimage comes to the fore (*BE* 53). During the period that *Blood Meridian* is set in, this ideology came by the name of "manifest destiny." Historically, the annexation of Texas and the acquisition of Oregon Country led to a revival of important motifs of the frontier myth. At the same time, it fueled the United States' ambition to form a nation "from sea to shining sea." In an 1845 article advocating the annexation of Texas, columnist John O'Sullivan had coined the term "manifest destiny," and thus given a name to the already widespread belief that the United States had been singled out by providence to extend its borders and spread American civilization and republican democracy. The effect was a conjunction of "imperialist ambition with that 'divine purpose' that had inspired the Puritans to found the 'redeemer nation' and the revolutionaries to establish the democratic 'last best hope of mankind'" (Cant 157).

Prophetic inspiration meshed with an essentially Darwinian view of social evolution. According to Slotkin, the consensus of conquering Mexico was rooted in a prevalent "belief in the concept of history as the story of the strife between advanced and primitive races," ideologues making it "the 'mission' of the Anglo-Saxon race to conquer the savage and make the New World the home of democracy and economic progress" (*FE* 174–75, 176). With the advent of the Mexican-American War , the federal government assumed the role of "an active and aggressive agent of expansion" (*FE* 165). Manifest destiny became a term used to promote and legitimize territorial expansion, conquest, and expropriation.

The Kid is drawn into these circles after brutalizing and likely killing a Mexican bartender in San Antonio de Béxar for being cheated out of a drink. As rumor of his prowess travels, he is sought out by a self-identifying "white and christian" (*BM* 28) recruiter to join a filibustering expedition into Mexico. Initially he refuses: "The war's over. [. . .] I aint lost nothin down there" (*BM* 29). The recruiter then tries to convince the ragged Kid of his cause by promising him an outfit, a "chance for ye to raise ye self in the world," and the prospect of becoming "a big landowner" (*BM* 29–30). To this appeal to central aspects of the American dream, long before it existed as a term, is added another distinctively American set of reasons in the Kid's meeting with Captain White. The Captain will also serve as the Kid's first mimetic model, while at the same time pointing toward other, more potent ones.

White's example can be interpreted as one of *external mediation*, drawing on the powerfully attractive aspect of sacrifice that comes by the name of heroism. In his analysis of "Heroic and Post-Heroic Societies," the German political scientist Herfried Münkler points toward central aspects that complement readings of *Blood Meridian* as a heroic epic, in a way that offers possibilities for integrating these aspects into the larger framework of mimetic theory. Münkler does so by pointing out both the centrality of sacrifice in attributing heroism and the indispensable nature of the religious element that comes with it:

> Only those who are ready to make sacrifices, including the ultimate sacrifice of their own lives, can become heroes. [...] Since the idea of sacrifice, in which one offers up himself to save the whole, cannot comfortably be conceived of without appealing to religion, heroic societies most often have a religious core. [...] Only societies that have the ability to symbolically transfigure death into an act of sublime meaningfulness can be understood as heroic societies. Conversely, preheroic or postheroic societies understand the dead of war and combat as the consequences of plain and simple slaughter. It is not the blood on his weapons that makes a hero out of the warrior, but his willingness to sacrifice himself, so that others may be saved. (2007, 742)

The transition to postheroic societies then would seem to run parallel with the collapse of mythologies, which elucidates our postmodern aversion to the heroic epic. Aside from religious and ideological factors, a more fundamental cause, Münkler suggests, may be demographics, as a reduction of birth rates in Western and industrialized countries and the resulting scarcity primarily of young men, but (perhaps concomitantly) also and increasingly of women whom, put bluntly, a society can afford to "sacrifice."[12]

By and large, the postheroic is the European condition, and increasingly so the American as well. Hence, most modern readers see through the emptiness and hypocrisy of White's rhetoric, just as most readers today see through the fantasmatic nature of the frontier mythos and the idealized, romantic world of classical Western movies, which as a genre have all but disappeared.[13] Judging by Sylder's statement to John Wesley that "they ain't no more heroes" (*OK* 214) or Sheriff Bell's guilt-ridden confession about "bein a war hero" to the public while in truth having abandoned his squad in World War II (*NC* 273–74), McCarthy seems to mistrust heroism as much as Girard does:

"Heroic models, understood as models that can be imitated, are now null. This is why totalitarian regimes have always tried to construct them. [. . .] Heroism is a value that is too corrupted for us to trust: in a way, scoundrels have always been infiltrating it, especially since Napoleon" (*BE* 102, 105). On a side note, it is perhaps worth pointing out that Antonio López de Santa Anna was called "the Napoleon of the West," and so reportedly referred to himself to Sam Huston in his surrender after the battle of San Jacinto. Yet the main point is that our perspective on these matters has shifted quite radically from 1950, 1936, 1914, 1883, or 1846.

The Texan Revolution took place in 1836, roughly a decade before the Mexican-American War and the events of *Blood Meridian*. Even a hundred years later, the dead of the Alamo could still be hailed as "heroes who sacrificed their lives," and who, animated by "the eternal spirit of sublime heroic sacrifice," perished "with flag still proudly waving [. . .] in the flames of immortality that their high sacrifice might lead to the founding of this Texas."[14] These words reflect a kind of founding violence, though perhaps not at its sacrificial purest, as the divine and monstrous binary nature of the transfigured victim has been split up: The dead on the American side are apotheosized, reflecting the beneficial side of the sacrificial victim. Conversely, the Mexican victims of the war that greatly expanded U.S. territory and ultimately resolved a decade of intermittent Texan-Mexican conflicts following the events of the Texan Revolution are disavowed, or, as in White's rhetoric, reviled.

It is hardly by accident that the Kid is recruited around San Antonio de Béxar, where the Alamo is located. In a case of external mediation, Captain White appeals to the Kid's patriotism both as an American and particularly as a Tennessean, who are the "bravest bunch of men under fire I believe I ever saw. I suppose more men from Tennessee bled and died on the field in northern Mexico than from any other state" (*BM* 33). While the Kid is comically ignorant of his countrymen's "heroic" sacrifice, his taciturn answers, modeled after the advice of the sergeant who recruited him, could equally bespeak insecurity, awe, resistance, or total indifference. White further invokes the heroic military aura of Mexican-American war hero Alexander William Doniphan and his legendary capture of Chihuahua in 1847. Following a rhetoric Jarrett tracks to editorials and speeches by expansionists like Stephen Douglass, John O'Sullivan, and William Swain (69–70), the appropriately named

Captain White interprets the Treaty of Guadalupe Hidalgo as a betrayal of the Americans who fought in the war and then "were sold out by their own country," specifically by "those mollycoddles in Washington" (*BM* 33–35).

White thus creates a line of American patriots and heroic models along which to situate himself and his men, who are to be "the instruments of liberation in a dark and troubled land" (*BM* 34). The liberation he envisions is one from the Indian "heathen horde" (*BM* 33) who terrorize the populace, but also of Mexicans *from themselves.* He denigrates them as "a bunch of barbarians [. . .] a race of degenerates" (*BM* 33–34), and as unfit for self-government: "There is no government in Mexico. Hell, there is no God in Mexico. Never will be. We are dealing with a people manifestly incapable of governing themselves. And do you know what happens with people who cannot govern themselves? That's right. Others come in to govern for them" (*BM* 34). While scholarship reflects the ideological nature of White's mix of religious, political, and racialist rhetoric—including the postmodern practice of wholesale condemning manifest destiny in the name of the ideals of liberty and democracy that it espoused—one element that deserves special attention is the act of scapegoating that this rhetoric performs.[15] Not only were Americans in doubt as to Mexicans' "racial status," their "benighted sister republic" (*BM* 34) was perceived as "a dark mirror in which Americans saw the features of their own culture" (*FE* 174). In a way, the rhetoric created in Mexico a kind of national scapegoat. This goes down to the level of the sacrificial victim's benign and malicious double nature, which are reflected in both the land and its people:

> The divisions of class and race, the political divisions between entrepreneurs and Jacksonian workingmen and paternalists, were reproduced in the depiction of Mexico, making that nation an unwilling testing ground for the definition and resolution of *Yanqui* ideological issues. The land and the people and the politics of Mexico were interpreted in terms of the current American vocabulary of myth and ideology. The United States was a nation that had grown great on the process of agrarian expansion into an Edenic wilderness. So Mexico, the new field of expansion, is seen as "an earthly paradise, wild yet beautiful." But modern America was now divided between a dwindling agrarian hinterland and a burgeoning Metropolis. So

in Mexico, the wilderness gives way to poor and crowded towns filled with "degraded" mestizos. (*FE* 174)

As news editorials of the time made efforts to depict the war à la Captain White as an act of liberation, its advocates envisioned a Spanish aristocracy enslaving the Mexican poor. Thereby, they unconsciously reproduced America's own enslavement of what were at the time about 2.5 million African Americans, as well as her oppression of other ethnic groups and the working classes. Thus, the spokesmen of manifest destiny went about the "ideologically necessary task of scapegoating Mexico for American sins" (*FE* 179). White himself reproduces this inconsistent and essentially mythological view by branding Mexicans as a "mongrel race, little better than niggers. And maybe no better" (*BM* 34), even as he purports, at some paternalistic level, to help them improve their lot and protect them from the "naked savages" to whom they have cowardly "paid tribute" (*BM* 33).[16] On the positive end of the spectrum, he praises Mexico's fertile lands and abundant riches in minerals, which makes it a kind of unspoiled paradise inviting young, ambitious Americans like the Kid "to make your mark in this world." Finally, he stresses the urgency of the mission by raising the rival specter of European powers, which will themselves colonize this desirable land "unless we act" (*BM* 35).

At the center of this seductive matrix of ideological imperatives, prospects of personal advancement, scapegoats, and heroic models, there is finally Captain White himself. Driven by delusions of white supremacy, White is a man of "sweeping moustaches," who scarcely even acknowledges his subordinates' presence, letting them wait, sometimes pausing for "measured minute[s]" (*BM* 32), a man who dusts his letters "with sand from a little onyx box" (*BM* 31), and wax-seals them with his ring like some warrior-aristocrat. Like his jingoist and racialist rhetoric, his every gesture oozes an overblown gravitas and style-consciousness reminiscent, Owens points out, of a George Armstrong Custer (29–30). To the Kid he may seem like a proper model to follow; to the reader, he cannot but come across as a satirical figure expressing the more ridiculous aspects of nationalist heroism.

Once the filibusters trespass into Mexican territory on a way compared to "the high road to hell" (*BM* 45), they enter the realm of the wilderness. But a few days in, they are ambushed by a horde of Comanches. What the

Captain arrogantly mistakes as "a little sport" (*BM* 51) turns into a total massacre. Barely surviving the slaughter and the following desert march, the Kid is arrested by Mexican authorities. Mirroring the historical end of the filibustering politician Henry A. Crabb in the Mexican Reform War of 1857, the body of Captain White is fed to the hogs, his severed head pickled and put on public display (Sepich 2008, 21). At this sight, even the narrator cannot resist a jibe at the Captain's expense, humoring White as "lately at war among the heathen" (*BM* 69).

The Kid's reaction to this humiliating deflation of White is a straightforward disavowal of the man who could have served as his model and who has now lost all attraction: "He spat and wiped his mouth. He aint no kin to me, he said" (*BM* 69). Later, he asserts sardonically: "Somebody ought to of pickled [his head] a long time ago. By rights they ought to pickle mine. For ever takin up with such a fool" (*BM* 70). Captain White's sudden, total defeat and gruesome demise at the hands of two peoples he regards as inferior not only proves fatally wrong his assumptions of racial supremacy, but effectively renders him a laughingstock. So it is with the ideology he represents. In *Blood Meridian*, there is no manifest destiny, and the sole providence seems to be that of superior violence. It is in this spirit that the Kid will join Glanton's scalp hunters, a group of new models infinitely more dangerous and attractive than White and his filibusters.

Doubles, Sacrifices, Mimetic Patterns

Even in the broad strokes I am painting here, the same patterns of mimetic rivalry and sacrifice that infuse *The Orchard Keeper* and *Child of God* cannot fail to resurface. In fact, they are magnified to a national scale. The sacrificial logic at the heart of the frontier myth suggests nothing less than the potential of rewriting the history of American continental expansion in terms of mimetic theory. Such a project is wildly beyond the scope of this work. The discussion so far allows merely for a tentative mapping of *Blood Meridian* in relation to both the mytheme of regeneration through violence and the history of manifest destiny. I have only begun to trace mimetic constellations on the textual level of the work itself. The case needs to be made that *Blood Meridian* truly is a novel as radically aware and revealing of mimetic dynamics and sacrificial structures as I make it out to be. Again, the aim of making this case is to show how this quality informs the novel's apocalypticism.

Therefore, it is worth temporarily suspending the investigation of American myth and history in order to establish the frequency with which mimetic figures and figurations appear in *Blood Meridian*. This applies all the more since scholarship has yet to take notice of them. This analysis began with a discussion of a paradigmatically McCarthyan image, casting the world as a bullet within the figurative bore of the sun and its moon replica, which I interpreted as a cataclysmic metaphor of conflictual mimesis. A similar celestial example is provided in a "false moon" that the gang spots one night. The appearance raises the question "if it were true that at one time there had been two moons in the sky." To this, the "expriest" Tobin responds that while "it may well have been so," God would have erased one of the moons to prevent "the proliferation of lunacy on this earth" (*BM* 244). This brief exchange can be read as a comment on the imperfection of creation, but the conjunction of double moons with the intensification of madness also suggests the frantic contagion of imitation to the loss of identity between mimetic rivals. Speaking of lunacy, the gang encounters and kills one of two German hermit brothers in the old mission church of San José de Tumacacori, of which one is judged "an imbecile" and the other "not altogether sane" (*BM* 225). Another brother, the "idiot" Two Bits, whom the Judge adopts, is fascinated on various occasions by his watery reflections (*BM* 258, 284).

Recalling Lester Ballard's Narcissus moment in *Child of God*, this last example points in the direction of doubles that are optical reflections of an often spectral quality. On reaching the ocean, the Kid watches the evening sky with its clouds as "a salmoncolored othersea" (*BM* 304). A more suggestive example is the doubling of a group of Apache horsemen crossing by the lakeside, which creates "in the dawn-broached sky a hellish likeness," an inverted horde of "howling antiwarriors pendant from their mounts" (*BM* 109). More straightforward reduplications pertain to the animal and human level, suggesting actual doubles. As has been pointed out, the bear that carries off one of the gang's Delawares "like some fabled storybook beast" (*BM* 137) finds a degraded and domesticated double in the dancing bear at Fort Griffin, each of them appearing, with reversed roles, in scenes drenched with sacrificial symbolism.[17] At another point in the narrative, we find the Kid staring into the sky "where very high there circled two black hawks about the sun slowly and perfectly opposed like paper birds upon a pole" (*BM* 213), a sight that immediately precedes his distant observation of the clash between two armies in the desert.

One could conceivably add a representational level with the Judge's anecdote of the old Hueco and his portrait. By drawing the Hueco, the Judge claims to have "chained the old man to his own likeness," so that "he could not sleep for fear an enemy might take it and deface it and so like was the portrait that he would not suffer it creased," until the distraught man sought out the Judge, "and they buried the portrait in the floor of a cave where it lies yet" (*BM* 141). By itself, the parabolic story is rather cryptic. One could shrug it off as just a tale of "primitive superstition." Yet such nonchalance is complicated in that the Hueco's sentiments mirror those of the scalphunter Marcus Webster. Webster insists on his difference from the "ignorant heathen savage" (*BM* 141), yet adamantly refuses to sit for a portrait for the Judge's ledger. It stands to reason that the Hueco's tale involves a kind of metaphysical fear that is somehow rooted in the Judge's supreme ability to produce "pictures like enough the things themselves" (*BM* 141). As if in variation on Oscar Wilde's *The Picture of Dorian Gray*, the Hueco fears damage and offense to the portrait as he would to himself. Consequently, he and the Judge hide and bury the portrait as a substitute for the man. The Judge's comment that "every man is tabernacled in every other and he so in exchange and so on in an endless complexity of being" (*BM* 141) could thus be read as reflecting a profound insight into the true object of human desires, that is, the *being* of the other.

Admittedly, these are relatively minor examples spread throughout a work of enormous poetic density, dissimilar in meaning and with little to no impact on the action. Put together though, they suggest a subtle pattern of doubles and reflections, sacrifice and substitution, rivalry and conflict. This pattern emerges fully once we take account of some of the more prominent and explicitly violent rival-doubles the novel puts forth. Frequently enough, the object of dispute is trivial, ephemeral, or hard to identify to begin with. This is apparent in the three pairings of the Kid and Toadvine, the aged Kid and young Elrod, and Black and White John Jackson.

In the Kid's first encounter with Toadvine in Nacogdoches, the clash is over the use of the narrow planks spread over the muddy ground and leading to the outhouses. With the Kid coming from one direction and Toadvine from the other, they literally become a *skandalon* (Gk. obstacle, stumbling block) to each other. To recall, the scandal designates a person rather than an object, namely "the model exerting its special form of temptation" (*TH* 418) that repels even as it attracts. Thus, it is Toadvine's "You better get out of my way" (*BM* 9) that irresistibly provokes the Kid. Like bedraggled versions of Oedipus's enemy sons Eteocles and Polyneices, they end up mimetic rivals: a kick in the jaw is reciprocated with the swing of a bottle, which is answered in turn with the slash of a knife. The rivals circle one another like the hawks that catch the Kid's eye on his desert journey. Both men end up indistinguishable and in the mud, from which they eventually emerge "like forms excavated from a bog" and "great clay voodoo doll[s] made animate" (*BM* 12–13). Ironically, it is against the third party of Old Sidney, who is potentially the man who eventually breaks up their fight by knocking them unconscious, that they are reconciled. They get their revenge by brutalizing the man and burning down the hotel.

In the twenty-third and final chapter of the novel, the Kid, who is now "the Man," clashes with Elrod, who is barely concealed as the Man's younger double. Again, it is not altogether clear what drives their conflict. The catalyst seems to be the scapular of Indian ears that the Man has kept and that serves as an increasingly amorphous and unrecognizable proof of past murders. Elrod thrice questions the authenticity of the grisly trophies, and so the veracity of the Man's war story. Jarrett rightly asks whether Elrod's "denial of the bloody origin of the scapular represent[s] a cultural and historical desire to repress the legacy of conquest in the history of the West" (87), but as Owens points out, the ears are also "a badge of merit earned by participation in primal violence" (24). First and foremost, it is his aggressive streak that links Elrod to the Kid. While the boy wants to hear nothing whatsoever of any kinship or familiarity with him, lashing out at the Man's conciliatory "son," Elrod is undeniably the younger Kid's likeness, not least in being the same age as him when he first got shot. His denigration of the Man—"I knowed you for what you was when I seen ye" (*BM* 322)—recalls the Kid's youthful repugnance at the weakness of filibuster Sproule: "I know your kind [. . .]. What's wrong with you is wrong all the way through you" (*BM* 66). Finally, faced with the threat of being shot, he repeats verbatim the Kid's self-affirmative words to Toadvine about being bested and killed in a fight: "They aint nobody done it yet" (*BM* 10, 322). In addition to the veracity of past atrocities, it is thus more immediately the man's warrior virtue, differently put his ability to incorporate the sacred violence that fueled these atrocities, that is put into question, and in this sense his very *being* at which the desire of his young rival is ultimately directed.

Finally, *Blood Meridian*'s exemplary rival-doubles are not difficult to spot, introduced as they are at the opening of chapter 7: "In this company there rode two men named Jackson, one black, one white, both forenamed John. Bad blood lay between them and as they rode up under the barren mountains the white man would fall back alongside the other and take his shadow for the shade that was in it and whisper to him" (*BM* 81). Once again, nothing truly accounts for the bad blood between the two men. The critical default reaction predictably diagnoses White Jackson's racism as the cause of aversion. This case is substantiated by setting sights on the two campfires that eventually serve as the scenery for the resolution of this conflict. It is upon the realization that the new recruits—among them the Kid as well as the Delawares and the Mexican John McGill, that is, Juan Miguel—are all gathered around one fire, and the veterans of the gang around the other, that the white denies the black his place: "You dont get your black ass away from this fire I'll kill you" (*BM* 106).

Against this straightforward case, Black Jackson points out that "Any man in this company can sit where it suits him," which is supported by the narrative comment that there were "no rules real or tacit" (*BM* 106) as to who should sit where. The internal segregation along racial lines and new recruits, then, is incidental. What is more, the gang's diversity by itself suggests that ethnic purity is not an issue, or at least not a priority. After all, this is a group on the warpath. They consistently present a united front not only to common foes, but also to civilians like the white saloon owner Mr. Owens, who is unceremoniously shot by Black Jackson when he tries to enforce segregation upon the group, or the sergeant who tries to arrest the murderer afterward.[18] Nor does anyone interfere or raise a word against the killing of White Jackson by Black Jackson. Consequently, the issue of race is largely exchanged for another: Glanton's gang is a company where a man's worth is not determined by the color of his skin but by his ability as a warrior.

As there is no other obvious cause for their conflict, nor much else by way of detail to characterize the relationship between Black and White Jackson, the one fact that stands out about them is that they are perfect namesakes and thus overtly construed as doubles. While racism may ex post facto graft itself onto their animosity, White Jackson seems to be first and foremost interested in Black Jackson *himself.* His whispering to the black and his crooning of "things that sounded like the words of love" (*BM* 81) intimates the kind of sometimes almost romantic attraction that Girard singles out as the central link between the disciple and the model-rival in a mimetic relationship. White Jackson's symbolic stepping on Black Jackson's shadow suggests the metaphysical quality of this attraction toward the other's *being*, "as if the white man were in violation of his person, had stumbled onto some ritual [. . .] whereby the shape he stood the sun from on that rocky ground bore something of the man himself and in so doing lay imperiled" (*BM* 81).

If the offense is of ritualistic quality, so is the resolution of the conflict. As Black Jackson steps up from behind White Jackson, he carries his bowieknife "in both hands like some instrument of ceremony" and decapitates his rival with a single stroke, whereupon "two thick ropes of dark blood and two slender rose like snakes from the stump and arched hissing into the fire" (*BM* 107). "This violent sundering," Adam Parkes points out, "bears witness to the self's insistently doubling motions, for the action of blood itself embodies the paring of opposites, giving the lie to the essentialist thinking that underlay the dead man's racism" (118). If the men's rivalry divided the group against itself, the impurity in its "communal soul" (*BM* 152) is thus purged in the purifying sacrificial flames, leaving the dead "like a murdered anchorite" (*BM* 107), which plays into the conjunction of violence and religion that will be discussed later on.[19]

In sum, these examples reveal a consistent pattern of conflictual doubles and sacrificial violence much as that present in McCarthy's earlier works. Like a bassline to a melody, this pattern underlies and subtly governs the novel's more explicit, thematic concerns. What is new for McCarthy is that we find the same patterns as characterizing intergroup relations as well. Given that the bulk of the novel follows their exploits, Glanton's scalp hunters take center stage in showing this.

Glanton's Scalp Hunters, or the Economy of Slaughter, Part 1

Demonstrably, *Blood Meridian* emerges as a work aware of and driven by mimetic dynamics. The novel sometimes broaches this issue in a straightforward manner. Acquisitive mimesis may well be at work in the figure of a priest in Jesús María, too, who is ridiculed and bullied by Glanton's gang and who in turn disdains the gold coins they fling at him, "until some small boys ran out to gather them" (*BM* 190), at which point he orders them to bring him the coins. The old hermit the Kid meets early on claims that "They is four things that can destroy the earth [. . .]. Women, whiskey, money, and niggers" (*BM* 18). The obvious interpretation is that the man is a chauvinist and a racist, driven into the wilderness by his misanthropy. Beyond the immediate repulsiveness of the man's views, they arguably contain a certain, ironic level of insight, too. For instance, the role of women as the objects of comedic or tragic romantic triangles, rivalries, duels, and even wars as in the *Iliad* is both an ancient literary trope and a manifestation of human acquisitive ambitions. In an early draft of the novel, Glanton sends Doc Irving "out for whores and drink," telling him to get "Enough to where they wont get fought over," to which Irving sardonically replies that "There aint that many in Mexico" (91/35/9, 274). Likewise, the Kid in his later travels sees "women fought over to the death whose value they themselves set at two dollars" (*BM* 213).

One does not have to look through either a gender or mimetic lens to see the dehumanizing reduction of both women and men into objects to be acquired, or the explosive potential in such reduction. The hermit confesses to being a former slaver, who earned well but "got sick of it" (*BM* 18). Needless to say, the contestation of the right to own another human being would be at the core of the bloodiest conflict in American history, the catastrophic Civil War that sometimes literally set brother against brother. Similarly lucrative prospects of making money by factually reducing human beings to body parts are what drove the scalp-hunting business. Following Girard though, the problem lies not in the object itself but in the competitors clashing around it, as the true "cannibalistic" desire is for the rival-model's *fullness of being.* What then of such cases where model and object actually fall together, as in actual cases of cannibalism or scalp hunting?

Following the Comanche massacre and his arrest by Mexican authorities, the Kid is transported to Chihuahua City. Reunited with his old acquaintance Toadvine, he joins John Joel Glanton's gang of professional scalp hunters. Upon their entrance, the scalp hunters appear as a group markedly different from the filibusters. Decorated as they are with the trophies of former victims, "the trappings of their horses fashioned out of human skin and their bridles woven up from human hair and decorated with human teeth and the riders wearing scapulars or necklaces of dried and blackened human ears" (*BM* 78), the group seems closer in spirit and manner to the Comanches who wiped out White's men. In fact, the group includes "a number of halfnaked savages [...], dangerous, filthy, brutal, the whole like a visitation from some heathen land where they and others like them fed on human flesh" (*BM* 78).

On top of the specter of cannibalism, one is reminded of Slotkin's assertion that in order to "beat the Indian" the frontiersman had to *imitate* him, an insight already present in Turner's thesis.[20] Their delusion of superiority and failure to imitate their enemies is essentially the fatal neglect of the decidedly "white" and purportedly "christian" (*BM* 28) filibusters. Quite beyond such notions, the gang is as ethnically diverse in its make-up of white, black, Delaware Indian, and Mexican members as the crew of Melville's *Pequod.*[21] This diversity is not purely of McCarthy's imagination, either, if Sam Chamberlain's *My Confession* can be believed: "There was Sonorans, Cherokee and Delaware Indians, French Canadians, Texans, Irishmen, a Negro and full blooded Comanche in this band of Scalp Hunters, with a miscellaneous collection of weapons, and equipment and a diversity of costume seldom seen in a regular organized body of volunteers for Indian warfare" (268).

Consequently, as in the conflict between the two Jacksons, the issue of race is displaced for another. Historically as well as literarily, Glanton's gang is a company where a man's worth is dependent on his warlike merit. Whereas the Pequot became "the first American Indian tribe to be slaughtered to extinction" (Wallach 2013, 40), Glanton's polyglot crew are themselves in the "business" of exterminating Indians. The myth-scenario of regeneration through violence demands a regress to a more primal state of existence. In terms of the quasi-Darwinian logic summoned by Judge Holden, it is a state apt to meet the unrelenting demands of the wilderness, the realm of the sacred, and of uncontrolled, indiscriminate violence. Adaptation is a key factor in the Glanton gang's journey: Their "absolute lawlessness [. . .] matches the absolute wilderness of the setting" (Guillemin 2004, 73). What is more, they also incorporate its absolute violence.

Before the gang eventually runs amok, they are introduced as a group not only of warriors, but also of businessmen. In this, they share the entrepreneurial virtues of the frontiersman, who by Slotkin's account is "a man of exploit, not of patient labor; a predator before he is a cultivator. He achieves [. . .] wealth not through drudgery and self-denial; but [. . .] through dramatic discovery and through violent struggle with a great antagonist" (*FE* 68). The scalp hunters are hired by Chihuahua's governor Angel Trias to protect the state against marauding bands of Indians. As McCarthy's epigraph from the *Yuma Daily Sun* indicates, the practice of scalping spans cultures, and it dates as far back as three hundred thousand years. On the North American continent, it apparently existed before the arrival of European settlers, and the scalp had value as an actual object of exchange and as a metaphysically charged object of spirituality and ritual. Nevertheless, "Europeans did play a significant role in promoting the practice," not only by adopting it themselves, but by contagiously spreading it, through paying bounty "to Indians who had previously never engaged in it or had done so sparingly" (Schimpf 2013, 27–28; see also Sepich 2008).

Historically, scholars like Sepich and Schimpf point out, scalp hunting in Chihuahua reached a high point around the middle of the nineteenth century, specifically during and after the Mexican-American War. A scalp then was worth up to $200. Hence, the killing of the indigenous people proved to be a lucrative business (Sepich 2008, 7), and businessmen is what scalp hunters like Glanton, James Kirker, or James Hobbs considered themselves: "We scalped the Indians, though some of the party said it looked barbarous; but I kept on scalping, saying that business men [*sic*] always took receipts, and I wanted something to show our success" (cit. in Sepich 1999, 125)." Glanton uses the same language when he tells one of the gang to "Get that receipt for us," and investigates an old Indian woman's scalp "the way a man might qualify the pelt of an animal" (*BM* 99). In the massacre of the Apaches, one of the Delawares emerges "with a collection of heads like some strange vendor bound for market" (*BM* 156), and the Judge, inquiring whether Glanton wants to continue his hunting for the Apaches, asks whether he intends to "drive that stock" (*BM* 160).

What comes to the fore here is perhaps the darkest aspect of the frontier myth. Referring readers to the extinction of the buffaloes whose bones become an important commodity in Fort Griffin, Wallach asserts that the heroic martial code, that superficially seemed to govern the Old West and that McCarthy demystifies, "has been reinscribed in a new, commercial guise of jingoistic capitalism" (2002a, 209), which already sanctions the scalp-hunting trade. On a fundamental level, humanity itself is commodified and subjected to the logic of ravenous capitalism, the American Indian reduced to "an aspect of the world of resources—a tree to be cleared off so the field can be farmed" (*FE* 17). Nowhere is this as blatantly obvious as in the business of scalp hunting.

What *Blood Meridian* puts into focus are the intricate ties between political interests, market economies, and violence. Accordingly, David Holloway sees at work in the novel an acute suspicion "that anarchic destruction is not simply an economic accident but an inner historical necessity, the very life blood of capitalist accumulation" (2000, 196). In an important essay on "The Questioning of Market Economies in Cormac McCarthy's Novels," Christine Chollier points out how, whereas usually "the so-called peace of the market must be ensured so that transactions can be freely carried out," *Blood Meridian* exemplifies "the substitution of violence for exchange." She continues:

> What is also interesting in *Blood Meridian* is that White's greed for gold and silver, which is hardly concealed by his mystic and religious arguments, is replaced [. . .] by a company which is first interested in financial reward but eventually loses sight of that former motivation. Murder generates murder, the novel shows, and general massacre replaces trade. However, the Judge argues that war is "[t]he ultimate trade awaiting its ultimate practitioner." [. . .] So, violence, which first appeared as complete annihilation of trade, is reestablished as the ultimate form of trade—its quintessence: as Patricia Nelson Limerick put it, "[c]onquest was a literal, territorial form of economic growth." (174–75)

As mimetic theory assumes the relative insignificance of the object, it is not surprising that the scalp hunters eventually lose sight of their financial goals, substituting the attraction of violence itself. If war is substituted for trade, that is, if the exchange of blows memorized in the object of the scalp is sub-stituted for the exchange of goods and symbolic monetary capital, this is at once a discovery of and return to the bloody roots of all symbolic exchange in the sacrificial victim. Andrew McKenna explains: "Any sort of thing can substitute for the victim precisely because the victim is always already a substitute, a signifier, a mark, in Derridean terms, of a deferral," and thus, too, "the sacrificial origin of money, as a substitute for the object of desire" (76), comes to the fore. The systems of barter and the archaic exchange of gift and countergift always threatened to devolve into excess and conflict as goods and gifts were compared. Thus, they were subject to complex rules and obligations aimed at dissimulating this danger.

In contrast, money provides a neutral means of symbolic exchange as it removes the factors of immediacy and comparability in reciprocity: "What symbolizes the link among people and prevents them from 'coming to blows' also has a sacred origin: money replaces the victim on whose head people used to find reconciliation. [. . .] We exchange goods so as not to exchange blows, but trading goods always contains a memory of trading blows" (*BE* 59). The Judge's claim that "All other trades are contained in that of war" (*BM* 249) is thus corroborated in macabre fashion. The force of the market both incubates and spreads the economically sanctioned contagion of violence. "Trade is a formidable form of war, especially since it results in fewer dead" (*BE* 58). Contrary to the common view of the global market as a guarantor of peace, however, the forces of the market and politics alike prove ultimately powerless in controlling the "ultimate trade." After all, the logic of work in trade, war, or any form of exchange is still that of *reciprocity*, which irresistibly reasserts itself.

In the end, it is crucial to realize that these are not merely flights of either literary imagination, mythical thinking, or scholarly abstraction, but patterns that characterize the interaction *between* individuals and larger groups. It would be a mistake to reduce the violence of these exchanges into some universal essence within humans, or perhaps males in particular. In an interview with Peter Josyph, Rick Wallach thus poignantly asks:

How do you classify the motives of a native people who are viewed as commodities on every level? Grab their land, their food supply, their *scalps*— their *bodies*, for God's sake. Is it viciousness to resist that? [...] There were conflicts among Native Americans long before Europeans arrived, but there were also nations, alliances, commerce—all the traffic of culture. [...] They learned a lot of what they knew from our illustrious ancestors. [...] If there's a point to be made about native viciousness, the infectiousness of the European brand ought to be stressed. (cit. in Josyph 2010a, 106)

Even in the market, there is no escaping the systemic logic of violent reciprocity, which is at best dissimulated and exported, yet may always stage a devastating return. Tracing the course of (American) violence backward in time, we shall find again and again different originators setting off new imitative cycles of acts and reaction, as causes multiply themselves. As we begin approaching the novel's apocalyptic dimension, it is thus inevitable to take a closer look at the contagion of European violence.

The Meaning of History:
Judge Holden and the Apocalypse

So far, I have dealt with *Blood Meridian* as a historical novel set in the era of manifest destiny and as a "revision" of central elements of the frontier myth, in other words as Bloom's "ultimate Western." Along the way, the novel has emerged as a work of proliferating doubles and characterized by sacrificial logic. In both respects, the American element is prevalent in the novel's unforgiving portrayal of U.S. history, even as we have yet to appreciate in full the myth-shattering dimension of how McCarthy reimagines frontier history. This chapter continues both of these lines of thought, but also recontextualizes them within an eschatological context. What McCarthy unveils, I argue, radically transcends the sphere of American culture and, potentially, that of the Western world, articulating instead a logic of the historical process of civilization and human nature as a whole.

As I have said, this logic is an apocalyptic one. While mimetic theory has always been implicitly eschatological,[23] it is only with *Battling to the End*

(2010) that René Girard, by his own admission, is able to spell out "the broad lines" of his anthropological theory "in its relation to history" (*BE* 1), to which the Apocalypse provides the *telos* and capstone. Surprisingly, Girard finds that "the apocalypse appropriate for our time is perhaps not longer Saint John at Patmos, but a Prussian general riding with his friends along the roads of Russia and Europe" (*BE* 135). The general in question is Carl von Clausewitz, a compatriot of whom the scalp hunters encounter in the historical personage of the weapons-trading "Prussian Jew" Albert Speyer (*BM* 82). It is Clausewitz's unfinished book *Vom Kriege* (1832) that Girard intends to complete, along with mimetic theory, in *Battling to the End*.[24]

Aiming to reform the Prussian military, Clausewitz wrote under the impression of a fundamental change in the way war was being waged by the introduction of a new element. The French Revolution had set a precedent by introducing compulsory military service, and Napoleon's total mobilization of the French citizenry into the *Grande Armée* saw him conquer Europe but also, in a kind of "poor man's response," spawned partisan and guerilla warfare. Whereas war before had been largely the field of aristocrats, mercenaries, and professional soldiers, the trend became one of the militarization of civil life. In Girard's words, Clausewitz perceived "what military theorists did not see: the fact that there was no longer any aristocracy, that modern war was no longer an art or game, but in the process of becoming a religion" (*BE* 155).

Clausewitz in the Southwest

At first glance, it may seem far-fetched to try and illuminate a Western novel set in the aftermath of the Mexican-American War with the strategic treatise of a Prussian general composed in the wake of the Napoleonic Wars and published 153 years earlier, one year before the fictional birth of the Kid. But whatever else it may be, *Blood Meridian* is also a novel of war (Sanborn 2013), and it is in this dimension that it finds its realization as an apocalyptic novel as well. In my view, both the Judge's views on and the novel's dramatization of war intersect and overlap with Clausewitz's reflections. In fact, we have already begun dealing with one of these overlaps in the discussion of war as the Judge's "ultimate trade." Clausewitz himself explicitly compared politics and trade to war, which can in turn be seen as "a kind of trade of a higher measure," as in each case one is engaged in "a conflict of human interests and operations" (136). Thus, Girard comments, the difference between trade and war is one of degree rather than nature. Trade is "constant low-intensity war" that can always intensify from a trade war into an actual war if "smooth settlement of exchanges degenerates into furious competition" (*BE* 59). In another parallel, the Judge compares war to games of sport and of chance, positing that "all games aspire to the condition of war, for here that which is wagered swallows up game, player, all" (*BM* 249).[25]

That said, the truly disconcerting challenge about the Judge's philosophy is to be found not in such ancillary analogies, but rather in his metaphysical conception of war. Holden's introductory words on the subject echo Heraclitus's famous fifty-third fragment, commonly translated "War is the father of all and the king of all; and some he has made gods and some men, some bond and some free."[26] Like Heraclitus, he proclaims war an original and enduring, a priori: "War was always here. Before man was, war waited for him. The ultimate trade awaiting its ultimate practitioner. That is the way it was and will be" (*BM* 248). War appears as an ancient kind of force or principle, akin to the Mennonite's sleeping wrath of God, which is above and beyond "what men think of [it]" (*BM* 248). As such, the Judge claims, it endures through time "because young men love it and old men love it in them," an explicitly mediatory or mimetic relation that, as in games, is fatally bound up in "the value of that which is put at hazard" (*BM* 249).

If, given the constancy of war in human history, we are inclined to grant the Judge's point, the obvious question is: Why is it, exactly, that men "love" war? An answer might be that as violence is perceived, in mimetic terms, as the ultimate mark of what makes humans godlike, and war is the totalization of violence, there is no greater assertion of man's divinity than war. Thus, in the Judge's view, Tobin, the former novitiate priest, "has put by the robes of his craft and taken up the tools of that higher calling which all men honor," to be "no godserver but a god himself" (*BM* 250). If old men love the love of war in young men, it is because it is the younger men's metaphysical fullness and their own remembrance of that fullness that this attraction to violence puts into focus.

In relation to this religious dimension, which is subsequently carried further, Judge Holden also draws an analogy McCarthy may have adopted from Clausewitz. In the first chapter of the first book of *On War*, the Prussian general characterizes warfare as a game of chance, a "play of possibilities and probabilities, good and bad fortune," rendering it "out of all branches of human activity, most akin to a game of cards" (44). Adopting this image, the Judge posits the following archetypal scenario:

> Suppose two men at cards with nothing to wager save their lives. Who has not heard such a tale? A turn of the card. The whole universe for such a player has labored clanking to this moment which will tell if he is to die at that man's hand or that man at his. What more certain validation of a man's worth could there be? This enhancement of the game to its ultimate state admits no argument concerning the notion of fate. The selection of one man over another is a preference absolute and irrevocable and it is a dull man indeed who could reckon so profound a decision without agency or significance either one. [...] This is the nature of war, whose stake is at once the game and the authority and the justification. (*BM* 249)

Evoking a line of thought associated with Arthur Schopenhauer and Nietzsche,[27] the Judge posits that behind the unfolding of events through time there is some kind of agency or *will* involved. This will is identified with both history and the force of war itself: "Seen so, war is the truest form of divination. It is the testing of one's will and the will of another within that larger will which because it binds them is therefore forced to select" (*BM* 249).

We thus arrive at the terrifying core of the Judge's metaphysics: "War is the ultimate game because war is at last a forcing of the unity of existence. War is god" (*BM* 249). War becomes the larger will that also serves as the supreme arbiter between individual human wills and that by choosing between two opponents locked in mortal struggle, asserts the value of the victor over the defeated. Against the objection that "might does not make right," the Judge asserts that such "decisions of life and death" take primacy, subsuming "all lesser ones [...] moral, spiritual, natural," as "a moral view can never be proven right or wrong by any ultimate test" (*BM* 250). The gang may proclaim that Holden is mad, yet as critics have been quick to point out, their deeds belie their words, as all they do is corroborate his awful thesis in their all-but amoral slaughter. The Judge continues:

A man falling dead in a duel is not thought thereby to be proven in error as to his views. His very involvement in such a trial gives evidence of a new and broader view. The willingness of the principals to forgo further argument as the triviality which it in fact is and to petition directly the chambers of the historical absolute clearly indicates of how little moment are the opinions and of what great moment the divergences thereof. For the argument is indeed trivial, but not so the separate wills thereby made manifest. (*BM* 250)

It is here that the "higher court" (*BM* 250) of history goes into session. War becomes "the primary instrument of historical law" (2013, 150) as Philip Snyder puts it, and Bryan Vescio similarly points out how the idea of "an impersonal and unknowable agency beyond all human will that determines our destinies" leads to the restoration of "the power of history—not history as experienced by individuals but what he describes to the Kid as an unknowable 'history of all'" (52). With war and history thus dogmatically ontologized as at once prior and external metaphysical determinants of whatever agency humans can lay claim to, the Judge's ideology assumes decisively fatalistic, totalitarian, and mythological qualities.

The Logic of the Duel and the Vanishing of War

In the Judge's metaphysics of war, we are confronted with a closed, totalitarian system that does not allow for freedom of choice. That man might authentically choose to resist war's violent gravitational pull does not seem to occur to the Judge. And indeed—following the truism that history is written by the victors, or else Schopenhauer's view that humans may do as they want, but cannot *will* what they want—it may appear that war is our perpetual, inescapable destiny.[18] Schopenhauer's contention aligns smoothly with the uncomfortable proposition that what we desire is less our choice but formed unconsciously by our models and environment. As the judge contends, the objects and arguments of conflict alike prove "trivial." The deciding factor is the terrible draw of the logic of the duel, which disintegrates the power of choice. In a related discussion, Rick Wallach connects *Blood Meridian* to *Beowulf* through their common depiction of "martial codes." Martial codes are those "structured social systems that justify and promulgate conflict, represent violence as craft, and conventionalize destructive activity" (2002a, 199), that shape the *heroic communities* (using Münkler's terminology) of Hrothgar's Heorot and the American mid-nineteenth-century Southwest. He judges that McCarthy's novel goes beyond the Old English poem by exposing "the psychological and cultural mechanisms behind the martial code instead of merely chronicling the code's effects" (Wallach 2002a, 200). These mechanisms, Wallach argues, are those of mimetic desire.

Before delving into this argument, I need to confront a conceptual problem: Generally, mimetic anthropology deals with the dynamics of individuals interacting *within* a community. How, then, can we theorize the interaction of two or more distinct social groups? How can we understand the transition from individual violence to sacred war? One answer is that in *Blood Meridian*, "the solipsism of mimetic desire disappears behind a masquerade of ennobled emptying of the self into a commonhood" that is "less an abnegation of desire than the abnegation of individual will" (Wallach 2002a, 202). Before the scalp hunters' massacre of the Apaches, they are fittingly described as a body composed of individuals united through a common purpose, "whose origins," fitting the Judge's views of war, "were antecedent" to them: "For although each man among them was discrete unto himself, conjoined they made a thing that had not been before and in that communal soul were wastes hardly reckonable more than those whited regions on old maps where monsters do live" (*BM* 152).

The question is whether we can translate the behavior of individuals into that of whole groups and even nations at war. By the Judge's profoundly Girardian contention, "What joins men together [. . .] is not the sharing of bread but the sharing of enemies" (*BM* 307), the straightforward answer would seem to be that, indeed, we can. Thus, Roberto Farneti and others have recently begun to utilize the implications of mimetic theory for political science and its understanding of interstate war. As Farneti argues in *Mimetic Politics: Dyadic Patterns in Global Politics*, mimetic theory's central tenet of the imitative dynamic of rivalry poses a serious challenge to political science's unquestioned paradigms of agency and autonomy, particularly to the "epistemological individualism according to which individuals, states, and organizations possess a distinct locus of agency and a capacity to act in isolation from other actors" (27).[29] In mimetic terms, once the warlike game of rivalry, of actions and reprisals is set in motion, it is excruciatingly difficult for its players to escape the dyadic logic of the duel—which is governed, reflexively, by the will of the other.

Girard himself only begins to consider war in such terms with his integration of Clausewitz into his theory, whom he credits with "intuitions very similar to [his] own" (*BE* 1).[30] In this undertaking, it is primarily to three central definitions of war within the first book "On the Nature of War"—the only one that Clausewitz regarded as finished—that Girard turns his attention. The first of these definitions is that of war as "a duel on a larger scale"; the second is the well-known dictum of war as the "continuation of politics by other means" (29, 47).[31] The third definition, by Clausewitz's estimation, comprises the other two. It conceives of war in religious terms, as a "wonderful" or "remarkable trinity" (Ger. *wunderliche Dreifaltigkeit*). Essentially another "grim triune," it consists, firstly, in the original violent element of war rooted in the variable passions of the peoples involved, secondly in the game-like element of chance and probabilities, which relates to the actions of the commander and the army, and thirdly in the governmentally set political objective to which war is subordinate (Clausewitz 49). A central role in both the second and third definitions is thus given to politics, which according to Clausewitz governs war in a means-to-ends relationship, in which akin to the Judge's view moral concerns are suspended: "violence, that is, physical force (for there is no moral force apart from the concept of state and law) is therefore *a means*; to enforce our will on our enemy is *the objective*" (29). Conversely, it is the first definition that Girard focuses on.

Like the Judge, Clausewitz conceives of war as a duel: "War is nothing but a duel on a larger scale. Countless duels go to make up war, but a picture of it as a whole can be formed by imagining a pair of wrestlers. Each tries through physical force to compel the other to do his will; his *immediate* aim is to *throw* his opponent in order to make him incapable of further resistance. *War is thus an act of force to compel our enemy to do our will*" (cit. in *BE* 4). The relation between the opponents within the duel is characterized by a tendency toward an utmost exertion of force—a reciprocal "escalation to extremes" (Ger. *Bestreben zum Äußersten*) that persists on multiple levels as parties by and by mobilize and exert the forces and means at their disposal, intensifying their efforts as their opponent responds in kind. Clausewitz literally calls this tendency a *law* (Ger. *Gesetz*), akin to the laws of nature.

If one side uses force without compunction, undeterred by the blood-shed it involves, while the other side refrains, the first will gain the upper hand. That side will force the other to follow suit; each will drive its opponent toward extremes, and the only limiting factors are the counter-poises inherent in war. [. . .] Even the most civilized of peoples, in short, can be fired with passionate hatred of each other. [. . .] The thesis, then, must be repeated: war is an act of force, and there is no logical limit to the application of that force. Each side, therefore, compels its opponent to follow suit; a reciprocal action is started which must lead, in theory, to extremes. (cit. in *BE* 5)

The latter entails not simply the defeat, but a tendency toward "absolute war" that will likely end in the exhaustion or destruction of one or both parties. Given the mimetic logic that characterizes the duel in all but name, it is scarcely surprising that the idea of the escalation to extremes that follows from it becomes the linchpin in Girard's apocalyptic reading of *On War*, which, I argue, finds its historically grounded but fictional exemplification in McCarthy's *Blood Meridian*. In the analysis of the duel as governed by recip-rocal action and tending to escalate toward extremes, Girard sees powerful analogues of his own concepts:

[R]eciprocal action both *provokes and suspends* the trend to extremes. It provokes it when both adversaries behave in the same way, and *respond immediately* by each modeling his tactics, strategy and policy on those of the other. By contrast, if each is speculating on the intentions of the other, advancing, withdrawing, hesitating, taking into account time, space, fog, fatigue and all the constant interactions that define real war, reciprocal action then suspends the trend to extremes. [. . .] Reciprocal action can thus be a source of both undifferentiation and of differences, a path to war and a road to peace. If it *provokes and accelerates* the trend to extremes, the "friction" of space and time disappear, and the situation strangely resembles what I call the "sacrificial crisis" in my theory of archaic societies. If, on the contrary, reciprocal action *suspends* the trend to extremes, it aims to produce meaning and new differences. However, [. . .] everything seems to indicate that violent imitation is the rule today, not the imitation that slows and suspends the flow, but the one that accelerates it. (*BE* 13–14)

Yet the consequence of the law of escalation, "absolute war"—which is what the Judge divinizes and the various factions of *Blood Meridian* mercilessly enact—for Clausewitz is but a concept, a kind of abstract fantasy to which actual wars logically tend, but that they do not practically reach. "Clausewitz does not say that reality is separate from the concept, but that real wars *tend towards that point*" (*BE* 6). This limit to violence is rooted in three things: war is not an isolated act devoid of sociopolitical context, it is neither a single decision nor a string of simultaneous decisions, and whatever decision is achieved is no complete and final decision (Clausewitz 33, 46). The reality of warfare thus provides modifications to its principle through factors of what Clausewitz calls *friction*, which slows down or even halts the escalation to extremes.[32] Simply put, it is these factors that Clausewitz tries to encompass in the more holistic concept of the "remarkable trinity" of populace, politics, and army and commander. In *Blood Meridian*, these are represented by Americans, Mexicans and Indigenous peoples, ideological forces like capitalism, manifest destiny, and the Judge's religion, and the various warbands of filibusters, Comanches, Apaches, Mexican *milicias*, and scalp hunters with their respective leaders like the chiefs Gómez and Mangas Colorado, Governor Angel Trias and General Elias, and of course Glanton and the Judge.

In the logic of the duel, what Girard metaphorically alludes to as the "social physics" (*BE* 184) of attacking, withdrawing, and inertia of response, escalation may be suspended if both parties imitatively agree to back down into what Clausewitz termed "armed observation." *Blood Meridian* does in fact feature such a moment when the gang confronts the Chiricahua Apaches of Mangas Colorado. Beforehand, Mangas's men have tortured and killed the gang's scouts, the last of the Delawares as well as whites who "had met with neither favor nor discrimination but had suffered and died impartially" (*BM* 227). The atmosphere is already tense as the gang comes upon the Apaches before the walls of Tucson, slowly riding through them "in a sort of ritual movement as if certain points of ground must be trod in a certain sequence as in a child's game yet with some terrible forfeit at hand" (*BM* 228). Again, the reference to games and rituals is striking. Things threaten to escalate when Glanton's horse bites the ear of one of the Indians' horses.

> [W]hen Glanton spun to look at his men he found them frozen in
> deadlock with the savages, they and their arms wired into a construction

taut and fragile as those puzzles wherein the placement of each piece is
predicated upon every other and they in turn so that none can move
for bringing down the structure entire. [. . .] Horseblood or any blood
a tremor ran that perilous architecture and the ponies stood rigid and
quivering in the reddened sunrise and the desert under them hummed
like a snaredrum. (*BM* 229)

The groups are so equally matched and so suddenly faced with one another
that the opposing forces of their violence cancel each other out. The scene
could almost serve as an allegory for the stand-off of the Cuban Missile
Crisis: all that is missing to bring down the "perilous architecture" and for
the situation to end in mutual destruction is a single misstep, the slightest
provocation. Only once the supreme commander of violence, Judge Holden,
steps in does the situation de-escalate to an "unratified truce" (*BM* 229), and
proper compensation for the horse's bloodied ear is promised.

Still, the logic of the duel remains primary: "The 'remarkable trinity'
does not place the duel under the control of politics: it sets it in time" (*BE*
56). A response may be suspended for a time, the escalation to extremes thus
seemingly halted, but usually so only to reemerge at a later time and with
heightened intensity, as is the case for instance with the scalp hunters and the
Yuma. Whereas Clausewitz may still have been "trying [. . .] to imagine war
as contained by politics" (*BE* 8), Girard finds the situation of war has evolved
again from the days the *Grande Armée* marched across Europe and Russia:

> We could also say that in Clausewitz's time the conditions were not ripe for
> the "trend to extremes," that he was not facing an apocalypse, but that we
> are tending more and more towards that absolute state of affairs which we
> find in his first definition of war. We could say that humans are in a sense
> not yet able to match real war with its concept, but that they will succeed
> some day. [. . .] I have the strange impression that Clausewitz, after his brief
> and frightening apocalyptic epiphany, returned, sobered, to ordinary, grim
> reality. (*BE* 7)

Today, the vantage point has shifted, the day of "war matching its concept"
drawn nearer. This is the anthropological meaning that Girard ascribes to the
Apocalypse: "The devastation will be all on our side: the apocalyptic texts

speak of a war among people, not of a war of God against humans. [. . .] It concerns *only* humanity, in a certain sense, and takes nothing from the reality of the beyond" (*BE* 48).[33] It is here that his argument assumes compelling urgency: Many of Clausewitz's points of "friction" that assured that "two adversaries will not move towards the extremes and will not respond to each other in the same way at the same time and in the same place" (*BE* 11) have been smoothed out by technological advances: modern transportation facilitates the mobilization of armed forces within days, even hours, and remote-controlled mass devastation is but the push of a button away.

Escalation goes beyond drone strikes and weapons of mass destruction. Girard finds Clausewitz predicting the ideological wars of the twentieth century, which are characterized, in Carl Schmitt's terms, by "a 'theologization' of war in which the enemy becomes an Evil that has to be eradicated" (*BE* 65).[34] What were the world wars, the Holocaust, and the other genocides of the twentieth century, if not an all-too real picture of an escalation to extremes? What was the Cold War, with its nuclear arms race and the governing deterrent-doctrine of *mutually assured destruction* (read, *m-a-d*), if not an escalating duel gone global? In a way, the "law" of escalation to extremes seems to approximate the second law of thermodynamics in being, Girard pessimistically asserts, potentially "irreversible" and "universal" (*BE* 100, 107). The only outcomes possible are exhaustion or destruction.

Wallach's discussion of the martial code in *Blood Meridian* proves elementary. Toward the end of it, he finds the novel dramatizes the "exhaustion of an entire epoch of the code" and its reinscription into something more radical and limitless (2002a, 209).[35] It is this process, too, that the Judge describes when he prophesies that "in the affairs of men there is no waning and the noon of his expression signals the onset of night. His spirit is exhausted at the peak of its achievement. His meridian is at once his darkening and the evening of his day" (*BM* 147–48). In portraying this exhaustion, McCarthy dramatizes a fundamental evolution of war itself. Paradoxically, the emergence of the duel, which is synonymous with the approach of "absolute war," is a consequence of the end of war as an institution. That is, war as something waged solely between nation states that used to be subject to codified rules: the necessity of actually declaring war, the treatment of wounded, of prisoners, the (non)use of certain weapons, the protected taboo status of civilians, and so on. Sociologists describe this modern phenomenon as *New Wars*, which "erupt in the empty space that separates the dwindling normative arrangements mandated by both the state and its international delegates, from normative and ideological configurations yet to come. No longer states or coalitions of states versus other states and other coalitions of states, but a disordered series of eruptions and "minor" conflicts in which identity, not territory, plays the pivotal justificatory role" (Farneti 30).

In this view, counterintuitive as it may sound, even the institution of war itself existed in order to contain violence. Could this be what the Judge alludes to as war becoming "dishonored and its nobility called into question" (*BM* 331)? As classical interstate war has largely disappeared, so have most of its rules. Similarly, the intermediary stage of ideological wars is largely gone, as such wars "are less convincing now because we no longer really try to justify violence" (*BE* 40).[36] The era of war today is one of violent contingency and undifferentiation. True peace is elusive, and it is no longer clear what "victory" would even look like. "We are thus more at war than ever, at a time when war itself no longer exists" (*BE* xvii). Pertaining not solely to Europe, but the world as a whole, the diagnosis is sobering:

> We have indeed entered into an era of ubiquitous, unpredictable hostility in which the adversaries despise and seek to annihilate each other. [...] This is not a question of believing in catastrophe at all cost or of comparing the number of dead today with that of yesterday in order to bring the seriousness of our time into perspective. We have to understand that the *unpredictability of violence* is what is new: political rationality, the latest form of ancient rituals, has failed. We have entered a world of pure reciprocity, the one of which Clausewitz glimpsed the warlike face, but which could also show the opposite countenance. [...] Today we are heading toward a form of war so radical that it is impossible to talk about it without making it sound hyper-tragic or hyper-comical, so unlimited that it can no longer be taken seriously. [...] Violence can no longer be checked. From this point of view, we can say that the apocalypse has begun. (*BE* 67–69, 210)

In light of this reflection, *Blood Meridian*'s violent substance comes into focus as conceived by McCarthy in a spirit of *prophecy*: "If I wrote about violence in an exaggerated way, it was looking at a future that I imagined would be a lot more violent. And it is" (Kushner).

Vietnam and Escalatory Violence, or the Economy of Slaughter, Part 2

Following Wallach's suggestion to investigate the European contagion of violence, we discover the universal reciprocity of the duel. In Barbara Ehrenreich's deceptively simple summary "war spreads from band to band and culture to culture because it is a form of contact that no human group can afford to ignore [. . .]. No warlike instinct, greedy impulses, or material needs are required to explain why war, once adopted by some, must of necessity be adopted by all" (133, 135). In light of the mimetic reading of Clausewitz, the internal determinants of this quasi-Darwinian relation become productive for analysis. From this view, it is noteworthy that the historical John Joel Glanton was allegedly greatly attracted to dueling, specifically with renowned fighters.[37]

Beyond such apocryphal pieces of trivia, it is worth recalling that by both Turner's and Slotkin's analysis, European settlers became like the Indians to survive in the New World. Concomitantly, one identifies Glanton's scalp hunters as the mirror image to the Comanches that wipe out White's filibusters. In turn, Glanton himself reportedly took up scalp hunting after Lipan Indians murdered and scalped a number of women and children of the Texas settlements he belonged to, among them his fiancée (Schimpf 2013, 33; Chamberlain 268–69). Still another episode that McCarthy likely adopted from Chamberlain sees the gang come upon five smoldering wagons of "dead Argonauts," whose bodies are "bristling with arrowshafts" and who are bearing "strange menstrual wounds between their legs and no man's parts for these had been cut away and hung dark and strange from out their grinning mouths" (*BM* 152–53). What initially appears to be a horrific, gender-undifferentiating atrocity by the Apaches turns out to be the deed of "white men who preyed on travelers in that wilderness and disguised their work to be that of the savages" (*BM* 153).[38] Likewise, in *My Confession*, one of the gang's feints to avoid dealing with the force of the Sonoran authorities is to mask their crimes against the Mexican people as those of Apaches, as some of them abduct a group of Sonoran women, rape them, and later kill them to avoid discovery (Chamberlain 272). It is as though we were lost in a blood-sprayed hall of mirrors!

None of this is to relativize the bloodshed, to point the revisionist finger, or to find out who first lit the fuse. In fact, the origins of violence, which intersects in individual and collective acts, become more elusive with each new act of reprisal and each passing generation. Rather, it is the dynamics of the exchange that need to be understood: By pointing out how whites disguise their crimes as "Indian savagery," not only do these episodes subvert the notion of an opposing savagery and civilization as essentially racial or cultural, they also emphasize the central role of *imitation* in the infectious spreading of violence. The great Comanche massacre and the many atrocities that follow do nothing if not reinforce this assessment: it is more than the lights of "a thousand unpieced suns" (*BM* 52) that the broken mirror-glass on the Indians' shields reflect. What must be realized is that the Comanches and the horrific violence they unleash on the filibusters are themselves already reflections of what Wallach calls the European brand of viciousness. This is apparent in how McCarthy has them overrun filibusters and readers alike:

> A legion of horribles, hundreds in number, half naked or clad in costumes attic or biblical or wardrobed out of a fevered dream with the skins of animals and silk finery and pieces of uniform still tracked with the blood of prior owners, coats of slain dragoons, frogged and braided cavalry jackets, one in a stovepipe hat and one with an umbrella and one in white stockings and a bloodstained weddingveil and some in headgear of cranefeathers or rawhide helmets that bore the horns of bull or buffalo and one in a pigeon-tailed coat worn backwards and otherwise naked and one in the armor of a Spanish conquistador, the breastplate and pauldrons deeply dented with old blows of mace or sabre done in another country by men whose very bones were dust and many with their braids spliced up with the hair of other beasts [. . .] and one whose horse's whole head was painted crimson red and all the horsemen's faces gaudy and grotesque with daubings like a company of mounted clowns, death hilarious, all howling in a barbarous tongue and riding down upon them like a horde from a hell more horrible yet than the brimstone land of christian reckoning, screeching and yammering and clothed in smoke like those vaporous beings in regions beyond right knowing where the eye wanders and the lip jerks and drools. (*BM* 52–53)

Akin to the Gadarene swine in *Outer Dark*, McCarthy's painterly prose casts the "wild frieze" (*BM* 53) of the Comanches as what one might call, with

Jean-Luc Marion, a *saturated phenomenon*—a kind of object so overwhelming in its sheer phenomenological "givenness" that it floods any one concrete object the eye can perceive or the mind can measure (Tin). Like the filibusters, the reader is steamrolled with a frantically paced and phrased impressionistic chaos, which only after a concerted reading effort yields some of its riches. Imminent violence is announced by the evidence of past murders and massacres, some of it spatiotemporally removed and enigmatic in its presence, such as the conquistador's armor, some of it recent and accumulated by the Comanches as indicated by their trophies and the blood that still clings to their clothes and weapons. A crimson red horse evokes the red horse of war in the book of Revelation, and the evocation of the Christian hell, too, gives the passage a vaguely apocalyptic tone. Much like the grotesque or, more appropriately, the sacred, the sensation such a phenomenon entails, for Marion, is religious in nature. Perhaps not unlike the reader's, the filibuster sergeant's reaction at this sight is an appropriately flabbergasted "Oh my god" (*BM* 53).

In conjunction with these impressions, the crucial element to recognize is the mimetic nature of violence, the root of its contagiousness. As Wallach points out, "the Indians are wearing western garb: top hats, wedding veils, dinner jackets. They have become our own darker selves" (Josyph 2010, 106). It is with this realization that my analysis rapidly approaches the violent, apocalyptic core of the novel. The carnage that follows delivers in excess of what the Comanche's appearance promised and prefigured:

> Everywhere there were horses down and men scrambling and [the Kid] saw a man who sat charging his rifle while blood ran from his ears and he saw men with their revolvers disassembled trying to fit the spare loaded cylinders they carried and he saw men kneeling who tilted and clasped their shadows on the ground and he saw men lanced and caught up by the hair and scalped standing and he saw the horses of war trample down the fallen and a little whitefaced pony with one clouded eye leaned out of the murk and snapped at him like a dog and was gone. Among the wounded some seemed dumb and without understanding and some were pale through the masks of dust and some had fouled themselves or tottered brokenly onto the spears of the savages. [. . .] [The Indians were] riding down the unhorsed Saxons and spearing and clubbing them and leaping

from their mounts with knives and running about on the ground with a peculiar bandy-legged trot like creatures driven to alien forms of locomotion and stripping the clothes from the dead and seizing them up by the hair and passing their blades about the skulls of the living and the dead alike and snatching aloft the bloody wigs and hacking and chopping at the naked bodies, ripping off limbs, heads, gutting the strange white torsos and holding up great handfuls of viscera, genitals, some of the savages so slathered up with gore they might have rolled in it like dogs and some who fell upon the dying and sodomized them with loud cries to their fellows. [. . .] Dust stanched the wet and naked heads of the scalped who with the fringe of hair below their wounds and tonsured to the bone now lay like maimed and naked monks in the bloodslaked dust and everywhere the dying groaned and gibbered and horses lay screaming. (*BM* 53–54)

Even in this abridged excerpt, the confusion of battle is palpable. Not providing the comfort of even minimal narrative distance, McCarthy practically drags the reader down into the midst of the chaos as seen, at least initially, through the eyes of the Kid. Consequently, any semblance of a fixed perspective is lost altogether. Sentences run on and on, rapidly enumerating bloody snapshots only connected by the coordinating *and*, creating a vertiginous panopticon of slaughter simultaneously surreal and realistic in its frantic, traumatic juxtaposition of fragmented bodies, dizzying gory details, and grotesque similes introduced by the comparative preposition *like*. Disorienting and chaotic as it presents itself, one might very well call this display one of *violentropic poetry*, ordered only somewhat through the energy put into its deciphering, yet retaining the overwhelming quality of undifferentiation inherent in the event described. Condensed into a single moment in time, this may well be what one imagines "escalation to extremes" to look like.

The narrative that follows does nothing if not cement this impression with its many massacres, singular murders, sites of slaughter, and violent little details, among which the bush hung with bloated and eyeless dead babies that the surviving Kid and Sproule stumble upon in the aftermath of the massacre is just one particularly gruesome example. Such is the consequence of the escalatory logic of the duel, and Glanton's scalp hunters provide a much more compelling mirror image to the Indians than did White's filibusters. As has been shown, their viciousness is initially driven by economic incentives.

Chihuahua pays for all scalps. Not even women and children are exempt from commercial slaughter. Therefore, Glanton's raids comply with the frontier scenario of the "savage war," the preemptively mimetic notion that since the "savage enemy" will slaughter without inhibition or discrimination, the "civilized race" is entitled and in fact required to respond with unrestricted violence and terror on its own part.

Slotkin describes this scenario in practically Clausewitzian terms: "A cycle of massacre and revenge is thus inaugurated that drives both sides toward a war of extermination" (*GN* 112), and only the victory of the civilized race can supposedly prevent actual genocide. McCarthy irrevocably discards the latter notion: in *Blood Meridian*, there is no constructive violence in the old sacrificial sense, and the only thing that follows upon a massacre is another massacre. Thus, the gang at one point passes "a place of bones where Mexican soldiers had slaughtered an encampment of Apaches some years gone, women and children, the bones and skulls scattered along the bench for half a mile" (*BM* 90). And while earlier it had been the Comanches who massacred the whites, roles are reversed in the gang's ambush on an Apache camp:

> The men were moving on foot among the huts with torches and dragging the victims out, slathered and dripping with blood, hacking at the dying and decapitating those who knelt for mercy. [. . .] one of the Delawares emerged from the smoke with a naked infant dangling in each hand and squatted at a ring of midden stones and [. . .] bashed their heads against the stones so that the brains burst forth through the fontanel and humans on fire came shrieking forth like berserkers and the riders hacked them down [. . .] and some lay coupled to the bludgeoned bodies of young women dead or dying on the beach. (*BM* 156–57)

There is no mercy, no restraint, and virtually no difference between the perpetrators of these atrocities. The images of rape and infanticide leave no doubt that this *is* a war of extermination, an escalation to extremes that allows for no moral high ground of the supposed representatives of civilization. In contrast to the Comanche massacre, the shock of this scene instead seems to be much the same as what the readers of *Time* must have experienced when they first saw Ronald Haeberle's photographs of the My

Lai massacre. The latter came to represent "the upsurge of an evil so 'mysterious' that it may well be limitlessly pervasive and may represent [. . .] a demonic potential inherent in our civilization, a 'madness' to which the home front is not immune" (*GN* 586).

Apart from *Moby-Dick*, *Blood Meridian*'s closest analogues are Joseph Conrad's *Heart of Darkness* and, perhaps more so than either, Francis Ford Coppola's masterful film adaptation of the latter in *Apocalypse Now*. The mythoclastic uncovering of Euro-American violence in the distant past merges with that of recent history and finally extends to a prediction of violence yet to come. McCarthy achieves this not only through either the Judge's or the narrator's musings, but by interspersing the overall narrative with small scenes and iconic reminders of the Vietnam War. Owens situates these scenes within the context of the reassessment of American violence during and after the war. In addition to a rising death toll abroad, Americans experienced a period of social transformation and upheaval at home. The years from 1967 to 1970 saw riots in Detroit and other major cities, the assassinations of Martin Luther King Jr. and Robert F. Kennedy, and the massacre at Kent State University. Suddenly, the war abroad resembled the war on American soil. Both wars the media covered with unprecedented images of violence and death: "As became apparent after the revelation of the My Lai massacre in 1969 [. . .] American soldiers routinely tortured, killed, and maimed not only Vietcong but also innocent villagers. A Girardian firestorm of violence spread from the battlefields to the streets of America as the fight for civil rights and antiwar protests ignited unstoppable crown fires" (Owens 20).

Shadows of My Lai weigh heavily upon the killings of the Glanton gang, as do the memories of the Washita, Sand Creek, or Wounded Knee massacres. The shock of My Lai consisted of the sudden role-reversal of the frontier myth's captivity/rescue paradigm that had been applied to Vietnam, forcing Americans to identify themselves as the savages that Vietnam had to be saved from. Another example, Glanton's murder of an old indigenous woman (*BM* 98), is a literary version of General Nguyên Ngoc Loan's photographically immortalized shooting of a suspected Vietcong during the Tet Offensive (Owens 22–23). The mutilations suffered by civilians, filibusters, scalp hunters, and Indians alike echo reports of mutilations dead American soldiers suffered at the hands of the Vietcong and vice versa. Finally, there is

the scapular of ears the Kid "inherits" from David Brown. It is like the ears
American veterans cut off the dead Vietcong to certify their body counts,
and later would bring home as trophies of war (*GN* 598). If a lesson of young
Elrod's questioning of the veracity of the trophies toward the end of the novel
is indeed "not to doubt the violent record of the past" as Kenneth Millard
says (85), surely the same has to be said about the novel as a whole. By linking
the violence of the distant frontier past to the more recent past of Vietnam,
McCarthy effectively dispels the notion that humanity has made any ethical
progress since.

In Vietnam, what began as a counterinsurgency soon escalated into a
war of attrition that ultimately exhausted American efforts. Likewise, what
makes the escalation of *Blood Meridian* Girardian instead of Clausewitzian,
and McCarthy's vision properly apocalyptic, is the fact that neither economics nor politics are finally able to control or halt the violence they have suck-
led and nursed. If there is indeed an economy of violence in it, its excesses
follow what Twain called the "spirit of massacre," which eventually explodes
the market built around violence. This seems to be the point of the Kid's
dream of the "false moneyer," who "seeks favor with the Judge," and tries to
create a coin with "a face that will pass, an image that will render this residual
specie current in the markets where men barter" (*BM* 310). Christine Chollier suggests that the cold forger tries to "establish a system where exchange
would no longer depend on barter but on currency" in order to limit the
spread of violence; but the Judge, seen as the embodiment of violence unending, "will not permit a trade other than war to dominate the market of predation" (175). In my view, the issue at hand is less the opposition between barter
and currency. Not to belabor the point, money and other symbolic means of
exchange are but a step or two from the more immediate form of barter that
while dissimulating violent exchange, always remains subject to it.

Simply put, there is no economic solution to the fundamental problem of
mimetic contagion. Carrying the 128 scalps and eight heads of their first raid,
Glanton and his men return to Chihuahua. Riding in under the admiring
gaze of hundreds of onlookers, including young girls and boys, who reach out
in fascination "to touch the grisly trophies" (*BM* 167), they receive a hero's
welcome and are invited to dine with the governor himself. The governor's
aides drink toasts to Washington and Franklin, and Glanton's men respond
"with yet more of their own country's heroes, ignorant alike of diplomacy

and any name at all from the pantheon of their sister republic" (*BM* 169).³⁹
What begins as an exuberant celebration of the scalp hunters' victory rapidly
deteriorates into something akin to the orgies in Euripides's *The Bacchae*: The
governor's kitchen is quickly exhausted, prostitutes invade the ball, fights
break out.⁴⁰ Governor Trias, like Johann Wolfgang von Goethe's *Zauberleh-
rling* to whom he is compared, is powerless to halt the rapid decline of his
city as bath houses become bordellos, cantinas "ghost taverns" (*BM* 171), and
stores begin to close. The gang's excesses continue for twenty-five nights. At
the end, the city walls are marked with citizens' scrawls professing "Mejor
los indios" (*BM* 171)—"rather the Indians." This holiday-gone-wrong repeats
itself in Ures and Coyame, where the gang are first "fallen upon as saints,"
but as they leave "three days later the streets stood empty, not even a dog
followed them to the gates" (*BM* 172).

   The gang's next step is to turn to murdering the people for whose protection they were hired. During the Apache massacre, the gang had already
taken to murdering Mexicans enslaved by the Apaches. Later, the peaceful
Tiguas, who even by Toadvine's admission "aint botherin nobody" (*BM* 173),
become victims of Chihuahua's historical inability to account for the origin
of most scalps.⁴¹ This is enough incentive for the further escalation, which
rapidly gives way to complete undifferentiation and does not even make halt
at the gang's own members as Glanton's shooting and scalping of the Mexican Miguel/McGill shows. The gang goes on a killing spree through remote
Mexican villages, their bloodlust excited at the "cries" and "visible frailty" of
villagers running from them "like harried game" (*BM* 181), and do not even
shy away from attacking Mexican soldiers. As an encounter with the Mexican
mercury miners shows, violence is finally not even committed for commercial reasons anymore, but simply for its mere availability (Millard 83), or else
because the miners are literally a *skandalon*, blocking the gang's path down
the mountain. Returning to Chihuahua for a second and final time, the gang
sells the governor the scalps of his own citizenry.

   At this point, the faintest notion that Glanton's men might somehow
serve a higher purpose must be discarded. Clearly, they are no representatives of manifest destiny or the lofty progress of civilization. Except for the
Judge, they seem to live in a state of nonculture. Save for their weapons, there
is "nothing about [them] to suggest even the discovery of the wheel" (*BM*
232). The gang may be thought to have regressed to an earlier evolutionary

stage—a process Theodore Roosevelt considered indispensable in the confrontation of wilderness and civilization—yet one would be hard-pressed to name any contribution they make to the advancement of society. Once they become outlaws, they cease to be even businessmen of their bloody trade. Nonetheless, the violence they practice is an undeniable part of America's frontier past. Its excessive and indiscriminate nature, paired with the illogic of self-exhaustion, dispels all romantic ideas of progress usually associated with the frontier.

Once their crimes are known, Glanton and his men become themselves "fugitives on some grander scale," a group hunted by the authorities, considering itself "well done" with "those things that lay claim to a man" (*BM* 248), and thus rid of whatever inhibition there might have been left. Instead of the pursuit of wealth or glory, it is now solely the unadulterated *sacred*, violence itself, that drives them. It is only initially surprising that once the troops of General Elias are breathing down their necks, the gang burns the valuable scalps they suffered and killed for. Characterizing the gang's behavior in light of George Bataille's concept of "nonproductive expenditure," Steven Shaviro thus succinctly asserts:

> Beneath the mask of a Darwinian struggle for survival, or a Hobbesian war of all against all, or even a lust for wealth and power and honor, they sumptuously, gratuitously squander their own lives—together of course, with those of many others—at every turn. They have no spirit of seriousness or of enterprise; they unwittingly pursue self-ruin rather than advantage. (156)

Once they assume control of Lincoln's ferry, after deceiving the Yuma that operated it before, the gang gradually begins to victimize even American citizens crossing the river on their way to California: "Travelers were beaten and their arms and goods appropriated and they were sent destitute and beggared into the desert. [. . .] Horses were taken and women violated and bodies began to drift past the Yuma camp downriver" (*BM* 262). Though they are still amassing riches, there are apparently no further plans for the gang, no economic rationale that still governs their "mindless rapacity." Only their own annihilation by the retaliating Yuma puts a stop to this rampage.

The gang's demise hardly signifies the end of violence, though. A huge pyre is erected for the slain, Glanton's dead body raised and borne "in the manner of a slain champion" (*BM* 275), and the guns, clothes, and amassed riches of the group divided among the victorious Yuma. As the burnt offering is set aflame, the Yuma "sat upon the ground each with his new goods before him and they watched the fire and smoked their pipes as might some painted troupe of mimefolk [...] for these people were no less bound and indentured and they watched like the prefiguration of their own ends the carbonized skulls of their enemies incandescing before them bright as blood among the coals" (*BM* 276). The "epilogue" to the gang's exploits thus becomes equal parts sacrificial ceremony and prophecy. What the novel says about violence pertains to past, present, and future. As if by the biblical proclamation that "all who take the sword will perish by the sword" (Mt. 26:52; Rv. 10:13) that McCarthy also quotes in the novel (*BM* 248), the text prefigures ever new cycles of violence. Shaviro's summary proves both apt and comprehensive: "The clash and testing of wills in which the Judge exults must end, not in the victory of one, but in the sacrificial consumption of everyone and everything. And such is finally our inmost, most secret and most horrific desire" (156–57). No metaphysics or divine wrath is finally required for this apocalypse: it is inherent within the desires and works of humanity itself.

It's Judgment that Defeats Us: *Blood Meridian* and Christian Failure

As we have seen, McCarthy probes the abyss of American myth and history with a penetrating and unflinching gaze. What he finds in this heart of darkness is absolute violence and war divinized. Unrivaled in American literature in its dispassionate and all-but-irresistible portrayal of these horrors, *Blood Meridian* is doubly apocalyptic. The novel's revelatory nature is reinforced by its employment of more esoteric sign systems such as alchemy and the tarot. Tarot symbolism has been discussed before, but never integrated into either mimetic or revelatory contexts, and it is here that we touch on the novel's metaphysical aspects, even as we keep our feet firmly planted in the mundane.[42] Insight into the tarot's function not only cements the novel's prophetic aspect, but serves to introduce the three final and inextricably related aspects that this apocalyptic reading of *Blood Meridian* has to account for. These are the figure of the Judge, the role Christianity plays in the novel, and finally, how it relates to the opposition that exists between the Judge and the Kid.

The Tarot and the Ruined Church

Leaving Chihuahua on their first expedition, Glanton and his men escort a family of circus folk. In a divinatory laying of the tarot, the woman of the group foretells the gang's fortunes. As John Sepich has established, many of the cards appear in one form or another throughout the narrative, foreshadowing or alternatively framing the events of the novel. The Kid is associated with a divided heart by the Four of Cups, which I will discuss later on. Black Jackson's fate, in which according to the Judge "lie our fortunes all" (*BM* 93), is framed by the Four of Wands (*BM* 274), which signifies "perfected work, settlement and rest after labor" (Sepich 2008, 107), and the group's ruin at the hands of the vengeful Yuma is prefigured by the "Carta de guerra, de venganza" (*BM* 96), that is, the inverted Chariot the old fortune teller sees drifting down a dark river.[43] For readers versed in either Spanish or the tarot, the gang's ending is thus foreshadowed in the first third of the novel.

Practically all of the tarot's major arcana, such as the Hanged Man, the Magician, the Hermit, the Tower, the Star, the Moon, and the Sun and of course Death, as well as some of the wands, coins, cups, and swords that make up the minor arcana are represented in the novel. Two cards are of special interest. The first is *el tonto*, the Fool. As the sole card not assigned a numerical value, the Fool is the most powerful card and in many ways the animating force of the tarot, signifying eternal movement. As Sepich and Stinson have shown, its association is with the Judge, the one among the ignorant scalp hunters who is clearly aware of all the meanings implied in the fortuneteller's laying of the cards. When queried, the Judge's answers are, as usual, obfuscating rather than illuminating. He assures the irritated Black Jackson that "All will be known to you at last. To you as to every man" (*BM* 93), hinting, one assumes, at some kind of universal revelation that by his ominously biblical phrasing, would seem to go beyond the certainty of death, which is suffered by all yet experienced individually. At the very least, the Judge seems to possess a special kind of insight into the workings that propel the novel's events, the nature of which has to be dealt with.

The second card of prophetic significance is present only in absentia as "the one card in the juggler's deck that they would not see" (*BM* 94). It identifies the fortune teller herself as the High Priestess: "The woman sat like that blind interlocutrix between Boaz and Jachin [. . .] true pillars and true card, false prophetess for all" (*BM* 94). There is an apparent paradox here: If cards and pillars are true, why is the old woman a "false prophetess"? Interpreting the card, Sepich draws on the work of Richard Cavendish. His Freemasonic reading connects the pillars to King Solomon's high temple in Jerusalem (1 Kgs. 7:15–22), and identifies the pillars' Hebrew meaning as "to establish" (Jachin) and "in strength" (Boaz), which together stand for "the balance of opposites of which reality is made [. . .] pillars of Mercy and Severity—and the opposites of the other, fatal tree which grew in Eden, the tree of knowledge of good and evil" (cit. in Sepich 2008, 110). Sepich connects these pillars to the opposites represented by the Judge and the Kid. To this, an apocalyptic layer of meaning is added when one calls to mind that the foundation of both pillars is the Judeo-Christian God and that Solomon's temple was destroyed in the time of the Babylonian exile. Hence the card hearkens back to the motif of ruined churches so prevalent in the novel, in fact doubly so, since the second high temple in Jerusalem was destroyed in 70 AD.

The first destruction and the Babylonian exile itself served as an inspiration for the book of Daniel, the prime apocalyptic text in the Old Testament. The second destruction features prominently in the New Testament in analogy to Jesus's death and resurrection and, even more centrally, as a sign heralding the beginning of the "times of the gentiles" (Lk. 21:24), which itself segues into the end times.[44] Girard thus extrapolates that

> the apocalyptic passages refer to a real event that will follow the Passion, but in the Gospels they were placed before it. The "time of the Gentiles" is thus, like the seventy years of servitude to the King of Babylon in Jeremiah, *an indefinite time between two apocalypses*, two revelations. If we put the statements back into an evangelical perspective, this can only mean that *the time of the Gentiles, in other words, the time when Gentiles will refuse to hear the word of God, is a limited time*. Between Christ's Passion and his Second Coming, the Last Judgment, if you prefer, there will be this indefinite time which is ours, a time of increasingly uncontrolled violence, of refusal to hear, of growing blindness. (*BE* 111)

While the role of Christianity in *Blood Meridian*'s apocalyptic has yet to be ascertained, its setting is surely one where the "word of God" remains largely unheard, or has been silenced. Though the old woman's reading of fortunes proves true insofar as the narrative that follows corroborates her predictions, it is perhaps only "for all" *of the gang*, who by extension represent Euro-American culture as a whole, that the old woman can be perceived as a "false prophetess." In one of the novel's quieter moments, the ex-priest Tobin tells the Kid that "it may well be that the voice of the almighty speaks most profoundly in such beings as lives in silence themselves" (*BM* 123). When the Kid—who is the character in the novel most strongly associated with silence, especially so as he gradually fades into the background while the gang's violence escalates—objects that "I aint heard no voice," Tobin tells him that "When it stops [. . .] you'll know that you've heard it all your life" (*BM* 123).

There is a connection here with what Girard deems a particular eschatological insight of the Bible texts: "Did Christianity predict its apocalyptic failure? A reasonable argument can be made that it did. This failure is simply the same thing as the end of the world. [. . .] The Revelation has failed: in a certain manner it has not been heard" (*BE* 47). Disregard or disavowal of Revelation—which should lead people to a serious ethical mobilization of practical commitment to one another and the sustainability of life on earth—is what facilitates the realization of its dark obverse, which is the end of the world. Indeed, judging by the conspicuous prevalence of ruined churches throughout the novel, Christianity in *Blood Meridian* has failed catastrophically. This failure represents the other side of the Judge's coin, the other half of the novel's apocalyptic dimension.

The novel's churches all too often become the sites of massacre. In San Antonio de Bexar, the first church the Kid sets foot in features an "array of saints [that] had been shot up by American troops," the statue of the virgin holds a headless baby Jesus, and in the sacristy, the Kid finds "the remains of several bodies, one a child" (*BM* 26–27). A church that the Kid and Sproule pass on their desert walk is "heaped with the scalped and naked and partly eaten bodies of some forty souls who'd barricaded themselves in this house of God against the heathen." The altar has been "hauled down," the "tabernacle looted," and "a dead Christ in a glass bier" lies "broken in the chancel floor." The "great pool of [. . .] communal blood" that has congealed "into a sort of pudding" and in parts has "cracked into a burgundy ceramic" (*BM*

60) signifies the fundamental blow that has been dealt to the institution of sacrifice, ironically by Christianity itself:

> The properties of blood [...] vividly illustrate the entire operation of vio-
> lence. [...] Blood that dries on the victim soon loses its viscous quality and
> becomes first a dark sore, then a roughened scab. Blood that is allowed to
> congeal on its victim is the impure product of violence, illness, or death.
> In contrast to this contaminated substance is the fresh blood of newly
> slaughtered victims, crimson and free flowing. This blood is never allowed
> to congeal, but is removed without trace as soon as the rites have been con-
> cluded. [...] The physical metamorphosis of spilt blood can stand for the
> double nature of violence. [...] Beneficial violence must be carefully dis-
> tinguished from harmful violence, and the former continually promoted at
> the expense of the latter. Ritual is nothing more than the regular exercise of
> "good" violence. (*VS* 36–37)[45]

In *Blood Meridian*, the differentiating, violence-diverting function of sacrifice has been suspended. Following mimetic theory, the culprit in this is none
other than Christianity. There simply is no such thing as generative violence
anymore.

It is not as though Americans are more respectful of the sanctuary the
church should provide. Glanton's gang mercilessly slaughters the Mexican
inhabitants of a mountain town who seek refuge in their church, "clutching
the altar" from which they "were dragged howling one by one and one by
one they were slain and scalped in the chancel floor" (*BM* 181). In the ruined
church of San José de Tumacacori, the gang not only kills one of the two
mad brothers who have settled there, but also finds four apparently ownerless
horses, which recall both the horsemen of the Revelation and the frightful
riderless horses of *Outer Dark* to similar implications: it becomes apparent
that the Apocalypse is less a mandate of theology than a consequence of
biblical anthropology.[46]

In any case, the gory pattern of violated churches and slaughtered Christians is too obtrusive to be overlooked. In a radical manner, it escalates the
more subtle overturning of Christian ethics found in *Outer Dark*. To recapitulate, Girard professes that archaic religion with its institution of sacrifice,

although (or rather because) it involves a misconception of violence, is society's most formidable protection against it: "[Religion] protects man from his own violence by taking it out of his hands, transforming it into a transcendent and ever-present danger to be kept in check by the appropriate rites" (*VS* 134). The dissolution of religious institutions is hence a clear sign of the cultural entropy that the sacrificial crisis entails. It bears repeating that the dynamic is radically altered by Christianity:

> The Greeks hid their scapegoats, which is very different. The Psalms reveal that violent people are not the ones who talk about violence but that it is the peaceful people who make it speak. The Judeo-Christian revelation exposes what myths always tend to silence. Those who speak of "peace and security" are now their heirs: despite everything, they continue believing in myths and do not want to see their own violence. The great paradox in all this is that Christianity provokes the escalation to extremes by revealing to humans their own violence. It prevents people from blaming the gods for their violence and places them before their responsibility. (*BE* 118)

Sacrifice, which is based on the scapegoat mechanism, has become culturally ineffectual with the Crucifixion and its revelation of the victim's innocence— "the stone that the builders rejected" (Mt. 21:42; *TH* 429) and on which the edifice of culture rests. This step signifies a transition from cyclical-sacrificial to linear-apocalyptic history. Part of the problem of escalation is that Christianity is still largely misunderstood, by both believers and nonbelievers, as sacrificial in a mythological sense. This misunderstanding elucidates what is an otherwise fairly enigmatic utterance by an old Mexican who approaches the Kid in a cantina: "Blood, he said. This country is give much blood. This Mexico. This is a thirsty country. The blood of a thousand Christs. Nothing. He made a gesture toward the world beyond where all the land lay under darkness and all a great stained altarstone" (*BM* 102). Evidently, the sacrificial blood that has been shed has failed to establish peace and order in Mexico.

Yet, following mimetic theory, this is only consistent: If one reads Jesus's death on the Cross as a kind of sacrifice, it is *the sacrifice to end all sacrifice*. The efficiency of sacrifice consequently evaporates, as knowledge of the victim's innocence becomes known and makes way for a gradual epistemological shift of perspectives. In Fleming's words, the increasing inefficiency of scapegoating correlates with an "inability adequately to *sacralize* violence" (145). This, however, results neither in "a decrease in the incidence [n]or in the severity of violence," but rather escalates both, because "as the surrogate victimage mechanism fails it needs to operate with greater levels of intensity to achieve the same ends" (Fleming 145). In this way, Western culture resembles a drug addict perpetually in need of increasing his dosage.

Another way of describing this is Clausewitz's *trend to extremes*. The Passion marks humanity's initiation into a time where it can no longer rely on the sacrificial system to unify itself, on "Satan casting out Satan," in other words, humanity's entrance into the end times. Deprived of an outlet allowing society to emerge revitalized from chaos, violence escalates to extremes, demanding ever more victims. This is the original anthropological solution Girard offers to Jesus's proclamation that he has "not come to bring peace, but a sword" (Mt. 10:34), which otherwise clashes so irreconcilably with the image of the loving and peaceful lamb of God. The problem contained in Jesus's words is exactly what constitutes the historical failure of Christianity:

> We cannot reduce Christianity to nothing but a venerable tradition to which we owe a message that is crucial for humanity's salvation. Christianity is also a historical current that finally led Pope John Paul II to an act of repentance during his visit to Yad Vashem and the Wailing Wall. It is a religion that very quickly returned to old sacrificial reflexes. In short, *it has not lived up to its message*, to the radically new information that it revealed: definitive knowledge of the mechanisms of violent foundations and radical demystification of the sacred, of the social organizations which it sanctions. Christ plunges us into knowledge of mimetic mechanisms. He thus indeed brings war not peace, disorder not order, because all order is suspect in a way: it always hides the one whose blood was shed in order to reconcile us. To denounce this, to chip away the paint of the "whitewashed tombs," was to disrupt the sacrificial mechanism forever. (*BE* 141)[47]

Historical Christianity's role, in Europe as in America, has been a decidedly conflictual one. It is thus decisively not as though Christianity were historically innocent.[48] Ever since it aligned itself with the forces of empire and turned to conversion by the sword, it has veered between adherence to its core message and falling back into archaic patterns of violence. Too often, it has done the latter.

In America, Christian religion served to justify the nation's expansionist claims, while being all-too-readily bent or cast aside where its ethics impeded the selfsame process. Manifest destiny, Schimpf points out, was at best "the relatively benign idea of exporting our democratic institutions to those who had the capacity for self-rule," while at its worst, "the doctrine amounted to a free pass for Americans to forcibly drag them into the modern world" (2008, 17). Open conflict thus emerged when Christians faced "the Indian," who already by the Puritans was "quickly demonized as the abject or evil Other, in contrast with their own righteous culture and beliefs" (Vieth 141).[49] Given "how completely the justifying myths of progressive territorial appropriation suffocated the Christian conscience" (Wallach 2013, 44), it is not all that surprising that the history of the Western reflects this, too. Thus, Jane Tompkins asserts: "What the Western shows us, among other things, is that Christianity had to be forcibly ejected. When the genre first appears on the scene, therefore, it defines itself in part by its struggling to get rid of Christianity's enormous weight" (cit. in Wallach 2013, 45). McCarthy is highly conscious of this problematic: his anti-Western should be read as a reflection on the unwitting, hypocritical ejection of Christian ethics *by* nominal Christians. As if it were not enough that churches turn into sites of massacre,[50] where it is not in ruins, the church is complicit in the novel's wars of extermination: Chihuahua's cathedral itself is decorated with "the dried scalps of slaughtered Indians" (*BM* 72).

In all of this, there lies a catastrophic failure, the outlines of which McCarthy sketched in *Outer Dark*. A true return to sacrificial ignorance being impossible, the problem in a sense is and perhaps always has been that "we are not Christian enough" (*BE* x). *Blood Meridian* is indeed a holocaust novel, yet "what is the Holocaust if not that terrifying failure? Christians have to assume their responsibility for that horror. They had been warned 2000 years ago and they have proven incapable of avoiding the worst" (*BE* 11). What else does the presence of the Delawares in Glanton's gang imply? Their origins, McCarthy tells us, lie in the "ashes at Gnadenhutten" (*BM* 138). In 1782, Pennsylvania militiamen slaughtered and scalped a whole village of

Christian Delaware/Lenape of the Bohemian-Moravian denomination. At the time, an essential part of the Moravian creed was a complete disavowal of violence, yet one could not guess it by the impression the Delawares make in the novel. Though they bear "christian names," they have "learnt war by warring," and while the world and its creatures are measureless and alien, nothing is more "alien" than "their own hearts [. . .] in them" (*BM* 138). In this violent alienation, they personify historical Christianity.

Finally, the agonizing truth of it all is embodied both in the Kid and, more immediately, in the figure of Tobin, the ex-priest. Against the Judge's divinization of war, the primacy of which negates the demands of ethics or morality, he offers exactly nothing:

> But what says the priest? [the Judge] said.
>
> Tobin looked up. The priest does not say.
>
> The priest does not say, said the Judge. Nihil dicit. But the priest has said. For the priest has put by the robes of his craft and taken up the tools of that higher calling which all men honor. The priest would be no godserver but a god himself. [. . .]
>
> I'll not secondsay you in your notions, said Tobin. Dont ask it.
>
> Ah Priest, said the Judge. What could I ask of you that you've not already given? (*BM* 250–51)

So, what McCarthy puts on display is the apocalyptic failure of Christianity. This failure correlates with and is partly responsible for the escalation of violence through time. In exposing it, *Blood Meridian* is more radical than *Outer Dark*, yet it simply spells out the logic that already guides Culla Holme's dream eclipse and, more explicitly, McCarthy's reimagination of the demonic Gadarene swine, which rise again in *Blood Meridian*. Finally, among the demons of *Blood Meridian*, the same man who would not ask anymore of Tobin than he has already given is at the epicenter of the cataclysm. If it were not obvious, one might have guessed so by his "lashless pig's eyes" (*BM* 310). We have begun to approach him in his philosophy of war, but only now are we rightly prepared to confront this character whom Bloom calls, with good reason, "the most frightening figure in all of American literature" (2000, 255). Only now are we ready to "face down" the "vast abhorrence" (*BM* 243) of the Judge.

A Void without Terminus or Origin

In discussing Judge Holden, critics have summoned a whole gallery of figures and characters. These range from the "historical" Holden of Chamberlain's *My Confession*, the dancing Hindu god Shiva, and the child-devouring Kronos of Greek mythology, to the archons of Gnostic religion and the tarot's Fool, from mythical tricksters and mundane confidence men to Nietzsche's *Übermensch*, Conrad's Kurtz, and Melville's Ahab *and* white whale, and from Yahweh, Faust, and the devil to finally a metatextual figure of writing itself. Some of these figures are of greater concern than others.

Even so, the text alerts us that McCarthy's creation is, in a way, all of them and more. As the Judge and his "adopted" imbecile approach the waterhole that the Kid, Tobin, and Toadvine have taken refuge at after the Yuma ferry massacre, they appear like another saturated phenomenon— "now quick with clarity and now fugitive in the strangeness of that same light. Like things whose very portent renders them ambiguous. Like things so charged with meaning that their forms are dimmed" (*BM* 281–82). The Kid's later fever dream, wherein the Judge casts his ominous shadow onto the coldforger, articulates as much and more: "Whatever his antecedents he was something wholly other than their sum, nor was there system by which to divide him back into his origins for he would not go" (*BM* 309). Taking a deconstructive approach, Wallach identifies in Holden "the fulcrum of *Blood Meridian*'s recursivity, an allegory of the text itself," and diagnoses:

> It is only because the narrative occasionally provides us with "banana peels," as Gabriel García Márquez once described metaphorical cul-de-sacs buried in a text—in this case, rational explanations for Holden's capabilities—and also because Holden's preternatural knowledge is hermeneutically encoded [. . .] that the possibilities for his true nature do not disseminate as wildly as the violence he provokes. Such semiotic contagion has been compared by Andrew McKenna to the contagion of mob violence, and mimetic violence always meets the violence of language whenever Holden's linguistic aggression breaks out. (2002b, 10–11)

Notwithstanding this tendency to disseminate, and at the danger of standing "at last darkened and dumb at the shore of a void without terminus or origin" (*BM* 310), no reading of *Blood Meridian* can ignore the Judge. From the moment the Kid sets eyes upon him as Glanton's men ride into Chihuahua, he is the dominant figure of the novel. An "enormous man [. . .] close to seven feet" (*BM* 6), albino-white of skin, and devoid of any body hair, the Judge stands out among the scalp hunters not just by appearance but as a complete frontiersman who is also a cosmopolitan: "He can cut a trail, shoot a rifle, ride a horse, track a deer. He's been all over the world. Him and the governor they sat up till breakfast and it was Paris this and London that in five languages [. . .]. The governor's a learned man himself he is, but the Judge . . ." (*BM* 123). To his multilingualism one has to add a seductive eloquence and verbal sophistry that Bloom compares favorably to the likes of Shakespeare's Ulysses and Iago (Josyph 2010b, 82). Round this off with his activities as explorer, scientist, and philosopher and what emerges is a complete Renaissance man, the apex of Western culture.

At the same time, there is a side to the Judge that makes him appear outright superhuman, perhaps even supernatural. Starting with the panicky Reverend Green, characters frequently compare him to the devil. Tobin describes him as a fantastic dancer able to "outdance the devil" and "the greatest fiddler I ever heard" (*BM* 123).[51] He possesses incredible strength, apparently crushing men's heads with his bare hands (*BM* 179) and lifting historical meteorites whose weight well surpasses that of current records.[52] Among his gifts also appear to be powers either of teleportation or else of unnatural speed. After the Kid and a random teamster have prudently evaded the chaos the Judge incites at Reverend Green's tent-meeting, which they leave at the first signs of trouble, they already find the Judge having a drink at the local bar. Similarly, in the Kid's final encounter with the Judge, who about thirty-one years after the scalp hunters' demise "seems little changed or none," he one minute sees him conversing with some patrons. Two short sentences and a single turn of the head later, he is simply "not there" (*BM* 325), only to reappear next to the Kid shortly after. Likewise, Tobin's recollection of the gang's first encounter with the Judge offers no explanation for his presence in the middle of "the greatest desert you'd ever want to see," sitting on "this rock like a man waitin for a coach," and apparently equipped with gold, silver, and weapons, but no canteen (*BM* 124–25). Everybody in Glanton's gang claims to have encountered the Judge in some other place before, and the Kid, in his later years, will likewise hear rumors of him wherever he travels (*BM* 313).

In addition to being an erudite scholar, which is true of Chamberlain's judge, he displays knowledge of things he could not conceivably know. Clearly able to divine the tarot fortunes, he predicts the hanging of David Brown when he offers to write him "a policy on your life against every mishap save the noose" (*BM* 161). Likewise, when he asks the Kid about the fates of Shelby, "whom you left [...] in the desert," and Tate, "whom you abandoned in the mountains" (*BM* 331), he reveals his awareness of events that he was neither present at nor could have heard of from anyone but the Kid himself. Some of these feats of body and mind can be rationally explained; others require considerable leaps of the imagination. In sum, they create the outline of a figure that is larger than life, and while perhaps not outright supernatural is at least "uncanny" (Josyph 2010a, 104). Still, since McCarthy is not writing a fantasy novel or "Stephen King western" (Josyph 2010a, 106),[53] the apparently superhuman character of the Judge is most likely to be read allegorically.

Faustian Patterns and the Judge

What possible meanings are entailed in reading the Judge as an allegorical figure? A strong argument can be made for reading him, as Cant suggests, as "a metaphor for culture itself," specifically a personification of the Western Enlightenment program and its tendency toward "megalomaniac anthropocentrism" (170–71). Along the same lines Bryan Vescio, who detects in the scalp hunters "manifestations of Western culture's irresistible urge to break with the past and to dominate the world," describes the Judge as "the personification of what [Paul] Valéry describes as the Western mind, so intoxicated with the intellect that it tries to remake the world in its own image" (51–52).

While this argument has considerable merits, it suffers from a similar reductionism as the supernatural interpretation. Certainly, the Judge sticks out in the gang as a man of culture and learning: in him, we find traits of the explorer, the historian, and the scientist. He combines these roles and projects them into a program often identified with the dark flipside of the Enlightenment. An explorer like Charles Darwin, Meriwether Lewis, and William Clark, the Judge collects archeological specimens, leaves, and plants, shoots birds, and catches butterflies, which he conserves or sketches into his ledger book. Asked for his purpose in this, he proclaims his will to ultimate knowledge: "Whatever in creation exists without my knowledge exists without my consent. [...] In order for [the world] to be mine nothing must be permitted to occur upon it save by my dispensation" (*BM* 198–99). It is the articulation of an aggressive intellectual imperialism that Bell deems the logical extreme of Enlightenment doctrine. Placing his hands on the ground, the Judge declares the world itself his claim, and in the same breath vows to "make war upon the unknown, to challenge destiny itself" (1988, 119), and become "suzerain of the earth" (*BM* 198). Though his claim echoes the biblical mandate to man to "subdue" the earth and "have dominion [...] over every living thing that moves on the earth" (Gn. 1:28), it is worldly in its reasoning: "The man who believes that the secrets of the world are forever hidden lives in mystery and fear. Superstition will drag him down. [...] But that man who sets himself the task of singling out the thread of order from the tapestry will by the decision alone have taken charge of the world and it is only by such taking charge that he will effect a way to dictate the terms of his own fate" (*BM* 199). If the Judge were the devil and hence another Mephistopheles, his quest to "single out the thread of order" would align him with the Faust of Goethe's *Gelehrtentragödie*. In this context, it is noteworthy that the Judge speaks Dutch, which he learned "off a dutchman" (*BM* 123). More importantly, like Faust, the Judge is or rather presents himself as a "worshipper of truth" (Bell 1988, 120). Yet, in contrast to Faust, who turns to magic, truth for the Judge is primarily defined by empirical science as that which can be positively known: "Your heart's desire is to be told some mystery. The mystery is that there is no mystery" (*BM* 252). The Judge's words and actions articulate a belief that man's claim to dominance is based on the prerequisite of knowledge. In order to "take charge" and control the world, you need to first know and understand the order of the world, put differently, its *truth*.

If he is indeed much like the devil, he is so partly because, like Lucifer, he is a "light-bearer"—only in the sense of the Enlightenment. Apart from his pranks, his main instrument in undermining Christian belief is that of science, especially when combined with warfare. The story of the Judge's gunpowder is of interest here as it makes a strong case for either of his respective mythoclastic roles, as devil *and* scientist. Tobin for one is convinced that

Glanton and the Judge have "a secret commerce. Some terrible covenant" (*BM* 126). It is the clearest allusion to the Faust legend in the book.[54] As Tobin tells the Kid, the gang first met Holden on a scalp hunt while out of powder and on the run from a group of "savages." Paths cross "about the meridian of that day," when the gang finds the Judge sitting all by himself in the middle of the wilderness, "his legs crossed, smilin as we rode up. Like he'd been expectin us" (*BM* 125). With two other members deserting only to die at the hands of the Indians, the Judge effectively joins as the group's thirteenth member. He leads them toward the mountains where they briefly split up again. Glanton's group lays a false track for their pursuers, thus giving Holden time to collect charcoal and bat guano, which he processes into saltpeter. As the gang picks him up, he directs them toward a hellish, volcanic malpais where Tobin and others believe they see "little cloven hoofprints" (*BM* 130). On top of the volcano, the Judge collects brimstone for sulphur and mixes all of the ingredients in a natural stone cauldron. Urinating into the pit, he cries out to the others "to piss, man piss for your very souls" and works the mass "into a foul black dough, a devil's batter" (*BM* 132).

Using the resulting powder, the gang annihilates the Indians. As Shane Schimpf rightly points out, the Judge thus "saves the Glanton gang via his knowledge of the land and his understanding of chemistry [. . .]. There is no praying to God; these men know better" (2008, 20). "Salvation" instead comes in the form of science, which assumes the form of a new kind of faith. At the foot of the volcano, the Judge holds a speech that reminds Tobin of a sermon, "but it was no such sermon as any man of us had ever heard before. [. . .] our mother the earth as he said was round like an egg and contained all good things within her" (*BM* 129–30). Parallel to the Judge's lecture on geology, which renders his listeners "right proselytes of the new order" (*BM* 116), the scalp hunters follow the Judge in his ascent to the mountaintop "like the disciples of a new faith" (*BM* 130). Once the powder is ready, the scalp hunters come forth to fill their horns, "one by one, circling past [the Judge] like communicants" (*BM* 134). Like a priest in the mass transubstantiates bread and wine into the body and blood of Christ, the Judge transforms his ingredients into gunpowder. His communal ritual concentrates and channels the destructive power in the chemical elements, which the gang then unanimously wields against the approaching Indians, their sacrificial victims.[55] Perversely, the Judge uses the Indians' own murderous desire against them as he channels it through his own person, appealing to their mercy and tricking them into a reckless attack by pretending that the rest of the gang have committed suicide (*BM* 134).

A supplementary interpretation is provided by Spurgeon, who observes that the transformation is brought about by "a symbolic and ritualistic rape, with all the men gang-raping the great vaginal hole in 'our mother the earth,' spewing piss instead of semen." The ritual thus appears as a perversion of "the sacred marriage and the eucharist of the wilderness contained within both the hunter myth and Christianity" (Spurgeon 88). Aside from the gendered implications, which present a still underappreciated side in the study of McCarthy and mythology as a whole, Spurgeon addresses something essential here. The coordinates of her insight need to be adjusted but slightly. After all, the Judeo-Christian tradition is at once continuous with archaic religion and mythology in its themes and radically different from them in its interpretation of these themes. From this perspective, the Judge at once perverts Christian rite and returns to the archaic essence of the eucharist of the wilderness. McCarthy thus lays open the violence that the myth dissimulates. It is at the surface only that this alliance of the products of scientific and mythological imagination seems paradoxical.

Demonstrably, Christianity in *Blood Meridian* is in the advanced stages of disintegration. The whole country seems caught in the wake of a sacrificial crisis. Many of the Mexican towns and cities have been abandoned or at least show evidence of rapid decay. Chihuahua City is filled with homeless, beggars, lepers, stray dogs, and orphans (*BM* 72–73). Notably, Girard points out that science and modern thought, by holding religion to be based on purely illusory bases and serving no real purpose whatsoever, have made it "a sort of scapegoat for all human thought" (*VS* 317).[56] In this respect, the mimetic perspective is in close agreement with that of Chris Dacus, whose analyses of "the west as symbol of the eschaton" (2009, 7) and "modernity as a political problem" (2013, 273) come closest to anchoring the apocalyptic in Western history as shaped by Enlightenment doctrine. Albeit in a footnote, Dacus references the thought of the French statesman and philosopher Joseph de Maistre, whose view that "the Enlightenment as a progressive ideology underestimates the socio-political importance of the Church" he sees reflected in *Blood Meridian*'s ruined churches. What is more many of Maistre's pronouncements on the metaphysical nature of war in the essay "On the Violent Destruction of the Human Species" sound eerily similar to those of the Judge. "History proves that war is, in a certain sense, the habitual state of mankind, which is to say that human blood must flow without interruption somewhere or other on the globe, and that for every nation, peace is only a respite." With this concept in mind, I would argue the Judge interpreted as the novel's epic hero in a post-Christian world is very much in accordance with Maistre's claim that the decline of the Church necessarily eventuates in violence and chaos. (2013, 281)[57]

In this respect, it seems only fitting that the Judge's war on Christianity takes the guise of science and technological progress, which, after all, has itself often been propelled by the forces to which today's military industrial complex is heir and that he likewise embodies.

At the same time, it has not gone unnoticed that Holden's own reasoning is often mired in apparent contradictions from one scene to another, nor is he above using deception or telling lies. Lecturing the gang on geology and the age of the world, he refutes those who quote from the Bible with a simple "Books lie," and then proclaims that God "speaks in stones and trees, the bones of things" (*BM* 116).[58] Once he has won the group over, he derides them as fools. Of course, he eventually reveals that *his* god is war. He may admit that "even in this world more things exist without our knowledge than with it," yet in the same breath affirmatively deny the existence of "men or creatures like them" elsewhere in the universe. His sole argument is that the vastness of creation is not bound "to repeat what exists in one part in any other part" (*BM* 245). Not bound perhaps, but maybe free to? Probabilistic arguments like the Drake equation would qualify the Judge's assertion as unlikely, but the simple truth of the matter is that he cannot know for sure.[59]

Perhaps, it is precisely *because* he cannot know that the Judge categorically denies the possibility of intelligent life in places beyond his reach, life that—like that of the birds that he would have "in zoos" (*BM* 199)—is autonomous. This totalitarian pursuit to absolute knowledge and control is fed by a certain rationality, though—like the metaphorical desert "land of some other order [. . .] whose true geology was not stone but fear" (*BM* 47)— the core of that rationality may just be some deep, indefinite dread: "These anonymous creatures, he said, may seem little or nothing in the world. Yet the smallest crumb can devour us. [. . .] Only nature can enslave man and only when the existence of each last entity is routed out and made to stand naked before him will he be properly suzerain of the earth" (*BM* 198).[60] A variation on the Faustian quest is thus revealed when Judge Holden declares that what order man finds in the world is finally the order "which you have put there, like a string in a maze, so that you shall not lose your way. For existence has its own order and that no man's mind can compass, that mind itself being but a fact among others" (*BM* 245). The Judge implies an important insight: the dichotomy between order and disorder is not so much dichotomous as asymmetrical as the appraisal of disorder and order alike can only be made from a state of order and sufficient knowledge of the object of our appraisal, lest the latter appear a chaos.[61] What is more, it requires conscious effort, an act of will, of "taking charge" of the world, as the Judge would say.

Given that ordering man's perception of the world is the basic function of myth, this utterance could signify that the Judge somehow shares in McCarthy's own mythoclastic agenda. Though myths may be designed to deny it, the order they provide, like themselves, is after all of *human* authorship, which is what the Judge expresses vis-à-vis the order of the world. Against this, Spurgeon rightly observes that Holden "deliberately cultivates a feel for myth, ritual, and religion and directs it toward his own ends. His goal is to harness the unconscious response to mythic heroes, invoke it [. . .], and reorder, or perhaps disorder, it on a deep and essential level" (79). This assessment perfectly describes the situation of the scalp hunters in relation to the judge; the situation of the readers, however, is different. On that level, the Judge's acts and words serve less to create a new myth than to reveal the profound disorder of which constant exposure, habit formation, and the formation of myths have drained a world in which truly "anything is possible":

> Had you not seen it all from birth and thereby bled [the world] of its strangeness it would appear to you for what it is, a hat trick in a medicine show, a fevered dream, a trance bepopulate with chimeras having neither analogue nor precedent, an itinerant carnival, a migratory tentshow whose ultimate destination after many a pitch in many a mudded field is unspeakable and calamitous beyond reckoning. (*BM* 245)

Nevertheless, it is probably only the Judge himself who can unflinchingly affirm and navigate this orderless world unhampered and with ease—essentially so because he is of the chimera (Gk. *khimaira*, she-goat) himself. In any case, we must not trust the Judge too far: the chaotic world he describes, apocalyptic teleology and all, is primarily his vision. The Judge's way of becoming suzerain, and the purest expression of his imperialism, then, is to impose his own mythic dis|order upon the world and his fellow beings.

Nietzschean Patterns and the Judge

It is insufficient to say that the Judge projects or pursues the ambitious, totalitarian program described above, as though he were merely some particularly delusional megalomaniac as the rest of the gang would have it when they call him mad. Rather, he radically embodies and personifies it, and in doing so holds up a mirror to Western civilization. The Judge's goal—*our* goal, McCarthy effectively says—is to become suzerain, which entails nothing less than the totalitarian, unobstructed imposition of (his/our) will. To be suzerain is to be like God. The sins of Satan, Adam, and Eve all originate in the same metaphysical desire for divinity. In the Judge, we find articulated that the *will to knowledge* and the *will to power* are one.

In the portentous triad of will, knowledge, and power, one is almost irresistibly put on the path of Friedrich Nietzsche, as a considerable number of critics have noted. Works such as *Zur Genealogie der Moral, Also Sprach Zarathustra*, and *Der Antichrist* all feature prominently in McCarthy scholarship.[62] Primarily, analyses have focused on three interrelated ideas, all of which have become hallmarks that Nietzsche's philosophy is associated with. These are (1) the death of God, which places us before the looming abyss of nihilism, (2) the need for positive assertion associated with the will to power and embodied by the *Übermensch*, or superman, and (3) the idea of Judeo-Christian ethics as slave morality born of resentment. Combining these ideas, Schimpf summarily argues that the whole of *Blood Meridian* presents

a meditation of a Nietzschean world where God has died [. . .] and consequently everything is in a state of chaos and steady decline both physically and morally. The point is to demonstrate how traditional religion, in the form of Christianity, has become stagnant and ineffectual, incapable of providing any sanctuary for those who seek it in times of crisis. What does flourish, however, is the transforming power of science and technology. (2008, 3)[63]

The problem that Nietzsche saw, however, is that the "triumph of the scientific paradigm comes at a cost and that cost is nihilism" (Schimpf 2008, 4). Pure science is decidedly *amoral* in that it is simply not concerned, nor according to Hume's law capable of dealing with, questions of ethics or with providing meaning to existence. With other ideas such as the eternal recurrence of the same, Nietzsche's coiner of illusory language, and his metaphysics of war also being discussed, it may appear that there is hardly a need for yet another Nietzschean interpretation of *Blood Meridian*. As I hope to show, however, these readings can be synthesized and productively extended upon—both to better understand the nature of the Judge and to integrate the novel's Nietzschean dimension into its apocalyptic, in which it plays a central role.

In many ways, the fulcrum of Nietzschean thought in *Blood Meridian* is constituted by his diagnosis of the state of modern man put forth in aphorism 125 of *Die fröhliche Wissenschaft*. The aphorism articulates the famous idea of the death of God. Simply put, this death as announced by the madman of the aphorism's parabolic narrative defines modernity as an era thoroughly without orientation, absolutes, or certainties either metaphysical or moral.

> Whither has God vanished? [. . .] I will tell you. We have killed him—you and I! We are all his murderers. But how did we achieve this? How did we manage to drink up the ocean? Who handed us the sponge to wipe away the whole horizon? What did we do when we unchained this earth from the sun? Whither is it moving now? Away from all suns? Are we not ever falling—backwards, sideways, forwards, and in all directions? Is there still an above and a below? Do we not stray through endless nothingness? [. . .] Has it not grown colder? [. . .] God is dead! God stays dead. And we have killed him. How do we console ourselves—we murderers of all murderers? The holiest and most powerful hitherto known in the world has bled to death under our knives—and who will cleanse us of this blood? What water could purify us? Which feasts of atonement and what sacred games shall we have to invent? Is not the greatness of this deed too great for us?

> Shall we not have to become Gods ourselves, just to seem worthy of it?
> (Nietzsche 1999b, 481)

Nietzsche articulates a diagnosis about the world and the position of humanity in it that has a lot in common with the Judge's vision of the world as a "migratory tentshow" in which "anything is possible" (*BM* 245). In simplified terms, what the madman laments is not the actual death of some personal, metaphysical entity, but the death of a concept of God, particularly the Judeo-Christian one. The latter, for Nietzsche, is fundamentally already an example of "resentment become productive"—with God on the side of the weak and victimized, as whose projection he is identified.[64] The death of this God, this concept, while partly attributable to the advances of natural science, the study of history, the critique of Christian morality, and other developments Cant summarizes under the label of "Enlightenment reason," for Nietzsche is already inherent in the values that it champions. As Nietzsche posits in his *Zarathustra*, the Christian deity's combination of omniscient witnessing with ideals such as mercy and forgiveness, which can be subsumed under the idea of a superabundant all-encompassing—that is, nondiscriminatory and thus *shameless*—love, corrodes the concept itself from within: such a God can no more be taken seriously.[65]

Yet, as the madman's crazed behavior indicates, the impact of the news he imparts is more upsetting than his listeners, whose contumely identifies them as atheists rather than believers, realize. With the death of God, the entire foundation of Western ethics and values gives way, as its indisputable metaphysical foundation crumbles, which leads "to the dead end of nihilism" (Cant 174).[66] Ending up in this dead end has always been a possibility in traveling the forking paths of McCarthy's literary labyrinth, so much so that early McCarthy criticism could still identify it as its one and only terminus. The death of God creates a dilemma that informs dominant modern and postmodern philosophies. Morally, it places Western man before the problem of devising viable alternatives to Judeo-Christian and other deist ethics, which are after all grounded in metaphysical absolutes.[67] More generally, it places humans before an ever-gaping void of meaning, before an emptiness that needs to be filled somehow. Finally, this is just what the Judge is trying to do.

Nietzsche asserts that modernity sickens man's spirit. His madman asks whether in order to endure the void opened up by the death of God, we have to become gods ourselves. In this, Girard would agree: "For two or three centuries this has been the underlying principle of every 'new' Western doctrine: God is dead, man must take his place" (*DDN* 57). But whereas Girard contends that the modern quest for metaphysical fullness, which unfolds along the vectors of mimetic desire, ends in perpetual disappointment, Nietzsche still posits "that the void can only be endured through positive assertion [. . .] of life itself" (Cant 174). Nietzsche's vision of the being that could bear the heavy awareness of insignificance and meaninglessness by creating his own values takes shape in the ideal of the *superman*.

In the Judge, McCarthy presents us with an unadorned image of what the superman could look like, essentially to "de-romanticize the idea" (Williamson 271; see also Schimpf 2008, 9, 29, 39; Hillier 2013, 60). More than by any physical or intellectual ability, the superman is finally characterized most of all by his overabounding vitality and *will to power*, which Woodson characterizes as "an effort to gain control over chaos, a stay against the brevity of human existence," as well as "a maintaining of the self against other people" (2002, 267). For this will to assert itself freely, Christian morality must be cast aside. Debating the subject of war, Black Jackson cites the Bible to the effect that "he that lives by the sword shall perish by the sword," to which the Judge candidly replies: "What right man would have it any other way?" (*BM* 248). Arguing from the position of theodicy, he provocatively asks, "If God meant to interfere in the degeneracy of mankind would he not have done so by now?" and simultaneously asserts that the proper way to raise children is to put them in pits with wild dogs, to make them use their wits to evade wild lions, and to test their *wills* by making them run "naked in the desert" (*BM* 147). Like his acts, Holden's values cannot but strike us as diametrically opposed to those of Christianity. It is fittingly the second passage of Nietzsche's *Antichrist* that best sets the parameters of this terrifying superman's values:

> What is good?—Whatever augments the feeling of power, the will to power, power itself, in man.
>
> What is evil?—Whatever springs from weakness.
>
> What is happiness?—The feeling that power *increases*—that resistance is overcome.
>
> Not contentment, but more power; *not* peace at any price, but war;

not virtue, but efficiency (virtue in the Renaissance sense, *virtu*, virtue free of moral acid).

The weak and the botched shall perish: first principle of *our* charity. And one should help them to it.

What is more harmful than any vice?—Practical sympathy for the botched and the weak—Christianity . . . [68]

As I will argue in the penultimate part of this chapter, it is the Kid's flawed Christianity that ultimately scandalizes and sets him at odds with the Judge. Echoing Nietzsche's critique of Western ethics in *Zur Genealogie der Moral*, Holden dismantles all objections the scalp hunters raise: "Moral law is an invention of mankind for the disenfranchisement of the powerful in favor of the weak. Historical law subverts it at every turn. A moral view can never be proven right or wrong by any ultimate test" (*BM* 250; Jarrett 82; Schimpf 2008, 23–24). For Nietzsche as for Judge Holden, Christianity's is a slave morality, born from the resentment harbored by the weak against the strong, or, as Fleming aptly puts it, "a most thoroughgoing cultural ennoblement of revenge fantasies against the victors of history" (125).

In the at least superficially positivist world of the Judge, which has excluded any authority like the God of Christianity from the equation, there can be no absolute against which to measure the right and wrong of a man's views or deeds (Williamson 265). The only higher court that the Judge accepts is that of history, "the repository of all that can be known" (Bell 1988, 120). Questions of moral right or wrong are made subordinate to questions of survival and victory, which the Judge reads as history's preference of one man (or race) over another. What lends the Judge's argument an unsettling credibility is the fact that in a universe with no other god or form of constancy, war appears as the one constant of human experience through time. Bell comments:

> Some other metaphysic would conceivably be preferable, some other system in which to believe and from which to infer and assign value. But man [. . .] has produced firm evidence in history that only violence recurs as the indisputable common denominator of his presence in time. War therefore must be [. . .] affirmed as being holy, for man's existence to have any sanctity at all. (1988, 121)[69]

In the words of the Judge: "If war is not holy, man is nothing but antic clay" (*BM* 307). While individual arguments of right or wrong are trivial in the Judge's eyes, it is the "separate wills"—in other words the force of opposing desires—that give the argument its life, that assume primacy, and history that records and asserts the preference of a "larger will" (*BM* 249): the Heraclitean *pólemos*, eternal war itself.

This escalatory assertion of the will of war itself represents not simply a rejection of Christianity, but the consequence of its breakdown. In his last meeting with the older Kid, Holden calls attention to another man in a repetition of the *ecce homo* motif of the novel's opening sentence: "See him. That man hatless" (*BM* 333). The picture the Judge paints is of a man whose life is "so balked about by difficulty" and "altered of its intended architecture" that he is "little more than a walking hovel hardly fit to house the human spirit" (*BM* 330). It bears more than a passing resemblance to Zarathustra's *last man*—that disaffected, mildly hedonistic being who personified Nietzsche's fear of what modernity would make of Western man.[70] As the Judge tells "the Man," the issue with that other man is not that life is hard but that "men will not do as he wishes them to. Have never done, never will do" (*BM* 330). This thought connects with the Kid's exchange with the old hermit he meets in the beginning of the book. The Kid asserts that "I can think of better places and better ways," to which the hermit responds by asking, "Can ye make it be?" (*BM* 19). Perhaps too rashly, the Kid concedes that he cannot, as most people likely would. If the earlier dialogue invokes Gottfried Wilhelm Leibniz's argument against theodicy that we are living in the best of all possible worlds, it turns out that the root of the man's lack of vitality is less his powerlessness than his unsettling view of a deeply amoral and meaningless cosmos. This feeling, the Judge insinuates, is ultimately harder to swallow than the feeling of being punished. Punishment, after all, would at least imply a sense of moral authority and order:

> Can he say, such a man, that there is no malign thing set against him? [. . .] What manner of heretic could doubt agency and claimant alike? Can he believe [. . .] [t]hat gods of vengeance and of compassion alike lie sleeping in their crypt and whether our cries are for an accounting or for the destruction of the ledgers altogether they must evoke only the same silence and that it is this silence which will prevail? (*BM* 330)

To interpret the hatless man's predicament as a simple case of ressentiment obscures the larger issue. The feeling that the cards are stacked against one, that the world is neither just nor fair, the Judge implies, is still preferable to seeing it for what it is—a desert that "calls for largeness of heart but [. . .] is also ultimately empty" (*BM* 330). In a way it defers the deeper, nihilistic terror of a universe without order or justice, in which "gods of vengeance and of compassion alike lie sleeping in their crypt," which echoes Nietzsche's madman's question of what churches are today, if not the tombs and burial monuments of God (1999b, 482). As we see everywhere, *Blood Meridian* turns the icons and churches of Christianity into ruins or sites of massacre, evoking a strong sense of divine putrefaction, the death or else—as in a variation of Ingmar Bergman—the mysterious and insufferable *silence* of God.

Other than perhaps the suicidal professor in *The Sunset Limited*, who like the Judge is associated with the atheist's color of choice (i.e., white), no character in McCarthy's work is as consciously aware of the looming existential vacuum as is the Judge. Whatever else may be known about him, the single most insightful moment has to be when he presses just this issue upon the older Kid in their final conversation. Having incited the slaying of the domesticated dancing bear, he describes the evening's proceedings as the orchestration of a ritual, a dance. Then, something truly extraordinary happens. As he seems to be gazing into the Kid's soul, the Judge, that albinic child-devouring devil, that ultrarational and yet uninhibitedly libidinal creature, perhaps inadvertently allows the reader a glimpse into his own: "We are not speaking in mysteries. You of all men are no stranger to that feeling, the emptiness and the despair. It is that which we take arms against, is it not?" (*BM* 329).

Not enough has been made of this moment, which may be nothing less than the most revelatory of the novel. One among few exceptions, James Dorson suggests in his poignant and erudite effort at "Demystifying the Judge" that

> the real horror in the novel is the horror of the Real—not the presence of the Judge, but what his presence hides. As Søren Kierkegaard aptly noted, "all the despair and all the horror of evil expressed in a word are not as terrible as silence." More terrible than the Judge's evil logic, then, is the silence between his words. Even worse than the novel's incantation of violence is

the profound stillness beneath its din. This silence, where all that is heard is the sound of our own inevitable demise, is what foments the rage for transcendental meaning. (115)

Despair of the silence of a godless, empty universe is the rage of metaphysical desire on a cosmic scale. Thus, one arrives at the core of the "new faith" the Judge brings to the scalp hunters, the substitute to fill the existential void left by Christianity. It is the very thing that religion protects man against. We have already seen in our discussion of the Clausewitzian escalation to extremes how for the Judge war itself becomes a religion, a god even. It is now that we see how, for the Judge, man himself becomes godlike to the extent that he is able to incorporate the corrupted sacred of war's absolute violence. Now, too, are we able to locate the germ cell of this escalation in the failure of Christianity itself.

Dionysus and Satan Dancing, or the Judge as Principle of Dis|Order

By and large, the discussion of how Nietzsche's philosophy informs the character, views, and actions of Judge Holden has moved within familiar coordinates. In the last argument, however, one touches upon something new, a more ancient dimension of the argument that is too easily overlooked among the vitriolic resentment that fuels the Lutheran pastor's son's polemic against the ethics of his upbringing.[71] In Nietzsche's words it concerns the opposition between Dionysus and the Crucified. Fleming writes:

> In asserting that Christianity was simply a politically opportune reheating of pagan religion, Nietzsche claimed that anthropologists and philologists missed the fact that, unlike the pagan/Dionysian version, Christianity in fact *stifled* life by its relentless promotion of resentment and its "morality of the slaves." Indeed, Nietzsche held that Christianity's lamentable doctrines which affirm the "equality of all souls before God" and the "sacredness of the human" merely function to repress both the most powerful members and the most powerful generative dynamics of culture. Christianity stood, therefore, not as a rehashing of the Dionysian, but as its chief antithesis, which—against biblical religion—upheld an unreserved affirmation of the will to destroy and celebrate life in all of its "violent intensity." (126)

There is something of this opposition between pagan religion and Christianity in the Judge's suggestion about the truth of the world, that is, its terrible silence, which the embittered man at the Fort Griffin saloon does not wish to see. As if he were quoting the old Mennonite, Holden's words imply that the gods may in fact not be dead, but only *sleeping*. What is more, the gods are not the same: They are "gods of vengeance and compassion alike"—that is, respectively, of vengeance *or* compassion.

Writing about Girard's reception of Nietzsche, Michael Platt points out that "unlike positivist students of mythology, most professors of anthropology, and modern atheist intellectuals, Nietzsche did not think the voluntary death at the center of Christianity was like all the violent sacrifices in so many founding mythologies" (362). Where the Cambridge anthropologists spearheaded by Frazer only saw Christianity as a kind of parasite grafting itself onto older rituals and myths, Nietzsche, like Girard after him, asserts that among such superficial continuities, there also exists a radical difference that comes down to an irreducible opposition between Dionysus and Jesus: "Dionysus versus the Crucified: there you have the antithesis. It is *not* a difference in regard to their martyrdom—it is a difference in the meaning of it. Life itself, its eternal fruitfulness and recurrence, creates torment, destruction, the will to annihilation. In the other case, suffering—the 'Crucified as the innocent one'—counts as an objection to this life, as a formula for its condemnation" (cit. in *GR* 247).[72]

While Nietzsche interprets "Dionysus cut to pieces" as "a *promise* of life" (*GR* 247) and eternal rebirth through destruction, he is "at least as convinced as Girard that the God of Jews and Christians is the God of victims *per se*" (Fleming 124). Dionysus, to recall, is the "god who mixed with men, the god of reciprocity, of mimetic doubles and contagious madness" (*BE* 102). As such, he personifies the transfiguration of violence and the victim through which society is reborn—or, in the Judge's words among the Anasazi ruins, that which "will be again [...]. And again. With other people, with other sons" (*BM* 147). Conversely, Nietzsche laments, two thousand years have passed since the inception of Christianity, and men have created "not a single new God" (1999a, 185). It is in this diagnosis of the roots of culture's religious infertility that one finds the most astonishing convergence between Girardian and Nietzschean thought. Nietzsche argues:

Through Christianity, the individual was made so important, so absolute, that he could not longer be sacrificed: but the species endures only through human sacrifice [. . .]. Genuine charity demands sacrifice for the good of the species—it is hard, it is full of self-overcoming, because it needs human sacrifice. And this pseudo-humaneness called Christianity wants it established that no one should be sacrificed. (cit. in Fleming 127)[73]

From this, it is apparent that Girard's and Nietzsche's views overlap in three important respects, though the third is implicit: first, the centrality of sacrifice for the revitalization of (archaic) cultures; second, the paradigm shifting role of Jesus as "the innocent one" who "dies against sacrifice" (*GR* 18), subverting its founding mechanism; and third, the grim prospect this opens up for modern man, although for Nietzsche this prospect is that of nihilism and the degeneracy of spirit whereas for Girard it is fully apocalyptic. Nietzsche can hence be credited with providing "a negative guide to the meaning of the Christian revelation" (*GR* 243). It is in their evaluation of this revelation that he and Girard part ways.

Up to this point, I have discussed a number of the disseminating roles that *Blood Meridian*'s Judge is identified with. My analysis has led from the straightforward, naïve reading that by his apparently supernatural abilities identifies him with the devil, to his multiple roles as explorer, scientist, archeologist, and sophist-philosopher, which, by extension, make him a representative of and metaphor for Western culture in his totalitarian, imperialistic drive to become suzerain of the earth. I have briefly alluded to his kinship with the chimera, which consists in his ability to thrive on the profound disorder that he regards as the world's true face, all the while he seeks to actively revitalize its archaic mythological order. The last two aspects in turn relate him to the Nietzschean superman who asserts his own will to power against both the threat of nihilism and the ethical confines of Christian ressentiment-values.

However, by themselves, these readings illuminate yet fail to fully encompass the "vast abhorrence" (*BM* 243) of the Judge. So, too, do readings that compare him to a Gnostic archon or else consciously strive to exclude metaphysics or allegory from the equation. Furthermore, there are sides to McCarthy's creation that I have barely touched upon—potentially metaliterary qualities such as his whiteness or his custom of destroying the artifacts he

sketches, his phallic nature, or his murderous, vaguely cannibalistic pedophilia. The superman's quest, however, has led us straight to the temple doors
of the one godhead whose model guides him on his way through the abyss of
modernity: the ancient, dancing Dionysus.

Could the god of wine, fertility, religious frenzy, and mob violence provide a more encompassing yet differentiated image of the Judge? McCarthy's
narrator suggestively likens him to "a great ponderous djinn," "an icon," and
finally "some great pale deity" (*BM* 96, 147, 92). Yet, to answer the question,
we may as well ask ourselves why it is *dancing* that the Judge is so closely associated with. Long before we see him take to the floor at the escalating festival
of Chihuahua, Tobin admiringly expresses that the Judge can "outdance the
devil himself" (*BM* 123). More than its enigmatic epilogue, the most lingering image of the novel is that of the Judge dancing and fiddling away among
the patrons and prostitutes of Fort Griffin's saloon:

> And they are dancing, the board floor slamming under the jackboots and
> the fiddlers grinning hideously over their canted pieces. Towering over
> them all is the Judge and he is naked dancing, his small feet lively and
> quick and now in doubletime and bowing to the ladies, huge and pale and
> hairless, like an enormous infant. He never sleeps, he says. He says he'll
> never die. He bows to the fiddlers and sashays backwards and throws back
> his head and laughs deep in his throat and he is a great favorite, the Judge.
> He wafts his hat and the lunar dome of his skull passes palely under the
> lamps and he swings about and takes possession of one of the fiddles and he
> pirouettes and makes a pass, two passes, dancing and fiddling at once. His
> feet are light and nimble. He never sleeps. He says that he will never die.
> He dances in light and in shadow and he is a great favorite. He never sleeps,
> the Judge. He is dancing, dancing. He says that he will never die. (*BM* 335)

In the Judge's dance, the pagan element returns with a vengeance. The preceding paragraph already introduces a kind of female double of the Judge in
the shape of an "enormous whore," half-naked like him in wearing "nothing
but a pair of men's drawers," just like the other prostitutes recall Glanton's
scalp hunters, draped as they are in "what appeared to be trophies—hats or
pantaloons or blue twill cavalry jackets" (*BM* 334). The mixture of dresses
not only signals a destabilization of gender identities but, in recalling the

bloody trophies of the scalp hunters, suffuses the ostensibly innocent exhilaration of the dance with the novel's ecstasy of bloodshed. If music and dance—traditionally seen as a mimetic art—are first among the bacchic rites, these women, too, are much like the raving maenads of Euripides's *The Bacchae*, celebrating horned Dionysus in the form of the Judge. The shift to the present tense and the parataxis of the final paragraph then create an almost musical, dizzying frenzy as language itself seems to be dancing with him. The prose approaches the quality of a vertiginous fugue suggestive of a continuous present, of an eternal recurrence whose chief expression is the Judge's terrifying boast: "He says that he will never die."

To recall, in an early draft of *Blood Meridian*, the Judge tellingly identified himself as the man "who knows how to make sleepers wake. The dead to dance if you'd believe it" (91/35/9, 465). Both passages constitute more than simply a nod to the medieval danse macabre. There is a definite link between dance and desire. In his analysis in *The Scapegoat* of how Salome's dance serves as a catalyst to unify the desires of Herod's birthday guests with the murderous model desire of Herodias,[74] Girard observes that dancing

> exacerbates desire, rather than suppressing it. What prevents us from dancing is not just the physical but the dreadful intertwining of our desires which keep us tied to the ground, and the *other* of desire always seems responsible for this misfortune; we are all like Herodias, obsessed with some John the Baptist. [...] Dance accelerates the mimetic process. It involves all the guests at the banquet in the dance, converging all the desires on the one object, [...] the head of John the Baptist on Salome's platter. [...] John the Baptist is first the scandal of Herodias and then becomes the scandal of Salome, who, through her artistic power, transmits the scandal to all the spectators. She gathers all the desires together and directs them toward the victim chosen for her by Herodias. The inextricable knot of desire must be loosened at the end of the dance, and this requires the death of the victim, who, for the time being, incarnates that desire [...]. The dancer and the dance are reciprocally generative. The infernal progress of the mimetic rivalries, the becoming *similar* of all the characters, the progress of the sacrificial crisis toward its denouement in a victim are all part of Salome's dance. (SG 134, 138)

In short, the same polarization of desire and violence at work in ritual is similarly effected by the dance that possesses the crowd, much like the demons of Gerasa to whom the Judge is connected by his "lashless pig's eyes" (*BM* 310), and directs it against the single victim that scandalizes it. It is not as if this sacrificial interpretation were accidental or alien to the text: In his encounter with the grown-up Kid at the Fort Griffin saloon, the Judge explicitly characterizes the dance as a ceremony and ritual, which to be true must include "the letting of blood [. . .] the tempering agent in the mortar which bonds" (*BM* 329).

Even the ancient motto *Et in Arcadia ego*, which is inscribed on the Judge's rifle, is not to be taken as a flat reference to the inevitability of death even in paradise. Rather, it is an indicator that the (temporary) peace of paradise is bought with bloody murder. Like the dance, it goes to show that to compare the Judge to Dionysus, ultimately, is to link him to both desire and the mob. In many respects, he recalls the triune of *Outer Dark*. We repeatedly see him skillfully manipulate crowds to his nefarious ends, be it the patrons and dancers of Fort Griffin's saloon, Reverend Green's tent meeting that he transforms into a lynch mob as his first act in the novel, the Indians whose bloodlust he uses to ambush them in the ritualistic transmutation of gunpowder, or the scalp hunters he initially saves only to ultimately deliver them to their own sacrificial death at the hands of the Yuma.[75] Clearly, the Judge knows how to rouse and channel men's desires. To the gang, he initially represents not simply salvation from their pursuers, but the traditional diabolic temptation of *aurum et argentum*, "gold and silver" (*BM* 125).[76] After the scalp hunters have been wiped out, he proceeds to buy Toadvine's hat and offers the Kid the exorbitant sum of $750 in exchange for his gun and powder. And if he is the only one who can soothe Glanton's frenzied spells of violence, it may be because he may be the one that induces them.

The Judge should be read as a principle cultural dis|order through desire and violence. Signs of this disseminate throughout the text. Thus, the novel's highly allegorical eleventh chapter is illuminating as it contains not only the short anecdote on the old Hueco and his portrait, but also the suggestive parable of the harnessmaker and his son, and finally the Judge's elaborations on the "dead fathers," the Anasazi. Firstly, the old Hueco's case can be seen as evidence of the Judge's supreme skill in rendering a lifelike portrait that becomes the object of feared rivalry as it is taken not as a representation but as containing the essence of the man. Secondly, the story of the harnessmaker formally resembles one of Jesus's parables; while missing a collective dimension, its elements can nonetheless be brought into meaningful relation with each other and the rest of the novel by adopting a mimetic perspective. Thus, the harnessmaker's imposture of Native Americans becomes striking as an imitative approach "to wheedl[ing] money" out of charitable wayfarers. The traveler with his message of taking "his brother into his heart" represents a messianic figure, urging that a passing "crazy black nigger," who is dressed in motley fashion "like a carnival clown" and suggestively drawing a funeral hearse, is "not less than a man among men" (*BM* 143).

The reasons for the violence of the tale are also meaningful: it is because the harnessmaker covets the traveler's money and watch, and perhaps a bit out of rivalry for the admiration of his own family, that he kills him, suggestively with a rock. After his father's deathbed confession, the harnessmaker's son goes to defile the traveler's grave because "he was jealous of the dead man" and consequently becomes "a killer of men" (*BM* 144–45). Finally, the Judge's tale contains the element of the victim's false transcendence. To the harnessmaker's wife, the traveler's grave becomes that of her own son, whereas to the traveler's son, his father becomes an "idol of perfection," a "frozen god" rather than a fallible man (*BM* 145). This idolization never allows him to "find his way," and, as the similar backstory of Elrod suggests, finally turns him into a killer as well.

Even the collective element asserts itself, in that the Judge's listeners "all beg[i]n to shout at once with every kind of disclaimer" (*BM* 145)—fighting over the truth of the mythical tale he has told them. Finally, the Anasazi ruins, according to the Judge, represent "the dead fathers" whose "spirit is entombed in the stone," leaving behind "ruins and mystery and a residue of nameless rage" (*BM* 146)—as well as a rival-model to which the generations of tribes now living in these lands cannot hope to measure up. Thus, in a double sense, the "dead fathers" are "not so dead" (*BM* 142).[77]

When, in Fort Griffin's saloon, the Kid argues that "everbody dont have to have a reason to be someplace," the Judge agrees with the caveat that "order is not set aside because of their [i.e., the patrons'] indifference" (*BM* 328). So he essentially points out that men's behavior may not always be deliberate but is nonetheless causally motivated. In a question directed as much at the reader as it is at the Kid, the Judge asks: "If it is so that they themselves have no reason and are indeed here must they not be here by reason of some other? And if this is so can you guess who that other might be?" (*BM* 328). One is tempted to fill in the blank with entities or, as the Judge says, "agencies" like God, death, the devil, or even the Judge himself. Yet, as McKenna points out in his crossreading of Derrida and Girard, "writing's capacity to represent anything derives from the fact that it represents nothing in particular" (30). Since the Judge is both a literary creation and a figure of writing itself, in a sense, all of the aforementioned items fit the bill. From a mimetic perspective, though, his question already contains its own answer, which in turn contains all others. The one whom the patrons and dancers "intend toward" (*BM* 329) is literally just "some other"—*any* other, but no one in particular, the *Other of desire*, which itself turns out to be the agency manipulating the dancers toward the sacrificial culmination of the ritual dance that follows.

Finally, in performing his wondrous coin-trick around the fire, the Judge is not simply playing the con man, he is providing a lesson in the inner workings of the human psyche that he knows so remarkably well: "The arc of circling bodies is determined by the length of their tether," he says, "moons, coins," and, significantly, "men" (*BM* 245–46). Whether one takes for its gravitational center the object or the rival, what the Judge describes here can serve as an allegory for mimetic desire itself. If this is so, the enormous, heavyweight judge, whose looming presence, much like that of Anton Chigurh in *No Country for Old Men*, is often linked with the appearance of coins and the imminent death of a character, is certainly the one holding the tether that is desire itself.[78]

A terrifying, phallic model and literally "a great favorite" in his final dance, the Judge both theorizes and personifies the mimetic workings of both desire and sacred violence. Ironically, the path of interpretation that mimetic theory lays out thus leads us back to one of our earliest associations. As Heraclitus says in fragment 127: "Hades and Dionysus, for whom they go mad and rage, are one and the same" (cit. in Otto 116). Essentially, this suggests that to compare the Judge to Dionysus is also to compare him to the devil: "Dionysos, in other words, is the same thing as hell, the same thing as Satan, the same thing as death, the same thing as the lynch mob. Dionysos is the destructiveness at the heart of violent contagion" (*ISS* 120).

There is a noteworthy distinction to be made, though. While Dionysus
and Satan are at base two names given to personify the same group of phenomena, the cultural context of the former still relates to cyclical time, a time
in which a community could yet be reborn through violence. Conversely,
the latter relates to the apocalyptic, linear time of a world in which victimization is radically demystified through the Crucifixion. Unlike Dionysus's
eternal return, Satan is therefore to be identified with the gradual *escalation
to extremes*, as communities can less and less rely on "Satan [to] cast out
Satan" (Mk. 4:8), that is, on the single-victim mechanism to be triggered
at the height of cultural disorder.[79] In sum, Satan *is* Dionysus in the Judeo-
Christian world. He is thus "the name of a decomposing structure," namely

> the very one that Saint Paul called "Powers and Principalities." [. . .] Christ
> replaced Dionysus, which is something that Nietzsche did not want to see.
> Violence now founds nothing; only resentment is constantly growing, in
> other words, mimetically, faced with the revelation of its own truth. [. . .]
> The linear time that Christ forced us to adopt makes the eternal return
> of the gods impossible, and thus also any reconciliation on the head of
> innocent victims. (*BE* 103)

If the devil is often portrayed as working in a legal profession, this can be
traced back to the meaning of the word itself. To recall, *Satan* in Hebrew
and *diábolos* in Greek both mean adversary and accuser. They signify "the
power of accusation and the power of the process resulting in blaming and
eliminating a substitute for the real cause of the community's troubles"
(Williams xii). Accordingly, the Judge's first act is to denounce Reverend
Green as an imposter, a wanted criminal, and a child molester, to which
the latter can only helplessly (yet ironically accurately) reply, "This is him.
The devil. Here he stands" (*BM* 7), before his tent meeting dissolves into
chaos. Shortly thereafter, the Judge openly admits that he never even heard
of Green. After the Yuma massacre, he claims to have denounced the Kid
to the Mexican authorities.

In this "legal context," my analysis is compatible, too, with Dorson's
identification of the Judge as a representative of the law in the sense of Walter
Benjamin's "Zur Kritik der Gewalt" (1921). A recurring mythical paradox is

the punishment and transgression of a law that the myth presupposes but only subsequently establishes through said punishment. As such, the foundation of law itself is interfused with violence: "Law exonerates and provides a legitimate basis for founding violence ex post facto, and this new legal ground covers up the original abyss from which it rises. Thus there exists a mutual legitimation between violence and law, each providing a cover for the other" (Dorson 108). Since the generative hypothesis, in variation of the Freudian primal murder, posits recurring acts of founding violence at the root of culture and so coincidentally of what can be called primal *law*, the worldly order, insofar as it derives from this murder and sustains itself by new acts of collective violence—the Judge's unifying "sharing of enemies" (*BM* 307)—can rightly be called *satanic*. "The function of violence is here to stay, because it is not exterior to order but the very function upon which our civilization rests" (Dorson 110).

It is important to realize that this attribution neither surrenders interpretive reason to metaphysical speculation, nor forces analysis into the logical cul-de-sac of mistrusting the Judge's supernatural or uncanny traits as traps of a text seen as complicit with him.[80] In fact, associating the Judge with Dionysus and Satan cuts deeper than any superficial markers of the diabolic routinely associated with him suggest. In a sense, that naïve equation was at once too literal and too metaphorical. The mistake is to think of the devil as a person. In James G. Williams's words, he instead has to be conceived of as "the 'principle' or 'first thing' of both order and disorder: of disorder because he is a figure representing rivalry and scandal; of order because he represents the mechanism that is triggered at the height of the disorder" (xii). For the Judge's aspiration to be suzerain, one can accordingly substitute one of the Bible's many titles of the devil: the prince of this world. There is a direct semantic link between Satan, the father of lies, and in some versions of liars, and the worldly and spiritual authorities opposed to the kingdom of God that the New Testament calls "powers and principalities" (KJV),[81] as it is the mythical lie the community of murderers tells itself about its victim that founds their social order for generations to follow (*TH* 191; *ISS* 42).[82] In this sense, the ignes fatui or will-o'-the-wisps of the desert with their "will to deceive that is in things luminous" (*BM* 120) can be said to be kin to the shining, albino-skinned Judge as well. And when he, having sketched and burned another of his artifacts, appears "much satisfied with the world, as if his counsel had been sought at its creation" (*BM* 140), that is so because, in a certain sense, it has been.

Read this way, as the personification of an alternatively disruptive and restorative principle of violence and desire, things about the Judge begin to fall into place: Why is it that everyone in the gang purports to have met the Judge somewhere before he first joins the group (*BM* 124)? Why, during his later traveling years, does the Kid hear "rumor" of him wherever he goes (*BM* 312)? And why, in depicting their encounter almost thirty years after their last confrontation, does McCarthy take pains to introduce the Judge as an entity both nigh omnipresent and beyond the grasp of time itself?

> [H]e was among every kind of man, herder and bullwhacker and drover and freighter and miner and hunter and soldier and pedlar and gambler and drifter and drunkard and thief and he was among the dregs of the earth in beggary a thousand years and he was among the scapegrace scions of eastern dynasties and in all that motley assemblage he sat by them and yet alone as if he were some other sort of man entire and he seemed little changed or none in all these years. (*BM* 325)

"Your heart's desire is to be told some mystery. The mystery is that there is no mystery" (*BM* 252), the Judge says. Following the line of argument I have drawn, there truly is "no mystery" to the Judge. In fact, the mystery of humanity's origins suddenly becomes explicable *through* him. The simple answer to all of these questions, to virtually everything that the Judge does or represents, is that he is not a person, but a principle. He can represent next to everything from the godhead and the devil to the Enlightenment, Western culture, and the text itself, or occupy every position within the mimetic process—because he embodies the founding principle, the mimetic dance of violence and desire itself, from which all else arises. This is why it is a fool's errand to search for "any ultimate atavistic egg" (*BM* 310) from which the Judge originates: He is that which always already animates the people of the crowd to cast out the at once bad-and-golden egg from which they hatch.

As I have pointed out in the discussion of *Outer Dark*, the identification of Satan with both the earlier and later stages of mimetic contagion conceives of him as an *intersubjective* phenomenon. This is why the Judge sits "by them [i.e., everyone] and yet alone" (*BM* 325). Existing solely between humans and rooted in their felt lack and unquenchable thirst for metaphysical fullness, he personifies that thirst. Tobin may assert that "no man is give leave of that [God's] voice" (*BM* 124), but the Kid rightly questions whether the voice speaks to the Judge, who, much the image of Nietzsche's modern man, admits that his experience of the universe is a terrifying silence. From this perspective, the Judge's whiteness, and the "empty slots" (*BM* 147) of his eyes become as suggestive as the mirror in Fort Griffin's saloon that might show the Judge but holds "only smoke and phantoms" (*BM* 325). Satan has "no actual being" (*ISS* 45); indeed, he is the very absence of being.

It is entirely conceivable that in that final encounter, the Judge exists only as a projection and temptation of the older Kid's psyche, coming to finally claim possession of him. To the latter's charge "You aint nothing," the Judge simply answers: "You speak truer than you know" (*BM* 331). Readers do not have to take the Kid's grammatical double negative as resulting in a positive, nor is the Judge's cryptic assertion necessarily to be interpreted this way. Following Wallach, evil "like inscription, [. . .] is simultaneously a negation and a real force and personality, behind which emptiness may be no more than intuited" (2002b, 11). Intuited, though, it may be. There is no denying the reality of the forces personified by the Judge, which according to Girard the Greeks called Dionysus and which the Bible calls Satan. Yet personal substance they have not.

Finally, the Judge may dance the dance of Dionysus, the dance that, as he says, "is the warrior's right" (*BM* 331), but the entirety of the text does nothing if not reveal the utter inertness of violence, which, deprived of its founding mechanism, can do nothing but escalate to produce ever diminishing returns of order, and finally nothing at all. In this lies one of the novel's major achievements. Surely, nobody who reads and understands *Blood Meridian* in this way will rightly be able to take up arms today in good faith, no matter what ideology is summoned to consecrate or justify war. "Literary emotion is an elixir that demystifies in the most honorable way. To understand war completely is to no longer be able to be a warrior" (*BE* 148). However, it is exactly the latter impossibility that the Judge wishes to negate:

> As war becomes dishonored and its nobility called into question those
> honorable men who recognize the sanctity of blood will become excluded

from the dance, which is the warrior's right, and thereby will the dance become a false dance and the dancers false dancers. And yet there will be one there always who is a true dancer and can you guess who that might be? [...] Only that man who has offered up himself entire to the blood of war, who has been to the floor of the pit and seen horror in the round and learned at last that it speaks to his inmost heart, only that man can dance. (*BM* 331)

The horror he speaks of is highly evocative of yet not simply identical to that of Conrad's Kurtz, nor that of Col. Kurtz's famous monologue in Coppola's *Apocalypse Now* (1979), to which it is even closer. Col. Kurtz still believes in the potential coexistence of morality and the horror of war. His is a necessary horror of means and ends that arises from a deep, presumed rationality of "what needs to be done" *regardless* of personal morality; it entails the use of one's "primordial instincts to kill without feeling, without passion. Without judgment. Without judgment. Because it's judgment that defeats us" (Coppola and Milius, 187–88).

Like Kurtz, Holden throughout emphasizes the primacy of the will— "perfect, genuine, complete, crystalline, pure" (Coppola and Milius, 187)— yet McCarthy's Judge is of course nothing if not a figure of *judgment*. As we have seen, morality does not concern him. His revelation is more disturbing: the horror he speaks of is one that—in the metaphysical abyss of desire and the implacable silence of God and the world—is an end to be asserted in itself, as it is finally, terribly discovered as the sole thing that "speaks to [one's] inmost heart." In this sense, to understand war today and yet affirm it as an end in itself—which, if we believe Girard, is what it finally is—becomes the apocalyptic gesture par excellence, making good on the prediction of *Zur Genealogie der Moral* in ways Nietzsche perhaps never intended: "Man will sooner desire *nothingness* than *not* desire" (2007, 412).

Scandal, Indifference, Conversion

In the Judge's dance we behold a horrific and exhilarating spectacle of death and desire, of violence and war escalating to extremes, that is but sound and fury signifying nothing. In this dance, the Judge himself is "the 'malign thing' that we conjure up in order to shelter us from the terrible silence of an 'unentailed' existence" (Dorson 115), and ultimately the apocalyptic expression of a will to nothingness itself. Yet it is only after his path of destruction has been cleared of all obstacles that the Judge can take to the floor.

Linking the dance to violence and desire almost inevitably calls forth the biblical notion of *scandal*: "Scandal and the dance are in opposition. Scandal is what prevents us from dancing" (*SG* 134). The *skandalon*, to recall, is literally a *stumbling stone*, which in the Bible is often directly associated and even identified with Satan himself, and in mimetic theory marks the position of the rival-obstacle that attracts even as it repels.[83] As such, it is noteworthy that the Judge, too, is associated with stones on two occasions. First encountered by Glanton's men in "the middle of the greatest desert you'd ever want to see" and sitting on a singular rock that Tobin compares to "a merestone for to mark him out of nothing at all" (*BM* 125), the Judge is both dancer wishing to clear the world of that which impedes his dance, and himself a formidable example of the skandalon both *in* and *of* the text. To this contention my reading testifies as much as any other attempt at making sense of him: the Judge is at once the supreme temptation and scandal of interpretation.

At the same time, it is not as if the Judge were without his own *skandalon*. The second case in point is the iron meteorite anvil of Tucson. Having analyzed and demystified the rock's origins, the Judge lifts and tosses it in a number of consecutive wagers. As Russel Hillier has convincingly shown, there is a meaningful link between the Judge's totalitarian will for dominion and his infanticidal pedophilia on the one hand, and the mysterious, heavenly anvil on the other (see 2013, 59–60, 62–63). The latter is suggestively described as a "molar" (*BM* 240), that is, both a grinding tooth and, literally, a millstone in Latin, which Hillier connects to Jesus's indictment of violence against children and its threat to drown the offender by having "a great millstone fastened around his neck" (Mt. 18:5–6).[84] Hence, the Judge's demystification and subsequent lifting of the celestial rock resonates with the murder or ominous disappearance of a number of children, such as the Apache boy that the "kidskin boots"–wearing judge (*BM* 79) scalps after having played with him another minute, or a Mexican boy whose body is discovered with a broken neck in juxtaposition to the image of the Judge "picking his teeth with a thorn as if he had just eaten" (*BM* 118).

Behind these infanticides, to which three or four more could be added,[85] Hillier uncovers a monstrous rationale of desire and scandal: "Like the meteorite and like the Kid, the children whom the Judge preys upon in *Blood Meridian* present to him a challenge, even an affront or a scandal by virtue of their very existence. The children are unconscious of the offense that they present to the Judge, because it is their natural state of being, their innocence which aggravates and mystifies him" (2013, 60). Differently put, the Judge's murderous pedophilia is at once an expression of his being repulsed by and attracted to the children's innocent, carefree, unentailed full-ness of being. In a twisted way, they embody qualities that the Judge himself exhibits. As McCarthy repeatedly reminds his readers, the obese and hairless judge resembles an "enormous infant," with "small hands" and a "serene and strangely childlike" face that features "oddly childish lips" (*BM* 6, 140, 335). He is a monstrous double of the children whose being he figuratively devours, like some Titan Cronos of the Old West.

Most of all, it is the Kid who seems to unite a "taste for mindless vio-lence" with an almost prelapsarian immaculacy of spirit in his "untouched" face and "oddly innocent" eyes (*BM* 3, 4), who irresistibly attracts the Judge from the moment he lays eyes on him, smiling approvingly.[86] The Judge's smile first shows itself as the Kid leaves Nacogdoches to the sight of a pillar of smoke rising from the hotel where he and Toadvine set a fire and brutal-ized two men. From then on, McCarthy takes care to point out whenever the Judge's gaze and smile does—or, in some cases, does *not*—fall upon the Kid, indicating the Judge's interest in him. In sharp contrast, his disappointment is palpable when he confesses, "I spoke in the desert for you and you only and you turned a deaf ear to me" (*BM* 307), and even openly admits it: "I recognized you when I first saw you and yet you were a disappointment to me" (*BM* 328). More than simply his antagonist, the Kid is the Judge's coun-terpart, his mirror image and the prime *skandalon* that needs to be either overcome or incorporated.

We will see whether this hypothesis can shed light on the complex relationship between the Judge and the Kid. The latter to this day remains one of the contested topics among McCarthy scholars. In my view, there are two questions at the core of this relationship that need to be addressed. The first question is asked so frequently that it has become something like the McCarthyan version of "Hamlet's Delay": Why does the Kid not shoot the Judge when he has the chance? A much less frequently asked question, by extension, concerns the mystery of what happens in the jakes of Fort Griffin's saloon. In the first, immediate step, however, this question is bound up with the conditions of the occurrence of that most unlikely of encounters between the Kid and the Judge, "the last of the true" (*BM* 327): Why, over thirty years after the events of the novel, does the Judge reappear when he does?

To begin with the Kid's failure of killing the Judge, one should start from the observation that the Kid has not just the opportunity, but also the skill and disposition to kill the Judge. After the Yuma massacre, he is the only one among a group of survivors comprised of himself, Toadvine, Tobin, the Judge, and the "imbecile" the Judge adopts, who is equipped with a weapon. The Kid thus emerges as the sole character with a chance of killing the Judge, provided he can realistically be killed.[87] Despite Tobin's pleading, which deserves attention by itself, the Kid decides not to shoot the unarmed man. Neither is he willing to sell the Judge his pistol, the Judge's exorbitant offer notwithstanding. If the Kid does not wish to shoot without provocation, ample cause is provided by the Judge's later attempt on his and Tobin's life, where he seriously wounds the ex-priest. Given that the Kid has proven a deadeye even at a distance of "over a hundred yards" (*BM* 278), shooting various of the pursuing Yuma, he probably would not miss the enormous judge as he repeatedly passes "before [his] gunsights" (*BM* 299).

Thus, practical considerations do not sufficiently explain the Kid's adamant refusal to shoot the Judge, which for all appearances costs him his life in Fort Griffin.[88] Neither does the Kid's refusal seem to be rooted in any moral objection. At least initially, his defining character trait is after all an inclination to excessive violence, which it evidently takes exceedingly little to incite.[89] For much of the book, he is clearly not above using violence and deadly force. Toward the end of the novel, however, none other than the Judge himself suggests another, new characteristic: "There's a flawed place in the fabric of your heart. [...] You alone reserved in your soul some corner of clemency for the heathen" (*BM* 299). Are we thus to infer that something has fundamentally changed about the Kid? To what extent is he alone different from the rest of Glanton's scalp hunters?

One point that Arnold raises is that although the Kid participates in the scalp hunters' raids, "we never actually see him scalping and hacking and raping" (1999, 64). Furthermore, many have pointed out that throughout the novel the Kid displays a distinct capacity for empathy and acts of kindness. One first such example is his work in a "diptheria [*sic*] pesthouse" (*BM*

5). Once he joins up with the Glanton gang, he repeatedly reaches out to help his companions, such as the wounded Miguel/McGill before Glanton shoots him. At different points in the novel, Sproule, Tate, and Tobin tell the Kid to "go on," essentially to abandon them and save himself. Yet he refuses. It is the Kid who helps the Judge kill one of the horses for food, and again it is the Kid who helps David Brown remove an arrow from his leg. In both cases, nobody else in the group moves a finger to help. Tobin warns him against helping the Judge and reprimands him for helping Brown: "Fool, he said. God will not love ye forever. [. . .] Dont you know he'd of took you with him?" (*BM* 163). In the quasi-Darwinian society of the scalp hunters, each man is supposed to fend for himself and survive on his own. Had the operation failed, Brown would have killed the Kid.

Finally, following the lottery of arrows, rather than kill him as intended, the Kid decides to spare and attempts to hide the wounded Shelby. He fills Shelby's flask with water from his own, even after the unarmed Shelby, who threatened he would shoot the Kid given a chance (*BM* 207), actually tries to snatch his gun. In contrast to Chamberlain, who in the corresponding scene of his *Confessions* is relieved to draw a blank, there is a sense, as Schimpf points out judging from the dynamics of the gaze, that the Kid consciously elects to be among the mercy-killers, perhaps as a way to oppose the Judge (2008, 35):

> When the Kid selected among the shafts to draw one he saw the Judge watching him and he paused [. . .]. He let go the arrow he'd chosen and sorted out another and drew that one. It carried the red tassel. He looked at the Judge again and the Judge was not watching. (*BM* 205)

Admittedly, with regard to the pursuing army of General Elias or the alternative of a slow, agonizing death by exposure, this supposed act of mercy may be the least merciful thing to do. Be that as it may, the Kid's actions undermine the scalp hunters' ideology of self-reliance and survival of the fittest and so belie his earlier ruthlessness. One only needs to compare the Kid's initial disdain of Sproule to his later care for the desperate and crying Shelby to see that something has changed. Guided by Emmanuel Levinas, one might say that the Kid has begun to claim the ability to escape the epistemological totality of violence and recognize "the face of the Other." In the words of Benoît Chantre:

> It is because adversaries do not want to see their growing resemblance that they embark on an escalation to extremes. They will fight to the death so as not to see that they are similar, and thus they will achieve the peace of the graveyard. However, if they recognize that they are similar, if they *identify themselves* with each other, the veil of the Same will fall and reveal the Other, the vulnerability of his face. I can lower my guard before the other-ness of the person I am facing. Confrontation is not inevitable. (*BE* 100)

In contrast, critics who read McCarthy as a nihilist have found the Kid's acts of kindness exiguous against the Judge's divinization of war, which the novel seems to enact virtually everywhere. Going further, Owens actually finds potentially redemptive attempts to "tease out the Kid's tenuous acts of 'clemency'" (12) to be detracting from the predominant theme of human depravity. On a different, yet similarly antirehabilitory note, Shaviro suggests that the Kid's attitude, rather than being merciful, is one of "passive resistance" through which he retains "the detachment of an observer" (151), and Guillemin finds the Kid simply "too indifferent to be merciless, for his failure to kill the wounded Shelby in the face of the advancing enemy is hardly charity" (2004, 90).

While it can be argued that rare and sometimes questionable as they may be, the Kid's acts of kindness are all the more significant against the backdrop of ubiquitous violence, the Kid's supposed *indifference* deserves attention as it leads back to the Judge's fascination with him. Perhaps even more so than his air of innocence, his indifference is exactly "what makes the Kid into an object of desire [...]. It is this indifference that irritates the will of the Judge, and that he seeks to master and appropriate; this seductive child's loneliness that he needs to baptize and give (re-)birth to" (Shaviro 152). Indeed, in the struggle of desires, indifference is an attitude that is neither innocent nor neutral. It is given rather as "the exterior aspect of a desire of oneself. [...] The indifferent person always seems to possess that radiant self-mastery which we all seek. He seems to live in a closed circuit, enjoying his own being, in a state of happiness which nothing can disturb. He is God" (*DDN* 106–7). While it seems unproductive to construe the Kid's indifference as a conscious strategy, it certainly helps to understand the Judge's fascination with him.

If the Kid's development can partly be viewed as a search for a father, as I have argued, the Judge is indubitably the model that literally as well as figuratively towers above all others. Everything he does—repulsive and abhorrent as it may be to the reader—seems to say: "Imitate me! Be my disciple! Worship me!" All of the scalp hunters fall under his spell, even Toadvine, who opts to stay at the waterhole and sells his hat to the Judge, and perhaps none more so than Tobin, who for all his opposition to him is the chief agent in mystifying the Judge. "Study the Judge," Tobin advises, and the Kid responds, "I done studied him" (*BM* 122). He is neither charmed nor fascinated nor, for the most part, afraid. In fact, it would be hard to pinpoint anything that the Kid wishes for or desires. He seems remarkably free of "those things that lay claim to a man" (*BM* 248), nor does he subscribe to the Judge's ideology. Though in the circulation of coins, ideologies, and desires "Everything's for sale" (*BM* 282), as the Judge would have it, this apparently does not include the Kid, or so it seems for the longest time.

To recall, McCarthy frames the Kid's journey as a sort of quest "to try whether the stuff of creation may be shaped to man's will or whether his own heart is not another kind of clay" (*BM* 4–5). On his journey he is presented with various temporary or lasting models to emulate and shape himself after: the hermit, Captain White, perhaps Glanton and Tobin, but most certainly the satanic Judge, who proposes his myth of violence and of war as the "truest form of divination" (*BM* 249). McCarthy, however, associates the Kid with another such form, specifically with the Four of Cups of the tarot. He first sees it on a wall in a ransacked Mexican town, and later draws the card when the Glanton gang have their fortunes told by the elderly circus woman. According to John Sepich's extensive notes on tarot symbolism, the Four of Cups associates the Kid "with the quality of mercy," or else "loving kindness," and significantly "suggests a divided heart" (2008, 106–7).[90]

Indeed, the card represents personal crisis, confused stagnation, and even disgust with oneself (Banzhaff 211; Golowin 252), or more specifically "a moment of contemplation of one's feelings during which one passes judgment and tries to determine one's own position" (Corte 2005, 41). Before going into interpretations of the card's arcane meanings, though, it is well worth taking a step back and simply looking at the allegorical image of the card itself. It presents a young man, sitting, cross-legged and arms folded below a tree with his head slightly bent, as if in meditation. On the ground before him, there are three cups, while to the right, another hand extends from a cloud, holding a fourth cup. Generally, the three cups are taken to represent the material world with all its treasures, whereas the cup from the cloud suggests spiritual riches and perhaps some kind of revelation.

Clearly, the card's symbolism brims with the dynamics of desire. The three cups can be taken to represent the temptations of the world, of the apparent desirability of the objects that our models alert us to, which, however, never fail to disappoint once they are actually attained—hence the potential dissatisfaction that the card implies. Conversely, if the cup from the cloud, which evokes the Holy Grail, represents not another illusory temptation, it may signify either potential insight or a "true" value, perhaps that of mercy or loving-kindness as Sepich suggests. In any case, the young man's is an attitude of contemplation and withdrawal from the world, from entanglement in temptation and scandal. In short, it evokes the kind of anchoritism that many of McCarthy's spiritually advanced characters have chosen, or, if it goes too far, the kind of pilgrimaging or restless searching that characterizes the Kid's later years. Yet even the moment of withdrawal and contemplation, passing as it well may be, in itself already contains the possibility of choice: either to become ensnared in the attempt of attaining the objects of desire that may set the subject at its rival's throat, or to attempt to reach the cup from the clouds, elusive as it may prove. And of course, there is always the potential of rejecting either possibility.

It may go against the traditionally static nature of the picaresque hero the Kid can be identified with, yet something about him really does seem to change. A number of critics have associated the Kid with the quality of heroism.[91] To do so comes with the territory of both heroic myth and the Western genre. Yet the shootout, the final duel between the hero and the villain that could reasonably be expected, does *not* happen. As in other works of McCarthy, *Blood Meridian* puts little trust in the heroic ideal. This may be so because McCarthy realizes that "[h]eroism cannot restrain the escalation to extremes" (*BE* 80), exactly because it is susceptible to corruption by ideology and mimetic contagion. Like Glanton's men, the Kid may have been "a hero anointed with the blood of the enemies of the [Mexican] republic" (*BM* 331), but McCarthy shows how quickly and devastatingly "heroic" violence spirals out of control and turns in on itself. Instead, I would argue that what the Kid's later development adumbrates, in Chantre's words, is the idea of "a passage from the sacred to the saintly," a "transformation of heroism into saintliness" (*BE* 98). The keyword, as Manuel Broncaro rightly points out, is that of *conversion* (42).

In tune with the potential of reading the journey narrative's progress in space as the literary externalization of an internal, psychological development in time (Freese 2015, 53), the process is likely a gradual one. Yet if one were to pinpoint a single episode, it would likely be the confluence of three scenes replete with mimetic figurations occurring shortly after the lottery of arrows. Separated from the scalp hunters, the Kid sees "two black hawks about the sun slowly and perfectly opposed like paper birds upon a pole," which is followed directly by the distant sight of "the collision of armies"—most likely Glanton's and Elias's troops—that passes "mute and ordered and senseless," and finally leaves behind not only "the shapes of mortal men who had lost their lives," but also a land that is "cold and blue and without definition" (*BM* 213). In the first image, one has a perfect expression of the rival doubles, the logic of which sets the stage for the emergence of the duel in history, the violent collision of the second image that while implying an order, is finally "senseless." What remains are dead bodies and a cold, indefinite emptiness.

Against this calm after the storm, McCarthy then sets a third image reverberating with religious symbolism. As the Kid makes his journey through the freezing cold of the nightly desert, he happens upon a wondrous sight:

> It was a lone tree burning on the desert. A heraldic tree that the passing storm had left afire. The solitary pilgrim drawn up before it had traveled far to be here and he knelt in the hot sand and held his numbed hands out while all about in that circle attended companies of lesser auxiliaries routed forth into the inordinate day, small owls that crouched silently and stood from foot to foot and tarantulas and solpugas and vinegarroons and the vicious mygale spiders and beaded lizards with mouths black as a chowdog's, deadly to man, and the little desert basilisks that jet blood from their eyes and the small sandvipers like seemly gods, silent and the same, in Jeda, in Babylon. A constellation of ignited eyes that edged the ring of light

all bound in a precarious truce before this torch whose brightness had set
back the stars in their sockets. (*BM* 215)

If God, as the Judge suggests, speaks in stones and trees, the scene indeed
carries the distinct marks of an epiphany. Petra Mundik calls to mind the
burning bush out of which God addresses Moses in Exodus 3:3, and directs
attention to the Kid's characterization as a "solitary pilgrim [...] traveled far
to be here," specifically as if he were to purposely join the "companies of lesser
auxiliaries" in their ritual circle and "vigil" (*BM* 215). It would seem that there
is something to be realized here, for the Kid as for the reader. Yet what exactly
the "spiritual significance" (Mundik 202) of the episode is remains nebulous,
unless its conjunction with the two sights that immediately precede it is
brought to bear upon the analysis. The sights of rival doubles and clashing
armies is radically opposed to the sight of a veritable desert menagerie of
deadly creatures, mortal enemies by nature, that are at least momentarily
joined in a "precarious truce." Rather than Exodus, this second image therefore evokes the prophetic promise of Isaiah 11:1–6, which opens with the
image of a sprouting tree:

> There shall come forth a shoot from the stump of Jesse, and a branch from
> his roots shall bear fruit. And the Spirit of the Lord shall rest upon him,
> the Spirit of wisdom and understanding [...]. The wolf shall dwell with the
> lamb, and the leopard shall lie down with the young goat, and the calf and
> the lion and the fattened calf together; and a little child shall lead them.
> The nursing child shall play over the hole of the cobra, and the weaned
> child shall put his hand on the adder's den. They shall not hurt or destroy
> in all my holy mountain; for the earth shall be full of the knowledge of the
> Lord as the waters cover the sea.[92]

In the prophetic vision, the image of the coming messiah takes hold first in
the tree, but secondly, some interpreters suggest, also in the form of a child
as befits the Kid's presence in the burning tree episode. What both passages
entail is the potential of a truce, of a reconciliation of enemies—signified in
both texts as wild animals—and, perhaps, of lasting peace.[93] In *Blood Meridian*, this potentiality is remarkably cast in the light of a fire that assumes a

quality less of the *sacred*—the elemental, violentropic, and uncontrollable fire that the Judge, like the satanic triune leader in *Outer Dark*, is said to be "somehow native to" (*BM* 9)—than of the *holy*, which represents a more spiritually enlightened, warming fire of promoting charity, community, or perhaps civilization itself that will rise to prominence in *No Country for Old Men* and especially *The Road*.

For the development of the Kid's character, the scene is of definitive importance, as is made clear during his reintegration into the ranks of the scalp hunters. Once he rejoins the group, Glanton "and his haggard riders star[e] balefully at the Kid as if he were no part of them" (*BM* 218). Adopting biblical language, it might be said that in finding the burning bush, the pilgrim has figuratively started out on the road to Damascus, where he meets Jesus, "whom [he was] persecuting" (Acts 9:5). The potential then, McCarthy suggests, is that the Kid can transform from Saul to Paul.

If the Kid's development is indeed a *conversion* to Christianity, it is logically anathema to the alternatively Dionysian or satanic judge and his Nietzschean ideology. Taking the part of prosecutor, the Judge's accusation against the Kid is thus substantiated: "You alone reserved in your soul some corner of clemency for the heathen" (*BM* 299). The Judge's use of the legal term "clemency" is not accidental. It expresses how in taking his steps, however tenuous, toward mercy and charity, the Kid represents a voice of dissent in the jury of the victors of history: "You were a witness against yourself. You sat in judgment on your own deeds. You put your own allowances before the judgements of history and you broke with the body of which you were pledged a part and poisoned it in all its enterprise" (*BM* 307). Again, we are reminded of Kurtz's psyche-shattering insight: "It's judgment that defeats us" (Coppola and Milius, 187–88). Fundamentally, the Kid's sense of (self-)judgment disturbs the hegemonic vision of the murderers necessary for regeneration through violence. So, when Bryan Vescio points out the inherent unreliability of the monolithic historical master narrative "due to partial or unreliable witnessing," against which the Kid represents true "redemptive possibilities" and even a potential for "a break with history" (47, 48, 55), it can be specified that the narrative is that of a history of violence, written by the community in the blood of their victims. In this regard, the Kid's conversion represents the introduction of new information into the system's historical program.

Several critics have interpreted the drawn-out conflict between the Judge and Tobin and the Kid in the desert as a "demoniac form of a temptation of Christ" (Josyph 2010b, 84; Mundik 207; Broncaro 54) during his forty days in the desert. Showing Jesus the kingdoms of the world, Satan, "desirous of taking God's place as an object of adoration" (*SG* 196), tempts Jesus with eternal, earthly dominion. "All these I will give you, if you will fall down and worship me" (Mt. 4:9), says the devil. "Dont you know I'd have loved you like a son?" (*BM* 306), says the Judge. And for a single moment, his disappointment seems to border on desperation as he reaches out for the Kid. What he desires more than anything is for the Kid to be his heir—heir to the world that belongs to the suzerain. Earlier, in his pseudo-biblical parables and his talk about the Anasazi, he had proclaimed: "It is the death of the father to which the son is entitled and to which he is heir more so than his goods" (*BM* 145). In the Judge's threefold passing "before your [the Kid's] gunsights" (*BM* 299), McCarthy inverts Peter's threefold denial of Jesus: here, it is Satan who is denied (Mundik 208). Along similar lines, Philip Snyder surmises that "it may also be that in that instant of choice, when the Judge passes before his gunsights, he refuses to sacrifice the Judge as a rejection of their demonic God/Abraham covenant, thereby moving himself outside the circular economy of the gang and thus rejecting the Judge's theory regarding war as the supreme human endeavor" (2013, 152–53).

Through his acts of kindness, through not fully sharing in the gang's unrestricted violence, the Kid renounces the Judge's thesis of "war as the telos of history" and "the cultural imperative of using violence to possess the continent" (Jarrett 85) as represented by Glanton's gang. Hence, "for the Kid to restrict the group's common ethos of murder by his own individual consciousness is a betrayal of history, the gang, and their 'communal soul'" (Jarrett 85–86). Unsatisfying though it may be for the reader expecting a final, heroic shootout, the Kid's neglect to kill the Judge may in the end present not so much a misstep, but a decision to spare his life. After all, what stronger renunciation could there be of a man whose faith and very being is a principle of boundless, indiscriminate, and self-perpetuating violence?

And how unfortunate is it, then, that the Kid's conversion proves a failure?

The Kid's Failure

"Christianity directs existence toward a vanishing point, either toward God or toward the Other. Choice always involves choosing a model, and true freedom lies in the basic choice between a human or a divine model" (*DDN* 59). In *Blood Meridian*, there is also a clear possibility, repeatedly taken up by scholarship, of reading the Kid as a messianic Christlike figure. McCarthy endows the Kid with this potential through a number of biblical signifiers and symbols. These range from the novel's opening evocation, respectively, of Pilate's *Ecce homo* (Jn. 19:5) and the Old Testament's Christ-prefiguring "behold, the child" (2 Kgs. 4:32), to the Kid's portentous birth under falling stars in 1833—thirty-three being the age of Christ when he was crucified—to his being wounded below the heart, and to his leaving Tennessee as "a shadowed agony in the garden" (*BM* 4), which evokes Jesus's lonely hour of anguished prayer and doubt in the garden of Gethsemane.[94]

Numerous parallels notwithstanding, straightforward readings of the Kid as a representative of Christian core values, or even as an analogue of Christ, run into the inevitable paradox of an "incompatibility between the Kid's messianic overtones and his depraved behavior" (Mundik 198).[95] Repentance, clemency, and charity are admirable, yet they do not by themselves make a saint, less so a messiah. For all parallels to Christ, and the potential of reading into the Kid's behavior a kind of *imitatio Christi*, there can be no doubt that McCarthy's creation is—at best—"a failed messianic figure rather than a genuine savior" (Mundik 199). Although my reading of key moments runs parallel to Petra Mundik's, in my view her interpretation of the Kid as a Gnostic *Salvator Salvatus*, who must first save himself through *gnosis* before he can impart his insight on others, only resolves the tension between the novel's messianic symbolism and the Kid's corrupt nature to exchange it for another problem. Like all gnostic interpretations of McCarthy, it cannot help but to reduce everything to a matter of knowledge and spiritual insight. In it, the problem of evil, the realities of human suffering, and the violence that so graphically marks the Kid as an inhabitant of a violent world—our world—are effectively factored out and forgotten, securely locked away in the ethical safe-deposit box of *gnosis*.

Conversely, the apocalypse that McCarthy places before us is not simply one of the spirit, but a possibility that concerns *this* world—past, present, and future. Violence is radically itself. To face it, conscious awareness *is* a necessity, but awareness alone is not sufficient to opt out of the Judge's dance. The novel's last thirty pages symbolically reinforce this impression with their sanguinary deconstruction of Christian iconography. The Kid is baptized, begins to carry a Bible "no word of which could he read" (*BM* 312), and is sometimes mistaken for a preacher. In a step up from his isolated acts of kindness, he begins to escort pilgrims through the desert. While the Kid may thus partially represent Christian values in the later part of the novel, the image of the ruined church that so ominously looms over the novel looms here as well.

The novel's final, bloody massacre of the Penitentes during their Holy Week reenactment of the Crucifixion, with its images of mutilated pilgrims, a fallen cross, and a disemboweled "alter-christ" (*BM* 315) provides a sobering outlook for the effectiveness of the Christian "good news." Finally, the Kid's quasi-confession into the ears of an elderly woman, an *abuelita* (Sp. grandmother), who by the quartermoons and stars on her shawl has been identified with the Virgin Mary, makes clear that Christianity is not only incapable of providing sanctuary, but has in fact been hollowed out.[96] There is no intervention by the virgin on behalf of the sinner, as the eldress turns out to be "a dried shell [. . .] dead in that place for years" (*BM* 315).

What needs to be kept in mind, however, is that the failure of Christianity is contingent upon the failure of *Christians*. This is why Broncaro's humble suggestion that "the Kid has metamorphosed into an essentially good individual—read Christian—who has learned the meaning of human fraternity amid universal destruction" (42), to me seems at once more accurate and more useful than all messianic readings, even if the messiah identified is a failed one. When McCarthy equips his illiterate kid with a Bible that he cannot read, he creates a most poignant representation of Western man and historical Christianity itself:

> The destruction will happen one day because of the growing imperium of violence; deprived of a sacrificial outlet, it is unable to establish the reign of order except by escalating. It will require more and more victims to create an ever more precarious order. This is the terrifying future of the world for which Christians carry the responsibility. [. . .] The relevance of the apocalyptic texts is therefore absolutely striking [. . .]. They say paradoxically that Christ will only return when there is no hope that evangelical

revelation will be able to eliminate violence, once humanity realizes that it has failed. (*BE* 118–19)

What dooms the Kid is that he never truly renounces violence. This can already be seen when he lashes out at the Diegueños of San Felipe who save Tobin and him on their flight through the desert. In fact, the narrative suggests that these "savages" (*BM* 301), who in Chamberlain are rightly identified as "*Cristianos* [. . .] trusty as Indians go" (296), are moved by a consciousness that is both Christian and apocalyptic.[97] Thus, despite their own destitution, they offer charity to "pilgrims" like Tobin and the Kid, flying "some savage pursuit [. . .] whether it be armies or plague or pestilence or something altogether unspeakable" (*BM* 301). In contrast, the Kid answers one Indian's—at worst curious—appeal to show him the gun by threateningly putting it against his head. Given the Judge's savage pursuit, this may be understandable in the heat of the moment. Yet even in his later years, the Kid still beats up a man who mistakes him for a male prostitute. In short, he remains a deeply flawed person with a divided heart. In this, he provides a reflection of Christianity as such.

What he does not do until the final chapter is kill again. Earlier, I discussed the rival-double relationship that characterizes the short exchange between the aged Kid, now called "the Man," and Elrod, whom McCarthy clearly sets up as the younger Kid's double and, implicitly, his "son" (*BM* 321). I argued that in questioning the veracity of the scapular of ears the Kid wears like an albatross around his neck, Elrod questions both the truth of victimization behind the course of empire and the man's pride, his *being* as a warrior. McCarthy leaves the exact nature of his further offenses nebulous, but it is likely because he is so much like the younger Kid that Elrod scandalizes the Man so profoundly that he threatens: "You keep him away from me [. . .]. I see him back here I'll kill him" (*BM* 322).

What has gone understandably unnoticed in a novel so full of bloody murder is that the bloodshed is by no means inevitable. Having temporarily chased off the orphans, the Man, anticipating trouble, moves his blanket away from the fire and into the bushes. Once Elrod returns with his rifle in hand, yet not necessarily murderous intent, he is completely exposed to the Man. As the Man calls the boy from the safety of darkness, "the boy swung with the rifle and [he] fired. / You wouldnt of lived anyway, the man said"

(*BM* 322). It is somewhat ambiguous who shoots first, indeed who shoots
at all. Depending on the edition of the text, of which the later, slightly corrected editions include the additional personal pronoun "he," the text suggests either that Elrod has effectively wasted his one shot, or that the Man
preemptively guns down his younger double (*BM* 323).[98]

In either case, Elrod hardly presents a threat. Not only does Elrod's
Sharp's rifle that the orphans later allege is "worth nothing" (*BM* 323) hold
no more than a single shot, he also is at a serious disadvantage at short distance against the Man's revolver and is completely exposed. Conversely, the
Man is practically invisible and acts with all the level-headed calculation
of a veteran. So Elrod is completely at the Man's mercy. Given the latter's
advantages, there is any number of alternatives to murder: The Man could
easily disarm the youngster. He could take away the rifle and chase him off.
He could tie him up and consequently leave him for his fellows to fetch in
the morning, or else deliver him to the authorities in Fort Griffin. He has
obviously anticipated Elrod's return, and so has had ample time to consider
what he would do. And what he does is shoot Elrod.

The mysterious antishowdown in Fort Griffin between the Man and
Judge Holden thus amounts to the Man's and implicitly historical Christianity's surrender to violence, its relapse into the corrupted sacred. When Sepich
casually suggests that "the sound of the shot that killed Elrod was heard by
the Judge" (2008, 132), he essentially answers the question of *why* the Judge
returns when he does. Rather than forgiveness or "clemency," the Kid ultimately chooses violence. From a Christian perspective, it is in this moment
that his conversion has failed. Accordingly, in the final pages of the novel,
Christian symbolism is displaced by the pagan imagery of the Judge's dance.
Having resisted for a long time, the Kid finally succumbs to the irresistible
mimetic attraction of his rival-double(s). Having done away with the boy he
calls his son, it is doubly appropriate that the albinic "man" who would have
been his father returns to assert: "You're here for the dance" (*BM* 327). From
the moment Elrod falls dead, the Kid is the Judge's, who thus comes to claim
him in the ironically fitting locale of Fort Griffin's jakes.

Whatever actually happens in the jakes that so shocks the hardy
patrons and continues to tickle imaginative scholars' predilection for
horror and scandal, metaphorically amounts to the same thing. The Man
may be cannibalized, he may be raped as a number of critics surmised, or

subjected—like Culla Holme in his dream—to a Dionysian *sparagmos*, which would be the equivalent of his being torn asunder by the devil as Faust is in some legends.[99] Whichever is the case, when the naked judge "gather[s] him in his arms against his immense and terrible flesh" (*BM* 333), he essentially absorbs the Kid's being into his own and consequently "emerges renewed and rejuvenated to join the dance" (Spurgeon 98). In a sense, the Kid may not even die. As I have argued, the Judge as either Dionysus or Satan is a *principle* rather than a person. Consequently, he may not be more than a figment of the older Kid's psyche, which, having lain dormant and silent for many years, now that the Kid's conversion has proved a failure, reasserts itself with terrible force. Perhaps the worst potentiality of reading McCarthy's enigmatic ending is thus that what is discovered in the jakes is not the mangled body of the Kid, but that of the dancing bear's young caretaker, the girl that has gone missing. Perhaps, it is that the Kid himself has become the ravenous, child-devouring Judge.

Judgment Day:
Two-Bits, the Paraclete, and the Implacable Choice

Reading *Blood Meridian* as an apocalyptic novel, I have tried to combine its historical with its mythical and biblical subtexts. The goal in this has been to provide an interpretation that firmly roots eschatology in observations about violence that are at once "true" to the historical course of empire and yet transcend such contexts—as mythical principles of cultural genesis and regeneration through violence. A key to this has been mimetic theory, which cannot but affirm yet help explicate what the novel says loudly and clearly about human violence: In the Judeo-Christian world, there is no Dionysian regeneration or eternal return. There is only the awareness of victimization and the Clausewitzian escalation to extremes, which places humans before an irreducible choice between renouncing violence without reservation or else facing the certainty of self-destruction, the novel's evening redness in the west.

Blood Meridian's apocalyptic is perfectly encapsulated in the opposition of its two central figures. On the one hand, there is the disseminating figure of the Judge, embodying everything from desire, violence, and scientific progress to the achievements of the Enlightenment and the West's long history of conquest and genocide. On the other hand, there is the Kid, who resists but ultimately fails to renounce violence. Half-hearted and ultimately muzzled as his conversion to Christianity may be, it contains within itself the epistemological shift toward the victims of history that destroys the hegemonic perspective of the mythico-historical narrative embodied by the Judge.

Seen so, Judge and Kid are figures at once of obfuscation *and* revelation. Their pairing embodies an apocalyptic conception of a war between violence and truth articulated in Blaise Pascal's Twelfth Provincial Letter: "It is a strange and tedious war when violence attempts to vanquish truth. All the efforts of violence cannot weaken truth, and only serve to give it fresh vigor. All the lights of truth cannot arrest violence, and only serve to exasperate it" (cit. in *BE* 80). With respect to the by now familiar theme of the revelation of the victim, which in this case takes the place of the truth, and the intensification that violence subsequently undergoes in order to dissimulate it, the conclusion lies close at hand that Pascal's observation offers yet another modality of the escalation to extremes. Adopting the terminology of early cybernetics, we could also describe it as a sort of feedback runaway effecting a catastrophic increase in *violentropy*.

McCarthy creates a direct parallel between the gang's massacres and the Judge's activities as researcher and archeologist. The Judge routinely destroys the original find after he has sketched it into his ledger book, scratching out, for instance, one of the Hueco tank drawings, which show monstrous visions "to justify every fear of man and the things that are in him" (*BM* 173). Similarly, an old Spanish piece of armor is crushed and pitched into the fire. However, it is explicitly not just the original artifacts of the violent past that the Judge aims to "expunge [. . .] from the memory of man" (*BM* 140) but, as he candidly declares, his notes and sketches as well. Both thermodynamic and informational entropy thus increase with the burning of the original and the future erasure of the records. McCarthy realizes this theme to greater effect in *The Road*, yet the process is complete here already and gains a more immediately human dimension when considering how the erasure of the Hueco drawings immediately precedes and parallels the gang's eradication of the peaceful Tiguas, leaving traces of violence and then, eventually, nothing at all:

> In the days to come the frail black rebuses of blood in those sands would crack and break and drift away so that in the circuit of few suns all trace of the destruction of these people would be erased. The desert wind would salt their ruins and there would be nothing, nor ghost nor scribe, to tell to any pilgrim in his passing how it was that people had lived in this place and in this place died. (*BM* 174)

If, as Andrew McKenna suggests, the yardstick of literary greatness lies in the ability of a given work to poetically reveal rather than reflect the relationships between the generation of meaning and the inner workings of society and its institutions (10), *Blood Meridian*, despite or rather because of its violence, amounts to as powerful a statement against violence as has been written. The Tiguas share the fate of so many victims forgotten by the victor's tale that historians have traditionally told. Conversely, on a metaliterary level, their fate is preserved by McCarthy's narrator, whose faithful and relentless recording of the gang's atrocities and its victims is the primary vehicle that allows us as readers to see the work's catastrophic implications. As Wallach points out, "the narrator holds the damage before the reader and keeps it there. [...] Thus, far from identifying itself with the Judge's amorality, the narrative voice of *Blood Meridian* consistently subverts his philosophy" (2002a, 212).

Does this mean that there is reason to be optimistic about the future? In a way, the figure of the mute imbecile James Robert Bell whom the Judge adopts for a while speaks as a representation of all humankind. Sepich's argument that Bell is "a saddening, chilling double of the idiotic world mass following leaders they can not possibly comprehend" (2008, 138) is certainly valid, but McCarthy's point seems less political than anthropological. First seen "smeared with feces" and "silently chewing a turd" in Tucson where his brother exhibits him as "The Wild Man Two Bits" (*BM* 233), Bell is repeatedly shown intently watching others and—in a scene reminiscent of both Narcissus and Lester Ballard—his own reflection in a pool of water (*BM* 284). Most of all, he is fascinated by fire. So in chapter 18, the shortest of the novel, he is freed by Sarah Borginnis and her companions. If these Christian women can be taken as another representation of Christianity, Bell's release from his cage, which they burn, could likewise be said to allegorize the freedom from the cycle of violence and scapegoating that the Crucifixion plunges humanity into. Yet, for all the women's assertions that "He knows" and "He

sees hisself in [the fire]" (*BM* 258), the next chapter sees him dancing drunk
around another fire on the eve before the Yuma massacre (*BM* 273).

While initially saved from drowning by the Judge in a scene reminiscent
of a "birth [. . .] or a baptism or some ritual not yet inaugurated into any
canon" (*BM* 259), James Robert's ultimate fate remains unclear. Last seen
with the Judge, he disappears somewhere in the desert. Identifying the idiot
with mankind and the Judge with science and nihilism, Schimpf accordingly
points out the essential dilemma that "while the Judge leads the idiot into
the abyss, the good Christian women [. . .] do him no good either" as they
fail "to understand the idiot's nature" (2008, 48–49). Still, it is only because
of the Christian women that there is an alternative to begin with. There is
no guarantee of salvation. The point, subtly articulated by the imbecile's
informationally suggestive nickname, "Two Bits," is that *there is a choice*. Two
fires, two bits. One or zero, Yes or No. Christ or Dionysus. Live or die.[100]
The imbecile's case is thus analogous to the Kid's failed conversion: "Christ
will have tried to bring humanity into adulthood, but humanity will have
refused" (*BE* 118).

Having himself elected, in the Judge's words, "to be no godserver but
a god himself," the ex-priest Tobin points out that the Kid is (still) "a free
agent" (*BM* 250, 284). As Edwin Arnold, one of the original proponents of
the moralist school of McCarthy scholarship, points out, the implication
is that the Kid has the ability to choose. Finally, whether it is, in Arnold's
words, "the lack of choice which damns the Kid" as he fails "to confront the
heart within, to 'face down' the Judge" (1999, 64), or whether he succumbs
to the Judge, as I have argued, what is important is that there is a choice
to begin with. Spoken with the opening epigraph from Paul Valéry's "The
Yalu," it is exactly not as though either "acts of pity or cruelty [. . .] were
irresistible." In graphically delineating the alternatives, in making them violently palpable, *Blood Meridian* offers its readers a degree of freedom that
may well be the pinnacle of what literary imagination can achieve. Choice
exists. Choice persists.

The novel's epilogue presents its readers with a final vista of a field of
buffalo bones, across which a man makes his way using an implement "striking the fire out of the rock which God has put there." He is followed by a
number of wanderers "in search of bones and those who do not search" (*BM*
337). Naturalistic readings have identified the epilogue with the closing of

the frontier and the "fencing in" of the West by means of posthole diggers. By extension, the progress of the wanderers hence constitutes an allegory of the progress of Western civilization, which here is opaquely characterized as "the verification of a principle, a validation of sequence and causality" (*BM* 337). In this reading, the epilogue validates what the novel has shown and is hence to be identified with the Judge and America's "national acceptance of [his] perverted antimyth" (Spurgeon 98–99; see also Sepich 2008, 66; Phillips 2002, 40). Conversely, Bloom asserts that the mysterious man leading the way may be an "opposing figure in regard to the evening redness in the west," a "new Prometheus [. . .] rising up against" the Judge (2000, 262–63). Likewise, the gnostic interpretations spearheaded by Daugherty (169) and Mundik (217–18), by the imagery of fiery sparks emerging from the rock, respectively identify the figure as a Gnostic pneumatic or *salvator* freeing the imprisoned spark of the divine through spiritual enlightenment.

In contrast, the mimetic reading accommodates all of these views while retaining the fundamental notion of history as an apocalyptic trial, the decision of which is bound up with the themes of witnessing and a concomitant, irreducible choice. As I have said earlier, there are at least two fires in the novel, one of which is the Judge's "nightfire" (*BM* 293) identified with the corrupted sacred, while the other, the burning bush, can be interpreted as a sign of the holy and of God. The field of bones and the walker's movement thus literally represent the West's march of empire, the "verified principle" of which turns out to be the ritual reenactment of scapegoating and sacrifice, which, however, does not guarantee "the pursuit of some continuance" (*BM* 337). The apocalyptic truth of the novel is one not of regeneration, but of *degeneration through violence.*

Insofar, the epilogue can be identified with the Judge. Yet, in the trial of history, there is also a figure standing against this accuser, a lawyer for the defense (Gk. *parakletos*) who—more closely to the Catholicism of McCarthy's youth—is likewise identified with tongues of fire. I am speaking of the Holy Spirit, who, in Girardian parlance, denotes the gradually spreading, revelatory awareness of the innocence of the victim through history:

> It is the Holy Spirit that teaches us that historical Christianity has failed and that the apocalyptic texts will now speak to us more than they ever have before. [. . .] [T]*he escalation to extremes is the appearance that truth*

now takes when it shows itself to humanity. Since each of us is responsible for the escalation, we naturally do not want to recognize this reality. The truth about violence has been stated once and for all. Christ revealed the truth that the prophets announced, namely that of the violent foundation of all cultures. The refusal to listen to this essential truth exposes us to the return of an archaic world that will no longer have the face of Dionysus, as Nietzsche hoped. It will be a world of total destruction. Dionysiac chaos was a chaos that founded something. The one threatening us is radical. We need courage to admit it, as we do to resist giving into the fascination of violence. (*BE* 103, 105)

A central player in the revelation, which is the same thing as the escalation, turns out to be the Judeo-Christian heritage.[101] However, as McCarthy and Girard both show, awareness alone is insufficient to ensure humanity's survival, let alone the lasting peace of a kingdom of heaven. It is only due to the revelation that there is a choice to begin with, yet there is ample reason to be pessimistic about humanity's renunciation of violence. After all, the "world of total destruction" may look eerily like that of *The Road.*

An Apocalyptic Journey

Revelation, Conversion, and the Different Ends of *The Road*

I am the way, the truth, and the life.

—John 14:6

Published in 2006, *The Road* marks another literary departure for McCarthy in exchanging the plains of the Southwest of his five previous novels for the American wasteland of a not-too-distant future. In contrast to most of his former work, the initial reception of the novel, which won the 2007 Pulitzer Prize for Fiction and inspired a film adaptation released in late 2009, was marked by almost universal approval. In the *New York Times*, Janet Maslin called it an "exquisitely bleak incantation—pure poetic brimstone" (2006), while Ron Charles of the *Washington Post* saw it as "a frightening, profound tale that drags us into places we don't want to go, forces us to think about questions we don't want to ask" (2006). Reactions abroad were more exuberant still. Reviewing the novel for the *Frankfurter Allgemeine Zeitung*, Hubert Spiegel called it "a masterpiece, perhaps the best he has ever written," and found that by looking at the world after its end, McCarthy had gone to "the outmost limits of what could be described" (2008). In the *Guardian*, Alan

Warner showed himself equally impressed. Drawing connections to events like the war in Iraq and the destruction of New Orleans by Hurricane Katrina, as well as the gothic worlds of McCarthy's earlier fiction, he wondered how the novel would fare in contemporary America's literary landscape and stated that "all the modern novel can do is done here" (2006).

Following Warner, *The Road* appears to present as much of a return to the atmosphere of McCarthy's early Southern works as does a departure from his twentieth-century Southwestern fiction. Critics had long suspected that underneath the themes of ecological decline and social disintegration of the Appalachian novels, there loomed the specter of some grander catastrophe. At the same time, the path outlined in the previous chapters is a long and winding one, connecting *The Road* to all of McCarthy's previous novels. If its catastrophic future seems hardly surprising a vision, it is because the portents McCarthy divined from the entrails of his more historically grounded work have always pointed toward this destination. In *The Road*, violence seems to have expended itself to the point of exhaustion. Direct exchanges of blows or bullets are rare, but their grim reminders are found everywhere. Myth, too, seems to have faded with the civilization that sustained it and was in turn sustained by its sacrificial narrative. What remains, though, is the profound need for narrative itself, for a meaningful story of life immanent in the face of the end itself.

Its end-of-the-world scenario notwithstanding, the generic classification of the novel may not be as straightforward as most readers assume when they describe *The Road* as apocalyptic or postapocalyptic, as though such labels were already explanations. Conversely, other critics have dismissed the significance of religious symbolism in the novel as anything other than ironic in meaning. After a brief revision of central aspects of apocalyptic writing and sample of apocalyptic elements of the works published between *Blood Meridian* and *The Road*, I propose a unifying view of McCarthy's apocalyptic as a highly syncretic blend of religious, popular/secular, scientific, and mystical conceptions of the end of the world and the narrative form of the journey. In the final part of this chapter, I will investigate the paradoxical sense of hope that permeates the novel in the face of total despair. This hope, I believe, is at one with the ethical stance implicit in McCarthy's vision. So—in the face of whatever revelations discussion of the recently published *The Passenger* and *Stella Maris* may yet hold in store—I read *The Road* as a true literary capstone to McCarthy's oeuvre. The lingering question in this undertaking, finally, is whether his literary imagining of encompassing liminality, of life in the end times, brings something new to the table, or whether it uncovers and puts into focus something that had been veiled and unclear heretofore.

Preludes to Ruin:
The Apocalyptic Genre and McCarthy's Works, 1986–2005

The story of *The Road* follows a father and his ten-year-old son on their way through the ruins of an American civilization that has been wiped out by an unspecified event. The story is told from a selectively omniscient third-person perspective frequently interspersed with free indirect discourse from the father's point of view. The world that he and his son pass through is covered by an all-encompassing blanket of ash that blocks the Earth from the sun. Society has collapsed, the biosphere has all but disappeared, and most humans have turned to cannibalism since all animal and plant life has become extinct. Faced with the prospect of being caught, raped, and cannibalized, the man's wife has committed suicide some time ago. Sustained solely by their love for one another, father and son make their way toward the ocean in the faint hope that it might be warmer in the south.

Since *The Road* is set after the world as we know it has come to an end, the postapocalyptic genre label is perhaps unavoidable. Given McCarthy's protean literariness and ambiguous stance in matters of religion, the critique of such attribution is equally inevitable (Woodson 2008; Phillips 2011). To see how far generic classification carries us, it is expedient to revisit the central historical parameters of apocalyptic literature explored at the outset of this study. A problem with the label is that it necessarily extends modern (mis)conceptions of the apocalypse itself, which has become a kind of passe-partout for any sort of large-scale catastrophe or end-of-the-world tableau. Literally, a postapocalyptic novel would be one set after the Apocalypse, or—as it is a label that applies predominantly to secular fictions like *Mad Max*, *The Day After*, or the *Fallout* video game series—its secular equivalents. While such fictions might embrace the utopian vision of lasting universal harmony of the Judeo-Christian concept, they rarely ever do so, for the same dramatic reasons that raise the popularity of dystopian fictions over that of their optimistic counterparts. Embracing catastrophe, (post)apocalyptic fictions must therefore simultaneously limit their cataclysms to a degree and a length of time at which narrative is still possible.

Since narrative, like human consciousness, exists ever and exclusively in passage, the end is thus rarely and truly the end: "Apocalypse depends on a concord of imaginatively recorded past and imaginatively predicted future, achieved on behalf of us, who remain 'in the middest'" (Kermode 8). As such, apocalyptic scripture transforms the traditionally oral mode of prophecy into a constitutively literary composition. It foretells and imaginatively documents the causes and manner in which "last things" play out, and the fate of those alive to witness the so-called end times. Like the collective stories of pagan myth, apocalypse thus implies a certain order to earthly events. Yet in contrast to archaic or Eastern religions' understanding of existence as an eternal cycle of life, death, and rebirth, Judeo-Christian eschatology regards human history as linear, finite, and irreversible, that is, as "a history of salvation moving purposively toward its predetermined end" (Freese 1997, 21).

Religious apocalypses thus differ from pagan myth with regard to the type of order they impose upon existence and the process of history, from which they derive a specific sense of purpose. Rather than the "correspondence with events in other cycles," it is the "unitary system" of salvation history that lends events their significance (Kermode 5). In the Bible, the paradigmatic example is the eponymous Revelation of St. John the Divine, which closes the Book as the Apocalypse conceptually closes that of history. Although it is not the be-all and end-all of such conceptions that concern me here, in shaping religious and literary models of history and its end, its influence on the genre is not to be understated, and so can be expected to leave its mark on *The Road* as well.

> John created both a powerful and many-leveled panorama of the final confrontation between God and Satan and a triumphant vision of "the promised end." And with the seven seals on the book of destiny and the four horsemen of the apocalypse, the grapes of wrath, the plague of locusts and the whore of Babylon, Gog and Magog as the embodiments of evil, the lake of fire and brimstone and the bottomless pit, he provided the central images which later writers would conjure up time and again. (Freese 1997, 21)

Though John's prophetic vision forecast the cataclysmic end of earthly life, shortly to arrive, it also predicted the Second Coming of Christ, the resurrection and judgment of the dead, and the utopian vision of a heavenly New Jerusalem illuminated by the glory of God. With the Reformation and the discovery of America as a potential site for this New Jerusalem, "the novel idea that history is moving toward a millennial regeneration of mankind became not only respectable but almost canonical" (Tuveson 17). For the pious Christian, the plot and arcane symbolism of Revelation emphasized catastrophic change, deliverance, and perfection, which were to be both feared and eagerly anticipated. Expectation manifested itself in the redemptive promise for the revelation of some grand truth that would provide the whole of existence with purpose. In this way, John poetically reinterpreted the Jewish sense of the historical discontinuity of the end and its tradition of perpetual deferral of the coming of the Messiah as a definitive and unified historical program in which believers could henceforth place themselves. The Apocalypse is thus radically set in time:

> In Revelation [. . .] the apocalyptic events are seen as beginning to occur contemporaneously [. . .]. But the apocalyptic time does not begin only with the Redemption. The fact that the images are largely taken from the historical and prophetic books of the Old Testament makes us see that *all* history finally is apocalyptic. The events in which we ourselves participate are parts of the pattern; we find ourselves in the Apocalypse. [. . .] John worked what had been detached dramatic moments into a cosmic unity. All that seemed mysterious and accidental, or isolated, is now revealed to have had its place in the great whole. (Tuveson 5–6)

In sum, the apocalyptic genre is defined primarily by the thematic elements of destruction and renewal, the epistemological element of uncovering something hitherto hidden, and the structural element of imposing a grander, meaningful design. Similarly, *The Road* can be said to provide a vantage point, a final itinerary of sorts in the journey through McCarthy's fiction. From that point, the work may now be perceived in full and is, perhaps, endowed with an overarching meaning that could only be surmised before.

I cannot offer a detailed analysis of the four novels and two plays that McCarthy published in the twenty-one years between *Blood Meridian* and *The Road* in these pages. Even so, a cursory sample shows that the same elements of myth, violence, and entropy continue to be at play in these works, to similarly apocalyptic implications. Certainly, the dialectic of mimetic antagonisms remains a presence. I have briefly discussed the underlying symmetry in the disparate pairing of young John Grady Cole and the dueña Alfonsa in their competition for Alejandra in *All the Pretty Horses*, as well as similar relations and their mythic transformation in *The Crossing*. In *Cities of the Plain* it is then John Grady's love for the young Mexican prostitute Magdalena that arouses the jealousy of her pimp Eduardo. In true Old Testament fashion, Eduardo describes Grady's advances as his "coveting of another man's property" (*CP* 240). After Magdalena's murder, John Grady's vengeful death-wish—his inability, in Eduardo's words, to "choose life"—drives him to confront his rival to "kill [him] or be killed" (*CP* 248). The rivalry culminates in a duel that ritualistically repeats John Grady's prison duel with a young "cuchillero" in the earlier novel. Whereas he had narrowly escaped with his life then, the later duel sees both men die at the points of each other's knives.

In *All the Pretty Horses*, John Grady functions as the *pharmakon* to the Mexican hacienda, the impure element that is initially desired and later expelled. In *The Crossing*, the she-wolf and the Indians are arguably scapegoats. Like his brother Boyd, Billy Parham is imbued with the scapegoat's double nature riding through town; he is described as that which the people "envied most and what they most reviled" (*CRO* 170). Yet, of the characters in the Border Trilogy, it is Magdalena who is most explicitly associated with a sacrificial victim. During one of her epileptic fits, the other prostitutes describe her as "una mujer diabólica" (Sp. a devil woman), who seems beset by "some incubus" (*CP* 72). The crowd of women she attracts comes armed with "a statue of the Virgin," "little figures [. . .] and votive shrines," and some dip "their handkerchiefs in the blood" (*CP* 72) on Magdalena's lips—not to help her, but to keep them as talismans. During their duel, Eduardo actually likens John Grady to the superstitious prostitutes, mocking his love as a metaphysical delusion "that craziness is sacred. A special grace. [. . .]. A partaking of the godhead" (*CP* 251).

It would seem that the microcosm of the brothel is caught in a mimetic crisis, brought on by the foreign elements of John Grady's love and Magdalena's defiance of her pimp. At one point, John Grady dreams of "a great confusion of obscene carnival folk," among whom he finds not only "painted whores" and "pale young debauchees," but also "youths in ecclesiastical robes," a "priest," a "procuress," and a "goat with gilded horns" (*CP* 103). The music suggests the quality of "some ancient rondel, faintly martial" and the "measure of something periodic [. . .] which only darkness could accommodate" (*CP* 104). At "the center of all" is "a young girl in white gauze dress who lay upon a pallet-board like a sacrificial virgin" (*CP* 104)—prefiguring Magdalena's body on a morgue table. The elements of a sacrificial crisis are thus present: chaos and confusion, a ritual quality, the martial repetitiveness of the violent proceedings, and the sacrificial victim at the center. As with McCarthy's other novels, it is unlikely that Magdalena's death brings a rejuvenation of order, nor is it a focus.

Cities, overall, is a novel replete with sacrificial symbolism. Perhaps the most significant case in point is another dream that is featured at length in the novel's epilogue. An aged Billy Parham meets another man whom he initially mistakes for death, and who will later call him his *cuate* (Sp. twin). The man tells Billy of a dream of some nameless traveler, who, "en tiempos antiguos" comes to spent the night at a rock that unbeknownst to the traveler, is a "bloodstained altarstone which the weathers of the sierra [. . .] had these millennia been impotent to cleanse" of "the stains of blood from those who'd been slaughtered upon it to appease the gods" (*CP* 270). Falling asleep, the dream-traveler then dreams himself. In this second-order dream, he meets a group of tribesmen in ceremonial garb. After drinking from a ritual cup, he "forg[ets] the pain of his life," and "become[s] accomplice in a blood ceremony that was then and is now an affront to God" (*CP* 280). Made an involuntary if nonresisting surrogate victim for a young girl hostage, the traveler attains the spiritual insight of "a great conspiracy" that is in "the world's silence" and that "he himself must then be a part of" (*CP* 282) and arguably becomes in his sacrificial death.

In the dream-narrator's view, there is a greater cost still than his dream-traveler's dream-death in the second-order dream. This cost is that of the mythical cover-up, namely "that this too would be forgot" (*CP* 280). Clearly, though, the communal erasure of the sacrificial foundations—which is the secret heirloom of the "world of our fathers" that "resides within us" yet (*CP* 281)—is at best a partial one. After all, the man who tells the story of his multilayered dream to Billy thereby spreads its knowledge, much in the way Girard conceives of the Holy Spirit. The dream-narrator's revelation is, at bottom, that of mimetic anthropology. Consequently, his report provides a final lesson of his and the traveler's insights that both diagnoses the secret, metaphysical nature of desire and the circularity of cultural regeneration, and formulates an antiacquisitive imperative:

> Of such dreams and of the rituals of them there can also be no end. The thing that is sought is altogether other. [. . .] These dreams and these acts are driven by a terrible hunger. They seek to meet a need which they can never satisfy and for that we must be grateful. [. . .] When I asked him to tell me what had happened he looked at me and he said: I have been here before. So have you. Everything is here for the taking. Touch nothing. Then I woke. (*CP* 287–88)

"Everything is here for the taking. Touch nothing." Some of McCarthy's wiser characters, like Black in *The Sunset Limited*, echo this profoundly antiacquisitive sentiment: "I think evil is something you bring on your own self. Mostly from wantin what you aint supposed to have" (67). The value of such insight is not to be understated, yet it is exceedingly rare. Black and Ben Telfair in *The Stonemason* espouse an antidote in the values of charity and hospitality (*SL* 93; *SM* 131). Yet for the most part, interpersonal relations in the Border Trilogy and *No Country for Old Men* are still governed by mimetic desire and the escalatory logic of the duel. The subjective, violent underpinnings of such antagonisms are put on display in the dramatization of prison economy, as experienced by John Grady in *All the Pretty Horses*. The state of the latter is close to the Hobbesian state of nature, which is, after all, a state of war and relative equality:

> The prison was no more than a small walled village and within it occurred a constant seethe of barter and exchange in everything from radios and blankets down to matches and buttons and shoenails and within this bartering ran a constant struggle for status and position. Underpinning all of it like the fiscal standard in commercial societies lay a bedrock of depravity and

violence where in an egalitarian absolute every man was judged by a single standard and that was his readiness to kill. (*APH* 182)

Devoid of the symbolic means of monetary exchange, relations within the prison hierarchy are ruled by the foreshortened and more immediate reciprocity of barter, which is less able to dissimulate the underlying violence of the dynamics of desire that underlies economic exchange. In the decades between the events of the Border Trilogy and *No Country for Old Men*, this more ancient mode of economics is then shown as becoming a part of the surrounding culture.

The latter novel's dramatization of the 1980s wars between Mexican drug cartels and U.S. authorities bespeaks, in the aging Sheriff Bell's words, a "breakdown in mercantile ethics" (*NC* 304) that must be considered a part of the escalation to extremes. From general mores to the decline of schools, social breakdown is pervasive.[1] It finds its representation in Anton Chigurh, who significantly decides the fate of his victims by a coin toss. While he pales in comparison to *Blood Meridian*'s Judge, he is mythically likened to the "bubonic plague" (*NC* 141) and, though himself "a nonbeliever," explicitly "model[s] himself after God" (*NC* 256), disassociating himself from any responsibility for his action through a strictly deterministic outlook.[2] Bell, who has an intuitive grasp of the larger escalation Chigurh's presence entails, calls him "a true and living prophet of destruction" (*NC* 4). Wisely, he wishes to avoid confronting him: "I always knew that you had to be willing to die to even do this job [...] I think it is more like what you are willin to become, and I think a man would have to put his soul at hazard" (*NC* 4). The logic he describes is that of the duel's escalatory violence, the unpredictability of which *No Country*'s sudden deaths dramatize.

Nor do the novels leading up to *The Road* leave much doubt as to the apocalyptic import of these developments. *No Country* has Bell assess that "nothing short of the second comin of Christ [...] can slow this train" (159), and sees his wife reading "St. John. The Revelations" (304). At once sacrificial and apocalyptic, *All the Pretty Horses* ends with the image of a "solitary bull rolling in the dust against the bloodred sunset like an animal in sacrificial torment" and the view of "the darkening land, the world to come" (302). *The Crossing* closes with the test of the first atomic warhead at Trinity Site. And *Cities of the Plain* directly evokes the looming cataclysm in its title, which

Bible & Point?

has been rightly related to the destruction of Sodom and Gomorrah. In its news of "wars and rumors of wars" (*CP* 61), it cites Christ's prediction of the end times in the Gospels (Mt. 24:6; Mk. 13:7). Finally in *The Sunset Limited*, which came out in the same year as *The Road*, White's death wish is driven by what he takes to be a "gradual enlightenment as to the nature of reality" (120), providing an ironic twist on the theme of revelation. At the bottom of this enlightenment is a profound cultural pessimism. White proclaims that "Western Civilization finally went up in smoke in the chimneys at Dachau," and that history is but "a saga of bloodshed and greed and folly the import of which is impossible to ignore" (*SL* 27, 112).[3] He diagnoses himself as much as the state of the world: "The things that I loved were very frail. Very fragile. I didnt know that. I thought they were indestructible. I've been asked didnt I think it odd that I should be present to witness the death of everything and I do think it's odd but that doesn't mean it's not so. Someone has to be here" (*SL* 26–27).

The Road ostensibly fulfills White's prediction, telling the story of those left to witness "the death of everything." Yet this is not the whole story, as the dialectic of apocalyptic writing always includes the twofold vision of looming destruction and the promise of salvation. This dialectic, ultimately, is captured better and more concisely in the final words of *Cities of the Plain*. Significantly, the latter ends in a "Dedication"—the first poem in McCarthy's work:

> I will be your child to hold
> And you be me when I am old
> The world grows cold
> The heathen rage
> The story's told
> Turn the page. (*CP* 293)

In the preludes to ruin presented by the texts following *Blood Meridian*, "Dedication" represents a coda and transition. The world of *The Road* is anticipated in the third line's vision of a freezing world while "the heathen rage"—setting up a relation between violence and the cooling of the world. Amid that entropic vision, something tender nonetheless comes to the fore. Depicting the loving care between child and parent, the first two lines present a relation of mutual affection. It predicts its later role-reversal and promotes the image of shared identities. The final two lines then predict the end of a story and include the imperative—implicitly to the reader—to begin another. Myth has run out. It is time for a new kind of story. We shall see to what extent this promise of "Dedication" is redeemed in *The Road*.

Syncretic Eschatology:
The Different Ends of *The Road*

Throughout this study, I have argued that McCarthy's work as a whole—concerned as it is with the revelation and sustained investigation of causes and consequences, things first and last—should be regarded as fundamentally apocalyptic. Demonstrably, the by now familiar interplay between mimetic dynamics and revelatory thought remains a current in the works after *Blood Meridian*, also. While this interplay is central to my understanding of McCarthy's apocalyptic, it is removed from what is generally understood by the term, nor does it exhaust what I have called his "unified poetic field." Now, of all his works, none has been as often and as explicitly associated with the genre as *The Road*.[4] As attributions of meaning vary, the secular, religious, and scientific facets of McCarthy's literary apocalyptic need to be explored and tested against the text, both on their own terms and against each other. In the following, I argue that these different parameters do not so much compete with as complement one another, offering an exceedingly versatile, syncretic eschatology. As the study of last things—of the destiny of humankind and the individual soul—the latter should embrace and blend religious, secular-social, and scientific concepts for a more encompassing vision suited to put the challenges of our age into view.

Biblical Apocalypse and Journey Form

As a mode of writing that has persisted through centuries and spouted ever new amalgamations with other genres and forms of writing, the apocalyptic is nothing if not adaptable: "It allows itself to be diffused, blended with other varieties of fiction—tragedy, for example, myths of Empire and of Decadence—and yet it can survive in very naïve forms" (Kermode 9). In contemporary imaginations, the naïve form or vehicle for visions of the end times is often that of the equally versatile journey narrative. For McCarthy, this is an obvious choice as well: at least half of his ten novels are explicitly structured around the itineraries of his traveling protagonists; the other half contain their fair share of roaming and rambling. Nomadic lifestyles are symptomatic of his heroes: social outcasts and vagabonds, young cowboys, vicious scalphunters, or refugees—whatever they may turn out to be, their anthropological blueprint seems to be that of *homo viator*, the traveling man, as much as it is that of *homo mimeticos* and *homo necans*.

In his 2007 TV interview with Oprah Winfrey, Cormac McCarthy traced the creation of *The Road* back to a trip to El Paso some years prior that he had gone on with his then four-year-old son John Francis. Standing by a window and listening to the sounds of distant trains passing in the night, he imagined what the town would look like fifty or a hundred years in the future: "I just had this image of these fires up on the hill and everything being laid waste, and I thought a lot about my little boy" (2007b). Perhaps such inspiration is not all-too-dissimilar from that which must have moved John on Patmos. Yet while *The Road* certainly retains generic qualities of apocalypse, as well as a fair share of biblical symbolism, its shape and most of all its perspectives differ sharply from John's. After all, though ever reluctant to discuss his intentions and while admitting that "obviously you can draw conclusions about all sorts of things," McCarthy also understatedly suggested that "I'd like to think it's just about the boy and the man on the road."

So, too, *The Road* is at base the story of the journey of father and son through the ruins of American civilization. Construed as one continuous whole, the text consists of mostly short paragraphs with wide spaces in between. In this way, it reflects the continual progress of the journey in the form of the narrative itself. Each paragraph represents one episode or station in the pair's journey. "The movement of the travelers and the movement of the text are one" (Cant 267). As I have mentioned, their journey evokes a sense of McCarthy revisiting his own earlier work. Although it is hard to pinpoint when exactly *The Road* is set, the wasteland of the novel is clearly that of an industrial America. Looking closer, father and son's journey evokes and revisits many of the locales and motifs characteristic of McCarthy's Appalachian period.[5] As a barn advertisement for Rock City, a natural tourist attraction near Chattanooga, indicates, father and son move through McCarthy's old home state of Tennessee for a time (*R* 18). On their way south, they pass the remains of an apple orchard similar to that of *The Orchard Keeper*. They find a dead family of suicides hanging from the crossbeam of a barn, which recalls Ballard's father's suicide in *Child of God*. An old, Southern mansion visited might as well be Suttree's abandoned childhood home. In a particularly horrific instant, the pair come across the corpse of a half-eaten, roasted baby, which recalls the nightmarish, sacrificial conclusion of *Outer Dark*. In part, the effect of such intertextual callbacks is to document both unsettling, catastrophic changes and similarly unsettling constants in the way humans confront the world.

As with many of McCarthy's earlier journeys, the nature of the pairs' passage itself is highly ambiguous. Taxonomically, such narratives materialize as an escape, as a quest, and as aimless wandering without definitive purpose.[6] In the first case, motivation can be described as *causal*, the movement away from something, with Israel's flight from Egypt and American captivity tales and slave narratives serving as examples. The quest journey is finally motivated by a specific goal, some sought-for object or mythical place, with Ulysses's ten-year-voyage for Ithaca or the chivalrous search for the Holy Grail as influential literary precursors. The picaro novel and the twentieth-century road trips immortalized by the beat generation exemplify the third form of directionless drifting, which makes the journey its own sake and inherent motivation (Freese 2015, 18). All three models are in fact easily blended and combined with one another.

> In concrete fictions [...] the need to escape from an old life might lead to a search for a new one, a failed search can end in an attempt to escape, a journey that spatializes an inner development might unfold as a teleological journey that gradually moves towards a harmonious ending or culminates in a sudden life-changing insight, or it might consist of aimless drifting that is an end in itself. (Freese 2015, 18)

In this respect, the journey of *The Road* is typologically overdetermined: father and son are "two hunted animals trembling like groundfoxes in their cover" (*R* 110), flying the deadly cold of the coming northern winter. Given the totality of the destruction, one may rightly ask whether any notion of either escape or quest is not necessarily a pure fiction. It easily appears that the pair's journey is but an end in itself, motivated simply by sustaining life as long as possible: "He said that everything depended on reaching the coast, yet waking in the night he knew that all of this was empty and no substance to it" (*R* 25).

This impression is relativized again, though, when taking into view the spiritual dimension of the apocalyptic mode and McCarthy's own framing of his heroes' journeys in particular. Here, yet another type of journey comes to the fore: from the scalphunters of *Blood Meridian* to father and son in *The Road*, his travelers are frequently referred to as "pilgrims," ascribing a spiritual component to their movements. John Cawelti even speaks of a "mythos of the pilgrimage" that McCarthy develops over the course of his work: "Each new book slightly shifts the grounds traversed by its predecessors" (165–66). While typologically, the pilgrimage can be defined as a quest with spiritual content, Cawelti observes that it is particularly difficult to decide whether the "pilgrimages" of McCarthy's heroes are best described in terms of a flight or search, as spatial or spiritual journeys, and whether they are directed toward the past or the future, damnation or salvation (165).

All of McCarthy's journey narratives are fraught with spiritual concerns. However, it is in *The Road* in particular that religious motifs are put front and center. Thus, father and son are not just fugitives, but also "pilgrims in a fable" (*R* 4) on their way to the ocean, where life on earth originated. Accordingly, Wieland Freund notes: "A troubled age has turned the pilgrimage into the road movie; McCarthy comes full circle and pilgrimages again. In spite of everything, *The Road* is of course a deeply religious novel—with a messiah at its center" (2007). The messiah Freund alludes to is the man's son, whose role will be discussed further on. For now, suffice it to say that among many examples, his literary transfiguration as a "golden chalice, good to house a god" (*R* 64) in particular points toward a religious kind of quest, invoking at once the novel's earlier working title as *The Grail* and the eponymous salutary vessel of Christian lore and Arthurian legend. Lydia Cooper thus proposes reading *The Road* as an "apocalyptic grail narrative" (2011a, 218), uniting both traditions by the common thematic denominator of redemption. Early on in the text, one thus begins to suspect that there is more at stake than mere survival.

Still, as always in McCarthy, the story is tightly yoked to the confrontation of life and death. While the end of the world offers a perfect background for these issues, the journey form provides an exceedingly versatile vehicle for their exploration. In *The Road*, the theme of the individual and collective journey of all life toward death is hence effectively as pressing as ever, and it is here, too, that the imagery of Apocalypse finds its most overt expression. A dominant, recurring image is that of the dead that father and son see on their way toward the ocean. Like themselves, the dead are frequently referred to as "pilgrims," yet their journeys have come to an end.

> The mummied dead everywhere. The flesh cloven along the bones, the ligaments dried to tug and taut as wires. Shriveled and drawn like latterday bogfolk, their faces of boiled sheeting, the yellowed palings of their teeth. They were discalced to a man like pilgrims of some common order for all their shoes were long since stolen. (*R* 21)

As the father remembers the days after the unspecified catastrophe, he recalls people "sitting on the sidewalk in the dawn half immolate and smoking in their clothes. Like failed sectarian suicides. Within a year there were fires on the ridges and deranged chanting. The screams of the murdered. By day the dead impaled on spikes along the road" (*R* 28). The father's memories provide a trace of the inexorable violence that occurred in the wake of the event. Apart from McCarthy's wording, the images themselves excite religious association. They evoke medieval depictions of hell akin to the paintings of Hieronymus Bosch or the *Inferno* of Dante Alighieri's *Commedia Divina* as much and more than the book of Revelation.

Many of the symbols from the latter text's catastrophic catalogue appear throughout the novel, providing a model for the barren wasteland that the world has been transformed into. It is worth pursuing some of these parallels. In Revelation, the opening of the sixth seal (Rv. 6:12) results in a great earthquake and solar eclipse. The sounding of the four trumpets (Rv. 8:7–12) summons a rain of hail, fire, and blood that burns a third of the plants and trees, a flaming mountain that destroys a third of the ships and of all life in the sea, a falling star that poisons a third of the earth's rivers, and the smiting of the sun that results in the darkening of day and night. The third and fourth of the last seven plagues (Rv. 16) eradicate all life in the sea and burn men with fire.[7]

In *The Road*, virtually all catastrophes have their counterparts. The earth is shaken with occasional tremors and quakes, and the banished sun now "circles the earth like a grieving mother with a lamp" (*R* 28). Rivers have been polluted and lightning- and firestorms have burned away almost all plant life and killed travelers on the road. When father and son eventually reach the ocean, they find a shipwreck. The beach is strewn with the bones of seabirds and "the ribs of fishes in their millions stretching along the shore as far as the eye could see like an isocline of death. One vast salt sepulcher" (*R* 187).

In the wake of such devastation, it is to be expected that war, pestilence, famine, and death—the four horsemen of the Apocalypse (see Rv. 6)—are a constant presence in the novel. The land is infested with bands of marauders, notably an army that wears scarves in the red color of war. There is a reference to a former cholera epidemic, the son is taken by fever at one point, and the father is continuously shaken by a vicious cough. Starvation has become a general condition, and death is all around. There are also a few more or less direct invocations of apocalyptic themes. On the verge of starvation, father and son's persistence is rewarded as they discover a hidden shelter filled with canned goods. This may represent the giving of "the hidden manna" promised to "him who overcometh" (KJB, Rv. 2:17), meaning those "who endur[e] persecution and sta[y] pure from defilement" (ESV 2466). As the father leaves the shelter, he finds the hatchway resembles "a grave yawning at judgment day in some old apocalyptic painting" (*R* 131). Another time, he wakes up from his sleep "like a man [...] in a grave" (*R* 180), only to recall an instant from his youth where he watched the relocation of several corpses in decomposing coffins. "The dead came to light lying on their sides with their legs drawn up and some lay on their stomachs" (*R* 180). The last examples evoke the resurrection of the dead and the reading of their names from the "book of life" in the Last Judgment (Rv. 20:11–15). In McCarthy's book of death, though, both judgment and resurrection have become precarious notions: even prophets lose their faith on the road.

Ely's Challenge, or the Limits of Revelation

The riches of scriptural references and motifs inspired by Revelation notwithstanding, skeptic readers are justified in questioning whether the imagery of *The Road* actually reflects a religious deep-structure, or whether it is not mere catastrophic window dressing. This uncertainty is due, on the one hand, to the cultural ubiquity of Revelation, watered down and reduced to surface imagery as its influence may often be. On the other hand, it is a result of McCarthy's narrative voice and the father's status as main focalizer, whose viewpoint frequently seems to bleed into that of the third-person narrator. As a result it is not always perfectly clear which of the story's many religious allusions originate with the father and which are presented through the voice of the narrator. Consequently, the ontological reliability of religious allusion within the world of the text can be called into question.

What is more, the epistemological limits of revelation—seen as received, literal prophecy—are explicitly questioned in *The Road*. In one of the novel's central encounters, the man and the boy meet an old, ragged, and half-blind man who introduces himself as Ely. He claims to be ninety and to have been on the road always, surviving on the things people give to him. He later reveals the last statement to be a lie, which leaves the question of how he survived all these years. An unlikely presence, Ely poses one of the more overt challenges of interpretation in *The Road*. Several critics have traced him to Elijah from the first and second books of Kings, in which God sends ravens to nourish the prophet in a time of drought (Freund; Wielenberg 2–3; Snyder 2008, 80–81). In *The Road*, it is the boy's pleading that persuades the father to share some of their food with him. "He looked at the old man. Perhaps he'd turn into a god and they to trees. All right, he said" (*R* 137). Beyond the themes of hospitality and divine nourishment evoked in this passage, which also find their referent in the mythic residue of the tale of Philemon and Baucis,[9] this scene calls attention to the eschatological role of the biblical Elijah: he is a prophet of the end times, said to return before the "Great Day of the Lord," a day "burning like an oven," and to "turn the hearts of fathers to their children, and the hearts of children to their fathers" (Mal. 4:1–6). So the prophecy of Elijah's return takes account both of the ashen wasteland of *The Road* and of the rising arc of genuine affection that the relationship between fathers and sons takes in McCarthy's work following *Blood Meridian*.

Yet similarities with the biblical text only go so far. A sort of prophet-in-retrospect, McCarthy's Ely proclaims: "I knew this was coming. [...] This or something like it" (*R* 142). Although the end was thus an expected one, Ely calls into question any divine rationale behind it: "People were always getting ready for tomorrow. I didnt believe in that. Tomorrow wasnt getting ready for them. It didnt even know they were there" (*R* 142). In this way, Ely exposes how strongly our days depend on the idea of "tomorrow," on the anticipation of a future that motivates present behavior and action. Strange at heart, the realization that there will not be any such future or tomorrow may take time to sink in. Once it does, one can expect the symptoms of mass panic experienced in times of great crisis and often put on display in apocalyptic fiction. In *The Road*, the descent into violence and bloodshed seems to occur "within a year" (*R* 28) of the catastrophe. Even biblical apocalyptic texts, associated with devastation as they may be, offer the messianic promise of the kingdom of heaven, which—as a perfected state—encapsulates at once an eternal tomorrow and the capstone of history. Judaism and Christianity are both fundamentally "religion[s] of expectation" (Tuveson 1). Thus, Ely's definitive foreclosure of tomorrow would also seem to foreclose anticipation of the Second Coming, Judgment Day, and so on. He refutes the very concept of the divine orchestration of history implicit in apocalypse.

The interpretation of the encounter with Ely is further complicated when the old man admits that Ely is not actually his true name. If he is a prophet of sorts, he is a failed one who has lost his faith: "There is no God and we are his prophets" (*R* 143), he confesses in a paradoxical variation of the Islamic *Shahada*.[10] While upon seeing the son, he initially believed he "had died," he later brushes off the father's quizzical suggestion of his son's divinity: "What if I said he's a god?"—"I'm past all that now. [. . .] Where men cant live gods fare no better. [. . .] So I hope that's not true what you said because to be on the road with the last god would be a terrible thing" (*R* 145).[11] Once again, God, nay, all gods, are reportedly dead, the sacrificial religion as exhausted as its unrealized Judeo-Christian resolution.

In a deconstructive sense, Ely's words—which link the existence of *any* god to the existence of the faithful—may be seen as the proclamation of the death of any sort of transcendental signified, any metaphysical presence or organizing principle providing order and meaning to the chaos of being. Alternatively, we shall yet see, *The Road* reflexively ties life to the persistence of such signifieds, which is already apparent in the man's question. Those survivors fallen from faith would be prophets, or perhaps witnesses to the failure of any system of meaning and order, professing it to the ones remaining believers. In this way, they would indeed be like Nietzsche's madman. Ely's warning against being on the road with "the last god" could hence be interpreted as commiseration with the one who will yet have to suffer an inevitable loss of faith. Perhaps this is still preferable to the more sinister,

Girardian foreboding, namely that the son himself, as the most good and most innocent, might be sacrificed and cannibalized for whatever dying community still exists.

Erik Wielenberg, one of the critics who have called into question the metaphysical foundation of ethics in *The Road*, correctly observes that God's existence in the novel remains consistently ambiguous. In citing the man's conditional proposition, "if [the boy] is not the word of God God never spoke" (*R* 5), he contends that the whole encounter with Ely points "toward the possibility that God never spoke. This old man has survived not through divine assistance but rather through random chance; he and all the other survivors of the catastrophe are prophets of atheism, bearing witness to the absence of God from the universe" (Wielenberg 3). Hence, Wielenberg proposes a straight and simple solution to the problem of theodicy. *The Road*, which has also been related to the book of Job, renders this problem more palpable than any other of McCarthy's works. Its most poignant formulation, though, comes in *The Sunset Limited*—which was also published in 2006 and has been considered a companion piece to *The Road*—in the final monologue of the nihilist White:

> I dont believe in God. [. . .] The clamor and the din of those in torment has to be the sound most pleasing to his ear. [. . .] And if [the] pain were actually collective instead of simply reiterative then the sheer weight of it would drag the world from the walls of the universe and send it crashing and burning through whatever night it might yet be capable of engendering until it was not even ash. (*SL* 137)

With his vision of a world burning in perpetual night and finally reduced to less than ash, White's words may actually present what little future there is still left in the burned world of McCarthy's tenth novel. Certainly, in the face of unbearable suffering, and the total annihilation witnessed in *The Road*, belief in an all-powerful and loving God becomes problematic, if not, as Dana Phillips contends, absurd (2011, 179). If not White's nihilism, Ely's paradoxical atheism thus appears as a position intellectually and emotionally plausible. This would be the case, at least, if the religious dimension McCarthy presented, his concept of the divine, were circumscribed by the limits of traditional religious doctrine. As I will show, this is not the case. Neither is

McCarthy's apocalypticism exhausted with Revelation, nor is his theodicy resolved by a simple negation of God—and thus the question itself.

Secular Conceptions of the End

Setting momentarily aside the complicated issues of theodicy and the condition of the divine, what can be asserted is that as the presence of God becomes problematic, so does the apocalyptic paradigm as a plan culminating in salvation as the end of history. For where there is no divine author, there is also no such plot, nor metaphysical foundation of meaning and purpose to history and human existence upon the earth. Popular apocalypticism, even as it gladly feeds on its aura, has shaken off the shackles of Revelation and largely dispenses with such issues. Tales of the end times are as popular as ever today. Only the parameters of these tales have changed considerably.

Aside from the revelatory implications the end carries in the Bible, it is exactly the framework of a divinely orchestrated course of history that has lost much of its persuasiveness. Conversely, with the Age of Enlightenment, the concept of *human agency* gradually emerged in its stead as the deciding factor shaping humanity's fate on this earth. The development of new technologies, Charles Darwin's theory of evolution, and advances made across scientific fields seemed to project the arc of human civilization as one bending, if not perhaps toward justice, then at least to ever loftier moral, intellectual, and technological heights. Carrying secularized traces of messianic enthusiasm, the faith in progress that characterized much of the nineteenth century was disappointed by the realities of the twentieth. Recent history may be told as one of humanity's scientific reach exceeding its ethical grasp, the progress of our consciousness being outpaced by that of our technology. Today, the very forces once thought to gentle the human condition—chief among them the unbridled demands and invisible snares of a global market—drive us at accelerating speed into a dead end.

Recent history comes into view. While the end of the Cold War led to a brief resurgence of a quasi-millennial but fundamentally secular optimism that is best encapsulated by Francis Fukuyama's notion of "the end of history" brought on by the apparent triumph of liberal-democratic capitalism as a socioeconomic version of the Kingdom, the early 2000s seemed to drive whatever utopian notions there might have been firmly into the ground:

> On 11 September 2001, the Twin Towers were hit. Twelve years earlier, on 9 November 1989, the Berlin Wall fell. That date heralded the "happy '90s," the Francis Fukuyama dream of the "end of history"—the belief that liberal democracy had, in principle, won; that the search was over; that the advent of a global, liberal world community lurked just around the corner; that the obstacles [. . .] were merely empirical and contingent [. . .]. In contrast, 9/11 is the main symbol of the end of the Clintonite happy '90s [*sic*]. This is the era in which new walls emerge everywhere, between Israel and the West Bank, around the European Union, on the US-Mexico border. The rise of the populist New Right is just the most prominent example of the urge to raise new walls. (Žižek 2009, 86–87)

In the shadow of 9/11, the temptation to speak of Samuel Huntington's scenario of the "clash of civilizations" as "politics at the end of history" (Žižek 2009, 120) may be great. In his Oprah interview, McCarthy himself related the success of his novel to a heightened public interest in "apocalyptic issues" since the attacks. Still, as *The Road* contains no reference to terrorism, Islamic or other, there may be little more in this line of thought than considering it as part of the "contemporary popular responses to 9/11, exploring [. . .] attributes of communal guilt, terror, and what, if anything, humanity can find that may provide a way out of the darkness both abroad and at home, that followed" (Cooper 2011a, 222). Nevertheless, the fluidity of cultural identity, the interdependency of exchange between civilizations, and the increasingly incalculable nature of violence suggest a more chaotic picture than Huntington's.[12]

> The threat of the escalation to extremes, which is one with the *continuity* of war, is always latent behind the discontinuities of real wars. [. . .] When differences between adversaries alternate with increasing rapidity [. . .] in other words, when the belief of adversaries in their difference from each other produces the alternation of defeats and victories and approaches reciprocity, then we are nearing what I call the sacrificial crisis. This is the

critical point when the group borders on chaos. Put nuclear weapons in the hands of the belligerents, and it will no longer be just the group, but the whole planet. (*BE* 14)

Alternatively, the mimetic prognosis of encompassing cultural undifferentiation and exacerbation of violence proceeds from an awareness of the fluidity of identity in cultural exchange and the conflictual potential inherent in the negotiation of *difference* and (in)equality on the grounds of the common and a shared market. Already, we see the thirty-year erosion of middle- and working-class diversity across the globe as the result of neoliberal market deregulation and predatory capitalism give way to populism and a reinvigorated neofascism with its usual scapegoating of marginal groups, as smaller and larger dyads of rivals emerge among domestic and geopolitical fault lines.[13] From this view, Huntington's essentialist conception of irreducible sociocultural difference only dissimulates the challenges of a shared world in which local acts provoke incalculable, *chaotic* effects on a national and international scale.

Whatever heuristic is adopted to map present challenges, it inevitably points at the displacement and partial reinterpretation of the biblical apocalyptic through secular lenses. Our own unfettered technologies and systems of political and socioeconomic organization appear now as the probable vehicles of mankind's collective demise (Grimm, Faulstich, and Kuon 9). A world economy in perpetual crisis, rising political fragmentation and extremism, global terrorism, and the realities of modern, technologically enhanced violence are but a few among many factors. Writing about *The Road*, Andrew Keller-Estes depicts modern apocalypticism as determined by the conglomeration of individual risks and various ecological disasters "into one 'environmental crisis' and the entire field of technological/nuclear/pandemic threats into one kind of generalized apocalyptic awareness" (195). The end is thus as immanent as ever but has largely been divested of its Judeo-Christian implications. It no longer offers either the uncovering of a hidden truth nor an interpretive model of history as imbued with inherent purpose.

Instead, secular apocalypticism serves as a placeholder for all possible models of the end, ranging from scenarios of viral pandemics, to environmental and economic collapse, to nuclear holocaust. Different though they are, these realistic or worldly models have one thing in common: be it by our mental incapability to keep up with our technological progress, or by our exploitation of nature and failure to adapt to the demands of a changing environment, it is *not* God, but rather humanity itself, that sows and reaps the fruits of "self-destruction as the final stage of secularization" (Grimm, Faulstich, and Kuon 9). Thus,

> mankind as the earth's most successful predator, continues to outcompete and out-kill other species to extinction in a monomaniacal swath, destroying whole ecologies and altering the global environment. [...] The ultimate extension of this crazed Babel of killing [...] is that we might finally engage in mindless violence to the point of extinguishing ourselves. [...] And this line of thought, this inevitable natural result of man's existence, is the naturalistic theme that McCarthy thrusts at us. (Owens 50).

The secular turn in contemporary apocalypses offers intriguing possibilities of critically investigating problems and developments of the present day by imaginatively projecting them into the disastrous future. In *The Road*, scholars have identified the memorable image of father and son pushing their shopping cart across their junkyard of a world as a sort of "dark mirror" reflecting excessive Western consumerism (Woodson 2008, 88). In the postapocalyptic world, the cart is repurposed, or perhaps functionally refocused, to storing and transporting the basic means of survival. Magically, a single can of Coca-Cola is "transformed from the most recognized trademark on the planet—the essence of banality—to a unique miracle," its consumption transfigured into an almost "sacred act"; brands and icons of consumer culture are hence freed from the current discursive burdens of "pollution, garbage, excess, obesity, environmental impact" (Keller-Estes 199–200). Simultaneously, the centering of bare necessities like shoes and food and the implication of the same consumer culture in its own exhaustion only encourages a critical stance.[14]

The changed nature of postapocalyptic consumption is a direct result of a radically altered environment. It is the nature of the blasted landscape father and son traverse that gives the novel its ecocritical force. Preceding any of the aforementioned effects of the text's self-referential callbacks to the early McCarthy, the state of the ecosystem here presents a disastrous, global escalation of the incipient environmental malaise depicted in the

Appalachian novels. While the latter were haunted by the pastoral specter of the machine in the garden, Tim Edwards summarily observes that "the machines have grown deadly, even universally deadly, having taken on new shapes in the form of chemical waste, air and water pollution, and of course nuclear technology and all of its attendant dangers" (56). The world is a cauterized wasteland, the country "barren, silent, godless" (*R* 4). At one point, father and son traverse a "rich southern wood that once held mayapple and pipsissewa," as well as ginseng and rhododendron, but save for a few morels they find in the dead forest, all plants have been burned away by gigantic firestorms. The trees are "twisted and knotted and black" (*R* 34), and in one episode come uprooted, almost crushing the two as they camp among them. Not unlike the polluted Tennessee River in *Suttree*, the rivers in *The Road* carry "skeins of ash and slurry" (*R* 43). The air itself is filled with so much ash that people wear protective masks. Visually, the ashen wasteland of the novel is hence inescapably dominated by the color gray, down to the pores of the print itself:

> It is impossible to read *The Road* without noticing how gray everything looks: days are gray; dusks are gray; dawns are gray; the light and the sky are gray; the landscape is gray; the city is gray; tree stumps are gray; the ash is gray; the slush, sleet, and ice are gray; the beach, sea, and hagmoss are gray; the water is gray; the window is gray; clothes are gray; the human body, both living and dead, is gray; hair is gray; teeth are gray; viscera are gray [. . .]—the heart is gray. The post-apocalyptic world of *The Road* has been grayed out, has moved from a brighter to a fainter shade. (Danta 10)

In contrast, the man's dreams and memories are still of a brighter, already autumnal yet subtly colored world of evergreens, yellow leaves, lilac, and blue mountains (*R* 11, 22, 17, 157), visually evoking the sense of loss as that world has vanished. Even the sun itself is blocked away, which recalls the unending eclipse of Culla Holme's nightmare in *Outer Dark*. And of course, animal life is all but extinct.

All in all, *The Road* thus presents a stark and haunting vision of "what would happen if the world lost its biosphere," as environmentalist George Monbiot observed (2007).[15] To say the world is dying would seem an understatement: the destruction could hardly be more complete. Yet the nature of the event that has so transformed the earth into this wasteland is clouded in mystery, and so continues to be the subject of debate. What is known for sure is only that the mother was pregnant with the boy at the time the event occurred, and that the actual story of *The Road* takes place about ten years later. Hollywood's disaster factory might propose the eruption of a supervolcano, or the impact of an asteroid or giant meteorite. Conversely, a number of critics seem to assume a nuclear holocaust and ensuing winter as the more likely scenario.[16] In the novel, the man witnesses the event as follows:

> The clocks stopped at 1:17. A long shear of light and then a series of low concussions. He got up and went to the window. What is it? she said. He didnt answer. He went into the bathroom and threw the lightswitch but the power was already gone. A dull rose glow in the windowglass. He dropped to one knee and raised the lever to stop the tub and then turned on both taps as far as they would go. (*R* 45)

The specter of nuclear warfare had entered the world of McCarthy's fiction some years earlier. At the end of *The Crossing*, in another quasi-epiphanic moment, Billy Parham witnesses the warhead test at Trinity Site, New Mexico. Waking in the early morning hours to find himself "in the white light of the desert noon," he gazes at the "darkening shapes of [a] cloud" on the horizon, only to return to the "inexplicable darkness" (*CRO* 425–26) and an implacable silence. In the pertinent scene of *The Road*, the concussions, the rose glow in the window, and the shear of light summon the image of nuclear explosions and the resulting mushroom clouds. The absence of power and failure of electronic equipment in the novel could be attributed to the effects of the electromagnetic pulse (EMP) waves a nuclear detonation emits. Other hints strewn throughout the text are more ambiguous. Old newspapers herald "curious news" and "quaint concerns" (*R* 24), yet it is not altogether clear whether they originate in a time shortly before or after the event. The man's presence of mind in saving drinking water in the bathtub right away suggests that the catastrophe itself is not entirely unanticipated, and the hidden subterranean shelter father and son discover recalls the public and private fallout shelters built at the height of the Cold War era.

Yet the single most powerful evocation of a nuclear explosion is the image of the stopped clocks, which are a reminder of the terrible symbolic weight of those clocks and watches halted in their cycle at 8:15 on Monday, August 6, 1945, the morning that "Little Boy" was dropped on the city of Hiroshima. Contemporary photographs of those watches may be the apocalyptic image par excellence of the twentieth century, freezing a moment when history would forever be changed. Time itself seems to have been stopped dead in its tracks, the progress of history and human civilization arrested. Alternatively, both Steven Frye (2009, 169) and Carl James Grindley (12) point out, the fact that the watches of *The Road* stop at 1:17 may hint at the biblical meaning of this event, as Revelation 1:17 details the theophany of Christ to St. John. Again, both conceptions are not essentially at odds, as the gravity of incomprehensible suffering frequently finds humans resorting to the language of religious symbol and metaphor: one recalls Robert Oppenheimer at Trinity Site, quoting the Hindu Bhagavad Gita—"Now I am become Death, the destroyer of worlds"—and once more in his MIT lecture, two years after Hiroshima and Nagasaki, asserting that with the bomb, "physicists have known sin, and this is a knowledge which they cannot lose."[17]

Was Oppenheimer too optimistic? Against the hypothesis of nuclear winter stands the fact that none of the few characters in the novel shows definitive signs of radiation sickness. The bloody cough that shakes the father and is also spread among the traveling marauders—some of whom wear "canister masks" and even a protective "biohazard suit" (*R* 28)—may indicate such illness but is far from conclusive. Doubts thus remain. As John Cant writes: "If this was a post-nuclear holocaust world then ubiquitous radioactivity, especially in the ash and dust, would have long since killed everybody" (268).[18] There does not seem to be a perfect explanation.

Discounting either a religious or man-made catastrophe in general, and nuclear war in particular, Dana Phillips argues for a "cosmic accident," specifically "the entry into the atmosphere of a massive meteor" (2011, 176), which he finds more consistent with the description of the event and has frequently been brought up as a probable scenario. Still, the possibility of a man-made apocalypse resonates strongly within *The Road*.[19] Thus, the father muses that "on this road there are no godspoke men. They are gone and I am left and they have taken with them the world" (*R* 27). Depending on how one interprets McCarthy's neologism "godspoke," the passage suggests the sinister possibility that the fanaticism of religious or political leaders—self-appointed representatives of the will of God—could have been responsible for the cataclysm. Alternatively, it may allude to the decline of faith in an apparently godforsaken world, or perhaps precisely the final failure of religious ethics—the human knowledge of "sin"—in staving off the worst.

Finally, the nature of the catastrophe is less significant than the consequence of life in its aftermath. McCarthy himself stated as much in his interview with the *Wall Street Journal*: "I don't have an opinion. At the Santa Fe Institute I'm with scientists of all disciplines and some of them in geology said it looked like a meteor to them. But it could be anything—volcanic activity or it could be nuclear war" (Jurgensen).[20] Whether or not the cataclysm—religious, environmental, nuclear, or cosmic in origin—was "brought on" or "merely exacerbated by human agency" (Phillips 2011, 176) is entirely within the scope of what Thomas Schaub calls "secular scripture" (153) and what I call syncretic eschatology. In sum, the indeterminacy of the singularity that causes the cataclysm is wholly deliberate, putting the focus instead on living in the end times. As we have seen, those indications that speak for a man-made cataclysm situate *The Road* in the context of the post-Enlightenment humanism. They are in accordance with the theme of escalatory violence that pervades his novels. Both reflect the pessimistic expectation that humans will be "destroying each other before an environmental catastrophe sets in" (Kushner). Hence, we can ask whether the nuclear holocaust scenario is not perhaps less a realistic setting than "a metaphorical explanation for the state of the world that McCarthy creates as his wider metaphor for the condition of man" (Cant 269). Yet how can we conceive of this condition in the literary marriage between theological, scientific, and secular meanings offered in *The Road*? For those truly desperate for a cause, McCarthy's work certainly offers a plethora of possibilities.

The Entropic End of *The Road*

If *The Road* represents McCarthy's return to his earlier work, its strongest referential point is *Blood Meridian*, McCarthy's apocalyptic Western. After all, the state of the world seems like the logical culmination of the developments exposed in the earlier novel. Furthermore, if the violence of *Blood Meridian* presented an astute example of what Girard, via Clausewitz, calls the mimetic law of the escalation to extremes, *The Road* presents the aftermath of this escalation. Though not as frequently as in the earlier novel, the path of father and son is still lined with images of violent death—with terrifying sights such as a frieze of human heads on a wall, immolated corpses on the road, cellars that cannibals have converted into a larder for human livestock, and most horrifically the roasted, half-devoured body of a newborn. Above all, it is the lifeless and grayed-out ashscape of *The Road* that resembles a monochromatic version of *Blood Meridian*'s deadly deserts, expanded to envelop the entire planet. As such, John Beck observes, these deserts are calamitous places charged with meaning:

> The desert reveals the beginning and the end, pre- and post-history, "fear in a handful of dust." Its granules expose the entropic movement of time toward a slow obliteration through erosion. [. . .] Deserts are disastrous places. They suggest an apocalypse that has already happened and which remains unredeemed. Deserts also seem to prefigure some future catastrophe that might befall places of habitation. [. . .] One way or another, deserts signal and invite annihilation. The desert is evidence of cosmic indifference or, worse, of an actual hostility toward human life, a mineral disdain for the vulnerability of the organic. (210)

It is not too hard to imagine the world of *The Road* as a "terra damnata," a "purgatorial waste" that father and son stumble through "like pilgrims exhausted upon the face of the planet Anareta" (*BM* 61, 63, 46).²¹ The effect of these disastrous landscapes and cosmic metaphors is one of paralleling the journey of humanity to the journey of the earth on its course through an indifferent cosmos. What was a figurative truth in *Blood Meridian* has become a literal truth in *The Road*, which exchanges sun-scorched, arenaceous deserts for an all-encompassing wasteland of ashes. Like the slow progress of the bone collectors crossing the buffalo graveyard plains in the epilogue of the earlier novel, the way of father and son here too articulates "the verification of a principle" (*BM* 337). Here, nothing is suggested, nothing prefigured. All has actually come to pass.

In the context of McCarthy's apocalyptic, it makes perfect sense then that Beck mentions the concept of entropy in direct juxtaposition with the apocalypse. Albeit in doing so, he implicitly conjoins two distinct, even contrasting Western traditions of thinking about the end: the first religious, prophetic, dating back more than two thousand years, envisioning the world's history as divinely preordained to end in cataclysmic destruction and subsequent perfection, and dramatizing said vision in narratives of arcane symbolism and revelatory intent; the second secular, scientific, and rather recent, predicting an end without new beginning, and set forth in mathematical equations representing ongoing natural processes the inevitable result of which is a universal tendency toward dissipation and disorder. In fact, Grimm, Faulstich, and Kuon list *entropy* as one of three essential structural motifs of modern apocalyptic literature, the other two being the inescapable *totality* of disaster and its *irreversibility*. But isn't entropy by definition both irreversible and total?

Entropy here means the "disintegration of all systems of governance and order," including "not only political but also social orders, also customs and morals, religion and philosophy" (Grimm, Faulstich, and Kuon 10). Certainly, such a designation fits superficial schematics. However, it is both too drawn-out in metaphoric extension and too removed from the science to detail or even recognize many of the implications present in the best work of a scientifically inclined artist like McCarthy. As with the religious and secular paradigms of "the end"—both of which have received far more critical attention in discussing *The Road*—it is thus worth exploring the physical and informational dimensions of "the entropic end."

To recall, entropy is the central value of the second law of thermodynamics. It measures the unavailability of usable energy within a closed system. Given that the amount of energy in the universe is limited, the inevitable dissipation of energy into unusable heat will eventually deplete all energy and result in a state of thermodynamic equilibrium close to absolute zero, what Helmholtz called the heat death of the universe. Since its formulation in the 1850s, the Second Law has come to represent *the* secular equivalent of the biblical Apocalypse, a scientific fact pertaining to believers as well as agnostics and atheists who formerly could dismiss talk of "the end" as mere religious superstition. What singles out the "entropic end" before other secular cataclysms like nuclear holocaust, global warming, or asteroid collision is that, like Judeo-Christian eschatology, it presents a finite, teleological model of time. Arthur Eddington thus identified entropy as an *arrow of time*. As McCarthy's friend, the physicist and complexity theorist Murray Gell-Mann explains:

The arrow of time is communicated from universe to galaxy to star and
planet. It points forward in time everywhere in the universe. On Earth it
is communicated to the origin of terrestrial life and its evolution and to
the birth and aging of every living thing. Virtually all cases of order in the
universe arise from order in the past and ultimately form the initial condition. That is why the transition from order to the statistically much more
probable disorder tends to proceed everywhere from past to future and not
the other way around. (220)

Like the Christian Apocalypse, the second law projects a universal, irreversible movement toward an end of all life and cosmic order. Unlike its religious
counterpart, it does not envision a new beginning after the end, or rather
the perfected completion of life as everlasting. In *The Road*, the notion of
entropy comes full circle. In the course of the mysterious event that has leveled civilization, the "cultural entropy" John Cant repeatedly speaks of has
approached its maximum. Yet so, too, has the *thermodynamic* entropy of the
physicist.[22] While the former has permeated McCarthy's work from the start
in the shape of social disorder punctuated with the signs of environmental
malaise, it is for the first time in his writing that the latter comes to full
articulation in all its universal consequence.

To begin with, there is the purely physical, or energy-concerned side
of the process: On the level of the individual, the struggle for food reflects
the basic need of the open system of the body to constantly feed on the low
entropy or energy of its surroundings in order to survive. On the global level,
and more fundamentally, we are exposed to the vision of a world that is "cold
and growing colder" day by day (*R* 12). In this cooling world, father and son
travel south in the hope that it might be warmer there. At more than one
instance, the pair is found huddled closely to one another in the deadly cold,
which McCarthy explicitly juxtaposes with the warmth of life. On finding
the hidden shelter, the father heats some water for a bath, which the boy
comments on with a delighted "Warm at last" (*R* 124). And as the father
wakes up in the night, he first seeks out his son in the dark: "He held his hand
to the thin ribs. Warmth and movement. Heartbeat" (*R* 98).

Some earlier drafts of the novel were even more explicit in connecting
warmth and energy consumption, the individual and the planet. A draft page
from the *The Grail* stage of the novel even injects Helmholtz's scenario of

the final heat death of the universe: "The days were growing shorter and the nights longer. The cold of space was pressing down upon them like a weight. Heatdeath. Everything settling out into a deadly repose. The earth itself now feeding upon its own protein. Waiting for a spring that would never come" (91/87/6, 219).[23] In another heavily corrected, abandoned fragment from the *Grail*-draft, the father ponders in equally metaphoric and physical terms that his "heart is cold with a dread that will not dissipate" (91/87/6, n.p.). Recalling the "heatdeath of the soul and of the heart" (91/97/1, n.p.) mentioned in *Whales and Men*, he is thus conceiving of the heart as another organ subject to an entropic force, which is "cold dread." While the deeper meaning of this specific metaphor requires explication, the simple and mundane tenor of *The Road*'s physical imagery could not be clearer: warmth signifies life, but the world itself is approaching the death of heat, and so both life and warmth are rapidly fading away.

The coldness is directly linked to the blanket of ash that shuts out the sun. In turn, the undifferentiation of ash voices the general theme of entropy as disorder.[24] Thus, the father is found awake in the night, contemplating "the cold and the silence. The ashes of the late world carried on the bleak and temporal winds to and fro in the void. Carried forth and scattered [. . .]. Everything uncoupled from its shoring" (R 9–10). The distinction of night and day has become blurry, and so has the distinction between yesterday and tomorrow. As the father explains to his son, there is no past, but at least for him, there is also "no later. This is later" (R 46). If entropy is the arrow of time, then this arrow's flight seems to have entered the final stages in its arc of descent. Even visually, the graying out of the ashen world represents a move toward the diminishment of luminance and color, a photographic reduction in contrast—or difference—that allows for the clear perception of the world. Thus, the icy cold nights are "dark beyond darkness and the days more gray each one than what had gone before. Like the onset of some cold glaucoma dimming away the world" (R 3).

Within the stark gray landscape of the text, it can already be discerned that the exploration of entropy does not exhaust itself in the physical. Watching from McCarthy's apocalyptic panopticon, a second aspect of his entropic vision thus comes into view with the process of informational entropy. Visually, there is manifestly less information than in his earlier works—both in its general, Batesonian description as a difference making a difference, or in its accepted general definition as well-formed and meaningful data. In 1988, Vereen Bell made a statement about McCarthy's work that from today's point of view appears as almost prophetic: "Metaphorically a road is the equivalent of a signifier in language or structure: It points us in a direction and leads us somewhere that could reasonably be anticipated to be a vicinity of meaning. But the roads of McCarthy's novels [...] do not do that" (1). The slow erosion of meaning in a world without order is precisely one of the main themes McCarthy thrusts at his readers in *The Road*.

It is worth considering how meaning might actually be conceived of *without* order. Since the signifying power of language rests upon the orderly, structural arrangement of letters or sounds, words and sentences, expressing entropic disorder in language is by necessity a paradoxical undertaking. To communicate disorder, the language has to be disorderly, yet the more disorderly it gets, the less it communicates. Nevertheless, because entropy is measured comparatively as the product of the progress from one state to another, *The Road* comes comparatively close: the novel's sparse, economic language is a far cry from the baroque Faulknerian omnipotence of language aspired to in McCarthy's earlier works, and still a reduction from the more Hemingwayesque style of the Border Trilogy. Structurally, all of McCarthy's novels prior to *The Road* were construed of chapters or textually motivated sections arranged into larger thematic parts. In comparison, the narrative of *The Road* is composed exclusively as a succession of short passages separated by huge spaces and shifting in perspective between a third-person narrator and the father's free indirect discourse, its linear progress in present tense broken up with infrequent glimpses into past and future.

Looking at the operative level of language and composition, the effect of McCarthy's choices here can be related to the aesthetic principle of *optical democracy* that characterized the prose of his early work and was consciously formulated in *Blood Meridian*. Yet whereas before, the paratactic leveling of elements was one of nouns, verbs, phrases, and clauses within a sentence, it is now one of whole sentences and even paragraphs, giving the whole an increasingly homogeneous, and—temporally speaking—eternally "present" kind of form. Essentially, while the novel's low level of structuration mirrors the itinerary nature of its protagonists' journey, it also reflects a comparative entropic lack of order in the way it is composed. Here, too, we have an escalation of trends to disorder.

Thematically, the loss of meaning is addressed directly as father and son come across "signs in gypsy language, lost patterns" (*R* 153) they cannot read, and billboards advertising goods that no longer exist. In terms of Shannon's mathematical theory of communication, one can still regard some of these artifacts as *information*, yet they certainly do not transmit any meaning to the pair. And while some markers, like a grisly array of heads on a wall, become significant as signs of warning, what signifiers of the lost world remain generally assume the character of *noise*. Or else, they are as the music the boy plays on the flute his father made, "a formless music for the age to come. Or perhaps the last music on earth called up from out of the ashes of its ruin" (*R* 66). Looking at their old road map, the father explains to the son that the state roads belonged to "what used to be called the states" (*R* 36) but cannot explain what happened to them. Maps in McCarthy's fiction are usually regarded as "simplifications that cannot signify the full complexity and variation of the changing world," as Cant points out, but the map father and son use represents "not much less than exists in the world, but now much more. It is the world that will not suffice" (275–76).

Assuming in Brillouin's terms that the entropy of a system is inversely proportional to the information it offers, and that the ruined civilization of *The Road* approaches maximum entropy, the information it offers approaches a minimum as the potential for human agency diminishes. Just as there is nothing to see through the man's binoculars from the hill in the river valley, there is—in a distinct echo of the famous antidramatic opening line of Samuel Beckett's *Waiting for Godot*—"nothing to be done" about the shopping cart's wonky wheels (*R* 7, 12). Simultaneously, taking a cue from Shannon, one could say that as the system's entropy irreversibly increases, the information needed to describe it grows proportionately to keep an overview, and that father and son simply cannot keep up with this demand. In this regard, their position is not unlike that of the readers, who lack a clear explanation of the event that set off the entropic runaway, and who are similarly confronted with the interpretive task, to cite Frank Kermode, "of making sense of the ways we"—writers, poets, artists, and humans in general—"make sense of our lives" (3).

Other reminders of "the richness of a vanished world" (*R* 117) punctuate the novel: golden Krugerrands, a grand piano in a decrepit manor, flower seeds the father takes with him against his better judgment. Most notable is a beautiful sextant he finds on the wreck of a ship that surrounded by the bones of seabirds and dead fish, is ironically named *Pájaro de Esperanza*, recalling the bordello Esperanza del Mundo in *Cities of the Plain*. After investigating the sextant, the father decides to put it back into its case and leave it behind. In the new world, it has no use because the celestial bodies, former points of orientation and symbols of the order of the cosmos, are hidden from sight. In this manner, McCarthy is laying a finger into the wounds of the information age, as his artifacts dramatize Jean-Pierre Dupuy's diagnosis that "ours is a world about which we pretend to have more and more *information* but which seems to us increasingly devoid of meaning" (1980, 3).

In particular, it is the entropic paradigm that charts the depths of this void of meaning in confronting the common death. Maps, phonebooks, advertisements, states—to be sure, these are signifiers without referents and thus increasingly without signifieds (Woodson 2008, 92). Yet a purely semiotic reading fails to grasp the totality both of the poetics of the unified field and of McCarthy's overall apocalyptic, wherein the entropic erosion of meaning constitutes but a part, albeit an important one.[25] Consequently, if one had to choose a single passage dramatizing the full extent of the state of the world in *The Road*, it would have to be this one:

> The world shrinking down about a raw core of parsible entities. The *names of things* slowly following those things into oblivion. Colors. The names of birds. Things to eat. Finally the names of things one believed to be true. More fragile than he would have thought. How much was gone already? The *sacred idiom shorn of its referents* and so of its *reality*. Drawing down *like something trying to preserve heat*. In time to wink out forever. (*R* 75)

In this passage, the full extent of McCarthy's syncretic eschatology is revealed in condensed form: the fall of a planet "trying to preserve heat" and "eating its own protein" against the scientific prognosis of approaching heat death, the catastrophic fall of civilization exposed in in all of its cultural fragility, and the spiritual abyss of meaning opening up before the last survivors as systems of meaning crumble—all these phenomena are inseparable from one another. In the philosophy and aesthetics of *The Road*, thermodynamic, cultural, and informational entropy form a programmatic (w)hole with its religious and secular apocalyptics.

The Salitter Drying, or Entropy and Mystic Panentheism

In the cold light of entropy, *The Road* easily appears as a product of McCarthy's keen scientific interest and the nihilist cosmology some readers still see at work in his novels. Once we widen the angle to be more receptive of McCarthy's syncretism, though, a narrow-minded scientism only makes for as impoverished an interpretation as do readings of *The Road* as a traumatic validation of "one's cynicism, skepticism, and nihilism" (Phillips 2011, 184). For one, such readings fail to seriously engage the theological concerns *The Road* is demonstrably invested with: all prayers to and curses of the divinity, all residue of Christian imagery amount to no more than the deluded, if all-too-human projections of a despairing father who has lost the world. So the novel's investigation of theodicy is certainly off the table. At the same time, the philosophical one-two punch of an indifferent *and* deterministic cosmos also excludes or at least curtails severely the potential for human agency prevalent in the more secular-humanist apocalypses. In conclusion, the end of the world is no more than "simply the end" (Phillips 2011, 188). *The Road*, then, leads nowhere remotely interesting.

Self-affirmatively nihilist exegesis thus programmatically precludes the possibility of redemptive readings, making of *The Road* but a "form of cosmic irony" (Phillips 2011, 188). Yet in declaring both religious and secular humanist perspectives void, such readings ironically presuppose the same one-dimensional framework that sustains the naïve apocalypticism they discredit. While on point in their critique of it, they miss the mark when it comes to foisting that framework onto McCarthy's fiction in the first place, if only to debunk it. Of course, one should neither confuse the religious dimension of his writing with a firm belief in or allegiance to any one specific creed. Given the democratic plurality of systems of knowledge and belief that McCarthy is interested in—some of which I have discussed in these pages—this short exchange between White and Black in *The Sunset Limited* makes for a plausible approximation of his view of religious doctrine and Christian orthodoxy:

White   Are you a heretic? [...]

Black   No more than what a man should be. Even a man with a powerful
        belief. I aint a doubter. But I am a questioner.

White   What's the difference?

Black   Well, I think the questioner wants the truth. The doubter wants to
        be told there aint no such thing. (67)

McCarthy's interview with Oprah Winfrey points in the same direction: Asked whether he had "worked the God thing out," McCarthy answered in sibylline fashion: "It would depend on what day you asked me. But sometimes it's good to pray. I don't think you have to have a clear idea of who or what God is in order to pray. You can even be quite doubtful about the whole business" (2007a). The problem with either—the widespread superficially apocalyptic reading of *The Road* and its negation—is a shared adherence to scriptural literalism and orthodoxy that would exchange a strawman for McCarthy's complex, "heretical" spirituality.

Singularly, all three—the straightforward apocalyptic, the purely scientific, and the purely secular-humanist reading—disregard the reflexivity and poetic adaptability of those systems of meaning and knowledge through which humans engage with the world and that are explicitly at stake in *The Road*. Of the latter, there is no example more suited to illustrate this than McCarthy's inclusion of obscure mystic thought, which coalesces with modern conceptions regarding entropy. Consider this moment of reflection:

> He walked out into the road and stood. The silence. The salitter drying from the earth. The mudstained shapes of flooded cities burned to the waterline. At a crossroads a ground set with dolmen stones where the spoken bones of oracles lay moldering. No sound but the wind. What will you say? A living man spoke these lines? He sharpened a quill with his small pen knife to scribe these things in sloe or lampblack? At some reckonable and entabled moment? He is coming to steal my eyes. To seal my mouth with dirt. (*R* 220)

The scene occurs close to the end of the book and poetically foreshadows the approaching death of the man. If not of dolmen stones, a grave will be made aside the road for him before long. McCarthy's words here assume an oracular quality. At the same time, it is not easy to make a clear cut between the musings of the man and those of the narrator. Both thematically and stylistically, the prose presents a self-referential commentary on the act of writing, which in a book such as *The Road* assumes the shape of prophecy. But perhaps the reference above is neither to McCarthy himself nor John of Patmos, but to another writer?

What comes to the fore is the obscure term *salitter*. In its usage, McCarthy adopts a concept of another "heretic"—the German shoemaker and mystic Jakob Böhme (1575–1624), whose *Six Theosophical Points* he had already quoted in *Blood Meridian*.[26] Providing a piece of the puzzle that is McCarthy's reading (of) the world, Böhme's thought warrants a more than cursory look. Phrased in a highly symbolic language, his spiritual thought collates cosmology, anthroposophy, theosophy, and christosophy through an appropriation of alchemy, Copernican heliocentrism, Paracelsianism, and Renaissance Neoplatonism (Principe and Weeks). Yet Böhme's driving force was mystical experience. The shoemaker of Görlitz believed he could glimpse an image of heavenly creation in imperfect, yet still divinely infused earthly forms. The result was an idiosyncratic Weltanschauung that often overlaps with, but is never fully congruent with, either orthodox Christianity or modern scientific concepts.

In *Aurora, oder Die Morgenröte im Aufgang*, Böhme, presumably inspired by the ongoing alchemical discussion of nitre (i.e., saltpeter) and other substances, designated *salitter*—varyingly spelled "salniter" and "salnitter"—as a divine *and* earthly substance, a sort of sap infusing all living things. Paradoxically, it contains at once "the seed of the entire godhood," and is simultaneously akin to "a mother who receives the seed and continually bears fruit"—specifically "the beautiful and lovely fruit of life" (1992, chap. 11.47, 212). Differently put, salitter is the "total force of the divinity, the compendium of all forces operating in nature and in the human psyche [. . .] the embodiment of a world conceived in organic terms" (Principe and Weeks 53).[27] Certainly, this is an appealing concept for a unified field approach of viewing the world, especially for a writer of diversified interests and heretic inclination.

Significantly, Böhme's panentheist cosmology differs from both the Manichean dualism of the Gnostics and the inclusive pantheist equation of God and the world: "Böhme could not have accepted Spinoza's *Deus sive natura*" (Wehr 1971, 91).[28] Concomitantly, the divine substance of *salitter* pervades multiple dimensions of the cosmos. In *Aurora*, the latter is identified with the "spoken" or "exhaled word" and is divided into at least three "natural" parturitions (Ger. *Geburt*). The geography or hierarchy of these parturitions is not easy to grasp, as they pertain to the world of matter as much as to that of the spirit. The first, "outermost parturition" is that of the material world as *physis*. The second is the so-called "sidereal parturition," which Böhme envisions as creating (biological) life within the first parturition and which represents the biosphere according to Wehr (1992, 39). Finally, the third "innermost parturition" is that of "the holy life," which exists between the other two and "stands in the power of love" (Böhme 1992, chap. 19.63). It is within this "center"—accessible solely through the spirit— that God is at once hidden and present (Böhme 1992, chap. 19.65), creating everything through the generative principle of "the speaking word" of which the "spoken word" of the other parturitions are iterations.[29]

It is from a doubly informed entropic and mystical position that the full weight of George Monbiot's praise of *The Road* as "the most important environmental book ever written" (2007) can fully be brought to bear. As man and boy cross through a field of weeds, the fixed forms of burned plants "fell to dust about them" (*R* 6). Later, they come to a "vast low swale where ferns and hydrangeas and wild orchids lived on in ashen effigies which the wind had not yet reached" (*R* 232). Formerly complex organic systems are reduced to granules of ashes, deadened and to be scattered by the wind. The earth of the novel is a planet that has apparently "lost its ability to reproduce life" (Palmer 65). According to James Lovelock, the measure of the latter is nothing else than its ability to reduce entropy: "Life is the paradoxical contradiction to the second law, which states that everything is, always has been, and always will be running down to equilibrium and death" (Lovelock 2000a, 23). Intriguingly, Lovelock's Gaia theory might be conceived as a scientific continuation and spiritual successor of Böhme's mystic vision. Whereas the geoscientist from Hertfordshire envisioned Gaia as a kind of superorganism we are all a part of, "a feedback or cybernetic system which seeks an optimal physical and chemical environment for life on this planet" (2000b, 10) by keeping it in homeostasis, the shoemaker from Görlitz envisioned his *salitter* as both a divine and mundane substance, constituting a "matrix of forces that generate life and awareness" and that, notably, "preserved the order of the cosmos" (Principe and Weeks 54).

Whether one puts the stress on the ability to sustain life or cosmic order, the association with the second law is close at hand. One might say that the ash-enveloped earth of *The Road* has for all intents and purposes become a closed system, unable to receive energy in the form of the warming rays of the sun that is now "banished" and "circles the earth like a grieving mother with a lamp" (*R* 28). As the Second Law describes, the entropy of such a system approaches a maximum at thermal equilibrium. Thus, it foretells of a time beyond time when the last star will have burned up and the universe will be all cold and darkness, "the very life" of which—Böhme is cited in one of *Blood Meridian*'s epigraphs—"are death and dying." Time is considered on a cosmic scale, measurable so long as things can yet move, though it be in the direction of disintegration, like an old train father and son happen upon, "decomposing for all eternity" (*R* 152).

With everything approaching the microscopic undifferentiation of dust, the man wonders whether the world's destruction will finally reveal "how it was made. Oceans, mountains. The ponderous counterspectacle of things ceasing to be. The sweeping waste, hydroptic and coldly secular. The silence" (*R* 231). What McCarthy may be offering here is thus another, scientific twist on the apocalyptic motif of Revelation in the observation of things falling apart, losing their order and structural integrity.[30] Yet what "truth" is it that the father glimpses and that now threatens to close the book of history?

> He walked out in the gray light and stood and he saw for a brief moment the absolute truth of the world. The cold relentless circling of the interstate earth. Darkness implacable. The blind dogs of the sun in their running. The crushing black vacuum of the universe. And somewhere two hunted animals trembling like groundfoxes in their cover. Borrowed time and borrowed world and borrowed eyes with which to sorrow it. (*R* 110)

The scientific twist here would be that there is no transcendental meaning nor hope of renewal. The entropic end is finally cold, secular, and absolute—or so it would seem. Writing about *Suttree*, Cawelti defined the world of

McCarthy as that of scientific rather than religious millennialism. "McCarthy views human life from the perspective of eternity, yet his version of eternity is the cosmic, geological, and biological immensity that derives from a purely naturalistic vision of the universe" (169). *The Road*, certainly, articulates this view in the concept of entropy and death as physical absolutes. Still, it would be a mistake to subsume all eschatology into it.

Ultimately, the eschatological blending, in this case of thermodynamics with seventeenth-century mysticism, offers a number of parallels in creating a more biocentric field of vision relating science and spirituality. It comes to a head though in the place, or rather the nonplace (Gk. *oú-topos*), assigned to metaphysics. To McCarthy's apocalyptic, Böhme's ideas prove illuminating in at least two ways, one of which will only come to the fore in the final part of this analysis. Thomas Schaub rightly points out that the drying of the salitter is yet another sign of withering life and casually speculates that it may express "the intensification of withdrawal from the earth of that divine immanence that Thoreau wrote of as the continual 'drenching of the reality that surrounds us'" (161). Demonstrably, *The Road* "links the possibility of the sacred to the existence of referents" (Schaub 155). Yet the text goes further, provided one takes seriously the consequences of panentheism, which offers a route out of the impasse between scientism and orthodoxy.

As Edwin Arnold has demonstrated, Böhme's conception of a divine matrix in his *Mysterium Magnum* (1623) constitutes a mystical substrate in the philosophical outlook of *The Crossing* as either the original substance or network of forces in existence. Like the salitter of which it is composed, the matrix suggests "the basic unity and interdependence of all elements," the fundamental insight being that "all forms hold an aspect of God, a divinity, within" (Arnold 2002b, 218, 222). In Böhme's vision, one thus finds a spiritual complement to McCarthy's artistic syncretism and the unified poetic field.

We might rightly, in fact, identify McCarthy as a mystical writer himself, a spiritual author who venerates life in all its forms, who believes in a source of being and order deeper than that manifested in outward show and pretense of human individuality, and who acknowledges the inevitability of death not as absurdity or tragedy but as meaningful transition from one plane of existence to another. (Arnold 2002b, 216)

The withering of the salitter as imagined by the father, then, aligns with Ely's notion of God dying with the last of men. Read this way, the death of world and humanity are less a sign of divine withdrawal than of the death of God. Unlike the death of God proclaimed by Ely or else in Nietzsche's *Die fröhliche Wissenschaft*, which referred to the decay of all systems that brought order and meaning to existence, this death assumes a more literal, organic shape. The world of *The Road*, in this sense, seems a place where God—understood as a divine substance and bonding agent that connects every living being, the all to the one and the one to the all, in short, the embodiment of life itself—may be in his death throes.

Certainly, to the religious mind, this possibility is infinitely more unsettling than anything in Revelation. There is, however, the caveat of confusing pantheism with panentheism. Formulating a partial answer to his own concerns with the problem of evil, Böhme believed the salitter of earth and the divine force of creation it embodies are corrupted from the start, even murdered through "wrath"—and so the earth is "burnt, frozen, drowned, and ossified" (1992, chap. 19.62, 372). Certainly, this is as good a description of the world of *The Road* as any. But in Böhme, the corruption pertains to the earth as pure *physis*, to the "outermost parturition" or layer of existence. It is the innermost parturition—that is, the center of the divinity—that extends the apocalyptic promise of resurrection: "For the earth will come alive again, because the godhood has born it anew in Christ" (1992, chap. 19.64, 372). Depending on how far Böhme's influence truly goes and complements the other aspects of McCarthy's apocalypse, there may thus be a chance for renewal. Still, if McCarthy tells us one thing, it is that piety alone, even a heretical piety, will not suffice.

What Do You Do Now?
Ethics in the Ruins of the Future

In the records of literary criticism, there is a certain "illness" that is sometimes diagnosed as ailing the highest echelons of the art. This is the illness of the "unworthy ending," that is, an ending that in what is otherwise considered a masterpiece, seems underwhelming and mundane, or worse yet, inconsistent and artificial. Great writers like Miguel de Cervantes, Stendhal, and Fyodor Dostoevsky were each, at various times, deemed misguided for ending their great novels with conclusions that all-too-often appeared as banal, forcibly conformist, and overly pious (*DDN* 291–94). Similarly, no passage of *The Road* has generated as much controversy as its twofold, multilayered ending. In turn, the ending seems to have colored the critical perception of *The Road* as a potential final entry in McCarthy's life's work, and an uncharacteristically gentle and even uplifting one at that. Mystified, one may ask with René Girard why otherwise accomplished novelists should consciously "disfigure the final pages of their masterpieces," and whether there is not perhaps a certain "unity displayed in novelistic conclusions" (*DDN* 292–93) that vexes the eyes of the critics. In the case of *The Road*, matters are complicated further for there being two endings.

A Problem of Two Endings and the Journey toward Death

The journey of father and son concludes with the son's admission into a new family, three days after the man's death. To some readers, this ending appears as a deus ex machina, starkly out of tune with all that has gone before, or else may ring hollow as in the dying world of *The Road*, this sudden resolution seems at best a temporary stay of the inevitable. Others may suspect that in the last pages of what could have been his last novel, moved by the experience of fatherhood in the autumn of his own life, McCarthy finally shied away from the darkness that his own incantations have summoned.[31] Following the conclusion to the narrative proper is a second ending or coda. The coda presents readers with the image that opened this study: an image of brook trout in mountain streams whose backs are "maps of the world in its becoming [. . .]. Of a thing which could not be put back. Not be made right again" (*R* 241). At first sight, the coda subverts all potential for hope there may be in the novel's proper conclusion. For a discussion of *The Road* to be reasonably complete, both of these problematic endings need to be addressed. I will begin with the second, the coda.

Interpretations of the trout's significance have produced a wide spectrum of responses. This spectrum ranges from fatalistic assertions of life's futility against the looming certainty of death, to a more optimistic belief in the possibility of new beginnings, to admonitory calls for a more environmentally sustainable and socially conscious behavior in the here and now.[32] McCarthy's comment to Winfrey on what he wanted his readers to take from *The Road* may indeed point toward the more moralistic and politically inclined interpretations: "Life is pretty damn good, even when it looks bad, and we should appreciate it more. We should be grateful" (2007a). To be sure, these words need not be taken as the gospel of interpretation, as some critics also deem any redemptive interpretations as misreadings in which the coda itself features as a literary decision that, on McCarthy's part, had better been avoided for inviting just such misreadings. So the trout coda remains ambiguous.

The validity of any interpretation of the passage hinges on its diegetic or extradiegetic status, on whether it is read as pertaining to the world of McCarthy's tale or the world of the reader. In the latter case, the coda confronts us with our abuse of the planet, the consequences of which we now begin to see and that will be visited in full only upon future generations. The coda thus becomes a call to action, to change the way we interact with the world, lest we pass the point of no return. McCarthy's intent as stated to Winfrey may be that "you should be thankful for what you have," yet he also admits that "I don't know who to be grateful to" (2007a). The agnostic position he adopts thus points us to the diegetic dimension. There, interpretation would seem to depend upon whether one reads the coda through the secular, entropic, or apocalyptic lens. Whether we deem life doomed to fade away, or extend a modest hope that "the earth will come alive again" as promised by Böhme and biblical eschatology, is dependent on the interpretive framework chosen.

Yet, as I have argued, in exploring the cataclysmic terrains of McCarthy's imagination, readers are well advised to chart the course of that apocalyptic journey by a map of equally spiritual, worldly, and scientific coordinates. In *The Road* as much as elsewhere, the dynamic force that propels all movement through the text is the dialectic of the confrontation and evasion of death. Even small details suggest this theme. In what has to be one of the shortest episodes in the early stage of the pair's journey, the son is found playing with a yellow toy truck he eventually places upon the tarp of their shopping cart (*R* 30). In a book visually dominated by the color gray, this otherwise fairly mundane moment is the more remarkable for its colorful rarity. Still, if not outright overlooked, the toy is likely to be deemed insignificant. To readers familiar with German poetry, though, the yellow color and placement of this truck upon the tarp of the cart may evoke Rudolf Baumbach's 1879 poem "Der Wagen rollt."[33] Unbeknownst to most Germans, who are likely more familiar with the 1920s *volkslied*-adaptation "Hoch auf dem gelben Wagen," Baumbach's poem functions as an allegory of life's progress toward death in the narrative frame of a journey atop a yellow stagecoach that for all of life's beauty, will not stop rolling toward its final destination.

Like the poem, *The Road* emerges as less of a realistic than an allegorical treatment of the existential issue par excellence. To convey it, McCarthy could hardly have chosen a better vehicle than the journey form, which perfectly suits the apocalyptic context. One of its types that has made its appearance in previous chapters but that I have avoided discussing here is that of the journey of initiation. Following the ritual stages of exit, transition, and reentry, initiation spatializes an internal development that often entails a loss of innocence through experience gained, especially, in confrontation of death. This confrontation may result in the symbolic rebirth or conversion of the initiate into some higher social order or spiritual stage of being (Freese 2015, 46). What emerges here is the structural twin-motif of revelation and conversion. Just like initiation, apocalypse entails a stage of transition and the unveiling of a profound, life-altering truth. In both cases, revelation leads to transformation—death and rebirth, destruction and restoration—ending in a perfected condition, which is what the process, in either case, is finally about. Whereas apocalypse encompasses the world at large, initiation elevates the individual, but in realizing both *as a journey*, McCarthy merges the static, panoptic, and quasi-divine perspective of the prophet with the mobile, immersed, and thus limited experience of the individual in passage.[34]

Incidentally, "deathbed conversion" is precisely the common thematic denominator of those great novels praised for their plots, characters, psychological or philosophical depth, and overall artistry, yet criticized for their conventional and forced conclusions. Frequently, the latter find the moribund protagonists renounce those ideals, dreams, and desires that formerly put them at odds with the world, and instead have the characters embrace it. This is true of Cervantes's *Don Quixote*, Stendhal's *The Red and the Black*, and several Dostoevsky novels. Frequently, the symbolism of the experience is a religious one. Relating conversion *and* initiation to the unity of conclusions in these works, Girard posits:

In reality, no purely intellectual process and no experience of a purely philosophical nature can secure the individual the slightest victory over mimetic desire and its victimage delusions. [. . .] The other experience, the conversion experience of the truly great writer [. . .], always retains the form of the great religious experiences. These can be shown to be all alike, whatever religion provides their framework. This experience can be picked up in the sacrificial framework of primitive religious institutions, where it forms what we refer to as initiation. It is always a question of breaking out of mimetic desire with its perpetual states of crisis, a question of escaping from the violence of doubles and the exasperating illusion of subjective difference in order to reach (through a kind of identification with the deity, particularly with his power of intercession) an ordered world defined in terms of a lesser violence, even if that is a sacrificial violence. (*TH* 399–400)

As I have shown, McCarthy's entire work is characterized by a deep awareness of the structures of the escalating *violentropy* of mimetic desire, its victims, and its apocalyptic consequences. Violence itself has long passed its zenith in *The Road*. Its results—real or metaphorical—are ubiquitous and plain to see. What remains to be seen, however, is whether McCarthy's conclusion—the last word that (discounting his one-off screenplay) he had put to the published page in sixteen years—bears out Girard's notion of the great, novelistic conclusion as well, and what interpretation the syncretic framework yields as to its implications.

Approaching the twin motif of revelation and conversion naïvely, two questions come to the fore in the context of eschatological syncretism and literary form: The first question is what "truth" it actually *is* that is "revealed" in *The Road*. Is it the naturalistic theme of man's base nature that emerges once the veneer of civilization is stripped away, that is, the revelation of an essential evil? Is it, more abstractly, a sociological and ecological accounting of that sacrificial escalation of *violentropy* seen in *Blood Meridian*, dispassionately documenting "how the world was made" in the "counterspectacle of things ceasing to be" (*R* 231)? After all, Linda Woodson rightly argues that McCarthy's narrative specifically "dismantles those human creations designed to avoid the truth of death, that which is created as a hold against death's inevitability" (2008, 91–92). From this view, all human endeavor appears vain and futile. Is McCarthy's revelation, therefore, simply the mere fact of death itself, or differently put, "the ultimate challenge of cosmic insignificance" (Cant 269) that arises in death's contemplation? Certainly, the moribund father's sudden assailment by "the absolute truth of the world" in the "crushing black vacuum of the universe" (*R* 216) can be read this way. The second question follows naturally from the first: In light of whatever revelation or initiation, what does conversion actually entail?

Theodicy and Anthropodicy

At a closer look, the choice between apocalypse and entropy finds its sublation within the syncretic framework. The discussion has shown that *The Road* supports both readings. It unifies them in its biocentric fusion of heretic mysticism and Lovelockian systems theory. Even if interpretation comes down wholly on the side of cold, secular scientism and the second law, not all is finally dark and gray, as the promise of unpredictable potentialities implicit in chaos theory and Prigogine's dissipative structures provide the legitimate hope that "self-organization can produce local order" (Gell-Mann 230). Even discounting such possibility, there is finally no denying the existence of "temporary islands of decreasing entropy in a world in which the entropy as a whole tends to increase" (Wiener 36). What does the formation of a new family at the end of the novel represent, if not just such an island with its own new order and small wealth of possibilities?[35]

That this island may be temporary does in no way preclude or constrain its significance. The centrality of human connections, of which the relation between father and son is one and that of the new family is another, points straight back to the earlier intuition that for all its preoccupation with death and apocalyptic issues, the end is not what *The Road* is finally about. Our thoughts may return to the wreck of the *Pájaro de Esperanza*, whose name and image may very well encompass the best that we, following the Kantian question, can hope for in the apocalyptic time. In the words of Norbert Wiener, the father of cybernetics: "In a very real sense we are shipwrecked passengers on a doomed planet. Yet even in a shipwreck, human decencies and human values do not necessarily vanish, and we must make the most of them. We shall go down, but let it be in a manner to which we may look forward as worthy of our dignity" (40).

Every road may end in death, as White professes in *The Sunset Limited* (137), yet that simple truth is not itself "the road," nor does the destination determine the meaning of the journey. Rather, the very image of the road begs the second, operative question of *life*—specifically, of *how to live*. So, again: If initiation leads to conversion, what, exactly, is the outcome of that conversion in the eschatological context? The telos of this question is an ethical one. Similarly, the reaction to cosmic insignificance, provided one accepts its validity as absolute, ought to be much like Sartre's answer to Ivan's famous question in another apocalyptic work and influence of McCarthy's, Dostoevsky's *The Brothers Karamazov*: If God were absent from the universe, all existence meaningless and everything permitted, such would be the starting point rather than the end of ethical inquiry.[36] What is more, this existentialist view of the human condition already presupposes a certain view of the deity as well. Both views must be questioned in the unified system of religious, scientific, and worldly eschatologies.

Such are the contested relations at the heart of McCarthy's apocalypse, the consequences of which must now be spelled out. Slavoj Žižek's contextual summary of Revelation in the light of the Crucifixion and Hiroshima provides a starting point:

As with Predestination, which condemns us to frantic activity, the Event is a *pure-empty-sign*, and we have to work to generate its meaning. Therein resides the terrible *risk of revelation*: what "Revelation" means is that God took upon himself the risk of putting everything at stake, of fully "engaging himself existentially" by way, as it were, of [. . .] exposing himself to the utter contingency of existence. True Openness is not that of undecidability, but that of living in the aftermath of the Event, of drawing out the consequences—of what? Precisely of the new space opened up by the Event. [. . .] the apocalyptic time is precisely the time of this indefinite postponement [. . .]: in some sense, we are already dead, since the catastrophe is already here, casting its shadow from the future—after Hiroshima, we cannot any longer play the simple humanist game of the choice we have [. . .]. Once the catastrophe has happened, we lose the innocence of such a position, we can only (indefinitely, maybe) postpone its happening again. (Žižek and Gunjević, 39–40, 70)

McCarthy's syncretic vision is his way of "adopting the properly apocalyptic stance [...] to keep a cool head" (71). While Žižek's "Event" refers specifically to the Crucifixion, which in both orthodoxy and mimetic theory demarcates the beginning of the end times, his techno-secular reconceptualization of the event through "the bomb" and its characterization as "pure-empty-sign" that compels us to "draw out the consequences" encompasses in full the interpretive openness of the catastrophe in *The Road*. This openness only begins with the catastrophe. Yet drawing out the consequences is no simple game, humanist or other. It is both a literary and literal endgame. It depends on the realization that like the man's suicidal wife, the human species is a "creation perfectly evolved to meet its own end" (*R* 50).[37]

What needs spelling out are the ethical consequences of living in the end times. As to the event's nature, McCarthy himself put it summarily and plainly: "It is not really important. The whole thing now is, what do you do?" (Jurgensen). This is precisely the position the father finds himself in. Constantly coughing blood, he is marked by death. Since his is the focal point of the novel, readers share in his experience as well. In his mind, the cold and gray reality of the present is constantly juxtaposed with the dreams and memories of a warm and colorful past—the world of the reader. All but for his son, his loss could not be more complete. The nadir of his existence is the suicide of his wife. While readers' sympathies may lie with the man, they should at least consider that in the world of *The Road* her choice is arguably a perfectly rational one. After all, the couple's final discussion shows her decisively dismantling all of his arguments for perseverance by pointing to its certain outcome:

> You cant protect us. You say you would die for us but what good is that? I'd take him with me if it werent for you. You know I would. It's the right thing to do.
> You're talking crazy.
> No, I'm speaking the truth. Sooner or later they will catch us and they will kill us. They will rape me. They'll rape him. They are going to rape

> us and kill us and eat us and you wont face it. You'd rather wait for it to
> happen. But I cant. I cant. [. . .] We used to talk about death, she said. We
> dont any more. Why is that?
>
> I dont know.
>
> It's because it's here. There's nothing left to talk about. [. . .] You have
> no argument because there is none. (R 47–49)

Monolithic as its influence stands, in relating eschatology to human relations, there are biblical texts more suited to reflect on *The Road* than the book of Revelation. The small apocalypses of the synoptic Gospels each feature passages directly preceding the Last Supper and Crucifixion, in which Jesus gives account of the end times (Mt. 24, Mk. 13, Lk. 21). Among the typical apocalyptic symbols—a darkened sun, falling stars, earthquakes, and famines—these passages markedly shift the focus from cosmic omens to human relations. So, in striking contrast to Revelation, Jesus speaks *not* of a war of God against man but of war among human nations, the decline of law and social institutions, the rise of hatred and the murderous breakup of family units—in short, the encompassing destructuration and internecine violence that characterizes the mimetic crisis and its escalation to extremes.

A special warning goes out to "women who are pregnant and for those nursing infants in those days! Pray that your flight may not happen in winter" (Mt. 24:19–20). One cannot but think of the fate of the mother in the ashen winter-world of *The Road*. The Gospels promise salvation to those who remain true and endure to the end. Yet this is no option for the mother. As Erik Wielenberg has convincingly argued (11–14), it is less the tribulations and hopelessness of the situation than her having lost all human connection to both her husband and her son that drives her to suicide: "My heart was ripped out of me the night he was born" (R 47), she says, and professes that the man's begging and crying do not mean anything to her. After years of coping daily with fear and privation, a final conversation fails to inspire a new reason to carry on. She departs without saying goodbye. Like the man and many a McCarthy character, she labors in "the heatdeath of the soul and heart," which has reached the maximum of what she could bear, leaving only the "coldness" of her decision as a "final gift" to father and son (R 49).

While perhaps not without its own points of friction, the application of revelation and entropy to social relations in the end times resonates powerfully. Even on a purely textual level, as before in *Blood Meridian* or *The Sunset Limited*, the conflict is set up as one between a truth that kills and a saving lie or illusion. Weakened to the breaking point by hunger, the boy suspects his father might be lying when he tells him that "we're not dying" (*R* 85–86). The father's claim that "everything depended on reaching the coast" is equally illusory, all of it "empty and no substance to it" (*R* 25). Even so, these fictions are an essential prerequisite of survival. Time and again, the man is close to desperation when he has to consider the necessity of killing his son in order to save him from a worse fate. After shooting a cannibal marauder who had surprised them in the woods and attacked the son, father and son are on the run from the man's companions: "A single round left in the revolver. You will not face the truth. You will not" (*R* 58).

The wife's "truth" is fully revealed in what is perhaps the most singularly horrific and eye-opening scene in uncovering the depths of all-too-human inhumanity. Close to the edge of starvation, father and son investigate the latched cellar of a seemingly abandoned house. A hideous smell pervades the air, and then they see it: a group of people, huddled and naked, one man on a mattress with half of his legs missing and the stumps burned to prevent bleeding out. The cellar is a larder where humans are kept to be killed and devoured, piece by piece. Moments later, they are on the run from the returning cannibals, powerless to answer the captives' pleas for rescue: "Help us, they whispered. Please help us" (*R* 93). Once again, the father is dreadfully close to "facing the truth":

> This is the moment. This is the moment. [. . .] Can you do it? When the time comes? When the time comes there will be no time. Now is the time. Curse God and die. What if it doesnt fire? It has to fire. What if it doesnt fire? Could you crush that beloved skull with a rock? Is there such a being within you of which you know nothing? Can there be? Hold him in your arms. Just so. The soul is quick. Pull him toward you. Kiss him. Quickly. (*R* 96)

The sequence of events pertains to two levels: the first is a purely human level, circumscribed by the actual (not just symbolic) objectification of other humans implied by cannibalism; the second is the level that relates humans to God. The conflict there is the same that is brought up in conversation with Ely. It is the same that is implied when in *Child of God*, Lester Ballard is called "so grievous a case against the gods" (188), and that Judge Holden asks in *Blood Meridian*: "If God meant to interfere in the degeneracy of mankind would he not have done so by now?" (147). Yet the father is neither Ballard nor the Judge. He is a latter-day Job. Like Job's, his answer to immense suffering is the embrace, or perhaps rather a desperate leap of faith when he has every reason to "curse God, and die" (Jb. 2:9). Perhaps he is worse off than Job, for like Abraham, he faces the terrible possibility of having to sacrifice his son: not *to* God, but to spare him from worse.

In depicting immeasurable loss and its dehumanizing effects, McCarthy joins his literary voice to one of the great debates of Western thought. Citing the book of Job, he invokes one of the original contributions that sought to reconcile the proposed omnipotence and all-goodness of God with the facts of evil and suffering. Describing this logical problem, Gottfried Wilhelm Leibniz had coined the term *theodicy* and declared the world—though imperfect—the best of all worlds possible. Voltaire, in light of the 1755 earthquake of Lisbon and the Seven Years' War, provided a satirical and pessimistic response in *Candide*, and Georg Büchner in *Danton's Tod* famously declared suffering itself the "rock of atheism" (3.1, 49). Generally speaking, theodicy is a contentious issue at the best of times, through the ages attracting thinkers from St. Augustine to Immanuel Kant and Jakob Böhme, all providing widely different answers as to the nature or existence of God, as well as the morality of theodicy itself in the face of mere suffering. McCarthy himself invokes Leibniz's dictum of "the best of all worlds possible" at various points in his work, predominantly in a critical light.[38] The consequence of the immersed, human perspective is a practical rather than a theoretical stance, altering between the resolved acceptance or the direct confrontation of evil and suffering. Consistent with Cawelti's description of McCarthy's characters as "god-haunted" (169), the man wrestles intensely with God. He is too steeped in sorrow to negate the issue with the privilege of critical distance: "He raised his face to the paling day. Are you there? He whispered. Will I see you at the last? Have you a neck by which to throttle you? Have you a heart? Damn you eternally have you a soul? Oh God, he whispered. Oh God" (*R* 10).

Theodicy converges with anthropodicy. The father's pleas and accusations show at once his desperation, his precarious faith, and the residue of the mindset that externalizes human violence and evil by projecting it onto the deity. Still, his theodicy is hardly one that disavows human freedom and agency as such, and thus does not play the blame game of shifting responsibility for all evil and suffering onto the deity, consequently to deny its omnipotence, goodness, or existence. In a reflexive way, the demand for God to speak, to intervene with the reality of suffering, is not just a reflection of morality, but also what brings morality into the suffering world. It has its reality in moral thought and acts alone. With the possibility of morality comes the possibility of failing to live up to it. The man may thus invoke Christ and God multiple times at the horrific revelation of the cannibals' simultaneous godlessness and inhumanity, which "permits" their acts. But the cruel irony is that the man's position with regard to the victimized humans in the larder, pleading for rescue, appears like that of God in relation to him: either unable to help or unwilling to do so.

In the end, God retains a foundational function in providing the man with his sense of mission. To avoid the death-spelling truth, he turns toward his son: "My job is to take care of you. I was appointed to do that by God. I will kill anyone who touches you" (*R* 65). Fatherly love and a sense of mission converge with the need for purpose and meaning. All is yoked to the life of the son, who, in a mimetic sense, unifies the functions of prized object and admired mediator as source of meaning. Thus, the threat of killing anyone who touches the boy reflects at once love and jealousy, and bears more than a hint of the fundamentalist's implicit inversion of Ivan Karamazov's thesis: "If God exists, everything is permitted" as "he perceives himself as His instrument, which is why [. . .] his acts are redeemed in advance, since they express the divine will" (Žižek 2006, 92). In this regard, the issue of theodicy and the Nietzschean murder of God as the foundation of value appear as two sides of the same coin: "The first death of God does not lead to the restoration of the sacred and ritual order, but to a decomposition of meaning so radical and irremediable that an abyss opens beneath the feet of modern man" (*BE* 93). For the man in *The Road*, the figurative abyss has become a reality. As his wife prophesizes, he will not survive for himself,

Words, Acts, and the Struggle for Meaning

If, as I claim, *The Road* represents the last stage in the ongoing journey of McCarthy's fiction, the now complete developmental logic or itinerary of this journey reveals that all along, this journey has been a literary pilgrimage. If so, the holy mountain ascended toward its end offers a panoramic view of ontology and ethics as fundamentally revolving around and evolving in relation to "the Other." This Other may be called God, or the world, or humanity. It may be glimpsed in a vibrant forest, or fish in a mountain stream, and most of all in the faces of other people. Ultimately, they come down to the same thing.

The fault lines of ethical relations with the Other emerge in the confrontation of words and acts. As father and son part ways with Ely, the prophet of atheism tells the father that had tables been turned, he would not have shared his food with them. In turn, the father admits that he would not have shared his food either, had it not been for the boy. Their short exchange brings up one of the central questions of the novel:

> Why did he do it?
> He looked over at the boy and he looked at the old man. You wouldnt understand. I'm not sure I do.
> Maybe he believes in God.
> I dont know what he believes in.
> He'll get over it.
> No he wont. (*R* 146)

To begin with, the question of the son's belief, that which he won't "get over," only points to the function of belief as such. Apart from the necessities of survival—shoes, warm clothes, food—both father and son need something to put their faith into, to derive meaning from, and to shape their journey upon. About two-thirds into the novel, the man watches the boy kneeling over their ragged and torn road map: "He thought he knew what that was about. He'd pored over maps as a child, keeping one finger on the town where he lived. Just as he would look up his family in the phone directory. Themselves among others. Everything in its place. Justified in the world" (*R*

154). The ordering function of such faith is other-centric. Even the wife's final advice to the man directs our attention to the importance of belief, though it be delusion: "A person who had no one would be well advised to cobble together some passable ghost. Breathe it into being and coax it with words of love" (*R* 49). A few pages later, the father himself echoes the mother's sentiment in a decidedly spiritual context when he likens the careful washing of another man's blood from the boy's hair to "some ancient anointing. So be it. Evoke the forms. Where you've nothing else construct ceremonies out of the air and breathe upon them" (*R* 63).

Though not necessarily or overtly religious, maps and phonebooks, like rituals and stories, are ways to impose order upon the world. In this particular respect, their function is essentially the same as that of those collective, historically adaptive, world-ordering stories we call myths. In *The Road*, the order of myth has finally collapsed, together with the social systems it reflected. Still, as Ron Charles observes: "With everything scraped away, the impulse to sanctify, to worship, to create meaning remains" (2006). In the words of the father: "Make a list. Recite a litany. Remember" (*R* 27). The need for order extends to that for a moral order as well. At the beginning of the novel, the man reads his boy tales out of a storybook, and tells him "old stories of courage and justice as he remembered them" (*R* 35). He does all in his power to give his boy the semblance of an education, to teach him how to survive, and last but not least to instill him with moral values. However, the position of ethics is precarious in a world in which all order and meaning—including that of myth and storytelling in general—are assailed by pervasive violence and entropic decline. It is the reality of "the death of everything" (*SL* 25)—humanity, God, the world, ethics—that looms over the pair like the proverbial sword of Damocles.

Part of the mythical heirloom the man passes on to his son is the black-and-white dichotomy between good guys and bad guys. Perhaps, this all-too-familiar metaphysics is the sole order that remains when all other systems have collapsed, circumscribing the full extent of postapocalyptic ethics. If so, it is a sorry state: the exclusive group of the good guys is strictly limited to father and son; the bad guys, that is *everybody else*. "There's a lot of them, those bad guys" (*R* 78), the son realizes, and the father later concedes, "I dont think we're likely to meet any good guys on the road" (*R* 127). It is the most basic form of what Girard calls the "underground motto"—*I am alone and they are everyone*—expressed in "a group of symbols and images intended not for communion but for universal separation" (*DDN* 261). That is to say, it is what has to be overcome. Following the father's logic, the pair constantly has to be "on the lookout." The central conflict of the book, and key to its ethical scope, is finally that between the man's compulsive xenophobia and the boy's desire to make contact with other human beings, "the rank self-centeredness necessary to survive as an individual and the altruism required to survive as a species" (Holcomb).

Assuming a Girardian point of view, it is exactly in the latter that *The Road* transcends the order of myth, which ever depends on the exclusion and sacrifice of the Other. One can begin to see why the father is not and cannot be the moral compass of the novel. Always, it is the boy who tries to help and befriend other people on the road, such as a moribund man who has been struck by lightning. Likewise, it is the boy who persuades his father to share the pair's dwindling food with Ely and who, in a second central encounter, pleads with his father to spare the life of a man who had previously robbed them of everything they possessed. It is here, too, that one approaches the core of what the son believes in and that clear differences emerge between him and his father. As the pair catches up with the thief, the father retaliates by making the starving man strip at gunpoint and taking his clothes, leaving him to die. His is the law of reciprocal violence, the Old Testament law of an eye for an eye: "I'm going to leave you the way you left us" (*R* 217). In contrast, the boy pleads for mercy, realizing the utter despair that drove the man: "He was just hungry, Papa. He's going to die. [. . .] He's so scared." The father insists: "I'm scared [. . .]. Do you understand? I'm scared"—yet it is exactly *because* he understands and is able to empathize that the son urges his father to "Just help him" (*R* 218).

The son's altruism is not merely naïve. In fact, he grows a lot on his journey. The father may warn him that "the things you put into your head are there forever" (*R* 10). But try as he might, he cannot protect the boy from the realities of the road.[39] As the father tries to shield him from the sights of the dead, he says: "It's okay Papa. [. . .] They're already there. / I dont want you to look. / They'll still be there" (*R* 161). Whereas in an earlier encounter, a marauder used the weakness he saw in the boy as the occasion for an attack, what the thief sees in the child is "very sobering to him" (*R* 215). Moments like these encourage reading *The Road* as an initiation narrative of the second degree. While the son's innate goodness is never lost, his innocence, to an extent, is—primarily so as regards his beloved father's capacity for evil. It bears repeating that initiation runs parallel to apocalypse: both of them entail the disillusioning, sometimes catastrophic revelation of a hidden truth. In the son's case, he gradually comes to realize that the stories his father tells him are not true, that the father's minimalist binary myth of good guys and bad guys does not match their actions. "They dont have to be true. They're stories," the father protests, and the son replies: "Yes. But in the stories we're always helping people and we dont help people" (*R* 225).

Constantly questioning whether they are still the good guys, the son realizes that it is not stories of good and bad, or who one may be underneath, but one's actions that define a person. After his pleas for mercy with the thief have long gone unheard, the father finally relents. But it is too late, as the thief is gone: "I wasnt going to kill him," the father apologetically assures his son, who simply responds, "But we did kill him" (*R* 219), remarkably including himself in his allocation of guilt. The implicit argument here could not be more timely or relevant: realizing the other's capacity of being the bad guy must in no way result in the type of politics of fear of the other that have recently reemerged all around us, once that picture is complemented by the troubling revelation of seeing oneself in the other's mirror image. In turn, one must realize the other's potential for being the good guy, and finally, the utter meaninglessness of all such labels on the proving ground of ethical action. In a subtle way, McCarthy shows where his sympathies lie: as predicted in "Dedication," it will be increasingly the son who takes care of his dying father. Whereas before, it was the father who marched ahead, it is now the son who will lead the way to the end of the road.

Carrying the Fire, or the New Messiah

We return, at last, to the end of *The Road* and the questions of what truths are revealed and what conversion means within the context of this revelation. "Truth is active throughout the great novel but its primary location is in the conclusion" (*DDN* 308). As the conclusion of the novel, the constitution of a new family at the end obviously has significant repercussions on how we interpret the entirety of *The Road*, and by extension McCarthy's work-spanning apocalypse. So: Is the positive turn at the end of the story and thus *The Road* as a whole the moment when Cormac McCarthy, having stared into the abyss for too long, finally blinks? Is this where, after spending the better part of four decades writing in dispassionate contemplation of human futility and insignificance, the author succumbs to cliché and saccharine sentimentalism? In fact, I argue, the opposite is the case: the light of *The Road* represents the necessary consequence of all the darkness that went before, the final sublation of the dialectics of life and death, good and bad—in short, of all that was ever inherent in McCarthy's work from his first stroke on the typewriter.

The journey father and son undertake is initially framed as a quest for survival. At the same time, the novel consistently reminds us that it is also a pilgrimage, and on this pilgrimage, there is finally something more at stake. That something is not the survival of mankind, but the survival of humanity as a value in the sense of *humanitas*. Contrary to the human evil chronicled in *Blood Meridian*, McCarthy remarks, *The Road* is fundamentally a book about human goodness (Jurgensen). Goodness resides within the boy, who in spite of all the death, desperation, and depravity he is confronted with, retains his altruism, even when it comes into conflict with the father's pragmatic survivalism. The latter becomes all the more problematic, since the boy's goodness is what the man is fighting for. "You're not the one who has to worry about everything," he reprimands his son, but the son insists, "Yes I am, he said. I am the one" (*R* 218). Indeed, he is "the pair's moral compass," and on more than one occasion, it is "only the boy's insistence [that] saves the pair's humanity" (Cleave 2006). Biblical association is close at hand: "the one" may thus become the One, that is, the Johannine vision of "the way, the truth, and the life" (Jn. 14:6).

Like McCarthy's other deserts, the wasteland of *The Road* is both "an actual and a metaphysical space which provides a testing ground for the moral positions assumed by his protagonists in the face of a universe apparently bent on destruction, and for his own narrative and formal concerns" (Beck 210). Narrative, formal, and moral concerns each have their bearings on one another, which is reflected in the twofold problem of informational and cultural entropy that *The Road* formulates. As far as the progressive erosion of meaning is concerned, the very existence of the novel stands in stark contrast to the violentropic tendencies of present-day civilization, the ongoing escalation and results of which it projects into a future that may be close at hand.

A piece of literary art, it represents what Freese calls "the most significant anti-entropic activity human beings are capable of, namely, the construction of meaningful messages" (2004, 344). Cant makes a similar point when he reads the novel as "an example of cultural vitality" even as it proclaims "the inevitability of cultural entropy" (280). In this existential manner, *The Road* poses the question of what morality and humanity there can be in an amoral and indifferent cosmos. This dilemma has plagued McCarthy's oeuvre from the start. Here, for the first time yet entirely consistently, he presents a hopeful answer. True to McCarthy's syncretic approach, the answer is complex.

On a secular and purely human level, *The Road*'s portrayal of a father–son relationship differs considerably from any such relationship found in McCarthy's earlier work, where the Oedipal conflict still looms large and dissimulates the underlying relation of mimetic rivalry. In *The Road*, it is characterized first and foremost by mutual love and care, as is evident throughout the novel. With everything else gone, father and son are "each the other's world entire" (*R* 5). On the deathbed his son has made for him aside the road, the father professes this love: "You have my whole heart. You always did. You're the best guy. You always were. If I'm not here you can still talk to me. You can talk to me and I'll talk to you" (*R* 235).[40] Complementing the emotionally shattering impact of loss that the novel articulates throughout, this unconditional love forms the second, positive half of the human core that differentiates *The Road* from a dispassionate work like *Blood Meridian*. On the level of statistical thermodynamics, McCarthy responds by casting the boy as the messianic center of a tale of the world that addresses both the entropic and the apocalyptic end. After all, the child's very birth is expressed in terms of statistical mechanics as an "improbable appearance" (*R* 50). He is the statistical, thermodynamic wonder of this novel. What ought not to be forgotten, though, is that so is finally every child ever born—every human and every form of life a natural and necessary, yet still precious exception to the second law.[41]

At the same time, and more extensively, the son is also enlarged with the signs of divinity. To his father, he is a "tiny paradise" (*R* 126), a "golden chalice, good to house a god" (*R* 64)—and thus essentially the Holy Grail, that sacred item of the knight errant's perilous quest and mystical cure of the ruined wasteland. In the dream that opens the novel and that is taken up again toward the end (*R* 3–4, 236), it is the boy who by the light of his candle leads the man through a dark cave that may represent the moral darkness of the world, the human condition as such: he is "the light of the world" (Jn. 12:8). Clearly, the symbolism McCarthy choses is predominantly Christian. Even from the beginning, the father is convinced of the son's divinity: "If he is not the word of God God never spoke" (*R* 4). While the conditional implies the possibility that indeed "God never spoke," the phrasing suggests the Word that both *is with* and *is itself* God (Jn. 1:1–5), and becomes flesh in taking a human form. As John's divine logos, this Word is the original source of "all things," of life and light, and so it is in Jacob Böhme's mystic vision of the generative, speaking, and breathing Word, of which the world is an exhaled manifestation. As is to be expected, one also detects echoes of the book of Revelation: "His eyes are like a flame of fire, and on his head are many diadems, and he has a name written, that no man knows but himself [. . .] and the name by which he is called is The Word of God" (19:13–14). The exact instance John speaks of here is the Second Coming of Christ, which, for all intents and purposes, is symbolically fulfilled with the appearance of the son in McCarthy's revelation.

Skeptics reasonably object that these passages present only the man's idealized view of his son. Yet, even after the man's death, the symbolism does not vanish. Finding his father dead, the son kneels down beside him and says "his name over and over again" (*R* 236). Since father and son remain nameless, and the son consistently calls his father "papa," the minute detail that the son refers to his father by name is significant, exactly because readers are not privy to it. In the light of the son's ostensibly divine nature and the novel's ties to Revelation, one may relate this act of naming to Jesus's promise to those that overcome the tribulations of the end times, that "I will never blot his name out of the book of life," but "confess his name before my Father" (Rv. 3:5). Add to this that—in contrast to the general namelessness of the boy and the man—McCarthy originally considered calling the mother "Mary" (91/87/6, n.p.), and these symbols become increasingly harder to discount as the delusion of the father or red herrings on behalf of McCarthy.[42] One may thus relativize or reinterpret the son's divinity but can hardly negate it outright. The lesson is one of universalism rather than particularism. Thus, the new mother at the end of the novel assures the boy—perhaps in an echo of Böhme's life-giving, breathing Word—that "the breath of God was his breath yet though it pass from man to man through all of time" (*R* 241).

Finally, the notion of this breath, connecting human beings, opens the doors to the innermost core of McCarthy's revelation. The effect of novelistic conversion, Girard claims, is that "the Self and the Other [. . .] become one in the miracle of the novel" (*DDN* 300). This is also the epiphany implied in the panentheist vision of Jacob Böhme: "For you must not ask: Where is God? Listen, blind human, you live in God, and God is within you; and if you lead a saintly life, you are yourself God. Wherever you may look, there is God" (1992, chap. 22.46). Readers of *The Crossing* might respond—quite rightly—with the hermit's indictment of the effectively pantheist priest, who was his younger self: "To see God everywhere is to see Him nowhere" (153). However, neither Girard nor Böhme believe that conversion is unconditional, nor does McCarthy usually allow for epiphany other than in confrontation of death. Putting an end to the violence of triangular desire, conversion implies neither the solitude of McCarthy's hermits, nor a mere return to the materialist world.[43]

Conversion can be seen, instead, as one that cleanses metaphysical desire of its mimetic trappings to its purest expression and essence, for which both *The Crossing* and *Whales and Men* have one word: longing. Longing—which is both "our true nature" as "arks of the covenant" (*WM* 133), and the source of that "wildness of heart" that drives the quest for God (*CRO* 153)—is the precondition of its own fulfilment. The latter is perpetually deferred and disappointed in mimetic desire and is only achieved in genuine conversion. Its essence, finally, is what the former priest talking to Billy Parham admits he was lacking when he was yet a priest, and that thus exposed him to the trappings of mimetic rivalry, confronting another hermit: "He thought there was love in his heart. There was not" (*CRO* 153).

In the dying father's eyes, the boy radiates with light, "glowing in that waste like a tabernacle" (*R* 230), the vessel that contains the Eucharist or Holy Communion of humans and God. As the son sustains the father and represents his last and fullest measure of *being*, the last sacred idiom unshorn of referent, the man's choice not to kill the boy and "take him with him" is not some selfish shying away from doing what is right, nor some final refusal to face the truth of the dead mother. Instead, it is the most altruistic gesture the father is capable of: his dying wish is that the son go on "carrying the fire" and "find the good guys" (*R* 234), something that is in stark opposition to the jealous xenophobia that has governed his actions throughout, all the more so as his son is now deprived of his sole protector.[44] The same point is driven home by Daniel Luttrull:

> The man, who formerly loved only the boy and would not hazard the boy's safety for anything, now embraces a broader charity, one that he seems to have learned from the boy. The man plans on leaving his son in the world not only because he "cant hold [his] son dead in [his] arms" but because he knows that the world needs his son to continue carrying the fire. (30)

In terms of Girardian psychology, novelistic conversion "puts an end to triangular desire [...]. Metaphysical desire brings into being a certain relationship to others and to oneself. True conversion engenders a new relationship to others and to oneself" (*DDN* 295). In giving his son up to light the world, the man's conversion, too, is thus "a victory over a self-centeredness which is other-centered, [a] renunciation of fascination and hatred [that] is the crowning moment of novelistic creation" (*DDN* 299). In contrast to the father, who stakes his being on the boy's life and so guards him both fearfully and violently, the son seems entirely free of the trappings of metaphysical desire and violence. He incorporates the "triumph over self-centeredness" that consists in "get[ting] away from oneself and mak[ing] contact with others" (*DDN* 298). It is exactly in this that the son can serve as the sole viable model of ethics in McCarthy's vision of the end time.

The core of this ethics is expressed in the other minimal "myth" of *carrying the fire*, which is the task of the good guys. It is both the pair's credo and the central image repeated throughout the text, yet it is never specified what exactly the fire is. The son himself questions its existence: "Is it real? The Fire? [...] Where is it? I dont know where it is" (*R* 234). One can only speculate on its nature. To be sure, McCarthy used this image before, and in a prominent position. It appears in Sheriff Bell's dream of a nightly journey at the end of *No Country for Old Men*, where his father carries "fire in a horn" and is "fixin to make a fire somewhere out there in all that dark and all that cold" (309). In the dream, Cant surmises, it stands for the heirloom of civilization that is passed on from one generation to the next. In *The Road*, he suggests it signifies "the mystery that is the spark of life itself and that needs no reason to exist" (Cant 271). Similarly, Luttrull interprets it as the mythical, Promethean fire of civilization. In thermodynamic terms, the boy's fire is

Graphic spark

heat differential incarnate, a powerful source of energy, capable of forming new structures. The latter is realized when he becomes part again of a larger and more complex system in the family comprised of people who are also "carrying the fire" and breathing the breath of God.

In such mystical matters, we are admittedly on shaky ground. Personally, I feel that all of these suggestions grasp only part of the truth. Yet these interpretations may be too modest in this context, as the reality that *The Road* enacts virtually everywhere is that of violentropy and the victory of death that extinguishes the spark of life. If the fire is to have any substance in this moribund world, I contend that—both by textual parallelism and substance—it would be that which the man speculates his own fathers seek:

> Do you think that your fathers are watching? That they weigh you in their ledgerbook? Against what? There is no book and your fathers are dead in the ground. [...] I think maybe they are watching, he said. They are watching for a thing that even death cannot undo and if they do not see it they will turn away from us and they will not come back. (*R* 165, 177)

At the end of the novel, the dying father tells his son that he carries the fire within himself: "It's inside you. It was always there. I can see it" (*R* 234). *The Road* is finally about what remains, that which "even death cannot undo." All of it is embodied in the boy, who—with his simple goodness, ability to forgive, share, and put his faith in others—becomes the justification and hopeful destination for traveling in the first place. In his example, one finds the seeds of a new yet old myth (or rather, antimyth) not inherently destructive, an Eros to challenge the reign of Thanatos.

In fact, rather than Eros, one should speak of *agape*—that is, the concept of "brotherly love, charity; the love of God for man and of man for God" (Liddell and Scott 4). This kind of love is "what remains after we assume the consequences of the failure of *eros*" (Žižek and Gunjević 38) in the Freudian sense, and *desire* in the mimetic sense. In the Christian context, *agape* is associated with the Holy Spirit, the paraclete, who at once inspires and symbolizes "the community of believers, linked by *agape*" (Žižek and Gunjević 38). Not to belabor a point made earlier on, it is altogether fitting that the Holy Spirit's symbolism is one of fire. Even in the unorthodox,

heretical mysticism of Böhme's _Clavis_, fire—as a phenomenological aspect
of epiphany—is deeply associated with divine love: "The burning fire is a
revelation of life and of divine love, through which that divine love kindles
the unity and sharpens itself as [or, for] a fiery work of the power of God"
(cit. in Wehr 1971, 78). In the _Aurora_, he further elaborates that "the same
fire is the true son of God, who is always born thus from eternity to eternity"
(Böhme 1992, chap. 8.82, 166).

Whether the paradigm chosen is thus orthodox or mystical Christianity,
entropic, or secular humanist amounts to the same thing. In the end, I agree
with Erik Wielenberg, "the point of it all is love" (12).[45] Love is the great
counterforce to violence. Like violence it surpasses cultural and interdividual
differences, which is what makes it possible to go from hate to love "by means
of an almost instantaneous conversion" (_TH_ 217). This conclusion may seem
trite and clichéd, even banal, yet in an oeuvre as ruled by violence as McCarthy, it is anything but that. Or, if banality it is, it is the same banality shared
by the greatest of secular and religious writers through the ages. Therefore:

> We should not deny that banality, but loudly proclaim it. [. . .] It is the
> absolute banality of what is essential in Western civilization. The novelistic
> dénouement is a reconciliation between the individual and the world,
> between man and the sacred. The multiple universe of passion decomposes
> and returns to simplicity. Novelistic conversion calls to mind the _analusis_
> of the Greeks and the Christian rebirth. In this final moment, the novelist
> reaches the heights of Western literature; he merges with the great reli-
> gious ethics and the most elevated forms of humanism those which have
> chosen the least accessible part of man. (_DDN_ 308)

Where I disagree with Wielenberg is in his apparent desire to purge the
novel's morality from Christian ethics and metaphysics. While the point to
free morality from the existence of God is well taken, Wielenberg mischar-
acterizes the highest Christian commandment to love God in that he omits
that the commandment is in fact a double-commandment, the second half
of which is "Love your neighbor." Considering the substrate of panentheist mysticism that informs _The Road_, the conclusion is that if you love your
neighbor, you love God also. In fact, the commandment goes even further as

the disciples of Jesus are also instructed—and perhaps set up for failure—to "[l]ove your enemies, do good to those who hate you, bless those who curse you, pray for those who abuse you," and further not to judge, nor to condemn, but to forgive and be charitable, all the while "expecting nothing in return" (Lk. 6:27–37). The commandment is thus at once antimimetic toward one's enemies, and mimetic insofar as Christians are encouraged to follow the *imitatio Christi*, and so to imitate God's love through the intermediary of Christ.

It is thus in love that humans come closest to the divine. It is through this capacity that the son—beyond all symbolism—most resembles Jesus: He is at once "the most outside yet also the most inside common humanity. He is *the most divine and the most human*" (*BE* 50). Even beyond symbolism, a single look at his actions is fully sufficient to reject Wielenberg's conclusion that "neither the man nor the child does particularly well" (18) by the standards of Christian morality as both misdirected and manifestly false. As Girard rightly states, loving God and loving your neighbor "are like one another because love makes no distinctions between beings" (*TH* 216). A call to more love, likewise, is the only practical response to either theodicy or anthropodicy. Ultimately, a Judeo-Christian or secular humanist ethics should amount to the same thing in fostering the treatment of the Other as sharing in the same kind of humanity and/or divinity that one shares in oneself: not sacred, but holy. It is this attitude that might yet save humanity—and at the same time justify its survival.[46]

Cormac McCarthy's apocalypse is thus finally one of transcendent love. This love is "at one and the same time the divine being and the basis of any real knowledge" (*TH* 277) as it is the same kind of universal love that guides Jesus's self-sacrifice on the Cross, the point from which revelation becomes possible. It is no literary accident that the father dies at a crossroads. Given the teleology not just of *The Road* but of McCarthy's oeuvre as a whole, I would argue it merely forces a fundamental choice that his work has been building up to the whole time: "You got two choices here," says the veteran who finds the boy, "you can stay here with your papa and die or you can go with me" (*R* 238). That is, the boy has the choice between certain death and taking a leap of faith in his fellow humans. Remarkably, when the son offers to give the veteran the pistol that his father entrusted to him, the veteran rejects it. Since violence is the prime shape that evil assumes in McCarthy's cosmos, this mutual disavowal of it by two people—a child and a grown man both of whom know violence—is a crucial gesture, impossible to overstate in its significance. The elementary and inevitable choice, in this case, may be the truth expressed by the black ex-convict in *The Sunset Limited* in his echo of W. H. Auden's "September 1, 1939": "That you must love your brother or die" (*SL* 121).

Conclusion

At the Crossroads of Life and Death

Near is
And difficult to grasp, the God,
But where danger threatens
That which saves from it also grows.
　　　—Friedrich Hölderlin, "Patmos"

Traversing the harsh terrains of Cormac McCarthy's fiction, readers are engaged in a complex and often unsettling exploration of how we, as humans, relate to the world and our fellow human beings. In this pursuit, our gazing eyes stray ever toward the horizons of what McCarthy calls "the various disciplines and interests of humanity" (Woodward 1992, 30–31). In his novels at their best, these interests and disciplines become part of a single, unified conception of the *world-as-tale*. Whatever questions are contemplated in the course of this literary journey come to a head in the confrontation of death. This confrontation, in turn, reaches its utmost urgency in the prospect not just of our own, personal deaths, but in that of the extinction of the species—and possibly the end of life on earth. In the words of T. S. Eliot's "The

Hollow Men," Western tradition has conceived of this latter, encompassing death alternatively as a violent, apocalyptic bang or an entropic whimper. Reading McCarthy, it now appears that the end may partake in the qualities of either death. In any case, the shape of things to come may now be seen more clearly.

So, to return to the beginning and the twofold introductory question of this study: Is the troubling vision laid out before us that of an *apocalypse*, specifically of an *American* apocalypse? Firstly, it will come as no surprise by now that, for all its watering-down, the end-time label is entirely justified here. Apart from McCarthy's personal, consistently pessimistic statements on the matter, his plots' investment in apocalyptic themes and symbolism, the irreversible totality of his catastrophes, and the model of history that informs them are all hallmarks of true eschatological contemplation. Yet these indicators only begin to describe McCarthy's apocalypse. With its thorough engagement of anthropology, history, religious and mystical thought, physics, and the earth and life sciences, his is a highly syncretic vision—suited to force the challenges of our age. Naturally, the generic shoe of *apocalypse* fits some of McCarthy's works more comfortably than others; from the syncretic perspective that informs this study, though, it is the one that best characterizes the unified vision of his life's work as a whole.

Secondly, the national character of this apocalypse has to be reconsidered within a global context. As much as McCarthy's fiction is invested with the national and local mythology and history of the United States, as vividly as its Appalachian and Southwestern settings ground his plots, and as indispensable as the English language in its American character is to the poetic forces McCarthy rallies—at heart, his central concerns and subjects are *not* specifically American. In respect of his literary eschatology, America is central first and foremost insofar as it is prototypical and perhaps ahead of the curve—providing a sight of "things hidden since the foundation of the world" that now gradually reveal themselves around the globe. Thus, both the Southern ideal of a permanent pastoral order and the ostensibly linear teleology of frontier myth and history have been shown to rely on the same sacrificial pattern of regeneration through violence. Characterized as they are by contagious violence and unexpected acts of kindness, the relations of McCarthy's characters—his fathers, sons, orphans, pariahs, criminals, murderers, hermits, philosophers, and travelers—likewise rely upon a certain, consistent dynamic. People, McCarthy seems to suggest, are by and large the same as they ever were—and wherever they come from.

It is these patterns that are important. In today's context, they must rather appear as an encompassing disintegration of order across spheres (social, political, moral, etc.) and nations. These trends go hand in hand with one of escalatory violence. Thus, the regenerative circulary of the pastoral and the upward teleology of the frontier myth now combine to reform as a downward spiral. The spiral radically transcends American and Western contexts: while the apocalyptic fabric of McCarthy's vision formally appears American, its structure and substance are woven from more ancient and more universal fibers.

Where Danger Threatens

Looking at the roles of myth, violence, and entropy—the main thematic and structural elements identified as key to McCarthy's apocalyptic scope—we are now able to see some of the "hidden seams" connecting everything in his tale of the world. McCarthy's brand of syncretic eschatology is particularly valuable today as a key not simply to spiritual concerns, but to those mundane and human relations, events, and processes threatening our survival. It provides an alternative to either the monopolization of apocalyptic scripture and discourse by fundamentalists, who cannot but conceive of human implication in "the end" other than in the guise of the sinfulness or essential evil of the heathens outside their respective circles, or the more pervasive, secular failure to heed the warnings and decisively act as one to confront the danger threatening us. In short,

> we have disregarded Revelation. [...] Today, violence has been unleashed across the whole world, creating what the apocalyptic texts predicted: confusion between disasters caused by nature and those caused by humans, between the natural and the man-made: global warming and rising waters are no longer metaphors today. Violence, which produced the sacred, no longer produces anything but itself. (*BE* x)

Certainly, recent developments give us cause to swallow the bitter pill of McCarthyan pessimism, even at its literary weakest, lowest dosage. As the character of Reiner points out in what became the tacky-but-true tagline to *The Counselor*: "Greed is greatly overrated. But fear isnt" (120). Across the globe, the rapacious greed unleashed by decades of neoliberal economics with its politics of market deregulation and uninhibited free trade has resulted in the impoverishment of the working classes. In many countries, it has led to the decline of the middle classes and the overwhelming affluence of an exceedingly small elite. Exacerbated by the struggle for natural resources, the destabilization or violent overthrow of regimes across the Middle East by the United States and its European allies has only created more violence.

In a physical sense, this escalation is reflective of the thermodynamic process: entropy must increase, its final projection being the heat death of the universe. Yet the way in which this teleology materializes is as a degrading cycle of energy and systems of alternating dis|order—from the single cell to the organism to the ecosystem and the planet. On the level of culture, at which one can metaphorically speak of cultural or social entropy, escalation is tantamount to a feedback runaway of alternating, mutually reinforcing impulses. This process describes the periodical outbreak of violence that retains the long-term logic of reciprocity. Theoretically, it knows no bounds other than its exhaustion, a breakdown of the system.

While cause and effect are obscured in its cycle, the escalation of subjective, systemic, and symbolic violence coincides with social fragmentation, the loss of institutional power, and the rise of extremist factions. In the context of intercultural relations and limited resources, escalating reciprocity is linked to the decline of the ecosphere and the increase of natural catastrophes. Old master-narratives, systems of meaning, and ethics disintegrate, or drown in a cacophony of noise, incendiary rumors, and symbolic violence. Perhaps the most concise formulation of this notion is John Grady's reflection that "the world's heart beat at some terrible cost and that the world's pain and its beauty moved in a relationship of diverging equity and that in the headlong deficit the blood of multitudes might ultimately be exacted for the vision of a single flower" (*APH* 282). Such is the social, physical, and informational effect of an escalation that I have described as part of an overall rise in *violentropy*.

All over Europe, we are now witnessing again the rise of authoritarian and frequently antidemocratic forces, as well as the reemergence of old Cold War fault lines that we had thought long overcome. As global temperatures and sea levels continue to rise, so does the frequency and number of natural catastrophes, humanitarian crises, and terrorist attacks. And in their wake will swell the newly mythologized "floods" of refugees to exacerbate the fears of the peoples in host countries, together with the old stereotypes of persecution and the voting success of the ideological heirs of 1933. Across the West, people are as divided as they have been in the past century, and the overall trust in the rule of law, in the integrity of our political representatives, as well as in the fourth estate is at record lows. All of it only pours water on the rumor mills of the new demagogues.

Things fall apart. In June of 2016, the majority of people of England and Wales voted for the UK to leave a union that had widely been regarded as a facilitator of peace and growth in Europe for over seventy years. Six years later, Russian tanks are rolling toward Kyiv as bombs are falling on barracks and hospitals alike. We may have to seriously reckon with the possibility voiced by ever greedy and hungry Malkina, the villain of *The Counselor*: before long, "there's not going to be a Europe" (177). And with the ascent and looming resurgence of one Donald J. Trump, the so-called "alternative right," and groups of unquestioning believers misled enough to try and overthrow the results of a democratic election, we may fear that before long, there may not be a United States of America, either. Even at his most blatantly ominous, McCarthy, in speaking through Malkina, may be proven right:

> I suspect that we are ill-formed for the path we have chosen. Ill-formed and ill-prepared. We would like to draw a veil over all that blood and terror. That have brought us to this place. It is our faintness of heart that would close our eyes to all of that, but in so doing it makes of it our destiny. Perhaps you would not agree. I dont know. But nothing is crueler than a coward, and the slaughter to come is probably beyond our imagining. (*COU* 183–84)

So, if this is where the road has led us, where do we go from here and what have we learned from the journey that lies behind us?

That Which Saves

In mapping out the apocalyptic challenge of McCarthy's work, this study has attributed a double nature to violence itself. Like the gods of mythology, it can assume both monstrous and beneficent traits. Like the blood spilled in murder or sacrifice, it may pollute or purify. Like the Greek *pharmakos*, it can spell both poison and cure for the community. When reciprocal, it is utterly destructive and socially entropic. When exacted unanimously, it is constructive and a force that can reintroduce order into the chaos of the sacrificial crisis. If mimetic theory is correct, it is at the origin of culture itself. In the context of Christian eschatology, it is also one of the prime threads in a web of interconnected dangers to our survival. This perspective finally offers a way of making sense of Cormac McCarthy's noted assertion, perhaps the most scandalous of all, that "[t]here's no such thing as life without bloodshed [. . .]. I think the notion that the species can be improved in some way, that everyone could live in harmony, is a really dangerous idea. Those who are afflicted with this notion are the first ones to give up their souls, their freedom" (Woodward 1992, 36).

At surface, McCarthy's statement goes radically against all modern pacifist conceits. Nevertheless, to interpret it as a surrender to violence at best and an advocacy of it at worst is a misreading. Instead, we should read it quite literally: McCarthy says that there *is* no such thing as life without bloodshed, not that a non- or at least less violent life is in principle beyond our grasp. What is clear is only that there is no simple cure, no straightforward way to improve human nature—an ideal that, at its worst, has resulted in eugenics and totalitarian horror. Yes, violence in its contagious forms is a fact of life. If anything, it is precisely the acceptance and wariness of this fact that enables us to choose *not* to be violent. And it is this possibility that makes us free—not because we are essentially better either as individuals or as a species, but because we are aware of the fact that we are not.

Consequently, McCarthy's statements, like Girard's, should be read as opposed to "giving polite lip-service to a vague ideal of non-violence" (*TH* 137), rather than to the ideal itself. Over the past two thousand years, we have become increasingly aware of the process of scapegoating and concomitantly more concerned for the victims we leave in our tracks as we march through history. As if by a physical law, this awareness historically correlates with an

escalation of violence, which demands ever more victims to hide its hypocrisy. Systemically, it is clearly tied to the corruption of politics, economics,
and the media.

> There is an indissoluble link between global warming and the rise in vio-
> lence. [. . .] [T]he confusion of the natural and the artificial [. . .] is
> perhaps the strongest thing in apocalyptic texts. Love has "cooled down."
> Of course, we cannot deny that it works in the world as it has never worked
> before, that the awareness of the innocence of victims has progressed.
> However, charity is now facing the worldwide empire of violence. (*BE* 216)

Time and again, the better angels among our artists, activists, and intellectual
and spiritual leaders have pointed to a "definitive renunciation of violence,
without any second thoughts" as the "implacable necessity" (*TH* 137) and
indispensable condition of our survival. And yet, we are rightly skeptical
of our ability—or willingness?—to effectively renounce either violence as
such, or the individual, national, or corporate claims to the world that are
at its roots. Given the multidimensional and protean nature of the problem
as subjective, systemic, and symbolic violence, the latter is a task we cannot
solve as individuals. Ironically, we know what we are doing, yet to make the
choices we must make, awareness alone is insufficient. Thus, dueña Alfonsa
asserts, "I dont believe knowing can save us" (*APH* 239), and McCarthy himself has offered the pessimistic prognosis that "we're going to do ourselves in"
(Kushner). What then, if anything, can save us?

Perhaps a little guidance. Apocalyptic writing, if it is genuine, will offer
the revelation of some important insight or else enunciate something that
may reasonably be called a *truth*. According to McCarthy, truth is precisely
what "writers must accomplish in their writing" (Wallace 138). For most of
this study, the truth revealed in McCarthy's writing has been that of the role
of imitation, desire, and above all violence in its mythic transformations in
the origin, persistence, and escalatory unraveling of Western civilization.
There is, however, a more subtle side of revelation, which, I suspect, functions more through affect and on the level of plot than through didactic
exposition. For the individual, it entails the kind of "mystical experience"
that McCarthy, back then, reportedly took as "a direct apprehension of
reality, unmediated by symbol" (Wallace 138). If truth is the writer's highest

calling, could it be, then, that the artistic rationale behind the literary path laid out in McCarthy's life work—though it remains necessarily mediated in his sanguinary signifiers—is to facilitate, as closely as possible, the kind of experience that would extend the possibility of attaining *truth*? Seen as a dialectical antithesis of violentropic escalation, it may even be that the one truth has to be suffered for the other to emerge. "Perhaps, we have to go through this" (*BE* 107).

Consequently, I hold the recurring moment in which epiphany is offered and conversion becomes attainable to be *the* critically underappreciated moment in McCarthy's fiction. In some cases, it takes the form of profound disillusionment, akin to a shock of initiation that provides individuation at the cost of socialization. An individual may gain a new sense of self in the process, yet their experience will result in self-imposed exile and a life on the road. Such is the case with John Wesley Rattner, Billy Parham in *Cities of the Plain*, and the various anchorites that populate the margins of McCarthy's novels. In other cases, revelation is repeatedly offered and rejected, as with Culla Holme, whose allegorical fate is one of purgatorial wandering. Often, the journey simply ends in death, as do those of Llewellyn Moss in *No Country for Old Men*, John Grady Cole in *Cities of the Plain*, and likely suicidal White in *The Sunset Limited*. All of them meet their ends because of their inability to escape the maelstrom of desire, violence, and personal vanity. In the case of *Blood Meridian*'s young protagonist, epiphany comes in the image of a burning tree and a precarious truce among predators. Conversion is within reach, but slips through the Kid's grasp when he murders his younger self in a boy he calls "son." In contrast, Lester Ballard takes the appearance of his younger self in a church bus as the sign to surrender himself to the law, dying both as his community's scapegoat and in acceptance of the responsibility for his crimes.

Finally, there are those characters who embrace epiphany, at the core of which they find conversion not to any specific religion, but to a new relationship toward "the Other." So Suttree, after obsessing over his uniqueness for much of the novel, significantly in conversation with his imaginary double, arrives at a realization of fundamental equality and shared humanity: "It is not alone in the dark of death that all souls are one soul" (*SUT* 414). After his own near death experience, he repeats this insight with an addendum:

"All souls are one and all souls lonely" (*SUT* 459). Finding his homeless friend the ragman dead—implicitly by his own will—he exclaims: "You have no right to represent people this way [. . .]. A man is all men. You have no right to your wretchedness" (*SUT* 422). He is speaking as much to himself as to his dead friend. Consequently, Suttree recants his former vanity together with his possessions, letting "everything fall away from him" until "there was nothing left of him to shed," and taking "for talisman the simple human heart within him" (*SUT* 468). Doing so, he is able to escape death and the destruction of Knoxville's McAnally Flats on the road westward.

Epiphany may change the course of a life, real or literary. Another example comes in one of the many tales and parables related to Billy in *The Crossing*. The story of the year-long rivalry between the narrating Mormon-turned-priest and the old hermit—whom some consider a lunatic and others a holy man—ends with the death of the hermit. On his death bed, the man articulates the same insight that moves Suttree: "He held the priest's hand in his own and he bade the priest look at their joined hand and he said see the likeness. This flesh is but a memento, yet it tells the true. Ultimately every man's path is every other's. There are no separate journeys for there are no separate men to make them. All men are one and there is no other tale to tell" (*CRO* 157). Like the tales contained within the larger tale of the world, we are distinct, yet also in a deeper sense at one upon a common journey—a pilgrimage perhaps—driven by a similar thirst, and caught in the same tales. McCarthy is ever in search of the universal, that which connects one and all. The recurring spiritual insight of the unity of souls equates anthropologically to that of fundamental kinship and *likeness*, which is the very soil and secret, common denominator of any emergent *difference*.[1] This relation defines at once the condition, origin, and vanishing point of mimesis and violence. Consequently, there is nothing substantial that separates us. The "absence of differences [. . .] or the nothing separating enemy brothers," also extends "the possibility of their union" (*BE* 46).

It may be pointed out that this realization, which is the essence of conversion, is neither inevitably nor exclusively Christian, though it is central in Christian ethics. Its core message and relation to orthodoxy is most clearly articulated by Black in *The Sunset Limited*. Through his conversion experience, he has been "cured of just about ever cravin" (39) and arrived at the secret, metaphysical core of mimetic relations. So, he posits:

> The whole point of where this is goin [. . .] is that they aint no Jews. Aint no whites. Aint no niggers. People of color. [. . .] At the deep bottom of the mine where the gold is at there aint none of that. [. . .] I would say that the thing we are talking about is Jesus, but it is Jesus understood as that gold at the bottom of the mine. He couldn't come down here and take the form of a man if that form was not done shaped to accommodate him. And if I said that there aint no way for Jesus to be ever man without ever man bein Jesus then I believe that might be a pretty big heresy. But that's all right. (*SL* 95)

All human beings, McCarthy's spiritual characters consistently propose, are not just alike, but share in a communal quality of the *divine* that unites them. This communion is diametrically opposed to the exclusory violence of the *sacred*.

To repeat once more the beautiful lines of an imperfect, perhaps rightly discarded text: "We are arks of the covenant and our true nature is not rage or deceit or terror or logic or craft or even sorrow. It is longing" (*WM* 130). Incidentally, the lines come in a letter by a character called "John." Following the image of the covenant, human longing may be identified as that for reconciliation with God. However, the latter, according to Jakob Böhme, is in every human being and, according to Christian belief, lives in the communion of humans led by *agape*. Such would also be the consequence of the panentheist ontology in McCarthy's work. At the bedrock of this ontology—which is grounded in the human dynamics described by Girard and spiritually informed by the Catholicism of McCarthy's upbringing as well as the mystical thought of Böhme and other heretics—one finds a sense not just of the equality and likeness of humans, but of their essential connection with the divine.

The caveat is that reconciliation and communion exist conditionally—as potentialities of acts that constitute what, speaking with the father in *The Road*, we may call goodness. Due to this conditionality, we must be skeptical about the father's assertion that "Goodness will find the little boy" (*R* 236). It does so, yes, but only because the boy and the veteran act on its potential. In the apocalyptic framework, the challenge that follows from mimetic anthropology and panentheist ontology, among others, is that of a radical *human* freedom and responsibility for our choices and actions. The metaphysical premise of this ineluctable responsibility is expressed by the dueña Alfonsa when she posits that the only constants in history are "greed and foolishness and a love of blood and this is a thing that even God—who knows all that can be known—seems powerless to change" (*APH* 239), and again in a short exchange between Ed Tom Bell and his uncle Ellis in *No Country for Old Men*:

> Do you think God knows what's happenin?
>> I expect he does.
>> You think he can stop it?
>> No. I dont. (269)

The ethical extension of panentheist ontology is an imperative that becomes the more urgent, yet also the more obvious the closer we get to the end. Goodness, grace, or God—to have an active presence in the world, depend upon the works of human beings. For this, we also need faith in one another. In the words of a former priest to young Billy Parham: "In the end we shall all of us be only what we have made of God" (*CRO* 158). The burden of reconciliation and redemption falls squarely on our shoulders.

In *The Stonemason*, Ben Telfair has an apocalyptic dream in which he finds himself standing at the "door of some ultimate justice" and subsequently confronted by "the God of all being" (112). God asks him a single and "terrible" question: "Where are the others?" (113). Ben's despair with his failure to keep his family together only highlights the truth he attains, which is that "we cannot save ourselves unless we save all ourselves. I had this dream and I did not heed it. And so I lost my way" (*SM* 113). Ben's condition of salvation will be recognized as the universalization of the choice Black articulates when he proclaims that "you must love your brother or die" (*SL* 121). Taking W. H. Auden's later disavowal of his words to heart, even love may not be enough.[2]

Certainly, it has often been easier to love humanity in the abstract than humans themselves, especially at their most inhumane. Love also needs to manifest in right action to shape the world. Whether or not we thus assume that a "Second Coming is at hand" (Yeats 577), that is, whether or not we approach the prospect of our collective end as believers, agnostics, or atheists, we must take to take to heart the lesson expounded by the atheist Žižek in his interpretation of the Crucifixion:

> There is no guarantee of redemption-through-love: redemption is merely given as possible. We are thereby at the very core of Christianity: it is God himself who made a Pascalian wager. By dying on the cross, he made a risky gesture with no guaranteed final outcome [. . .]. Far from providing the conclusive dot on the "I," the divine act rather stands for the openness of a New Beginning, and it falls to humanity to live up to it, to decide its meaning, to make something of it. (Žižek and Gunjević, 39–40)

As Chigurh proposes in *No Country*: "Every moment in your life is a turning and every one a choosing. Somewhere you made a choice. All followed to this" (259). Staying within the frame of the journey and following the travels of McCarthy's characters, we find ourselves at a crossroads, at which, looking backward, we must choose how we proceed.[3] In confronting the encompassing *violentropy* of our age, both the awareness and the acceptance of our responsibility are essential: they alone open up the space of a genuine choice between life and death. However, that choice cannot be defined in purely negative terms. Acknowledging and relinquishing violence—even, nay especially, our own—are necessary but finally insufficient gestures. If the dire prospects of global conflagration or the violentropic "heatdeath of the soul and heart" are to be avoided, the alternative to violence cannot merely be nonviolence: "All men are equal, not under law, but in fact. We must thus make decisive choices: [. . .] We have to destroy one another or love one another, and humanity, we fear, will prefer to destroy itself" (*BE* 48–49).

Contemplation of the worst facilitates nothing so much as the supreme necessity of the good—for us, personally, of doing the best we can, and doing so together. Epistemologically, it facilitates the uncovering and disarmament of the violence at the dark heart of our oldest myths and the telling and retelling of those narratives that help define and encourage healthier and more sustainable relations to the world and to each other. Pragmatically, good models, real and fictional, are key in inspiring not just resistance to violence and injustice but the kind of positive reciprocity that fulfills the otherwise empty promise of words like *forgiveness*, *charity*, and *love* above all. Besides his flawed and distinctly human characters, McCarthy also provides us with models of what is best in us—none more so than the boy in *The Road*. Sharing, for one, we are told, is the law of the road (*CP* 267), and good will a thing of "power to protect and to confer honor and to strengthen resolve and [. . .] to heal men and to bring them to safety long after all other resources [are] exhausted" (*APH* 219). Grace, finally, is a thing given freely "without reason or equity" (*SM* 131).

In literary criticism, to speak of such matters while seeking to alarm or to encourage without succumbing either to a cynical pessimism, false objectivity, or a naïve and saccharine moralism is a balancing act that, by rule of thumb, is better left to the poets. Therein lies, then, a task for poets of the apocalypse through all ages: to impart what danger threatens, and tend for all to that which saves from it. As Hölderlin knew, these two become clearer in relation to one another.[4] Thus, in one of the final flashbacks from the ruined wasteland of *The Road*, the father remembers how, years after the cataclysm,

> he'd stood in the charred ruins of a library where blackened books lay in pools of water. Shelves tipped over. Some rage at the lies arranged in their thousands row on row. He picked up one of the books and thumbed through the heavy bloated pages. He'd not have thought the value of the smallest things predicated on a world to come. It surprised him. That the space which these things occupied was itself an expectation. (*R* 158)

Like the messianic religions, great literature should finally be taken to imply a certain expectation. This expectation may be that of the reader toward the work, yet it is also ever that of the piece of art toward its reader. At its most basic, it may simply be this, that there be a future in which we will continue the telling of the tales that, McCarthy suggests, are all part of the universal tale of the world, of our world. In the image of the ruined library, that expectation has been given the lie and has thus in turn given way to "rage" directed at that same implicit, messianic expectation, that the future be better. Expectation, however, is reflexive—and anger thus finally misplaced—for it is the implicit expectation of great art, which serves as the purest representation of what it is to be human in the world, that the reader him- or herself tends to the space in which it may continue to extend its promise. Thereby, we retain the chance to make good on it. Following *The Road*, it is up to us to carry the fire.

"In reality the way of the world is not fixed in any place. [. . .] We ourselves are our own journey" (*CRO* 413–14).[5] We are, then, at a crossroads. Neither the artist's words nor the Word of God will, by themselves, save us from ourselves. Such awareness forces an implacable choice: It is entirely up to us to steer the course of history, in which there are finally "no control groups" (*APH* 239). However, that there is and never was "no might have been" (*APH* 239) does not bar the view of a world in its unfolding, or stifle the pen from drafting new maps to find what other world it may yet be. "I know that one life can change all life. The smallest warp in the fabric can tilt all of creation to run anew. Choice is everywhere and destiny is only a word we give to history" (*WM* 129). True, we may be "free to act only upon what is given" (*CP* 195)—yet what is given, the best of our models show us, is a potential that may well be limitless. It is through confronting the end and dispassionately contemplating the worst that the choice of a different, better way opens up before us. The test, then, is one of our willingness to walk it—and of our faith to do so without guarantee of success. And so, toward this at least temporary end of McCarthy's apocalyptic journey, one finds that the individual journey of (a) life becomes the journey of *life*, of life itself, and the wanderer at once the way and its destination.

In life rather than death.

Notes

INTRODUCTION:
AN AMERICAN APOCALYPSE?

1. Abrams lists five defining criteria of biblical apocalypticism: (1) a *finite teleology*, articulated in (2) a *plot* "with a beginning, a middle, and an end," written by (3) a hidden, *providential* author who determines the "apparent order and connections of things [. . .] and the prepotent but hidden order of Providence," which is shaped by (4) singular *key events*, which are "abrupt, cataclysmic, and make a drastic, even an absolute, difference," connecting (5) the loss of the original paradise before the Fall to the perfected paradise-to-be in a *symmetrical pattern* (35–37). Literarily, Grimm, Faulstich, and Kuon call apocalyptic such works that imply "a specific, literary model of interpreting reality and history," that is, "such works as imagine—sometimes by having recourse to the stock of Judeo-Christian imagery and symbolism—a progressively dissolving order moving inexorably toward downfall and catastrophe" (9).

2. Thus, part of the book of Daniel was written while the Hebrews were persecuted under the Hellenistic king Antiochus IV Epiphanes (175–164 BC) and the ensuing Maccabean revolt, whereas the Christian book of Revelation is usually dated to fall into the reign of either Nero or, more likely, Domitian (81–96 AD) during which Christians were similarly persecuted (ESV 1582–84, 2453–54).

3. A 2010 study by Pew Research Center showed a majority of Evangelicals (58%) and a still considerable number of mainline Protestants (27%), Catholics (32%), and unaffiliated believers (20%) predicting that Christ would "probably" or "definitely"

return before 2050 (Pew Research Center 15). In 2014, a survey of the Public Religion Research Institute and the American Academy of Religion found that, though Americans were overall more likely to interpret natural disasters as the result of natural causes, such as climate change (62%), a substantial and increasing number (49%) saw such disasters as signs of "'the end times' as described in the Bible." According to the authors, "Americans from different religious backgrounds vary in their willingness to attribute the severity of recent natural disasters to the biblical end times. White evangelical Protestants are substantially more likely to attribute the severity of recent natural disasters to biblical end times (77%) than climate change (49%). While nearly three-quarters (74%) of black Protestants also agree that natural disasters are a sign of the apocalypse, they are about as likely to see these natural disasters as evidence of climate change (73%). Substantially fewer Catholics (43%), white mainline Protestants (35%), and religiously unaffiliated Americans (29%) see recent natural disasters as evidence of the biblical end times" (Jones, Cox, and Navarro-Rivera 23).

4. In a rarely covered interview, Matussek muses that "like the preachers in his novels, Cormac McCarthy is a moralist. Less fanatical, more resigned. When he speaks of the downfall, he speaks not of ecological or economic catastrophes, but of the death of 'the human within,' of the death of meaning. 'How can you live without morality?' he says at one point."

5. McCarthy voiced the same sentiment more amicably fifteen years later: "There are a lot of people out there—a lot who grew up in the Sixties and are still flower children—who imagine you can just get people to stop being violent [. . .]. They pretend that the world they live in is that world, but it's not [. . .] and probably never will be" (Kushner). One is tempted to identify McCarthy's position as rooted in a conservative outlook, as indicated in a note from the Cormac McCarthy Papers: "Liberalism is the ideology of the rebel, the radical. But those who would make the world new seldom have any sense of how much worse it can get" (91/87/5, n.p.).

6. I do not offer detailed analyses of *Suttree* (1979), the novels of the Border Trilogy (1992–98), or *No Country for Old Men* (2005), nor any of the dramatic texts. The reasons for their exclusion are both pragmatic and content related. For one, literary criticism is unavoidably reductionist, tending to sacrifice context and distort content to suit its interest. Against this, I wish to maintain as much as possible the integrity of the literary work. While my selection is motivated by literary substance, the works excluded could be shown to fit my argument as well. In addition, as the inclusion of *The Crossing* above already shows, I draw on these works where it seems particularly illuminating, without claiming to offer full interpretations. However, in my assessment, the works in question offer little that is substantially new in advancing the lines of McCarthy's apocalypse, instead exploring grounds similar to those covered in the works selected for analysis. On the other hand, the integrative reading I wish to offer by necessity hinges upon an extensive amount of close reading and the inclusion of scholarship that has been done to realize its explanatory potential, to achieve breadth as well as depth. Regarding the length of the resulting analyses, it is unavoidable to select.

7. In the 1970s and 1980s, mimetic theory consistently expanded from literature and

anthropology to psychology, history, economics, and other related fields. Apart from its unfashionable aspiration to grand theorism, what likely kept it from achieving the same level of influence attained, for instance, by structuralism and deconstruction was Girard's eventual outing as a Christian: "In France [Girard] was a *cause célèbre* or a *bête noire*, because his argument for a universal anthropological theory, combined with the position that the deepest insights of Western culture stem from biblical revelation, shocked and alienated those who held to the assumption of the all-encompassing nature of language and who tended to ignore Christianity or view it with contempt" (*GR* 4).

CHAPTER 1. SANGUINARY SIGNIFIERS:
THE DIS|ORDERLY LANGUAGE OF MYTH, VIOLENCE, AND ENTROPY

1. Girard originally adopted this myth from Roger Bastide's summary in *Ethnologie Générale* (*SG* 48–49), but a more focused treatment can be found in Girard's essay "Disorder and Order in Mythology" (1984).

2. Stylistically, the meeting of divergent mythic and folkloric traditions has its counterpart in McCarthy's polyglot merging of faithfully rendered Southern and Southwestern vernacular and the increasing use of Spanish with what fellow author Madison Smartt Bell identifies as McCarthy's "high style." The latter is characterized by its "demanding vocabulary," "sonorous tone," "archaic diction," and "long rolling run-on sentences" built around the "repetition of conjunctions" and the use of "linked independent clauses rather than subordinate clauses" (2000, 5). As this high style would not seem out of place next to the epic poetry of Homer, both of McCarthy's styles can be said to reflect the origins of myth and folklore, which, as oral traditions, are syntactically marked by simplicity and repetition.

3. The connection between myth and literature is as old as it is intimate. Aristotle, in his *Poetics*, built his theory of tragedy around the representational imitation of action, specifically the composition of events resulting from the acts of dramatic agents—the *mythos* or "plot" (1449b–1450a). Even Plato, otherwise known for his distrust of the poets, often resorted to mythic stories, the more effectively to educate his pupils.

4. For instance, "[m]ythology has been interpreted by the modern intellect as a primitive, fumbling effort to explain the world of nature (Frazer); as a production of poetical fantasy from prehistoric times, misunderstood by succeeding ages (Müller); as a repository of allegorical instruction, to shape the individual to his group (Durkheim); as a group dream, symptomatic of archetypal urges within the depths of the human psyche (Jung); as the traditional vehicle of man's profoundest metaphysical insights (Coomaraswamy); and as God's Revelation to His children (the Church). Mythology is all of these" (Campbell 1993, 382). To this, one may add Campbell's own idea of a universal *hero-* or *monomyth*, Lévi-Strauss's interest in myth's invariant structures, or Barthes's critique of contemporary myths. What distinguishes these theories are the respective relations they establish between myth and such fields as religion and ritual, science, philosophy, psychology, sociology, history, ideology, and art.

5. *Cosmogony* or creation myth is the most pronouncedly religious paradigm. It is
   likely the oldest as well since "for the world to be lived in, it had first to be founded"
   (Coupe 58). *Fertility myth* associates the death, resurrection, or replacement of a god
   or king with the vegetative cycles of nature and the state of the realm. *Heroic myth*
   tells of a hero who accomplishes often superhuman feats, such as the slaying of a
   monster and the founding or the regeneration of his community. Finally, *deliverance
   myth* encompasses narratives such as the Hebrews' exodus from Egypt or the
   pilgrims' migration from Europe to found their "shining city upon the hill," as well as
   teleological models of history such as the Apocalypse, or the historical materialism of
   Marx and Engels. It envisions an imperfect state of things, a people's liberation from it,
   and its movement toward a more perfect state (Coupe 1–5). These ideal types are often
   mixed, as the hero may turn out to be the new king in a community he has regenerated,
   or the founder of a community born at the end of deliverance.

6. John's use of *logos* may be said to subsume, reunite, or blend the Greek mythos and
   logos, which originally overlap in meaning. The creation in John can thus be read as
   equally mythical, philosophical, and religious.

7. That this view is, in fact, still McCarthy's is confirmed by his 2017 essay on the
   unconscious and the origin of language: "At some point the mind must grammaticize
   facts and convert them to narratives. The facts of the world do not for the most part
   come in narrative form. We have to do that" (29).

8. In conceiving myth as a primitive proto-science, nineteenth-century mythographers
   posited that its purpose was to explain the world. Eliade argues that in addition
   to explaining the world, myth teaches humans to live in it by providing models
   for "a simple physiological function such as eating" to "social, economic, cultural,
   military or other activity" (98). Leeming posits that myth is instrumental in forming
   "cultural identity" and in expressing "any given culture's literal or metaphorical
   understanding of various aspects of reality" (xi–xii), whereas Armstrong roots myth in
   the awareness of death, deeming it "designed to help us to cope with the problematic
   human predicament. It helped people to find their place in the world and their true
   orientation" (6).

9. This is a point frequently argued in mythography. Armstrong asserts that myth "puts us
   in the correct spiritual or psychological posture for right action" (4). In more concrete
   terms, it can be argued, as Eliade does, that the "supreme function" of myth is "to 'fix'
   the paradigmatic models for all rites and all significant human activities," which are
   dramatized in the "paradigmatic gestures of the gods" (98). This type of relationship
   is characterized by what Girard calls *external mediation*, the process through which
   humans learn to follow the ideals, aspirations, and desires set by the example of their
   distant and admired models; only here, the imitative imperative emitted by the
   mythological model is not simply *individual*, as in Don Quixote's admiration for
   Amadis de Gaulle, but principally *collective*, affecting a culture in its entirety.

10. If the idea of an imitative ideological imperative exerted by myth seems too outlandish
    a hypothesis, one need only consider the language used by soldiers and officials during
    the Vietnam War (1959–75). Thus, President Lyndon B. Johnson could encourage

American troops in Vietnam to "bring the coonskin home" and to "nail it to the barn" (cit. in *GN* 496). In an interview with *Time*, journalist Hugh Sidey compared the situation in Vietnam to the battle of the Alamo, another powerful metaphor in the frontier myth. U.S. Ambassador Maxwell Taylor explained setbacks experienced in the war along similar lines: "It is very hard to plant corn outside the stockade when the Indians are still around" (cit. in *GN* 495). Finally, a veteran judged that the governing idea that infused American soldiers was the *Indian idea*, "the only good gook is a dead gook," and compared the taking of the ears of dead Vietcong to that of taking scalps "like from Indians. Some people were on an Indian trip over there" (*FE* 17). In Vietnam, the communist reds replaced the "redskins" of the American continent. For all appearances, the mythic Indian war metaphor of frontier times was indeed the more or less conscious field manual for soldiers and politicians alike.

11. The phrase "the fatal environment" was not in the original poem, which appeared in the *New York Tribune* on July 10, 1876, as "A Death Sonnet for Custer." It is to be found in the retitled versions published in *Leaves of Grass*, following the 1881–82 and later editions.

12. It is worth pointing out the subversive potential ascribed to *stories* by Arendt (Levinson 2003; Schutz 2003) and Morales (115–16). Stories of resistance or revolution provide models, too. So, myths may be turned on their heads, yet such stories lack myth's collective investment, belonging more in the realm of individual, literary creation. The exception are myths belonging to Coupe's *deliverance* paradigm, which includes the Marxist myth of revolution. Nonetheless, Barthes asserts that myth on the left, which "defines itself in relation to the oppressed," though potentially transformative, tends to be artificial and impoverished (148).

13. Archetypes include central events, such as birth, death, and marriage, as well as motifs, such as creation, flood, and cataclysm, and figures such as anima, shadow, hero, wise elder, child, trickster, and many others (Coupe 140–46). In *The Hero with a Thousand Faces* (1949), Campbell combines Jungian archetypes with Arnold van Gennep's structuring of initiation rites by arranging both according to the template of the monomyth and thus links the task of individuation to the cultural role of myth. Yet to say that such archetypes exist in a collective unconscious requires a metaphysical leap that Coupe associates with "the universal and eternal forms of Plato" (145). Whether such forms exist or not, their axiomatic conjecture only displaces the problem: Archetypes literally are just patterns of which copies are made. Archetypes are begging the question.

14. Violence was thus long considered wholly irrational. Recently, this view has been challenged by evolutionary anthropology, which suggests that it may in fact be a conscript in the service of our "selfish genes." If one can draw insights from the behavior of our closest relatives—the great apes, who engage in deliberate murder, organized raiding, rape, and infanticide—human procreational success, too, may have depended on such strategies. Though limited in how far these findings can illuminate violent phenomena in human *culture*, the idea of violence serving specific ends adds to the complexity of the issue. Thus, Carl von Clausewitz defines the violence of war as a

natural extension of political action. Conversely, Hannah Arendt conceives of it as opposed to the collective power of action that is genuine politics. Maintaining that violence is "ruled by the means-end category," she also asserts that characteristically, the "end is in danger of being overwhelmed by the means" (1970, 4). Differently put, violence takes over where the power of acting together fades away.

15. Mirror neurons are "multimodal association neurons that increase their activity during the execution of certain actions and while hearing or seeing corresponding actions being performed by others" (Keysers R971). It has been suggested that they are "involved in understanding the meaning and intentions of observed actions, learning by imitation, feeling empathy, formation of a 'theory of mind,' and even the development of language" (Dinstein et al. R13). Fleming points out that these theses "have some interesting potential to corroborate the increasing functional role of imitation in the evolution of primates and humans" (176). For specific discussions of the intersections between mimetic theory, developmental psychology, neonatal and infant imitation, neurophysiology, and the topic of mirror neurons, see the contributions by Vittorio Gallese, one of the discoverers of mirror neurons, as well as by Meltzoff, Garrels, and others in *Mimesis and Science* (2011).

16. In his *Poetics*, Aristotle posited that from the early days of childhood, human beings have a proclivity to imitation exceeding that of other animals (see 1448b). Some nineteenth-century works, notably Gabriel Tarde's *Les lois de l'imitation* (1890) and William James's *Principles of Psychology* (1890), paid attention to the social role of imitation. Tarde defined it as an irreducible fact of social interaction—active or passive, intentional or not. Prefiguring Girard, James even speculated that a link existed between human imitation and the dynamics of the violence of crowds: "Man is essentially *the imitative animal*. His whole civilization depends on this trait, which his strong tendencies to rivalry, jealousy, and acquisitiveness reinforce. [. . .] [T]here is the more direct propensity to speak and walk and behave like others, usually without any conscious intention of so doing. And there is the imitative tendency which shows itself in large masses of men, and produces panics, and orgies, and frenzies of violence, and which only the rarest individuals can actively withstand" (1950, 408).

17. Both model and disciple are oblivious of their respective roles, the double imperative, or that they can enter into competition at all. This is especially true for little children, who follow the order to imitate innocently. Again, Girard comments on Freud. For him, the wish to commit incest and patricide does not come from the child, but is an attribution that "spring[s] from the mind of the adult, the model. In the Oedipus myth it is the oracle that puts such ideas into Laius' head, long before Oedipus" is even born (*VS* 175).

18. Like the object of mimetic rivalry, the *objet petit a* exists "in a kind of curved space—the nearer you get to it, the more it eludes your grasp (or the more you possess it, the greater the lack)" (Žižek 2008a, 21). It is "the leftover which embodies the fundamental, constitutive lack," something sought for in vain "because it has no positive consistency—because it is just an objectification of a void," the "original lost

object" that "coincides with its own loss" because it "is precisely the embodiment of this void" (Žižek 2008b, 54, 104, 178).

19. For a detailed analysis, see "'It's More True, But It Ain't as Good': Searching for Truth in the Death-Deferring Dialogue of McCarthy's *The Sunset Limited*" (Wierschem 2014).

20. De Tocqueville observes in *Democracy in America* (1835): "When all the privileges of birth and fortune are abolished, when all professions are accessible to all, and a man's own energies may place him at the top of any one of them, an easy and unbounded career seems open to his ambition [. . .]. But this is an erroneous notion, which is corrected by daily experience. The same equality that allows every citizen to conceive these lofty hopes renders all the citizens less able to realize them; it circumscribes their powers on every side, while it gives freer scope to their desires. Not only are they themselves powerless, but they are met at every step by immense obstacles, which they did not at first perceive. They have swept away the privileges of some of their fellow creatures which stood in their way, but they have opened the door to universal competition; the barrier has changed its shape rather than its position. [. . .] Hence the desire of equality always becomes more insatiable in proportion as equality is more complete" (660–61; also *DDN* 120). In this, de Tocqueville is close to Hobbes, who reasons that in the state of nature, an "equality of ability" among humans results in an "equality of hope in the attaining of our ends" (83).

21. Girard traces this limitation of our perspective to Plato. In *The Republic*, Socrates famously calls out the poets of his time for ascribing base emotions to the gods, depicting divine and heroic crimes and petty conflicts. In his view, their stories and myths provide bad examples for the youthful, future guardians of the just state, and should instead offer uplifting tales promoting civic virtue (377e–379b). During their education, the guardians should imitate only those models and virtues appropriate for brave, level-headed, pious, and free men (395a–e, 500a–d). Girard asserts that in his "fear of mimesis" Plato is "closer than anyone to what is essential," but also finds him deceived by mimesis as he allegedly truncates "the essential dimension of acquisitive behavior, which is also the dimension of conflict" (*TH* 8). Girard may be too sweeping in his criticism, though. While Plato does not directly articulate the idea of acquisitive mimesis, its spirit arguably lives in the prohibitions of the just state explored in *The Republic*. After all, a central requirement of its guardians and political leaders is that they own no private property (416a–417b). The formula "to each his own," which encapsulates but oversimplifies Plato's idea of justice, is logically tied to a prohibition against acquiring what is not one's own or striving toward a position one is not suited for (441c–442c).

22. Sophocles's *Oedipus* is a prime example of this: Looking for the cause of the Theban plague, Creon, Oedipus, and Tiresias are all unwittingly drawn "into the structure of violent reciprocity—which they always think they are outside of, because they all initially come from the outside" (*VS* 69). Another striking example is the second scene of Molière's *Le Bourgeois gentilhomme*, in which a philosopher sets out to settle a dispute between masters of dance, music, and fencing as to the nobility of their

respective arts, only to end up asserting the nobility of his own and starting a brawl with the other three (McKenna 1–3).

23. In general, countermeasures can be described according to categories of prevention, compensation, and the type of arbitration of a judicial system. The latter limits vengeance to a single, publicly administered act of reprisal, which modern societies call justice. Based on the "recognition of the sovereignty and independence of the judiciary" (*VS* 22–23), judgment falls with such authority that no reprisal is possible. Strategies of compensation and prevention predominate in tribal societies. Compensation accords the injured parties "a careful measure of satisfaction" (*VS* 21) to placate their desire for vengeance without inspiring it in others.

24. The same point is made by Žižek regarding Islamic fundamentalism and Huntington's idea of a clash of cultures: "The problem is not cultural difference (their effort to preserve their identity), but the opposite fact that the fundamentalists are already like us, that, secretly, they have already internalized our standards and measure themselves by them" (2009, 73).

25. To Girard, music evokes structure. He is not alone in this, as Boris Gunjević points out: Music, from "Augustine and the whole Hellenistic and Christian tradition up to Descartes," was seen as "the measure of the soul's relation to the body through which we are able to participate in eternal harmony. Just as the soul can recognize in disharmonious music its own distortions and mistakenness, in the same way music can articulate imbalances in the psychological, political, and even cosmic orders" (Žižek and Gunjević 217).

26. Yet this is not the whole story. One of the prima donna's companions posits that there is a secret involved in the conflict that the clown knows—specifically "el secreto [. . .] que en este mundo la máscara es la que es verdadera" (*CRO* 229), that in this world the mask is that which is the truth. The interpretation of this statement hinges upon what referents and meanings we assign to the terms "world," "mask," and "truth." Does "this world" refer merely to the world of the play, to the real world, or perhaps both, insofar as one reflects the other? Regarding "mask," we are prone (as good postmodernists) to take it as a signifier of the malleability and protean construction of personal identity, which leaves no true core or essence of personality behind. The truism goes that we are always wearing a mask, or, in fact, many. In a way, the mask would be the truth, as there is nothing else in either the theater or the "real" world. From a Girardian angle we may associate the mask of self-sufficiency and metaphysical fullness that narcissists and coquettes project strategically toward others by their indifference and arrogance. Also, we must identify the masking operations of mythological imagination in the masks of the gods, heroes, and monsters communities create. Truth, in this sense, amounts to a pragmatic narratological effect: a story is brought to bear upon the world that it effectively shapes to comply with its fiction. At the same time, the prima donna adds that "for the wearer of the mask nothing is changed. The actor has no power to act but only as the world tells him. Mask or no mask is all one to him" (*CRO* 230). Whether a culture turns its victims into monsters or gods, for the victims the outcome is indeed the same. Finally, we can cast ourselves as the actors in the mythic drama enacted.

Hence, we are compelled to "act as the world tells us"—yet that world is ever also of our own making.

27. Among other examples, Girard cites the stories Abraham and Isaac, the episode of Ulysses as captive of Polyphemus, and Sophocles's *Ajax*. He finds that in each of these narratives "an animal intervenes at the crucial moment to prevent violence from attaining its designated victim" (*VS* 6). God sends a ram to be sacrificed instead of Isaac, Ulysses and his men escape the man-eating Cyclops tied to the bellies of his sheep, and as Ajax is denied the fallen hero Achilles's armor, he furiously slaughters a herd of sheep that Athena tricks him into believing are the Greek leaders who offended him. What these cases have in common is that violence does not fall upon the intended victim, but rather on an animal replacement. One might make mention, too, of the story of Cain and Abel. Cain, "a worker of the ground," murders his brother Abel, "a keeper of sheep" (Gn. 4:2–8) after God has rejected his offerings but accepted his brother's. Significantly, the murderer is "the one who does not have the violence-outlet of animal sacrifice at his disposal" (*VS* 4).

28. Initial criticism of Girard charged that he relied on marginal examples of sacrificial practices, taken out of context to fit his theory. While he admits to his idée fixe, the research conducted by both Girard and other scholars has since largely dispelled what validity allegations of cherry-picking held at the publication of *Violence and the Sacred*. Simply put, if you pick cherries for forty years, you end up with a reasonably impressive mountain of cherries. Reflecting the old opposition of particularist and universalist reasoning, the charge of obfuscating cultural contexts is not so much unwarranted as misdirected, for universalism is, in fact, the point. It is true that Girard views "violence as grounded in notions of universal and essential human nature" (Lawrence and Karim 334). Yet the observation that humans imitate one another and so one another's desires is barely more essentialist than the claim that humans breathe, sleep, eat, excrete, and communicate. So when Lawrence and Karim claim that Girard "begs the question [...] of the violence of the 'modes of domination,' specifically the modes of racism, xenophobia, sexism, classicism, homophobia, and ageism that are integral to systemic violence" (334), they are themselves presupposing these modes, ignoring the question of their genesis and underlying principles. Girard's generative hypothesis pertains to the beginnings of culture. Specific modes of domination, which emerge in particular cultures, are shaped by the principles he sees at work, but only channel violence in certain ways (e.g., sexism, racism), without fundamentally altering the underlying pattern.

29. Again, these attributions are mythological. While Girard says much about why a victim *must* be chosen by survivalist necessity and *how* the choice is determined, an open question is what compels humans to choose, i.e., why they actually *do* choose. Hans Blumenberg's *Arbeit am Mythos* may fill in a blank here. As deficient beings, he posits, early humans are thrown into a world that seems vast and silent, amorphous and empty—in McCarthy's words "a land of some other order [...] whose true geology [is] not stone but fear" (*BM* 47). The unknown fills man with constant dread and paralyzing terror. Psychologically, this tension must eventually be relieved. Again, myth serves to impose symbolic order upon the threatening chaos, and it does so by

designating and naming the unknown, thus putting it at a certain distance. The forms that emerge may be monsters, but the transformation at least makes it possible to temper fear by addressing and in a sense banishing them (Blumenberg 194–95). In German, the difference is between diffuse "Angst" and concrete "Furcht." Applied to the sacrificial crisis, it becomes clear why a narrowing down of the universal threat is necessary and evolutionarily possible. While Girard grants that prohibition is motivated by "the fear of violence" (*VS* 221), it plays a central role in ritual, too: the designation of victims, who are attributed with markers of monstrosity, may be seen as a psychologically necessary step in containing and concretizing an unsustainable, diffuse angst.

30. Indeed, one is well advised to recall Nietzsche's warning that physics and the sciences are themselves less an explanation of the world (*Welt-Erklärung*) than another way of interpreting (*Welt-Auslegung*) and arranging (*Welt-Zurechtlegung*) it according to how humans see it (Nietzsche 2007, 28). The problem of insufficient knowledge in observing and theorizing about the world comes to a head in the discussion about the ontological and epistemological nature of order and disorder. If the impression is one of randomness and disorder, the problem is "that randomness contains uncertainty about its own nature, that is, an uncertainty on the nature of uncertainty" (Morin 103).

31. In *Warped Passages*, McCarthy's first name is misspelled "Cormack." Other associates of McCarthy's include theoretical physicist and biologist Geoffrey West, paleobiologist and *Extinction* author Douglas Erwin, geochemist and climatologist Daniel Schräg, and chaos and complexity theorist J. Doyne Farmer.

32. Some contributions in this vein are offered by various ecocritical studies (e.g., Keller-Estes 2013), Ciarán Dowd's work on geophysiology and complexity (2013), Julius Greve's investigation of Lorenz Oken's philosophy of nature in McCarthy (2015), as well as the work of Patrick O'Connor.

33. The reference to "Heatdeath" in *The Road* is found in a passage that has been crossed out on a page still marked *The Grail*. The page is numbered on the top left-hand side with the number 21/219 and the date 21 AUG, and a circled 5 on the bottom left.

34. Admittedly, it is scientifically imprecise to speak of heat and work as different forms of energy, which itself is "the capacity of a system to do work" (Atkins 18). Rather, the terms "work" and "heat" represent transfer processes of energy, which make use of the uniform or random motion of atoms in the surroundings.

35. It is generally presumed that the universe is an isolated system. Barring the entrance of comets and meteorites into the atmosphere, or the launching of crafts and satellites into space, the earth itself can be considered a closed system, as can a closed pot of water boiling on a stove. Take away the lid, and you get an open system, which is the category of living organisms. Additionally, once processes of communication and social organization enter into consideration, these categories assume an increasingly metaphoric character.

36. Entropy is a negative term, the measure of a loss. Seeking for a positive counterpart indicating the ability of a system to do work and grow more ordered, Felix Auerbach,

among others, suggested *ectropy*, and Ernst Schrödinger put forth *negative entropy*, which Léon Brillouin shortened to *negentropy*. Such linguistic confusion involved in the terminology of entropy is a topic all to itself (Freese 1997, 96–98).

37. The closest modern correspondence to McCarthy's concept here may be found in ideas such as Wilhelm Ostwald's *Energetik*, which held "all material, psychological, and spiritual reality" to be "based on 'energy' and therefore subject to the First and the Second Law of Thermodynamics" (Freese 1997, 150). It is worth noting, too, that the semantics of Aristotelian *dynamis* and *energeia* are much broader than the modern term "energy."

38. John Grady's loss of Alejandra to her grandmother is similarly expressed in entropic terms. It is not simply John Grady's defeat to Alfonsa, but the void of desire that is experienced as "something cold and soulless enter[ing] him like another being" (*APH* 254). Two pages later, the "pain of the world" is similarly described as "some formless parasitic being seeking out the warmth of human souls" (256)—indicating that the suffering of the world may be related to the parasitic, entropic force that I will identify with mimetic contagion and the exhausting violence that results from it.

39. In those instances when the entropy theorem left the domain of physics to make its way into the humanities, it was interpreted in terms of a sweeping pessimism that came naturally to the decades that followed the fin de siècle and witnessed the conflagration of Europe in World War I. In works such as *A Letter to American Teachers of History* (1910), *The Degradation of the Democratic Dogma* (1919), and *Der Untergang des Abendlandes* (1918), Henry Adams and Oswald Spengler applied the second law to history, using it as a rationalization of their prognoses of general sociocultural decline (Freese 1997, 164–71; Decker 82–91). In psychoanalysis, Freud tentatively connected entropy to his death drive (Freese 1997, 117–18).

40. Herbert Spencer cast evolution as a cycle of construction, sustainment, and dissolution that in sum progressed in the general direction of higher complexity. Henri Bergson opposed entropy to his notion of an élan vital, an extraspatial, psychological vital force that was not subject to the laws of physics and so curtailed the universality of Clausius's principle. Friedrich Nietzsche rejected the notion of any sort of final state of equilibrium for his structurally and traditionally mythic idea of *eternal return*. He reasoned that in an eternal universe with limited matter and energy, every possible arrangement of states would have been produced an infinite amount of times. The second law to him constituted an at best provisional hypothesis (Nietzsche 1988, 14[188]). Providing a mathematical version of Nietzsche's argument, Ernst Zermelo applied Henri Poincaré's *recurrence theorem* to suggest that in time any state in a mechanical system will eventually recur. Unfortunately, the time required was a lot older than the universe itself (Freese 1997, 113).

41. Consequently, the second law became associated with things that though not impossible, "are just too improbable to happen" (Freese 1997, 111). For the organization of molecules in a more ordered state is not impossible—it is just extremely improbable. Henry A. Bent expressed as much in an analogy that became as famous as it is memorable: "At room temperature [. . .] conversion of a single calorie of thermal

energy completely into potential energy is a less likely event than the production of Shakespeare's complete works fifteen quadrillion times in succession without error by a tribe of wild monkeys punching randomly on a set of typewriters" (29). Alternatively, to cite another popular analogy that any parent will relate to, it is highly probable that the orderly arrangements of toys, children's books, etc. in a tidied-up playroom will soon give way to disarray once the disordering agent of a child is introduced. This is so simply because there are infinitely more arrangements that can be called untidy or disorderly than can be called orderly (Bateson 3–8).

42. Molecules, for instance in a gas, exist at different energy levels. Depending on variables such as the size and temperature of the system—in this case the container holding the gas—there is a limited number of possible microstates. The higher this number is, that is, the higher the system's energy, the less likely one is to predict a microstate. At low temperature, a high number of molecules in the gas will concentrate at the lower energy levels. So, when one blindly selects a molecule, it is relatively *probable* to predict correctly that it will come from one of these states. Conversely, at higher temperatures, the molecules of a system spread across the higher levels, and the probability of selecting a molecule from any specific energy level decreases: "This increased uncertainty of the precise energy level a molecule occupies is what [physicists] really mean by the 'disorder' of the system, and corresponds to an increased entropy" (Atkins 53).

43. Shannon's paper was republished one year later, under a slightly altered title that significantly adopted the direct article, and included an expository essay by Warren Weaver. More than sixty years later, Luciano Floridi warns that "[w]ork on the concept of information is still at that lamentable stage when disagreement affects even the way in which the problems themselves are provisionally phrased and framed" (2).

44. Von Neumann reasoned that "first, the function is already in used in thermodynamics under that name; second, and more importantly, most people don't know what entropy really is, and if you use the word 'entropy' in an argument you will win every time!" (cit. in Freese 1997, 198). The question of whether informational and thermodynamic entropy are identical or analogous, or whether the formulas are only symbolically isomorphic but otherwise unrelated is still subject to debate (Freese 1997, 197–202). Floridi argues: "In thermodynamics, the greater the entropy, the less available the energy. This means that high entropy corresponds to high energy deficit, but so does entropy in MTC: higher values of entropy correspond to higher quantities of data deficit. Perhaps von Neumann was right after all" (47).

45. In this, information "relates not so much to what you *do* say, as to what you *could* say," and thus designates "a measure of one's freedom of choice" (Shannon and Weaver 8–9) among possible messages. The probability of a certain message is calculated against the probabilities of all possible messages one could select and *has* selected in the past. Conversely and more intuitively, contemporary information theory defines information as made up of data that are not just well-formed but also meaningful (Floridi 21), and thus defines it as *negentropy*—as "a measure of order or of organization" (Bertalanffy 42).

46. To acknowledge some of the problems involved, in addition to the question of (1) whether information must be considered as the direct or the inverse correlative of a system's entropy, it is subject to debate (2) whether one understands it as a measure of randomness or of organization, (3) whether one considers *potential* information, as does Shannon, or *actual* information, as does Brillouin, and finally (4) whether one considers the information contained in a system or the information required to describe it. Rudolf Arnheim illustrates what happens when both concepts are mixed: "What sequence of events will be least predictable and therefore carry a maximum of information? Obviously a totally ordered one, since when we are confronted with chaos we can never predict what will happen next. The conclusion is that total disorder provides a maximum of information; and since information is measured by order, a maximum of order is conveyed by a maximum of disorder. Obviously, this is a Babylonian muddle. Somebody or something has confounded our language" (15).

47. In the decades to follow, Nicolas Georgescu-Roegen unmasked the (implicitly mechanist) capitalist view of the economy as a *perpetuum mobile* and argued for a new "minimal bioeconomic program" that included various measures to increase the sustainability of life on earth. Influenced primarily by the informational view of entropy, Lila L. Gatlin translated it into genetics by relating such concepts as uncertainty, variety, and storage to the sequential information of the DNA. In James Lovelock's Gaia theory, the ability of a system to reduce its internal entropy became a central criterion in the definition of life itself.

48. Cant repeatedly uses the metaphor of "cultural entropy" in his monograph (2008). More specifically, Georg Guillemin notes that McCarthy's pastoralism in *Suttree* "subjects the symbol of intruding industrialism itself to destruction, as if to suggest a shared tendency to entropy" (2004, 15), and Jay Ellis in his "Keynote Address to the Knoxville Conference" identifies "the idea that any world arises out of iterative and yet locally mutable creative force on the brink of ever-present entropy and destruction" (2008, 37).

49. As Fleming points out, Jean-Pierre Dupuy, Henri Atlan, and others have likewise tentatively explored "parallels between the morphogenetic scope of Girard's theory and theories of self-organization in the physical sciences" (172). As far as I am aware, most of these inquiries were restricted to the first half of the 1980s, the high point of inquiry being represented by a joint symposium at Stanford University, in 1981, which was documented in the collection *Disorder and Order* (1984).

50. To these formal connections, less substantial yet fascinating analogies may be added that allow for connections between the Girardian language of social disorder and "the language of order through disorder in contemporary science." Examples are such words as "disturbance," "turbulence," and "trouble," all of which stem from the Latin *turba*, which designates a crowd, specifically "the mob on the rampage." Another word is "fluctuation," which suggests "the important role played by the flood in mythology"—one of Girard's *symbols of desymbolization* that may be "symbolic of the disturbed mob." Finally, the etymology and connotations of *noise* correlate both entropy and information to violence and the operation of myth: "in French, *noise*,

which means 'quarrel' [...]; such words as *bruit, rumeur*, 'rumor' in English, all [...]
carry negative implications in regard to the sound they designate. A 'rumor,' or a
'noise,' interferes malignantly with the only sound that should really be heard, the one
regarded as the message, the official message. Now, it is remarkable that on the margins
of a great number of cultural traditions one hears the same 'rumor' in regard to the
death of a primordial hero, the original legislator or founder of the cultural order. The
official message is that he was miraculously taken up to heaven, or some such story, but
according to the 'rumor' he was killed by the entire group of those who benefited most
from his death" (Girard 1984, 86–87).

51. Whether one believes in it or not, it cannot be denied that complications in vocabulary
that come from adopting alien paradigms have been at the helm of past breakthroughs,
or lead to new perspectives. As we have seen, Girard himself occasionally employs the
cybernetic language of feedback and runaway (*TH* 292), and discusses analogies like
those above. One may also surmise, with Lévi-Strauss, "the kinds of procedure which
Nature uses at one level of reality are bound to reappear at different levels" (1995, 10).
Projects such as those of Georgescu-Roegen, Lovelock, or Gatlin actively endorse this
view. The obvious objection to Lévi-Strauss's claim is that, with no accessible book
of nature, we have no way of knowing the sum total of nature's repertoire, nor the
malleability and generative productivity of its procedures.

52. In *Blood Rites*, Barbara Ehrenreich similarly hypothesizes that myths represent and
memorize a transformation, the evolutionary transition of human ancestry from prey
to predator. She asserts sweepingly that there is "no question" that sacrifice reenacts
"the predation of animals on humans" (51). Although Ehrenreich quotes *Violence
and the Sacred*, her treatment of Girard's theory indicates that her engagement with it
is cursory at best. Instead of identifying the pronounced centrality of mimesis in his
work, she wrongly reasons that Girard assumes "the existence of an aggressive instinct"
(29) akin to Freud's death drive, which is patently wrong and explicitly rejected by
Girard. Yet it is worth noting that Ehrenreich's *from-prey-to-predator* hypothesis itself
has some merit and shows similarities with Girard's when it comes to questions of
the rise of civilization and process of hominization, the threat of the common foe
that unites the group, the institutionalization of violence in ritual, or the double-face
of the predator/victim as both provider and destroyer. On closer examination, both
hypotheses may turn out to be at least partially concurrent.

53. Thus, in a letter to James Madison, Thomas Jefferson wrote: "I think our governments
will remain virtuous [...] as long as they remain chiefly agricultural; and this will be as
long as there shall be vacant lands in any part of America. When they get piled upon
one another in large cities, as in Europe, they will become corrupt as in Europe" (cit. in
Hofstadter 27). Again, a lack of distance is seen as breeding conflict.

54. The same spirit hovered over the face of Wounded Knee, Sand Creek, or, for that
matter, My Lai. Slotkin's assertion that the Puritan "could never understand [...] the
relationship between these two faces of his character, and he was certainly unable to
see this as proof of his human kinship with the Indians" (*FE* 137), reinforces that

mimetic doubles caught in mutual antagonism are utterly incapable of perceiving their sameness.

55. In fact, Theodore Roosevelt would rationalize such acts of violence into a systematic historiographical scenario. In true myth-fatalist fashion, he envisioned the West as a quasi-Darwinian arena in which the violent "succession of savages by civilized races" would bring about a "return to the life of an earlier historical stage" (*GN* 38) that would ultimately renew the vigor of the Anglo-American race. The effects of regeneration through violence can thus be traced historically from the local Greek community to the intercommunal level of the young American nation. The mechanism, too, is exactly that of scapegoating writ large—with one crucial difference: few are as unapologetic and open in their justification of violence as Roosevelt.

56. This is partly because we tend to view myths as fantastical. Even where we grant that myth contains a certain truth, we view it in philosophical or spiritual terms. A second factor in our changed reception is that "medieval and modern persecutors do not worship their victims, they only hate them. They are therefore easy to identify as victims. It is more difficult to spot the victim in a supernatural being who is a cult object" (*SG* 112).

57. Girard's argument resembles that of Nietzsche in *Zur Genealogie der Moral*. Nietzsche posited an original order of powerful masters, whose natural morality of "good-bad" was supplanted by the oppressed slaves' ressentiment morality of "good-evil." The latter Nietzsche identified with the morality of Judeo-Christianity; particularly, the crucified god of Christianity was the god of victims per se. In works like *Der Antichrist*, Nietzsche saw the conflict of the West as that between Greek classicism and Christianity, personified as that between Dionysus and the Crucified. Ironically, the converted Catholic is in agreement with the patron saint of nihilism.

58. With the revelation of My Lai, Americans were suddenly forced to perceive themselves as the "savages" of the frontier myth, as Slotkin explains: "After Mylai [*sic*], the logic of the captivity/rescue myth required us to identify ourselves as the Indians, and by that logic our mission now became one of rescuing Vietnam from 'us,' or (better) of rescuing us from ourselves" (*GN* 588). All too often, however, the countermyths thus created do not lead to any serious demythologization, but become mere inversions of the original myth from which they "draw nourishment [. . .] rather like worms feeding on a corpse" (*VS* 206).

CHAPTER 2. DISSOLVED IN A PALE AND BROKEN IMAGE: PASTORALISM, MIMESIS, AND DIS|ORDER IN *THE ORCHARD KEEPER*

1. For a detailed account of McCarthy's relationship to Erskine, see King (2011).

2. Several minor characters serve as occasional focalizers, most notably John Wesley's father, Kenneth Rattner. Other examples are June Tipton, the barman Cabe, and Mr. Eller the storeowner. In most of these instances however, the reader is allowed but the shortest of glimpses into the perception of these characters.

3. As David Paul Ragan suggests, the latter aspect may be seen as an example of the adaptability of living nature that John Wesley needs to emulate in contrast to the failing antinomianism of Ownby and Sylder (26).

4. Several critics, among them Luce, Prather, and Cant have identified John Wesley as the narrator, or at least as an influence on the more abstract narrative voice of the novel. This is only the more likely due to the evidence of "Wake for Susan": John Wesley's prototype, Wes, imagines the story of Susan in a parallel narrative situation to the frame of *The Orchard Keeper* sitting by her tombstone in a graveyard (Cant 60).

5. Some scholars connect the ruin of the orchard with the First World War. This would account for the lack of fruit pickers (Luce 2009, 31). However, Rattner is killed in 1934, likely in August, and Ownby's reflection on the orchard takes place six years later (see *OK* 52). Depending on local factors, peach harvest takes place in a period from May to August, which puts the time of the orchard's ruin in late spring to early summer of 1920—at least one and a half years after the end of World War I.

6. In the end, the inn does not collapse down the precipice (though its porch does) but, in one of the unexplained mysteries of the novel, burns down on the ritualistically significant date of winter solstice 1936. Luce suspects that the fire may have been laid by members of the temperance movement glimpsed on John Wesley's excursion to Knoxville, though the text provides little evidence either way.

7. More so, they are a danger to himself. The tire of his Ford coupe blowing up gives Kenneth Rattner the chance to assault him, the accident of his Plymouth on the creek bridge will necessitate his rescue by John Wesley, and water in the gas tank of his third car eventually leads to his arrest.

8. For an opposing view, see Natalie Grant's essay on "Man and the Natural World in *The Orchard Keeper*" (2002).

9. For a more detailed exploration of the TVA's effect on the region, see Luce (2009, 18–23). One of the specificities of eastern Tennessee is that the Lost Cause of the Confederacy is not part of regional mythology. Plantation work dependent on slavery was an economic nonfactor, most slaves were domestic, and the sentiment predominantly in favor of the Union, which was also supported militarily. The complicated history of the region is alluded to in Warn Pulliam's statement that "back then this was the North" (*OK* 145).

10. According to Luce, Charles Joseph Sr. was in fact "the chief attorney responsible for processing the condemnation of [the] properties" (2009, 22) of the families displaced by the TVA.

11. Apart from secondary characters, several elements such as settings and particular details of description were inspired autobiographically. For instance, an actual Brown Mountain orchard with a pit "four feet deep and bottomed with green slime" used as "a natural vat for mixing insecticide" must have served as a model for the Red Mountain orchard of the novel (Gibson 26).

12. Sylder himself seems to identify with the figure of the heroic outlaw, as is evidenced by

his singing of the W. C. Handy song "Long Gone John (from Bowling Green)" as he evades the police on his tours (*OK* 76).

13. In 1934, Sylder owns a fast, new coupe, which is later identified as a Ford (*OK* 45) and thus likely a Model 40 build with a V8 motor. Rattner does not specify his made-up model of the V8.

14. What Luce omits is the aspect of symmetry as Rattner "looks back" through the mirror.

15. McCarthy may be subtly referring to one of the most influential stories concerned with the monstrous double, Robert Louis Stevenson's *Strange Case of Dr. Jekyll and Mr. Hyde*. Like Rattner, Hyde evokes disgust among those who meet him and, as Sylder's view of the terror on Rattner's face, an unspecified notion of "physical deformity" (*OK* 38). Similar to Sylder's assessment, Hyde is morally singled out by Jekyll: "Edward Hyde, alone in the ranks of mankind, was pure evil" (Stevenson 81).

16. This pattern repeats itself with Sylder's later protégé John Wesley, who rejects the sexual advances of the precocious Wanita Tipton and becomes a part of the community through his growing awareness of death, the hunt, and the disillusioned loss of innocence as he is confronted with the new order's callous utilitarianism.

17. As in other instances, McCarthy may be playing with the readers' expectations. Sylder does not actually vomit, suggesting the contamination remains. At the least, Sylder's journey follows Arnold van Gennep's tripartite ritual initiation pattern of separation, transition, and reincorporation, with regard to his loss of a job, his departure from Red Branch, and his return after the murder. His journey involves at least four of five elements that Freese identifies as central in the American story of initiation (1998, 171–77): discovery of evil within himself and without (i.e., his double Rattner), loss of innocence and gain of experience (i.e., the traumatic murder), incorporation into society (i.e., his return to Red Branch), and self-discovery (i.e., settling down and maturation).

18. The only act of violence against another person we see him commit is his nightly assault on Gifford. Luce assumes that Sylder's act is limited to the single punch actually featured in the book (2009, 54); however, Sylder's swollen fist and comment about Gifford's continuous "astin who it was" (*OK* 168) indicate that the beating may have extended beyond the single hit. Be that as it may, the act is committed in the name of protecting John Wesley and the community itself from Gifford, whose "selling out" of his neighbors destroys social cohesion, which, in the communal ethics of the early McCarthy, amounts to a cardinal sin.

19. After "A Drowning Incident," this is the second time McCarthy makes use of the Oedipal conflict between father and son. The latter, Cant has traced, intensifies throughout the novels up to *Blood Meridian* and then goes through a phase of relaxation until evolving into a positive relation with *No Country for Old Men* and especially *The Road*. Following the mimetic pattern, this theme is less important, given that the Oedipal rivalry is another mimetic relation involving but a few additional complications.

20. Incidentally, Legwater is described as a "spodomantic sage divining in driven haste

the fate of whole galaxies against their imminent ruin" (*OK* 240). Spodomancy is the ancient art of divination from cinders, soot, and ashes, especially such as involved in ritual sacrifice.

21. For a detailed investigation of heroism in connection to McCarthy's use of narrative perspective and character interiority, see Cooper (2011b, 1–23).

22. Scout, whom Ownby got as a pup in trade for a "broken shotgun" (*OK* 93) thus becomes a surrogate victim to an entirely irrational act of violence. Also, Brickmann writes: "In a community named Red Branch, the killing of a hound, Cuchulain meaning 'the hound of Culain,' must signify an incredible betrayal" (63).

23. For details on the historical Lemuel Ownby, who became a local legend for his resistance to the displacement policy enacted in the wake of the national park creation, and who only died in 1984 at age ninety-five, see Luce (2009, 15–18). Ragan (1999) compares Ownby to Leatherstocking as well as Merlin and Prospero, Hall sees him as "a Caucasian Uncle Remus" (72), Luce (2009) also associates him with Thoreau and again Natty Bumppo, Frye (2009) with Thoreau and Emerson, and Domsch (2012) once more with Thoreau.

24. Though Rattner's corpse is most likely discovered some days or even weeks after Sylder disposes of it, Ownby cuts his staff on the night following the murder, unwittingly preparing for his role as keeper (*OK* 46).

25. Luce suggests that Ellen was pregnant and had a miscarriage (2009, 40).

26. Sanborn's study of animals in McCarthy's fiction identifies the cat—also known as cougar, mountain lion, or "ghost cat"—as both "fact and fiction, hunter and haunter" (2006, 28) and the only animal that is able to strike fear into the hearts of men, even if present only as a rumor, which provides occasion for the practical joke Ownby plays on his fellow Red Branchers for being unable to tell a hoot-owl's scream from that of a panther. "Man must respect the panther, and as such, man as mythmaker, mythologizes the feline at the highest position of the feline hierarchy" (Sanborn 2006, 28).

27. Another possibility is that he kills his rival in the confrontation or afterward. This may be the implication of Ownby's internal monologue in the asylum (*OK* 228). Based on the assumption of a limitation of criminal liability in time, after seven years, he assumes Rattner's killer is free of (legal) persecution or (spiritual) retribution. He recalls his conversation with some lawyer and refers to a nine-year period of his own "scoutin" in the wilderness, which clearly does not refer to the seven years he tends to Rattner's body (Luce 2009, 42).

28. This process could also be described as the destruction of Ownby's masochistic self, understood in the existential sense that Girard attributes to the term and that is primary to any sexual relation but rather implies the constant search of the "slave" for an insurmountable obstacle, the master, to the fulfillment of his metaphysical desire (*DDN*, 176). Other than Girard's masochist, who is aware of the relation between his unhappiness and his desire, Ownby's self-imposed solitude would seem to signify his renunciation of desire itself by renouncing the world. Like Black in *The Sunset Limited*, he is cured "of just about ever cravin" (39).

29. Due to its relevance, I wish to mention the consequential theory that associates the tank with Oak Ridge and the Manhattan Project, which is proposed among others by Natalie Grant, Chris Walsh, and Wade Hall, who suggest the tank is a storage facility for "atomic waste atop a nearby mountain—like an ironic cathedral tower announcing itself to a fallen world" (Hall 72; see also Grant 78, and Walsh 2009, 46, 53). Cant takes up this suggestion and establishes a link of the tank to the TVA, which supplied Oak Ridge with electrical power. He goes on to claim that "the Manhattan Project, and its Oak Ridge installation were in place by 1940, the year in which the tank is attacked" (Cant 67). However, though the fear of nuclear annihilation resonates both with McCarthy's Border Trilogy and the decade in which *The Orchard Keeper* was written, and despite Cant's assurance to the contrary, this idea is in fact "a chronological impossibility" (Cant 67). As Richard Rhodes establishes in *The Making of the Atomic Bomb*, the Oak Ridge town and area were indeed acquired and established as late as September 1942 (486). This is two solid years after Ownby shoots the tank, which is to say nothing of the unlikelihood that even as early as 1940, nuclear waste would be stored above ground and unguarded. Wesley Morgan provides an overview of the range of interpretations. He is also the one who identifies the apparent real-life model of the tank as a navigational installation of the Federal Aviation Administration, regulating both civilian and military air traffic. As this installation would not have been in place before the 1950s, Morgan judges McCarthy's employment of the tank an anachronism (2012).

30. The association of the mythological wasteland with the tank could also relate Arthur Ownby to either the mystical King Arthur or Anfortas, the wounded fisher king. Motifs from grail legend certainly sit well with the overall framework of myth in McCarthy's work.

31. We may add to this that as if to evoke the gun shells Ownby prepares and fires into the tank (*OK* 94, 97), the senior who makes the remark is identified, uncharacteristically for such usually nameless peripheral characters, as John Shell (115).

32. As Sanborn notes and Schlosser acknowledges in her account, there is an Anglo-version of the tale in which a witch preying on cattle in a cat form is caught by the townsmen mid-transformation and thus transfixed in that form. Reportedly, the tale inspired Ambrose Bierce's story "The Eyes of the Panther" (1897).

33. The word *hootnanny* yields additional clues. First reported in the 1920s, its origin is unknown, though it may be related to and adopted from the Scottish New Year's Eve, *hogmanay*—itself a tradition dating back to pagan Norse or Gaelic origins—into the Appalachian vernacular. Today, the word is often used as a placeholder like *thingumajig*—a function word carrying little to no semantic content, which seems quite apt for the ill-defined and vague nature of the tank. According to the *Oxford English Dictionary* (Simpson and Weiner 1989), it also refers to "informal session or concert of folk music and singing" (374). The online *Urban Dictionary*, which allows users to define words in the ways in which they actually use them, is potentially more informative: among other things, the *hootenanny* is a regional musical festivity that "tends to be wild, uninhibited and Dionysian" (Chris Cliche, July 12, 2004), and

hootnanny is further described as a "gathering that involves mischief, paganism, or other heinous acts." It would seem that this type of communal folk festival potentially bears exactly the qualities that following Émile Durkheim, revitalize cultural order and reproduce the experience of its genesis, which for Girard makes festivals a kind of reenactment of the sacrificial crisis (*VS* 120). Finally, Chapman's *New Dictionary of American Slang*, relates it to the word *hewgag* that similarly describes a musical instrument and, more significantly, "an indeterminate unknown mythical creature" (215).

34. Functionally, the grotesque in Kayser's thought works much in the same way that the revelation of the sacred, i.e., *hierophany*, works in Eliade's and to an extent in Girard's thought. The former might be regarded as a pale reflection of the latter in the secular world, in other words, to the disenchanted, modern mind that no longer has any conception of *the sacred*, yet still experiences, on occasion, its sublime and terrifying manifestations.

35. The interplay of different kinds of perception (of space vs. sacred time vs. profane time) is so complicated that while perhaps bearing "a closer relation to the infinite complexity of actuality, the matrix of human experiences [. . .] than would a conventional Jamesian narrative," is all-too-easily lost on the reader and may thus—here I agree with Cant—be considered "a weakness" (61) of the novel.

36. Again, I do not wish to infer that McCarthy consciously drew on Girard's theories. In fact, writing on *The Orchard Keeper* began at least a year before the French *Mensonge romantique et verité romanesque* was published, and more than a decade before its English translation. Rather, it points in the direction of a burgeoning mimetic awareness that McCarthy shares with the great writers that inspired Girard's theories, and whom McCarthy counts among his favorites as well, particularly Fyodor Dostoevsky and Shakespeare.

37. The overall aesthetic has resulted in much speculation as well as in a surprising number of mistakes in scholarship. For instance, conjectures such as Luce's that Ownby's wife was pregnant, that Sylder is aware of Kenneth Rattner's identity, or that his beating of Gifford is limited to a single strike, though possible, often go unsupported by textual evidence. Another example is the question of what John Wesley did in the years between the end of the story proper and his return to Red Branch in 1948. Some have suggested he joins the army in World War II, becoming the war hero his father was claimed to be (see Prather 39; Hage 127–28), which seems statistically unlikely as he would only have turned eighteen in 1945. Other claims challenge the bounds of what seems possible or are demonstrably wrong. Thus, Jarrett (1997) writes that Ownby is apprehended at Eller's store when the clerk is identified as a man called Huffaker and the store likely located closer to the Harrykin area. Ellis speculates the feral cat of the novel may be a bobcat before admitting that a predator "that can carry up a bobcat would be rare but death does not bother with proportion" (2006, 54), and Hage goes a step further by identifying the cat as a panther (37). Prather assumes Ownby told a lawyer that "a man frequenting the orchard" (39) dumped the corpse in the pit, but this would run completely counter to Ownby's antinomian character, and the text does not

indicate him telling on Sylder either, which would have been problematic also since Ownby never sees Sylder dispose of the body. Domsch (31) writes that people decide not to tell John Wesley of the corpse's identity when the boy has been gone for months and the corpse is never definitively identified.

38. The hypothesis of John Wesley as narrator accounts for the novel's flaws, jumps, and open questions. Assuming the identity of the narrative voice with the grown-up John Wesley's is problematic, not only for the level of detail and insight into the characters' psyches, but also for the narrative voice's verbal power that seems out of character for the otherwise rather quiet boy, as well as his apparent lack of school education, and finally his position as a character not just in the narrative proper, but in the prologue as well, assuming the young man watching the workers is in fact John Wesley.

CHAPTER 3. ORDER IN THE WOODS AND IN MEN'S SOULS: GOTHIC PSYCHOMYTHOLOGY AND SCAPEGOATING IN *CHILD OF GOD*

1. In a thoughtful review, Gerard Raymond, acknowledging the "extreme" nature of the subject material, judges that the movie is not "an entertainment with added shock value," but rather "a portrait of a truly disturbed man who reflects human nature back to us, albeit through a very distorted glass" (2013).

2. The full quotation of the priest, a Reverend Engelmann, goes as follows: "I'm a Christian minister and Mr. Gein is a *child of God*. [. . .] God may be nearer to Mr. Gein than the rest of us because God comes closer to people in dealings with life and death. Mr. Gein is closer to such things than the rest of us" (cit. in Luce 2009, 146). Engelmann's compassion for Gein is especially striking when compared to the constant rejection and demonization of Gein's literary counterpart Ballard by his community, including its churchgoers.

3. Other than Gein, another source to which the motifs of necrophilia and isolation in the novel are often traced is the infamous limerick: "There once was a hermit named Dave, / Who kept a dead whore in his cave. / 'I know it's a sin,' / said Dave with a grin, / 'but think of the money I save.'"

4. Exceptions to this are the Joycean *Suttree*, which frequently lapses into free indirect discourse and stream of consciousness, or the first-person reflections of Sheriff Bell in *No Country for Old Men* and the father in *The Road*.

5. Ellis posits that the young Lester is unlikely to have paid taxes on his family land in the years between his father's death and his eviction. As Ballard is about twenty-seven years of age when he finally is evicted, the question of why he is not evicted earlier still stands. A possible answer is that his father may have had some financial assets used to pay the taxes, which may have been used up by the time of Lester's eviction.

6. McCarthy's novel shares this aspect both with the Blevins case, as Blevins confessed to voyeuristic activities much like Lester's, and Hitchcock's *Psycho*, which playfully reflects the cinema audiences' gaze at the screen with scenes of Norman Bates as a peeping tom and more or less abstract eye-imagery (Luce 2009, 147–52).

7. Luce adopts these largely self-explanatory categories from R. E. L. Masters and Eduard Lea's *Sex Crimes in History* (1963), which she identifies as another possible source for McCarthy (2009, 135–45).

8. On a side note, since Ciuba's lucid analysis focuses almost wholly on mimesis and violence, it neglects some of the novel's narrative features that McCarthy interweaves with mimetic dynamics, such as the voyeuristic play of perspectives, as well as thematic features, e.g., Lester's trauma, or his position within the American pantheon of myth. It is the interplay of these levels that makes *Child of God* more than a case study in mimetic rivalry. In the words of Giles, who provides another syncretic reading using some mimetic insights, Lester "cannot be understood on a purely mythic level" (129)— he is a character with an inside, even if we are not privy to it.

9. Like Ballard's, the status of the child is indefinite. It is referred to as "the thing in the floor" (*CG* 77), insinuating that even the narrator may be in doubt about its status. Yet, while mother and daughter are disgusted at the child's biting off the legs of a robin Ballard brought as a gift intended to impress the daughter, Ballard seems to understand the child's logic: "He wanted it to where it couldn't run off" (*CG* 79). The scene thus establishes a parallel between Ballard and his dead girlfriends and baby Billy and the bird. It also parallels people's averse reactions to either: So in the course of his clumsy courtship, Ballard again finds himself flat-out rejected, insulted, and verbally emasculated by the girl: "You're crazy as shit [. . .]. You ain't even a man. You're just a crazy thing" (*CG* 117). Ballard responds first by mockingly parroting the girl's threat to "tell Daddy on you" (*CG* 117), and eventually by shooting her and setting the house on fire, purposefully repeating the accidental fire that leads to the loss of his second wood cabin home to erase evidence of his crime.

10. Ironically, the car radio is playing a song "for all the sick and the shut-in," the lyrics of which foreshadow the necrophilic turn Lester's desires will soon take and the "divine" authority he will assume: "Gathering flowers for the master's bouquet. Beautiful flowers that will never decay" (*CG* 86).

11. In Nell Sullivan's feminist interpretation of the "dead girlfriend motif" (2000) in McCarthy's early work, *Child of God* is a prime offender in what is seen as signs of misogyny on the side of both character *and* author. The charge has since been reiterated frequently. In contrast, Ellis, who acknowledges the general importance of feminist readings of McCarthy's works, finds such charges "monosemantic" and asserts that Sullivan "sometimes fails to distinguish between McCarthy, his putative intent, and the reasonable inferences one may make from his novels" (2006, 93–94; also Gamblin 28–29).

12. Berry takes his information from a 1981 report surveying eighty counties on the loss of land by the Appalachian Land Ownership Task Force: "The committee documented the decline, placing heavy emphasis on the role absentee timber and coal interests played in the transition of Appalachian population from a modest but independent yeomanry to an impoverished people unable to save from destruction the land from which they draw their sustenance" (62).

13. Other possible dates are the flood years of 1963 and 1965.

14. Later, Ballard sells the watches of his victims at a store in the neighboring county. Significantly, the store owner declines to buy any, showing Ballard a collection of his own watches that have gathered dust under the counter for years. In Southern literature, the watch is often a symbol of time and modernity, the things that the South tried to shut out, as for instance in Quentin Compson's chapter in Faulkner's *The Sound and the Fury*.

15. Likewise, Slotkin asserts that because the yeoman "possesses a share of property (and therefore of political power) he is a sturdy defender of property as an institution, and of the social system that authorizes [...] property holding" (*FE* 70).

16. Constantin François de Chasseboeuf Volney too observes: "The American hunter, who had daily occasion to kill and eat the slain [...] has imbibed [...] an errant, wasteful and cruel disposition. [...] He unites with his fellows in troops, but not in fraternities. A stranger to property, all the sentiments springing from a family are unknown to him. Dependent on his own powers, he must always keep them on the stretch: and hence a turbulent, harsh, and fickle character; a haughty and intractable spirit hostile to all men" (cit. in *REG* 383).

17. Luce relates this and other references to the stars to the creation myth of Plato's *Timaios*. In the myth, each star is assigned to one soul, offering a vision of celestial order and the potential for humans to understand it through observation. However, "when Lester looks at the stars, he sees them as voyeurs like himself [...]. Lester cannot perceive a creative order in the world, inferring only the principle that 'all things fought,' a principle that both McCarthy and Plato acknowledge, but that both would view as a half-truth or worse" (2002, 186).

18. Echoes of Thoreau gain additional weight when considering Gibson's assertion that the novel is likely set in the Sevier County area of Walden's Creek, which was home to a real-life Ballard clan. Phonetic association close at hand, the man whose forest cabin Ballard occupies is named Waldrop (Gibson 30; Luce 2009, 164).

19. This failure may also be read ecocritically, as a historical consequence of the kind of exploitation that represents the extreme of the divine Adamic mission to subdue the earth and "have dominion [...] over every living thing" (Gn. 1:28), more than a subtle hint of which has sedimented into the imperialist aspirations inherent in the British notion of the "white man's burden" and the American concept of manifest destiny.

20. The convertibility of energy is already inscribed within the measurement unit of the calorie, the everyday use of which indicates the amount of energy we consume with our food, but that in physics specifies the amount of energy required to increase the temperature of a single gram of water by one degree Celsius. Nature's tendency toward disorder not only manifests itself, in the novel, in the messy state of the cabin but is doubly encoded within the image of the collapsed and decomposing outhouse. Of course, the fact that the sinkhole now gives growth to various weeds that sprout "in outsized mutation" (*CG* 13) is evidence that at a more microscopic level nature is able to break down and convert even the degraded energy of fecal matter and use it for

more highly organized structures, once again highlighting the relative epistemology of apparent disorder.

21. Ellis elaborates in at once thermodynamic, mimetic, and spatial terms: "This sacrifice of the outside enclosure of the grounds around his found house foreshadows its inevitable loss: the natural order is inverted here, with fencing brought outside to fuel the heating of the inside" (2006, 86).

22. Again, Girard's apocalyptic turn is never brought up in any of the mimetic readings of McCarthy's work. This is a consequence of their stopping halfway, with *Violence and the Sacred*, without taking into account that there may be sand in the gearbox of the scapegoat mechanism, represented by the revelation of the victim's innocence, as Girard has argued in consecutive works.

23. In this, there lies more than a hint of the commonly voiced concern that our media-fueled fascination with Ballard's relatives—be they fictional like Hannibal Lector, Patrick Batemen, or TV's Dexter, or real serial killers like Ed Gein, Jeffrey Dahmer, John Wayne Gacy, or Ted Bundy—actually lends an aura of infamy to these figures. The fear is much the same as with giving media attention to school shooters and is very much a mimetic one: that the glorious infamy we endow these figures with will inspire the desirous imitation of others, causing more suffering and bloodshed.

24. Guillemin claims that the novel's middle landscape—the space between city and wilderness—is "shown to be in perfect order" (2004, 40). Aside from my examples above, Berry's (2002) meticulous investigation of the novel's ecological dimension shows this to be a misperception.

25. Ironically, yet in keeping with Girard, Reubel is humorously unaware of the workings of mimesis in either his or his daughter's behavior: "I don't know what makes them girls so wild. Their grandmother was the biggest woman for churchgoin ever seen" (*CG* 38).

26. To quote another example, Ballard suspects that his double, the "idiot child," is the offspring of the Lane girl he is courting and her own father; judging by the girl's abashed and fearful reaction, he may be right. This goes to show that in the novel, incest is not a rare exception, the sacrificial crisis not limited to the junkyard.

27. Thus, John Cant posits that the White Cap reference is part of McCarthy's attempt "to write into American discourse forgotten, ignored or suppressed aspects of American history" (92), an agenda that is pursued to much greater effect in *Blood Meridian*.

28. In addition, the city is apparently not even Sevierville, but probably Memphis (*CG* 194).

29. Luce (2002, 190) traces the blacksmith episode to the myth of the birth of iron in the Finnish *Kalevala*. From the mimetic perspective, one might mention here the liminal role of metalworkers in certain African tribes: Since metal has potential for good and evil, the metalworker is seen as the master of the violence it can embody; he enjoys privileges, but is also considered a somewhat sinister pariah (see *VS* 260–61).

30. Guillemin ties this scene to the resurrection of Christ, citing the presence of the Sunday church bus, as well as Ballard's emergence from the grave-like caves after three days (2004, 48). Arnold also states Ballard's time in the caves as three days (1999, 57). While

the opening of the chapter indeed states that Ballard explores the first cave for three days, it is clearly specified that at the time of his emergence, "he had not eaten for five days" (*CG* 190). Since he spends little time with the vigilantes and certainly did not go hungry for two days in the hospital (*CG* 177) before his abduction, this is a flaw in the resurrection reading. Another frequent suggestion is that the scene represents a kind of diabolical transfer, suggesting that Lester's evil may live on in the boy. This supernatural interpretation can be traced to the familiar tropes of the Hollywood slasher-horror genre, yet hardly bears out in the context of this reading.

31. On a side note, while it fits exceedingly well with the novel's Narcissus theme, Girard would criticize the mirror stage concept as such: "The whole imagery of mirrors and the imaginary rests (as does the Freudian thesis) on the myth of Narcissus, who looks at himself in the mirror of the pool and allows himself to be captivated by his own image, as he was captivated by the sound of his own voice in the Echo episode. [...] These metaphors always conceal doubles; in endowing them with an explanatory value, you are still working along the lines of mythology. The mirror stage is a naïve resurgence of mythology" (*TH* 403–4).

CHAPTER 4. A SENSE OF JUDGMENT:
MYTH, CHRISTIANITY, AND COSMIC DISORDER IN *OUTER DARK*

1. Thus Russell M. Hillier (2006) suggests that the novel constitutes a "dark parody of Bunyan's *The Pilgrim's Progress*," while Christopher Metress (2001), in an attempt to dissolve tensions between the nihilist and religious schools of McCarthy criticism, reinterprets its characters' journeys as the *via negativa* of apophatic theology, emphasizing the (un)knowability of God in negative terms—through what God is not.

2. The novel actually opens with a one-page vignette detailing the appearance of the nightmarish triune, which, in suggestively Girardian fashion, sets out in "spurious sanctity" (*OD* 3) and eventually breaks into a spontaneous fight that ends as abruptly as it begins.

3. See in particular Guillemin (2004). One problem with these interpretations is that the narrator's linguistic capacities by far exceed anything the practically illiterate Culla is capable of.

4. Bell comes close when, in an earlier essay, he identifies the dream as "a parable of the promise of life" (1983, 36) and the breaking of this covenant as brought about by God, who is consequently rejected by all.

5. This reading is corroborated by what is perhaps the earliest version of the dream scene, which is still written in first-person perspective: "Then the crowd turned upon me, a ragged horde of bodies, bonebags in rags and tatters, and began to tear me to pieces" (91/8/2, 8).

6. In keeping with my argument that the novel actually features Christianity reverting to these mythic patterns of violence, the early draft is further remarkable as identifying the

prophet as "a bearded man in a white robe whom [Culla] soon perceived to be Jesus" (91/8/1, 157).

7. Thus, after the auguries are received by both Remus and Romulus, in book 1:7, a scuffle ensues and Remus is "struck down in the affray," literally "ibi in turba inctus Remus cecidit" (Livy 24–25). In book 1:16, the mysterious disappearance of Romulus himself is preceded by storms and confusion and followed by a sunny and serene day, "postquam ex tam turbido die serena et tranquilla lux rediit" (Livy 56), and while the senators next to Romulus ("qui proximi steterant") proclaim he has ascended as a god, "[t]here were some, I believe, even then who secretly asserted that the king had been rent in pieces by the hands of the senators" (Livy 59).

8. In *Suttree*, Suttree's father writes letters criticizing his son's drop-out lifestyle among "the helpless and the impotent," and in which he advocates a career "in the law courts, in business, in government" (*SUT* 13–14). These letters are sometimes cited in support of such autobiographical takes on the precarious father–son relationships that dominate McCarthy's early to middle period. So is the aforementioned vision in which Suttree is threatened by a dark figure whom he first takes to be his father but later finds to be his son.

9. With regard to the scene involving the unearthed, robbed, and rearranged corpses that set the town on edge, Cant suggests that McCarthy is casting himself as a grave robber conscious of his debt to Faulkner, figuratively acknowledging "that, as a writer, he is wearing a dead man's clothes" (86, 271).

10. Schafer contrasts the tinker with the shepherd who adopts Oedipus (112). For more specifically Oedipal interpretations of incest in *Outer Dark*, see also Hall (72), Ellis (2006, 118), Cant (76), and Giles (111).

11. A pitiable yet unsympathetic figure, the tinker is unlikely to inspire much trust in the readers. Earlier versions of the text made his deplorable intentions more explicit yet, in having him make advances toward Rinthy and coercing her into sexual intercourse by dangling the promise of her child before her (91/8/1, 162, 165–66).

12. According to the testimony of a surviving eyewitness, and in fact various other sources, Laius fell at the hands of *many* robbers and not just one, whereas Oedipus acted on his own. As Oedipus exclaims, if the witness's story matches the oracles' as well as Jokasta's and the Thebans', "I will have escaped disaster. [. . .] Laios was killed by bandits. [. . .] One man cannot be many" (ll. 972–75). Like Girard, Goodhart thus suggests Oedipus may in fact not have killed Laius. After the first half of the play has put great emphasis on the exoneration this one witness's testimony could mean for Oedipus, the questioning of the servant curiously never follows up on this central point. Rather, the question of the homicide has been displaced by the question of Oedipus's heritage. Hence, Goodhart judges: "Rather than an illustration of the myth, the play is a critique of mythogenesis, an examination of the process by which one arbitrary fiction comes to assume the value of truth" (67).

13. If incest did in fact occur, another question would be: How is it that the child so horrifies Culla as to see no other solution than killing it? The child is born in a remote

place, with no visible defects. And with apparently nobody knowing the Holmes, a convincing lie could conceivably be fashioned, casting either Culla as Rinthy's legitimate husband, or making up a deceased husband as Rinthy then does in her conversation with the lawyer.

14. At one point, Culla is seen dismantling his father's shotgun, claiming that it "ain't daddy's gun" (*OD* 30).

15. Against my argument, attention can be called to another early draft. There, Culla explains to the newborn child that "It wont be your fault [...] I caint be your daddy. We'd be some kind of double kin" (91/8/1, 14). This proves that McCarthy initially conceived of the situation as a case of incest. Still, the fact that he decided to erase all such definitive evidence from the final novel opens an interpretive space to support my argument.

16. According to Girard, "the Latin word *decidere* means etymologically to divide by the sacrificial knife, to cut the throat of a victim" (*SG* 238).

17. Two of the inbuilt flaws of the system were an often lengthy bureaucratic process of appeal that was often more damaging to the defendant than the penalties, and the fact that the judges received "no salary and were compensated only when a defendant was found guilty" (Luce 2009, 130, 128–30).

18. In addition, Arnold interprets the mute, nameless member of the triune as "the grown double of [Culla's] own unclaimed child" (1999, 50).

19. On the theme of blindness, see Arnold (1999, 52); Ellis (2006, 124); Frye (2009, 38). Metress (2001) and Luce (2009) also relate the theme to that of metaphysical and or gnostic ignorance.

20. One might speculate that it was more likely the resentful tinker, rather than the triune, who mutilated the child, given that the child's wound has already healed and not too much time seems to have passed between the triune's murder of the tinker and their second encounter with Culla.

21. Likewise, the crone Rinthy meets is concerned with not "breakin the Sabbath" and whether she has been "saved" (*OD* 109), but does offer her hospitality nonetheless, indicating the positive mimesis Rinthy inspires.

22. Sanborn articulates a contrasting view. He posits that Rinthy "directly through incest, or indirectly through inaction is responsible" for the child's death, and that she "has failed as a mother in the duty to protect her child" (2006, 58). This assertion is puzzling, if only for the fact that Rinthy passes out from the exhaustion of labor and thus cannot possibly prevent Culla's abduction of the child. Further, Sanborn's view of the incest as a cause of death ignores that the child would not even be born if there had been no sexual intercourse, incestuous or not, effectively blaming the life-creating act itself for the eventual death of that life.

23. Luce's gnostic analysis of the implications of light and dark in the novel provides an extensive and insightful reinterpretation of these dynamics, and the novel's solar

imagery in particular, far from the mainstream associations of the sun and light with the divine, truth, or enlightenment.

24. Much of contemporary theology tends to interpret this parable and the master's behavior—which is difficult to reconcile with the image of a forgiving and benevolent deity—as Jesus's encouragement to make the most of one's talents, both in the sense of one's wealth and (God-given) abilities. The punishment is then seen less as coming from God than as a consequence of one's inaction caused by debilitating fearfulness.

25. In fact, both can be seen as parts of the same process. As the Protestant ethic historically defines desire for earthly wealth and success as a desire for spiritual salvation, it may present a step in the formation of the modern elevation of *metaphysical* desire for the divinized model-mediator's fullness of being. As a countermovement to capitalist exploitation and critique of the illusory religious Überbau, Marxism in turn shares in the rise of this same culture that has allegedly killed God and put man in his place. Further understanding, as Ernst Nolte and Girard do, the rise of National Socialism in Germany as a reaction and countermovement to the rise of communism, and Stalinism as a response to Hitlerism, the apocalyptic bend of the historical process that Christianity, capitalism, and communism all form a part of violently comes to the fore (*BE* 40).

26. I am indebted to Stephen McKenna for pointing me toward this little deconstructive gem. It is necessary to point out that this interpretation involves a visual sleight of hand, as the Latin *P* is not the same as the Greek *P*, which is the *rho*, really the *r*. However, this inconsistency has its precursor in the interpretation of the ☧ itself, as the latter was later also interpreted as the *Pax Christi*—the peace of Christ.

27. Skeptics and critics of this interpretation often see it as a poetic addition of the gospel author in the sense of a prophecy ex post facto. Conversely, mimetic theory frees the passage of the (metaphysical) necessity of referencing preternatural foresight on the part of Jesus, instead simply suggesting the logical consistency of these events from an awareness of the workings of mimetic violence and the *skandalon* that Jesus represents.

28. What sets McCarthy apart even from writers like Miguel de Cervantes and Dostoevsky is that *novelistic writers*, aware as they are of mimetic rivalry, "as a general rule, do not reach the unanimous victimage mechanism" (*DBB* 200). McCarthy articulates this principle clearly in *Outer Dark* (1968)—four years before the French publication of *La violence et le sacré* and nine years before its English translation. As it is also the first apocalyptic work in McCarthy's oeuvre, this turn predates Girard's spelling out of the apocalyptic implications of his theory in *Things Hidden* (1977/1987), and its historical application in *Battling to the End* (2007/2010).

29. A possible historical counterpart to McCarthy's vision may also have been provided by the "miracle of the sun" that occurred on October 13, 1917, in the Portuguese town of Fatima before a crowd of tens of thousands of believers and nonbelievers. The miracle had been prophesied by three children, who said they had been visited by an angel and the Virgin Mary. Given the theme of child murder in *Outer Dark*, the apocalyptic background of World War I and a country that at the time was ruled by a

largely anti-Christian Masonic government assume significance, too. The children were abducted and put under the threat of death to reveal their secret, yet each remained steadfast. I am grateful to Ann Astell for alerting me to these parallels.

30. To name just two, Adalbert Stifter's "Die Sonnenfinsternis am 8. Juli 1842" and Mark Twain's *A Connecticut Yankee at King Arthur's Court* both provide good examples of apocalyptic texts and the dread inspired by a solar eclipse. Stifter presents the account of an awestruck narrator witnessing the eclipse, Twain has his "enlightened," time-traveling Yankee use his knowledge of a coming eclipse to frighten the Arthurian court into submission. Looking at myth, it is worth noting that, thematically and structurally, Culla's dream is not far from two accounts discussed by Girard—the Aztec myth of Teotihuacan and the pagan miracle tale of Apollonius of Tyana. In the first story, two gods engage in semivoluntary self-sacrificial competition to determine which of them shall lighten the yet dark world as the moon and who as the more prestigious sun (*SG* 57–65). In the second story Apollonius lifts a plague from the city of Ephesus by inciting its inhabitants to stone a beggar who subsequently is revealed to be a demon and the true cause of the plague (*ISS* 49–57). While the Aztec story is a true myth, the second tale is only a half-transformed account of scapegoating.

31. See for instance the Amplified and the Common English Bible translations.

32. The horsemen are empowered "to kill with sword and with famine and with pestilence and by wild beasts of the earth" (Rv. 6:8). These forces are represented by the lynchings and the triune's murders, Culla's hungering for food and drink, the epidemic in his dream as well as actual cholera deaths (*OD* 138, 104), and the deaths caused by snakes, horses, and hogs (*OD* 120, 165–66, 213–15).

33. For discussion of the scene, see Schafer (112), Grammer (36), Cant (85), Greenwood (36–37), and Giles (116–17). Luce points out the imagery of turbid water in this scene and elaborates on the historical background of Tennessean hog drives (2009, 131–33). Sanborn analyzes the role of hogs as heralds of human death in *Outer Dark*, but leaves out any discussion of the biblical details (2006, 61–62).

34. Matthew's variation that there are two demoniacs who forcibly block the road for any traveler, rather than the one-man legion, relates the demoniacs to the *skandalon* or stumbling block, the rival-obstacle of the crisis: "Possession is not an individual phenomenon; it is the result of aggravated mimeticism. [. . .] Matthew turns to the minimal mimetic relationship, to what might be called its basic unit. He endeavors to return to the source of the evil. [. . .] Matthew exteriorizes the demon in a real mimetic relationship between two real individuals" (*SG* 172). However, in exchanging duality for multiplicity, Matthew loses both the collective aspect and the correspondence between a horde of demons and a herd of swine.

35. In the Kristevan reading, the original abject, which keeps on threatening the integrity of the subject, is the mother. Consequently, Fisher-Wirth argues that in Rinthy's journey, *Outer Dark* aims to "represent from within, the story of the abjected 'feminine.' [. . .] Only in *Outer Dark*, that is to say, does McCarthy attempt [. . .] to write the story of that Other who/which has been abjected, upon whom/which so

much terror, loathing, and desire have been projected by the (male) subject" (132–33). For a thorough investigation of Kristevan psychoanalysis through a Girardian lens, see Reineke (2014).

36. As Spencer observes, this blurring of lines extends to the typography of the novel, too. The triune at first appears solely in the italics of the interchapters—apparently so as "to posit evil as a nightmarish force outside of humanity"—but then increasingly enters the proper, roman-type chapters, shattering "the illusion of the separateness of evil" (85–86).

37. Another influence in the poetic conception of the triune may have come from Ingmar Bergman's movie *The Virgin Spring* (1960), which features three raping and murdering goatherds, one of them an entirely mute child, another impaired in his speech for having his tongue removed. Similarly to *Outer Dark*, the movie is concerned with the opposition of paganism and Christianity, which is swept aside by retributory vengeance.

38. It is noteworthy that in an early draft, McCarthy relates the triune leader to Uriah the Hittite, one among King David's elite Gibborim guard, whom David himself envied as his rival for the love of Uriah's wife Bathsheba, and consequently had murdered (2 Sam. 11). David's desire not only brings turmoil upon his own house with the death of their first child, but also, some exegetes claim by the prophet Nathan's curse, the civil war of David's son Absalom, who attempted to wrest the kingship from David and had public intercourse with ten of his father's concubines. The biblical tale thus already contains most elements of mimetic rivalry and ensuing crisis, a propagation of desires and conflicts between a king and his elite soldier, and later his own son, as well as the theme of child-death. McCarthy himself clearly picks up on several of these themes, emphasizing sacred violence, desire, and revenge over the New Testament values of love and forgiveness. The leader asks: "What is a murderer but one who usurps the power of God? And how could Uriah usurp the prerogative of forgiveness when no God himself forgives. No, not God himself, else there'd be no hell. He forgives on condition only. He swaps. But for Uriah to forgive he would have had to be greater than God because he had nothing to swap" (91/9/2, 153). The leader thus presupposes the ambiguous, vengeful God of the Old Testament, and perhaps even older, pagan gods, still. Connecting forgiveness to swapping, he may even subtly invoke the principle of sacrificial substitution. In any case, he identifies with Uriah, claiming the latter was saved exactly "because he wouldnt forgive, because he knew better, because his heart was foul with loathing for old David" (91/9/2, 153) In a half typed, half pencil-written, and barely legible note, he exclaims: "Uriah, that's my name, and every man that has something I want, that man is David to me. I'm sick with revenge it [illegible] me inside" (91/9/2, 153). Even at the stage of writing his second novel, McCarthy was clearly attuned to mimetic dynamics.

39. One is reminded of Ralph Ellison's discussion of the power of names to shape reality: "[I]t is through our names that we first place ourselves in the world. Our names, being the gift of others, must be made our own. [. . .] We must learn to wear our names within all the noise and confusion of the environment in which we find ourselves;

make them the center of all of our associations with the world, with man and with nature. We must charge them with all our emotions, our hopes, hates, loves, aspirations. They must become our masks and our shields and the containers of all those values and traditions we learn and/or imagine as being the meaning of our familial past" (147–48). In declining to name his son, Culla denies his son even the chance to make it his own, and simultaneously both his past and his future. McCarthy himself realized this power when he dropped the Charles Jr. and became Cormac. It is worth mentioning that McCarthy and Ellison were connected through Albert Erskine, their joint editor. Ellison early on lent his support to the aspiring author when he praised him as "a writer to be read, to be admired, and quite honestly—envied" (*OK* blurb).

40. Finally, Rinthy disappears from the narrative in a "frail agony of grace" (*OD* 237) in the lighted glade, resting next to her dead child. Cooper finds that her love and indomitable quest have earned her the empathy and kindness of the narrator, to whom she is a "little sister" (*OD* 238); supposedly, in a case of what might be called "metaleptic mimesis" between narrator and reader, she attains the reader's empathy as well (2011b, 49).

41. Along parallel yet inverted lines, Luce's gnostic reading interprets the child's sacrifice as a failed poisoning of the archon's darkness, yet judges that it does not "seem to accomplish the vanquishing of Darkness from within, despite enacting one version of the gnostic salvation myth" (2009, 92).

42. Concurrently, Guillemin points out the novel's "replication of plot structures" that results in the ritual progression of the siblings' circular journeys and symmetry of recurring situations (2004, 63).

CHAPTER 5. DEGENERATION THROUGH VIOLENCE: THE APOCALYPTIC LOGIC OF *BLOOD MERIDIAN*

1. In 2005, *Time* placed it on its list of "100 Best English-language Novels from 1923 to 2005," and the *New York Times* 2006 critics and writers' poll of the Best Works in American Fiction placed it third behind Toni Morrison's *Beloved* and Don DeLillo's *Underworld.*

2. For readings of the novel as historical romance, revisionist or anti-Western, see Robert L. Jarrett (1997), Inger-Anne Søfting (1999), and John Sepich (2008). Georg Guillemin (2004) characterizes the novel as picaresque. A variety of readings and new perspectives are opened up in the casebook of the McCarthy Society, *They Rode On: "Blood Meridian" and the Tragedy of the American West* (2013). Whereas the volume's title may suggest a modern preference for the mode of tragedy, both Oliver Mort and Chris Dacus stress the epic qualities of the novel in "Are We Still the Good Guys? Cormac McCarthy and the Postmodern Heroic Quest," and "Borderline Insanity: Modernity as a Political Problem in Cormac McCarthy's *Blood Meridian*," while Ronja Vieth reads the novel in the gothic tradition of McCarthy's earlier novels in "A Frontier Myth Turns Gothic."

3. For a discussion of the novel's "mimesis of perception" and cognitive manipulation effected by McCarthy's visual style, see Christopher White, "Reading Visions and Visionary Reading in *Blood Meridian*" (2013).

4. A problem of the influential gnostic readings of McCarthy is their tendency to desanguinate, abstract, and relegate matters of misery, poverty, or violence into the metaphysical realm of matters such as archontic *heimarmene* or the fleshbound divine spark. They obstruct addressing these problems on a human level. This impasse is radically put into focus by Peter Josyph's emotional appeal after peeking into Harrogate's hole in "A Walk with Wesley Morgan through *Suttree*'s Knoxville": "Harrogate is fiction, but somebody was living in here for Christ's sake, so . . . it's . . . it's 2010 and [. . .] somebody is *in* here. [. . .] You see, that's . . . that's what . . . that's what all of these critics, these bullshitters, they don't understand with their *Gnosticism* [. . .]. Somebody has to *come in here* at the end of the day! I was homeless . . . once . . . and I know what it's like . . . It's not *Gnosticism*, I'm telling you . . . They're just out of their minds . . . They have to get out of their houses and see this—this is what it's about, the whole book [. . .] and [McCarthy] found it, and he understood it, and he *nailed* it" (2011, 48).

5. In chapters 19 and 21 of *Moby-Dick*, Ishmael and Queequeg meet the madman, or, alternatively, the prophet Elijah, who implores them not to join Ahab (Bloom 2000, 258). Melville's Elijah may also have inspired the figure of Ely in *The Road*. For more parallels between *Moby-Dick* and *Blood Meridian*, see Polasek (2013).

6. Several episodes of *Blood Meridian*, such as the arrow lottery, Glanton's epileptic fits, the Judge's lectures on geology, and the Kid's escape from the historical Yuma Ferry Massacre, find their counterpart in *My Confession*. So do historical figures and characters such as Angel Trias, John Joel Glanton, Sarah Borginnis, the ex-priest Ben Tobin, Marcus Webster, and notably Judge Holden, for whose existence Chamberlain's historically often questionable autobiography provides the only source. For detailed accounts of Chamberlain's influence on McCarthy and other historical sources, see Rick Wallach's "Sam Chamberlain and the Iconology of Science in Mid-19th Century Nation Building" (2013), and John Sepich's *Notes on "Blood Meridian"* (2008).

7. An earlier draft of the novel further actually identifies the Kid's father as Irish (91/35/3, 1).

8. Tracing this phrase to Alexander Pope's "Behold the child, by Nature's kindly law" from the second epistle of his *Essay on Man*, Barcley Owens comments that McCarthy's image of humanity "will overturn the Enlightenment's motif of the innocent child and hopes for civilized man" (3). Alternatively, the opening has been traced to Pilate's presentation of Jesus to the crowd—"Behold the man!" (Jn. 19:5)—and Nietzsche's *Ecce Homo: How One Becomes What One Is* (1908).

9. Shane Schimpf tracks the phrase to Joshua 9:21–23, in which the Gibeonites are made bondsmen of the Israelites (2008, 60). Beyond the reference to menial work and with regard to the Kid's fate, it seems significant that the Gibeonites are cursed. The phrase also occurs in Deuteronomy 29:10–29, which threatens punishment of those

unfaithful to the covenant, including the destruction of the land. This brings to mind the blasted deserts of *Blood Meridian* and may characterize the Kid as one who has broken the covenant with God.

10. Schimpf links the rainbow in the poem to the rainbow in Genesis 9:14–15, which is the sign of God's covenant with man after the flood (2008, 62). The late draft also includes the image of the child "bearing a tottery armload of firewood like a man goin to an altar" (91/35/3, 1), subtly evoking the tale of Abraham and Isaac.

11. For a discussion of the role of (hyper)masculinity in *Blood Meridian*, see Josef Benson's "An Ironic Contention: The Kid's Heroic Failure to Rebel against the Judge's Hypermasculinity in *Blood Meridian*" (2013).

12. Postheroic societies make up for their lack primarily through technology, which finds expression in the increasing asymmetry of modern warfare. Münkler points to the work of sociologist and genocide scholar Gunnar Heinsohn, whose work "shows impressive correlations between population growth and the intensity of violence a society develops toward the inside as well as the outside" (2007, 751).

13. Naturally, the critique of the romantic vision of the form can be traced back at least from Clint Eastwood's *Unforgiven* (1992), through Arthur Penn's *Little Big Man* (1970), to John Ford *Searchers* (1954), and beyond. Filmmakers often pursued mythoclastic projects aimed at particular dimensions of the myth (e.g., race, class, gender, empire), as Richard Slotkin shows in *Gunfighter Nation*. Truly, the Western has never disappeared. Of the modest, recent resurgence, films like Quentin Tarantino's *Django Unchained* (2012) and *The Hateful Eight* (2015) tackle issues of ethnicity, whereas Antonia Bird's *Ravenous* (1999), or the Australian film *The Proposition* (2005) articulate potent critiques of Western imperialism. *The Proposition*, directed by John Hillcoat who also adapted McCarthy's *The Road* (2009), and Alejandro Iñárritu *Revenant* (2015) come closest to putting a McCarthy Western on screen and are replete with imagery and constellations that would warrant mimetic analysis.

14. The citation stems from the front and back inscriptions of the Alamo Cenotaph, a.k.a. *The Spirit of Sacrifice*. Located at Alamo Plaza, the monument was commissioned in 1936, a hundred years after the battle.

15. Chris Dacus writes: "Manifest Destiny was not as bad as some would like us to believe; for if it were bad in all respects, we would be forced to conclude that extending democracy and liberty was bad too. This conclusion is not something very many people are willing to concede, above all those who now criticize Manifest Destiny, for such criticism is usually made in the name of democracy and liberty. [. . .] McCarthy ironically distances himself from the contemporary critique of Manifest Destiny because the critique itself is no less imperialistic metaphysically" (2013, 277).

16. For details on the history of relations between Apaches, Comanches, and Mexicans, see Shane Schimpf, "A Short History of Scalping" (2013).

17. Spurgeon compares the bear to an avatar of the wilderness, ascribing to him a role similar to the sacred hunter of myth (89–92). An early draft describes the situation as "a sacrifice to something out there altogether unreckonable" (91/35/9, 188).

18. Interestingly, the use of the word "nigger" in the novel applies to blacks, Mexicans, Indians, and even whites. When Black Jackson shoots Mr. Owens, Davy Brown's comment—"Most terrible nigger I've ever seen" (*BM* 236)—seems to refer to the dead Owens rather than Jackson. Among the scalp hunters, the pejorative seems primarily to denote something along the lines of "enemy" or perhaps "victim."

19. Similarly, in the next chapter, Glanton commits Grannyrat's belongings into the fire in lieu of the man himself, who has deserted and likely been killed by the Delawares for breaching his contract with the group.

20. Thus, Turner wrote: "The wilderness masters the colonist. It finds him a European in dress, industries, tools, modes of travel and thought. It takes him from the railroad car and puts him in the birch canoe. It strips off the garments of civilization and arrays him in the hunting shirt and the moccasin. It puts him in the log cabin of the Cherokee and Iroquois and runs an Indian palisade around him. Before long he has gone to planting Indian corn and plowing with a sharp stick; he shouts the war cry and takes the scalp in orthodox Indian fashion. In short, at the frontier the environment is at first too strong for the man" (4).

21. The gang's cannibalistic description evokes that of the *Pequod*: "She was a thing of trophies. A cannibal of a craft, tricking herself forth in the chased bones of her enemies. All round, her unpanelled, open bulwarks were garnished like one continuous jaw, with the long sharp teeth of the sperm whale, inserted there for pins" (Melville 70). See also Jarrett (76).

22. This is another point where *Blood Meridian* recalls yet diverges from the heroic epic. As Münkler points out, the hero relies on the narrative of his deeds told by the poet. Poet and hero rely on each other, as the poet has nothing to tell without the hero and the hero cannot exist as a hero other than through the poet's words. The trophy is merely a substitute in case no poet or journalist is present, and it is a poor substitute in that it tells little of the manner in which the foe was conquered or the greatness of the deed itself (2007, 743).

23. The penultimate chapter of *Deceit, Desire and the Novel* is already entitled "The Dostoyevskian Apocalypse."

24. Its French title is after all *Achever Clausewitz* (2007). For a critique of the book in juxtaposition with the influential reading of Clausewitz by Raymond Aron, see Stephen L. Gardner, "The Deepening Impasse of Modernity" (2010).

25. Early on, McCarthy introduces this theme in view of the novel's rival-doubles par excellence when one scalphunter proposes a bet "as to which Jackson would kill which" (*BM* 86). Clausewitz, comparing war to games of chance and probability, asserts that "luck in war is of higher quality than luck in gambling" (cit. in *BE* 149). Another parallel emerges when Clausewitz's advice to hire experienced, battle-hardened officers to educate new recruits is read along the initiation narratives Freese (1998, 37–38) identifies in war novels like Stephen Crane *Red Badge of Courage*. Girard suggests that veteran officers "are able to model an effective relation to war, [...] proper access to something sacred because they are still in contact with it. [...] For Clausewitz,

becoming accustomed to war is an initiation experience. War is the only field in which craft and mysticism are completely united at the most crucial points" (*BE* 94).

26. I have referred to the fragment and the dimensions of *pólemos* as strife, generally as a reaction between opposing forces. McCarthy's notes clearly show his awareness of the fragment, as an unnumbered typescript page contains the quote "'War is the father of us all and our king. War discloses who is godlike and who is but a man, who is a slave and who is a free man.' (Heraclitus)" as well as a memorandum to "see other translation. Let the Judge quote this in part and without crediting source" (91/35/1, n.p.).

27. Scholars have taken note of these resonances. Thus, Jarrett reads the Judge both as a representative of reason's will to knowledge and Western man's will to power, replacing the Hegelian "spirit driving history by a unitary will" (82).

28. Thus, Albert Einstein paraphrased a sentence from Schopenhauer's *Preisschrift über die Freiheit des Willens*. The German original reads: "Du kannst thun was du willst: aber du kannst, in jedem gegebenen Augenblick deines Lebens, nur ein Bestimmtes wollen und schlechterdings nicht Anderes, als dieses Eine" (58–59).

29. Farneti writes: "Autonomy is neither a psychological fact about agency, nor a mere attribute of rationality; it is a complex notion entailing the ability to give oneself the rule whereby we act. [. . .] *Mimetic* agents are, admittedly, poor introspectors; they can either give or acknowledge reasons, but their knowledge of reasons is not genuine. They inhabit a world of expedient rationalizations that shelter and suppress their mimetic psychologies. Mimetic agents fail to give an account of themselves, for they have little access to the reflective sources of their judgment. The structure of their agency challenges the two fundamental underpinnings of the autonomy thesis and shows that the normative qualifications that define agency are somehow suspended" (18–19).

30. Similar to Turner's argument about the Indian frontier as a unifying force for American identity, Girard argues that it was compulsory military service that truly unified France, whereas Prussian and German nationalism arguably arose in opposition to Napoleon and France (*BE* 33, 154).

31. English translations use *duel* for the German "erweiterter Zweikampf" (Clausewitz 29), which is less evocative of codification and military ritual than what one might associate with the word "duel."

32. Among others, these are factors like practical impediments against a "*simultaneous concentration of all forces*" (*BE* 7), the human tendency to delay decisions and not to go all in with one's resources, varying degrees of involvement and hostile feeling on the part of the populace, the opposite polarity of attack and defense, and finally the political objective that governs the military one. While occasionally fading into the background as Clausewitz does not deny, politics will reassert itself as the "trend to extremes" slows down. In sum, these factors theoretically allow for wars of "all degrees of importance and intensity, ranging from a war of extermination down to simple armed observation" (*BE* 9).

33. The texts Girard has in mind are less the book of Revelation, which is a striking

omission of his, than the passages in the synoptic Gospels preceding the Crucifixion, i.e., Matthew 24, Mark 13, and Luke 21.

34. In this sweeping claim similarly held by Ernst Nolte, National Socialism becomes a mimetic response to Bolshevism, Stalinism a response to Hitlerism (*BE* 40), the Second World War a delayed escalation of the First, and all of it traceable to the hereditary enmity between France, Prussia, and later Germany, and a man Hegel famously called "the world spirit on horseback," the emperor Napoleon. Similarly, in the total militarization of civil life, a connecting line can be drawn between the *soldat-citoyen* of the Napoleonic era, the Spanish and Russian partisans that opposed Napoleon, and the phenomenon of modern terrorism (*BE* 66–69), which can be seen as the "mimetic double" of today's asymmetrical wars and surgical strikes (*BE* 91). With regard to suicide attacks, Girard argues that they represent "a monstrous inversion of primitive sacrifices: instead of killing victims to save others, terrorists kill themselves to kill others" (*BE* 67). For a complementary view of the connection between terrorism and technology, see Münkler (2007, 751–52).

35. Concomitant both with Wallach's exhaustion of the martial code and with Münkler's hypothesis about the shift from heroic to postheroic societies, with which it shares a symptomatic decline in birth rates and population growth, Girard posits the consequence of the trend as one of (national) exhaustion. Total mobilization, as Münkler points out, is a condition that includes "all material and psychic resources" resulting in an exhaustion of these societies that results in their turn from heroic to postheroic societies (2007, 749). Over the course of 150 years, French-German enmity exhausted Europe, which "no longer puts up much resistance to terrorism" (*BE* 212). In simplified terms, Prussia exhausted itself against Napoleon, France did so against Germany in 1870 and WWI, Germany did so in WWII, and the USSR exhausted itself against the United States during the Cold War. If declining birth rates in the United States and its catastrophic expenses in two recent catastrophic and counterproductive wars in Afghanistan and Iraq, which produced ISIS and destabilized the region, are any indication, America may be in the process of doing the same: "The West is going to exhaust itself in its fight against Islamic terrorism, which Western arrogance has undeniably kindled" (*BE* 209–10).

36. Thus, Girard judges "the fact that we speak of 'rogue states' proves how far we have left behind the codification of inter-state war. Under the guise of maintaining international security, the Bush administration has done as it pleased in Afghanistan, as the Russians did in Cechnya. In return, there are Islamist attacks everywhere" (*BE* 67). Another example is the torture scandal of Guantanamo that "demonstrates the contempt for the laws of war. Classical war, which included respect for the rights of prisoners, no longer exists" (*BE* 67).

37. Chamberlain writes: "During the civil wars between the Regulators and Moderators, Glanton would join neither party, but with the utmost impartiality picked a quarrel with some famous fighter of one or the other party and 'rubbed him out'" (269).

38. The episode from Chamberlain that likely inspired McCarthy reads: "A broken waggon, skeletons of cattle and horses, the remains of an American emigrant man

on the ground, while in the wagon was the bodies of a woman, a little girl and boy, all killed by arrows and scalped. [...] One of our men, Mountain Jim, who had been examining the arrows, said, 'This is the work of white men. No doggone red niggers carry so many kind of arrows and leave them behind'" (275).

39. Chamberlain mentions a similar episode on a military expedition to California that stops in Chihuahua. "In honor of the Governor [Angel Trias], a grand review was given by Colonel Washington, which concluded with a sham fight in which His Excellency was shown the way we whipped his *paisanos* (countrymen); this no doubt proved quite satisfactory, for he expressed himself as highly delighted" (246).

40. This is at once an escalation of the festival and a return to its origins, as McKenna points out: "We are regaled with the thematics of transgression, of overturning traditional values, and so on, without any recollection that the carnival played on the margins of Ash Wednesday, that Mardi Gras was a prelude to the Passion, as Saturnalia was to sacrifice. We can desire to perpetuate the seemingly emancipatory antivalues of the festival against repressive institution only if we forget that the very free play of its antistructuring proclivities is a sacrificial institution. It is only in relatively modern times that such free-play is not the foreplay to bloodletting" (35).

41. According to Sepich, this inability presented "a temptation to which John Glanton, historically, succumbed" (1999, 127). Chamberlain also reports Glanton selling the authorities Mexican scalps (275).

42. For comprehensive discussions of McCarthy's use of tarot symbolism, see Sepich (2008, 110–17), and Emily J. Stinson's "*Blood Meridian*'s Man of Many Masks: Judge Holden as Tarot Fool" (2013).

43. Sepich points out the presence of the sphinxes on the card that he connects to Fort Griffin by the shared chimeric quality of the lion's body in both sphinx and griffin (2008, 109). With regard to Cant's identification of the sphinx with a circular model of history, at least in the popular Rider-Waite-Smith tarot, the sphinxes on the card are actually drawing the war-chariot. The Judge, who will be identified with Dionysus and Nietzsche's idea of *eternal return*, is associated, too, with the circular, sacrificial model of history that evokes the dance he speaks of. However, this depiction of the card constitutes an anachronism, as the Rider-Waite-Smith cards were only published in 1910. Yet the older Tarot of Marseilles does not fit either, as its High Priestess does not include the pillars of Boaz and Jachin. So it is unclear which tarot deck McCarthy has in mind.

44. In the synoptic Gospels, Jesus's prophecy of what the end of days will look like is introduced by the foretelling of the destruction of the temple where "there will not be left here one stone upon another that will not be thrown down" (Mt. 24:2; Mk. 13; Lk 21).

45. On blood imagery, see Jarrett (68).

46. Some of this sacrilegious violence may, once again, have been inspired by a tiny detail in *My Confession* that occurs after a massacre of Mexicans by American volunteers, the historical veracity of which has been called into question. Chamberlain notes: "A rough

crucifix was fastened to a rock, and some irreverent wretch had crowned the image with a bloody scalp" (88).

47. The whitewashed tombs Girard mentions, which designate both "the tombs of the prophets whom your fathers killed" (Lk. 11:47) and the metaphorical tomb where the sacrificial victim is hidden from sight, recall both the city that reminds Conrad's Marlow of "a whited sepulchre" (9), and from where he will journey into the eponymous *Heart of Darkness* and, more immediately, the "whited regions" called up twice in *Blood Meridian*, once as places where men go "to hide from God" (*BM* 44) and a second time as places "where monsters do live and where there is nothing other of the known world save conjectural winds" (*BM* 152).

48. It may be objected that in McCarthy's West, Christian virtues like "mercy and kindness will much more likely get you killed" (Schimpf 2008, 3), and that "true Christians would soon be extinct like the 19th century Shakers" (Pastore 109). This argument involves a *petitio principii*: taking the violence of the other as the condition for one's own "regrettable" inability of acting with kindness and mercy, it already follows the fatal logic of the duel. While the situation at that point may indeed comply with this dilemma, one has to ask how it turned out that way, if it could have been different had one not resorted to violence initially.

49. Vieth's analysis involves a slight confusion in assuming that "the gang members feel their behavior justified by their Christian ideology and condemn the 'savages,' saying 'Damn if they aint about a caution to the christians'" (142). As it is Sproule of Cpt. White's command who utters these words, having survived the Comanche massacre, this notion cannot be attributed to the gang, who care even less about Christian appearances than White's deluded troop (or, troupe). What is more, in speaking of "the christians" rather than, say, "us Christians," "Christendom," or "Christianity," Sproule puts a certain distance between himself and that religion, as if he does not count himself among its followers. Neither might Glanton's men, even as some may refer to "the good Book" at times. The irony "in which those who profess to be most civilized and Christian commit the most repellent crimes" (Vieth 143) thus rings only half-true.

50. The tendency of churches becoming the sites of massacre is not allegorical or metaphorical, either, but another historical reality. A recent example that came to light only about sixty years after the fact is the SS massacre of a whole village, Sant'Anna di Stazzema in Tuscany, on the August 12, 1944. As in *Blood Meridian*'s many atrocities, most of the 120 to 140 victims were women, children, and elderly people, who were rounded up at the church and then gunned down and subsequently incinerated, together with the village.

51. The association of musicians, specifically violinists, with the devil is a common trope. One possible allusion is to Niccolò Paganini, who due to his brilliant technique was sometimes thought to be in league with the devil. An American example is the country song "The Devil Went Down to Georgia" by the Charlie Daniels Band, which was a chart success in 1979 and features a violin duel between the devil and a young man.

52. The Judge wins a near impossible wager to lift and carry a meteorite used as an anvil,

The historical counterpart of said stone was estimated to weigh either 600 or 2000 pounds, i.e., 273 or 910 kg respectively (Sepich 2008, 63–64). Both estimates beat the current, 2004 clean-and-jerk world record of 581 pounds (263.5 kg).

53. In his interview with Peter Josyph, Wallach argues that the Judge is "the very icon of ambiguity" inherent in language, and speaks against flat readings of him as supernatural, pointing toward an early version of the script: "McCarthy played with that kind of closure in an early draft of the novel, wherein the Judge at the bar in Fort Griffin effectively admits to the Kid that he's some kind of immortal being—inferentially the devil himself. By the second draft, McCarthy had written it out" (2010a, 107). Instead, Wallach believes, "There's a rational explanation for everything he does that seems inexplicable at first" (Josyph 2010a, 104). For instance, he points out that we do not know how much time passes between the collapse of Green's tent show and the Kid's entrance into the bar, and that the Judge may only appear unchanged to the Kid. Likewise, as to the Judge's supernatural knowledge, one *could* assume that his jesting yet correct prediction of Brown's survival of all massacres and final execution may be lucky coincidence—hanging is after all a common fate of the Western outlaw—and that his knowledge of Shelby's and Tate's fates, barring the Kid actually telling him about it without McCarthy showing it, simply springs from a supreme psychological insight into the minds of men. Another argument, which I will come to later, is that the Judge may be a projection of the Kid himself.

54. The covenant can be said to find its fulfillment in the ultimate annihilation of all of the gang. For more on devil covenants and the Faust legend, see Sepich (2008, 121–27).

55. Two further possible referential points of this pivotal scene shall briefly be mentioned here. In a Yale lecture on "The American Novel since 1945," Amy Hungerford suggested that the scene mirrors Satan's invention of gunpowder and cannon in Milton's *Paradise Lost*, book 6, lines 469–91 (137–38). In addition, this particular scene might be an inversion of the delightful union of spirits that Ishmael experiences in chap. 94 of *Moby-Dick*, squeezing out the impurities in the sperm of a whale, a representative of nature. Whereas Holden's ritual leads to a massacre of the Apaches, Ishmael feels all enmity and borders between him and his polyglot coworkers dissolved "into the very milk and sperm of kindness" (Melville 323). A mimetic-ecocritical interpretation of the episode would be that the whale itself is the sacrifice uniting the sailors.

56. In particular, he criticizes ethnology as represented by Sir James Frazer. "His writing amounts to a fanatical and superstitious dismissal of all the fanaticism and superstition he had spent the better part of a lifetime studying" (*VS* 318). In this, Girard argues, Frazer shares in the unwillingness of science to be enlightened about its own misconceptions regarding the role of religion or, for that matter, philosophy. Decades after Frazer's death and the writing of *Violence and the Sacred*, it is hard to avoid seeing the dogmatic extremism and theological ignorance of the New Atheist movement, which cannot allow the thought that religion might have any positive impact whatsoever, as anything but a mimetic response to the dogmatic extremism and scientific ignorance of nominally Christian fundamentalists, who see science as the

work of the devil while reading the Bible literally lest it challenges their bigotry. Both sides would like nothing better than to see the other disappear and are yet informed by the same, literalist interpretations of Scripture. In light of the apocalyptic trend to extremes, what supreme irony is it then that the figureheads of New Atheism—Richard Dawkins, Christopher Hitchens, Sam Harris, and Daniel Dennett—have dubbed themselves "the four horsemen"?

57. That Girard also draws on de Maistre and that Dacus in turn quotes Clausewitz, albeit only in passing, supports the impression that Dacus's analyses are close to my own.

58. In the claim that books (always) lie, we find a metatextual variation on the classical liar's paradox. If taken as absolute, the claim, which is printed *in a book*, would have to be false to be true. Not to involve such a paradox, the Judge's statement would have to be either refuted or else limited to a statement such as "*some* books *sometimes* lie," insofar as they may say things that are not true in a factual sense. The statement gets more complicated when opposed to the Judge's later claim that "a false book is no book at all" (*BM* 141). The second statement contradicts the first, unless further limitations are imposed: if a book's lies or falsehoods did not necessarily render the book as a whole false, its ontological status as a book could still stand.

59. Another way of looking at the Judge's inconsistencies and contradictions is to see them as part of an agenda to render the distinction of truth and falsehood void, infecting and subverting it in a manner that could be called deconstructionist or perhaps antimaieutic, but is perhaps more mundanely described as what philosopher Harry G. Frankfurt nonchalantly calls *bullshit* (33–34, 51–53). In this claim, my discussion intersects with readings of the Judge as a confidence man, like Bernhoft's.

60. Again, one is reminded of Blumenberg's attribution of the ordering function of fear itself that may provide an explanation for the necessity of selecting a scapegoat in the overall chaos of social crisis. In *The Stonemason*, the line is said by Ben Telfair who thereby justifies sharing his thoughts and worries with his wife Maven (119). The quotation reappears in *The Counselor* (52), where it is attributed to Henry Miller. Wes Morgan on the McCarthy Society Forum has traced it to Miller *Colossus of Maroussi*. The original reads: "Whatever we cling to, even if it be hope or faith, can be the disease which carries us off. Surrender is absolute: If you cling to even the tiniest crumb you nourish the germ which will devour you" (69). The various uses of the phrase emphasize either the necessity of knowledge out of fear, or the abolishment of attachments.

61. To this epistemological argument, an ethical layer is added by including a similar argument, made by a blind man to Billy Parham in *The Crossing*, that involves the same asymmetry: "The order which the righteous seek is never righteousness itself but is only order, the disorder of evil is in fact the thing itself" (293). Righteousness, in this case, is a reaction to the sobering revelation of profound, true evil, a case of ressentiment.

62. Jarrett (1997), Cant (2008), Schimpf (2006), Hillier (2013), and Benson (2013), all provide substantial readings of elements of *Blood Meridian* through the lens of Nietzsche's philosophy. Apart from the ideas named above, Woodson (2000 and 2002)

has fruitfully associated the coldforger of the Kid's fever dream with Nietzsche's coiner of illusory language from "On Truth and Lies in a Nonmoral Sense," though perhaps the image of the workshop where ressentiment values are forged like coins in the fourteenth chapter of book 1 of *Zur Genealogie der Moral* (2007, 281–82) relates more immediately. Williamson (2013) devotes an essay to discussing the Judge's metaphysics of war through a Nietzschean lens. Shaviro (149), Ellis (2000, 165), Millard (85), Vanderheide (2000, 182), Phillips (2002, 20), and Guillemin (2002, 244 and 2004, 95) refer to Nietzsche and Nietzschean concepts such as eternal return, will to power, or the superman in passing.

63. On the same issue, compare Bell (1988, 120–21) and Jarrett (82–84).

64. Without going into too much detail, in this view, God is a projection of slave morality, born of resentment of the slaves against the noble masters. The latter effects a reevaluation of values effected by the priest caste to gain power over the warrior caste. Hence, the formerly good and noble become evaluated as "evil," which as a term replaces the (more or less) descriptive "bad" that applied to the state of the slaves, which now in turn evaluate themselves as "good" (Nietzsche 2007, 266–74).

65. In the fourth part of the book, Zarathustra first meets the final pope (Nietzsche 2002, 321–32). He asks him whether it is true that it was God's love and pity for crucified man that caused his death. The final pope sketches the evolution from the harsher Old Testament image of God to that of the loving God of the New Testament, which ultimately clashed with his role as judge and authority, making him more like an old grandfather, a grandmother even, than a father. Zarathustra then encounters the "ugliest man" whom he identifies as God's murderer. It is God's pity that offends man so much in its totality and "shameless" inclusivity. As revenge against God, the overly curious and intrusive "witness," he transforms into so ugly and miserable a creature that its evil and ugliness doom God, who cannot look away. Christianity's focus on forgiveness of the "evil" of man not only renders life itself contemptible, but ultimately man himself, which in turn exhausts the concept of divine forgiveness, the supreme image of which is the crucified Christ. In the words of *Der Antichrist*, pity is practical nihilism—and Christianity the religion of pity (cf. Nietzsche 1999a, 172–73). Concerning the implications of the death of God, see also Figal (176–79).

66. In *Götzendämmerung*, Nietzsche asserts that by abolishing Christian belief, one also pulls the carpet from under Christian morality, as the truth and authority of its metaphysical foundation gives way (1999a, 113–14).

67. The greatness of the task is affirmed by Jürgen Habermas, himself an atheist: "For the normative self-understanding of modernity, Christianity has functioned as more than just a precursor or catalyst. Universalistic egalitarianism, from which sprang the ideals of freedom and a collective life in solidarity, the autonomous conduct of life and emancipation, the individual morality of conscience, human rights and democracy, is the direct legacy of the Judaic ethic of justice and the Christian ethic of love. This legacy, substantially unchanged, has been the object of a continual critical reappropriation and reinterpretation. Up to this very day there is no alternative to it. And in light of the current challenges of a post-national constellation, we must draw

sustenance now, as in the past, from this substance. Everything else is idle postmodern talk" (150–51).

68. The translation of *The Antichrist* used is H. L. Mencken's (i.e., Nietzsche 1918, 43); for the original, see Nietzsche (1999a, 170). See also Williamson (265).

69. All in all, the Judge's philosophy resembles the racialist historiography of historians like Theodore Roosevelt who conceived of history as a "Darwinian arena" that would prove one race, the Anglo-Saxon, superior to all others. However, the Judge does not presuppose any such supremacy.

70. Simply put, the last man is an apathetic being without higher aspiration, strength of will, or sense of wonder, yet puzzled by such questions as "What is love? What is creation? What is longing? What is star?" He lives in a small world, presumably because his view of it is narrow, and he in turn renders everything else small, preferring equality, sameness, and stability over difference, individuality, and originality, being entertained to being challenged. Nietzsche (2002, 19–20).

71. Romano Guardini hence asserts: "When N. speaks about Christianity it is as if a paroxysm came over him. [. . .] [H]e loses all measure of truth and even decency. The untruth of his attack is all the more vehement because he sees so much that is right. [. . .] At the same time, such a breath of closeness blows through all of N's struggle against Christ and Christianity that one cannot avoid the conclusion: he is turning against something which—he knows in his innermost heart—is good" (cit. in Platt 359).

72. The original is "Nachgelassene Fragmente 1888. 14[89]" (Nietzsche 1988, 265).

73. The original "Fragment 1988 15[110]" reads: "Der einzelne wurde durch das Christentum so wichtig genommen, so absolut gesetzt, daß man ihn nicht mehr *opfern* konnte: aber die Gattung besteht nur durch Menschenopfer [. . .] Die echte Menschenliebe verlangt das Opfer zum Besten der Gattung—sie ist hart, sie ist voll Selbstüberwindung, weil sie das Menschenopfer braucht. Und diese Pseudo-Humanität, die Christentum heißt, will gerade durchsetzen, daß *niemand geopfert wird*" (Nietzsche 1988, 469).

74. John the Baptist scandalizes Herodias in his condemnation of her marriage to Herod, the brother of her former husband Philip. Salome expressly asks her mother what she should wish for, while Herod is bound to his "exorbitant offer" of anything she wants—which is really expressing his own "desire to be possessed" (*SG* 141)—by his oaths and his guests, whose individual desires are likewise channeled through Salome.

75. In the first meeting of Yuma and scalp hunters, it is thus also only the Judge who seems to take seriously the strange, somewhat clownish figures of Caballo en Pelo and his men (*BM* 254–55).

76. In the side story of David Brown's flight from San Diego, Brown likewise uses the promise of money to seduce the soldier Petit into freeing him from prison, only to shoot him from behind (*BM* 268–69).

77. Research into the Anasazi's mysterious disappearance posits that either additionally or alternatively to climatological reasons, violence and religion may have played a

decisive role: "Belying the popular image of the Anasazi as a peaceable kingdom of farmers and potters, some of the new research puts the blame for the collapse on a bloody internecine war. Other researchers are trying to combine archeological evidence with anthropological studies of the modern pueblo Indians to make the case that the Anasazi were roiled by a religious crisis" (Johnson 1996).

78. In addition to the Kid's dream of the cold-forger, one can cite the case of Black Jackson, who on the evening before his death is last seen standing on a rise next to the Judge and, immediately before being riddled with arrows, bows to pick up "a small coin," "perhaps once lodged under the tongue of some passenger" (*BM* 273). What is more, the older Kid, just before he sees the Judge again in the Fort Griffin saloon, pays the barman with "a silver coin" (*BM* 324), and the Judge's presence among the patrons is likewise juxtaposed with the owner of the dancing bear walking about and "shaking the coins in his hat" (*BM* 325). Quite clearly, there is a pattern at work that immediately connects a given character's fate, usually his death, to the image of the coin. As several scholars have connected the Judge to Anton Chigurh, who decides the fate of his victims by a coin toss, the implications of this motif potentially transcend *Blood Meridian*.

79. Interestingly, whether by design or numerological coincidence, by taking the digit sums provided by the Judge's weight in stones (i.e., 24) and the separate sums of the first and second two digits of its metric conversion (i.e., 154.2 kg), one arrives at the proverbial "number of the beast" (Rv. 13:18): 666.

80. Iain Bernhoft convincingly casts the Judge as a confidence man. He argues that "the narrative is also complicit with the Judge, his mystifications and his claims. [. . .] [T]he text itself plays the straight man for the Judge's confidence games" (74–75). Bernhoft assumes that the "plain truth" is that there is nothing at all supernatural or superhuman to the Judge, by whose own words "there is no mystery," and that he is a mere man. This position is problematic for a number of reasons. First of all, it seems to assume that in approaching the novel as "historically grounded," interpretations have to remain firmly within the field of the nonfantastic historical reality. In discrediting Tobin as the prime offender in mystifying the Judge and more or less explicitly charging critics who read him as the devil, a god etc., with the same mistake, Bernhoft posits that such things do not exist. Worse, should one take the Judge as anything demonic or partly supernatural, one automatically disavows history, which is a history of violence: "Mystifying the Judge occludes the historical realities of the text, and in turn risks turning the novel's violence into an aestheticized spectacle that can be consumed at a safe distance and without implication" (75). But this is not necessarily the case, and not at all true for the Girardian conception of Satan, which roots all mystification in real, actual violence. Second, there are a lot of things that are hard to explain about the Judge on a purely rational level. Bernhoft's answer for this is that the text itself is complicit in the Judge's deception. In essence, he extends the postmodern dictum "Don't trust the teller, trust the tale" to "Better don't trust the tale, either." In that, the meaning of the text as a whole becomes highly arbitrary, or else can only rely on foregone materialist-historical conclusions that fit the author's a-metaphysical stance. Finally, the assertion involves a contradiction: If we should not trust the Judge, then why should we trust him when he

tells us "there is no mystery"? Following this logic, reading the novel must become an exercise in *ex falso quodlibet sequitur*—in a falsehood from which anything may follow.

81. The phrase occurs primarily in the King James Version in Paul's letters, i.e., Rm. 8:37–39; Col. 1:16, 2:15; Eph. 3:10–11, 6:12. For mimetic theory, Colossians 2:15 is of special importance, as it states that in the Crucifixion, Jesus "disarmed the rulers and authorities and put them to open shame, by triumphing over them in him." The ESV authors note: "The cross of Christ marks the decisive defeat of the demonic powers. On the cross, they were stripped of their power to accuse Christians before God" (ESV 2297). Girard interprets this passage as direct reference to the deconstruction of founding violence at the expense of scapegoats through the Crucifixion. Depending on the translation, one may find alternative terms such as "rulers," "forces," "authorities."

82. Conversely, Stephen Pastore dogmatically asserts that readings of the Judge as either Gnostic archon or satanic figure are false, "as can be easily proven by even a cursory reading of the text" (108). His two main arguments are first that the Judge "does no lying" and second that he is "not charming" as one would expect the devil to be (108). Though Pastore's own identification of the Judge with the Old Testament Yahweh is noteworthy, neither of his two refutations holds up to scrutiny. While the first claim is somewhat dependent on what qualifies as lying, there are multiple instances where the Judge is prominently involved in the intentional circulation of untruths. He would clearly seem to speak *contra mentem* when he accuses Reverend Green of sodomy and child molestation, as he later admits to never having heard of Green before. He legally represents Glanton and Black Jackson in their denial of Jackson's murder of Owens toward the authorities. In the gunpowder tale, he lures the Indians into carelessly attacking by falsely claiming to be the last one alive. He partakes in the whiskey barrel swindle with Mangas Colorado as well as the Yuma ferry swindle. Finally, he likely either falsely accuses the Kid to the local authorities of having conspired with the Indians in the ferry massacre, or else lies to the Kid about having done so. Pastore's second claim is equally shaky when one considers how the Judge is the center of attention practically everywhere he appears, and in the final dance of the novel is literally and repeatedly described as "a great favorite" (*BM* 335).

83. An important example is Peter's attempt to dissuade Jesus from accepting crucifixion and death. Jesus replies: "Get behind me Satan! You are a hindrance [literally: a scandal; stumbling block] to me" (Mt. 16:23).

84. The next sentence, "Woe to the world for temptations to sin!" (Mt. 18:7), implicitly strengthens the link between scandal and Hillier's millstone, as the Greek original once again uses the word *skandalon*.

85. Apart from these two cases, there are those of the girl that goes missing in Jesús María during the feast of Las Animas (All Souls), another girl that is mentioned as abducted in Tucson just before the Judge's meteorite wager, a girl of twelve that is discovered naked but alive in the Judge's quarters at the Yuma massacre, and the young girl caring for the dancing bear at Fort Griffin who mysteriously disappears (*BM* 191, 239, 275, 333). It seems worth pointing out that the Mexican boy's death as well as all of the girls'

cases except for the Tucson one are either symbolically or contextually dramatized as sacrificial deaths.

86. The Kid arouses the desire and interest of others than the Judge. Thus, the old hermit he meets early on at night is found "bent over him and all but in his bed," and toward the end of the novel, he is "taken for a male whore" (*BM* 20, 311).

87. A possible exception to this is Toadvine, who, in a brief moment of moral outrage, puts his gun against the Judge's head after he has scalped the young Apache boy, and criticizes the slaughter of the Tiguas.

88. Bernhoft argues that the Kid "considers firepower, not demonic power, in gauging his chances" (74). In chapter 9, the Kid's gun is identified as "a big Walker revolver" (*BM* 109), which was about the largest and most powerful hand gun at the time with a maximum effective firing range of about one hundred yards.

89. Apart from the sailors he fights in New Orleans and from Toadvine whom he fights simply because he presents an obstacle on the way to the outhouse, he presumably murders the men in the Nacogdoches hotel. Incarcerated after White's ill-fated filibuster, he imitates the acts of other prisoners who throw stones at a group of boys pestering them from atop the prison walls; he "cleanly" drops "a small child" who vanishes from sight to a "muted thud" (*BM* 71). Later in the novel, it seems to be the Kid who first responds to "a muttered insult" (*BM* 178) in the Narcori cantina that erupts into a fight and small massacre, leaving thirty-six men dead. In his flight from the Yuma, the Kid drops several assailants with his revolver.

90. The quality comes from kabbalistic interpretation of the fours among the minor arcana, which associates it with the Hebrew word *khesed* or *chesed*, which Sepich notes as mercy, though more common translations of the word are the noted loving-kindness as well as compassion, grace, love, or covenant-love.

91. See Bloom (2000, 262). Benson (2013) offers a nuanced treatment of the kid as an *ironic hero*.

92. The ESV notes: "Isaiah uses the imagery of his time to make one point: the earth shall be full of the knowledge of the Lord. The One whom Israel rejected as unhelpful renews the world [...]. In Isaiah's time, Judah was to the nations [...] as prey to fierce predators. Messiah's benevolent rule would change all that. [...] In the context of once-predatory imperial powers coming under the Messiah's sway and thus learning to be peaceable [...] some interpreters understand these fierce animals as images for these larger nations [...]. Understood this way, Isa.11:9 speaks of the future messianic age when the predatory nations will no longer hurt or destroy God's people" (1262).

93. If one needs any more evidence to strengthen this mimetic interpretation, one might consider as a fourth element the "demonic tracks of javelinas," also called peccary or skunk pigs, which the Kid encounters directly after the desert epiphany, "drinking at a standing pool of water" (*BM* 215). Like the demons of Gerasa at the presence of Christ, they run off once the Kid comes close.

94. To my knowledge, McCarthy's reference to the agony in the garden has so far gone

unnoticed. It is significant both to my analysis of Christianity in the novel and by itself, as it became a major motif in Western art, depicted by El Greco, William Blake, Heinrich Hoffmann, and other painters, as well as in an oratorio by Ludwig van Beethoven. In this respect, the motif thus rivals the *ecce homo*, which was perhaps first identified in McCarthy by Guillemin (2004, 92). Elisabeth Andersen is to be credited with the extension to the Old Testament's story of Elisha's resurrection of a child, which is said to prefigure Christ's resurrection, but relates the source to Isaiah 41:1, which contains no mention of a child nor the Latin phrase *ecce puer* (89). The error is reproduced by Mundik (197). Manuel Broncaro correctly relates the phrase to 2 Kings 4:32 (37).

95. For other Christian and messianic readings, see Schimpf (2008), Andersen (2008), and Pastore (2013).

96. Sepich notes the woman resembles depictions of Mary's appearance as Our Lady of Guadalupe and goes on to stress that a pact with the devil could be terminated "in pre-Reformation Faust tales [by] a last-minute plea to the Virgin" (2008, 123). See also Spurgeon (95) and Mundik (202).

97. The Kumeyaay tribes of California and Baja California were Roman Catholic and only became uprooted during secularization after Mexico became independent from Spain.

98. The "he" is included, for instance, in the 25th anniversary edition of *Blood Meridian* (2010, 336).

99. To name a few, Mundik suggests cannibalism (213); Shaw (117–18) and Spurgeon (97–98) identify rape. Regarding the Kid's end, Sepich suggests that in accordance with Christopher Marlowe's *Doctor Faustus* and other Faust tales, the Man is "torn asunder" by the Judge (2008, 125). It is worth mentioning that the griffin is a sometime symbol for Jesus Christ. In an alternative interpretation of the Kid's end, John Vanderheide thus reads the constellation of the jakes and male witnesses as an analogy to Christ's tomb and the two Marys' learning of his resurrection. In this reading, the mortal aspect of the Man is "literally *eliminated* in the apotheosis," and the one witness's apparent shock is simply a result of a terrible odor emanating from the outhouse (2000, 181).

100. Another, suggestively Nietzschean pair would be the Judge's "Will or nill" (*BM* 330). Of course, depending on whether one sides with Nietzsche or Girard, Christianity may in turn be interpreted as the life-denying choice, yet given the infertility of violence in *Blood Meridian*, choosing Dionysus is clearly no alternative.

101. Toadvine, in his own moment of deciding whether to stay with the Judge or join the Kid and Tobin, is seen making "a tripod of three fingers" that he then turns around to make "six holes in the form of a star or hexagon" (*BM* 285) that he then rubs out again. It has been speculated that this is the Star of David, and that Toadvine may be Jewish. If my reading is correct, this implies that in close ties to Christianity conferring the choice on the Kid to renounce the Judge, Toadvine essentially has the same ability to choose.

CHAPTER 6. AN APOCALYPTIC JOURNEY:
REVELATION, CONVERSION, AND THE DIFFERENT ENDS OF *THE ROAD*

1. With Bell's reflections providing a fairly conservative point of view, the whole novel's pessimism cannot but feel reactionary, though this quality plays out mostly on the level of *mores*. One example is the decline of schools, which—according to a forty-year-old survey, used to deal with "talkin in class and runnin in hallways. Chewin gum. Copyin homework," and now are faced with "Rape, arson, murder. Drugs. Suicide," leading Bell to conclude that "the world is goin to hell in a handbasket" (*NC* 196). Narcotics—which Bell describes as a satanic invention liable to "bring the human race to its knees" (*NC* 218)—are as much a part of this process as "Mammon," the "false god" of "real money" (*NC* 298, 182). One might suspect a larger critique of economic policy, specifically neoliberal economics and Reaganomics, somewhere in *No Country's* pages. While poverty and unemployment are set against the corporate backdrop of drug cartels and the business ethics of mercenaries like Chigurh, it is hardly a business novel. Its inherent arguments are personal and moral rather than socioeconomic. Thus, Llewellyn Moss's greed and pride are what ultimately costs his life, and result in the additional deaths of his wife and a young hitchhiker.

2. In this sense, Chigurh represents the exact opposite of Black in *The Sunset Limited*, who similarly claims to have "no choice" in saving White and further claims not to have got "a original thought in my head" (9, 13), modeling his behavior after that of Jesus. *The Stonemason*, likewise, features a positive relation of mimesis in Ben Telfair's emulation of Papaw—in fact, the play's first spoken words are "I always wanted to be like him" and the amusing memory of Ben "walk[ing] like him. And he was eighty-five years old" (6–7). Positive mimesis is also at the heart of the relation of Ed Tom Bell and his father, as well as his dead daughter.

3. Here, White echoes Edward Gibbon's *Decline and Fall of the Roman Empire*, where Gibbon famously describes history as "little more than the register of the crimes, follies, and misfortunes of mankind" (102).

4. About nine in ten articles about the novel label it as either apocalyptic or postapocalyptic. To name a few, Carl James Grindley explicitly compares *The Road* to the book of Revelation, suggesting the novel takes place "post-Rapture" (13). Other scholars use the term loosely: Ashley Kunsa speaks of "post-apocalyptic Naming" in *The Road* (2009), and Tim Edwards looks at the "post-apocalyptic waste land" of the novel through the lens of pastoralism (2008). Conversely, Linda Woodson has argued that *The Road* is not principally apocalyptic, but rather a post-postmodern journey narrative in the tradition of American road literature (2008). A middle ground is presented by Lydia Cooper. Based on the novel's earlier title, *The Grail*, she relates it to T. S. Eliot's *The Waste Land* and Arthurian literature, reading the novel as an "apocalyptic grail narrative" (2011a).

5. For more explicit treatments of McCarthy's return to his early work and the journey through Tennessee, see the respective essays of Chris Walsh, who examines the novel's "post-southern sense of place" (2008, 48), Wesley G. Morgan's examination of "the

route and roots" of the novel (2008, 39), and Louis Palmer's thesis that McCarthy is going "full circle" in rewriting *The Orchard Keeper* (62).

6. For a thorough taxonomy and overview of the journey of life in American literature, see Freese (2015); for a concise study of the journey in McCarthy, see Wierschem (2015b).

7. For another consideration of *The Road* in the light of Revelation, see Grindley (2008).

8. It should be pointed out, though, that this particular lineup of the horsemen already involves a modern popularization. The nature of the first, white rider in particular is subject to debate, sometimes being interpreted as a representation of Christ himself, sometimes as the Antichrist, or a bringer of civil war and destabilization that calls forth the other riders "to kill with sword and with famine and with pestilence and by wild beasts of the earth" (Rv. 6:8; ESV 2471–72).

9. In book 8 of Ovid's *Metamorphoses*, Philemon and Baucis house the disguised Zeus and Hermes, and the food and drink they serve are miraculously replenished all the time. The gods then warn them of the impending destruction of the city. On their death, they are turned into a pair of intertwining trees. For a general discussion of hospitality in *The Road*, see Snyder (2008).

10. That is, the Islamic credo, "There is no God but God. Mohammed is the prophet of God." There is a paradoxical sense, too, in which the authority of Ely's denial of God's existence depends exactly upon his authority as a prophet of the nonexistent. McCarthy's wording implies a literary sleight of hand. To take Ely's word, as it were, would be to have one's atheist cake and eat it religiously.

11. A refutation of Ely's prophetic role is provided by Phillips, who points out the commonality of biblical names in the South and that "[a]mateur eschatology is a southern pastime" (2011, 180). To Phillips, any allusive interpretation is misguided, the plethora of biblical motifs in the text a nihilistic irony of McCarthy's.

12. McCarthy seems acutely aware of the theoretical shortcomings of the Huntington thesis. An undated, partially pencil corrected note from a 2005 draft records the following excerpt; where corrections affect content, I have provided the original in square brackets: "The answer to the problems with the Muslim terrorists would seem to be to halt fossil fuel consumption—by whatever means—and let the Arabic countries descend into that very poverty which will proscribe the purchase of armaments to use against The West [us]. But this only puts off the problem to a future date. You would have to go to the jungles of Brazil to find a human being who does not understand that the true tools for the destruction of Islamic fundamentalism [the Muslim cultures] are everywhere at hand. They are blue jeans, rock and roll music, Hollywood movies, McDonald hamburgers, DVD's [*sic*], color television. The people of Islam [These people] are not fighting for world domination. They are fighting for their lives. They are fighting for the survival of a three thousand year old culture which in their hearts they may well know is doomed. A constantly evolving world pop techno culture [This] is an historical imperative of a scope Spengler could only dream of" (91/87/5, n.p.). It is unclear whether these are private musings of McCarthy's, notes potentially adopted

from another source, or original prose or dialogue intended for a character in *The Road* or another work, though the last two seem unlikely.

13. For an analysis of mimetic dynamics in economics, see Paul Dumouchel's classic "The Ambivalence of Scarcity" (2014), and Jean-Pierre Dupuy's *Economy and the Future* (2014).

14. In this regard, one can begin to discern in such moments in *The Road* an example of what Boris Gunjević has in mind in calling for a theologically rooted critique of capitalism as such: "If we accept Walter Benjamin's assertion that capitalism is a religion, would not the most radical critique [. . .] of capitalism be one articulated by religion? [. . .] The capitalist matrix within which imperial practices function can be criticized relevantly only if the critique embraces a certain theology, for Empire will otherwise always prevail, as it has until now, thanks to its diabolic adaptability to the market" (Žižek and Gunjević 100).

15. McCarthy was also included on the *Guardian*'s list of "50 People Who Could Save the Planet" (Vidal et al. 2008), an optimistic appraisal he would probably be the first to call into question.

16. Snyder describes the setting as one ravaged by nuclear winter (2008, 69), Greenwood mentions "nuclear holocaust" (77), and Edwards identifies the cause of the catastrophe as "[t]he Bomb itself" (56).

17. The first quotation, taken here from Richard Rhodes's *Making of the Atomic Bomb* (1986, 676) is also interesting for often being translated exchanging "time" for "death." The second quotation stems from Oppenheimer's 1947 MIT Lecture "Physics in the Contemporary World," on which he later elaborated: "I meant that we had known the sin of pride. We had turned to [affect] . . . the course of man's history. We had the pride of thinking we knew what was good for man, and I do think it had left a mark on many of those who were responsibly engaged" (Day 109, brackets in the original).

18. Upholding a realistic angle, one might object that range and effect of nuclear fallout are diminished in case of high altitude explosions. At the same time, the higher the altitude of the nuclear detonation, the greater the range of the resulting EMP which is potentially capable of covering a whole continent the size of the United States. The absence of working electronic equipment in the novel is thus theoretically consistent with the lack of evidence of fallout and radiation sickness.

19. Conversely, Phillips tends toward the meteor-hypothesis, as his view of the text as "ironic" discourages its reading as a "cautionary tale" and the role of human agency within it. At a closer look, the disavowal of human agency in the catastrophe turns out to be a step in Phillips's discrediting of the theodicy issue in *The Road*. In this way, the problem of evil and suffering evoked in the wake of a cosmic event can be shifted, so to speak, onto God's shoulders, rather than mitigated by the theological view of evil as a free choice of moral agents, which is the consequence of a reading assuming nuclear war or man-made environmental catastrophe. The consequence of this "dilemma" would then be that of denying God's presence in *The Road*, making short work of its

religious themes and symbolism as negligible or, at best, the father's pathological self-delusion.

20. Interestingly, McCarthy implicitly contradicts or at least strongly relativizes an earlier assertion by Kushner that McCarthy "suggests that the ashcovered world in the novel is the result of a meteor hit" (2007).

21. As Leo Daugherty explains, *Anareta* (Gk. destroyer) is a planet that in the Renaissance was believed to be destructive of life (163).

22. Strictly speaking, one would have to distinguish between the sum total of entropy, which tends toward maximum, and the current entropy generated in ongoing processes. In the latter sense, the world we see in *The Road* is not actually one of high physical entropy. Rather, it is one that has already expended or "lost" most of its entropy in the massive exhaustion of energy and warmth involved in the event and the ensuing burning of the biosphere, which, physically, would have been the time of highest entropy. Now, with nary a natural process going on or much energy being exchanged, current production of entropy would be comparatively low, simply because there is nothing left to produce it.

23. The crossed-out page is numbered on the top left-hand side with the number 21/219 and the date 21 Aug, and a circled 5 on the bottom left.

24. In choosing this image, McCarthy may have drawn on an otherwise (for him) unexpected source, namely F. Scott Fitzgerald's *The Great Gatsby*, an earlier title of which was *Among Ash-Heaps and Millionaires*. In the chapter dealing with Gatsby's death, Tom Buchanan recalls reading how "the sun's getting colder every year" (113), and Nick Carraway retrospectively contemplates how "we drove on toward death through the cooling twilight" (130), lines evoking both the second law and McCarthy's favorite trope of life's journey toward death. More significantly, McCarthy's world of ashes is prefigured in Fitzgerald's famous valley of ashes. The latter in turn was likely inspired by Henry Adams's *Degradation of the Democratic Dogma*, which applied the second law to history cast as an ever increasing ashheap (Freese 1997, 175).

25. For an insightful discussion of the role of language in *The Road*, see Linda T. Woodson "Mapping *The Road* in Post-Postmodernism" (2008).

26. For someone interested in experiences of spiritual epiphany and heretical thought as McCarthy, Böhme—whom Hegel called the first German philosopher—provides a fascinating case study. Mystical experiences, which offered him views into the "innermost being of nature" and the world, punctuated his life and were the inspiration of his writings. Such is the case with an experience in 1610, which led to the composition of the *Aurora* in 1612. It would not see official publication until long after Böhme's death. Instead, friends of his copied and spread the work in secret, after the then high priest of Görlitz caught wind of it. A strict Lutheran worried about the orthodoxy of his flock, he rebuked the shoemaker in his homilies and reported Böhme to the magistrate, who seized and forbade further publication of the *Aurora* (Wehr 1971, 23–24).

27. Principe and Weeks provide a concise treatment of the term, which comes in a divine

and a mundane variety, as well as the historical alchemical discourse and concepts Böhme was probably aware of.

28. God's being is compared to that of a wheel that contains and connects various other wheels turning upward, downward, and crossways, so that it is possible to learn something of its wondrous shape in glimpses of its movement (Böhme 1992, chap. 21.61).

29. *The Stonemason* is another text that contains a fair share of mystical thought. Thus, Papaw's lessons to Ben are that true masonry is held together "by the stuff of creation itself," that there is a kind of mystical "sap in the stone. And fire"(10), and that within the "blackness unknown and unknowable [...] God and matter are locked in a collaboration that is silent nowhere in the universe" (67)—which is a resonance that guides the true mason in his work of building the world. See also Wehr (1971, 90–92; and 1992, 36–39).

30. Similarly, when the sociopathic character of Malkina asserts in *The Counselor*, "that truth has no temperature" (*COU* 21), it could merely be read as her invocation of the pathetic fallacy to justify her lack of attachment to people, whom she puts on the level of things. Yet as she continues, "There it goes," and the action direction states the referent of her sentence as "the sun flar[ing] out beneath the horizon" (*COU* 21), McCarthy subtly evokes the same, entropic truth of the heat death as a truth both scientific and total in its scope.

31. Dedicated to John Francis McCarthy, *The Road* is after all also a deeply personal book, in Winfrey's words a "love story" (2007b) to his son, who, according to McCarthy, served as a practical coauthor of the book in inspiring much of it (Jurgensen).

32. Various readers have offered pessimistic readings of the passage. Willard Greenwood contends that in this image "the standard theme of the apocalyptic genre, in which the natural world continues to work and return to 'normal' in the absence of human interference, has been turned upside down" (80–81). Tim Edwards concludes that "*The Road*, in the end, is a prophetic hieroglyphic of horror, an American jeremiad more terrifying than even the Puritan imagination could conjure" (60). Conversely Ashley Kunsa, in her otherwise astute discussion of "Post-Apocalyptic Naming in Cormac McCarthy's *The Road*," tellingly omits the problematic line "not be made right again." In reading the boy as a new Adam and the coda as harkening back to the dawn of creation, she optimistically judges that "the end and the beginning are inseparable in *The Road*. For it is the end of the old world that signals the possibility of a new one" (68). Paying attention to the grammar of the passage, Thomas Schaub locates the initial "once" of the paragraph as "the time of the reader" and points out that "the thing which could not be put back is 'the world in its becoming,' not the world accomplished and destroyed" (165). That world is naturally gone for the characters of the novel, with what possibilities it held significantly reduced to those of the world we read about. But that world itself may still retain a modicum of possible futures, while our own retains yet more. Many have also offered more optimistic, redemptive interpretations. From Schaub's, it is perhaps but a small step to Randall Wilhelm's suggestion that the coda and other images, in conjunction with "the father's actions in the novel [...]

offer a thinly-veiled political stance on human stewardship of the physical world as well as the codes of human conduct" (141). Finally, Louis Palmer sees in it "an icon of hope, a recognition of what we have not yet lost, but still may," arguing that if consolation is denied, it may be "to suggest that we have certain personal, cultural and historical responsibilities," and wondering whether "perhaps McCarthy is an activist after all?" (66–67). Shifting the scales back toward the negative, Dana Phillips in his antiapocalyptic reading of the novel judges readings of the brook trout as "allegorical, symbolic, mythic or otherwise charged with greater meaning" as misguided, if to be explained simply by the ways in which both readerly expectations and genre conventions operate, and he concludes that "perhaps in this one instance McCarthy really 'ought not have done it'" (2011, 186).

33. The lyrical persona is sitting on a yellow stagecoach aside the driver. He experiences the beauty of life only to realize that he cannot stay to enjoy it as the coach keeps rolling. In the last stanza, the persona sits aside a skeleton holding a scythe and hourglass and says farewell to his loved ones. McCarthy has demonstrated his familiarity with German writers and thinkers, from the renowned like Johann Wolfgang von Goethe, Friedrich Schiller, Thomas Mann, Martin Luther, Arthur Schopenhauer, and Friedrich Nietzsche, to the lesser known such as Theodor Storm and the comparatively obscure such as Jakob Böhme or the nineteenth-century natural historian and philosopher Lorenz Oken (Greve). Hence, it is hardly a stretch to suggest McCarthy's familiarity with a text so in tune with one of the central themes of his work, especially given the folksong.

34. Governed by the father's viewpoint and without any social order to speak of that the son could be initiated into, *The Road* may not immediately appear as initiatory. Critics have argued that part of the natural philosophy that underlies McCarthy's nature writing is a constant questioning and decentering of anthropocentric viewpoints, and even the composition of more "biocentric maps" (Keller-Estes 214–16). In this light, it is not surprising that the individually focused journey of initiation may also be sublimated into articulating or at least accommodating a larger perspective, without falling for the green utopianism of abandoning all human points of view. Concomitantly, the effect of juxtaposing disastrous landscapes and celestial imagery is that of allegorically paralleling the journey of humanity as represented by the nameless protagonists to the journey of the planet on its course through the cosmos. It may be added too, that while initiation is always also a social act, apocalypse likewise can be seen as interlocking two eschatologies—of "the individual soul, and of the world [...] the first making possible the second" (Tuveson 4).

35. Regarding *The Road* as a journey of initiation for the son, one may also say that through his personal growth against the backdrop of a long-lasting experience of death, he is symbolically resurrected after three days and consequently initiated into the social structure of the new family.

36. The quote is found, in varying translations, in part 4, book 11, chapter 4, "A Hymn and a Secret," of *The Brothers Karamazov*. Following Lacan's formula that for the atheist, God is in fact not dead but *unconscious*, Žižek posits a first inversion of Dostoevsky:

"What characterizes modernity is no longer the standard figure of the believer who secretly harbours doubts about his belief and engages in transgressive fantasies; today we have, on the contrary, a subject who presents himself as a tolerant hedonist dedicated to the pursuit of happiness and whose unconscious is the site of prohibitions: what is repressed is not illicit desires or pleasures, but prohibitions themselves. 'If God doesn't exist, then everything is prohibited' means that the more you perceive yourself as an atheist, the more your unconscious is dominated by prohibitions that sabotage your enjoyment" (2006, 92). He later adds a second, religious fundamentalist inversion of Dostoevsky: If God exists, everything is permitted—permitted, that is, to the self-perceived instrument of his will.

37. The author frequently summoned in this context is not Faulkner or Herman Melville, but Samuel Beckett (see, e.g., Charles, Warner 2006, Greiner). To be sure, there is a distinct echo of the famous first words of *Waiting for Godot* in the man's contemplation of a broken shopping-cart wheel—"What to do about it? Nothing" (*R* 12)—which here expresses the futility of man's efforts in the tide of larger forces. However, such comparisons are largely limited to the bleak settings of Beckett's early plays, especially *Waiting for Godot* and *Endgame*, as well as certain views about the human condition both authors seem to share. Stylistically, there are vast differences between McCarthy's baroque language and Beckett's linguistic minimalism, and neither do McCarthy's novels share Beckett's intricate play with and use of form and structure.

38. Aside from *Blood Meridian*'s early dialog between the Kid and the hermit, musing about better worlds and their existential restriction to the realm of the imagination, a flashback in *The Road* finds the father muse about how "if he were God he would have made the world just so and no different" (185). Most explicitly, Leibniz theodicy informs White's exclamation in *The Sunset Limited*: "I'm at a loss as to how to bring myself to believe in some most excellent world when I already know that it doesnt exist" (133). For detailed discussions of theodicy and atheism in *The Road* and *The Sunset Limited*, see Vanderheide (2008) and Wierschem (2014, 339–44).

39. In this, there is perhaps more than a bit of McCarthy's ambiguous feelings of insufficiency in raising his son John Francis: "I tell people that he is so morally superior to me that I feel foolish correcting him about things, but I've got to do something—I'm his father" (Jurgensen).

40. In this context, one cannot help but draw autobiographical connections to McCarthy's becoming a father for the second time in 1999. *The Road* is dedicated to his son John Francis, whom McCarthy describes as "the best person I know, far better than I am" (Woodward 2005, 104). In his interview with Winfrey, he openly acknowledged he would not have written the novel had it not been for John Francis's birth: "[Having a child as an older man] wrenches you up out of your nap and makes you look at things fresh [. . .]. It forces the world on you, and I think it's a good thing" (2007b).

41. Conservative estimates project the existence of between one hundred and two hundred billion galaxies in the universe, with newer estimates making claims of up to two trillion. With roughly seven billion people on planet Earth in 2015, this would put the ratio of galaxies to human lives at somewhere between 14.3:1 to 285.7:1. As far

as we know, and against all universal odds, we constitute the rarest "substance" in the universe.

42. Given the mother's originally intended name, and the son's nature as a Jesus-analog, we might even hazard the father's spoken yet undisclosed name to be McCarthy's own, original middle name: Charles *Joseph* McCarthy Jr. In this regard, McCarthy's choice of leaving his protagonists unnamed was certainly the right one.

43. Another important parallel between the thought of Girard and Böhme is contained in the *Aurora*'s explanation of the presence of evil in the world, though the latter is still somewhere between mythical, mystical, and humanist thought. While the devil is the one who corrupts creation, human evil manifests itself in what Böhme calls the "four sons" of the devil, which are, in order, pride, miserliness (which is akin to avarice), envy, and finally wrath (Ger. *Hoffart, Geiz, Neid, Zorn*). Wrath is what finally sets the world of the outer parturition aflame. These concepts by themselves are suggestive of mimetic desire and its consequences (Böhme 1992, chap. 16.79–88). Böhme further implies that the ultimate root of it all is pride, i.e., the prime manifestation of romantic self-absorbedness that is metaphysical in its illusion of originality and self-sufficiency. He exhorts his audience to "leave strife behind and do not spill innocent blood, and do not therefore waste land and cities as is the devil's will. Instead, put on the helmet of peace and gird yourselves with love for one another and be gentle to one another. Leave behind pride and avarice, and none should envy another's stature. Do not be ignited by the fire of wrath, but live in gentleness, chastity, friendliness, and purity, and thus you shall all be and live in God" (Böhme 1992, chap. 22.45).

44. The father's former paranoia may have given way to a more modest caution, yet still holds a certain grasp over him, only now it seems much more concerned with the son's life itself than with the son's life as the purpose of his own. Thus his commandment "you need to find the good guys" retains the form of a double-bind, as it comes with the warning "but you cant take any chances" (*R* 234). Strictly speaking, to join the veteran and his family, the son will have to take a chance, so the father's commandment is paradoxical; perhaps it should hence rather be simply interpreted as a warning not to be too reckless.

45. In fact, even the minutest of details is geared toward the revelation of this simple truth. Such a detail is, for example, the missing card Two of Clubs in the card game (*R* 45). For a reader familiar with McCarthy's use of the tarot in *Blood Meridian*, where cards as the Four of Cups feature prominently, the instant association would be to the (phonetically close) Two of Cups, a card sometimes known as the Lord of Love and associated with reciprocal love, reconciliation, growth, and meaningful relationships. One may of course object that that card is missing, though this is clearly a case of *absence présente*, that is, the very thing that makes it stick out and thus facilitates the association is that the card is missing. More negative interpretations could focus on the imagery of the card, two lovers, and relate it to the dead mother, who is beyond reconciliation.

46. On the interdividual level, conversion effects the abandonment of the kind of "deviated transcendency" associated with the human models of desire, and their concomitant

repudiation, which calls "for symbols of vertical transcendency whether the author is Christian or not" (*DDN* 312). In this regard, it may be worth adding that Böhme likewise believed in the essential sameness of all humans—either in love or hate: pride, avarice, envy, and wrath govern every man, and hold sway in Christendom as well, yet the opposite is also true. "I am not alone, but all humans are alike, be they Christians, Jews, Turks or heathens; whosoever is filled with love and gentleness, is filled by God's light as well" (1992, chap. 22.52). Thus, we can also interpret the father's thoughts, shortly after he has laid down to die: "Look around you, he said. There is no prophet in the earth's long chronicle who's not honored here today. Whatever form you spoke of you were right" (*R* 233).

CONCLUSION:
AT THE CROSSROADS OF LIFE AND DEATH

1. After all, for difference to be diagnosed, the premise of comparability and thus of sameness in some relation has to be granted. Performatively, this is the case as soon as we begin to compare. Naturally, other relations may be brought to bear. Yet, on an anthropological level, the basic, comparative relation of the human would consequently be primary to any perfunctory difference that results from cultural construction.

2. So, at various points, Auden either chose to change the words of "September 1, 1939" to "We must love one another *and* die," to omit the problematic stanza, or to disassociate himself from the poem entirely (Lenfield).

3. When regarding such global problems as that of climate change, it may in truth well be that the moment of choice has passed us by, or else that we have missed the point at which our choice would have yielded a different outcome. In this case, we are more like the dreamer toward the end of *Cities of the Plain*—finding that "there are no crossroads. Our decisions do not have some alternative. We may contemplate a choice but we pursue one path only. The log of the world is composed of its entries, but it cannot be divided back into them" (286). In matters of life and death, there is neither a foregoing nor a revision of decisions we may have postponed or put on someone else's head, once the decisive moment has passed.

4. The translation of Hölderlin's "Patmos" quoted here and in the epigraph follows that of Michael Hamburger (Hölderlin 1994, 483). The original reads: "Nah ist / Und schwer zu fassen der Gott. / Wo aber Gefahr ist, wächst / Das Rettende auch" (Hölderlin 2008, 197, ll. 1–4).

5. Jim Campbell's translation of McCarthy's original Spanish.

Bibliography

MATERIALS FROM THE MCCARTHY ARCHIVE

McCarthy, Cormac. *The Orchard Keeper*. Correspondence. Southwestern Writers Collection 091: The Cormac McCarthy Papers. Wittliff Collections, Texas State University, San Marcos, TX. 91/1/1.

———. *Outer Dark*. Various typescript and holograph pages. Southwestern Writers Collection 091: The Cormac McCarthy Papers. Wittliff Collections, Texas State University, San Marcos, TX. 91/8/1.

———. *Outer Dark*. Typescript early draft. Southwestern Writers Collection 091: The Cormac McCarthy Papers. Wittliff Collections, Texas State University, San Marcos, TX. 91/8/2.

———. *Outer Dark*. Early Draft. Southwestern Writers Collection 091: The Cormac McCarthy Papers. Wittliff Collections, Texas State University, San Marcos, TX. 91/9/2.

———. *Whales and Men*. First draft. Typescript with holograph corrections in pencil. Irregular pagination. 225 leaves. Southwestern Writers Collection 091: The Cormac McCarthy Papers. Wittliff Collections, Texas State University, San Marcos, TX. 91/97/1.

———. *Whales and Men*. Final draft. Printout with no corrections. 133 pages. Southwestern Writers Collection 091: The Cormac McCarthy Papers. Wittliff Collections, Texas State University, San Marcos, TX. 91/97/5.

————. *Blood Meridian*. Correspondence editorial notes: photocopy and typescript pages. Southwestern Writers Collection 091: The Cormac McCarthy Papers. Wittliff Collections, Texas State University, San Marcos, TX. 91/35/1.

————. *Blood Meridian*. Bert Krantz to McCarthy, June 24, 1985. ANS, 1 p. Includes 121 pages of "late draft" photocopy manuscript pages. Southwestern Writers Collection 091: The Cormac McCarthy Papers. Wittliff Collections, Texas State University, San Marcos, TX. 91/35/3.

————. *Blood Meridian*. Typescript. Heavily corrected in pencil and black ink. Pages 1–169 are absent; includes many additional pages numbered as inserts and additions. So-called "First Draft" (374 leaves). Irregular pagination. Southwestern Writers Collection 091: The Cormac McCarthy Papers. Wittliff Collections, Texas State University, San Marcos, TX. 91/35/9.

————. *The Road*. Drafts 2005, n.d. Photocopy of corrected typescript pages in folder marked "Xeroxes of 7 and 8 not mailed but carried to US." 29 leaves. Southwestern Writers Collection 091: The Cormac McCarthy Papers. Wittliff Collections, Texas State University, San Marcos, TX. 91/87/5.

————. *The Road*. Typescript draft, unnumbered pages in folder marked "*The Road*—1st draft." Heavily corrected in pencil. 302 leaves. Southwestern Writers Collection 091: The Cormac McCarthy Papers. Wittliff Collections, Texas State University, San Marcos, TX. 91/87/6.

PUBLICATIONS

Abrams, Meyer Howard. 1971. *Natural Supernaturalism: Tradition and Revolution in Romantic Literature*. New York: Norton.

Andersen, Elisabeth. 2008. *The Mythos of Cormac McCarthy: A String in a Maze*. Saarbrücken: VDM.

Andreasen, Liana Vrajitoru. 2013. "*Blood Meridian* and the Spatial Metaphysics of the West." In *They Rode On: "Blood Meridian" and the Tragedy of the American West*, edited by Rick Wallach, 166–95. N.p.: Cormac McCarthy Society.

Arendt, Hannah. 1970. *On Violence*. Orlando, FL: Harcourt.

————. 1997. *The Origins of Totalitarianism*. San Diego, CA: Harcourt.

Aristotle. 1994. *Die Poetik*. Edited and translated by Manfred Fuhrmann. Stuttgart: Reclam.

Armstrong, Karen. 2006. *A Short History of Myth*. Edinburgh: Canongate.

Arnheim, Rudolf. 1971. *Entropy and Art: An Essay on Disorder and Order*. Berkeley: University of California Press.

Arnold, Edwin T. 1999. "Naming, Knowing and Nothingness: McCarthy's Moral Parables." In *Perspectives on Cormac McCarthy*, edited by Edwin T. Arnold and Dianne C. Luce, 45–69. Jackson: University Press of Mississippi.

———. 2000. "Cormac McCarthy's *The Stonemason*: The Unmaking of a Play." In *Myth, Legend, Dust: Critical Responses to Cormac McCarthy*, edited by Rick Wallach, 141–54. Manchester: Manchester University Press.

———. 2002a. "The Mosaic of McCarthy's Fiction." In *Sacred Violence*, vol. 1, *Cormac McCarthy's Appalachian Works*, edited by Wade Hall and Rick Wallach, 1–8. El Paso: Texas Western Press.

———. 2002b. "McCarthy and the Sacred: A Reading of *The Crossing*." In *Cormac McCarthy: New Directions*, edited by James D. Lilley, 215–38. Albuquerque: University of New Mexico Press.

Arnold, Edwin T., and Dianne C. Luce. 1999. "Introduction." In *Perspectives on Cormac McCarthy*, edited by Edwin T. Arnold and Dianne C. Luce, 1–16. Jackson: University Press of Mississippi.

Atkins, Peter. 2010. *The Laws of Thermodynamics: A Very Short Introduction*. Oxford: Oxford University Press.

Atlan, Henri. 1984. "Disorder, Complexity and Meaning." In *Disorder and Order: Proceedings of the Stanford International Symposium (Sept. 14–16, 1981)*, edited by Paisley Livingston, 109–28. Saratoga, CA: Anma Libri.

Auden, W. H. 2003. "September 1, 1939." In *The Oxford Anthology of English Poetry*, vol. 2, edited by John Wain, 696–99. Oxford: Oxford University Press.

Bandera, Pablo. 2019. *Reflection in the Waves: The Interdividual Observer in a Quantum Mechanical World*. East Lansing: Michigan State University Press.

Banzhaf, Hajo. 1990. *Schlüsselworte zum Tarot*. München: Goldmann.

Barthes, Roland. 1972. *Mythologies*. Translated by Annette Lavers. New York: Hill and Wang.

Bataille, George. 1988. *The Accursed Share: An Essay on General Economy*. Vol. 1. New York: Zone Books.

Bateson, Gregory. 2000. *Steps to an Ecology of Mind*. Chicago: University of Chicago Press.

Beck, John. 2000. "'A Certain but Fugitive Testimony': Witnessing the Light of Time in Cormac McCarthy's Southwestern Fiction." In *Myth, Legend, Dust: Critical Responses to Cormac McCarthy*, edited by Rick Wallach, 209–16. Manchester: Manchester University Press.

Bell, Madison Smartt. 1992. "The Man Who Understood Horses." *New York Times*, May 17, 9–11.

———. 2000. "A Writer's View of Cormac McCarthy." In *Myth, Legend, Dust: Critical Responses to Cormac McCarthy*, edited by Rick Wallach, 1–11. Manchester: Manchester University Press.

Bell, Vereen M. 1983. "The Ambiguous Nihilism of Cormac McCarthy." *Southern Literary Journal* 15.2:31–41.

———. 1988. *The Achievement of Cormac McCarthy*. Baton Rouge: Louisiana State University Press.

Benjamin, Walter. 1965. "Zur Kritik der Gewalt." In *Zur Kritik der Gewalt und andere Aufsätze*, 29–65. Frankfurt am Main: Suhrkamp.

Bennett, Charles H. 1987. "Demons, Engines and the Second Law." *Scientific American* 257:88–96.

Benson, Josef. 2013. "An Ironic Contention: The Kid's Heroic Failure to Rebel against the Judge's Hypermasculinity in *Blood Meridian*." In *They Rode On: "Blood Meridian" and the Tragedy of the American West*, edited by Rick Wallach, 232–45. N.p.: Cormac McCarthy Society.

Bent, Henry A. 1965. *The Second Law: An Introduction to Classical and Statistical Thermodynamics*. New York: Oxford University Press.

Bernhoft, Iain. 2013. "'Some Degenerate Entrepreneur Fleeing from a Medicine Show': Judge Holden in the Age of P. T. Barnum." In *They Rode On: "Blood Meridian" and the Tragedy of the American West*, edited by Rick Wallach, 65–81. N.p.: Cormac McCarthy Society.

Berry, K. Wesley. 2002. "The Lay of the Land in Cormac McCarthy's Appalachia." In *Cormac McCarthy: New Directions*, edited by James D. Lilley, 47–73. Albuquerque: University of New Mexico Press.

Bertalanffy, Ludwig von. 1969. *General Systems Theory*. Rev. ed. New York: George Braziller.

Bloom, Harold. 1992. *The American Religion: The Emergence of the Post-Christian Nation*. New York: Simon and Schuster.

———. 2000. *How to Read and Why*. London: Fourth Estate.

Blumenberg, Hans. 2003. "Arbeit am Mythos." In *Texte zur Modernen Mythentheorie*, edited by Wiflried Barner, Anke Detken, and Jörg Wesche, 194–218. Stuttgart: Reclam.

Böhme, Jakob. 1921. *Sex Puncta Theosophica, oder von Sechs theosophischen Punkten hohe und tiefe Gründung*. Leipzig: Insel.

———. 1992. *Aurora oder Morgenröte im Aufgang*. Edited by Gerhard Wehr. Frankfurt am Main: Insel.

Boyer, Paul. 1998. "Apocalyptic Literature." In *A Companion to American Thought*, edited by Richard Wightman Fox and James T. Kloppenberg, 36–37. Malden, MA: Blackwell.

Brickmann, Barbara. 2000. "Imposition and Resistance in *The Orchard Keeper*." In *Myth, Legend, Dust: Critical Responses to Cormac McCarthy*, edited by Rick Wallach, 55–67. Manchester: Manchester University Press.

Brickner, Richard P. 1974. "*Child of God*." *New York Times*, January 13, 334.

Broncaro, Manuel. 2014. *Religion in Cormac McCarthy's Fiction*. New York: Routledge.

Brown, Angela K. 2007. "Texas Teacher Suspended after Book List Complaint." *New York Sun*, October 23. http://www.nysun.com.

Broyard, Anatole. 1973. "'Daddy Quit,' She Said." *New York Times*, December 5, 45.

Bruhm, Steven. 2002. "The Contemporary Gothic: Why We Need It." In *The Cambridge Companion to Gothic Fiction*, edited by Jerrold E. Hogle, 259–76. Cambridge: Cambridge University Press.

Büchner, Georg. 1961. "Dantons Tod." In *Sämtliche Werke*, 7–77. Berlin: Tempel.

Campbell, Jim. n.d. "A Translation of Spanish Passages in *The Crossing*." Cormac McCarthy Society. http://cormacmccarthy.com.

Campbell, Joseph. 1993. *The Hero with a Thousand Faces*. London: Fontana.

Campbell, Neil. 2000. "Liberty beyond Its Proper Bounds: Cormac McCarthy's History of the West in *Blood Meridian*." In *Myth, Legend, Dust: Critical Responses to Cormac McCarthy*, edited by Rick Wallach, 217–26. Manchester: Manchester University Press.

Cant, John. 2008. *Cormac McCarthy and the Myth of American Exceptionalism*. New York: Routledge.

Cawelti, John G. 1997. "Cormac McCarthy: Restless Seekers." In *Southern Writers at Century's End*, edited by Jeffrey J. Folks and James A. Perkins, 164–76. Lexington: University Press of Kentucky.

Chamberlain, Samuel E. 1956. *My Confession: The Recollections of a Rogue*. New York: Harper and Brothers.

Chapman, Robert, ed. 1986. "Hoot(e)nanny. | Hootananny, *n.*" In *New Dictionary of American Slang*, 215. London: Macmillan.

Charles, Ron. 2006. "Apocalypse Now." Book World, *Washington Post*, October 1, 2006. http://www.washingtonpost.com.

Chollier, Christine. 2000. "'I Aint Come Back Rich, That's For Sure,' or the Questioning of Market Economies in Cormac McCarthy's Novels." In *Myth, Legend, Dust: Critical Responses to Cormac McCarthy*, edited by Rick Wallach, 171–76. Manchester: Manchester University Press.

Ciuba, Gary M. 2002. "McCarthy's Enfant Terrible: Mimetic Desire and Sacred Violence in *Child of God*." In *Sacred Violence*, vol. 1, *Cormac McCarthy's Appalachian Works*, edited by Wade Hall and Rick Wallach, 93–102. El Paso: Texas Western Press.

———. 2007. *Desire, Violence and Divinity in Modern Southern Fiction*. Baton Rouge: Louisiana State University Press.

Clausewitz, Carl von. 2012. *Vom Krieg*. Hamburg: Nikol.

Cleave, Chris. 2006. "A Harrowing Portrait of a Futurist America." *Telegraph*, December 11. http://www.telegraph.co.uk.

Conlon, Michael. 2007. "Writer Cormac McCarthy Confides in Oprah Winfrey." Reuters, June 5. http://www.reuters.com.

Conrad, Joseph. 2006. *Heart of Darkness*. Edited by Paul B. Armstrong. New York: Norton.

Coomaraswamy, Ananda K. 2007. "Symplegades." In *The Underlying Religion: An Introduction to Perennial Philosophy*, edited by Martin Lings and Clinton Minnaar, 176–99. Bloomington, IN: World Wisdom.

Cooper, Lydia R. 2011a. "Cormac McCarthy's *The Road* as Apocalyptic Grail Narrative." *Studies in the Novel* 43.2:218–36.

———. 2011b. *No More Heroes: Narrative and Morality in Cormac McCarthy*. Baton Rouge: Louisiana State University Press.

Coppola, Francis Ford, and John Milius. 2001. *Apocalypse Now Redux: Original Screenplay*. London: Faber and Faber.

Corte, Julia. 2005. *Tarot. Schicksale und Zukunft deuten*. Wien: Tosa.

Coupe, Laurence. 1997. *Myth*. London: Routledge.

Crèvecoeur, J. Hector St. John de. 1986. *Letters from an American Farmer and Sketches of 18th-Century America*. Edited by Albert E. Stone. London: Penguin.

Dacus, Chris. 2009. "The West as Symbol of the Eschaton in Cormac McCarthy." *Cormac McCarthy Journal* 7:7–15.

———. 2013. "Borderline Insanity: Modernity as a Political Problem in Cormac McCarthy's *Blood Meridian*." In *They Rode On: "Blood Meridian" and the Tragedy of the American West*, edited by Rick Wallach, 273–81. N.p.: Cormac McCarthy Society.

Danta, Chris. 2012. "'The Cold Illucid World': The Poetics of Gray in Cormac McCarthy's *The Road*." In *Styles of Extinction*, edited by Julien Murphet and Mark Steven, 9–26. London: Continuum.

Daugherty, Leo. 1999. "Gravers False and True: *Blood Meridian* as Gnostic Tragedy." In *Perspectives on Cormac McCarthy*, edited by Edwin T. Arnold and Dianne C. Luce, 159–74. Jackson: University Press of Mississippi.

Day, Michael A. 2016. *The Hope and Vision of Robert J. Oppenheimer*. Singapore: World Scientific Publishing.

Decker, William Merrill. 1990. *The Literary Vocation of Henry Adams*. Chapel Hill: University of North Carolina Press.

Dinstein, Ilan, Cibu Thomas, Marlene Behrmann, and David J. Heeger. 2008. "A Mirror Up to Nature." *Current Biology* 18.1:R13–18.

Ditsky, John. 1981. "Further into Darkness: The Novels of Cormac McCarthy." *Hollins Critic* 18:1–11.

Domsch, Sebastian. 2012. *Cormac McCarthy*. Munich: Edition Text + Kritik.

Doniger, Wendy. 1995. Foreword to *Myth and Meaning: Cracking the Code of Culture*, by Claude Lévi-Strauss, vii–xv. New York: Schocken Books.

Dorson, James. 2013. "Demystifying the Judge: Law and Mythical Violence in Cormac McCarthy's *Blood Meridian.*" *Journal of Modern Literature* 36.2:105–21.

Dowd, Ciarán. 2013. "The Hum of Mystery: Parataxis, Analepsis, and Geophysiology in *The Road.*" *Cormac McCarthy Journal* 11.1:23–43.

Dumouchel, Paul. 2014. "The Ambivalence of Scarcity." In *The Ambivalence of Scarcity and Other Essays*, 3–96. East Lansing: Michigan State University Press.

Dupuy, Jean-Pierre. 1980. "Myths of the Informational Society." In *The Myths of Information: Technology and Postindustrial Culture*, edited by Kathleen Woodward, 3–17. London: Routledge.

———. 2014. *Economy and the Future: A Crisis of Faith.* Translated by M. B. DeBevoise. East Lansing: Michigan State University Press.

Durant, William, and Ariel Durant. 1968. *The Lessons of History.* New York: Simon & Schuster.

Edwards, Tim. 2008. "The End of the Road: Pastoralism and the Post-Apocalyptic Waste Land of Cormac McCarthy's *The Road.*" *Cormac McCarthy Journal* 6:55–61.

Ehrenreich, Barbara. 1997. *Blood Rites: Origins and History of the Passions of War.* New York: Metropolitan Books.

Eliade, Mircea. 1987. *The Sacred and the Profane.* Translated by Willard R. Trask. Orlando, FL: Harcourt.

Eliot, T. S. 1975. "*Ulysses*, Order and Myth." In *Selected Prose of T. S. Eliot*, edited by Frank Kermode, 175–78. London: Faber & Faber.

———. 2004a. "East Coker." In *The Complete Poems and Plays of T. S. Eliot*, 177–83. London: Faber and Faber.

———. 2004b. "The Hollow Men." In *The Complete Poems and Plays of T. S. Eliot*, 83–86. London: Faber and Faber.

Ellis, Jay. 2000. "McCarthy Music." In *Myth, Legend, Dust: Critical Responses to Cormac McCarthy*, edited by Rick Wallach, 157–70. Manchester: Manchester University Press.

———. 2006. *No Place for Home: Spatial Constraint and Character Flight in the Novels of Cormac McCarthy.* New York: Routledge.

———. 2008. "Another Sense of Ending: The Keynote Address to the Knoxville Conference." *Cormac McCarthy Journal* 6:22–38.

Ellison, Ralph. 1995. "Hidden Name and Complex Fate." In *Shadow and Act*, 144–66. New York: Vintage.

English Standard Version Study Bible. 2008. Wheaton, IL: Crossway.

Euripides. 1968. "The Bacchae." In *The Complete Greek Tragedies*, translated by William

Arrowsmith, edited by David Grene and Richmond Lattimore, 141–220. Chicago: University of Chicago Press.

Evenson, Brian. 2002. "McCarthy's Wanderers: Nomadology, Violence, and Open Country." In *Sacred Violence*, vol. 1, *Cormac McCarthy's Appalachian Works*, edited by Wade Hall and Rick Wallach, 51–59. El Paso: Texas Western Press.

Farneti, Roberto. 2015. *Mimetic Politics: Dyadic Patterns in Global Politics*. East Lansing: Michigan State University Press.

Fiedler, Leslie. 1958. "From Redemption to Initiation." *New Leader* 26 (May): 20–23.

Figal, Günter. 1999. *Nietzsche: Eine philosophische Einführung*. Stuttgart: Reclam.

Fisher-Wirth, Ann. 2002. "Abjection and 'the Feminine' in *Outer Dark*." In *Cormac McCarthy: New Directions*, edited by James D. Lilley, 125–40. Albuquerque: University of New Mexico Press.

Fitzgerald, F. Scott. 2000. *The Great Gatsby*. Stuttgart: Klett.

Fleming, Chris. 2004. *René Girard: Violence and Mimesis*. Cambridge: Polity Press.

Floridi, Luciano. 2010. *Information: A Very Short Introduction*. Oxford: Oxford University Press.

Foerster, Heinz von. 1984. "Disorder/Order: Discovery or Invention?" In *Disorder and Order: Proceedings of the Stanford International Symposium (Sept. 14–16, 1981)*, edited by Paisley Livingston, 177–89. Saratoga, CA: Anma Libri.

Frankfurt, Harry G. 2005. *On Bullshit*. Princeton, NJ: Princeton University Press.

Frazer, James George. 2009. *The Golden Bough*. Oxford: Oxford University Press.

Freese, Peter. 1994. *"America": Dream or Nightmare? Reflections on a Composite Image*. Essen: Die Blaue Eule.

———. 1997. *From Apocalypse to Entropy and Beyond: The Second Law of Thermodynamics in Post-War American Fiction*. Essen: Die Blaue Eule.

———. 1998. *Die Initiationsreise: Studien zum jugendlichen Helden im modernen amerikanischen Roman*. Tübingen: Stauffenberg Verlag.

———. 2004. "From the Apocalyptic to the Entropic End: From Hope to Despair to New Hope?" In *The Holodeck in the Garden: Science and Technology in Contemporary American Fiction*, edited by Peter Freese and Charles B. Harris, 334–56. Normal, IL: Dalkey Archive Press.

———. 2015. "The 'Journey of Life' in American Fiction." In *The Journey of Life in American Life and Literature* Heidelberg: Winter.

Freud, Sigmund. 1950. *Totem and Taboo: Some Points of Agreement between the Mental Lives of Savages and Neurotics*. Translated and edited by James Strachey. New York: Norton.

———. 1961. *Civilization and Its Discontents* Translated and edited by James Strachey. New York: Norton.

Freund, Wieland. 2007. "Cormac McCarthys Hölle auf Erden." *Die Welt*, March 19. http://www.welt.de.

Frye, Northrop. 1971. *Anatomy of Criticism: Four Essays*. Princeton, NJ: Princeton University Press.

Frye, Steven. 2009. *Understanding Cormac McCarthy*. Columbia: University of South Carolina Press.

Gallese, Vittorio. 2011. "The Two Sides of Mimesis: Mimetic Theory, Embodied Simulation, and Social Identification." In *Mimesis and Science*, edited by Scott R. Garrels, 87–108. East Lansing: Michigan State University Press.

Gamblin, Hillary. 2011. "Discovering the Romantic in a Necrophiliac: The Question of Misogyny in *Child of God*." *Cormac McCarthy Journal* 9.1:28–37.

Gans, Eric. 1981. *The Origin of Language: A Formal Theory of Representation*. Berkeley: University of California Press.

Gardner, Stephen L. 2010. "The Deepening Impasse of Modernity." *Society* 47.5:1–22.

Garrels, Scott R. 2011a. "Human Imitation: Historical, Philosophical, and Scientific Perspectives." In *Mimesis and Science*, edited by Scott R. Garrels, 1–38. East Lansing: Michigan State University Press.

———. 2011b. "Mimesis and Science: An Interview with René Girard." In *Mimesis and Science*, edited by Scott R. Garrels, 215–53. East Lansing: Michigan State University Press.

Gauss Jackson, Katherine. 1965. "Books in Brief (Book Review)." *Harper's Magazine*, 112.

Gell-Mann, Murray. 1995. *The Quark and the Jaguar: Adventures in the Simple and the Complex*. London: Abacus.

Gibbon, Edward. 1994. *The History of the Decline and Fall of the Roman Empire*. Vol. 1. Edited by David Womersley. London: Penguin.

Gibson, Mike. 2002. "Knoxville Gave Cormac McCarthy the Raw Material of His Art. And He Gave It Back." In *Sacred Violence*, vol. 1, *Cormac McCarthy's Appalachian Works*, edited by Wade Hall and Rick Wallach, 23–34. El Paso: Texas Western Press.

Giemza, Bryan. 2012. "Toward a Catholic Understanding of Cormac McCarthy's Oeuvre." In *You Would Not Believe What Watches: Suttree and Cormac McCarthy's Knoxville*, edited by Rick Wallach, 158–73. N.p.: Cormac McCarthy Society.

Giles, James R. 2009. "Discovering Fourthspace in Appalachia: Cormac McCarthy's *Outer Dark* and *Child of God*." In *Cormac McCarthy*, edited by Harold Bloom, 107–31. New York: Infobase Publishing.

Girard, René. 1976. *Deceit, Desire and the Novel: Self and Other in Literary Structure*. Translated by Yvonne Freccero. Baltimore, MD: Johns Hopkins University Press.

———. 1977. *Violence and the Sacred*. Translated by Patrick Gregory. Baltimore, MD: Johns Hopkins University Press.

———. 1978. *To Double Business Bound: Essays on Literature, Mimesis and Anthropology*, 136–54. Baltimore, MD: Johns Hopkins University Press.

———. 1984. "Disorder and Order in Mythology." In *Disorder and Order: Proceedings of the Stanford International Symposium (Sept. 14–16, 1981)*, edited by Paisley Livingston, 80–97. Saratoga, CA: Anma Libri.

———. 1986. *The Scapegoat*. Translated by Yvonne Freccero. Baltimore, MD: Johns Hopkins University Press.

———. 1987. *Things Hidden Since the Foundation of the World*. Translated by Stephen Bann and Michael Metteer. Stanford, CA: Stanford University Press.

———. 1991. *A Theater of Envy: William Shakespeare*. Oxford: Oxford University Press.

———. 2001a. *The Girard Reader*. Edited by James G. Williams. New York: Crossroad Herder.

———. 2001b. *I See Satan Fall Like Lightning*. Translated by James G. Williams. New York: Orbis.

———. 2010. *Battling to the End: Conversations with Benoît Chantre*. Translated by Mary Baker. East Lansing: Michigan State University Press.

Goethe, Johann Wolfgang. 2003. *Faust: Texte*. Frankfurt am Main: Insel.

Golowin, Sergius. 1983. *Die Welt des Tarot*. Basel: Sphinx Verlag.

Goodhart, Sandor. 1978. "ΛηστὰςʹΕφασκε: Oedipus and Laius' Many Murderers." *Diacritics* 8.1:55–71.

Grammer, John M. 1999. "A Thing against Which Time Will Not Prevail: Pastoral and History in Cormac McCarthy's South." In *Perspectives on Cormac McCarthy*, edited by Edwin T. Arnold and Dianne C. Luce, 29–44. Jackson: University Press of Mississippi.

Grant, Natalie. 2002. "The Landscape of the Soul: Man and the Natural World in *The Orchard Keeper*." In *Sacred Violence*, vol. 1, *Cormac McCarthy's Appalachian Works*, edited by Wade Hall and Rick Wallach, 75–82. El Paso: Texas Western Press.

Greenwood, Willard P. 2009. *Reading McCarthy*. Santa Barbara, CA: Greenwood Press.

Greiner, Ulrich. 2007. "Am anderen Ende der Geschichte." *Die Zeit*, March 29. http://www.zeit.de.

Greve, Julius. 2015. "Another Kind of Clay: On *Blood Meridian*'s Okenian Philosophy of Nature." *Cormac McCarthy Journal* 13.1:27–53.

Grimm, Gunter E., Werner Faulstich, and Peter Kuon. 1986. "Einleitung." In *Apokalypse: Weltuntergangsvisionen in der Literatur des 20. Jahrhunderts*, edited by Gunter E. Grimm, Werner Faulstich, and Peter Kuon, 7–13. Frankfurt am Main: Suhrkamp.

Grindley, Carl James. 2008. "The Setting of McCarthy's *The Road*." *Explicator* 67.1:11–13.

Guillemin, Georg. 2002. "'See the Child': The Melancholy Subtext of *Blood Meridian*." In

Cormac McCarthy: New Directions, edited by James D. Lilley, 239–65. Albuquerque: University of New Mexico Press.

———. 2004. *The Pastoral Vision of Cormac McCarthy*. College Station: Texas A&M University Press.

Guinn, Matthew. 2000. "Ruder Forms Survive: Cormac McCarthy's Atavistic Vision." In *Myth, Legend, Dust: Critical Responses to Cormac McCarthy*, edited by Rick Wallach, 108–15. Manchester: Manchester University Press.

Habermas, Jürgen. 2006. *Time of Transitions*. Malden, MA: Polity Press.

Hage, Erik. 2010. *Cormac McCarthy: A Literary Companion*. Jefferson, NC: McFarland & Company.

Hall, Wade. 2002. "The Human Comedy of Cormac McCarthy." In *Sacred Violence*, vol. 1, *Cormac McCarthy's Appalachian Works*, edited by Wade Hall and Rick Wallach, 61–73. El Paso: Texas Western Press.

Hayles, N. Katherine. 1990. *Chaos Bound: Orderly Disorder in Contemporary Literature and Science*. Ithaca, NY: Cornell University Press.

———. 1991. "Introduction: Complex Dynamics in Literature and Science." In *Chaos and Order: Complex Dynamics in Literature and Science*, edited by N. Katherine Hayles, 1–33. Chicago: University of Chicago Press.

Hedges, Chris. 2002. *War Is a Force that Gives Us Meaning*. New York: Public Affairs.

Hesiod. 2008. *Theogony and Works and Days*. Translated by M. L. West. Oxford: Oxford University Press.

Hicks, Granville. 1965. "Six Firsts for Summer." *Saturday Review*, June 12, 35–36.

Hillier, Russell M. 2006. "'In a Dark Parody' of Bunyan's *The Pilgrim's Progress*: The Presence of Subversive Allegory in Cormac McCarthy's *Outer Dark*." *ANQ: A Quarterly Journal of Short Articles, Notes and Reviews* 19.4:52–59.

———. 2013. "The Judge's Molar: Infanticide and the Meteorite in *Blood Meridian*." In *They Rode On: "Blood Meridian" and the Tragedy of the American West*, edited by Rick Wallach, 58–64. N.p.: Cormac McCarthy Society.

Hobbes, Thomas. 2008. *Leviathan*. Edited by J. C. A. Gaskin. New York: Oxford University Press.

Hofstadter, Richard. 1961. *The American Political Tradition*. New York: Vintage.

Holcomb, Mark. 2006. "End of the Line." *Village Voice*, August 29. http://www.villagevoice.com.

Hölderlin, Friedrich. 1994. "Patmos." In *Friedrich Hölderlin: Poems and Fragments*, translated by Michael Hamburger, 483. London: Anvil Press.

———. 2008. "Patmos." In *Friedrich Hölderlin: Gesammelte Werke*, edited by Hans Jürgen Balmes, 197–203. Frankfurt am Main: Fischer.

Holloway, David. 2000. "'A False Book Is No Book at All': The Ideology of Representation in *Blood Meridian* and the Border Trilogy." In *Myth, Legend, Dust: Critical Responses to Cormac McCarthy*, edited by Rick Wallach, 185–200. Manchester: Manchester University Press.

———. 2002. *The Late Modernism of Cormac McCarthy*. Westport, CT: Greenwood Press.

Horton, Matthew R. 2002. "'Hallucinated Recollections': Narrative as Spatialized Perception of History in *The Orchard Keeper*." In *Cormac McCarthy: New Directions*, edited by James D. Lilley, 285–311. Albuquerque: University of New Mexico Press.

Ives, Stephen, dir. 1996. *The West*. Episode 8, disc 4. "One Sky Above Us." Episode 8. PBS/Polyband.

James, Caryn. 1985. "Is Everybody Dead Around Here?" *New York Times*, April 28, 31.

James, William. 1950. *The Principles of Psychology*. Vol. 2. New York: Dover.

Jarrett, Robert L. 1997. *Cormac McCarthy*. New York: Twayne Publishers.

Jefferson, Thomas. 1984. *Writings: Autobiography, Notes on the State of Virginia, Public and Private Papers, Addresses, Letters*. Edited by Merrill D. Peterson. New York: Library of America.

Jillet, Lou. 2013. "*Blood Meridian* and the Archive." In *They Rode On: "Blood Meridian" and the Tragedy of the American West*, edited by Rick Wallach, 1–9. N.p.: Cormac McCarthy Society.

Johnson, George. 1996. "Social Strife May Have Exiled Ancient Indians." *New York Times*, August 20. http://www.nytimes.com.

Jones, Robert P., Daniel Cox, and Juhem Navarro-Rivera. 2014. *Believers, Sympathizers, & Skeptics: Why Americans Are Conflicted about Climate Change, Environmental Policy, and Science*. Washington, DC: Public Religion Research Institute.

Josyph, Peter. 2011. "A Walk with Wesley Morgan through *Suttree*'s Knoxville." *Appalachian Heritage* 39.1:21–49.

———. 2010a. "Blood Bath: A Conversation with Rick Wallach about *Blood Meridian*." In *Adventures in Reading Cormac McCarthy*, 93–110. Lanham, MD: Scarecrow Press.

———. 2010b. "Tragic Ecstasy: A Conversation with Harold Bloom about *Blood Meridian*." In *Adventures in Reading Cormac McCarthy*, 77–91. Lanham, MD: Scarecrow Press.

Jung, Carl Gustav. 2009. "Über die Archetypen des kollektiven Unbewußten." In *C.G. Jung: Archetypen*, edited by Lorenz Jung, 7–43. Munich: DTV.

Jurgensen, John. 2009. "Hollywood's Favorite Cowboy." *Wall Street Journal* November 20. http://online.wsj.com.

Keller-Estes, Andrew. 2013. *Cormac McCarthy and the Writing of American Spaces*. Amsterdam: Rodopi.

Kelly, James. 2010. "All-Time 100 Novels." *TIME*, January 6, 2010. http://entertainment. time.com.

Kermode, Frank. 2000. *The Sense of an Ending: Studies in the Theory of Fiction*. Oxford: Oxford University Press.

Keysers, Christian. 2009. "Mirror Neurons." *Current Biology* 19.21:R971–73.

Keysers, Christian, and Valeria Gazzola. 2010. "Mirror Neurons Recorded in Humans." *Current Biology* 20.8:R353–54.

King, Daniel. 2011. "Albert Erskine at Random House: The Cormac McCarthy Years." *Comparative American Studies* 9.3:254–72.

Kirk, G. S., J. E. Raven, and M. Schofield. 2006. *The Presocratic Philosophers: A Critical History with a Selection of Texts*. Cambridge: Cambridge University Press.

Kristeva, Julia. 1982. *Powers of Horror: An Essay on Abjection*. New York: Columbia University Press.

Kunsa, Ashley. 2009. "'Maps of the World in Its Becoming': Post-Apocalyptic Naming in Cormac McCarthy's *The Road*." *Journal of Modern Literature* 33.1:57–74.

Kushner, David. 2007. "Cormac McCarthy's Apocalypse." *Rolling Stone*, December 27. http://www.davidkushner.com/article/cormac-mccarthys-apocalypse/.

Lacan, Jacques. 2006a. "The Instance of the Letter in the Unconscious, or Reason Since Freud." **Écrits**: *The First Complete Edition in English*, translated by Bruce Fink, 412–41. New York: Norton.

———. 2006b. "The Mirror Stage as Formative of the Function of the I as Revealed in Psychoanalytic Experience." *Écrits: The First Complete Edition in English*, translated by Bruce Fink, 73–81. New York: Norton.

———. 2006c. "Science and Truth." In *Écrits: The First Complete Edition in English*, translated by Bruce Fink, 726–45. New York: Norton.

Lang, John. 2002. "Lester Ballard: McCarthy's Challenge to the Reader's Compassion." In *Sacred Violence*, vol. 1, *Cormac McCarthy's Appalachian Works*, edited by Wade Hall and Rick Wallach, 103–11. El Paso: Texas Western Press.

Lask, Thomas. 1968. "Southern Gothic." *New York Times*, September 23, 33.

Lawrence, Bruce B., and Aisha Karim, eds. 2007. *On Violence: A Reader*. Durham, NC: Duke University Press.

Leeming, David. 2005. *The Oxford Companion to World Mythology*. Oxford: Oxford University Press.

Lenfield, Spencer. 2015. "Why Auden Left: 'September 1, 1939' and British Cultural Life." *Journal of the History of Ideas* Blog, December 9, 2015. https://jhiblog.org.

Lessing, Gotthold Ephraim. 1998. *Laokoon. Oder: Über die Grenzen der Malerei und Poesie*. Stuttgart: Reclam.

Levinson, Natasha. 2003. "'But Some People Will Not': Arendtian Interventions in Education." In *Philosophy of Education 2002*, edited by Scott Fletcher, 200–208. Urbana, IL: Philosophy of Education Society.

Lévi-Strauss, Claude. 1963. *Structural Anthropology*. Translated by Claire Jacobson and Brooke Grundfest Schoepf. New York: Basic Books.

———. 1995. *Myth and Meaning: Cracking the Code of Culture*. New York: Schocken Books.

Lewis, R. W. B. 1966. *The American Adam: Innocence, Tragedy and Tradition in the Nineteenth Century*. Chicago: University of Chicago Press.

Liddell, H. G., and Robert Scott. 1963. *An Intermediate Greek-English Lexicon: Founded upon the Seventh Edition of Liddell and Scott's Greek-English Lexicon*. Oxford: Oxford University Press.

Lincoln, Kenneth. 2009. *Cormac McCarthy: American Canticles*. New York: Palgrave Macmillan.

Livy, Titus. 1998. *History of Rome: Books I and II*. Translated by B. O. Foster. Cambridge, MA: Harvard University Press.

Lovelock, James. 2000a. *The Ages of Gaia*. Oxford: Oxford University Press.

———. 2000b. *Gaia: A New Look at Life on Earth*. Oxford: Oxford University Press.

Luce, Dianne C. 2002. "The Cave of Oblivion: Platonic Mythology in *Child of God*." In *Cormac McCarthy: New Directions*, edited by James D. Lilley, 171–98. Albuquerque: University of New Mexico Press.

———. 2009. *Reading the World: Cormac McCarthy's Tennessee Period*. Columbia: University of South Carolina Press.

Luttrull, Daniel. 2010. "Prometheus Hits *The Road*: Revising the Myth." *Cormac McCarthy Journal* 8.1:20–33.

Madsen, Michael. 2011. "The Uncanny Necrophile in Cormac McCarthy's *Child of God*; or, How I Learned to Understand Lester Ballard and Start Worrying." *Cormac McCarthy Journal* 9.1:17–27.

Marx, Leo. 1981. *The Machine in the Garden: Technology and the Pastoral Ideal in America*. Oxford: Oxford University Press.

Maslin, Janet. 2006. "The Road through Hell, Paved with Desperation." *New York Times*, September 25. http://www.nytimes.com.

Matussek, Matthias. 1992. "Die Abendröte des Westens." *Spiegel* 36:190–98.

Maxwell, James Clerk. 1878. "Diffusion." In *Encyclopedia Britannica*, 9th ed., vol. 7, 220. New York: Samuel L. Hall.

McCarthy, Cormac. 1959. "Wake for Susan." *Phoenix*, 3–6.

———. 1960. "A Drowning Incident." *Phoenix*, 3–4.

———. 1992a. *All the Pretty Horses*. New York: Knopf.

———. 1992b. *Blood Meridian, or The Evening Redness in the West*. New York: Vintage.

———. 1992c. *Suttree*. New York: Vintage.

———. 1993a. *Child of God*. New York: Vintage.

———. 1993b. *The Orchard Keeper*. New York: Vintage.

———. 1993c. *Outer Dark*. New York: Vintage.

———. 1994a. *The Crossing*. New York: Vintage.

———. 1994b. *The Stonemason*. New York: Vintage.

———. 1996. *The Gardener's Son*. Hopewell, NJ: Ecco Press.

———. 1998. *Cities of the Plain*. New York: Knopf.

———. 2005. *No Country for Old Men*. New York: Vintage.

———. 2006a. *The Road*. New York: Knopf.

———. 2006b. *The Sunset Limited*. New York: Vintage.

———. 2010. *Blood Meridian, or The Evening Redness in the West*. 25th anniversary ed. New York: Modern Library.

———. 2013. *The Counselor*. London: Picador, 2013.

———. 2017. "The Kekulé Problem: Where Did Language Come From?" *Nautilus* Mar/Apr: 22–31.

McKenna, Andrew. 1992. *Violence and Difference: Girard, Derrida, and Deconstruction*. Chicago: Illinois University Press.

Meltzoff, Andrew. 2011. "Out of the Mouths of Babes: Imitation, Gaze, and Intentions in Infant Research—the 'Like Me' Framework." In *Mimesis and Science*, edited by Scott R. Garrels, 55–74. East Lansing: Michigan State University Press.

Melville, Herman. 2002. *Moby-Dick*. New York: Norton.

Metress, Christopher. 2001. "Via Negativa: The Way of Unknowing in Cormac McCarthy's *Outer Dark*." *Southern Review* 37.1:147–54.

Millard, Kenneth. 2000. *Contemporary American Fiction*. New York: Oxford University Press.

Miller, Henry. 2010. *The Colossus of Maroussi*. New York: New Directions.

Milton, John. 2003. *Paradise Lost*. Edited by John Leonard. London: Penguin.

Monbiot, George. 2007. "Civilisation Ends with a Shutdown of Human Concern: Are We There Already?" *Guardian*, October 30. https://www.theguardian.co.uk.

Morales, Helen. 2007. *Classical Mythology: A Very Short Introduction*. Oxford: Oxford University Press.

Morgan, Wesley G. 2008. "The Route and Roots of *The Road*." *Cormac McCarthy Journal* 6:39–47.

———. 2012. "The 'Government Tank' in *The Orchard Keeper*." *Cormac McCarthy Journal* 10.1:93–96.

Morin, Edgar. 1984. "The Fourth Vision: On the Place of the Observer." In *Disorder and Order: Proceedings of the Stanford International Symposium (Sept. 14–16, 1981)*, edited by Paisley Livingston, 98–108. Saratoga, CA: Anma Libri.

Mort, Oliver. 2013. "Are We Still the Good Guys? Cormac McCarthy and the Postmodern Heroic Quest." In *They Rode On: "Blood Meridian" and the Tragedy of the American West*, edited by Rick Wallach, 246–55. N.p.: Cormac McCarthy Society.

Mulvey, Laura. 1975. "Visual Pleasure and Narrative Cinema." *Screen* 16.3:6–18.

Mundik, Petra. 2013. "This Luminosity in Beings So Endarkened: Gnostic Soteriology in *Blood Meridian*." In *They Rode On: "Blood Meridian" and the Tragedy of the American West*, edited by Rick Wallach, 196–223. N.p.: Cormac McCarthy Society.

Münkler, Herfried. 2007. "Heroische und postheroische Gesellschaften." *Merkur* 61.8/9:742–52.

———. 2013. "Mythic Sacrifices and Real Corpses: *Le Sacre du Printemps* and the Great War." In *Avatar of Modernity: The Rite of Spring Reconsidered*, edited by Hermann Danuser and Heidy Zimmermann, 336–55. Basel: Boosey & Hawkes.

New York Times. 2006. "What Is the Best Work of American Fiction of the Last 25 Years?" May 21. http://www.nytimes.com.

Nietzsche, Friedrich. 1918. *The Antichrist*. Translated by H. L. Mencken. New York: Alfred A. Knopf.

———. 1988. *Nachgelassene Fragmente 1887–1889*. Edited by Giorgio Colli and Mazzino Montinari. Kritische Studienausgabe 13. Munich: DTV/deGruyter.

———. 1999a. *Der Fall Wagner / Götzen-Dämmerung / Der Antichrist / Ecce Homo / Dionysus-Dithyramben / Nietzsche Contra Wagner*. Edited by Giorgio Colli and Mazzino Montinari. Kritische Studienausgabe 6. Munich: DTV/deGruyter.

———. 1999b. *Morgenröte / Idyllen aus Messina / Die Fröhliche Wissenschaft*. Edited by Giorgio Colli and Mazzino Montinari. Kritische Studienausgabe 3. Munich: DTV/deGruyter.

———. 2002. *Also Sprach Zarathustra*. Edited by Giorgio Colli and Mazzino Montinari. Kritische Studienausgabe 4. Munich: DTV/deGruyter.

———. 2007. *Jenseits von Gut und Böse / Zur Genealogie der Moral*. Edited by Giorgio Colli and Mazzino Montinari. Kritische Studienausgabe 5. Munich: DTV/deGruyter.

O'Shea, Sean. 1970. *Voyeurismus: Psychologie, Ursprung und Motive einer Perversion*. Munich: Heyne.

Otto, Walter F. 1965. *Dionysus: Myth and Cult*. Bloomington: Indiana University Press.

Oughourlian, Jean-Michel. 1984. "Mimetic Desire as a Key to Psychotic and Neurotic Structure." In *Disorder and Order: Proceedings of the Stanford International Symposium (Sept. 14–16, 1981)*, edited by Paisley Livingston, 72–89. Saratoga, CA: Anma Libri.

Ovid. 1922. *Metamorphoses*. Translated by Brookes More. Boston: Cornhill.

Owens, Barcley. 2000. *Cormac McCarthy's Western Novels*. Tucson: University of Arizona Press.

Palmer, Louis. 2008. "Full Circle: *The Road* Rewrites *The Orchard Keeper*." *Cormac McCarthy Journal* 6:62–68.

Parkes, Adam. 2002. "History, Bloodshed, and the Spectacle of American Identity in *Blood Meridian*." In *Cormac McCarthy: New Directions*, edited by James D. Lilley, 103–24. Albuquerque: University of New Mexico Press.

Pastore, Stephen. 2013. "Judge Holden: Yahweh on Horseback." In *They Rode On: "Blood Meridian" and the Tragedy of the American West*, edited by Rick Wallach, 108–11. N.p.: Cormac McCarthy Society.

Peterson, Dale, and Richard Wrangham. 1996. *Demonic Males: Apes and the Origins of Human Violence*. New York: Mariner Books.

Pew Research Center. 2010. "Life in 2050: Amazing Science, Familiar Threats." https://www.pewresearch.org/wp-content/uploads/sites/4/legacy-pdf/625.pdf.

Phillips, Dana. 2002. "History and the Ugly Facts of *Blood Meridian*." In *Cormac McCarthy: New Directions*, edited by James D. Lilley, 17–46. Albuquerque: University of New Mexico Press.

———. 2011. "'He Ought Not Have Done It': McCarthy and Apocalypse." In *Cormac McCarthy: "All the Pretty Horses," "No Country for Old Men," "The Road,"* edited by Sara L. Spurgeon, 172–88. London: Continuum.

Pinker, Steven. 2011. *The Better Angels of Our Nature: The Decline of Violence in History and Its Causes*. New York: Allen Lane.

Planck, Max. 1915. *Eight Lectures on Theoretical Physics*. New York: Columbia University Press.

Plato. 1991. *Der Staat*. Translated by Rudolf Rufener. Munich: DTV.

———. 2010. "Timaios." In *Sämtliche Werke*, vol. 3, edited by Erich Loewnthal, 93–191. Heidelberg: Lambert Schneider.

Platt, Michael. 2009. "René Girard and Nietzsche Struggling." In *Nietzsche und Frankreich*, edited by Clemens Pornschlegel and Martin Stingelin, 351–75. Berlin: DeGruyter.

Polasek, Cassie. 2013. "'Books Are Made Out of Books': Herman Melville's Moby Dick and Cormac McCarthy's Judge Holden." In *They Rode On: "Blood Meridian" and the Tragedy of the American West*, edited by Rick Wallach, 82–94. N.p.: Cormac McCarthy Society.

Porush, David. 1991. "Fiction as Dissipative Structures: Prigogine's Theory and

Postmodernism's Roadshow." In *Chaos and Order: Complex Dynamics in Literature and Science*, edited by N. Katherine Hayles, 54–84. Chicago: University of Chicago Press.

Prather, William. 2000. "'Like Something Seen through Bad Glass': Narrative Strategies in *The Orchard Keeper*." In *Myth, Legend, Dust: Critical Responses to Cormac McCarthy*, edited by Rick Wallach, 37–54. Manchester: Manchester University Press.

Prescott, Orville. 1965. "Still Another Disciple of William Faulkner." *New York Times*, May 12, 45.

Prigogine, Ilya. 1984. "Order out of Chaos." In *Disorder and Order: Proceedings of the Stanford International Symposium (Sept. 14–16, 1981)*, edited by Paisley Livingston, 41–60. Saratoga, CA: Anma Libri.

Prigogine, Ilya, and Isabelle Stengers. 1984. *Order Out of Chaos: Man's New Dialogue with Nature*. New York: Bantam Books.

Principe, Lawrence M., and Andrew Weeks. 1989. "Jacob Boehme's Divine Substance *Salitter*: Its Nature, Origin, and Relationship to Seventeenth Century Scientific Theories." *British Journal for the History of Science* 22.1:53–61.

Ragan, David Paul. 1999. "Values and Structure in *The Orchard Keeper*." In *Perspectives on Cormac McCarthy*, edited by Edwin T. Arnold and Dianne C. Luce, 17–27. Jackson: University Press of Mississippi.

Randall, Lisa. 2006. *Warped Passages: Unraveling the Mysteries of the Universe's Hidden Dimensions*. New York: Harper Perennial.

Raymond, Gerard. 2013. "New York Film Festival 2013: *Child of God* Review." *SLANT*, September 24. http://www.slantmagazine.com.

Regenbogen, Arnim, and Uwe Meyer, eds. 1998. "Chaos." In *Wörterbuch der philosophischen Begriffe*, 121–22. Hamburger: Meiner.

———. 1998. "Mythos." In *Wörterbuch der philosophischen Begriffe*, 436. Hamburger: Meiner.

Reineke, Martha J. 2014. *Intimate Domain: Desire, Trauma, and Mimetic Theory*. East Lansing: Michigan State University Press.

Rhodes, Richard. 1986. *The Making of the Atomic Bomb*. New York: Simon and Schuster.

Russell, Richard R. 2009. "A Keatsian Echo in Cormac McCarthy's *The Orchard Keeper*." *Cormac McCarthy Journal* 7:34–35.

Sanborn, Wallis R., III. 2006. *Animals in the Fiction of Cormac McCarthy*. Jefferson, NC: McFarland, 2006.

———. 2013. "'War Is Your Trade, Is It Not?': *Blood Meridian* as American Novel of War." In *They Rode On: "Blood Meridian" and the Tragedy of the American West*, edited by Rick Wallach, 256–60. N.p.: Cormac McCarthy Society.

Sansom, Dennis. 2007. "Learning from Art: Cormac McCarthy's *Blood Meridian* as a Critique of Divine Determinism." *Journal of Aesthetic Education* 41.1:1–19.

Schafer, William. 1977. "Cormac McCarthy: The Hard Wages of Original Sin." *Appalachian Journal* 4.2:105–19.

Schaub, Thomas H. 2009. "Secular Scripture and Cormac McCarthy's *The Road*." *Renascene* 61.3:153–67.

Schimpf, Shane. 2006. *A Reader's Guide to "Blood Meridian."* Princeton, NJ: BonMot Publishing.

———. 2013. "A Short History of Scalping." In *They Rode On: "Blood Meridian" and the Tragedy of the American West*, edited by Rick Wallach, 25–37. N.p.: Cormac McCarthy Society.

Schlosser, S. E. 2004. "The Wampus Cat." In *Spooky South: Tales of Hauntings, Strange Happenings, and Other Local Lore*, 92–98. Guilford, CT: Globe Pequot.

Schopenhauer, Arthur. 1978. *Preisschrift über die Freiheit des Willens*. Hamburg: Felix Meiner.

Schutz, Aaron. 2003. "Stories vs. Practices: Education for Political Action." In *Philosophy of Education 2002*, edited by Scott Fletcher, 209–11. Urbana, IL: Philosophy of Education Society.

Segal, Robert A. 2004. *Myth: A Very Short Introduction*. Oxford: Oxford University Press.

Sepich, John. 1999. "'What Kind of Indians Was Them?': Some Historical Sources in Cormac McCarthy's *Blood Meridian*." In *Perspectives on Cormac McCarthy*, edited by Edwin T. Arnold and Dianne C. Luce, 123–43. Jackson: University Press of Mississippi.

———. 2008. *Notes on "Blood Meridian."* Austin: University of Texas Press.

Shakespeare, William. 2007. "Troilus and Cressida." In *William Shakespeare: Complete Works*, edited by Jonathan Bate and Eric Rasmussen, 1456–535. Houndmills: RSC/Macmillan.

Shannon, Claude E., and Warren Weaver. 1998. *The Mathematical Theory of Communication*. Urbana: University of Illinois Press.

Shaviro, Steven. 1999. "The Very Life of the Darkness: A Reading of *Blood Meridian*." In *Perspectives on Cormac McCarthy*, edited by Edwin T. Arnold and Dianne C. Luce, 145–58. Jackson: University Press of Mississippi.

Shaw, Patrick W. 1997. "The Kid's Fate, the Judge's Guilt: Ramifications of Closure in Cormac McCarthy's *Blood Meridian*." *Southern Literary Journal* 30.1:102–19.

Simpson, John, and Edmund Weiner, eds. 1989. "decide, v.1." In *The Oxford English Dictionary*, vol. 4, 329. Oxford: Clarendon Press.

———. 1989. "Hoot(e)nanny. | Hootananny, n." In *The Oxford English Dictionary*, vol. 7, 374. Oxford: Clarendon Press.

———. 1989. "pandemonium, n." In *The Oxford English Dictionary*, vol. 11, 129. Oxford: Clarendon Press.

———. 1989. "paraclete, n." In *The Oxford English Dictionary*, vol. 11, 181. Oxford: Clarendon Press, 1989.

Simpson, Lewis. 1975. *The Dispossessed Garden*. Athens: University of Georgia Press.

Simpson, Philip L. 2000. *Psycho Paths: Tracking the Serial Killer through Contemporary American Film and Fiction*. Carbondale: Southern Illinois University Press.

Slotkin, Richard. 1973. *Regeneration through Violence: The Mythology of the American Frontier, 1600–1860*. Norman: University of Oklahoma Press.

———. 1985. *The Fatal Environment: The Myth of the Frontier in the Age of Industrialization, 1800–1890*. Norman: University of Oklahoma Press.

———. 1998. *Gunfighter Nation: The Myth of the Frontier in Twentieth-Century America*. Norman: University of Oklahoma Press.

Smith, Henry Nash. 2009. *Virgin Land: The American West as Symbol and Myth*. Cambridge, MA: Harvard University Press.

Snow, Charles Percy. 1968. *The Two Cultures and a Second Look*. Frankfurt: Diesterweg.

Snyder, Phillip A. 2008. "Hospitality in Cormac McCarthy's *The Road*." *Cormac McCarthy Journal* 6:69–86.

———. 2013. "The Gift of Death in *Blood Meridian*." In *They Rode On: "Blood Meridian" and the Tragedy of the American West*, edited by Rick Wallach, 146–56. N.p.: Cormac McCarthy Society.

Søfting, Inger-Anne. 1999. "Desert Pandemonium: Cormac McCarthy's Apocalyptic 'Western' in *Blood Meridian*." *American Studies in Scandinavia* 31:14–30.

Sophocles. 2011. "Oedipus the King." In *The Complete Plays of Sophocles*, translated by Robert Bagg and James Scully, 387–491. New York: Harper Perennial.

Spencer, William C. 2002. "Cormac McCarthy's Unholy Trinity: Biblical Parody in *Outer Dark*." In *Sacred Violence*, vol. 1, *Cormac McCarthy's Appalachian Works*, edited by Wade Hall and Rick Wallach, 83–91. El Paso: Texas Western Press.

Spiegel, Hubert. 2008. "Cormac McCarthys Romane: Das dunkle Zentrum der Welt." *Frankfurter Allgemeine Zeitung*, June 7,. http://www.faz.net.

Spurgeon, Sara. 2002. "The Sacred Hunter and the Eucharist of the Wilderness: Mythic Reconstructions in *Blood Meridian*." In *Cormac McCarthy: New Directions*, edited by James D. Lilley, 75–101. Albuquerque: University of New Mexico Press.

Stevens, Wallace. 1990. "The Idea of Order at Key West." In *The Collected Poems*, 128–30. New York: Vintage.

Stevenson, Robert Louis. 2005. *The Strange Case of Dr. Jekyll and Mr. Hyde*. Peterborough, ON: Broadview Press.

Stinson, Emily J. 2013. "*Blood Meridian*'s Man of Many Masks: Judge Holden as Tarot Fool."

In *They Rode On: "Blood Meridian" and the Tragedy of the American West*, edited by Rick Wallach, 95–107. N.p.: Cormac McCarthy Society.

Sullivan, Nell. 2000. "The Evolution of the Dead Girlfriend Motif in *Outer Dark* and *Child of God*." In *Myth, Legend, Dust: Critical Responses to Cormac McCarthy*, edited by Rick Wallach, 68–77. Manchester: Manchester University Press.

Sullivan, Walter. 1965. "Worlds Past and Future: A Christian and Several from the South." *Sewanee Review* 73.4:719–26.

Tin, Mikkel B. 2010. "Saturated Phenomena: From Picture to Revelation in Jean-Luc Marion's Phenomenology." *Filozofia* 65.9:860–76.

Tocqueville, Alexis de. 2000. *Democracy in America*. New York: Bantam.

Turner, Frederick Jackson. 2008. *The Significance of the Frontier in American History*. London: Penguin.

Tuveson, Ernest Lee. 1968. *Redeemer Nation: The Idea of America's Millennial Role*. Chicago: University of Chicago Press.

Urban Dictionary. n.d. "Hootenanny, *n.*" http://www.urbandictionary.com.

Vanderheide, John. 2000. "The Process of Elimination: Tracing the Prodigal's Irrevocable Passage through Cormac McCarthy's Southern and Western Novels." In *Myth, Legend, Dust: Critical Responses to Cormac McCarthy*, edited by Rick Wallach, 177–82. Manchester: Manchester University Press.

———. 2008. "Sighting Leviathan: Ritualism, Daemonism and the Book of Job in McCarthy's Latest Works." *Cormac McCarthy Journal* 6:107–20.

Vescio, Bryan. 2013. "'On Parallax and False Guidance in Things Past': Valéry and the Uses of History in *Blood Meridian*." In *They Rode On: "Blood Meridian" and the Tragedy of the American West*, edited by Rick Wallach, 46–57. N.p.: Cormac McCarthy Society.

Vidal, John, David Adam, Jonathan Watts, Leo Hickman, and Ian Sample. 2008. "50 People Who Could Save the Planet." *Guardian*, January 5,. https://www.theguardian.co.uk.

Vieth, Ronja. 2013. "A Frontier Myth Turns Gothic." In *They Rode On: "Blood Meridian" and the Tragedy of the American West*, edited by Rick Wallach, 133–45. N.p.: Cormac McCarthy Society.

Vondung, Klaus. 1988. *Die Apokalypse in Deutschland*. Munich: DTV.

Wallace, Garry. 1992. "Meeting McCarthy." *Southern Quarterly* 30.4:134–39.

Wallach, Rick. 2002a. "From *Beowulf* to *Blood Meridian*: Cormac McCarthy's Demystification of the Martial Code." In *Cormac McCarthy: New Directions*, edited by James D. Lilley, 199–214. Albuquerque: University of New Mexico Press.

———. 2002b. "Judge Holden, *Blood Meridian*'s Evil Archon." In *Sacred Violence*, vol. 2, *Cormac McCarthy's Western Novels*, edited by Wade Hall and Rick Wallach, 1–13. El Paso: Texas Western Press.

————. 2013. "Sam Chamberlain and the Iconology of Science in Mid-19th Century Nation Building." In *They Rode On: "Blood Meridian" and the Tragedy of the American West*, edited by Rick Wallach, 38–45. N.p.: Cormac McCarthy Society.

Walsh, Christopher. 2003. "There's No Place Like Holme: The Quest to Find a Place for McCarthy's Southern Fiction." In *Cormac McCarthy: Uncharted Territories / Territoires Inconnus*, edited by Christine Chollier, 31–42. Reims: Presses Universitaires de Reims.

————. 2008. "The Post-Southern Sense of Place in *The Road*." *Cormac McCarthy Journal* 6:48–54.

————. 2009. *In the Wake of the Sun: Navigating the Southern Novels of Cormac McCarthy*. Knoxville, TN: Newfound Press.

Warner, Alan. 2006. "The Road to Hell." *Guardian Review*, November 4. https://www.theguardian.co.uk.

Warner, Marina. 1994. *Managing Monsters: Six Myths of Our Time*. London: Vintage.

Watt, Ian. 1984. "Order and Disorder in the Arts and Sciences: A Historical Restrospect." In *Disorder and Order: Proceedings of the Stanford International Symposium (Sept. 14–16, 1981)*, edited by Paisley Livingston, 34–40. Saratoga, CA: Anma Libri.

Wehr, Gerhard. 1971. *Jakob Böhme*. Reinbek: Rowohlt.

————. 1992. "Jakob Böhme und sein Erstlingswerk." In *Aurora oder Morgenröte im Aufgang*, 11–45. Frankfurt am Main: Insel.

Whitbourn, Christine J. 1974. "Introduction." In *Knaves and Swindlers: Essays on the Picaresque Novel in Europe*, edited by Christine J. Whitbourn, ix–xix. London: Oxford University Press.

White, Christopher. 2013. "Reading Visions and Visionary Reading in *Blood Meridian*." In *They Rode On: "Blood Meridian" and the Tragedy of the American West*, edited by Rick Wallach, 177–90. N.p.: Cormac McCarthy Society.

Whitman, Walt. n.d. "From Far Dakota's Cañons." Walt Whitman Archive. http://www.whitmanarchive.org.

Wielenberg, Erik J. 2010. "God, Morality, and Meaning in Cormac McCarthy's *The Road*." *Cormac McCarthy Journal* 8.1:1–19.

Wiener, Norbert. 1988. *The Human Use of Human Beings: Cybernetics and Society*. Boston: DaCapo Press.

Wierschem, Markus. 2013. "The Other End of *The Road*: Re-Reading McCarthy in Light of Thermodynamics and Information Theory." *Cormac McCarthy Journal* 11.1:1–22.

————. 2014. "'It's More True, But It Ain't as Good': Searching for Truth in the Death-Deferring Dialogue of McCarthy's *The Sunset Limited*." In *Imaginary Dialogues in America*, edited by Till Kinzel and Jarmila Mildorf, 327–47. Heidelberg: Winter.

————. 2015a. "'Some Witless Paraclete Beleaguered with All Limbo's Clamor': On

Violent Contagion and Apocalyptic Logic in Cormac McCarthy's *Outer Dark*."
Contagion: Journal of Violence, Mimesis and Culture 22:185–202.

———. 2015b. "At a Crossroads of Life and Death: The Apocalyptic Journey(s) of Cormac
McCarthy's Fiction." In *The Journey of Life in American Life and Literature*, edited by
Peter Freese, 159–85. Heidelberg: Winter.

Wilhelm, Randall S. 2008. "'Golden Chalice, Good to House a God': Still Life in *The Road*."
Cormac McCarthy Journal 6:129–46.

Williams, James G. 2001. Introduction to *I See Satan Fall Like Lightning*, by René Girard,
translated by James G. Williams, ix–xxiii. New York: Orbis.

Williamson, Eric Miles. 2013. "Cormac McCarthy's *Blood Meridian* and Nietzsche: The
Metaphysics of War." In *They Rode On: "Blood Meridian" and the Tragedy of the
American West*, edited by Rick Wallach, 261–72. N.p.: Cormac McCarthy Society.

Winfrey, Oprah. 2007a. "Cormac McCarthy on Writing." Oprah.com. http://www.oprah.
com.

———. 2007b. "Oprah's Exclusive Interview with Cormac McCarthy Video." Oprah.com,
June 5. http://www.oprah.com.

Wood, James. 2005. "Red Planet: The Sanguinary Sublime of Cormac McCarthy." *New
Yorker*, July 25. http://www.newyorker.com.

Woodson, Linda T. 2000. "'De los Herejes y Huérfanos': The Sound and Sense of Cormac
McCarthy's Border Fiction." In *Myth, Legend, Dust: Critical Responses to Cormac
McCarthy*, edited by Rick Wallach, 201–8. Manchester: Manchester University Press.

———. 2002. "Leaving the Dark Night of the Lie: A Kristevan Reading of Cormac
McCarthy's Border Fiction." In *Cormac McCarthy: New Directions*, edited by James D.
Lilley, 267–84. Albuquerque: University of New Mexico Press.

———. 2008. "Mapping *The Road* in Post-Postmodernism." *Cormac McCarthy Journal*
6:87–97.

———. 2013. "Cormac McCarthy's Spanish." In *They Rode On: "Blood Meridian" and
the Tragedy of the American West*, edited by Rick Wallach, 121–32. N.p.: Cormac
McCarthy Society.

Woodward, Richard B. 1992. "Venomous Fiction." *New York Times Magazine*, April 19,
28–31, 36, 40.

———. 2005. "Cormac Country." *Vanity Fair*, August 1, 98–104.

Wordsworth, William. 2008. "My Heart Leaps Up When I Behold." In *The Major Works*,
246. London: Oxford University Press.

Yeats, William Butler. 2003. "The Second Coming." In *The Oxford Anthology of English
Poetry*, vol. 2, edited by John Wain, 576–77. Oxford: Oxford University Press.

Žižek, Slavoj. 2006. *How to Read Lacan*. London: Granata.

———. 2008a. *The Fragile Absolute. Or Why Is the Christian Legacy Worth Fighting For?* New York: Verso.

———. 2008b. *The Sublime Object of Ideology.* New York: Verso.

———. 2009. *Violence.* London: Profile Books.

Žižek, Slavoj, and Boris Gunjević. 2012. *God in Pain: Inversions of Apocalypse.* New York: Seven Stories.

Index